JANE'S
LAND-BASED AIR DEFENCE

SECOND EDITION

EDITED BY
TONY CULLEN and CHRISTOPHER F FOSS

1989-90

ISBN 0 7106-0890-X
JANE'S DEFENCE DATA
"Jane's" is a registered trade mark

Copyright © 1989 by Jane's Information Group, 163 Brighton Road, Coulsdon, Surrey CR3 2NX, UK

All rights reserved. No part of this publication may be reproduced, stored in retrieval systems or transmitted, in any form or by any means, electronic, mechanical, photocopying, recording or otherwise, without the prior written permission of the publishers.

In the USA and its dependencies
Jane's Information Group Inc, 1340 Braddock Place, Suite 300,
PO Box 1436, Alexandria, Virginia 22313-2036, USA

Alphabetical list of advertisers

A

Aerospatiale/Tactical Missiles
1, rue Beranger, 92320 Chatillon, France .... [10]

AB Bofors
S-691 80 Bofors, Sweden .... [3]

B

Breda Meccanica Bresciana SpA
Via Lunga 2, 25162 Brescia, Italy .... inside front cover

British Aerospace (Dynamics) Ltd
Six Hills Way, Stevenage, Hertfordshire SG1 2DA,
UK .... bookmark

E

Euromissile
12 rue de la Redoute, 92260 Fontenay-aux-Roses,
France .... outside back cover

H

Hollandse Signaalapparaten BV
PO Box 42, 7550 GD Hengelo, The Netherlands .... [5]

M

Marconi Command & Control Systems Ltd
Chobham Road, Frimley, Camberley, Surrey GU16 5PE,
UK .... outside front cover

N

NFT
PO Box 1003, N-3601 Kongsberg, Norway .... [16]

O

Officine Galileo
Military Systems Division, Via A Einstein 35,
50013 Campi Bisenzio, Florence, Italy .... inside back cover

OTO Melara Spa
Via Valdilocchi 15, 19100 La Spezia. Italy .... [8]

S

SATT Communications AB
Tellusborgsvagen 90, PO Box 32701, S-126 11 Stockholm,
Sweden .... [12]

T

TERMA Elektronik AS
Hovmarken 4, DK-8520 Lystrup, Denmark .... [14]

Thomson CSF/DSE
1 rue des Mathurins, BP10, 92222 Bagneux, France .... [10]

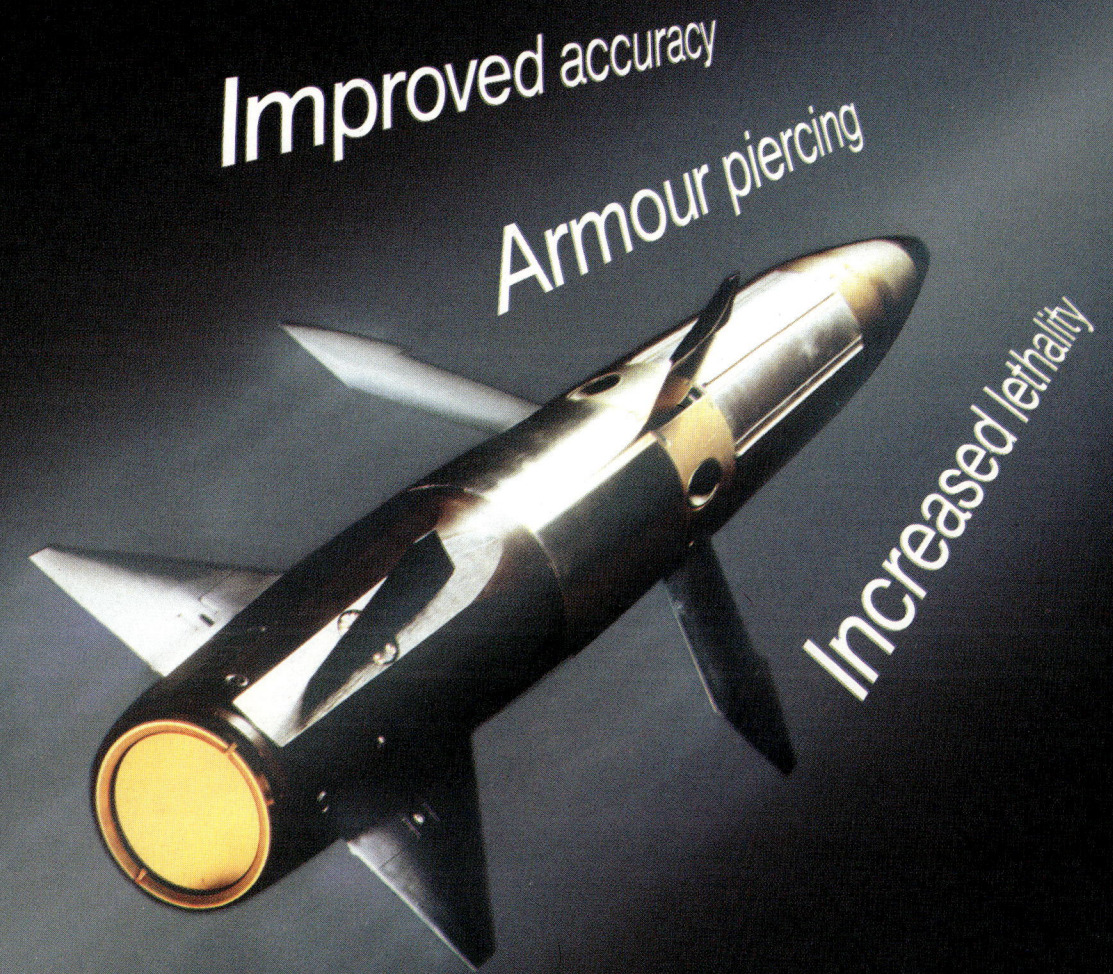

Extended range

Improved accuracy

Armour piercing

Increased lethality

RBS 70. All-target Missile System. Now with new Missile Mk 2

Classified list of advertisers

The companies advertising in this publication have informed us that they are involved in the fields of manufacture indicated below:–

Airborne Search and Rescue System
Officine Galileo

Anti-Aircraft Gun Turret
Breda Meccanica Bresciana
Marconi Command & Control Systems
Officine Galileo
OTO Melara

Anti-Tank Weapon Systems
Euromissile

Data Links
Hollandse Signaalapparaten

Fire Control Systems
Hollandse Signaalapparaten
Marconi Command & Control Systems
NFT
Officine Galileo
SATT Communications

Fire Control Radars
Hollandse Signaalapparaten
Marconi Command & Control Systems

Fuzes
Bofors
British Aerospace

Gun Control Equipment
Breda Meccanica Bresciana
Hollandse Signaalapparaten
Marconi Command & Control Systems
Officine Galileo
SATT Communications

Manportable Surface-to-Air Missiles
Bofors
British Aerospace

RWR-Self Protection Systems (EW) for Firstline Aircraft
SATT Communications

RWR-Self Protection Systems (EW) for Combat Helicopters
SATT Communications

Search Radars
Hollandse Signaalapparaten

Self-Propelled Anti-Aircraft Guns
Bofors
OTO Melara

Self-Propelled Surface-to-Air Missiles
Bofors
Aerospatiale
British Aerospace
OTO Melara

Semi-Mobile Surface-to-Air Missiles
Aerospatiale
British Aerospace

Simulators
British Aerospace
Marconi Command & Control Systems
Officine Galileo

Static Surface-to-Air Missiles
Aerospatiale

Systems Integration
Marconi Command & Control Systems

Test Equipment
Marconi Command & Control Systems

Thermal Imagers/FLIR
Officine Galileo

Towed Anti-Aircraft Guns
Bofors
Breda Meccanica Bresciana

Training Equipment
British Aerospace
Marconi Command & Control Systems

Upgrade & Refurbishment of Existing Systems
Breda Meccanica Bresciana
Marconi Command & Control Systems
Officine Galileo
TERMA Elektronik

Weapon Systems
Aerospatiale
Breda Meccanica Bresciana
OTO Melara

THE FLYCATCHER

Modern air attackers are fast and will mask their approach.
A defender hardly stands a chance. The defender who relies on Flycatcher, does; it will catch all that flies.

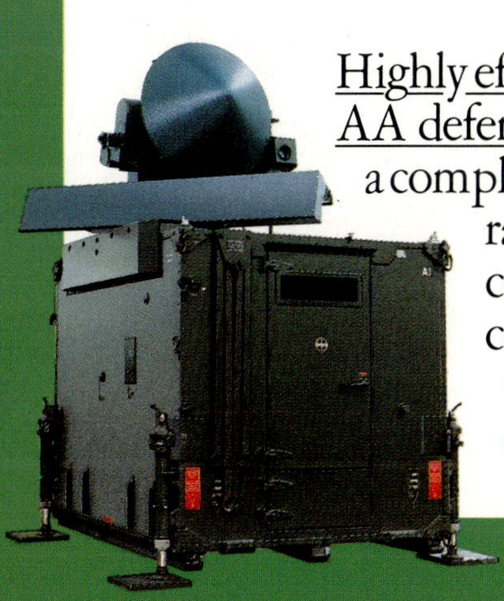

<u>Highly effective all-weather AA defence.</u> Flycatcher is a complete, self-contained radar/weapon control unit. It can control several types of medium-calibre guns and guide short-range missiles.
The use of two separate radar bands ensures accurate tracking, also at low levels and under all weather conditions.

Flycatcher is easy to deploy by helicopter or truck and simple to operate. Flycatcher catches all that flies, by early detection and instant reaction. Ask for more information.

Hollandse Signaalapparaten BV
P.O. Box 42, 7550 GD Hengelo,
The Netherlands. Telex 44310

TACKLE THE FUTURE WITH SIGNAAL INTEGRATED SYSTEMS

In mid-1989 OTO Melara completed the first SIDAM 25 quadruple 25 mm self-propelled anti-aircraft gun systems for the Italian Army, mounted on a modified M113 series armoured personnel carrier. This turret is also being offered for installation on a wide range of other chassis including the Spanish BMR-600 (6 × 6) and the ENGESA EE-11 Urutu (6 × 6). Until the introduction of the SIDAM 25, the Italian Army had no self-propelled air defence weapons of any type in service.

JANE'S
LAND-BASED AIR DEFENCE
1989-90

FOUR 25 mm KBA OERLIKON AUTOMATIC CANNONS
DAY AND NIGHT OPTRONIC FCS **RATE OF FIRE: 2,400 RPM**

THE *SIDAM 25* SYSTEM, HERE ON A M113 APC, IS DESIGNED AND MANUFACTURED UNDER SPECIFICATION OF THE ITALIAN ARMY

4 x 25 'SIDAM 25' TURRET
OTO MELARA MOBILE AA SYSTEMS
76/62 'OTOMATIC' TANK

AUTONOMOUS AA WEAPON SYSTEM - RATE OF FIRE: 120 RPM
RADAR AND OPTRONIC SEARCH & TRACKING CAPABILITY
FULLY STABILIZED FIRE CONTROL SYSTEM

GRUPPO EFIM — FINANZIARIA E. BREDA

OTO MELARA SpA, ITALY (I 19100) LA SPEZIA, 15 VIA VALDILOCCHI
TEL (39-187) 530 111 - TLX 270368-281101 OTO I - TELEFAX (39-187) 530 669

A Company of the OTO MELARA - BREDA M. B.- OFFICINE GALILEO - S. M. A. Consortium

Contents

Foreword [11]

Land-Based Air Defence

National and International Air Defence Systems 1

Manportable Surface-to-Air Missile Systems 26

Self-Propelled Anti-Aircraft Guns 54

Self-Propelled Surface-to-Air Missiles 106

Towed Anti-Aircraft Guns 154

Towed Anti-Aircraft Gun Sights 230

Static and Towed Surface-to-Air Missile Systems 241

Inventory 288

Index 305

THE FUTURE OF NATO'S AIR DEFENSES
AN ALLIANCE DILEMMA?

In less than a decade, NATO's current air defenses will no longer be able to cope with hostile technologies scheduled to enter service between now and then.

To counter this threat, two European defense technology leaders have pooled their expertise to produce a family of surface-to-air missiles unprecedented in agility and operational effectiveness, and able to neutralize attacks of up to ten supersonic/maneuvering intruders simultaneously.

Real-time threat analysis and fire control are coordinated by Thomson-CSF's Arabel multi-function radar system.

Aerospatiale's twin-stage Aster missiles will home in on the target with remarkable accuracy — and at high supersonic speeds.

This partnership results in a system so potent that it has already been chosen for procurement by a major Western European navy.

And represents the single system of its kind presently under development in the free world that is capable of assuring the vital defense requirements of the Western Alliance.

Foreword

During the last 12 months or so of *perestroika* and *glasnost*, the Soviet Air Defence forces have quietly and effectively continued an across-the-board upgrading programme of battlefield and rear-area air defence systems.

The basis for upgrading has been the Soviet military planners' ability to evaluate the Warsaw Pact-NATO conventional force balance in a strategic-operational context. They have a deep understanding of the underlying philosophy of military science that allows them to take into account and assess not only the quality and quantity of forces and equipment, but also whole systems and all the associated principles and variables that effect the way a war is fought, such as surprise, rates of advance, manoeuvre capability and the nature of the opponent.

In this way the Soviet planners calculate the forces and equipment of the Warsaw Pact and the opponent in a broad context and also, how they support the principles of warfare. The process is dynamic in nature and constantly leads to changes in the organisational structure of the Soviet forces to accommodate developments in equipment, training and tactics to counter the introduction of new enemy tactics and technology.

Thus, despite the handicap of a poorer overall economic performance and technology base than the West, the Soviet Union still produces weapon systems in less time and, very often, at less cost than NATO, which are designed to minimise these disadvantages.

The technologies involved in an individual system may seem to the West to be simple and, in some cases, inferior but when they are combined together to meet the requirement of the planners they are usually found to be more than adequate to fulfil the mission for which the system has been designed.

A recent US General Accounting Office Report highlighted this by giving the example of NATO's aircraft effectiveness. When a wide range of factors such as quality of equipment, quality of personnel and aircraft ground control are considered, the effectiveness of NATO aircraft in relation to those of the Warsaw Pact is estimated to be in the ratio of five to one in NATO's favour. However, the ratio is actually one of parity because of the Warsaw Pact's overwhelming superiority in anti-aircraft defence systems.

Moreover, in the Warsaw Pact's combat scenario of the European battlefield, the potential capability of NATO to use airpower on a significant scale across its Corps boundaries is perceived as a major threat, as this can effect the ground battle on an operational scale. Thus any political subterfuge or military measure that is assessed by the Warsaw Pact's planners as having the capability to reduce and/or eliminate aspects of the NATO aircraft supremacy, will be used in trying to shift the balance decisively towards the Warsaw Pact side of the equation.

It should also be noted at this point that unless NATO has initiated a complete mobilisation before commencement of hostilities, then in the critical opening phases of the conflict the only significant means which the NATO commanders have of affecting the ground battle is the judicious use of airpower; otherwise the last resort is tactical nuclear weapons.

Hence the Soviets' introduction during the 1980s of the SA-16 manportable SAM, the mobile SA-12a, SA-12b, SA-15 and SA-17 SAM systems, the 2S6 gun/SAM system and the targeting of forward deployed long-range SA-5 missile complexes against AWACS-type targets. The recent reduction in Warsaw Pact tanks-for-NATO aircraft should also be viewed collectively in the light of what has been outlined above.

It is hoped by now that the reader will have begun to grasp just how important land-based air defence has become in the overall military picture of both sides in Central Europe.

To give further examples, NATO is countering, to a certain extent, the Warsaw Pact operational plans by investing significant resources in developing air defence assets and airbase facilities. The upgrading of systems like Rapier, Crotale and Roland coupled with the widespread deployment of Patriot and the various concept studies such as the MSAM for the I-HAWK follow-on programme are all good examples which, by implication, substantially enhance NATO's deterrence capability against any Warsaw Pact aggression.

In the West, considerable effort is also being devoted to developing a viable Anti-Tactical Ballistic Missile (ATBM) system. The US Army's long-range Patriot system in Europe is undergoing the PAC-1 Anti-Tactical Missile (ATM) upgrade and will receive the follow-on PAC-2 improvements. In the longer term the US/West German Advanced Tactical (AT) Patriot missile variant will take over this role in the mid- to late-1990s. Shorter range terminal defence ATBM systems such as the BAe Wolverine concept are also under consideration.

In a unique partnership outside of the NATO framework, the US DoD has also placed a contract with Israeli Aircraft Industries (IAI) to produce its Chetz (Arrow) ATBM system in demonstrator form which, if successful, will then be taken through to the production stage to fill major air defence gaps for both countries.

It is taken as a matter of fact by the authors that the Soviet Union has already evaluated the ATBM area and fielded the appropriate mix of short-/long-range defensive ATBM-capable SAM systems within its current air defence enhancement programme.

Although both the Western and Eastern power blocs feel that the primary tactical ballistic missile threat comes from each other, a major stimulus for the ATBM work has been provided by the widespread use of such weapons during the recent Gulf War. In nine years, Iran fired approximately 120 'Scud B' (including one against Kuwait), 330 *Oghab* and five IRAN-130 missiles. Iraq launched 67 FROG-7 and 361 'Scud B', *Al Hussein* and *Al Abbas* rockets/missiles at Iranian military and civilian targets.

Other combat users of heavy rockets/missiles include Afghanistan (30–40 'Scud B' in late 1988 through 1989 against mojahedin guerrilla positions), Egypt (some 20-30 FROG-7, *Al Tin* (formerly the *Al Kafir*) and *Al Zeitoon* (formerly the *Al Zafir*) unguided rockets and three 'Scud B' against targets in Sinai) during the 1973 Yom Kippur War, Libya (at least two 'Scud B' against the Italian Mediterranean island of Lampedusa in April 1986), Syria (approximately 20 FROG-2/3/7 against northern Israel, including two which ultimately landed in Jordan during the 1973 Yom Kippur War), and South Yemen (several 'Scud B' during the recent civil war there).

It is the availability of these weapons, coupled with the newly developed nuclear, chemical and biological warfare capabilities within many non-NATO/Warsaw Pact countries and the willingness of certain nations to use the systems without constraint against outside agencies, which is causing the greatest concern to the Super Powers and their allies, as one day the armed forces, military bases or civilians they deploy around the world could be the target of such an attack.

The data contained in the accompanying table illustrates this point by showing collated information on the tactical ballistic missile/rocket and warhead capabilities of the non-Warsaw Pact/NATO nations.

After some years of relative inactivity, there has been a renewed interest in self-propelled air defence systems in some countries.

A considerable amount of information has now become available on the new Soviet 2S6 self-propelled air defence system which is now in service with the Group of Soviet Forces Germany (GSFG) as the replacement for the ZSU-23-4 system which first entered service with the Soviet Army as far back as 1965.

The 2S6 is a much more capable system than the one it replaces as it has both tracking and surveillance radars and is armed with both guns and missiles. The missiles would probably be used to engage targets at longer ranges while the twin 30 mm guns are used to engage targets at shorter ranges. The 2S6 is likely to be a highly effective system against both tactical aircraft and helicopters. Its high cost and the large number of ZSU-23-4 needing to be replaced, not only in the Soviet Army but also within the Warsaw Pact, indicate a long production run.

Late in 1988 Marconi Command and Control Systems received its first order for its private venture Marksman twin 35 mm air defence system from Finland, where the turrets will be installed on existing T-55 MBT chassis. This is the first sale of a system of this type in the West for well over 10 years.

"Why's everyone always picking on me?"

"Cheer up, old bat. A good dose of electronics will soon get you in shape."

New update package to make your Super-Fledermaus super again.

A joint venture by SATT Communications AB and Philips Elektronikindustrier AB, Sweden and TERMA Elektronik AS, Denmark, has developed an update package to give the Super-Fledermaus state-of-the-art performance. News that will prove very welcome on the market, particularly in view of the fact that a new system with equivalent performance can cost three to four times as much as the update package. Deliveries of upgraded Super-Fledermaus units are already in work in Europe.

The update package involves using a new, decentralized digital computer to replace the electron tubes and electromechanical components of the old system and fitting a new Ku band frequency agility radar with MTI capability.

These improvements will boost hit probability by factors of 5 to 8 and cut reaction time to as little as 5 seconds. And if the poor availability of the system has been a source of irritation in the past, we can guarantee an MTBF of more than 500 hours for our update.

So stop picking on Super-Fledermaus. Pick up the phone for more information on the update package.

 **SATT Communications AB**

Box 32701, S-126 11 STOCKHOLM, Sweden. Telephone: Int +46 8 726 86 00. Telex: 15325 SATCOM S

FOREWORD

While some countries insist that missiles alone can meet their battlefield air defence requirements, a number of countries firmly believe that a mix of highly mobile gun and missile systems is by far the best solution. For manning and financial reasons however, other nations have chosen to rely on missile systems only.

For many years the United States Marine Corps (USMC) has been able to field equipment tailored to meet its specific requirements in a fraction of the time taken by other forces. A good example of this is its requirement for an air defence version of its Light Armored Vehicle (LAV) of which some 758 have already been delivered in various versions.

The USMC have awarded competitive contracts to two United States companies; General Electric and FMC, which will each deliver two prototypes of the Light Armored Vehicle — Air Defense this year. These will then be subjected to extensive trials and hopefully one will be selected for production in the first quarter of FY 1990. Like the Soviet Union, the Light Armored Vehicle — Air Defense will have a mix of guns and missiles to engage multiple targets at different ranges.

Following the cancellation of the Sgt York twin 40 mm Divisional Air Defense Gun (DIVAD) system, the US embarked on the West's most ambitious air defence system modernisation package under the overall name of the Forward Area Air Defense System. Although, because of budget constraints, there are some doubts as to whether the US Army can procure sufficient quantities of all of the systems required, which cover both sensors and weapons, there is little doubt that progress is being made. Late in 1988, the first production examples of the Pedestal Mounted Stinger (PMS) were completed by Boeing Aerospace and if tests are successful the ADATS system is expected to enter service in the early 1990s.

In the UK, the Shorts Starstreak High Velocity Missile (HVM) is probably the most advanced system of its type in the world, and its introduction into service with the British Army mounted on the Alvis Stormer armoured vehicle will be a much needed air defence boost to the British Army of the Rhine.

Many of today's battlefield air defence systems rely on radar to provide key target information, but a number of countries are looking at other passive systems to provide this information. The British Army will be the first country in the West to field a passive detection system. It has been developed by THORN EMI and is called the Air Defence Alert Device (ADAD). The system will be employed by air defence units of the Royal Artillery in two versions; tripod-mounted and self-propelled. The latter will be part of the Shorts Starstreak HVM system, so enabling each unit to be independent of other battlefield sensors.

This second edition has a number of important changes. First, a section has been added on National and International Air Defence Systems. This section provides key information on the overall air defence systems of many countries of the world, the types of radar and command and control systems used, and planned improvements.

The *Towed Anti-Aircraft Gun Sights* section is also new. Many countries are now upgrading their older air defence guns with new sights and improved ammunition to enable them to have an enhanced capability against the evolving threat. Most of these sights can either be fitted onto new production guns or retrofitted to older weapons.

The *Static and Towed Surface-to-Air Missile Systems* section now also includes information on anti-tactical ballistic missile systems which are likely to become more important in the years to come.

The editors would like to take this opportunity of thanking the many manufacturers, defence forces and individuals who have contributed to this edition of *Jane's Land-Based Air Defence*. Special thanks are due to Bernard Blake who compiled the first section and Duncan Lennox for his input on anti-tactical ballistic missile defences. Special thanks are also due to Terry Gander, David Isby, James M Loop and Steve Zaloga for their most valuable assistance.

Additional information and photographs for the third edition should be sent to the editors at Jane's Defence Data, Sentinel House as soon as possible.

Tony Cullen
Christopher F Foss
March 1989

Non-Warsaw Pact/NATO Tactical Missile/Rocket and Warhead Capabilities[1]

Country	System	Range (km)	Status[2]	Payload (kg)	HE	ICM	CW	BW	NU
Algeria	FROG-4	48	S	363	Y	N	Po	N	N
	FROG-7	70	S	550	Y	Y	Po	N	N
Afghanistan	'Scud B'	280	S	1000	Y	Y	Pr	N	N
Argentina	Condor II*	1000	D	500	Y	Y	Po	N	Po
Brazil	SS60	60	P	150	Y	Y	Pr	Po	N
	SS300	300	D	1000	Y	Y	Po	N	Po
	SS1000	1000	D	1000	Y	N	Po	N	Po
China, People's Republic	M9/M11	200/600	P	ca 1000	Y	Y	Y	Pr	Y
	M1/M1B	80/100	P	150	Y	Y	Pr	Po	N
Cuba	FROG-5	35	S	454	Y	N	Y	N	N
	FROG-7	70	S	550	Y	Y	Y	N	N
Egypt	FROG-7	70	S	550	Y	N	Pr	Po	N
	'Scud B'	280	S	1000	Y	N	Pr	Po	N
	Sakr-80	80	P	200	Y	Y	Po	Po	N
	Badr-2000*	1000	D	500	Y	Y	Po	Po	N
India	*Agni*	2000	D	ca 1500	Y	Pr	Po	Po	Pr
	Prithvi	250	P	1000	Y	Po	Pr	Po	Pr
	Indian Type 1	150	D	ca 500	Y	Y	Pr	Po	Po
Iran	'Scud B'	280	S	1000	Y	N	Y	Pr	N
	Iran-320[3]	320	P	1000	Y	N	Y	Pr	N
	Shahin 2	130	P	180	Y	Po	Pr	Po	N
	Oghab	75	P	70	Y	Po	Po	Po	N
	Nazeat	100+	P	150	Y	Po	Po	Po	N
Iraq	FROG-7	70	S	550	Y	N	Y	Pr	N
	'Scud B'	280	S	1000	Y	N	Y	Pr	N
	Condor II*	1000	D	500	Y	Y	Pr	Pr	Po
	Al Hussein	650	P	135	Y	N	N	N	N
	Al Abbas	900	P	1000	Y	Pr	Y	Pr	N
	Al-Faw	150	P	ca500	Y	Y	Pr	Po	N
	Al-Ababeel	50	P	ca250	Y	Y	Pr	Po	N
	Al-Sijeel	35	P	ca250	N	Y	Pr	Po	N
Israel	MAR-290	25	P	320	Y	Y	Pr	Po	N
	MAR-350	75	P	150	Y	Y	Pr	Po	N
	Lance	121	S	454	N	Y	Y	Po	Y
	Jericho I	650	P	500	Y	Y	Y	Po	Y
	Jericho II	4500	P	1100	N	N	Y	Po	Y
	Jericho II	7500	P	500	N	N	Y	Po	Y

[13]

JANE'S·INFORMATION·GROUP

Leading suppliers of impartial, factual, professional information to the defence, aerospace and transport industries.

The Group's unique capabilities for research and analysis enables it to provide the most comprehensive information from a single source.

Products and Services:
Marketing Forecasting
Subscription Services
Yearbooks and Directories
On-line Services
Journals and Newsletters
Confidential Market Research
Electronic Databases

JANE'S INFORMATION GROUP
the unique answer to your intelligence requirements

Jane's Information Group Sentinel House 163 Brighton Road Coulsdon Surrey CR3 2NX United Kingdom Tel: 01-763 1030	Jane's Information Group International Center Cointrin 20 route de Pre-Bois PO Box 636 1215 Geneve 15 Switzerland Tel: 022-980505	Jane's Information Group 1340 Braddock Place Suite 300 Alexandria VA 22313-2036 United States Tel: 703-683-3700

TERMA Elektronik AS

Updating, modification and "reverse-engineering"

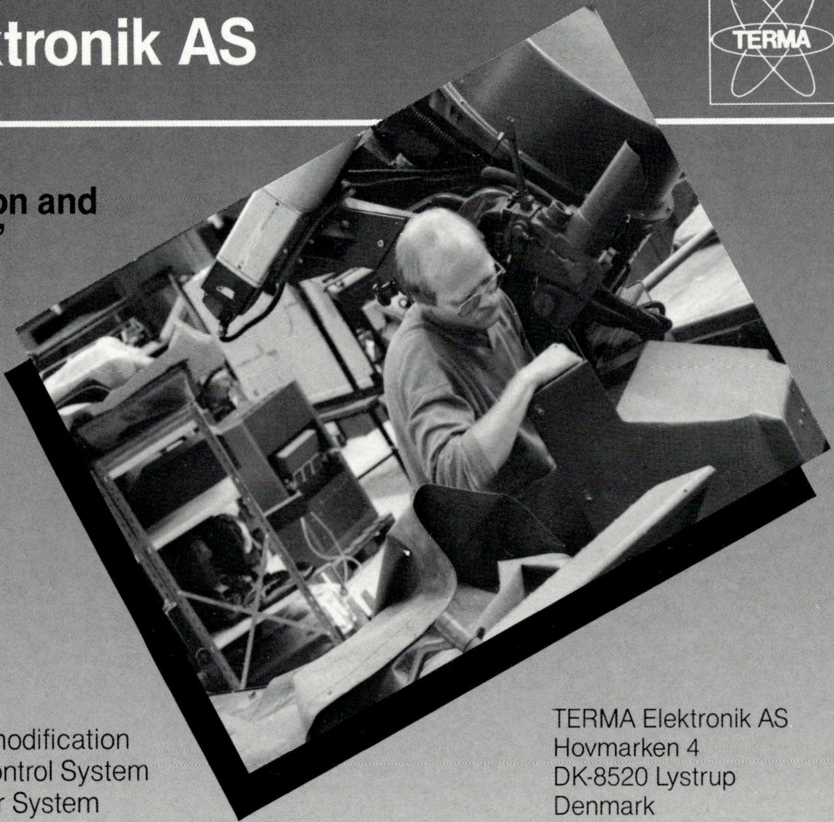

Equipment currently under modification
- Super-Fledermaus Fire Control System
- QUAD and GCA Par Radar System
- Hawk Missile System
- Surveillance Radar System

TERMA Elektronik AS
Hovmarken 4
DK-8520 Lystrup
Denmark
Telephone +45 6 222 000
Telex 68109 terma dk

FOREWORD

Country	System	Range (km)	Status[2]	Payload (kg)	HE	ICM	CW	BW	NU
Korea, North	FROG-5	35	S	454	Y	N	Y	Y	N
	FROG-7	70	S	550	Y	Y	Y	Y	N
	'Scud B'[4]	280	S	1000	Y	N	Y	Y	N
	'Scud PIP' 5	650	P	1000	Y	N	Y	Y	N
Korea, South	Honest John	37	S	680	Y	Y	N	N	N
	Nike Hercules	160	S	500	Y	N	N	N	N
Kuwait	FROG-7	70	S	550	Y	Y	N	N	N
Libya	FROG-7	70	S	550	Y	Y	Y	Po	N
	'Scud B'	280	S	1000	Y	N	Y	Po	N
Pakistan	Haft-I	80	D	500	Y	Pr	Pr	Po	Po
	Haft-II	300	D	500+	Y	Pr	Pr	Po	Po
Saudi Arabia	DF-3	1600	S	2040	Y	N	N	N	N
Syria	FROG-7	70	S	550	Y	Y	Y	Pr	N
	SS-21 'Scarab'	120	S	700	Y	Y	Pr	Pr	N
	'Scud B'	280	S	1000	Y	N	Y	Pr	N
Taiwan	*Ching Feng*	120	P	454	Y	Y	Pr	Po	Po
Yemen, North	'Scud B'	280	S	1000	Y	N	N	N	N
	FROG-7	70	S	550	Y	N	N	N	N

Legend:
HE — High Explosive
ICM — Improved Conventional Munitions (ie Cluster Type)
CW — Chemical Warfare
BW — Biological Warfare
Nu — Nuclear
S — System in service
P — System in production
D — System in development
Y — Yes, a warhead of this type exists in country for weapon
N — No warhead of this type exists in country for weapon
Pr — Probable warhead of this type exists in country
Po — Potential technology is available to produce warhead of this type in country

Notes:
* Condor II and *Badr*-2000 are essentially the same missile being developed under a technology co-operation programme
1. A recent CIA report indicates that by the year 2000, at least 15 countries will be producing their own ballistic missiles. In addition, a total of 20 countries have either already produced or are in the process of developing a capability to manufacture their own chemical warfare agents. Ten of these countries, including Iran, Iraq, Libya and North Korea, are also known to be actively working on biological warfare agent programmes.
2. Other sources have differing information as to the status of these missiles
3. Iran-320 is a locally built derivative of 'Scud B'
4. 'Scud PIP' is a locally built North Korean product improved 'Scud B' with increased range and enhanced accuracy

NORWEGIAN ADAPTED HAWK (NOAH)
Ground-based Air Defence System

The Royal Norwegian Air Force (RNoAF) ordered the NOAH system in 1984 for airfield defence. The first battery, in triad configuration to provide effective radar coverage and adequate ECCM capability, was deployed three years later. Today, all NOAH batteries are operative and additional systems have been delivered for use as tactical radars providing target data for L70 guns.

THE ART OF HITTING THE TARGET

The NOAH programme is the first major application of the mobile Acquisition Radar and Control System (ARCS), jointly developed by NFT and Hughes Aircraft Co. The latter contributes its Low Altitude Surveillance Radar (LASR) and NFT the Fire Distribution Centre (FDC) based on its multi-function console, KMC 9000.

NOAH has the communication capability of netting information from two or more sensors, thus providing an integrated tactical air picture, eliminating blind zones, affording early warning and enhancing battle control. LASR automatically detects fixed-wing aircraft and helicopter targets infiltrating below the protective umbrella provided by long- and medium-range air defence radar sensors and gives autonomous radar coverage for short-range air defence. LASR employs a unique combination of 3-D pencil-beam scanning, very high stability signals, and target doppler-signal processing to reject land, sea, rain clutter and chaff. LASR's completely automatic digital signal processing and target extraction enable rapid data reporting in virtually any format. NFT's KMC 9000 multi-function console is a compact and self-contained unit designed for both fixed sites and tactical applications. Its prime functions are tactical surveillance and operational management, and involve air/surface surveillance, target tracking, threat evaluation and weapon assignment. ARCS is a general purpose air defence subsystem that can equally well be used with other missile systems or subsystems.

Norsk Forsvarsteknologi as
P.O.Box 1003, N-3601 Kongsberg
Telephone (+47 3) 73 82 50

JANE'S
LAND-BASED AIR DEFENCE 1990

☐ **YES!** Please send me next year's edition of JANE'S LAND-BASED AIR DEFENCE 1990.

NAME _____

TITLE/RANK _____

ORGANISATION _____

ADDRESS _____

CITY _____

STATE/ZIP/COUNTRY _____

If you sign and return this order card, we will register your subscription to next year's edition, and invoice you prior to publication so that the book can be sent to you without delay.

However, we will hold the price of next year's edition at the current level if you send a remittance with the order card, and we receive it by 31 October 1989.

PLEASE COMPLETE BOTH SIDES OF ORDER FORM

JANE'S
LAND-BASED AIR DEFENCE 1989

☐ **YES!** Please send me _____ additional copy(ies) of this edition of JANE'S LAND-BASED AIR DEFENCE 1989.

NAME _____

TITLE/RANK _____

ORGANISATION _____

ADDRESS _____

CITY _____

STATE/ZIP/COUNTRY _____

US PRICE
$120.00

UK & REST OF WORLD PRICE
£70

PLEASE COMPLETE BOTH SIDES OF ORDER FORM

OTHER PRODUCTS FROM JANE'S INFORMATION GROUP

*	Title	Price US$	Price £	Qty
JANE'S DEFENCE AND AEROSPACE YEARBOOKS 1989				
	Jane's Military Communications 1989	$140	£80	
	Jane's Military Logistics	$190	£100	
	Jane's Fighting Ships 1989-90	$170	£100	
	Jane's Radar and EW Systems 1989-90	$140	£80	
	Jane's Infantry Weapons 1989-90	$170	£95	
	Jane's Avionics 1989-90	$170	£95	
	Jane's Underwater Warfare Systems 1989-90	$140	£80	
	Jane's NBC Protection Equipment 1989-90	$135	£80	
	Jane's Battlefield Surveillance 1989-90	$120	£70	
	Jane's C³I Systems 1989-90	$140	£80	
	Jane's Armour and Artillery 1989-90	$145	£85	
	Jane's AFV Systems 1989-90	$145	£85	
	Jane's All The World's Aircraft 1989-90	$170	£100	
	Jane's Security & Co-In Equipment 1989-90	$110	£65	
	Jane's Military Training Systems 1989-90	$135	£80	
	Jane's NATO Handbook 1989-90	$110	£65	

*	Title	Price US$	Price £	Qty
JANE'S DEFENCE AND AEROSPACE BINDER PRODUCTS 1989				
	Jane's Strategic Weapon Systems	$300	£175	
	Jane's Defence Appointments (Pacific Rim)	$1050	£600	
	Jane's Defence Appointments (NATO Europe)	$1050	£600	
	Jane's Air-Launched Weapons	$300	£175	
	Soviet High Command	$935	£550	
	Jane's Naval Weapon Systems	$300	£175	
	Warsaw Pact High Command	$825	£500	
INTERAVIA DIRECTORIES 1989				
	Interavia ABC Aerospace Directory 1989	$295	£175	
	Interavia Space Directory 1989-90	$140	£80	
	International Defense Directory 1990	$365	£230	

☐ Please send me a complete list of all JANE'S INFORMATION GROUP products.

*Please indicate products required ✓

PLEASE COMPLETE BOTH SIDES OF ORDER FORM

☐ I enclose a cheque payable to JANE'S INFORMATION GROUP

☐ Please invoice my Company/Organisation
Purchase Order No. _____

_____
SIGNATURE

Send US orders to:

> JANE'S INFORMATION GROUP
> Department Yearbooks
> 1340 Braddock Place, Suite 300
> P.O. Box 1436
> Alexandria, VA 22313-2036
> (703) 683-3700
> 800 243-3852

Send UK & Rest of the World orders to:

> JANE'S INFORMATION GROUP
> Department DSM
> Sentinel House
> 163 Brighton Road
> Coulsdon
> Surrey CR3 2NX
> United Kingdom
>
> International (+441) 763 1030
> de la France 19..05.90.83.98 (appel gratuit)
> aus der B.D.R. 0130-81 01 53 (Nahtarif)
> in UK 0800 282 455 (toll free)
> or UK 01-763 1030 (not toll free)

☐ I enclose a cheque payable to JANE'S INFORMATION GROUP

☐ Please invoice my Company/Organisation
Purchase Order No. _____

_____
SIGNATURE

Send US orders to:

> JANE'S INFORMATION GROUP
> Department Yearbooks
> 1340 Braddock Place, Suite 300
> P.O. Box 1436
> Alexandria, VA 22313-2036
> (703) 683-3700
> 800 243-3852

Send UK & Rest of the World orders to:

> JANE'S INFORMATION GROUP
> Department DSM
> Sentinel House
> 163 Brighton Road
> Coulsdon
> Surrey CR3 2NX
> United Kingdom
>
> International (+441) 763 1030
> de la France 19..05.90.83.98 (appel gratuit)
> aus der B.D.R. 0130-81 01 53 (Nahtarif)
> in UK 0800 282 455 (toll free)
> or UK 01-763 1030 (not toll free)

DELIVERY DETAILS

NAME _____

TITLE/RANK _____

ORGANISATION _____

ADDRESS _____

CITY _____

STATE/ZIP/COUNTRY

Send US orders to:

> JANE'S INFORMATION GROUP
> Department Yearbooks
> 1340 Braddock Place, Suite 300
> P.O. Box 1436
> Alexandria, VA 22313-2036
> (703) 683-3700
> 800 243-3852

PAYMENT METHOD

☐ I enclose a cheque payable to JANE'S INFORMATION GROUP

☐ Please invoice my Company/Organisation
Purchase Order No. _____
(All prices include shipping by surface mail. Air mail rates on application)

_____
SIGNATURE

Send UK & Rest of the World orders to:

> JANE'S INFORMATION GROUP
> Department DSM
> Sentinel House
> 163 Brighton Road
> Coulsdon
> Surrey CR3 2NX
> United Kingdom
>
> International (+441) 763 1030
> de la France 19..05.90.83.98 (appel gratuit)
> aus der B.D.R. 0130-81 01 53 (Nahtarif)
> in UK 0800 282 455 (toll free)
> or UK 01-763 1030 (not toll free)

National and International Air Defence Systems

Note: Many countries now have an air defence system based primarily on long- and medium-range radar equipments. The size of these systems depends to a large extent on what individual countries can afford and also the degree of likely threat. There are some highly comprehensive and sophisticated systems such as those forming the defensive shields of the United States and Soviet Union which incorporate several different types of radar and air defence missiles, and are intended to counter the threat of ballistic missile, cruise missile and manned aircraft attacks. Another comprehensive network is NADGE (NATO Air Defence Ground Environment), which covers most of Western Europe. National systems tend to be somewhat simpler and can vary from one or two radar equipments placed at strategic points on the periphery of the particular country to more complex systems such as Britain's UKADGE, the French STRIDA and the Saudi Arabian Peace Shield.

Air defence is a particularly sensitive subject and consequently information on some nations' systems and equipment is somewhat limited. Political as well as military reasons frequently are the cause of manufacturers' reluctance to divulge the destination of equipments such as radar or computers, which might otherwise enable assessments of the air defence provisions of particular countries.

ABU DHABI

Although peace talks between Iran and Iraq are now in progress, the situation in the Gulf is still tense. Because of this, Abu Dhabi has initiated an urgent requirement for an air defence system which includes both radar and the necessary communications links. Equipment to the value of around $700 million is involved and the United States, United Kingdom and Soviet Union have had discussions with Abu Dhabi. These discussions started during 1987 and no announcements have been made as to their progress or the type of equipment being sought. Since Abu Dhabi is part of the United Arab Emirates (see later) it is almost certain that any air defence requirements will form part of an overall UAE system.

SOUTHERN AFRICA

This area covers Angola, Botswana, Malawi, Mozambique, Namibia, Tanzania, Zambia and Zimbabwe. It does not include the Republic of South Africa. Angolan air defence is described under a separate entry.

In general, Southern Africa has been supplied with both ground and airborne air defence equipment from Soviet sources, although in some cases Chinese aircraft and AA guns are in operational use. Although there appears to be no centralised air defence the area is well supplied with surveillance radar systems, most of which are Soviet types, and it is assumed that each country operates its own air defence centre. The accompanying diagram gives locations of those sites that have been identified, together with their coverage on 1 m² target at 20 000 ft. Soviet radars in operational use include Barlock, Spoon Rest, Flat Face, Side Net, Odd Pair, Squat Eye and Thin Skin. Most of the SAMs deployed are also of Soviet types, including SA-2, SA-3, SA-6, SA-7, SA-8 and SA-9, plus a variety of AA guns of various types and calibres.

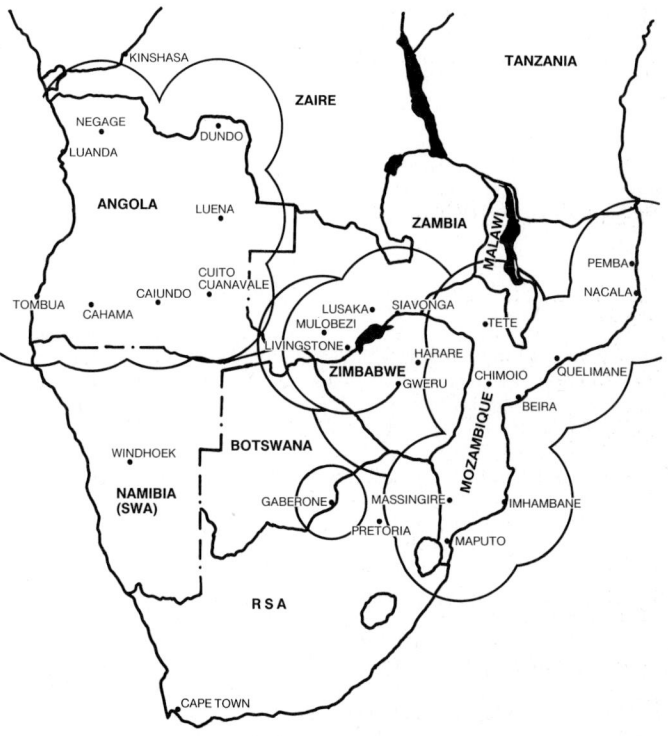

WORLD AIR DEFENCE SYSTEMS / Angola-Australia

ANGOLA

For reasons that are not difficult to understand, very little is known about the air defence systems operating in Angola. Virtually all radar systems and other military equipment have been supplied by the Soviet Union and much of it is operated by Cuban personnel. Over 20 radar sites using a variety of Russian surveillance and search radars have been identified including Tall King, Spoon Rest, Bar Lock, Flat Face, Squat Eye and Side Net systems. The accompanying diagram gives location of the radar sites that have been identified, with the coverage up to 20 000 ft.

With the current situation in the south-western area of Africa, whereby the Republic of South Africa and the government of Angola have agreed terms for the evacuation of Namibia by both sides and the holding of free elections, it is not easy to see what will happen to the air defence system should all the Soviet and Cuban personnel withdraw. The probability seems to be of an 'uneasy peace' with the air defence network being maintained by 'foreign technicians'.

The Angolan Air Force, maintained and operated largely by Soviet and Cuban personnel, consists almost entirely of Soviet aircraft with a sprinkling of other types. The main strike force consists of MiG-17, MiG-21 and MiG-23 aircraft with deliveries of Su-22 ground attack aircraft. The strike force appears to number about 100 aircraft. In addition there are large numbers of helicopters, mainly of French and Soviet manufacture, and a mixture of transport types.

Surface-to-air missiles in operational deployment include SA-2, 3, 6, 7, 8, 9, 13, 14 and 16.

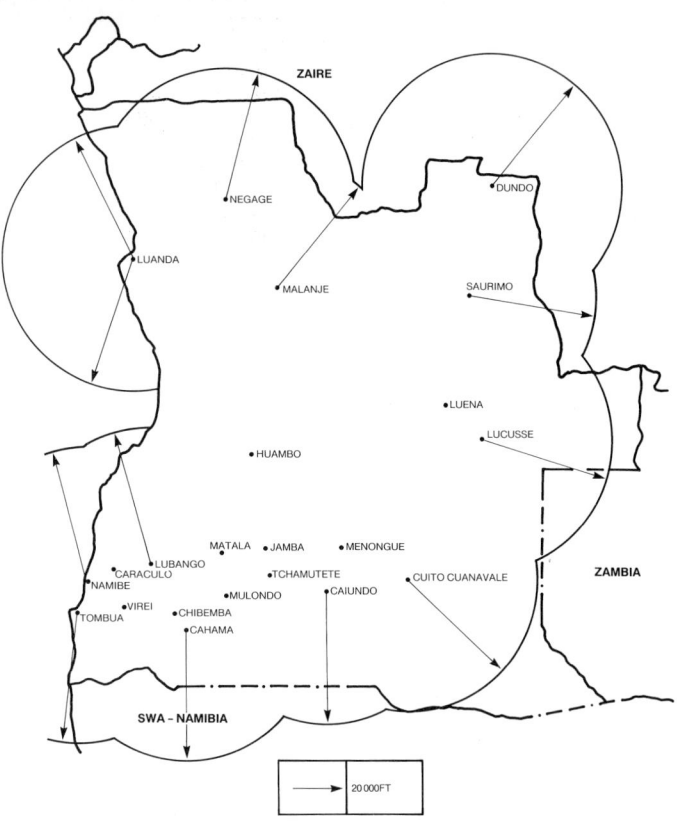

ARGENTINA

With the changes in government after the Falklands campaign against the United Kingdom, very little has emerged from Argentina on the subject of air defence. It is known that a programme for an integrated air defence/ATC was being carried out in the 1970s by Thomson-CSF of France but the extent of this has not been made public. It is believed that it is similar in principle to that provided for Brazil. In 1985 the President of Argentina introduced a new plan to reorganise the defence of the nation, with a new National Defence Council to replace the former military committee. The council was established in 1988 and will be responsible for carrying out wide-ranging defence structure and planning. Until the Anglo/Argentine hostilities in 1982, Argentina was spending somewhere in the region of eight per cent of its GNP on defence - by far the highest proportion in South or Central America.

During the late 1970s three Westinghouse AN/TPS-43 radars were procured, and a number of Cardion-built AN/TPS-44 systems were also supplied. No official information has been disclosed but it seems likely that these systems were deployed to afford cover for the main naval and air bases near Buenos Aires, Port Belgrano, Commodoro Rivadavia, Santa Cruz, Rio Gallegos, Rio Grande and Ushaia. In 1982 one of the AN/TPS-43 radars was deployed in the Falklands and was subsequently captured by the British forces. After being refurbished in the UK it returned to the Falklands and is now based at Port Stanley. It seems likely that early steps were taken to replace this item following Argentina's withdrawal from the Falklands, either with another AN/TPS-43 or a similar type such as the Thomson-CSF TRS-2215 or TRS-2230. It has also been reported, although not confirmed, that Argentina has recently placed an order for a number of Selenia RAT-31S radar systems.

The Argentine Air Force is quite extensive and includes the A-4 Skyhawk, Mirage IIIEA/IIICJ and IAI Dagger A/Mirage V, as well as two COIN squadrons equipped with Pucara aircraft. Updated versions of the Pucara have now been delivered, and it is understood that Argentina will obtain about 40 AMX strike fighters in due course. The procurement of Pucara and AMX aircraft will replenish the losses suffered in the Falklands campaign.

The surface-to-air missile force is operated by the Argentine Army Marine Corps and consists of a variety of French, British and Soviet missiles, including Roland, RBS 70 and Tigercat, plus the manportable SA-7 and Blowpipe.

AUSTRALIA

A wide-ranging defence strategy was outlined in a Defence White Paper produced in March 1987. It committed Australia to high quality intelligence together with flexible, long-range capabilities for maritime surveillance and interdiction, aimed at denying effective use of the sea or air to the north of the country to any hostile nation. In accordance with a statement made by the Australian Minister of Defence in September 1987 a sum of $704 million was budgeted for 1987-88 fiscal year, providing an average real growth in defence spending of 1.7 per cent a year over the five years of the Hawke government. The key elements are the development of the Jindalee OTH radar, the upgrading of the P-3C maritime surveillance aircraft, the strike force of F/A-18 and F-111 aircraft, plus ground and naval forces. In addition the Australian Defence Minister announced in July 1988 that the country intends to go ahead with the procurement of up to four airborne early warning aircraft. Three airframes are believed to be under evaluation: the Boeing E-3A Sentry with its AN/APY-1 radar, the Lockheed P-3 Orion, and the Lockheed C-130. The latter two would be fitted with the AN/APS-138 radar.

The original air defence system was known as Hub Cap and provided three-dimensional airspace surveillance and fighter control to intercept hostile aircraft over a wide area. It operates from fully mobile air-conditioned shelters designed for deployment by C-130 aircraft. Since the sparse population and continental size of Australia combine to make a conventional static air defence organisation similar to that of the USA an unrealistic proposition, an effective compromise was achieved by the combination of two Hub Cap systems, with the search radars and part of the infrastructure needed for the control of civil and military air traffic serving the main population centres of the country. The new strategy will update Hub Cap, and implementation is being carried out currently and for the next few years. The original Hub Cap radars were replaced by three Westinghouse AN/TPS-43 radars, and the sites were subsequently rewired with fibre optic cabling for enhanced operator safety. A tactical air defence system, also supplied for Westinghouse, is operational and allows for radar-directed control of defensive fighter operations wherever the system is deployed.

The use of digital computing allows automatic tracking of targets from primary radar, while plot extraction from the secondary radar returns is used to reinforce the primary radar auto-tracking. For the RAAF requirements the computer is programmed to take account of aircraft characteristics, perform an assessment of an interception situation when supplied with the relevant data on weapon availability, and provide a number of alternative intercept solutions for selections by the controller. Comprehensive communication facilities are also provided with the Hub Cap system.

Construction of a backscatter over-the-horizon (OTH-B) radar for the detection of aircraft, ballistic missiles and ships was first revealed in 1974. Code name for the project is Jindalee. An experimental narrow beam Jindalee system, operated from a site near Alice Springs, indicated that the future surveillance of the Australian coast and offshore regions could be undertaken by this technique. As a result of these tests a larger and more powerful version, with greater transmitter power and a larger receiving antenna, was constructed and produced highly successful results. It has now been confirmed that a network of three, and possibly four, Jindalee OTH radars will be constructed at a cost of some US$400 million. Studies are currently in progress on their precise location and, in addition to the Alice Springs station, other sites are being investigated in the north and north-west of Queensland. Another site will be in Western Australia and a fourth may be constructed in the Northern Territory. In September 1988 it was announced that the prime contractors for development of the first operational installation would consist of Amalgamated Wireless (Australasia) PTY Ltd, Broken Hill Proprietary Co and Telecom.

The Royal Australian Air Force is equipped with F-111C long range attack aircraft which have recently been upgraded with the Pave Tack target acquisition and tracking system. The Mirage III strike/interceptor force has been replaced by 75 F/A-18s. For SAM applications the Army operates Rapiers equipped with Blindfire radar, and manportable Redeye which is being replaced with the Bofors RBS 70.

AUSTRIA

In the mid-1970s Austria commenced the planning of an integrated civil/military air surveillance system. The military part of the system was given the project name of Goldhaube, and both military and civil parts are fully operational. The Goldhaube system consists of six medium-range 3D fixed radar stations, each equipped with SSR interrogators for use in the ATC role. Three of the radars are military and three civil, although all are used for military air surveillance as well as ATC purposes. The stations are at Kolomannsberg, Steinmandl, Speikkogel, Koralpe, Feichtberg and Buschberg. Two mobile radars were also acquired and feed into the overall network. These mobile systems can also operate autonomously and each is fully equipped with its own processing and display subsystem in an operations shelter. The radar data is transmitted via narrow-band data links to an Air Defence Operations Centre and an Air Traffic Control Centre.

The six fixed radar stations are Selenia RAT-31S systems and the two mobile stations consist of the Selenia MRCS-403 which incorporates the RAT-31S as the basic radar. The main characteristics of the RAT-31S system are simultaneous range, azimuth and elevation measurements of targets at all altitudes, good ECCM performance, and high resistance to ground/weather clutter.

The system produces an air situation picture which is transmitted back to the superior command centres via a narrow-band data link, together with functions such as automatic track initiation, automatic tracking, automatic and/or manual height measurement and automatic track reporting. The system can process three-dimensional low- and medium-altitude air situations, and is also able to perform autonomous control functions such as identification, interceptor control and missile control (although at present Austria has no SAMs).

The operations shelter contains a dual computer, three display consoles, a communications control unit, and ground-to-air facilities. The computer is integrated locally with the three-dimensional surveillance radar, and for remote IFF/SSR inputs the system is equipped with a data link interface for receiving plots. The computer-processed information is fed to the display subsystem as synthetic/alert track information and to remote centres as track information via a data link.

There is no Austrian air force as such, since all aircraft are part of the Army. In line with the Austrian neutral stance, there have been no fighter/interceptor aircraft in the past: only types mainly devoted to army support and reconnaissance. However, the Army is now taking delivery of a number of refurbished J-35D Draken aircraft.

The first Austrian site to be equipped with Selenia's MRCS-403/RAT-31S air defence radar

Internal view of a Selenia MRCS-403 system operational shelter supplied to the Austrian MoD

BRAZIL

Brazil is in the late stages of the development of an integrated civil/military airspace surveillance and control system which will be the culmination of a series of systems known as DACTA I, II and III. These represent stages of evolution of the complete system and comprise a vast radar and operations centre network covering most of the Brazilian airspace, with Thomson-CSF in partnership with Brazilian industry. The complete system is under the control of CISCEA (Commissao de Implantacao do Sistema de Controle do Espaco Aereo). DACTA I was initiated in 1972 covering the central part of Brazil. This led to a series of phased extensions and updating programmes (DACTA II, DACTA III and Amazonia) to expand the coverage and to modernise the original DACTA I at a later stage.

DACTA I uses the Thomson-CSF LP-23M long-range surveillance radars and RS 870 SSRs, supplying data to the Brasilia Regional control centre which provides radar control over the Rio/São Paulo/Brasilia triangle. The DACTA II phase relates to the introduction of TRS-2230 3D radars and more RS 870s to provide coverage and control over military and civil traffic in the southern part of the country from Curtiba centre. The completion of these two phases gives unbroken coverage of about four million square kilometres. DACTA III will extend this coverage over the north-eastern region with a new regional centre at Recife. Two-dimensional primary radars with SSR are used in this phase of the programme. In total the DACTA II and III phases entail the supply of a large number of long-range 3D radars, four approach radars, and operations centres equipped with 20 to 30 consoles each. The final stage of the project is the implementation of the Amazonia phase which includes the provision of new surveillance radars and two new autonomous regional centres at Manaus and Belem.

Concurrent and interconnected with the project are numerous other radars (civil and military) which have been ordered and installed during recent years. Among such items are a number of Selenia RAT-31 3D surveillance systems, and various airfield surveillance and terminal area radars of French and Italian manufacture. A number of French height-finding radars were installed during the earlier years of DACTA I and it is likely that a significant proportion of these are still operational. At the Brasilia control centre, target data from search, height finder and SSR sensors are received via microwave links and processed by two automatic data processing systems. The computer programming is fully integrated and its functions include tracking of military and civil aircraft, interception for air defence, and flight plan processing for ATC purposes. The centre consists of separate operations rooms for ATC and for air defence, and there is an automatic switching centre for message management and communications.

It is understood that both the DACTA I and DACTA II phases have now been completed, and work on the upgrading of DACTA I and construction and installation of DACTA III is well under way. These phases involve replacement of some of the original radars: for example the LP-23M and Volex 3D equipments are being replaced by TRS-2230 systems. The number of these latter systems being supplied during the DACTA III phase is uncertain but is at least 12. The original LP-23M and Volex radars could be used elsewhere such as the regional control centres at Manaus and Belem in the Amazonia phase of the programme. Completion of the Amazonia phase and implementation of the full five-centre system is estimated to take several more years, although by the end of the 1988 radar coverage extended over the centre, south and north-east of Brazil, as well as part of Amazonia.

Technology transfers have been such that Brazilian industry is a full partner in the project. The consoles, totalling more than 100, the secondary and approach radars, and the telecommunications and launching aids facilities were manufactured in Brazil with Thomson-CSF partnership. Brazilian contractors involved in the project include ESCA (Engenharia de Sistemas de Controle e Automatacao) SA, ELEBRA Controles SA, and Tecnasa Eletronica Profissional SA.

The Brazilian President manages the country's national security with the help of a National Security Council and the respective Service chiefs. There is no overall ministry responsible for defence matters. The strike/interceptor force of the Brazilian Air Force consists mainly of Northrop F-5E aircraft and Mirage IIIEBR, and it has been reported that Brazil is acquiring more of these types. Eighty eight AMX fighters have been ordered and the first of these are due for delivery in the Spring of 1989. In addition Brazil operates a large COIN aircraft group with over 100 aircraft of various types. For SAM purposes, the Army deploys four Roland systems. The Brazilian Army is currently undergoing a five-year modernisation programme in deployment and equipment which is designed to last until 1992.

A comprehensive radio, telephone and microwave link system co-ordinates the extensive radar and communications network needed for Brazilian ATC/air defence control purposes

TRS-2230 three-dimensional surveillance radars and RS 870 SSRs like this will cover the entire southern Brazilian airspace when the Siscea ATC/air defence network is completed

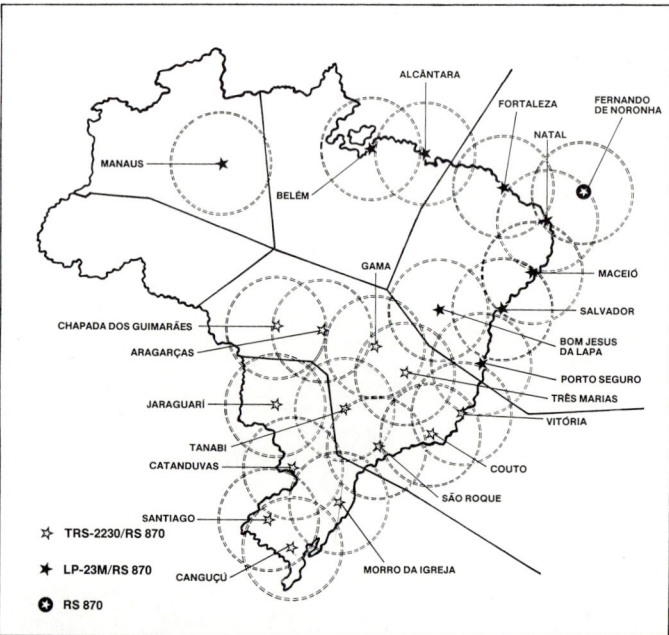

Map showing the full extent of the Brazilian integrated air defence/ATC radar network when the Siscea programme is completed. The six air defence zones, with headquarters at Belem, Recife, Rio de Janeiro, São Paulo, Porto Alegre and Brasilia, are served mostly by LP-23 M surveillance radars in the north and TRS-2230 3D radars in the south of the country

CANADA

The air defence of Canada is inextricably tied in with that of the United States, and the 1985 North American Air Defence Modernization (NAADM) accord between the two countries underlines the joint requirements. After the Canadian national elections in November 1988 the two countries have drawn even closer economically by a free trade agreement which will eventually abolish import and export controls between them.

A white paper produced in June 1987, entitled *Challenge and Commitment,* outlined Canadian defence policy for the rest of the century and emphasised the basic tenet that the country's defence policy 'will continue to be based on a strategy of collective security provided by the North Atlantic Treaty Organisation, including the continental defence partnership with the United States. Canadian forces are committed to the direct defence of Canada, the collective defence of North America, and to peacekeeping.'

The basic NAADM project consists of: a new North Warning System (NWS) to replace the elderly DEW line, including new radar sites in Canada; the OTH-B sites in the USA; and the use of USAF AWACS aircraft. This latter accord included the setting up of dispersed operating bases for the E-3s, and also for the provision of forward operating locations for interceptor and tanker aircraft when "in the judgement of the Canadian government the international situation so warranted." The NAADM programme is funded jointly by the United States and Canada.

The new NWS radars are being positioned in Alaska, North Canada and down the Labrador coast, and consist of both long-range AN/FPS-117 and short-range gap-filler AN/FPS-124 surveillance systems. Installation of the former was completed in December 1988. Details of the system and its present status are contained in the relevant entry under the United States. Canada is responsible for the project management, system integration, new facility design and construction, operation and maintenance of the system in Canada, and is also supplying the complex communications network of NWS. In Canada, CANAC/Microtel has been selected to co-ordinate the project.

Canada is also procuring a new low level air defence (LLAD) system for the 1990s, the cost of which is likely to exceed C$1 billion. The project is a most ambitious plan to equip the Canadian armed forces with the Martin-Marietta/Oerlikon developed ADATS, the Contraves Skyguard fire control system, and the Oerlikon GDF-005 twin barrel 35 mm anti-aircraft gun. Initial deliveries have commenced and are spread over the next two or three years. The LLAD system is scheduled to be fully operational by 1991.

Canada is most unusual in that it is completely unified with no distinct services as such. The strike/interceptor part of the air force segment consists of CF-18 aircraft, of which three squadrons are based in West Germany as part of the NATO force. A total of 138 CF-18s were ordered and nearly all of these have been delivered, equipped with AIM-7 Sparrow air-to-air missiles.

CARIBBEAN AREA

To fill a gap in the air defence long-range surveillance radar coverage, the USAF is developing a radar network in the Caribbean basin to provide an enhanced capability to US Atlantic and Southern commands. Under Project 3159 (Caribbean Basin Radar Network) the USAF plans to erect the radars at various undisclosed locations. Eight sites have been planned. The USAF is buying the systems and operating them, and will share data with the host countries. Bids were requested for the radar systems and the Westinghouse AN/TPS-70 was selected. The first system has been installed in Panama and is believed to be operational. No information regarding the time scale of the other seven stations has been released.

CHINA, PEOPLE'S REPUBLIC

The armed forces of the People's Republic of China are nominally under the control of a National Defence Council of approximately 100 members, but authority is really invested in the Communist Party Central Committee, with operational direction provided by its military commission. A separate Defence Command is responsible for all aspects of air defence.

No details of Chinese air defence systems have been released but there are some known statistics regarding their size. Until comparatively recently the Chinese were reported to have some 100 surface-to-air missile units in service and about 16 000 AA guns of various types. The Chinese Air Force operates over 6000 aircraft, of which about 4000 are interceptors (mainly of marginal effectiveness). Associated with these aircraft are about 1500 air defence radars, but little is known of the detailed employment of these systems other than that the network provides airspace surveillance and control, and an early warning system for the detection of hostile missiles. Most of these radars are Soviet systems originally built under licence, or more recent developments of these equipments.

The most recent information, however, suggests that the country's defences are being substantially, albeit slowly, modernised. New radars are being designed and improved versions of the SA-2 Guideline missiles, which the Chinese acquired originally from the Soviet Union, are being produced as the HQ-2B/J. Despite this, the overall air defence network appears to be subject to major weaknesses, such as an outmoded command, control and communications system. Certainly, China lacks a centralised and computerised air defence system, and responsibility for airspace control appears to rest largely with local area headquarters.

In the mid-1980s it was reported that a French company had supplied six long-range radars, three terminal area radars, and control centres for airspace management of the Shanghai/Beijing region. There has been no official confirmation of this but, if true, it could well mean that China is manufacturing Western-type radars under licence, as well as being engaged in an indigenous surveillance radar development programme. Certainly at least one very large phased-array has been constructed in the west of the country, presumably as part of the missile warning system. China has also stated that an OTH radar programme was being implemented.

In proportion to size and population the defence budget of the People's Republic of China is very small. The territory is so vast that an integrated defence system will take many years, and an immense sum of money, to implement. Implementation of new air defence systems will undoubtedly be concentrated in the major areas of population and to safeguard military targets. The general impression, however, is that spending on the more sophisticated items of defence is a relatively low priority to more urgent economic reforms, and that China is content for the moment to rely upon its large conventional forces for protection.

DENMARK

As part of NATO, Denmark's air defence system is fully integrated into NADGE (see later). As part of the NATO updating programme, two Marconi Martello S723 three-dimensional radars have been installed in Denmark. In addition Denmark and Norway, funded by NATO, have awarded contracts to Hughes Aircraft Company for an automated command and control information system for NATO's northern Europe command. The system is due to be operational in 1989.

To improve detection of low-flying intruders a Coastal Radar Integration System (CRIS) was instituted in 1984 to link data from the Danish radars surveying the Kattegat and Western Baltic. In mid-1986 THORN-EMI Electronics of the UK installed this coastal radar integration system in Denmark to feed information from the coastal radar network to the Danish elements of NADGE.

The Royal Danish Air Force operates a number of fighter/ground attack squadrons equipped with F-16A/B aircraft and a fighter/reconnaissance squadron with RF-35 Drakens. An Air Defence Group operates a SAM battalion equipped with Improved HAWK batteries.

EGYPT

Egypt has four armed services, one of which is dedicated to air defence. As a result of a somewhat chequered background in dealing for some years with the Soviet Union and later with various nations, Egypt's inventory comprises an extremely varied selection of hardware.

During the early 1980s four General Electric AN/TPS-59 and eight Westinghouse AN/TPS-63 air defence radars were delivered at a cost of some $154 million. In addition 12 AN/TSQ-143 mobile automated operations centres, which interface with the radars, were provided for operation of HAWK missile batteries. Each operations centre has four OJ-560 display consoles, two main computers, 12 high-density microprocessors and an audio/video recorder that files all track data, displays and operator actions. These are now fully operational. In mid-1986 Egypt signed an agreement with Westinghouse to co-produce the AN/TPS-63 system. The deal was stated to be worth over $190 million over seven years and covers the joint production of 34 radars by Westinghouse and Benha Electronics of Egypt, the first of which was completed in December 1988.

In December 1983 Hughes Aircraft Company received a $210 million contract for the first phase of a new Egyptian national air defence system which was intended to integrate all existing radars, missiles batteries, air bases and command centres into an automated command and control system. In late 1987 on-site testing of this phase began and subsequently Hughes has received another $159 million to further expand the system. This includes additional command and control sites, operational software, control displays, large screen displays and computers.

The complete network will enable detection and monitoring of unidentified aircraft approaching the borders and enables fast initiation of defensive measures, including the use of fighter interceptors and missile batteries. Egypt has also taken delivery of five Grumman E-2C Hawkeye early warning aircraft equipped with AN/APS-138 series radars, which form part of the network to detect low level aircraft at long range.

With the move away from Soviet equipment to Western systems (largely American and French), Egypt operates a mixture of both East and West. The split air defence system means that the Air Defence Command operates a mixture of MiG-21MFs and F-16s, while the Air Force operates fighter/ground attack F-4Es, Mirage Vs, Mirage 2000s, Su-7s and Shenyang F-6s (Chinese version of the MiG-19). SAMs include a large number of SA-2, SA-3, SA-6, Crotale, Improved HAWK, and Skyguard/Sparrow batteries. These last missile systems are made under licence in Egypt and are known as Amoun. The Army uses the SAM-7 Sakr Eye manportable missile.

FINLAND

Late in 1988 Finland selected a modified copy of the French Thomson-CSF Crotale system to meet its low level air defence requirements. These will be based on a Finnish SISU XA-180 (6 × 6) APC chassis and will use the new LTV VT-1 missile, which was originally developed to meet the requirements of the US Army in the FAADS-LOS-RH competition. When delivered the system will be located at the most northerly air base at Rovaniemi, near Helsinki, and close to the Karelia base in the east.

The fighter segment of the Finnish Air Force is equipped with about 75 aircraft: J-35 Drakens and MiG-21s. Forty BAe Hawk 51 trainers are also part of the force, and no doubt these could be converted quickly to the ground attack role. SAM batteries include the SA-3, SA-7, SA-14 and SA-16.

FRANCE

France is not part of the NATO alliance although it co-operates with NATO. Since General de Gaulle took France out of the alliance in 1966, the country has had a chequered history of co-operation with NATO, although it has always been committed to the defence of Western Europe. However, during the past two years France has been extending its involvement with NATO, and although French forces will not come under the direct command of the NATO supreme commander in the event of hostilities, they will obviously co-operate to the fullest extent. This, however, does mean that much of the French air defence organisation is set up on national grounds as is evidenced in the STRIDA network outlined below, although STRIDA is interlocked with both NADGE and Britain's UKADGE.

The Strategic Air Command of the French Air Force is the nuclear strike force, and is designed to carry the ASMP tactical nuclear stand-off missile. The force will eventually consist of 18 Mirage IVs, 75 Mirage 2000Ns, plus 24 Super Etendards from the Naval Aviation. The Air Defence Command has approximately 300 Mirage F-1C, 2000C and IIIC interceptor aircraft operating within the STRIDA air defence system. The Tactical Command operates a variety of Mirage aircraft and about 45 Jaguars. Over 300 Mirage 2000s have been ordered to replace the older aircraft. France has also ordered four Boeing E-3 AWACS aircraft. The first of these will be delivered in 1991 and the complete fleet will eventually be phased in with the STRIDA network and the overall NATO command.

STRIDA

STRIDA (Système de Traitement et de Representation des Informations de Défense Aérienne) is the French national air defence data handling system. It consists of a network of stations covering French territory, with the following main functions:
(a) detection and identification of aircraft in French airspace
(b) threat evaluation and dissemination of early warnings. The air situation is centralised and synthesised in the air defence operational centre (ADOC)
(c) updating of active means (aircraft and missiles) status in every sector operational centre (SOC)
(d) weapons selection, engagement and automatic interceptor guidance
(e) aircraft recovery to air bases
(f) control of military operational and training flights
(g) co-ordination with the air traffic control system to ensure identification and spacing of operational military flights with general air traffic
(h) progressive integration of the information reported by air base radars for improving the low altitude coverage.

STRIDA consists of different types of operational centres (ADOC, SOC/CRC, CRC, ARP) which exchange digital messages by a special telecommunication network, the Air 70, associated with electronic switching stations. At ARP and CRC levels, signals coming from 2-D and 3D long-range radars and height finding systems are used to provide the labelled air instructions needed at SOC/CRC and ADOC levels. All information and orders to be exchanged between these different centres for command and control purposes are transmitted through the Air 70 network.

The STRIDA network is connected to NADGE, to the 412L network and to Combat Grande to provide complete coverage of western continental Europe. It is also connected to the STRAPP (STRIDA-APPROCHE) system which integrates recovery radars, and to the French ATC CAUTRA system for co-ordination of military and civil air traffic control.

The data handling equipment of a typical latest generation CDCS station consists mainly of:
(a) an EMIR radar data extractor using a programmed extraction concept
(b) a high power processing system using IBM 370 series computers
(c) a display subsystem including from 20 to 30 operational positions
In some centres special equipment is found; in the air defence operational centre a large screen display, and a piloted aircraft simulator generates a video signal corresponding to up to 12 aircraft in the centre of intercept controller training. This signal can be mixed with the live video of the radar for simulation.

Each operator position or console designed for one operator and his assistant is composed of:
(a) a plan view display for presenting raw video (local radar raw video) and data generated by the processing system (synthetic view of the air picture - mainly tracks). A 40 cm diameter screen is used
(b) one or several monochrome or colour screen(s) (diagonal from 13 to 35 cm and capacity up to 4000 characters) for presenting detailed information on certain subjects (tracks, intercepts) or data received in alphanumeric form (operational status, flight schedules)

A STRIDA air defence reporting centre and communications node co-located with a 3D radar in the Alps

(c) several keyboards and a rolling ball (or joystick) for selecting the data presented and entering data and functions
(d) control keyboards and panels for communications (radio, telephone, interphone) and secondary radar.

Status: The research and development programme for STRIDA began in 1956 under the responsibility of Services Techniques des Télécommunications et d'Equipments aeronautiques (STTE). The first stations were fitted with specialised IBM/CAPAC real-time computers and Sintra VISU II display subsystem. They became operational in 1963. Since that date there has been a continuous programme of improvements and upgrading for both hardware and software during the implementation of the whole military programme, every new centre having to be interoperable with the others. Medium and high altitude coverage is achieved.

The low level coverage with STRAPP system is now near completion.

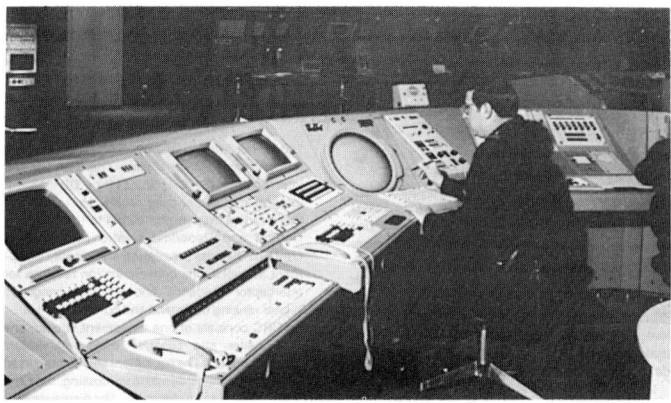

VISU IV consoles produced by the Sintra subsidiary of Thomson-CSF for the STRIDA air defence system

The next step entails the extension of low level coverage of the system by the integration of tactical operations radars and SAM activities.

In 1980 Sintra was chosen to supply the STAC (Système de Traitement Automatique en Caliue) and to design the AL 73 (Adaptateur de Liaisons 73) for tactical radar processing and HAWK activities management at each mobile tactical and SAM control centre. Data to and from STRIDA main centres are automatically processed and transmitted by the STAC and the AL 73 system.

Contractor: Thomson-CSF, Division Systèmes Défense et Contrôle, 18 Avenue du Marechal Juin, 9253 Meudon-la-Forêt Cedex, France (following the merger of Sintra with the Thomson Group).

GERMANY, WEST

As part of NATO, the forces of West Germany are fully committed to the alliance, and the country is covered by the air defence networks of NADGE and GEADGE (see below). Since the defence forces were re-activated during the period of occupation after the Second World War they can only operate as a part of the overall NATO force. The West German Air Force has undergone a major re-equipment programme which was to replace the obsolete F-104 fighter/ground attack aircraft with Panavia Tornados. Most of the latter have now been delivered. The force also operates about 175 close-support Alpha Jet aircraft. Air defence equipment includes three air defence regiments with Roland II SAMs, Patriot SAMS, Improved HAWK and manportable Redeye Stinger systems.

GEADGE

GEADGE is the acronym for German Air Defence Environment and is the network for the southern part of West Germany. The system, for which Hughes Aircraft Company was nominated the prime contractor in 1979 under a contract worth more than $150 million, replaced an older radar network operated by the West German Air Force. The system integrates new and existing long-range surveillance radars into a single network based on four centralised command centres, and is now fully operational. It embraces manned and unmanned fixed and transportable radar systems.

GEADGE now receives data directly from E-3A AWACS early warning aircraft. The southern part of West Germany was not included in the original NADGE system but GEADGE fills the gap left in that system and interconnects directly with it. In addition to fixed and transportable gap-filler radars, the new system uses two of four new permanently located radars known by the manufacturer's name of HADR (Hughes Air Defence Radar). This is an advanced 3D, multi-role system which will automatically detect, classify and report targets intruding into its coverage.

In the GEADGE system, Hughes has also supplied HMP-116 minicomputers, H-5118M central computers, and HMD-22 display and control consoles, as well as being responsible for software, installation and integration. The HMD-22 consoles are built under licence by AEG and the communications equipment for the system has been supplied by Tekade.

More recently, the GE AN/FPS-117 long range radar has been selected for NATO use. A contract for three systems has been awarded by West Germany for NATO infrastructure application.

TLVS System

TLVS (Taktisches Luftverteidigungssystem) is a conceptual study for a new medium-range tactical air defence system, with anti-tactical missile capabilities, designed to be in operation from the year 2000 onwards as a successor to the HAWK system. It is being developed in a joint programme by MBB, AEG and Siemens as a SAM system incorporating radar, communications network, and a comprehensive command and control station. It is designed for all-sector, all-weather defence against a variety of airborne threats, including tactical ballistic missiles, and can operate in dense ECCM environments with a high simultaneous fire power.

The multi-funtion radar is intended to detect low-flying objects with small radar cross-section, as well as high-diving missiles. The TLVS SAMs will be fitted with an active seeker head to provide for multiple simultaneous engagement of several airborne targets. Mid-course guidance will be provided by the radar. A 'fire and forget' capability will exist for close-range targets.

The command and control will incorporate sophisticated weapon system processors to enable rapid decisions to be made in complex situations. The provision of artificial intelligence methods is being investigated. The communications network will be jam-proof, and will be backed up by alternative fibre-optic links.

A West German captain monitors the air traffic over the southern portion of West Germany at a GEADGE site

TMLD Low Level Reporting and Control System

The air defence of West Germany is intimately bound up with the overall NATO air defence ground environment (NADGE) system of radars, communications and data processing and control centres, and to varying degrees with systems employed by allied nations present in Europe, such as the American 407L air weapons control system. However, because of limitations in the low level cover of parts of the former systems and because the AFCENT sector of the Central European NATO area is particularly subject to the threat of low flying surprise attacks, the Luftwaffe has set up the TMLD (Tiefflieger-Melde-und-Leitdienst) low level reporting service, additional and supplementary to the other radars.

This is part of the combat operational system of air defence and is designed particularly for the monitoring of low level airspace. The TMLD radars are located in the area near the border, the individual sites being chosen to ensure continuous surveillance. When the radar detects a target, the information is converted into data messages and immediately transmitted to the low level reporting centres, TMLZ (Tiefflieger-Melde-und-Leitzentralen), and on to the user. The whole TMLD is completely mobile so that changing tactical and operational circumstances can be accommodated. The main tasks of the TMLD are:

(1) monitoring the lower levels of airspace in selected areas
(2) processing the low level air situation in the control centres (TMLZ) and passing the information on to the air defence control centres (eg NADGE, GEADGE)
(3) preliminary warning and target forecasting for HAWK SAM units
(4) control of air operations.

The TMLD units are combined into two sections, and are employed in the 2 ATAF and 4 ATAF areas. In each case they come under the command of the commander of a Type B signals regiment. It is planned to assign them as a NATO command force. The main elements of such a unit are:

(1) a radar crew to operate the radar equipment
(2) an evaluation crew to man the control centre
(3) a radio relay crew for setting up communications links
(4) a maintenance crew for the maintenance and repair of equipment.

In peacetime the TMLD mainly limits its activities to monitoring the area in the immediate vicinity of the border, in a quasi-static role.

At other times, however, monitoring of airspace must be extended to a greater area, making use of the system's mobility and flexibility. In this it will be supported by the Army's AAD command and control systems, which will be employed in monitoring the airspace over the combat area.

The principal hardware used in the TMLD system comprises: MPDR 30/1 mobile pulse Doppler radars; TM control centre; CRC TM display unit; radio link set. The radar consists of two 5-ton trucks, each with a 1½-ton trailer containing a generator, with one truck serving as an equipment carrier and the other as the antenna carrier. In the TM centre all the information provided by all the radar equipment within one sector is processed and displayed. Linked users include the NADGE/GEADGE air defence control centres and Improved HAWK SAM batteries.

Operation

Information on air targets supplied by the TM radar is converted into messages for transmission to the TMLZ. The data transmitted contains the positions of the target as X/Y co-ordinates and the target identification. Two operating modes are planned for the preparation of this information: automatic, and semi-automatic.

Automatic Operation: this is regarded as the normal mode for peace time. Targets detected are automatically evaluated on the basis of whether or not they emit a valid IFF/SIF code, and they are reported accordingly. In addition, the operator in the radar truck (acting on instructions from the control centre) can insert further symbols manually in order to give prominence to certain targets of particular significance.

Semi-automatic Operation: this mode is of special importance when automatic operation with the radar signal processor is not possible for technical or tactical reasons. In this mode the operator can mark targets identified on the radar display with the aid of a rolling ball, using symbols that he can superimpose on the target blip. Transmission of targets to the TMLZ or the user is again performed automatically. For this purpose various types of symbol are available, to each of which a particular meaning is assigned to assist the responsible air defence officer in reaching decisions.

Status: The system has been fully operational since 1977.

Manufacturer: Siemens AG, Radio and Radar Systems Division, Landshuterstr.26, 8044 Unterschleissheim, Federal Republic of Germany.

A Siemens MPDR-30 radar of West Germany's low level air defence system deployed in the field

ICELAND

The first phase of an interim air defence system which began operations in July 1988 has closed the gap that existed between defence systems in the United Kingdom and European NATO countries with the Joint Surveillance System in the USA and Canada. The system incorporates the two Bendix AN/FPS-93 ground radars used in the earlier system, positioned at Rockville and Stokksnes in the south-west and south-east corners of Iceland respectively, to detect and monitor all traffic in the area around Iceland, and also has extended surveillance coverage through links with US and NATO E-3 AWACS early warning aircraft. Two northern radar/communications sites at the north-east and north-west corners were scheduled to be operational by the end of 1988. Operated by the USAF, the new system ties in directly with the combined US/Canadian facilities at Griffiss AFB, New York and North Bay, Ontario. It replaces a manual system which was more than 30 years old.

The interim system, provided by Hughes Aircraft Company, incorporates two computer networks, one of which acts as a 'hot' spare and can be switched in to take over from the primary. Twelve operator consoles, each having a 19-inch monochrome CRT and a smaller screen for data displays, are provided. Digitised radar tracking data from the AN/FPS-93 systems plus information from heightfinding radars is presented. Another part of the interim system, the Iceland Command and Control Enhancement (ICCE), is due to become operational in mid-1989 and will improve links between ground command and control and the AWACS aircraft.

A new NATO-Icelandic air defence system (IADS) is planned for the 1990s and will include four GE AN/FPS-117 radars, which will be installed at sites on the four corners of the island by 1990, at Rockville, Bolungarvik, Gunnolfvikursfjall and Hofn. The two northern radars are being installed and the two southern ones will replace the older radars at the southern sites. A team has been formed by Lockheed Missiles and Space Company and Standard Elektrik Lorenz AG (SEL) of West Germany to compete for elements of this new generation air defence system. As a prime contractor Lockheed would integrate the C[3] system and take responsibility for the automated air defence funtions, including application software using ADA programming language. SEL would serve as the major sub-contractor and would provide the communications subsystems. A consortium of Boeing Aerospace, Thompson-CSF and Plessey has announced that it will compete in the NATO-funded programme to develop improved C[3] capabilities. Hughes is also understood to be bidding for this system. A contract award by the USAF Electronics Systems Division is likely to be made in mid-1989.

Iceland itself is a member country of NATO and as such has NATO airfields and radar sites on its territory. It does not, however, have any defence forces of its own other than a Coast Guard and a limited number of paramilitary security personnel.

INDIA

The existing Indian IADGES (Indian Air Defence Ground Environment System) is understood to consist of a miscellaneous assembly of radars of varying origin, reflecting India's changing international associations and allegiances over the past 40 years. This includes British, French, Soviet and Italian systems, and possibly other types. In the 1970s the system was installed along the Indian northern and western borders (with China and Pakistan), and a communications system for use in the air defence of a limited area along the northern border built with American equipment. In addition, at least 24 long- and medium-range radars of Italian design were installed, ostensibly for ATC purposes, but clearly so that data from some could be used for air defence. Most of these radars are D-band equipments, eight being the ATCR-2 and the remainder ATCR-4Ts. Licensed production of the latter was carried out in India by Bharat Electronics.

In 1984 Thomson-CSF announced a contract to supply four TRS-2215D three-dimensional radar stations to India, and the construction under licence of at least five more. India is now developing an indigenous air defence radar industry largely based on co-operation between Thomson-CSF and Bharat Electronics.

India has very considerable numbers of Soviet fighter aircraft and missile systems. The latter includes SA-2, SA-3, SA-6, SA-7, SA-8, SA-9, SA-11 and Tigercat surface-to-air missiles. These missiles will almost certainly rely upon the appropriate Soviet and Western fire control radar, such as Long Blow, Straight Flush etc, for guidance.

A very ambitious programme, aimed at self-sufficiency in missile design and production, has been initiated by India and the first results are now becoming evident. In the surface-to-air field two weapons are in development: the Akash which is a long-range SAM, and the Trishul which is a short-range low level SAM system for the army. The latter is stated to be at an advanced stage of user trials.

The Indian Air Force is divided into a number of regional commands to cover a vast country of some three and a quarter million square kilometres. The battle order reflects the split loyalties of India between east and west, and the air defence squadrons consist of MiG-21s, MiG-23s and MiG-29s. The fighter/ground attack force includes Mirage 2000s, Jaguars, MiG-23s and MiG-27s. Large numbers of aircraft are still on order.

ISRAEL

A computer-controlled air defence system has been installed in Israel but no official details have been made public, and indeed no official confirmation of its existence has ever been made. It appears to be generally accepted that Hughes Aircraft Company was awarded the contract after completing a study for the new system, and it is also understood that the system is based on main control centres situated near Tel Aviv and in the Western Negev. There are probably subsidiary centres elsewhere, and the existence of a tactical operations centre with a PPI display of the entire Israeli airspace for viewing by the Cabinet has been claimed. The complete system has been in operation since the mid-1970s.

It is believed that there are many similarities with the USAF 407L tactical command and control system, and it has been reported that Hughes 4118 digital computers, as used in the 407L, are employed for data processing. Sensors are understood to include two Westinghouse AN/TPS-43 3D radars and several AN/FPS-100 systems. In addition there are almost certainly other radars of UK, French and Israeli design which have been incorporated in the system. Elta Electronics manufactures a range of mobile and static surveillance radars based on the original EL/M-2205 design, and it would appear very probable than some of these are incorporated in the system, perhaps as replacements for the AN/FPS-100 equipments which would now be rather obsolete. For the airborne element, four Grumman E-2C early warning aircraft were delivered during the late 1970s, each equipped with AN/APS-125 radar. This may have been updated with the later variant, the AN/APS-138. Grumman also caried out a contract to make the E-2C data link compatible with the Israeli air defence network to enable the exchange of data between ground and air sensors, as well as integrating the AEW element into the overall system.

In the early 1980s a major communications control system for air defence sites, known as the MCCS-800, was supplied by Electronics Corporation of Israel in co-operation with Elbit Computers. Alternatively known as ACCESS, the system provides each one of a large group of

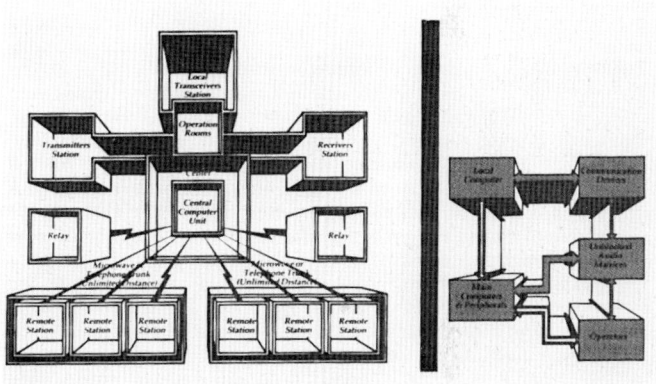

System architecture (left) and block diagram (right) of the ACCESS system

operators with fast and reliable access to up to 1000 communication devices located in the control centre vicinity or in remote communications stations.

The Israeli defence forces are unified, with their cost largely underwritten by the United States which contributes a large amount of foreign aid to the country, either in the form of equipment or in financial terms. The air force segment operates mainly American built aircraft with F-15s, F-16s, and F-4s, and more F-16s on order. Also part of the interceptor force are some of the 100 plus Kfirs. With the cancellation of the Lavi aircraft on economic grounds it would appear likely that a substantial number of additional F-16s are likely to be ordered. For ground air defence some 15 SAM battalions with Improved HAWK are deployed.

INDONESIA

Considerable modernisation of Indonesia's air defence network has taken place during the 1980s. Thomson-CSF of France has been heavily involved in this updating and originally supplied two TRS-2215D radar systems, followed by 12 TRS-2230Ds. By the mid-1980s Thomson-CSF had provided four centres for air traffic control purposes, and had installed several TA 10 or TA 23 primary radars, RS 770 or RS 870 secondary radars and 10 regional control centres. These systems could also be used to augment the air defence network. More recently Indonesia decided to update its air defence for the central area, and instituted a competition to which several companies responded. No further information has been released on this subject, although Thomson-CSF has recently announced its involvement in a new integrated airspace coverage system in co-operation with local industry. Thomson-CSF has also installed TRS-34005 maritime surveillance radars on the Strait of Malacca.

The Indonesian Air Force is relatively small in numbers. It operates two attack squadrons with A-4s and an interceptor squadron with F-5Es. On order are some F-16s.

ITALY

The Italian national air defence system forms part of the NATO NADGE (see separate entry). The most recent development in that area has been the acquisition of two Hughes HR-3000 3D radars which were ordered by NATO to upgrade the cover in the southern flank of NATO. Much of the national air defence network is based on the Selenia RAT-31S radar which is operated by the Italian Air Force, both in its transportable role and in a mobile tactical form as part of the MRCS-403 command and control centre. A version of the RAT-31S, known as the RAT-31SL, has been developed by Selenia in co-operation with Sperry (now part of the Unisys Corporation), and 10 of these systems were due to be ordered by the Italian Air Force at the end of 1988.

A new integrated command, control and telecommunications system, known as CATRIN, is in the early development stage with operational deployment scheduled for 1993. It is primarily for battlefield use and is part of an overall modernisation programme for the Italian Army, from helicopter gunships to C^3I systems. The system consists of three subsystems: a telecommunications network (SOTRIN), a surveillance/ground target acquisition and fire control system (SARAO), and a low/very low air surveillance subsystem with tactical command and control of AA guns and aircraft (SOATCC).

The SOATCC subsystem comprises a radar network, a command and control system and an information/logistics network. The radar network uses both 3D and 2D sensors to identify low and very low flying targets. Using this data the command and control centres evaluate the threat, co-ordinate air defence, and control the airspace and missions of friendly aircraft.

The CATRIN project began in June 1987 when the Italian MoD commissioned a consortium of companies to produce the system. The consortium consists of Aeritalia, Agusta, Italtel, Marconi, Italiana, Selenia and Telettra. A six-year programme is envisaged, with pre-prototype testing scheduled to take place in 1990.

As a member country of NATO, Italian forces form a substantial part of NATO's Southern Command. The Italian Air Force has been re-equipping with Tornados, although it still has a large number of F-104S Starfighters in service. For close air support a substantial number of MB-339s are being procured, and deliveries of the joint Italian/Brazilian AMX fighter aircraft have now commenced. The main SAM batteries are equipped with Improved HAWK with procurement, by licensed production, of the Mistral and Patriot.

JAPAN

The Japanese air defence system, BADGE (Base Air Defence Ground Environment) is a computerised air defence system which provides umbrella protection against air attack on the Japanese mainland. The system consists of radars which will automatically detect, track and identify airborne targets over Japan and the surrounding ocean, computers to process data and furnish information on weapon availability, and interception data. The system was built largely in Japan for the Japanese Self Defense Force, with Hughes Aircraft Company of the USA as the prime contractor, and became operational in 1969. Much of the original equipment and system design was supplied by Hughes but most of the subsequent manufacture has been indigenous.

BADGE sites extend from the northernmost tip of Hokkaido to the southern extremity of Okinawa Island, and there are at least 28 fixed surveillance radar sites. Japanese airspace is divided into four air defence sectors with a direction centre for each.

In 1982 Japan initiated an extension programme known as BADGE-X which was intended to increase its coverage and also provide for the integration of the Japanese HAWK surface-to-air missile batteries with the existing defence systems. In early 1983 the NEC Corporation was selected as prime contractor to undertake this extension programme, with Hughes as a major sub-contractor for systems design, management and licensing of hardware. There were five phases of this operation, although the precise order was not known:
(1) updating and expanding BADGE to improve coverage
(2) linking BADGE to the Patriot/Improved HAWK batteries via the JAN/TSQ-51B distribution systems being built by the NEC Corporation under licence from Hughes
(3) development of an airborne early warning system
(4) further extension of BADGE to cover key areas such as Okinawa
(5) replacement of the Bendix AN/FPS-20 and GE AN/FPS-6 radars with three-dimensional systems.

Installation and construction of the extension programme commenced in 1985, with the first system installed at the HQ of the Middle Air Defense Force, and completion was scheduled for late 1988.

The BADGE system computers have all now been replaced and/or duplicated, and additional computers and peripheral equipment have been added. Older early warning and fighter radars have been replaced by modern 3D types. The equipment selected has the JASDF designation of J/FPS-2, but is also known as the F3D. It is produced by the NEC Corporation and is understood to be based on a mobile radar known as the J/TDS-100, the first example being installed in 1979. The J/FPS-2 is an electronically scanned phased array radar using mechanical rotation for azimuth scan and extensive ECCM facilities. The JASDF is believed to have at least seven of these systems in operation, plus a number of the mobile J/TDS-100 radars. It would appear that these radars are variants of the NEC NPG-880 or its mobile version, the NPM-510.

The Japanese government has also decided to purchase an over-the-horizon (OTH-B) system from the United States. Incorporation of this system into the overall OTH-B networks that may some day include sites in the Aleutian Islands and Guam would fill a gap in the Pacific area. According to Japanese sources, one of the Nansei Shoto islands will host the radar. Proposed locations within that area originally included Okinawa and Iwo Jima, but the latter has been ruled out because of its volcanic activity.

In addition to the ground-based air defence system Japan has acquired an airborne early warning force of eight E-2C aircraft, all of which are operational and feed information into the BADGE network.

The Japanese armed forces are designated as Self Defense Forces to avoid any possibility of being thought of as offensive military arms. The Japanese Self Defense Force is equipped entirely with American aircraft which consist of F-15s and F-4s for interceptor purposes. A version of the F-16, known as the FS-X, is intended to replace about 50 F-1 fighter/bomber aircraft. About 130 of the FS-X type are planned.

JORDAN

Jordan's air defence is based on F-5 and Mirage F-1 aircraft, and Improved HAWK SAMs supported by AA guns. The main command and control element is the Litton Data Systems AN/TSQ-73 air defence missile control and co-ordination centre. To augment its air defence network, Jordan tried to obtain mobile Improved HAWK batteries plus a number of F-16C or F-20 aircraft, but the request was blocked by opposition from the US Congress. Contracts have now been signed with France for 20 Mirage 2000 aircraft and with the UK for eight Tornados.

A number of radars of western origin, including some Westinghouse AN/TPS-43 equipments, are currently operational, and the Royal Jordanian Air Force has placed a contract with Marconi for new Martello 3D air defence radars. The contract also includes modernisation of existing radar facilities.

Redeye, SA-7, SA-8, SA-13 and SA-14 SAMs are in operational service, and Shorts Javelin and BAe Rapier SAMs are possibly on order. The air defence command of the Jordanian Air Force comprises F-5 and Mirage F-1 aircraft.

KOREA, NORTH

North Korea has a comprehensive air defence system which has been radically upgraded during the past three years. The number of deployed SAM battalions has been expanded to cover the entire country, and the range, quality and type of radar coverage has been increased. This has resulted from a Soviet agreement to modernise what was an obsolete system in exchange for port privileges and overflight rights. MiG-23 fighters have been supplied, and more recently SA-5 Gammon SAMs have arrived. An estimate of total SAM force indicates a total of 1200 deployed (SA-2s, SA-3s and SA-5s), with a similar number in strategic storage.

North Korea is believed to be the only country outside the USSR to have deployed the advanced Tin Shield early warning/GCI target acquisition radar system. Depending upon its location, Tin Shield can provide coverage of large parts of South Korea as well as North Korea.

Barlock A GCI systems and Fan Song A missile control radars are also in use. Early warning, target acquisition and GCI radars are deployed in large underground bunker complexes consisting of an access tunnel, control room and crew quarters, protected by steel blast-proof doors and nuclear, biological and chemical filtration systems. The radar antennas are mounted on elevators which raise them to the surface when required.

The entire country comprises a single air defence district, controlled by the Korean People's Air Force (KPAF) with its headquarters in Pyongyang. The district is divided into three sector commands, although the defence of Pyongyang itself is believed to be provided by a special subsector. Each sector command consists of an HQ, air defence direction centre, early warning radar regiment, at least one fighter division, several SAM regiments, and one AA artillery division.

KOREA, SOUTH

South Korea already possesses an air defence system which is primarily orientated along its northern border with North Korea and the coastal waters to the south-west. No details of this system have been made available.

A new overall air defence system to provide for target assignment, early warning and co-ordination of other air defence forces such as interceptors is being developed. Two variants of the Westinghouse AN/TPS-63 are currently employed, a dualised AN/TPS-65 version which combines two AN/TPS-63 radars in one system, and a dual-band version which combines the technology of the AN/TPS-43 and the AN/TPS-63.

Improved HAWK surface-to-air missiles are being supplied and the country is also procuring the related AN/TSQ-73 system for command and control. The fighter force of the South Korean Air Force includes three squadrons of F-4Ds, F-16s and F-4Es, plus 12 strike squadrons with F-5Es.

KUWAIT

The air defences of Kuwait have for some years operated Mirage F1 interceptors, A-4 Skyhawks and eight battalions of Improved HAWK surface-to-air missile systems. In mid-1988 Kuwait announced that it was negotiating with the USA for the sale of 40 F/A-18 fighters and an undisclosed number of Stinger missiles, as well as a number of Mirage 2000 aircraft. This requirement stemmed from the increased threat from the Gulf War between Iraq and Iran. Whether, in view of the peace agreement between those two countries, the requirement is still valid remains to be seen.

Kuwait has acquired a number of radar systems over the past few years, including AN/TPS-32 radars from ITT-Gilfillan. It has also been reported that one or more Plessey AR-3D radars have been supplied but this has never been confirmed. For command and control of the I-Hawk missiles two Litton AN/TSQ-73 systems were procured and have been operational for some years.

In November 1983 Thomson-CSF was awarded a contract to modernise the low-altitude defences and set up an integrated command system for the entire air defence infrastructure. Gradual implementation has involved the supply of the TRS-2230 3D radars, and in March 1985 Thomson-CSF announced a further contract for the Kuwait Air Force Air Defence command, control and communications programme to modernise the air defence network. This included a series of radar stations around the country's borders and a central command post. In addition it was announced in early 1988 that Kuwait is to operate a Westinghouse Low Altitude Surveillance System (LASS), consisting of a tethered aerostat equipped with a modified AN/TPS-63 radar with a range of about 160 nm.

During the 1987/88 period Kuwait approached various Western nations for discussions on air defence network upgrading and various suggestions were made. Arrangements have been made for data link facilities to allow Kuwait to share data obtained from Saudi Arabian E-3 AWACS aircraft, and use of the information for the direction of HAWK missile batteries. Kuwait also appears to be very interested in procuring the Amoun air defence system from Eygpt.

LIBYA

Over a period of several years companies from a number of countries, including the USA, UK, Italy and France have competed for the task of modernising the Libyan air defence network but these efforts have been thwarted by political obstacles. With the almost total lack of contact between Libya and the Western coutries, air defence of the former is understood to be based on Soviet principles, and relies upon equipment from the same source. The Libyan Air Force fighter and interceptor force consists of some 350 aircraft, two-thirds of these being MiG-21/23s with the remainder Mirage F-1/5Ds and MiG-25 Foxbats.

Libya has a separate Air Defence Command as part of the air force, with a command and control system known as SENEZH. No details are available, although it is likely that the radar network consists of a mixture of older French and Italian equipments, with the later systems being of Soviet origin. The armed forces operate a large number of Soviet surface-to-air missiles, equipped with their fire control radars, including the SA-2, SA-3, SA-5, SA-6, SA-7, SA-8, SA-9, SA-10, SA-13, as well as the French Crotale system.

MALAYSIA

With the withdrawal of the UK forces from the Far East in 1971, the Malaysian government procured three Marconi S600 mobile radar units to meet the country's immediate needs and to support the RAAF detachment of rotated F-18 aircraft through the base.

In the early 1980s Malaysia instituted the Malaysian Air Defence Ground Environment (MADGE) programme with Hughes Aircraft Company as the prime contractor. This system is now operational and provides air surveillance and identification services for civil and military aircraft in all airspace of interest to Malaysia. It uses modern data processing equipment, large screen displays, new communications and Hughes air defence radars (HADR), used in conjunction with earlier existing radars, to provide target data for the entire country. Control of radar sensors, aircraft and other air defence assets is exercised from a number of control centres.

Malaysia is known to be considering an update of its air defence capability by the acquisition of a number of assets, including AWACS aircraft, new fighters, low level air defence radars, various surface-to-air missiles and low level air defence guns, although some of these plans have had to be shelved because of budgetary restraints. Malaysia has received Congressional authority to buy 12 F-16 aircraft from the USA.

MOROCCO

A comprehensive air defence network was initiated in 1977 and is currently operational. The principal contractors were Westinghouse, Burroughs (now part of the Unisys Corporation) and Ford Aerospace under a contract assessed at about $100 million. Westinghouse provided the primary radars and integrated the entire system while Burroughs supplied large scale B-6700 computers for processing tracks, ATC data, identification and plot extraction. Ford Aerospace provided the microwave communication links.

The complete system is based on 16 AN/TPS-43 radars at early warning and coastal sites. A centralised command and control facility directs Moroccan air defence aircraft, which are Mirage F-1s. These are complemented by SA-2, SA-7 and Chaparral missiles.

NATO

The NATO Air Defence Ground Environment (NADGE) is a multi-national programme involving 14 NATO countries (as far as funding and contracts are concerned) in the updating and co-ordination of the air defence systems of 10 European members of NATO. They are Norway, Denmark, West Germany, Netherlands, Belgium, Italy, Greece, Turkey, Spain and Portugal. The British air defence network, UKADGE (see later), interfaces with NADGE. French participation is limited to use of, and contribution to, the reporting and control functions via STRIDA (see earlier), and that country's defence forces will not normally be directed against hostile targets by NATO. The members of the original six-nation consortium which evolved NADGE are Hughes Aircraft Company, USA; Marconi Radar Systems, UK; AEG Aktiengesellschaft, West Germany; Thomson-CSF, France; Selenia SpA, Italy; NV Hollandse Signaalapparaten, Netherlands. There are also numerous sub-contractors from all the participating countries which are receiving orders in relation to their own country's contribution to the funding of the project.

NADGE was conceived as an overall plan for the improvement of existing hardware and the provision of new equipment in certain areas. The history of the programme and details of improvements and upgradings have been described in successive issues of *Jane's Weapon Systems*. Improvements to individual national air defence networks are in train in several NATO countries and these will all be engineered to complement and enhance the overall NADGE capability. Portugal is obtaining three Hughes HADR H-3000 3D radars and Norway has also acquired three HADRs. Norsk Forsvarsteknologi (Hughes and Kongsberg) are producing 18 AN/TPQ-36 derived Low Altitude Surveillance Radars (LASR) to form a low level acquisition radar and control system (ARCS) of air defence. The computer-based ARCS is used with the HAWK missile system where it replaces three radars and multiple control centres. West Germany has selected the AN/FPS-117 radar for three NATO defence sites under a $65 million contract.

The NATO E-3 AWACS fleet is now in full operation and both the United Kingdom and France have agreed to buy these aircraft for their own early warning system and co-operation with the NATO fleet. The first of seven aircraft for the UK are due for delivery in 1991. France had ordered four aircraft on approximately the same time scale. The Airborne Early Warning/Ground Environment Integration Segment (AEGIS) programme provides for the controlled exchange of air surveillance data between the NADGE system and the AWACS aircraft by augmenting existing ground facilities. It enables the processing of in-flight AWACS radar data for dissemination to command control installations throughout Europe from Scandinavia to Turkey. The first two AEGIS ground stations, in Denmark and West Germany, became operational in 1983, and the complete system was due to become operational in late 1988. In addition, automated command and control information systems have been installed in a number of countries to give NATO commanders current information on the disposition and readiness of their forces in the field, and provide information on enemy air activities through the use of high speed computers.

A NATO requirement for a number of D-band 3D surveillance radars for Italy, Greece, Turkey and Portugal to upgrade the NATO southern flank has been met by the order of 10 Hughes HR-3000 systems, three each for Portugal and Turkey, and two each for Italy and Greece.

To improve detection of low-flying intruders, Denmark has installed the Coastal Radar Integration System (CRIS) which links data from Danish coastal radars surveying the Kattegat and the Western Baltic. In mid-1986 THORN EMI Electronics installed this system to feed information from the coastal radar network to the Danish elements of NADGE.

The NADGE system is continuously evolving and, in addition to the ACCS programme described below, a number of other updating plans

An air defence commander in a West German NADGE (NATO Air Defence Ground Environment) centre provides instructions to the E-3A AWACS early warning aircraft through the digital manual input station (MIS) under new capabilities provided by AEGIS (Airborne Early Warning/Ground Environment Integration Segment)

are in progress. Turkey has a requirement for airspace control which probably requires updating or replacing about 12 radar stations. Turkey also needs a new major communications network, known as the Turkish Air Force Integrated Communications System (TAFICS). Selenia has won contracts to improve the Italian national air defence network with an Argos-10 long-range surveillance system in Sicily, and has provided 14 RAT-31S E/F transportable 3D radars. West Germany has developed a low level system to meet national requirements consisting of Siemens DR 641 radars in a TRMS mobile system. Most of these programmes are national in concept but all contribute to the overall NADGE system.

Air Command and Control System

NADGE was originally conceived as a purely defensive system against manned aircraft. However, new threats have emerged and these, together with future threat evolvement, need to be met by a completely integrated defensive and offensive system. An on-going study has been carried out within NATO for the Air Command and Control System (ACCS) to provide a NADGE update which will ultimately provide overall air control of all types of air activity within Allied Command Europe (ACE). It is intended that this should be evolutionary in nature, starting with existing facilities and types of organisation for NATO air force control, and proceeding from that point to meet future requirements in a number of stages. By the year 2000, or shortly after, NATO intends to have vastly improved the command and control system of its air forces by implementing a system that will bring together, expand, modernise and automate all relevant subsystems and components of control.

The ACCS programme is currently in the planning stage, and a NATO ACCS team has been established, with the actual creation of ACCS commencing in 1991. The execution of ACCS will be based on a five-part master plan, and in view of the importance of the ACCS programme, both politically and economically, industry has co-operated to form two international consortia, ACCSCO (ACCS Company) and AMS (Airspace Management System). The first consists of Siemens, AEG-Telefunken, Marconi, Plessey, MBLE, Selenia, Hollandse Signaalapparaten, Thomson-CSF and Hughes Aircraft Company. The second consortium comprises Boeing, Westinghouse, ESG, SEL, Thomson-CSF, ISR, Racal Radar, Logica and Italtel. The two consortia differ to some extent in their approach to the ACCS programme in that AMS believes in the early introduction of new technology and operational doctrines, while ASSCO believes in using the existing system as a foundation on which new equipments and technologies can be built.

To date four contracts, worth a total of $10 million, have been awarded to the two consortia for the ACCS Multi-sensor Integration Study and the Communication and Automated Data Processing Design Options Study. In addition, AMS has won a contract for the ACCS Data Base Implementation and Automated Data Processing Support Tools Study.

NETHERLANDS

As with most other West European nations the Dutch national air defence system forms an integral part of the NATO NADGE network (see separate entry).

One interesting system, produced by Hollandse Signaalapparaten, is an integrated coastal surveillance, command and control network, known as Watchdog. Its primary objective is collecting, processing and presenting clear information in order to evaluate continuously the coastal situation, and safeguard against low level air attack maritime intruders. In its most extended configuration, the primary sources of information are coastal radar stations, direction finding stations and thermal imaging posts. Target data and other tactical information are fed into the system computer and continuously updated, correlated, stored and distributed to other users, as well as being presented on operator displays together with computer-generated geographical maps of the area concerned.

The Royal Netherlands Air Force forms part of NATO's Second Tactical Air Force. The fighter/bomber element consists of F-16 aircraft and NF-5s. More F-16s are being delivered and by 1992 the total force should consist of over 200 of these aircraft. SAM forces comprise 12 squadrons with I-HAWKs and four Patriot squadrons.

Operator's console at the harbour operations centre, Ymuiden

NIGERIA

In the mid-1980s Nigeria continued a programme of refurbishment and upgrading of its national air defence infrastructure, including the airspace control service. A Selenia RAT-31S was procured and has been in operation at Lagos for civil/military purposes, including control of nearby AA units consisting of guns and Roland SAM units. Elsewhere in Nigeria, ATC radars that had been shut down for many months were reactivated.

Since 1985, however, with the considerable decline in oil revenues the Nigerian economy has been in a parlous state and savage cuts had to be made in defence expenditure during 1986 and 1987. In 1988 the government announced a considerable rise in the defence budget to offset the two previous years. It seems doubtful, however, if any of the budget will be used for procurement of new air defence equipment. Main air defences consist of MiG-21MFs, plus 16 Jaguars and 16 Roland SAMs, with SA-7 and Blowpipe manportable SAMs.

NORWAY

As part of NATO, Norwegian air defence systems are integrated into the NADGE system and Norway has recently acquired three Hughes air defence 3D radars to enhance facilities for the NADGE network. These radars are used in shelters positioned on the top of mountains, and are mounted on elevators so that the antennas can be retracted into the environmentally controlled silos for routine maintenance. In addition, Norway and Denmark are acquiring an automated Command and Control Information System (CCIS) for NATO's northern Europe command.

For defence against low level air attacks, Norway is introducing the NOAH (Norwegian Adapted HAWK) programme to lengthen the operational life of the HAWK weapon system beyond the year 2000. This includes a new generation of mobile air defence radars developed by Hughes. The AN/TPQ-36A, also known as the Low Altitude Surveillance Radar, is deployed with a fire distribution centre developed by Norway's Kongsberg Vaapenfabrik as part of a new Adapted HAWK missile system called the Acquisition Radar and Control System (ARCS). A joint venture company, Norsk Forsvarsteknologi A/S, has been formed and will deliver a total of 24 ARCS systems.

A single ARCS is able to replace the three radars and two control units currently needed to operate the three launchers in the Improved HAWK battery configuration. NOAH has the communications capability to net information from two or more sensors, thus providing an integrated tactical air defence picture giving early warning and battle control.

The Norwegian Army is currently engaged on tests on its NALLADS (Norwegian Army Low Level Air Defence System) radar unit, mounted on a Hagglund Bv 208 vehicle. The system is designated NO-MPY-1 and controls the army's Bofors RBS 70 surface-to-air missile system.

As a member nation of NATO, the Royal Norwegian Air Force assigns much of its strength to that organisation. The strike/interceptor force consists of F-16A/Bs and F-5A/Bs.

OMAN

The air defences of the Sultanate of Oman have undergone two major modernisation and improvement programmes, one in the early 1970s and the second in 1985. The first of these, carried out by British Aerospace, provided a highly mobile and accurate integrated air defence system capable of protecting civil or military installations from air or ground attack and able to intercept intruders within Oman or its surrounding waters. The hardware selected for these tasks consisted of 28 Rapier fire units, equipped with Blindfire radars, and Jaguar tactical and strike aircraft. The current combat aircraft strength amounts to 23 Jaguars and 8 BAe Strikemasters, plus 14 Hunters. Eight Tornado F.2 air defence versions are on order. The radar and communications networks needed to provide adequate early warning, and command and control links to the defence forces, were supplied and installed largely by Marconi.

In mid-1985 it was announced that Marconi had received a £38 million contract to extend and update the air defence network. The major items of new equipment were two Martello S713 long-range 3D radars with their asscociated display and handling systems. These have now been delivered and are fully operational. Part of the contract also included updating and expanding existing Sector Operations Centres (SOC), and Control and Reporting Centres (CRC), as well as provision of a new CRC.

Marconi Radar S600 series search and heightfinder radars deployed in the desert

The communications system has two main centres connected by terminal and repeater stations. These link the air defence operations centre with the two SOCs, each of which has its own surveillance radar station. Defence centres in the vicinity of Muscat in the north and along the border with Yemen in the south are linked by a tropospheric scatter system. This network is used to convey processed data and communications from radar sites and SOCs to the main operations centre.

PAKISTAN

Pakistan is in the course of setting up a new air defence system based on a ground radar chain with stations at Karachi, Lahore, Pasni, Islamabad, Rahimyarkham and Jiwani. The radar systems are being supplied by Thomson-CSF of France but no information on the types of radar concerned have emerged, although they are probably of the TRS-2215 and/or TRS-2230 type (mobile and fixed/relocatable systems respectively). Six radars are reported to have been ordered but there are no indications as to whether any part of the system will be locally manufactured. Already in service are a number of Westinghouse AN/TPS-43 radars, as well as one old AN/FPS-100.

In addition, a number of West German secondary surveillance 'gap filling' radars are employed. The majority of these older radars are deployed near the Indian border and it is understood that the new French systems are likely to be similarly deployed. Pakistan also has some Giraffe battlefield radars. For airborne surveillance, Pakistan is interested in procuring a number of Boeing E-3 AWACS aircraft and negotiations with the USA are under way.

Since the announcement of this new air defence system in early 1988 a new government has been elected following the death of President Zia. Whether this will have any effect on the procurement of the equipments remains to be seen.

The Pakistan Air Force consists of a mixture of American, French and Chinese aircraft. The main interceptor force consists of F-6s (Chinese built MiG-19s) and F-7s, and the fighter/ground attack fleet includes F-16A/Bs, Mirage IIIs, Mirage Vs and Shenyang A-5s (Chinese built derivative of the MiG-19). The SAM force uses Crotale, HQ-2, Stinger and the RBS 70.

PHILIPPINES

Although independent since 1946, the Philippines has relied almost entirely on the United States for its defence, and this is reflected in the inventory of the Philippine forces. The USA enjoys important base facilities in the country, notably at Subic Bay naval base and Clark Air Force Base. Two Selenia ATCR-3T radars supplied for ATC purposes at Manila and Mactan in 1972 can be used in a supplementary surveillance role. Four ITT-Gilfillan 320 Series 3D transportable air defence radars have also been delivered.

The US base facilities at Subic Bay and Clark AFB provide a guarantee against external attack but the leases expire in 1991. Negotiations had been deadlocked for some time, with the United States offering a substantial increase in the lease terms for the two years remaining and the Philippine government demanding a great deal more. Agreement has now been reached and, presumably, talks about renewing the lease after 1991 will commence in the near future. The United States had threatened to pull out altogether if the Philippine government did not moderate its requirements, possibly rebasing on the island of Guam. Had this occurred there is a strong possibility that the Soviet Union would have endeavoured to have a presence in the area, a possibility which undoubtedly focused the minds of the American negotiators to reach a settlement! It is of interest to note that the USSR has already made a proposal to close Soviet bases in Vietnam if the US will close its bases in the Philippines. The exact terms of the settlement between the US and Philippines have not been revealed but it is noteworthy that the Philippine defence budget for 1989 has been increased by 30 per cent, an increase which must have been made possible by the new military bases deal.

The Philippine Air Force is quite small, consisting of one interceptor squadron with F-5 aircraft and one fighter squadron with F-8s. A relatively large number of COIN aircraft is operated and the extra 30 per cent in the 1989 budget will probably be used largely to augment this force to deal with the country's internal security problems.

PORTUGAL

As a member of NATO, the Portuguese air defence system has become part of the NADGE network (see separate entry), and in 1985 a Hughes HR-3000 radar was ordered by NATO for installation in Portugal to supplement the NADGE chain in southern Europe. Since then Portugal itself has ordered a further two HR-3000 systems. More recently the US has delivered five tracked Chaparral SAM systems and associated alerting radars. An Improved HAWK battery is also being supplied.

The Portuguese Air Force is quite small and consists mainly of A-7 strike aircraft and G-91s for fighter-bomber work.

SAUDI ARABIA

The original Saudi Arabian air defence network was provided in the 1960s and was based on UK and US radars. A succession of improvements have been grafted on to this basic system over the past 20 years, either for overall system enhancement or as adjuncts or essential elements of a new weapon system. A considerable amount of defence equipment was purchased from France and included a Thomson-CSF T.ACCS (Thomson Air Command and Control System) for air defence purposes. In 1980 the US supplied four Westinghouse AN/TPS-43 3D radars, and in 1981 AN/TPS-43G radars were ordered, in addition to modifying the original systems to the 43G standard. At the time the US deployed a number of AWACS aircraft to serve as an airborne command post based in Saudi Arabia.

To further strengthen air defences in the area, defence ministers from six Arab states in the Gulf area agreed in principle to establish an air defence system based on Saudian Arabian airborne warning and control aircraft. The states concerned are Saudi Arabia, Kuwait, United Arab Emirates, Bahrain, Qatar and Oman. The overall project is known as Peace Shield and was finalised to include five E-3 AWACS aircraft, eight Boeing KE-3A tanker aircraft, a command, control and communications complex with underground command centres, data processing and communication links, and a new ground network of 17 GE Aerospace AN/FPS-117(V)3 long-range radars, similar to the North American North Warning System. Work on the programme, which was estimated to cost $8.5 billion, commenced in 1981 and by 1988 the centralised command operations centre had been constructed and work on building and connecting five sector command and operations centres had been completed. The first E-3 aircraft was delivered in June 1986 and all 13 E-3 and KE-3A aircraft are now in operation. The Royal Saudi Arabian Air Force is also receiving Tornado ADV/IDS and BAe Hawk aircraft. The main SAM force consists of Improved HAWK, Crotale and Shahine systems.

SINGAPORE

During 1980 an integrated civil/military surveillance system based on the LAR II D-band radar with associated data handling equipment, manufactured by Hollandse Signaalapparaten of the Netherlands, was supplied. Most of the hardware is located at Changi International Airport and the data stored in this system is available to both civil and military authorities. In 1982, in a move seen in some quarters as a preliminary to the formation of a regional air defence system embracing five ASEAN states (Indonesia, Malaysia, the Philippines, Singapore and Thailand), Singapore ordered four E-2C early warning aircraft. These aircraft are now operational with the Singapore Air Force and provide airborne surveillance over much of South-East Asia's airspace. SAM defence comprises Bloodhound, Rapier and RBS 70.

SPAIN

Combat Grande is the name of the programme of automation of the Spanish air defence system by the USAF for the Spanish government, supplied by a jointly owned Spanish-American company registered in California. Funding for the first two phases of this programme has been provided by the US, which may also approve funds for the third and fourth phases. Combat Grande will be linked into the NATO NADGE network.

The original programme was intended to automate Spain's manual air defence system by developing a combat operations centre, sector operations centres, and modernising a number of long-range radar and communications sites. The programme also called for the improvement and enlargement of an existing microwave communications system. Included in the radar enhancements have been the provision of new IFF/SIF facilities, video extractors and modems. A capability for remote operation of the radar site ground/air communications was also provided.

The system employs the Hughes H5118M computer, and the Radex system developed by Hughes in an earlier defence programme provides video extraction and signal processing facilities.

The second phase of the programme, unofficially known as Combat Grande II, has made additions to the radar facilities, and new microwave communications have been installed to improve network data exchange services. Between 1980 and 1982 Collins data transmission equipment replaced outdated hardware at 44 sites being modernised to improve transmission of data to Torrejon Air Base for use in the combat operations centre. A large search radar at Brabanza Mountain in the north-west of Spain was handed over to the Spanish Air Force by the USAF Electronic Systems Division in 1984, and was the eighth air defence site to be modified.

Prime contractor for the update is COMCO Electronics Corporation, a company owned jointly by Hughes Aircraft Company and CESELSA. Each of the parent companies has a 50 per cent holding in COMCO. Hughes built the computers and designed the communications equipment for the programme; CESELSA manufactured the communications

One of the seven long-range radar sites in the Combat Grande Spanish air defence system. Also known as SADA, Sistema Semi-Automatico de Defensa Aerea, it was produced by a jointly-owned Spanish-American company, COMCO

subsystems and managed the civil engineering construction.

The Spanish Air Force consists of four major commands, the air defence being handled by Combat Air and Tactical Air Commands. These consist of a variety of aircraft, including EF-18 Hornets, F-4Cs, Mirage IIIs, Mirage F-1s and F-5s. The SAM force includes Nike Hercules and Improved HAWK systems.

SWEDEN

The Swedish automatic air surveillance and operational control system, known as STRIL, is operated by the Royal Swedish Air Force. It is based on four air defence sectors, each having a sector operations centre (SOC) which receives radar data from static and mobile control and reporting centres (CRC). Inputs to the system come mainly from high and low level air surveillance radars, but a visual backup reporting service is included to supplement radar data and to replace it if necessary. Information from all these sources is fed into a central data store, from where it is extracted for selective presentation to controllers having specific territorial assignments.

When a threat is detected the STRIL controllers, who also have state-of-readiness information on available forces and weapons, decide with which kind of available weapon the threat can best be countered and assign that weapon to the task. In appropriate cases, eg surface-to-air missiles, they will also control the operation. Currently the forces controlled by the system are the SAAB Draken and Viggen interceptor aircraft, AA guns and Improved HAWK SAMs. Most of the control and reporting centres, and the display and computing equipment at the local operations rooms at radar sites, has been delivered by Datasaab, which also participated in the overall system development of STRIL.

The STRIL centre is also linked to the civil defence organisation and can alert them and warn industry and the civil population.

If the threat cannot be countered by the forces under the control of one centre but can be countered by those of another centre, the system provides both voice and transmission links for giving information to other centres. Both narrowband and broadband microwave links are employed for exchange of data between centres.

Although primarily an air defence system, STRIL also is linked to coastal anti-aircraft artillery and missiles.

The original STRIL-60 system has been the subject of a sustained development and improvement programme throughout its operational life and work is now continuing towards a STRIL/C-90 standard. The most recent, and as far as is known, the most extensive modernisation is currently in progress. Sixteen 3D primary radars have been installed to supplement and/or replace older types and Datasaab has supplied new advanced computerised display systems with such facilities as automatic tracking. The older radars were the Thomson-CSF Palmier 3D types which were used in the original NADGE system, but these have now been replaced by the ITT/Gilfillan AN/TPS-32 (Swedish designation PS806) with the antennas installed on retractable 25 m masts operated from mountain silos. Some of these sites have chambers which can house mobile control and reporting centres, with multi-processing and display subsystems provided by Marconi.

Low level surveillance is carried out by a chain of PS15 radars, developed and built by Selenia in the late 1960s. These are being replaced or supplemented by ITT/Gilfillan systems (Swedish designation PS870). Delivery of these commenced in 1987 and the programme completion is scheduled for 1993/94.

The two main examples of the of the Datasaab family of transportable air defence operations centres (TADOC) used in the STRIL system are the TADOC 311 and 431. The latter is the more sophisticated with regard to the operational functions and computing power. These centres can be moved to new locations easily if strategic plans are changed or if it becomes necessary to replace other centres destroyed by enemy action.

TADOC 311

Normally, the TADOC 311 interacts with radars in the ASCC system. Data from the radars is sent automatically to the CRC without any operator intervention. The primary radar can be of the 2D or 3D type and automatic transmission ensures fast target detection within the entire ASCC system and thus a short system response time (essential in modern air defence systems). However, since systems that may have to be used in wartime must have fall-back modes of operation, the TADOC 311 can exercise a certain amount of control in addition to its normal reporting role. This permits independent operation, should the CRC or its ground-to-ground communication fail. In addition to its 'own' local radar, the TADOC 311 can make use of a remote radar (either a military gap-filler radar or a civil radar). This remote radar delivers extracted radar data via a narrow-band, telephone-type channel such as a radio link.

The TADOC 311 can also serve as a centre for visual reporting posts (VRP). Their data can be filtered by the centre and transmitted to the CRC.

Main operational tasks of the TADOC 311 include:
(1) Producing target information and transmitting it to the CRC. This is normally automated for radar data (transmission of extracted radar data or plot messages). There is, however, a manual backup function that can be used if the radar or extractor function is degraded. The

Sweden / **WORLD AIR DEFENCE SYSTEMS** 17

Operational console in a TADOC 311 air defence control cabin

manual backup function can also be used to filter and transmit target information obtained from VRPs
(2) ECCM control, which entails evaluation of the ECM situation and the taking of appropriate countermeasures to eliminate or alleviate the consequences of jamming
  Secondary operational tasks include:
(3) Autonomous airspace surveillance, which is carried out within the area covered by the connected radar station(s) in the event that ground communication to the CRC or the CRC itself is out of action
(4) Weapons control; primarily, control of fighter aircraft in the situations cited above
(5) Producing target information and transmitting it to nearby SAM/AAA units. This can be performed using the manual backup function mentioned earlier.

TADOC 431
Normally the TADOC 431 serves as a tactical operations centre such as a CRC in the ASCC system. The TADOC 431 is responsible for all tactical operations within an air defence sector. Sensor information from radars and control and reporting posts (CRP) is transferred automatically to the TADOC 431, which can also receive information from visual reporting posts (VRPs) either directly or via a CRP (in which the information is filtered to some extent). The received airspace information forms the basis for weapons control. The TADOC 431 also reports the airspace situation to a co-ordination centre (CC). This reporting is automatic so that the CC will receive an accurate and up-to-date airspace situation picture of the sector in question. However, since systems that may have to be used in wartime must have fall-back modes of operation, the TADOC 431 can take over some CC functions should the CC or its ground-to-ground communication fail.

The main operational tasks of the TADOC 431 include:
(1) Airspace surveillance: this is carried out utilising information obtained from connected sensors of different kinds and from subordinate centres. An airspace situation picture of the air defence sector is compiled and presented in the TADOC 431 itself and can be reported to a superior centre such as a CC
(2) Weapon control, which involves: evaluation of the threat situation; assignment of the appropriate weapon system (fighter, SAM or AAA); allocation of specific fighter aircraft or SAM/AAA unit and weapon controller; interception and recovery control of fighter aircraft or allocation of targets to SAM/AAA units. Weapons control is exercised throughout the air defence sector and is based upon the airspace situation picture
(3) Civil defence telling and base alerting: this is carried out by issuing warnings to threatened civil targets, such as highly populated areas, industrial areas etc. Warnings are also issued to threatened air bases. Moreover, general airspace situation information is distributed to different 'customers'
(4) Co-ordination of military and civil air traffic control by co-ordinating military and civil air traffic activities in the air defence sector to ensure safety and facilitate identification of civil flights
  Secondary tasks include:
(5) Close air support and reconnaissance supervision: for the most part, this entails supervision of reconnaissance flights and supervision and/or direction of close air support aircraft. The objectives are to keep track of these aircraft and be ready to warn them of hostile aircraft
(6) Naval support and co-ordination by co-ordination of naval and air force activities in the air defence sector to minimise the risk of inadvertent firing on friendly units. This can also include the exchange of selected target information between the TADOC 431 and a naval command centre.

STRIL C/90
STRIL C/90 is scheduled to enter full operational service in the mid-1990s. It is intended to be a very flexible and highly automated system, able to operate with current and forseeable sensors and communications. A complete upgrading of the SOCs and CRCs with new data processing and displays, and their associated software, together with new narrow-band data link communications is under way. This will also phase in with the introduction of the new SAAB Gripen interceptor aircraft.

The new Swedish Gripen multi-role combat aircraft has now flown, albeit some two years later than planned. Operational testing is now going ahead and the aircraft will enter service into the Royal Swedish Air Force. Until that date, the RSAF air defence force comprises six ground attack squadrons, equipped mainly with Viggens, and 11 interceptor squadrons with Viggens and Drakens. In addition, three fighter/reconnaissance squadrons with Viggens are operational. Improved HAWK and RBS 70 SAMs form the main part of the air defence missile strength.

Status: As was stated earlier, work is in progress to update the STRIL system with a new project entitled STRIL/C 90, which is scheduled to enter full operational service in the mid-1990s. This is intended to be a very flexible, highly automated system, able to operate with current and foreseeable sensors and communication systems. It will certainly entail a complete upgrading of the SOCs and CRCs with new data processing and display systems and their associated software, together with new narrow-band data link communication links. It will also phase in with the introduction of the new Swedish Gripen interceptor aircraft. Requests for tenders have been issued to both indigenous and international companies and the successful bidder was to have been chosen by the end of 1987.

Manufacturers: Prime contractor for the STRIL system is Datasaab AB (formerly Stansaab Elektronik AB), 175 86 Järfälla, Sweden. Datasaab is also responsible for the creation of similar systems in Denmark and elsewhere.

WORLD AIR DEFENCE SYSTEMS / Switzerland-Tunisia

SWITZERLAND

The Swiss air defence system, known as Florida, was designed and installed by Hughes Aircraft Company in the early 1970s. It is a fully computerised system consisting of a number of military radar stations with 3D radars and air defence centres. Information from the sensors is fed into conversion equipment in underground air defence centres, and processed in turn by a high-speed general purpose computer. This computer automatically establishes speed, heading and altitude of unidentified intruders, and display consoles present a constantly updated picture of the aircraft's track, as well as information on the various weapons available, their launch ranges, velocities, armament, restrictions and 'time-to-kill'.

The radar used is a long-range 3D type with a planar array antenna, using the Hughes elevation frequency scanning technique. An IFF subsystem is incorporated. The processed raw data is fed to air defence direction centres where it is accepted by a computer which also accepts information from the missile sites, airfields and other military installations. It can also simulate air battles for training and instruction and can be used as a general purpose data processing centre.

The Florida system became operational officially in April 1970. About 10 years later the Swiss government studied the methods of updating the system, particularly in the sphere of providing air surveillance and ground control of interceptor aircraft in the lower airspace. Field tests and evaluations were held of competing systems, among them being the Hughes VSTAR and the Selenia MRCS-403 mobile air defence system with its 3D radar RAT-31S. In early 1982 it was announced that under a Swiss air defence programme called Taflir, a version of the Westinghouse AN/TPS-70(V) radar, known as Vigilant, had been ordered and was delivered in 1984 for evaluation. These trials were understood to be successful and it was reported that an order was placed for systems to be delivered in the late 1980s. However, no confirmation of this has been made.

SYRIA

It is known that a major upgrade of the Syrian air defence system has been carried out with the assistance of Soviet equipment and technicians, but virtually no details have been disclosed. A command and control network, codenamed Swamp, is part of the upgrade. It has been reported also that a number of Big Bird early warning radars have been supplied by the USSR.

Inevitably, the Syrian Air Force is composed almost entirely of Soviet aircraft. The strength, particularly considering the relatively small population of 11 million, is large with some 300+ aircraft in the interceptor/fighter category alone. These consist of MiG-17s, MiG-21s, MiG-23s, MiG-25s, MiG-27s, Su-20s and Su-22s. In addition, about 80 MiG-29s are being delivered. The SAM force is operated by the army with air force and army manpower and comprises SA-2, SA-3, SA-5, SA-6, SA-7, SA-8, SA-9, SA-11 and SA-13 batteries.

TAIWAN

Taiwan is currently engaged in the development and implementation of an integrated air defence system known as Sky Net. This system is similar to those produced by Hughes Aircraft Company for Japan, Switzerland, Spain and Israel, and will include an upgraded Hughes Air Defense Ground Environment with advanced multi-mode radars. Whilst no definite information has been released it would appear likely that the radars will be a variant of the Hughes HADR (HR-3000) system.

Taiwan is developing a new surface-to-air weapon system with technological assistance from the USA. It is believed that the system, known as Chang Bai (Long White), is currently under test and is intended to be a land-based SAM system, similar in concept to the US shipborne AEGIS, employing a phased-array radar, with assistance from RCA. Taiwan's Sky Bow 1 SAM, which uses a Patriot launcher and HAWK electronics, will be used with the system. Taiwan already has nearly 2000 SAMs, including HAWKs, Chaparrals and Nike Hercules, which are almost certainly operated by Westinghouse AN/TSQ-73 automated air defence centres. A number of Westinghouse AN/TPS-43 radars are also in operation.

Inevitably, the Taiwan Air Force is totally equipped with American aircraft. The interceptor/fighter strength consists of more than 300 F-5s and about 200 F-104s. A new light fighter, the Ching-Kuo, is in development.

THAILAND

A programme to automate and modernise the Royal Thai Air Defence System (RTADS), at an estimated cost of $207 million, is now in progress. The work, in three phases, will be financed by US Foreign Military Sales Credits, and the USAF Electronic Systems Division is acting as contracting agent for the Royal Thai Air Force. It involves modernisation of the RTAF's present radar network and also the Central Air Defence Sector command, control and communications system.

The first phase links radars in the central plain, including areas bordering Kampuchea, and will improve coverage of Thailand's northern and eastern border regions. This also provides interoperability with US forces. Phase 1 also includes upgrading the existing long-haul communications system in the central sector's terminal and repeater stations. Radars will be modified with data extractors to support centralised tracking and weapons control. The second and third phases will come later. At present the radar network consists of two Westinghouse AN/TPS-43 systems delivered in 1980 and three AN/TPS-70 systems ordered in 1985/86, and these will form part of the first phase of automation. In addition, a number of Sanders mobile Low Level Air Detection Systems (LLADS) have been delivered. The Contraves Skyguard low level defence system has been delivered.

The Systems Development Group of Unisys (formed by a merger of Burroughs and Sperry) is prime contractor and system integrator for the first phase, and has completed live test demonstrations using data relayed by satellite from Thailand to the company's ground station in California. The Mitre Corporation is providing engineering support.

The Royal Thai Air Force operates F-5 aircraft in the fighter/interceptor role. A number of F-16s are also being delivered. The Selenia Spada SAM system has been delivered to protect the new F-16 bases.

TUNISIA

Very little is known about Tunisian air defence other than the fact that Thomson-CSF is reported to have supplied four TRS-2100 Tiger radars and two TRS-2215 systems. Tunisia still maintains strong ties with France since its independence and it is most likely that other equipment, such as control centres, will have been supplied from that country. The Tunisian Air Force is very small and operates a few F-5s and MB-326s in the fighter/strike role.

TURKEY

As a member of NATO, Turkish air defence is integrated with that organisation. The system currently in operation is somewhat outdated and is being modernised, both from a national point of view and with the funding of NATO itself. Three Hughes HR-3000 3D surveillance radars are being supplied and the command, control and communications network is being updated. Further information on the NATO network is given in the NATO section earlier. A requirement also exists for updating or replacing about 12 radars systems, and the government has already asked for proposals from a number of companies. It is also proposed to update the Turkish Air Force communications network, with NATO funding.

Turkey is also modernising its low level air defence system and has asked for proposals. Of the six bids received, three had been eliminated by December 1988, leaving Oerlikon with its ADATS system, Euromissile with Roland and Thomson-CSF with Crotale. Surface-to-air missile systems operated currently include Rapier and Nike Hercules. In addition, 160 F-16C/D aircraft have been ordered and are being delivered, and will eventually supersede the F-104s in service at the moment.

UNION OF SOVIET SOCIALIST REPUBLICS

The Soviet Union maintains an elaborate and extensive air and space defence network consisting of a variety of organisational levels equipped with a multiplicity of sensors, systems, and command and control levels which are frequently interdependent and overlap to provide redundancy.

Early Warning
What is claimed as the world's most comprehensive early warning system provides separately for detection and alerting to both ballistic missile attack and conventional air attack by missiles and aircraft within the atmosphere. The current ballistic missile early warning system consists of a launch detection satellite network, over-the-horizon (OTH) radars, and a series of large phased-array radars on the periphery of the Soviet Union.

The launch detection satellite system can give a warning of any US ICBM launch, as well as determining the area from which it was launched. Two large radars of the OTH type are in operation facing US ICBM sites and could provide up to 30 minutes warning of attack. Two additional OTH systems have joined them to improve coverage and monitor US ship and aircraft movements in the Pacific area, and also cover the eastern border of the USSR with China. It is not known how effective these radars are but, judging from the problems that the US has had with the development and operation of its own OTH programme, perhaps too much emphasis should not be put on their capability.

The next layer of ballistic early warning facilities consists of 11 Hen House large detection and tracking radars located at six sites on the Soviet periphery, and these can confirm the warning of an attack given by the satellite and OTH networks and give an indication of its scale. The Hen House radars are also able to provide certain target tracking data in support of ABM deployments.

The construction of new large phased-array radars is continuing with three new systems being built on the periphery of the USSR. It is also believed that there are nine engaged in the upgrading of the ballistic missile defences, including the controversial radar at Krasnoyarsk in Siberia. The entire network of large phased-array radars will form almost a complete circle around the USSR, with the complete system being operational by 1990. This will provide ABM battle management beyond Moscow.

The new phased-array radars duplicate or supplement the 11 existing Hen House systems at six locations on the USSR periphery. They are believed to be able to track more attacking missiles with greater accuracy than the existing network, covering almost all approaches to the Soviet Union. This will allow the USSR to establish a national ABM network system rather than the one based on Moscow at present. In the past 10 years the Soviet Union has probably spent in the region of $150 billion on strategic defence, a sobering thought and one reason for the recent emphasis on the reduction of nuclear and conventional arms.

Ballistic Missile Defence
Throughout the past 10 years or so the Soviet Union has been working to upgrade the Moscow ABM system. The original single-layer ABM system included 64 reloadable launchers above ground at four complexes for the Galosh ABM-1b, six Try Add guidance and engagement radars

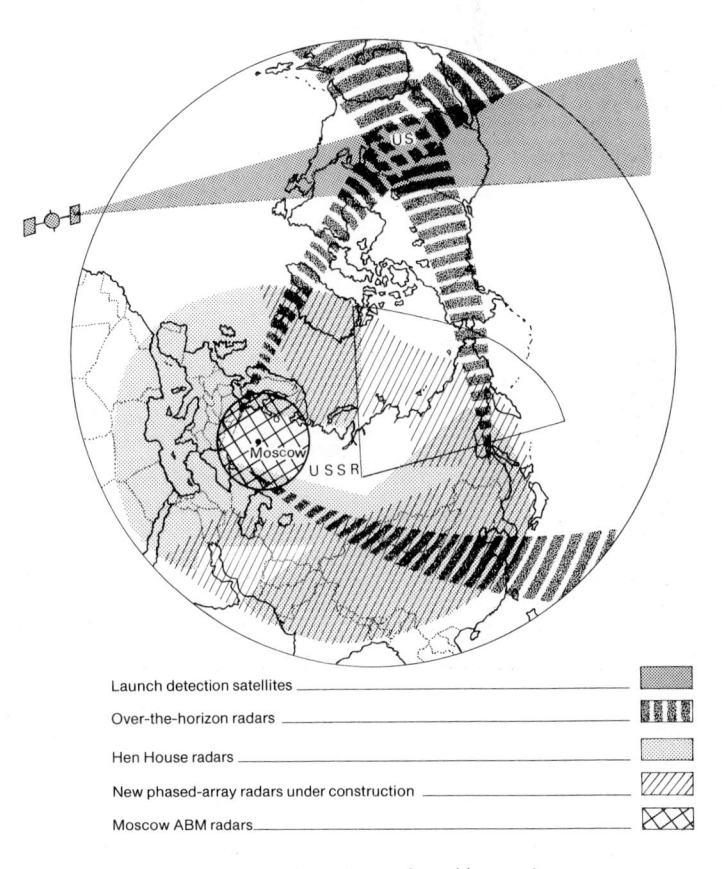

Moscow ABM system map

Coverage of ballistic missile detection and tracking systems

WORLD AIR DEFENCE SYSTEMS / USSR

Map summary of principal Soviet strategic assets

at each complex, and the Dog House and Cat House target tracking radars to the south of Moscow. This system is now being upgraded to the 100 launchers allowed by the 1972 treaty; in the interim there have been only 16 Galosh deployed. The system was due to be completed by the end of 1988 and is now a two-layered system consisting of: silo-based long-range modified Galosh interceptors designed to engage targets outside the atmosphere; silo-based high-acceleration SH-08 Gazelle interceptor missiles to engage targets within the atmosphere, associated engagement and guidance radars; and the massive new Pill Box four-sided, phased-array radar at Puskino, north of Moscow, designed to control ABM engagements.

The SA-10 Grumble SAM has now been deployed at nearly 100 sites, many of which are near Moscow. A mobile version, the SA-10b, is also being deployed. Also in operational use is the SA-12a Gladiator mobile SAM, while a longer-range, higher-altitude version, the SA-12b Giant, is about to enter service. This latter SAM is reported to be capable of intercepting aircraft at all altitudes as well as cruise missiles and tactical ballistic missiles.

Air Surveillance

There are an estimated 10 000 air defence radars deployed at about 1200 sites. These provide virtually complete coverage at medium to high altitudes on the Soviet airspace, and in some cases for many hundreds of kilometres beyond the national borders. Limited cover against low-altitude targets is concentrated in the west of the country and in certain high priority areas elsewhere. Existing air surveillance radars are being improved, with several new types in development. In addition, the data networks are being improved to enhance the exchange of data throughout the surveillance network. The programme of improvements is understood to include the partial integration of strategic and tactical defences, upgrading of early warning and surveillance facilities, and the installation of improved communications networks.

In addition to the ground surveillance systems, the Soviet Union operates a large number of airborne early-warning aircraft. The original Tu-126 Moss AEW aircraft has now been superseded by the IL-76 Mainstay which uses a rotodome antenna radar similar to that employed by the Boeing E-3.

The Soviet Air Force is the largest in the world and is divided into four main parts, known as Long Range Aviation, Air Defence Force, Frontal Aviation (Tactical Force), and Air Transport Aviation.

Each part has its own role, organisation, command structure and equipment. Approximately 2250 air defence interceptor aircraft are dedicated to strategic defence, with an additional 2000 interceptors which could be drawn for this purpose. Most of these additional aircraft would come from the tactical air forces segment which has more than 5000 aircraft at its command.

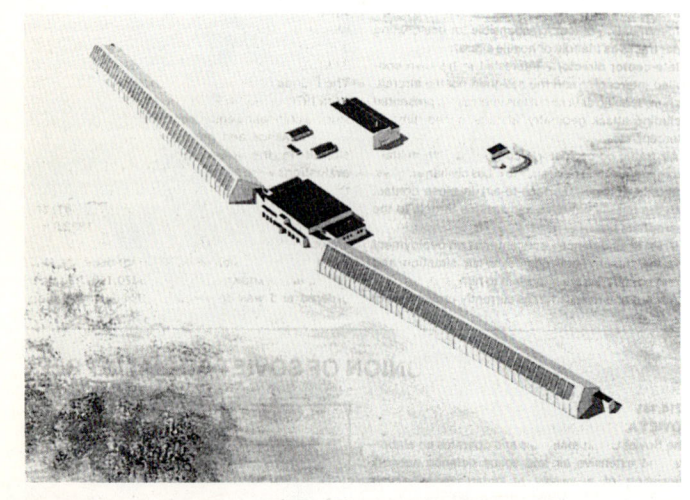

Eleven of the large Hen House ballistic early warning radars are located at six sites around the periphery of the Soviet Union

Artist's impression of the phased-array ballistic missile detection array and tracking radar at Pechora in the north of the Soviet Union

US artist's impression of the Soviet Dog House ABM battle management radar

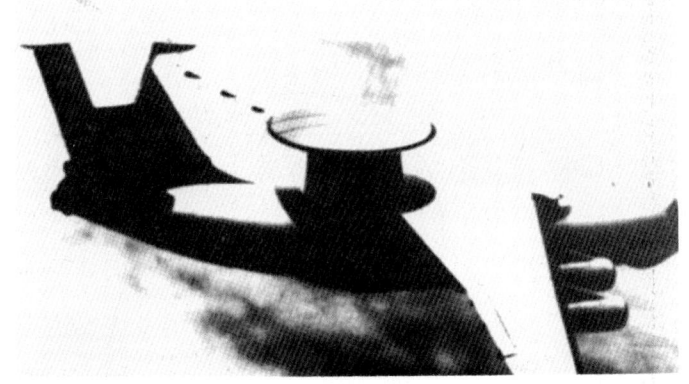

The Soviet Union is deploying the Mainstay AWACS aircraft which is based on the IL-76 Candid transport

PVO Strany

PVO Strany (*Voiska Protivovzdushnoy Strany*) is the national air defence command of the Soviet Union, with an underground headquarters on the outskirts of Moscow. There are four operations/systems commands:
(1) RV-PVO (*Radio teknicheski Voisk-PVO*) radio-technical troops
(2) ZA-PVO (*Zenitnaya Artilleriya-PVO*) anti-aircraft artillery
(3) ZRV-PVO (*Zenitnaya Raketmye Voiska-PVO*) anti-aircraft missile troops
(4) IA-PVO (*Istrebitel 'naya Aviatsiya-PVO*) fighter aviation forces.

The 10 000 or so air defence radars are the responsibility of the RV-PVO, while missile systems and AA guns are in the hands of the ZA-PVO and ZRV-PVO commands. Fighter aircraft are managed by IA-PVO.

Operationally, the Soviet air defence network is divided into four levels of command responsibility: Air Defence (AD) Districts or Rayons, AD Zones, AD Sectors, and 'frontal' AD sub-units defending specific point targets. The rayons are sub-divided into at least two AD zones and these are in turn divided into SAM defence sectors. Each level has a particular command function and operational mission. At rayon level these include search and entry, long-range target identification, designating air threats to lower command echelons, and authorisation of fighter intercepts or missile engagements. Twenty two rayons cover the USSR from the eastern border with China to the Warsaw Pact states of Eastern Europe.

The AD districts are divided into AD zones, some districts having as many as four zones, and these are under IA-PVO operational command. The command responsibilities at this level embrace target identification friend or foe (IFF), GCI radar operation, and fighter intercept of hostile/unknown aircraft.

An AD sector is a specific, relatively small scale section of airspace under the control of Air Defence Launch Command Centres, and their defence is based on SAMs and their associated target tracking and guidance radars.

Passive Defence

The Soviet Ministry of Defence controls the nation-wide civil defence programmes of the USSR. The Chief of Civil Defence is a Deputy Minister of Defence and General of the Army. Full-time civil defence staff exist at each echelon of the Soviet administrative structure. Civil defence staff also exist at significant industrial, utility and other installations. In wartime, the civil defence administrative structure, assimilated into an integrated command system, would play a significant role in maintenance of the government and the economy. This goal is supported by the protection provided for the leadership through deep, hard, urban sheltering and an extensive network of hardened relocation sites outside the cities, with redundant communications systems. The programme also provides for continuity of support for the economy in wartime through the protection of the essential workforce by sheltering at work and by the dispersal of off-shift workers to areas away from work sites.

UNITED ARAB EMIRATES

The United Arab Emirates plans to spend more than $700 million in radar and communications equipment and has recently acquired three AN/TPS-70 surveillance radars. Westinghouse has also agreed to supply command and control equipment to communicate, correlate and display real-time data from these radars. An operations centre and system to integrate air defence in the area is also planned and it is believed that Hughes Aircraft Company is negotiating with the UAE. A number of aircraft and weapon systems are currently on order, including Mirage 2000 aircraft, Improved HAWK missiles and Skyguard air defence radar systems.

UNITED KINGDOM

The United Kingdom Air Defence Region (UKADR) forms one of four regional commands of the NATO integrated air defence system and stretches about 2000 kilometres in an arc from north of the Faroe Islands to the western flanks of continental Europe. The systems for warning of attack on the UK are BMEWS (described under the USA), and the UK Air Defence Ground Environment (UKADGE), the former being concerned with ballistic missiles and the latter with aircraft. UKADGE is also coupled into the continental air defence systems by its links with six NADGE stations.

A programme of improvement, known as improved UKADGE (IUKADGE) was instituted in 1984 and the structure of the system is illustrated in the accompanying map. Centralised command of air defence operations in the UK air defence region is exercised from the Air Defence Operations Centre (ADOC) which is linked to four combined sector operations centres and command and reporting centres (SOC/CRC), with, in turn, links to command and reporting centres, and reporting posts. Links are established with the French STRIDA system at Tours and Doullens, NADGE at six sites, NATO and RAF AWACS aircraft, certain naval vessels and various defence assets such as fighter bases.

At the core of the programme is the IUKADGE Command and Control System (ICCS), which is the biggest software-based system in Europe linking command and control with land-based sensors, operational sites, aircraft and warships. The ICCS system should have entered service in 1987 but delays put this date back to 1988. As far as is known, the system is now operational. IUKADGE will be supported by the GEC Uniter communications network which is largely based on the System X telephone system developed by GEC and Plessey. Stage 1 was completed in 1986 and Stage 2 is due for completion in 1990.

As far as the IUKADGE ground radar systems requirement was concerned, this called for 12 transportable systems capable of being set up at pre-surveyed sites and going into operation within six hours of arrival. This has been met by three different equipments: two D-band GE AN/TPS-592s, four D-band Marconi S723 Martellos, and six E/F-band Plessey AR-320s. Of these 12 systems, the two AN/TPS-592s, two of the Martellos, and three of the AR-320s were funded by NATO. The remaining five were funded by the UK government. The two AN/TPS-

22 WORLD AIR DEFENCE SYSTEMS / UK-USA

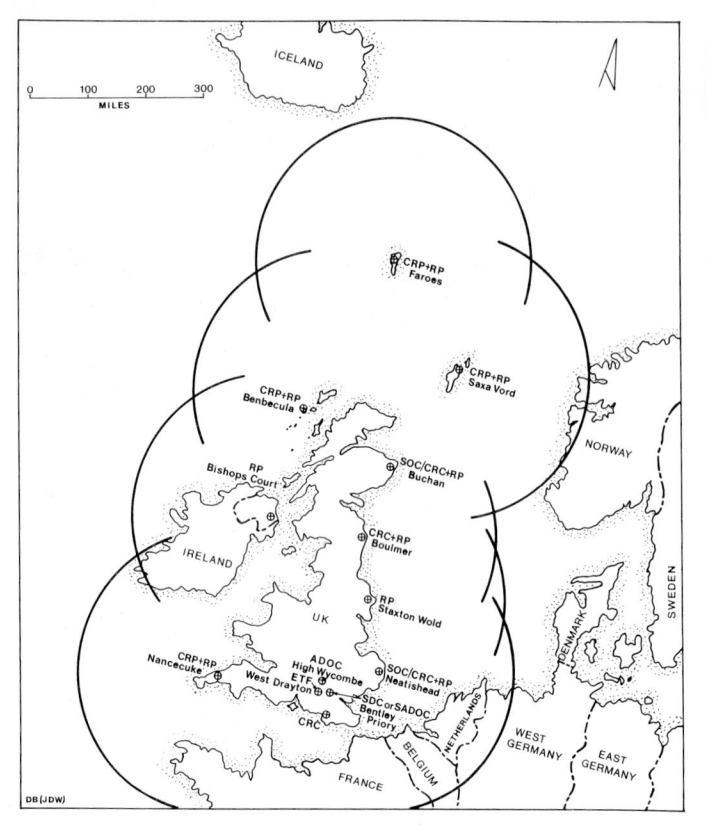

Map of major IUKADGE sites in the British Isles (Jane's Defence Weekly)

RAF personnel check out computer displays for IUKADGE, undergoing final test at Hughes Aircraft Company, Fullerton, California. Displays shown include Marconi text monitors (left), a Plessey air status display (centre), and a rear-projected HDP-4000 large screen display provided by Hughes. The improved system is produced by UKADGE Systems Ltd

592s have been installed at the Buchan and Benbecula sites and are operational. The four Martellos have been delivered and are also operational at various sites. Delivery of the six AR-320s began in 1987 and is believed to be complete. A fifth Martello, an S713 version, has also been delivered and is probably being used as an operational spare.

The United Kingdom has now ordered seven Boeing E-3 AWACS aircraft, the first of which is due to be delivered in 1991. These will replace the ageing Shackleton aircraft which are still maintaining airborne early warning. Construction and installation of a network of UK data link stations has been completed to enable the use of interim, and later full, JTIDS.

In August 1987 a consortium headed by ICL was awarded a £37 million contract to develop and build a new computer-based command, control and information system (CCIS), to improve the ability to control air operations strategy. The project is jointly funded by NATO and the UK MoD. It will link UKAIR HQ, and a standby HQ, to major RAF and USAF sites in the UK with facilities to enable UKAIR CCIS to interoperate with other UK and NATO systems, including the Central Region CCIS, UK Maritime CCIS and IUKADGE.

As with any air defence system updating UKADGE is a continuing affair and even when the complete IUKADGE system is operational there will be additional upgrading to cope with new technologies and/or threats. The complete system, including the radars, communications networks, full JTIDS, etc, will probably become fully operational in 1992/93. The cost of the full updating of the UK's air defences has been around £7 billion, with the cost of IUKADGE itself about £1 billion.

As a member nation of NATO, the United Kingdom contributes a large part of the Royal Air Force to that organisation. The major aircraft types in current service for interceptor, strike/attack and offensive support are the Tornado IDS/ADV, Jaguar, Phantom, and Harrier. Surface-to-air missile systems include Bloodhound and Rapier with Blindfire radar.

UNITED STATES OF AMERICA

The land-based air defence network of North America consists of a number of interlocking systems to protect both the United States and Canada against ballistic missile and aircraft attack. Together, they constitute the most sophisticated air defence system in the world, with its centre in the North American Air Defense Command (NORAD) Combat Operations Center within the Cheyenne Mountain complex. The main systems are BMEWS, the North Warning System, Joint Surveillance System, SLBM Detection System, Spacetrack, Navspur and the OTH radar system. Research and development for future systems is being conducted under a programme known as the Air Defense Initiative. Details of the various systems are given below.

Ballistic Missile Early Warning System (BMEWS)
The BMEWS system consists of a small chain of very large radars for the detection of a ballistic missile attack on North America from the general direction of the USSR. There are three operational sites: at Thule, Greenland; at Clear, Alaska; and at Fylingdales, UK. Information on all BMEWS targets is transferred by a communication network to the NORAD UK Combat Operations Center.

Three types of radar were used in the original system. At Thule there were four AN/FPS-50 detection radars and one AN/FPS-49 tracking radar, at Fylingdales there are three AN/FPS-49 systems, and at Clear there are three AN/FPS-50 and one AN/FPS-92 (an improved version of the AN/FPS-49). Upgrading of the system is in progress and includes replacement of the older AN/FPS-49 radars by a version of the Raytheon AN/FPS-115 Pave Paws.

The BMEWS sites have been in operation since 1962 and have proved very reliable. In conjunction with early warning satellites, the BMEWS radars comprise the principal means of warning of an attack. Additional warning of SLBM attack is provided by the SLBM Detection System, which also uses the AN/FPS-115 radars, and is described later.

The upgrade programme for BMEWS consists of the incorporation of new computers, new software, increased bandwidth and larger raid tracking capability. New communications facilities for links with NORAD are being installed. The programme also includes the replacement of the missile impact predictor sets (MIPS) at all three sites by replacing the original on-site IBM 7090 computers with redundant CDC 170-876 processors. ITT was awarded a contract by the USAF Space Command in late 1987 to operate and maintain the BMEWS system.

The system at Thule has been upgraded with a version of the AN/FPS-115 and became operational in 1986. A $166 million contract for the Fylingdales update, funded jointly by the USA and UK, was given to Raytheon in June 1988 and work has commenced. Apart from updating the computers, software and communications, the main work at

USA / WORLD AIR DEFENCE SYSTEMS

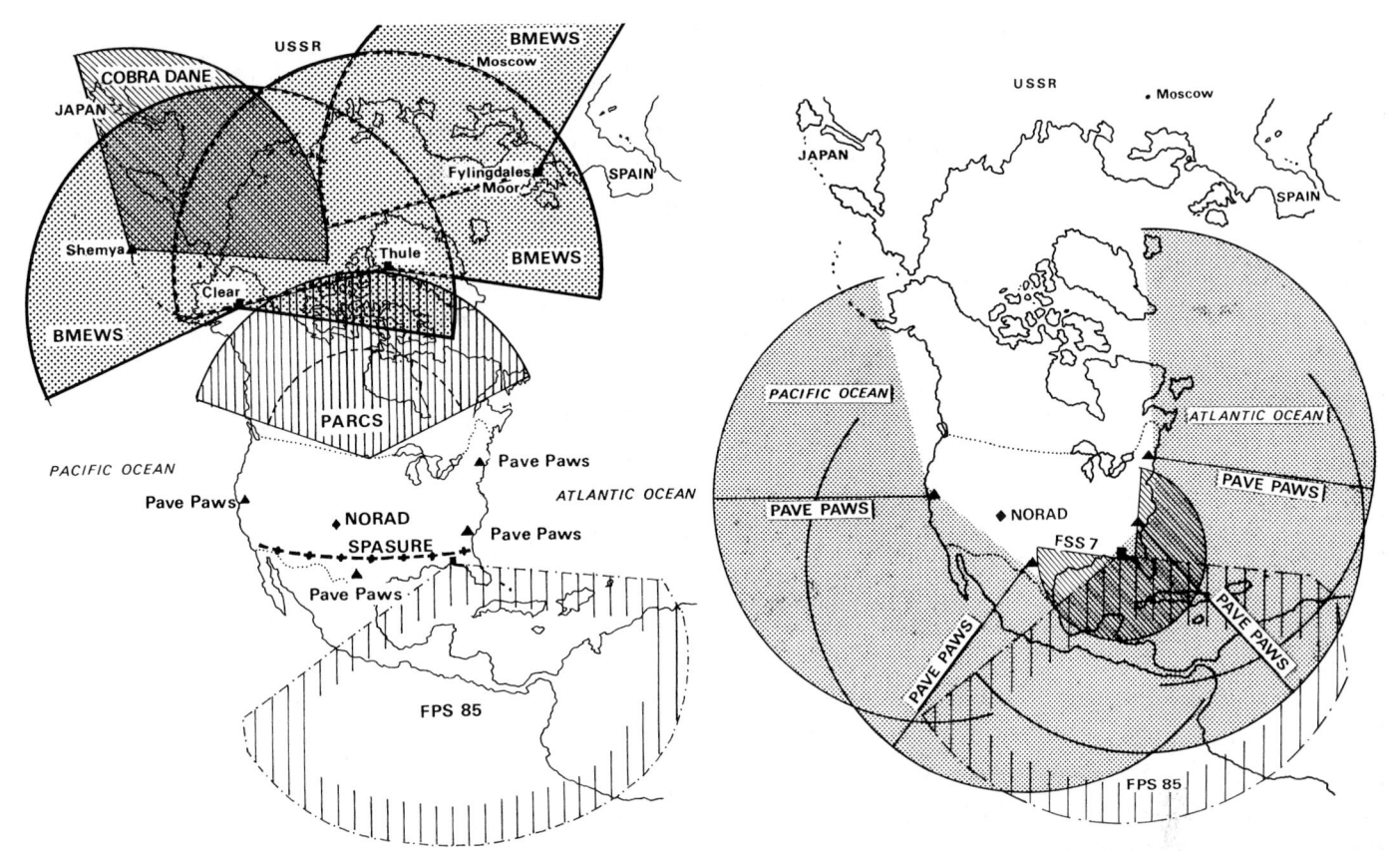

Main elements of the American ICBM warning facilities protecting North America, showing the coverage of BMEWS stations, PARCS (Perimeter Acquisition Radar Attack Characterisation System), and the FPS-85 phased-array radar and SPASUR network in the south. All four Pave Paws radars are now operational

Only one AN/FSS-7 SLBM detection radar needed to be retained after the Pave Paws phased-arrays on the East and West Coasts of the USA entered service. Previously there were three FSS-7s on each coast. Although all four Pave Paws radars are now operational, the last FSS-7 and the FPS-85 will be retained for the moment

Fylingdales is on the radar sensor, where the three AN/FPS-49 systems are being replaced by a version of the AN/FPS-115. This particular version has three solid-state phased-array antenna faces as opposed to the two faces of Thule and the SLBM Pave Paws systems. The third BMEWS site at Clear is to be upgraded in the 1990s.

The new systems will be more accurate, have a larger track capacity, and provide better prediction facilities. The radars, and the associated processing equipment, will also provide far more accurate detection and analysis of the larger number of smaller warheads in a multiple independently targetable re-entry vehicle (MIRV) attack. In addition to its ICBM related functions, the Fylingdales site will improve warning of missile attacks on NATO territory, and of SLBM attacks against North America, while enhancing surveillance of objects in space.

North Warning System

The North Warning System, previously known as the DEW (Distant Early Warning) line is one of the earlier parts of the complex of radar systems designed to warn of hostile aircraft or missile attacks on North America. It is an array of radars stretching across the northern areas of North America from Alaska, via Canada, to Greenland. The project was originally implemented as programme 413L.

The main radars of the system have been the AN/FPS-19 and the AN/FPS-30. The number in the original DEW line was 60 but this was reduced to 35 (31 in Canada and Alaska, and 4 in Greenland). This figure is being maintained while an extensive updating programme is carried out.

The updated North Warning System will consist of 13 GE AN/FPS-117 long-range radars (11 in Canada and 2 in Alaska) and 39 short-range, unattended Unisys AN/FPS-124 gap-filler radars. Of the 13 AN/FPS-117 radars, 10 use old DEW lines sites and three are on new sites in Canada (two in Labrador and one on Baffin Island). Computer systems, software and communications upgrades in support of the new network are also part of the improvement programme.

Unisys is responsible for the overall system engineering, the development of the short-range radars and the communications architecture. The updating programme is proceeding under a joint cost and responsibility arrangement between the United States and Canada as part of the 1985 North America Defense Modernization accord between the two countries (see entry under Canada).

As of December 1988, 10 of the AN/FPS 117 radars were operational, and the three built on new sites had been installed and handed over for operational testing. The second phase, the installation of the 39 short-range radars, is under way and procurement of these has started. Full operational status of the new North Warning System is currently scheduled for 1992.

SLBM Detection System

This system, which became operational in 1971, is designed to detect missiles launched by submarines operating either in the Atlantic or Pacific Oceans. It originally consisted of seven radars, with three located on each coast and one in Texas. The main radar used was the ANN/FSS-7, but in 1972 it was decided to supplement these radars with about 20 per cent of the surveillance capability of the AN/FPS-85 radar which is otherwise assigned to the Spacetrack programme, and which can provide coverage over Central America and the Caribbean.

The system has now been completely upgraded by the use of the AN/FPS-115 Pave Paws which have been installed at Otis AFB in Massachusetts, Beale AFB California, Robins AFB Georgia and Eldorado AFB California. All four sites are operational, and these four, together with the PARCS radar in North Dakota, complete a planned five-site phased-array radar SLBM warning complex. Raytheon was awarded a contract in August 1988 to provide upgrades to the first two Pave Paws systems, those in Massachusetts and California, giving them the same enhanced data processing capabilities as the two later systems. It is understood that when these are complete in 1989 the USAF plans to de-activate the AN/FPS-85 radar at Eglin AFB.

In addition to the Pave Paws programme, the USAF is developing a long-range surveillance radar programme in the Caribbean area (see entry under Caribbean).

Joint Surveillance System

Under USAF programme 968H the Joint Surveillance System (JSS) was developed as a successor to the SAGE/BUIC system which had been the mainstay of the North American defence surveillance for some 25 years. The expression 'Joint' stems from Canadian participation and also by virtue of the fact that in the USA there is joint provision of sensors and data on the parts of the civil and military air authorities (FAA and USAF). Some hardware from SAGE/BUIC is incorporated in JSS but the latter essentially replaces the former system in performing the peacetime air sovereignty mission.

JSS centres (ROCCs) are located at Griffiss, March, McChord and Tyndall AFBs, and they receive data from 46 radar sites. Fourteen more sites feed data to another ROCC in Alaska at Elmendorf AFB, and two radar sites supply data to another ROCC in Hawaii. Twenty-four air surveillance radar networks in Canada feed data to two ROCCs located at North Bay, Ontario.

The function of the ROCCs is to accept data from multiple sensors, automatically process this data, and display data for detection, tracking, and identification of air targets, and the assignment and direction of interceptor aircraft to ensure peacetime sovereignty. In time of war or

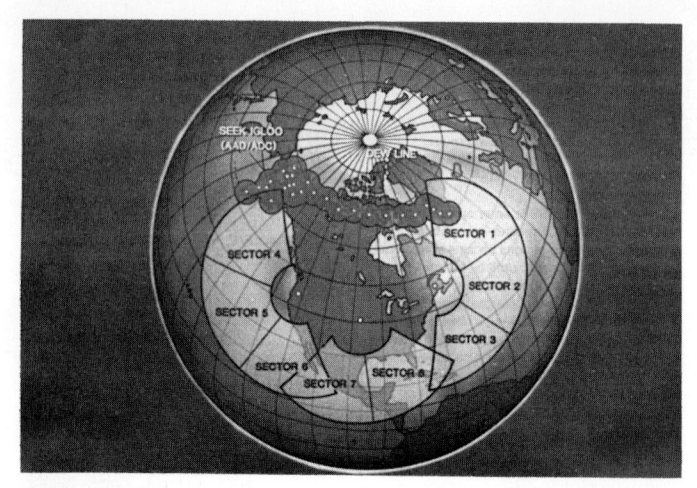

WORLD AIR DEFENCE SYSTEMS / USA

North American air surveillance systems, showing OTH-B sectors for east, west and southern cover and improved DEW Line to north

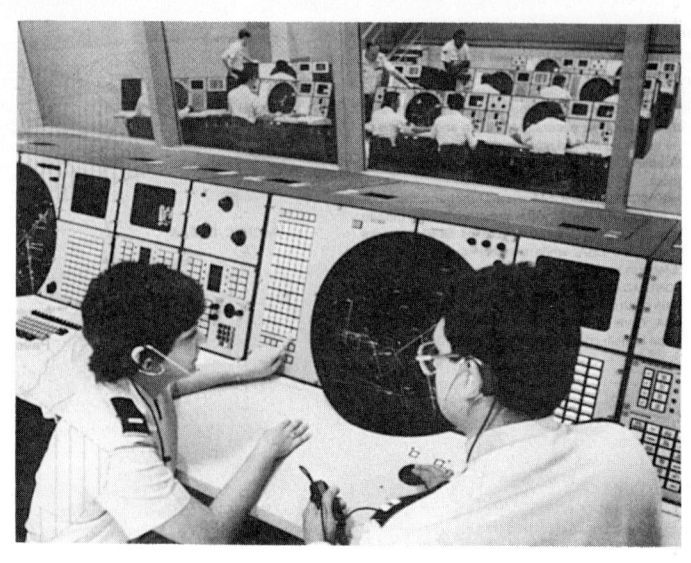

Console operators in the JSS Region Operations Control Centres receive information from up to 20 military and civilian radars

emergency, JSS ROCCs serve as a means of transferring the command and control functions to E-3 AWACs aircraft, and would continue as a backup to AWACS. In peacetime, six of these aircraft are assigned to co-operate with JSS.

The North American Air Defense Command (NORAD) Combat Operations Centre (COC) to which ROCC information is passed has been undergoing modification under PE 12311F, which provides for command, control and communications support to HQ NORAD. Within this PE is the NORAD Cheyenne Mountain Complex Improvement Programme (427M), and acquisition programmes to update the data processing, display and communications elements of the NORAD COC and the Space Defense Center part of the Aerospace Defense Command (ADCOM) Spacetrack system.

All regions of the JSS were operational by the end of 1984.

Over-the-horizon Radar Systems

The continental over-the-horizon backscatter radar (CONUS OTH-B) system has been developed under US Programme 414L by GE, under the auspices of the USAF Electronic Systems Division. The system is designed primarily as a defence against hostile aircraft and low-flying cruise missiles and will increase the warning of attack by air-breathing threats by extending US surveillance coverage from the American east and west coasts. It will provide all-altitude capability. A system with certain similarities, being developed by Raytheon for the US Navy, is known as ROTHR (Relocatable Over-the-horizon Radar).

The eastern segment of the CONUS OTH-B, which covers the whole of the North Atlantic approach areas over a 180° arc, has achieved limited operational status, and operational trials are being carried out currently. The western section, which will cover the Pacific area in three 60° segments, is under construction. A third two-segment section to cover the southern approaches is in the planning stage. A fourth section, based in Alaska, is in the early pre-planning stage, and is designed to cover the northern Pacific along the Aleutian island chain. In addition, the USAF plans to have more systems on various islands in the Pacific in due course. There have also been a number of unconfirmed reports that the USA is negotiating with the UK to install a system in western Scotland to monitor the eastern and north-eastern part of the Atlantic Ocean. A detailed description of the design and operational status of both CONUS OTH-B and ROTHR is given in the *Jane's Radar and Electronic Warfare Systems* yearbook.

Spacetrack

Spacetrack is the USAF worldwide system for the detection, tracking and identifcation of all objects in space. It consists of radar, optical and radiometric sensors located around the globe and its control centre maintains a catalogue of all objects. Information from Spacetrack is fed to the Space Defense Operations Centre (SPADOC), located at NORAD Cheyenne Mountain complex, and is part of the centrally-managed Space Defense programme involving four functional areas: anti-satellite, space surveillance, space systems survivability, and command and control.

Main sensors of the systems are the AN/FPS-85 radar at Elgin AFB, the Cobra Dane radar at Shemlya AFB, and the passive AN/FSR-2 optical and radiometric sensors. The AN/FPS-85 is an electronically steerable radar operating in the UHF band and giving three-dimensional information on all satellites and similar objects passing over it. The complete network of Spacetrack radar sites, in addition to the AN/FPS-85 and Cobra Dane, includes the BMEWS sites at Thule, Clear and Fylingdales (see BMEWS entry above). Other radar sites in the system are positioned at Pirinclik, Turkey and Kaena Point, Hawaii. The Pave Paws radar at Eldorado AFB, Texas also feeds information into the Spacetrack network.

The current Spacetrack optical system is a four-site Baker-Nunn camera system at San Vito, Italy; Sand Island in the Pacific; Mount John, New Zealand; and Edwards AFB, California. It is capable of tracking and identifying satellites out to synchronous orbit altitudes of more than 35 000 kilometres. Improvements continue to be made to Spacetrack sensors. The long term intention is to convert Spacetrack into a near real-time space-based system with less dependence on sites overseas.

Navspur

Navspur is the US Navy Contribution to the overall NORAD space detection and tracking system. It detects and tracks satellites which pass through a 'detection fence' consisting of a fan-shaped radar beam extending in an east-west direction from San Diego, California to Fort Stewart, Georgia. A central transmitter is located at Lake Kickapoo, Texas. There are a total of nine stations - six receiving and three transmitting. The beam cannot be steered and detections are made when objects pass through a stationary beam. There is a single Baker-Nunn camera at Cold Lake in Canada. The Navspur headquarters and computation centre is at Dahlgren, Virginia and the nine field stations extend across the southern part of the USA along a great circle inclined at about 33° to the equator. The largest transmitter is at Lake Kickapoo and the two smaller ones at Gila River, Arizona and Lake Jordon, Atlanta. The six receiving stations are situated at: San Diego; Elephant Butte, New Mexico; Red River, Arkansas; Silver Lake, Missouri; Hawkinsville, Georgia; and Fort Stewart. Other sensors feeding into the system are the three BMEWS radar stations, the USAF eastern test range radar on Ascension Island, the Space and Missile Test and Evaluation Center at Vandenberg, and the Malvern radar in the UK.

GEODSS

A major segment of the Spacetrack augmentation programme is the GEODSS (Ground Electro-Optical Deep Space Surveillance) system. An experimental prototype was developed by Lincoln Laboratory at White Sands Missile Range, New Mexico by August 1975 and has subsequently become part of the overall GEODSS system. It consists of: two telescopes, a 31-inch surveillance and a 14-inch tracker, operating in tandem; associated electro-optics; a computer system with ancillary electronics; and communications equipment. The project has five sites: White Sands, Choe San Jong in South Korea, Maui in Hawaii, Diego Garcia, and one in Portugal. The first four sites have now been deployed and are operational, and the Portuguese site is due to be completed in 1989. The Maui site is a separate project in its own right and is developing techniques for rapid and accurate calibration of Spacetrack radars using US Navy transit satellites.

The computer provides for on-line analysis and initial presentation, and it also includes an automatic alarm on detecting unknown space objects. The telescope can detect objects in space which are 10 000 times below the threshold of the human eye. A form of MTI is used to control the movement of the telescopes, this being arranged to correspond with either the motion of the target or the star field.

SPADOC

SPADOC has evolved in phases from a totally manual system in 1979 to the current semi-automatic capability. A phase IV upgrading programme is being carried out by Ford Aerospace under a USAF contract and is being accomplished in three blocks. Block A provides the basic architecture and executive software, Block B increases the NORAD Space Surveillance Center capability, and Block C incorporates a number of improvements such as semi-automated space warning, countermeasure management, evasive manoeuvre detection, and strike assessment. It is intended that the complete SPADOC system will reach full operating capability by 1992.

Air Defense Initiative
The Air Defense Initiative project is in the exploratory development stage and is intended to develop ground, airborne and space-based system concepts, and the necessary technology, for USAF future surveillance missions. Major development technology includes new surveillance radars, countering of low radar signature threats, cruise missile surveillance, and ECCM techniques against anti-radar missiles.

Little unclassified information on this project has been released by the USAF but it is understood that a number of design technologies have been completed, including a lightweight phased-array space-based radar antenna using solid-state transmitter modules, a conformal array radar for an advanced airborne surveillance radar, a lightweight surveillance radar decoy, and a number of associated hardware systems.

Although there are a large number of both contractual and USAF in-house efforts involved in this programme, the project is still in the very early design and development stage. Time scales are unknown but the project appears to be aimed at the mid- to late-1990s.

VENEZUELA

The Venezuelan forces include a number of weapons specifically intended for anti-aircraft applications, including a number of Roland systems. No details of a dedicated air defence network have been made public but two Italian-built long-range ATC radars are situated at the western and eastern extremities of the country and could be used in the air defence role. A Selenia ATCR-2 is located at Maracaibo in the west, while in the east there is a Selenia ATCR-3. It is understood that Westinghouse has supplied air defence equipment, which probably includes the AN/TPS-43 radar system. A tri-service evaluation committee has considered the development of a national air defence system but no decision appears to have been made. As with other oil-producing states, the substantial downturn in revenue from this source has probably curtailed the defence budget.

The Venezuelan Air Force is relatively small and consists mainly of three fighter squadrons with F-5A/Bs, F-16Bs and Mirage III/Vs. Roland and RBS 70 SAM batteries are used for ground air defence.

YUGOSLAVIA

Yugoslavia has relied in the past on Soviet and Warsaw Pact sources for much of its military equipment. It does, however, manifest a stoutly independent line in certain areas of its defence equipment. Although there is a preponderance of Warsaw Pact systems such as SA-2, SA-3, SA-6, SA-7, SA-8, SA-9 and SA-11 SAMs, some elements of Western hardware appear in its inventory. Examples of this include six Westinghouse AN/TPS-70 3D radar systems which were acquired in the early 1980s, and the local manufacture of SA-341 Gazelle helicopters. The Yugoslavian Air Force is composed mainly of Soviet types, such as the MiG-21 with about 200 in operational service and MiG-29 with about 40-50 in service, but a locally produced light attack aircraft, the Galeb/Jastreb, and strike aircraft, the Orao, have been produced in quantity.

Manportable Surface-to-Air Missile Systems

BRAZIL

Orbita MSA-3.1 Low Altitude Surface-to-air High Velocity Missile System

Development/Description
The Brazilian companies of Embraer and ENGESA have joined together to form the company of Orbita Sistemas Aerospacias SA which has a Military Division assigned to the development and production of missile systems for the Brazilian armed forces.

One of the projects is a shoulder launched surface-to-air high velocity missile, the MSA-3.1, which is being developed in conjunction with British Aerospace as a follow-on from that company's Thunderbolt design. The MSA-3.1 will normally have a launch team of two. It is guided by an automatic command-to-line-of-sight system which utilises a digital coded laser link to the missile with a stabilised sight and auto-tracker that follows a flare at the base of the weapon. Upon firing, the missile is initially boosted out of its launcher-container to a point clear of the gunner where its solid propellant rocket motor can cut in to increase its speed to a maximum of 1300 m/s (or Mach 3.9).

The nose of the missile contains the gyro package, thermal battery, motor ignition delay unit, command link detector, receiver and decoder units, guidance command processing unit and the single kinetic energy warhead with a tungsten annular cutter.

Variants
A version known as the MSA-3.2 is planned for use on the ENGESA EE-9 (6 × 6) Cascavel wheeled AFV.

A naval variant is also under consideration.

SPECIFICATIONS
TYPE	single stage, high velocity low altitude
LENGTH	1.510 m
DIAMETER	0.060 m
WEIGHT	
complete system	18.7 kg
missile plus launch tube	12.5 kg
sight and guidance unit	3.2 kg
WARHEAD	single kinetic energy dart with a tungsten annular cutter
MAX SPEED	Mach 3.9
MAX EFFECTIVE RANGE	6000 m

Status: Development phase.

Manufacturer: Orbita Sistemas Aerospacias SA, Engexco Exportadora SA, Avenue Tucunare, 125/211, PO Box 152, 06400 Barueri-SP, Brazil.

CHINA, PEOPLE'S REPUBLIC

HN-5 Series Manportable Anti-aircraft Missile System

Development
The HN-5 is a reversed engineered version of the Soviet SA-7 (Grail) manportable surface-to-air missile system which is fully described later in this section.

The current production model, the HN-5A, is an improved variant which is capable of making tail-on engagements against jet aircraft or head-on engagements against propeller-driven aircraft and helicopters under visual aiming conditions. It has been used in combat by Iran during the Gulf War.

The main improvements of the HN-5A (Strela-2M copy) over the original HN-5 (Strela-2 copy) include a greater detection range of the IR homing seeker (made possible by providing cooling to the IR detector), reduced susceptibility to IR background sources such as bright clouds by the incorporation of a background noise rejection device into the IR seeker and a more powerful HE warhead.

Description
The system consists of a launch tube which serves as an aiming device and launcher as well as a carrying case; a gripstock firing unit (designated SK-5A), mounted under the forward part of the launcher which provides launch information and ensures correct firing of the missile and, lastly, a thermal battery mounted on the forward part of the gripstock to provide power.

The missile itself is composed of four sections: the infra-red seeker section which is fitted with both cooling and background noise rejection devices; the control actuator which contains a gas generator; the warhead and fuze; and the rocket motor with rear fins attached. The infra-red seeker is designed to detect the thermal radiation emitted from the target and converts this into missile steering commands to guide the missile by proportional navigation to an intercept point.

The China Precision Machinery Import and Export Corporation also offers the CH-3A integral test and measuring vehicle based on a 6 × 6 cross-country chassis to complement the HN-5 as well as a training system.

The CH-3A integral test and measuring vehicle has a target simulation table with an IR source attached, an integral tester and a self-contained power unit.

The training system includes a tubed dummy missile and firing unit for use in operating, aiming and firing practice; a reusable battery; a monitor score recorder and a moving target simulator.

The HN-5C is essentially an HRB-230 (4 × 4) truck chassis, on the rear of which is mounted a pedestal with four HN-5A SAMs either side

Close-up of front end of HN-5A manportable SAM system with end cap removed

Variants

The HN-5C designation is used to describe a vehicle-mounted HN-5 system. The first shown was a HRB-230 (4 × 4) cross-country vehicle with a forward control fully enclosed cab which contains the fire control electronic equipment. To the rear of the cab is a pedestal on either side of which is mounted a bank of four HN-5 or HN-5A missiles in the ready-to-launch position. Between the two banks of missiles is the fire control system which consists of an infra-red tracker, a rangefinder and a TV camera. Detecting and tracking the target and launching the missile can be accomplished either manually or automatically.

Although the prototype system is mounted on an HRB-230 truck, it can be mounted on other chassis as it only weighs 2000 kg. Eight reserve missiles are carried in addition to the eight missiles in the ready-to-launch position. Evaluation trials of the HN-5C were completed in June 1986 but it is understood that production has yet to start.

The main roles of the system can be summarised as follows: protection of mechanised units; air defence for forward units and air defence for high value targets such as airfields.

During the 1987 Paris Air Show a model of the WZ 523 (6 × 6) armoured personnel carrier was shown fitted with the HN-5C launcher system on the vehicle's roof.

Chinese gunner taking aim with HN-5A manportable SAM system

Status: Production of the original HN-5 is complete and it is in service with the Chinese armed forces and North Korea. The more recent HN-5A is in production and in service with the Afghanistan Mojahedin, the Chinese armed forces, Iran, Iraq, North Korea, Nicaraguan Contras, Thailand and Pakistan. HN-5C is still at prototype stage.

Manufacturer: Chinese state factories with export marketing being carried out by China Precision Machinery Import and Export Corporation, 17 Wenchang Hutong Xidan, Beijing, People's Republic of China.
Telephone: 895012
Telex: 22484 SPMC CN

SPECIFICATIONS

TYPE	single stage, low altitude
WEIGHT (including launcher)	16 kg
MAX OPERATIONAL ALTITUDE	2500 m
MIN OPERATIONAL ALTITUDE	50 m
MAX SLANT RANGE	4000 m
MIN SLANT RANGE	800 m
MAX SPEED OF TARGET (in tail-on engagements)	260 m/s (950 km/h)
MAX SPEED OF THE TARGET (in head-on engagement)	150 m/s (550 km/h)
REACTION TIME	not more than 5 s
LAUNCHER	manportable single round disposable with grip-stock

EGYPT

Sakr Eye Low Altitude Surface-to-air Missile System

Development

The Egyptian Army has been using the Soviet supplied Strela-2/Strela-2M (SA-7 Grail) manportable low altitude surface-to-air missile for many years but for a number of reasons Egypt can no longer obtain spare parts or replacement missiles from the Soviet Union.

In the late 1970s, a reversed engineered and improved version of the SA-7b was placed in production and subsequently called the Sakr Eye (Eye of the Falcon). It is manufactured by the Sakr Factory for Developed Industries at Almaza. The weapon was developed with the technical assistance of Thomson-Brandt Industries as prime contractor, Thomson-CSF and SODETEG.

Qualification occured in 1982 and it was first shown in public in late 1984 with pre-series production commencing in March 1985. Full production started in 1986 following extensive Egyptian Army trials with initial operational capability being achieved in 1987. Egyptian sources indicated that it cost $180 million to develop Sakr Eye with all funding coming from the Egyptian Defence Ministry.

Description

In general, the method of operation is similar to the Soviet Strela-2 series which is fully described later in this section. The information provided here is from Egyptian sources who also claim that the system is more reliable than the original Soviet weapon.

The Sakr Eye system comprises two main components; the missile itself and the grip-stock. The missile is transported and launched from an expendable launch tube which is made of glass fibre and is also fitted with two aiming sights positioned on the left forward side, an acquisition indicator lamp and a thermal battery mounted under the front which has sufficient power for 40 seconds. The thermal battery can be replaced in the field if required.

The missile is a fire-and-forget type and consists of an infra-red (IR) homing head, guidance and control section and warhead and propulsion

MANPORTABLE SAM SYSTEMS / Egypt

Sakr Eye SAM system fitted with night sight and IFF system

Sakr Eye SAM system without IFF or night sight

sections. The grip-stock combines the firing mechanism and the logic circuits and when attached to the launch tube carries out the firing sequence and authorises ejection of the missile in either the manual or automatic modes. Once a target has been engaged, the launcher tube is discarded and the grip-stock attached to a new launcher.

In the absence of an integrated IFF system a typical target engagement sequence is as follows: the gunner acquires the target and aligns the weapon using the open sight and then selects either manual or automatic firing mode; audio and visual cues are given to the gunner to indicate when the target is within the weapon's engagement envelope. The trigger is then squeezed according to the selected mode and the missile is ejected from the launch tube by a small rocket motor. Then, after a short delay, the booster accelerates the missile until the sustainer motor is ignited to propel it to the target. If a target is not encountered within 4400 m Sakr Eye destroys itself. Homing is by means of a passive infra-red seeker which was developed by Teledyne and is more sensitive than the original. The HE warhead is detonated by a contact fuze that also provides for graze initiation of the warhead.

The Sakr Eye ammunition container has two missiles fitted with thermal batteries plus two spare batteries while the grip-stock container has one grip-stock. It takes 10 seconds to be prepared for action and can engage aircraft travelling at a maximum speed of 280 m/s in a pursuit or flying at a maximum speed of 150 m/s head on. Successful trials have also been carried out with Sakr Eye fitted with the US CA-563 optical sight.

This incorporates increased magnification ($\times 2.75$ with a 22° field of view) with advanced sighting techniques that include a direct computer sight digital interface with the missile, so that positive acquisition and confirmation of specific target lock-on can occur.

The optical magnification is incorporated to improve identification at extended ranges. Light Emitting Diode (LED) cueing is provided to indicate system status such as uncaged seeker or an out-of-tolerance condition. A night vision module can also be incorporated into the CA-563 optical sight. Optional equipment includes a Thomson-CSF PS-340 IFF unit, which is attached to the right side of the launcher with the interrogator electronics unit hanging on the operator's belt, and a night vision sight.

The Egyptian Army Sakr Eye is normally operated by a three-man team comprising the commander, gunner and wireless operator with a long wheelbase Jeep (4×4) light vehicle carrying two missile teams.

Variants

Pedestal Mounted Sakr Eye

In addition to the standard manportable version the prototype of a pedestal-mounted version has been built and installed on a Jeep. Both ship-launched and helicopter-mounted versions have also been proposed.

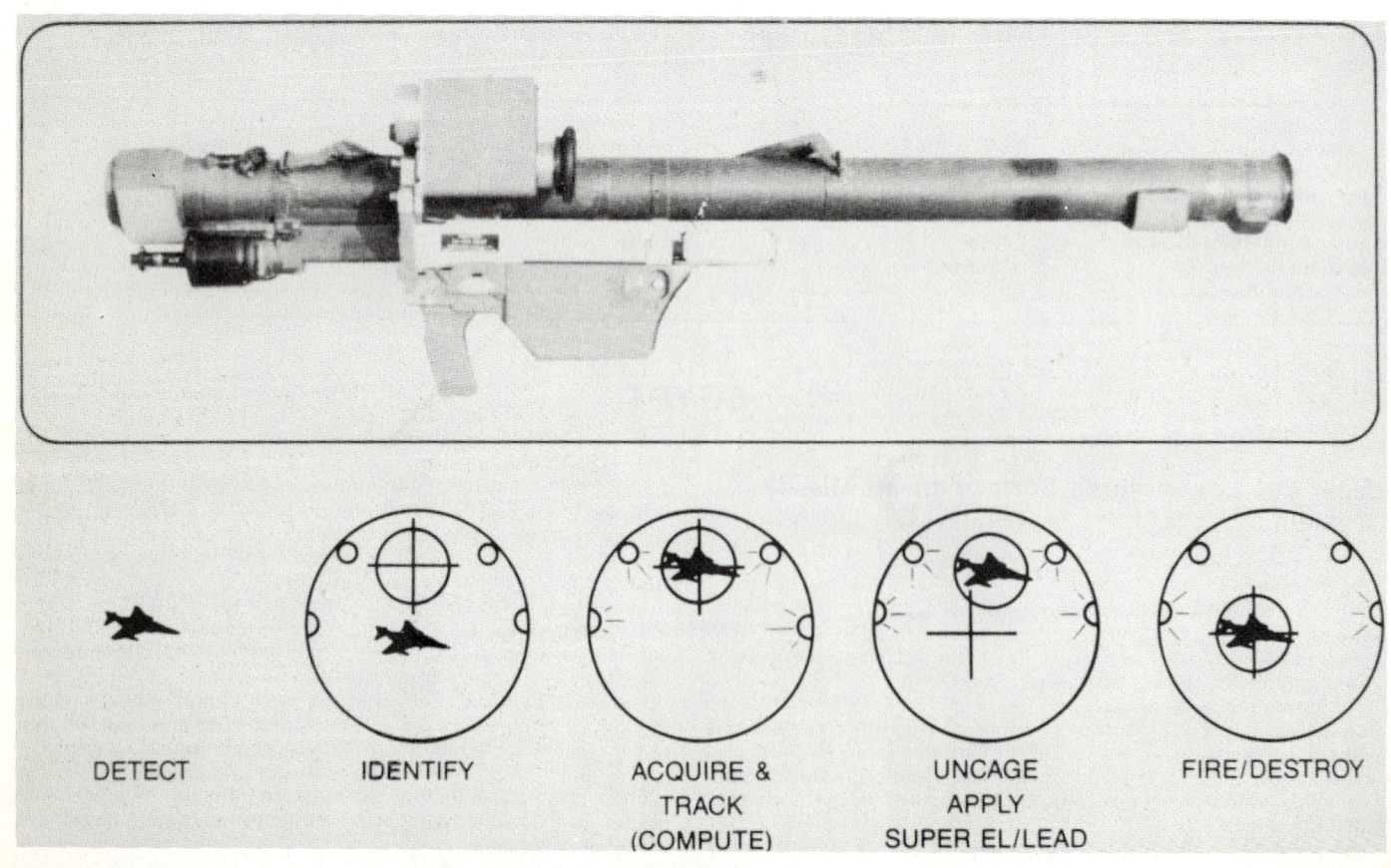

DETECT — IDENTIFY — ACQUIRE & TRACK (COMPUTE) — UNCAGE APPLY SUPER EL/LEAD — FIRE/DESTROY

Sakr Eye SAM fitted with CA-563 optical sight (top) with typical target engagement (bottom)

M113A2 mounted Sakr Eye

The Electronique Serge Dassault Sinai 23 twin 23 mm self-propelled air defence system mounted on an M113A2 chassis is also armed with Sakr Eye surface-to-air missiles, details of which are given in the *Self-propelled Anti-aircraft Gun Systems* section. Sinai was selected for service with Egypt following extensive trials with this system and the Thomson-CSF Nile 23 twin 23 mm self-propelled air defence system, which is also mounted on an M113A2 chassis.

Status: In production. In service with the Afghanistan Mojahedin and Egyptian Army.

Manufacturer: SAKR Factory for Developed Industries, Heliopolis, Cairo, Arab Republic of Egypt, POB 33.
Telephone: 963 239/962 227/965 252
Telex: 92175—92770 CERVA UN

SPECIFICATIONS

TYPE	two-stage, low altitude
LENGTH OF MISSILE	1.3 m
DIAMETER OF MISSILE	0.072 m
WEIGHT OF MISSILE	9.9 kg
WEIGHT OF COMPLETE WEAPON	
without CA-563 sight	15 kg
with CA-563 sight	18 kg
PROPULSION	solid fuel booster and solid fuel sustainer rocket
WARHEAD	HE smooth fragmentation with contact and graze fuzing
MAX EFFECTIVE RANGE	4400 m
MAX EFFECTIVE ALTITUDE	2400 m
MIN EFFECTIVE ALTITUDE	50 m (150 m for a helicopter)
LAUNCHER	manportable single-round disposable with grip-stock
RELOAD TIME	6 s

FRANCE

Matra Mistral SATCP Low Altitude Surface-to-air Missile System

Development

In 1977 a technology group formed by the French Joint Chiefs of Staff and the Délégation Générale pour l'Armement (DGA, French Weapons Procurement Authority) began a study of different short-range gun and missile point defence surface-to-air systems to meet a tri-service requirement. By 1979 the study had been narrowed to the procurement of a new third generation missile system to be known as the Sol-Air-Très Courte Portée (SATCP, surface-to-air very short-range) and an operational programme index was established that year by the Direction des Engins/Délégation Générale pour l'Armement (Missile Division of the French Weapons Procurement Authority) to develop a weapon common to all the three services.

In March 1980 an evaluation trial was held to examine the proposals put forward by five competing firms. These were quickly narrowed down to the projects proposed by Matra, Aerospatiale and Thomson-Brandt and in September that year, following further technical and feasibility studies, Matra was named as the firm responsible for developing and producing the SATCP weapon system.

On 1st December 1980 the development contract for the basic manportable tripod-launched version was placed with the firm naming Matra as the prime contractor and the Société Anonyme de Télécommunications (SAT, for the homing head), Société Européenne de Propulsion (SEP, for the rocket motor), Société Nationale des Poudres et Explosifs (SNPE, for the solid propellants), SAFT (for the thermal batteries) and Manurhin (for the warhead, safety arming device and missile container-launcher tube) as the main subcontractors.

Test firings were started in 1983 and the last of the 37 scheduled launches of what has been named the Mistral by Matra were completed in March 1988. The first production systems were delivered to the French Army and French Air Force during late 1988. The French Army requires 500 launchers and some 5000 missiles in the SATCP, AATCP and Santal versions while the French Air Force needs some 400 SATCP launchers and 4000 missiles.

Current French Army deployment is likely to group the SATCP Mistral launchers in three Corps-level air defence support regiments. These will each deploy a number of batteries that will comprise four to six sections, each of six launchers and a Samantha alerter system. Each section will normally adopt a triangular field configuration with a pair of launchers at each apex of the triangle, approximately 2.5 km from the other two pairs.

The three Force d'Action Rapide (FAR) divisions, the 4th Airmobile, 11th Parachute and 27th Alpine, will each have their own SATCP launchers equipped with an integral Thomson-LMT IFF device but not linked to a Samantha. The remaining two FAR divisions, the 6th Light Armoured and the 9th Marine Infantry, will each have a battery of about 20 of the mobile Santal systems which will be used in sections of four.

The French Air Force will use its SATCP launchers for defence of its airfields.

Description

The Mistral system comprises the missile in its container-launcher tube, the vertical tripod stand, a pre-launch electronics box, a daytime only sighting system and the battery/coolant unit. A FLIR thermal sight for night-time firing and an IFF interrogation system are under development.

The whole of the basic assembly can be broken down into two 20 kg loads—the containerised missile and the pedestal mount with its associated equipment for carriage by the missile team commander and the gunner respectively. However, in operational use the system will normally be transported in a light vehicle to the deployment area where it will be manpacked to the firing site by the team.

Matra Mistral SATCP missile being launched during trials

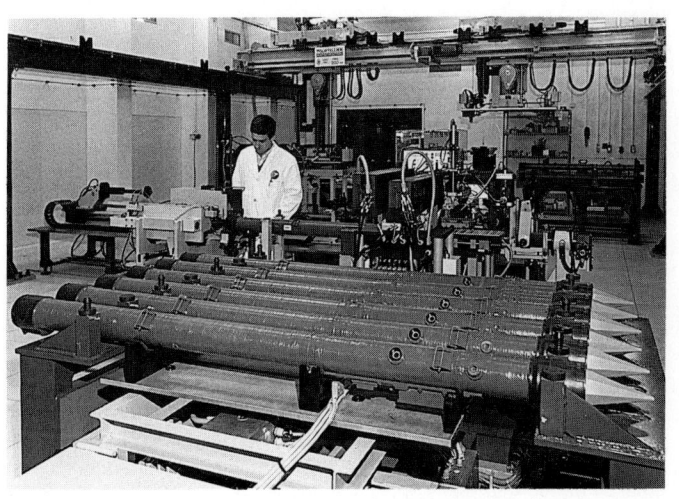

Matra Mistral surface-to-air missiles in their launchers on the production line

MANPORTABLE SAM SYSTEMS / France

Matra Mistral SATCP system deployed in ready-to-fire position

The missile itself is a slim two-stage cylindrical type with a booster motor to eject it from the launch tube and a sustainer rocket motor to accelerate it to its maximum speed of Mach 2.6. Flight control is exercised by two pairs of movable canard control surfaces located in the weapon's front region. The 2.95 kg HE-fragmentation warhead uses 1 kg of explosive and layers of tungsten balls to achieve increased penetration of the target surface and is fitted with both contact and proximity fuzes to ensure detonation. The Matra Manurhin Défense proximity fuze is an active laser type and has a 1 m precise cut-off distance for use against oncoming or very low level targets. This is an advantage over other types of proximity fuzing which are prone to causing premature detonation due to false target returns.

The cooled passive infra-red (IR) seeker is derived from technology used on the Matra R550 Magic 2 air-to-air missile programme and has a multi-element sensor with digital processing of incoming signals in both the 3-5 µm IR and ultra-violet (UV) regions of the spectrum. This results in a considerable enhancement of the seeker's sensitivity (almost 3.5 times that of the Magic 2) and allows a non-afterburning jet combat aircraft to be acquired at ranges of 6000 m or so and light combat helicopters with reduced IR signatures at ranges of 4000 m or more. In both cases the incoming target angle does not matter as the seeker head can move through ±38° with a narrow field of view after lock-on.

An IR transparent magnesium fluoride pyramidal-shaped seeker cover was used so as to appreciably reduce the drag factor normally found at the upper end of the speed range with more conventional cover shapes. This increases the Mistral's manoeuvring capabilities considerably during the terminal phase of the flight, up to the point where it can tackle targets that use 8 *g* evasive manoeuvres.

In combat, the team commander is in charge of liaison with the section fire control centre, identifying the target and ordering the engagement. The gunner then carries out the firing sequence of target acquisition, system lock-on and firing.

At a launch site the firing post is erected first, using its adjustable legs on terrain with a gradient of up to 12 per cent, to level both the attached height-adjustable gunner's seat and the two-handed firing grip. The latter is fitted with a safety lever to avoid accidental operation of the seeker activation lever, a homing head unlocking button to unlock the seeker from a target which is not to be engaged, a seeker activation lever to initiate battery power, a detector cooling and missile gyroscope spin-up button and, lastly, a firing trigger.

The missile in its container-tube is then fitted together with the battery/coolant unit, the sighting device and the pre-launch electronics box. The box carries out the following function during an engagement: it determines the search field and sensitivity of the seeker using the target data derived from the head looking at the aiming point, then, it either automatically rejects it as a false target or confirms it as valid by calculating target correction information for the launch. The battery/coolant unit supplies the electrical power required by the missile before its launch and supplies the coolant necessary to cool the detector cells of the seeker head for lock-on. Once initiated the unit operates for a period of 45 seconds and then has to be replaced which takes a short time to do. It takes approximately 60 seconds to assemble the Mistral system in the ready-to-fire state at a firing site.

The target can be designated in one of three ways: by the team commander, using information passed over a radio net from an off-site observation network or visually, by himself, using binoculars etc, or via information passed to the firing post's azimuth alignment display from a module connected to the section fire control system, or lastly, by the gunner himself using his own sighting system.

Once a target is designated in azimuth the gunner acquires it in elevation with his ×3 magnification telescope and begins tracking it. All the aiming data is continuously displayed luminously via a clear collimator system which allows the gunner to follow the pre-launch sequence and assess the target's future azimuth and elevation lead angles whilst at the same time tracking the target. He then releases the safety lever and engages the seeker activation lever. This causes the battery/coolant unit to energise and release the detector coolant. After two seconds the system is sufficiently stabilised for the seeker to lock-on to the target and feed its data to the pre-launch electronics box which checks it in the manner described previously. If a validated target is signalled and is within range then the gunner depresses his firing trigger. This causes the SNPE SD double-base extruded propellant booster motor to ignite which accelerates the missile to a muzzle velocity of 40 m/s. Before the entire missile emerges the motor burns out in order to protect the gunner from blast effects. Once free of the launch tube and in its coasting phase the weapon's wrap-around tail fins and control surfaces fully deploy. At 15 m from the launcher the booster motor falls away and the 2.5 second burn composite fuelled sustainer motor fires to accelerate the missile to its maximum speed. The weapon is then guided to the target's exhaust plume by the onboard passive IR/UV homing system whereupon in its immediate vicinity the missile adopts a final forward correction to its flight profile so as to pass close to/hit the target thus activating its warhead. Maximum total flight time possible is 12 seconds (including the 2.5 second sustainer motor burn period). As soon as a round is fired the expended

France / MANPORTABLE SAM SYSTEMS

launch tube is discarded and a new one fitted in approximately 10 seconds. Total engagement time from firing sequence initiation to weapon launch can be less than five seconds without early warning of a target and around three seconds if a warning is provided. This allows a single firing post to undertake multiple engagements of targets if required.

A total of 78 light cross-country vehicle-mounted Samantha alerting systems have been ordered by the French Army for delivery from 1991 onwards for use with the Mistral SATCP air defence sections.

A Samantha system consists of a Stratagèmes data processing system, a PR4G secure combat radio transmission system and a Thomson-CSF TRS2630 Griffon upper E/F-band radar with a coherent frequency-agile solid-state emitter and dual-frequency digital pulse-compression receiver mounted within a high gain planar antenna array. The radar has a range of 19.7 km against aircraft/helicopters flying at speeds of 40-850 m/s and uses specific horizontally polarised emissions to monitor for hovering helicopters out to a range of 11 km.

Samantha is designed to be the first level in the French Army's projected three-level hierarchical Command, Control and Alerting (C^2A) airspace management network known as MARTHA (Maillage Antiaérien des Radars Tactiques contre Hélicoptères et Avions). It can also be used with other missile systems such as SANTAL and Roland and, if required, will be able to take over control of additional firing platforms from other missile sections whose alerting system has been damaged or destroyed by enemy action.

Variants

Alamo Light Vehicle Mounted System

The basic single-round Mistral launcher system has been adapted to fit on light vehicles such as the Peugeot-Mercedes jeep, the FL-500 Lohr all-terrain vehicle, the VLRA ACMAT 4 × 4 light truck and the Matra Poncin all-terrain vehicle.

ALBI Lightweight Twin-round Mobile System

The lightweight Mistral twin-round ALBI system is designed for use on light armoured vehicles such as the Panhard VBL to protect both units on the move and vital points (VPs).

Consideration is being given by the French Army to the possibility of adopting the system as part of its Mistrale acquisition programme.

Santal Armoured Vehicle Turret System

For armoured vehicles the six-round ready-to-fire all-weather Santal turret version has been developed (see *Self-propelled SAM* section for a full description).

AATCP Air-to-air System

For air-to-air use the Mistral becomes the Air-Air Très Courte Portée (AATCP, air-to-air very short-range) missile which uses up to four 70 kg two-round groups of missiles on weapons pylons with an internal electronics box to arm helicopters. The French Army is buying it for its armed helicopters.

SADRAL Naval System

For naval use it becomes the 1500 kg all-weather six-round Système d'Autodéfense Rapproché Anti-aérien Léger (SADRAL, light short-range anti-aircraft self-defence system) for use on surface ships of all sizes. This version has been adopted by the French and Abu Dhabian navies.

Simbad Lightweight Twin-round Naval System

This is a navalised lightweight twin-round launcher designed primarily for installation on various types of smaller vessels, logistics vessels and

Matra Mistral SATCP system showing tripod launcher

support ships to provide them with a degree of autonomous anti-aircraft self-protection.

The Simbad system can be fitted to any type of 20 mm cannon mounting.

Mygale Air Defence System

Mistrale has been adopted for use with the Mygale low level short-range co-ordinated air defence system, a full description of which appears in the *Self-propelled SAM* section of this book.

In 1985 Gabon ordered a Mygale section of one warning and fire control vehicle, five firing post vehicles and associated Mistral missiles. The section was delivered during 1988.

Status: Production. On order for or in service with Abu Dhabi (SADRAL), Belgium (SATCP, 714 missiles ordered in November 1988 contract worth BFr 3.5 billion with 300 further missiles on option), France (Army and Air Force, initial order for 2300 missiles placed in March 1988), Gabon (Aspic), Italy (75 per cent licence production of SATCP by OTO Melara, Snia BPD and Selenia negotiated for production of 600 launchers and 5000 missiles) and Jordan (reported purchase 1984).

Manufacturer: Prime contractor and system integration Matra, Military Branch, B.P.1, 78146 Velizy-Villacoublay Cedex, France.
Telephone: (3) 946 96 00
Telex: MATRA 698.077 F

SPECIFICATIONS

TYPE	two-stage low altitude
LENGTH	
missile	1.81 m
container-launcher tube	1.85 m
DIAMETER	
missile	0.0925 m
WING SPAN	0.19 m
WEIGHTS	
missile (launch)	18.4 kg
container-launcher (with missile)	21.4 kg
PROPULSION	solid fuel ejector rocket motor with solid fuel sustainer rocket motor
GUIDANCE	infra-red/ultra-violet passive homing
WARHEAD	2.95 kg HE-fragmentation with contact and active laser proximity fuzes
MAX SPEED	Mach 2.6
MAX EFFECTIVE RANGE	4-6000 m depending upon target type
MIN EFFECTIVE RANGE	300 m
MAX ALTITUDE	4500 m
MIN ALTITUDE	15 m
LAUNCHER	manportable or vehicle-mounted single-round disposable, vehicle-mounted twin-round disposable

MANPORTABLE SAM SYSTEMS / Japan-Sweden

JAPAN

Keiko Low Altitude Surface-to-air Missile System

Development
In 1979 the Japanese Defence Agency authorised its Technical Research and Development Institute (TRDI) to develop a novel type of manportable low altitude surface-to-air missile system that would have a unit cost of less than 10 million yen and be considerably more accurate than contemporary weapons currently in service with the Japanese Ground and Air Self Defence Forces.

Following the allocation of nine billion yen in the Fiscal Year 1988 Defence Budget, responsibility for the programme was transferred from the TRDI in February 1988 to the Toshiba Corporation, with the final development phase scheduled to be completed during 1990. The first operational deployments are due to follow in 1991.

Demonstration rounds using the system technology were evaluated by the US Army in 1986.

Description
The missile is believed to be of standard configuration using separate current technology booster and sustainer rocket motors. The homing system, however, is of a dual-mode imaging type which uses both infra-red and visual light region guidance wave-lengths. All the operator has to do is to lock the head onto the target whereupon a high resolution charge coupled device (CCD) 'memorises' its appearance and causes the weapon to follow an all-aspects attack flight profile that is very resistant to any defensive countermeasures that may be employed.

No other details are available at present.

Status: Development prototypes.

Manufacturer: Toshiba Corporation, 1-1, Shibaura 1-chome, Minato-ku, Tokyo 105, Japan.
Telephone: (03) 245 3050

SWEDEN

Bofors RBS 70 Series and RBS 90 Low Altitude Surface-to-air Missile Systems

Development
In late 1967 the Swedish Army's Commander-in-Chief gave a special Air Defence Committee the assignment to review the country's air defence requirements and recommend what equipment should be developed or bought to meet them.

On the given economic and strategic grounds the Committee chose a combination of Saab JA-37 Viggen interceptors and short-range missile systems. The latter had to be cheap enough to be procured in large numbers yet still be able to operate under very adverse ECM conditions. The Committee also recommended that the chosen system should replace the 20 mm cannon and General Dynamics Redeye (known locally as the Rb69) shoulder-launched SAM at the brigade level and the Bofors 40 mm and 57 mm anti-aircraft guns at the divisional level.

After reviewing all the alternatives available, a development contract for one of the systems studied by the Committee, the RBS 70, was placed with Bofors in mid-1969. It was intended at this stage to procure only the missile in its container-launcher tube, the control system and the sight and stand, with target detection being carried out visually.

However, the studies carried out by the Committee and later by the Commander-in-Chief of the Army, showed that a more effective system would be produced if a search radar and IFF system were included. Therefore, in mid-1972 development contracts were also placed with SATT Electronik AB for the PI-69 IFF system and for the RBS 70 and with LM Ericsson for its PS-70/R search radar (now known as the Ericsson Radar Electronics AB PS-70/R Basic Giraffe radar).

The first delivery of RBS 70 systems for trial purposes was made in late 1973 with user trials conducted between 1974 and 1975. In a three-phase evaluation programme the Swedish Army fired more than 100 complete test rounds fitted with telemetry heads. In 1975 the programme was completed satisfactorily and in June of that year the first production orders were placed for the Rb70 missiles, sights, stands and PI-69 IFF sets. The first order for production of Basic Giraffe radar sets was not placed until 1978. The first production day-only RBS 70 sets were delivered to Swedish Army training units in 1976 with the first operational units being formed the following year. The first production radar sets were delivered in 1979.

Currently, each of the Swedish Army's 11 Type 77 infantry, nine Type 66 and four Norrland brigades have an air defence company equipped with the RBS 70 manportable SAM system. Each company consists of a HQ element (with four cargo and one tow truck(s)), three missile platoons (each with three RBS 70 launcher stands) and a radar platoon (with two Saab-Scania Type 40 4 × 4 cross-country vehicles mounting PS-70/R Basic Giraffe radar sets).

In the late seventies Bofors completed development of the RBS 70+ system which uses the same equipment as the basic RBS 70 but fires the Rb70 Mk1 missile with a new laser guidance beam sensor unit that

Bofors RBS 70 SAM being launched during winter trials in Sweden

Bofors RBS 70 SAM deployed in firing position

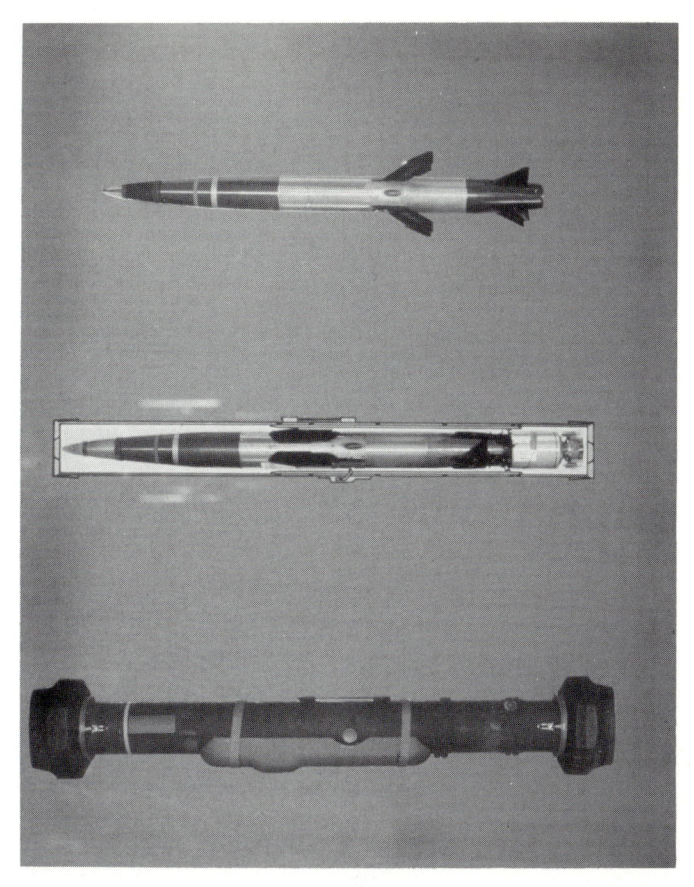

RBS 70 missile in flight, cutaway of missile in launcher/transport tube and missile in launcher/transport tube as carried in field

Bofors RBS 70 SAM system deployed in the field, from rear

enlarges the engagement envelope by between 30 to 50 per cent depending upon the tactical situation. Protection of the four Swedish Army armoured and mechanised brigades is provided for by similar strength air defence companies to the infantry units but equipped with the RBS 70+ version using converted Ikv-102 and 103 armoured tank destroyers as the Lvrbv 701 launch platform (see *Self-propelled surface-to-air missile system* section for full details).

To complete the RBS 70 family Bofors was awarded a development contract in 1984 by the Swedish Defence Procurement Administration (FMV) for the RBS 70M Mörker, (Swedish for night) day/night missile system. Contracts were also placed with Ericcson Radar Electronics AB for complementary search and tracking radars and a thermal imaging system for the weapon and to Hägglund Vehicles for the conversion of its Bv206 articulated tracked vehicle as the fire unit.

Now known by the designation RBS 90 the first systems are due to be delivered in 1991-92 with the first unit becoming operational in 1993. The RBS 90 system is due to supplement the RBS 70 rather than replace it and will be deployed at the divisional level in battalion units of three companies. These will comprise a central surveillance/Command, Control and Communications (C³) combat control platoon with an Ericsson PS-90 (Giraffe 75) vehicle mounted 13 m high antenna mast mounted G-band radar and four to six fire units. The frequency-agile radar has a 75 km range/12 500 m altitude capacity and is able to automatically detect/track up to 20 targets simultaneously due to its Moving Target Indicator (MTI) and automatic hovering helicopter detection facilities. The companies may be detached as required to defend either field forces such as the Norrland brigades in northern Sweden or high value targets such as airbases. Although a completely new system, the RBS 90 is compatible with existing Rb70/Rb70 Mk1 rounds but will be deployed with the newly developed Rb70 Mk2 missile.

Exports of the basic RBS 70 system have been via several routes to the following countries: Argentina, Australia, Bahrain, Eire, Indonesia, Norway, Pakistan, Singapore, Tunisia, United Arab Emirates (Dubai), and Venezuela. Most of these countries, including Norway, Tunisia and Singapore have purchased the Basic Giraffe radar set to complete the system.

A modified version of the Giraffe has been developed under a contract placed in 1983 for the Norwegian Army. Known as the Norwegian Army Low-Level Air Defence System (NALLADS) project the updated Giraffe 50 AT (All Terrain) radar contains a specially designed data-processing unit and is known under the Norwegian designation NO/MPY-1 radar system. It is installed on a Bv206 tracked vehicle with the power generator and communications equipment in the front car and the radar and command and control units in the trailer car. The G-band radar and back-to-back IFF antenna can be raised up to a height of 7 m on an extendable arm. The frequency-agile radar provides automatic location, identification and evaluation of threats and can handle up to 20 targets simultaneously with automatic track initiation. The derived data can then be sent to terminals at each one of up to 20 RBS 70 launch stations through a specially developed communications system. Up to three NALLADS can be linked together to defend an extremely large area. The software for the system was developed by Ericsson in conjunction with Nordic Electronic Systems while the weapon-control terminals come from Siemens (Norway). The first prototype system was delivered to the Norwegian Army in 1987 and if a procurement decision is reached shortly after the trials are finished then the first production unit could be operational in 1990.

Target detection performances are: 70 km range/7000 m altitude against a 10 m² target; 50 km range/5200 m altitude against a 3 m² target; 37.5 km range/4000 m altitude against a 1 m² target; and 22.5 km range/2200 m altitude against a 0.1 m² target.

The Singapore Air Force uses both manportable and vehicle-mounted RBS 70 systems. The latter uses a launcher stand mounted in the rear compartment of a Cadillac Gage (4 × 4) wheeled V-200 APC.

Description
The basic Rb70 round is a two-stage solid propellant rocket motor powered type. It is never removed from its container launcher tube when in the field and once fired the tube is discarded. Both impact and active laser proximity fuzes are fitted with an HE-fragmentation warhead that is surrounded by numerous tungsten pellets. The warhead has a shaped charge and therefore, an armour piercing capability. On detonation this produces over 3000 fragments. The proximity fuze is set for short-range activation so as to avoid premature detonation during operations close to reflecting surfaces such as ice, snow and water. For very low altitude targets, such as helicopters flying nap-of-the-earth flight profiles or behind natural obstacles such as trees, it can be disabled before launch by means of a switch on the gunner's left-hand aiming grip, so that the weapon actually needs to hit the target with its contact fuze in order to score the kill. In a head-on attack the double fuzing arrangement ensures that the warhead detonation is on the front end of an aircraft from where only two of the tungsten pellets are required to hit a pilot

MANPORTABLE SAM SYSTEMS / Sweden

Bofors RBS 70 Mk 2 SAM in flight

in order to incapacitate him. The shape charge can penetrate all aerial armoured targets as well as light armoured vehicles and surface targets.

In addition to the essentially smokeless Imperial Metal Industry's sustainer rocket motor, the missile body also houses a receiver unit which senses deviation from the laser line-of-sight and a small computer which converts these deviation signals into guidance pulses that command the missile to automatically follow the centre of the laser beam. Maximum engagement altitude is around 4000 m whilst the minimum altitude is effectively ground level.

The Rb70 Mk1 missile is essentially the same as the basic Rb70 but uses a laser guidance sensor unit which increases the rearward field of view to 57° from 40°. This considerably enlarges the available engagement envelope.

The Rb70 Mk2 is markedly different internally but remains the same in terms of overall size and weight. The electronics have been considerably miniaturised in order to fit a larger motor and warhead. The new sustainer increases both the missile velocity profile and the maximum range and altitude (up to 7000 m as opposed to 6000 m of the other round types against slow moving targets and from 3000 to 4000 m altitude). The maximum velocity is reached slightly earlier and once in the coasting phase the velocity decreases more slowly so that when the missile reaches its maximum range it is flying slightly faster than the earlier round types. It also has an armour piercing capability which allows engagements of both armoured ground and surface targets as well as armoured aircraft/helicopters. The basic firing unit comprises two major parts; a stand and the sight. Each constitutes a one-man pack with a third team member carrying a missile in its container-launcher tube. The IFF equipment, if used, forms another portable pack as does the target data receiver terminal which is used in conjunction with the Giraffe search radars.

For an engagement the tubular stand assembly is removed from its carrying harness and the three legs unfolded and roughly levelled by adjustments to one of them. The operator's seat is then unfolded from the vertical central tube and the gyro-stabilised sight, power supply, IFF unit and launcher-container missile tube attached. All the electrical connections are made to these units, the operator's headset and the data receiver terminal if present. A well trained crew will take only 30 seconds to complete all these procedures.

When the Basic Giraffe PS-70/R vehicle-mounted G-band pulse Doppler radar is networked with the launcher unit, before operations can begin, a prismatic compass is set up behind the vehicle pointing at a mirror located on the edge of the radar's cabin roof. The angle between true north and the radar reference direction is read from the compass and set into the radar by means of a switch on the control panel to ensure that the Position Plan Indicator (PPI) scan is orientated to the north. A point at least 20 km to the south and east is then chosen on the map of the area and the radar's position is read and its co-ordinates, relative to the chosen point, are inserted on the control panel by a thumb wheel. Each firing unit attached to the radar is then also orientated to true north by prismatic compasses at each site and the relative positions of the radar and firing units established on a common grid purpose for command and control reasons. For defence of an area containing a number of high value targets the firing units are deployed around 4000 to 5000 m apart thus allowing a company to defend an area of approximately 200 km².

The radar has MTI facilities and is fitted with an antenna that is elevated on a hydraulically operated mast to a height of 12 m. The operating cab houses three operators who detect and track targets on the digital PPI with another man plotting the air situation as updated by higher echelons on a map which is used by the commander as the basis for his orders.

RBS 70 VLM based on Land Rover (4 × 4) chassis with one RBS 70 SAM in ready-to-launch position and reserve missiles carried in rear of vehicle

A radar search is initiated on receipt of a radio report from the higher air defence echelons which indicates that a potential target is approaching. The maximum detection range of 30–1800 m/s targets is 40 km and target tracks are started at 20 km. Up to three can be handled simultaneously between the radar's altitude limits of very low level up to 20 000 m. The target's speed, course and direction is then passed up to a maximum of nine firing units by radio or cable link to the data receivers as required by the radar vehicle commander. With the radar vehicle's aid the firing unit can engage to the maximum range of the missile. The target data receiver unit computer takes the information sent, applies a parallax correction, displays the required angle of traverse and range to the target on a small screen and transmits an acoustic signal to the gunner who slews his sight and launcher assembly using two aiming handles until he hears a pulse tone on his headset. This indicates that the sight is aligned with the approaching target in azimuth and the gunner then starts to search in elevation until he acquires it. Once the target is in missile range, indicated again by the target data receiver, the gunner fires the weapon by depressing a button with his left thumb.

The laser guidance unit is activated and a Bofors booster motor on the missile is ignited to propel it out of the tube. For operator safety the motor cuts out before the end of the missile leaves the tube. The booster motor is jettisoned at a point several metres from the muzzle and the round's four centre body fins and four rear cruciform control surfaces unfold. The sustainer motor ignites and the guidance receiver on the missile starts to sense the modulated laser guidance beam. The on-board computer then translates these signals received into commands for moving the electrically operated control surfaces. Once at maximum velocity the sustainer cuts out and the missile continues on course in its coasting mode. To ensure a hit the gunner has only to keep the target in the middle of the crosshairs of his sight by using a thumb joystick.

If no search radar is available an observation post has to be established to provide early warning. The gunner then has to search for the target himself. When he has slewed the system onto the rough bearing of the target he releases the weapon's safety-catch, activates the electronics for missile launch some five seconds later and commences fine aiming with a reticule sight. The IFF equipment, if fitted, is automatically activated at the same moment and this transmits an interrogation signal. If a friendly response is received the firing circuit is overridden and visual signal lamps in the arming sight indicate that this has happened. The gunner then

Sweden / **MANPORTABLE SAM SYSTEMS** 35

Bv 206 all-terrain articulated vehicle with Bofors RBS 70 SAM system mounted on roof of rear unit

Bofors RBS 70 SAM installed on a Cadillac Gage V-200 (4 × 4) Commando APC chassis as used by Singapore

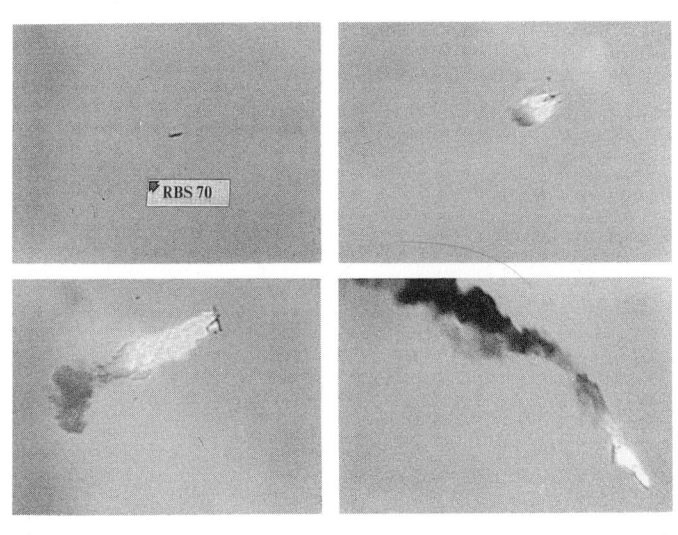

Sequence of RBS 70 SAM engaging a small drone launched from RBS 70 VLM

Bofors VLM on Panhard VCR (6 × 6) APC chassis with launcher deployed for engaging a target

discontinues the action and resets the safety device. The ×7 magnification sight he uses for the fine aiming has a 9° aperture. The range is gauged by means of a graticule with a head-on fighter-sized target which is indicated as being in range when it appears to be bigger than half the central gap in the graticule. If it is twice as large as this space then it is too close for effective engagement. Once the gunner is satisfied that the conditions are correct he launches the missile, maintaining his aim to the missile impact by guiding the gyro-stabilised optical sight with his thumb joystick.

Reloading takes less than 10 seconds and the empty tube is discarded. The padded end-caps of a new container-launcher are removed and this is hooked onto the stand and secured by a lever which also connects the electrical contacts for the pre-launch power supply to the missile and the firing signal from a battery in the sight unit.

Variants

RBS 70 VLM

There is a vehicle-launched version of the RBS 70 system available under the designation RBS 70 VLM. The launcher platform can be a light all-terrain vehicle with the stand assembly mounted at the rear. This version is also offered on the Panhard VCR (6 × 6) APC, Bv206 tracked vehicle and Cadillac Gage V-200 series APC with one missile in the ready-to-fire position and six to eight others in reserve.

RBS 70 SLM

The system has also been adopted for use on small naval vessels. In this guise it is known as the RBS 70 SLM, either in a basic version or in a containerised version.

RBS 70/M113A2 Vehicle-mounted System

In response to a mid-1980s requirement from the Pakistan Army for an RBS 70 installation to defend mechanised units, Bofors adapted its VLM system for use with the FMC M113A2 tracked APC. A full description of the system is given in the *Self-propelled missiles* section.

RBS 70 Modular Concept

The RBS 70 Modular concept is intended for integration with either vehicle- or ship-mounted air defence systems as an add-on or new-build addition. The integrated system can then be tailored to the tactical requirements depending upon the weaponry and selected sensors of the vehicle or ship.

In the former case the weapon system can be fitted on either light cross-country or heavy armoured vehicle designs with Bofors providing the RBS 70 missile launcher modules (one to four, depending upon fit, 500 × 450 × 1750 mm in size with each containing two ready-to-fire missiles and weighing 80 kg in the light vehicle module version and 100 kg in the heavy vehicle module version), the missile control unit (300 × 250 × 250 mm in size and weighing 10 kg), a freon container (300 × 200 × 200 mm in size and weighing 8 kg including the container), missile sequencer unit (350 × 300 × 200 mm in size and weighing 8 kg) and guidance beam transmitter.

All the moveable parts are mounted on a servo-controlled pedestal or turret. Depending upon the complexity required, the customer can then integrate these Bofors modules with various types of his own chosen modules/systems as deemed necessary for the system's tactical role. For example a high technology approach by a purchaser might involve networking the vehicle system to an external surveillance system for target detection and assignment, so that it can be operated either manually or automatically for the engagement of the assigned target.

The co-partner would then provide for the vehicle the purchaser's own choice of laser rangefinder, TV and/or FLIR sensor modules, pedestal/turret servo drive systems, fire control computer, automatic tracking system and operator control panel with monitor facilities. The sensors and Bofors guidance beam transmitter assembly would then be mounted on a joint structure for aiming at the target.

RBS 90

The latest version, the RBS 90, will use two Bv206 tracked vehicles as the basis of the fire unit. The first carries the disassembled missile stand equipment and three men in addition to the driver in its two cabins. The

MANPORTABLE SAM SYSTEMS / Sweden

other Bv206 carries a driver and up to five further personnel in the front cab together with a fire controller (who doubles as the fire units radar operator), gunner and engagement co-ordinator in the trailer's cab. The fire controller receives target data either from a company level central search and early warning radar or from his trailer's own roof-mounted PS-91 Ericsson Radar Electronics AB H/I-band low probability of intercept 20 km range, 7000 m altitude capability radar, a derivative of the 3D pulse Doppler HARD search and acquisition radar set.

This radar provides aircraft bearing, elevation and range for him to select targets for engagement from up to eight being tracked. The information provided is sufficiently accurate for the aircraft to be acquired by the launcher's own tracking sensors. In poor visibility a target can be tracked by the radar until it becomes visible through these optronic systems.

The gunner himself is seated in front of a TV screen which includes outputs from either the thermal imager or daylight TV camera tracking systems installed on the remotely-controlled, power-operated twin-tube missile launcher stand. He has only to keep his sight aiming mark on the designated target handed over to him by the fire controller.

The boresighted laser guidance system remains with the launcher stand which weighs 185 kg complete when assembled and can either be deployed on the ground, as with the basic RBS70 system, or mounted in or on a vehicle such as another Bv206. Deployment time for the ground role engagement is less than five minutes. Once fired the engagement sequence is essentially the same as described earlier.

RBS 70/REPORTER

The day-only RBS 70 systems can also be interfaced with the Dutch Hollandse Signaalapparaten REPORTER radar system in place of the Giraffe set. This uses a portable operations room shelter mounted on the rear of any 1½-ton military vehicle, a generator unit and a 5-m extendable radar antenna mounted on a two-wheel trailer towed by the radar truck.

Bofors RBS 90 deployed in field

The 2D I/J-band radar is fitted with an integrated IFF system and has a 40 km detection range on targets flying between 15 and 5000-m. A MTI facility is fitted and the system can track up to 12 targets automatically from a 20 km range. The information derived is then routed automatically via a one-way data transmission system to all the firing units in the field to ensure their positions are not revealed. An unlimited number of such units can receive this data. The total time from target detection by the radar operator to the actual reception of an alarm at a firing unit can be as little as four seconds.

SPECIFICATIONS

TYPE	two-stage low altitude
LENGTH	
missile	1.32 m
container-launcher (with end caps)	1.745 m
DIAMETER	
missile	0.106 m
container-launcher	0.152 m
WING SPAN	0.32 m
WEIGHTS	
Rb70/Rb70 Mk 1 missile (at launch)	16.5 kg
Rb70 Mk 2 (at launch)	16 kg
container-launcher (with Rb70/Rb70 Mk 1 missile)	26.5 kg
(with Rb70 Mk 2 missile)	26 kg
stand (with carrying harness)	25 kg
sight with pads and carrying harness	35 kg
PROPULSION	solid fuel booster and solid fuel sustainer rocket motor
GUIDANCE	modulated laser-beam riding
WARHEAD	Rb70/Rb70 Mk 1 1 kg HE-fragmentation with contact and active laser proximity fuzing Rb70 Mk 2 larger with similar fuzing
MAX SPEED	supersonic
MAX RANGE	
basic Rb70/Rb 70 Mk 1	
high speed targets	5000 m
low speed targets	6000 m
Rb70 Mk 2	
high speed targets	6000 m
low speed targets	7000 m
MIN RANGE	about 200 m
MAX ALTITUDE	
Rb70/Rb70 Mk 1	3000 m
Rb70 Mk 2	4000 m
MIN ALTITUDE	ground-level
LAUNCHER	RBS 70/70+ manportable or mobile single round trainable stand RBS 90 mobile twin round trainable stand

Status: In production. By early 1989 total production of the RBS 70 system amounted to over 1000 launchers and 10 000 missiles with Norway being the largest customer. In service with the following countries:

Argentina
A small quantity has been delivered to the Marine Corps.

Australia
Early in 1985 the Australian Army selected the RBS 70 following an evaluation with the Shorts' Javelin and General Dynamics Stinger as the replacement for its ageing Redeye SAMs and a contract was placed with Bofors for the supply of 60 launchers and support items. A Memorandum of Understanding (MoU) was also drawn up between Australia and Sweden which provides for assurances on non-interrupted product support for the system. It also allows Australian industry to participate in the development and production of the next generation missile system. In addition, Australian industry would become involved in the manufacturing of locally designed high technology products for sale by the Bofors world-wide marketing organisation.

The first contract was valued at SEK 87 million with additional orders being subsequently placed.

Bahrain
The Bahraini Army purchased some 60 RBS 70 launchers and over 500 missiles in 1979 with the first deliveries being made in 1980.

Ireland
The Irish Army purchased four RBS 70 launchers in the late seventies.

Indonesia
A number of RBS 70 launchers have been delivered for use by the Indonesian Army.

Norway
Following a Norwegian Army competitive evaluation in the late seventies for a manpads missile system a contract was placed worth SEK 400 million for 110 RBS 70 launchers and 27 Basic Giraffe radars. These were used to reorganise the air defence batteries of six field brigades with three Basic Giraffe radars, 18 RBS 70 launchers and twelve 20 mm light anti-aircraft guns each.

In 1984 a second manpads evaluation contest was held for a system to re-equip the rest of the field brigades. The RBS 70 again won and a SEK 700 million contract was placed with deliveries to take place between 1987 and 1990. The contract also involved a long-term maintenance agreement between Bofors and the Norwegian Ministry of Defence and the participation by Norsk Forsvarsteknologi (NFT, formerly Kongsberg Vaapenfabrikk) in manufacturing some of the electronic components of the system and undertaking the final assembly and testing of the sights.

The contract also contained an option which has been taken up for additional systems for use by the Norwegian Coastal Defence Force. Most of these systems have already been delivered.

In April 1988 Norway awarded a further SEK 500 million contract to Bofors for the Rb 70 Mk 2 missile as the third phase of its RBS 70 procurement programme for its Army and Coastal Defence Force. The missiles are scheduled for delivery between 1990-92 with the contract including options for additional missile batches as required.

Pakistan
In 1984 Pakistan ordered 680 missiles and 144 RBS 70 launchers with Basic Giraffe radar systems. These were delivered from 1986 onwards and include M113A2 APC installations.

Singapore
The Singapore Air Force operates one squadron of RBS 70 launchers that are carried on Cadillac Gage Commando V-200 (4 × 4) APCs. The Singapore Army also uses a number of the portable launchers. A total of 240 missiles plus between 20-40 launchers were purchased in 1982.

Sweden
The Swedish Army deploys a large number as described in the development section of this entry. In December 1988 the Swedish Armed Forces placed a SEK 200 million contract for Rb 70 Mk 2 missiles.

Tunisia
In 1979 the Tunisian Army ordered 60 RBS 70 launchers and 12 Basic Giraffe radar systems which were delivered in 1980-81.

United Arab Emirates
In 1979 Dubai placed an order for a number of RBS 70 launchers and 304 missiles which were delivered from 1980 onwards.

Venezuela
A number of RBS 70 launchers have been delivered for use by the Venezuelan Army.

Manufacturers: RBS 70/70+/90 systems and systems integration
AB Bofors, S69180 Bofors, Sweden
Telephone: (0) 586/8100,
Telex: 732 10 bofors,
Fax: 46 586 58145

PS-70/R Giraffe, PS-90 Giraffe 75 and PS-91 radars
Ericsson Radar Electronics AB, Surface Sensors Division
PO Box 1001, S-431 26 Mölndal, Sweden.
Telephone: (31) 671000
Telex: 20905 ericras

REPORTER Radar
Hollandse Signaalapparaten BV, Zuidelijke Havengweg 40,
PO Box 42, 7550 GD Hengelo, Netherlands.
Telephone: 074-488111,
Telex: 44310 sign nl.

UNION OF SOVIET SOCIALIST REPUBLICS

SA-16 Low Altitude Surface-to-air Missile System

Development/Description
In the 1987 edition of the US Department of Defense Soviet Military Power publication it was revealed that the Soviets were fielding a third type of PZRK (perenosniy zenitniy raketniy kompleks: portable air defence system) with their armed forces. Given the US designation SA-16 the only other information offered was that it was considered to be a highly accurate weapon and was replacing the SA-7 in some units on presumably a one-for-one basis.

Known by the Soviets as Igla (Russian for needle), examples have been captured in Angola by UNITA and South African Defence Forces. It is a futher development on the SA-14 with a changed shape around the shoulder rest, a frangible nose cap and a modified firing mechanism.

In the Finnish Army the system is called the 86 Igla and is linked to external target acquisition and control systems. These modifications include the use of a locally made infra-red target finder with an automatic search mechanism designed by Altim Control. A fire command unit, developed by the Nokia Group, allows firing instructions to be relayed electronically from the command vehicle to the gunner. This vehicle will be a modified troop transporter and a target location radar will be mounted on a Pasi cross-country vehicle to complete the system set-up. Training on the 86 Igla is being undertaken by the Rovaniemi Air Defence Battalion.

Status: In production. In service with Angola, Finland and Soviet Union.

Manufacturer: Soviet State Factories.

SA-16 manportable SAM system with operator positioned on top of an armoured vehicle (Soviet Military Power 1988)

SA-16 manportable surface-to-air missile system deployed

MANPORTABLE SAM SYSTEMS / USSR

SA-14 Gremlin Low Altitude Surface-to-air Missile System

Development
The PZRK (perenosniy zenitniy raketniy kompleks: portable air defence system) Strela-3 (Russian for Arrow) was given the US designation SA-14, NATO designation Gremlin, when it entered operational service in the late seventies.

The Gremlin has replaced the earlier SA-7 series weapons on a one-for-one basis in many front line units such as the organic anti-aircraft missile squads (each of three operators with grip-stocks) of BTR-60/70/80 (8 × 8) equipped Motorised Rifle companies, Soviet Naval Infantry companies and BMD equipped Airborne companies, the organic anti-aircraft missile platoons (each of nine operators with grip-stocks) of BMP equipped Motorised Rifle battalions and Soviet Army and Navy Spetsnaz special forces.

Examples of the SA-14 were captured by the Uniao Nacional para a Independencia Total de Angola (UNITA) movement in southern Angola during the October 1987 Lomba river battles against the MPLA and Cuban mechanised units.

Description
Compared to the SA-7 series the SA-14 has an uprated rocket motor, a more powerful warhead and an improved cooled passive infra-red homing seeker with proportional guidance so it can deal with both approaching and receding aircraft and other targets manoeuvring at up to 8 g. It is also believed to incorporate IR signal processing to defeat common IR countermeasures such as flares and modulated IR 'hot-brick' type decoys. The missile is similar to the SA-7 but heavier. The grip-stock assembly has a ball-shaped battery at the front in contrast to the rear mounted can-type battery of the SA-7. The weapon can also be fitted with a passive radio-frequency direction finder antenna system. Maximum effective engagement range against an approaching target is said to be 4000 m and a receding target 6000 m. The minimum effective range is said to be 600 m. The maximum and minimum effective engagement altitudes are above and below that of the SA-7.

A close-up of the nose ends of the three missile launchers showing the different sights, battery and coolant assemblies on the three launchers. The SA-16 (right) has a conical nose cone, and a battery/coolant assembly mounted below and at an angle from the launcher tube. The SA-14 (centre) has a flat nose cover, similar to the SA-7, and a battery/coolant assembly mounted parallel to the launcher tube. The SA-7 has a quite different battery/coolant assembly below the launcher tube

SA-14 (Gremlin) manportable surface-to-air missile system captured in Angola by UNITA forces late in 1987

This illustration shows the launcher tube assemblies for the three missiles without the battery/coolant assemblies fitted. SA-16 is on the right, SA-14 is in the centre and SA-7 at left.

The similarity between the SA-7 and the SA-14 launchers is quite marked, while the SA-16 launcher differs in many aspects, including different flip-out aiming sights which are arranged more on the side of the launcher

---

SPECIFICATIONS (provisional)

TYPE	two-stage low altitude	GUIDANCE	infra-red homing
LENGTH		WARHEAD	2 kg HE-fragmentation with contact and graze fuzing
missile	1.4 m		
DIAMETER		MAX SPEED	600 m/s
missile	0.075 m	MAX EFFECTIVE RANGE	6000 m
WEIGHTS		MIN EFFECTIVE RANGE	600 m
missile	10.5 kg	MAX EFFECTIVE ALTITUDE	5500 m
launcher	4.5 kg	MIN EFFECTIVE ALTITUDE	10 m
PROPULSION	solid fuel booster and solid fuel sustainer rocket motor	LAUNCHER	manportable single-round disposable with grip-stock

---

Status: In production. In service with Angola, Czechoslovakia, Cuba, Finland, East Germany, Hungary, India, Jordan, Nicaragua, Poland, Soviet Union and Syria.

Manufacturer: Soviet State Factories.

SA-7 Grail Low Altitude Surface-to-air Missile System

Development

Development of the PZRK (perenosniy zenitniy rakentniy kompleks: portable air defence system) Soviet Military name Strela-2 (Russian for Arrow, Soviet factory index number 9M32 US, designation SA-7a, NATO designation Grail Mod 0) was begun in 1959 by the Turopov OKB-134 design bureau at Tushino in order to provide a manportable passive infra-red homing surface-to-air missile system capable of engaging the enemy's battlefield support aircraft and helicopters. Development was completed in 1965 and the SA-7a entered Soviet Army service in 1966. Because of its fairly primitive lead sulphide seeker head it was only able to engage a target when it was fired from directly behind at the very hot exhaust area. This tail-chase situation resulted in it only being able to engage aircraft flying at less than 925 km/h with the preferred target being one flying at 462 km/h or less. This early-type uncooled seeker was also easily saturated by false targets as it did not have any filter system to screen out spurious heat sources. Thus the missile seeker could not be pointed within 20° of the sun (as it would home on to this rather than the target) or fired at an elevation of less than 20-30° (as it could pick up geothermal heat from sun-baked rocks on the ground and home on that). It could also be saturated by solar reflection from clouds and go wildly off course. These faults also made the Strela-2 very vulnerable to countermeasures such as infra-red decoys and flares and made it unable to engage low-flying targets. In order to rectify these faults the Soviets fielded the Strela-2M, (US designation SA-7b, NATO designation Grail Mod 1), (Soviet factory index number 9M23M), in 1971 which included a more sophisticated seeker with a filter to exclude spurious and countermeasure heat sources and an improved warhead to give greater uniformity in the fragmentation pattern. Although still a tail chase weapon the SA-7b can be fired from up to 30° either side of the target's tail and still have a good chance of hitting it. The Strela-2M can also be used with a small passive radio frequency (RF) antenna fixed to the front of the operator's helmet. This picks up the emissions from aircraft radars and radar altimeters and feeds a set of small headphones so as to provide the gunner with an audio warning of the approach of an aircraft and its rough direction.

For the Soviet Spetsnaz special forces the Strela-Blok version of the Strela-2M was developed. This uses a special launcher device in place of the grip-stock with an integral timer that allows the system to be emplaced near the likely flight paths of enemy aircraft and helicopters in rear areas and at airbases. Once the time delay ends an acoustic sensor is activated which is gated to a preset noise level. When this is achieved the missile is launched.

In the mid-seventies an improved version of the Strela-2M was produced. This, known by the US designation SA-7c and NATO designation Grail Mod 2, has a new grip-stock with a vertical handhold and a small paddle assembly just behind the thermal battery. The paddle arrangement is a more sophisticated RF detector to replace the previous helmet-mounted device.

The first recorded combat use of the SA-7a was in 1969 during the 1968-70 Egyptian-Israeli War of Attrition when around 100 or so firings caused a small number of Israeli jet fighter-bombers to be damaged in the jet pipe area. At the same time as this happened the SA-7 was given to the North Vietnamese Army to counter the American mass use of helicopters, however, it was not used widely in combat until the 1972 invasion of South Vietnam when the weapon scored a number of kills against both American gunship and transport helicopters and slow-flying fixed-wing aircraft such as the Cessna O-2 observation plane, the Douglas A-1 Skyraider piston-engined fighter-bomber, the Lockheed C-130 Hercules transport and the Lockheed AC-130 Hercules gunship. During the period 30 March to 30 June 1972 it shot down a total of 10 US and six South Vietnamese planes and helicopters. By the end of the American involvement in January 1973 a total of 528 missiles had been fired at US and Vietnamese planes scoring 45 kills (including 1 F-4, 7 O-1s, 3 O-2s, 4 OV-10s, 9 A-1s, 1 CH-47, 4 A-37s, 4 AH-1s and 9 UH-1s) with another six seriously damaged. During the first six months of 1973 some 22 SA-7 launches were detected by South Vietnamese aircraft, destroying six planes and three helicopters. In the remaining six months of 1973 and 1974 another 19 South Vietnamese aircraft/helicopters fell victim to the missiles. In the following year the SA-7 was seen to have spread to all four Military Regions of South Vietnam and was continuing to take a steady toll of South Vietnamese Air Force assets including Cessna A-37 and Northrop F-5 jet fighter-bombers causing the switching of many bombing missions to medium altitude rather than low altitude for which

SA-7 (Grail) manportable surface-to-air missiles in service with East Germany Army (US Department of Defense)

Close-up of SA-7 (Grail) manportable surface-to-air missile system showing trigger arrangement

Close-up of Polish SA-7 (Grail) manportable surface-to-air missile system with Pelangator (Soviet name for an R/F direction finder) on his helmet

MANPORTABLE SAM SYSTEMS / USSR

the Air Force had been trained. The weapon was also instrumental in providing air defence to the fast moving North Vietnamese army columns during the last months of South Vietnam's existence in 1975.

However, it was two years prior to this that the SA-7 series saw major action when some 4356 were launched by both Syrian and Egyptian troops against the Israeli Defence Force Air Force over the 19 days of the Yom Kippur War. These scored two confirmed kills, assisted in the destruction of five other aircraft and caused damage to the tailpipes of 28 others. Of the latter only a few suffered sufficient damage to ground them for longer than a day.

The SA-7 has also seen combat use in the 1982 Falklands War (with Argentinian Air Force personnel, no kills), the 1982 Invasion of Lebanon (with Syria), the Gulf War (by both Iraq and Iran), Angola (by the MPLA and Cuban troops against South Africa with 255 fired between 1978-1986 and well over 300 by September 1988 destroying one Impala jet and damaging four other aircraft including a C-47 Dakota), in Nicaragua (by both the Sandinistas and the Contras against each other's aircraft and helicopters), in South Yemen during the January 1986 Civil War, on the Thai-Laotian and Thai-Kampuchean borders (by Laotian, Kampuchean and Vietnamese forces) and in the Chad region (by Libya against French aircraft).

The relative simplicity of the SA-7 has also resulted in the widespread distribution of the weapon to various guerrilla and terrorist groups throughout the world. As such, it has been used by the Palestinians in Lebanon and Jordan, the Polisario Front in Morocco, Mauritania and the Spanish Sahara, the Mojahedin in Afghanistan (against the Soviet and Afghan Air Forces) and other groups in Iraq, Angola, Mozambique (Frente Libertaçao de Moçcambique or FRELIMO between 1973-1974), Guinea-Bissau (Partido Africano de Independência da Guiné e Cabo Verde or PAIGC in 1973), Rhodesia (damaging one Hawker Hunter, one BAe Canbera and destroying two civilian Vickers Viscount airlines), the Philippines, Sudan, Oman (23 launches between 1970-76 destroying one BAe 167 Strikemaster, one Hawker Hunter and a helicopter), Nicaragua (at least one Mi-8 Hip in 1985), Iran and Chad. In practically all cases it has caused the destruction of both civilian and military aircraft or helicopters.

In Soviet service the SA-7 is operated by a team of two. The gunner carries the grip-stock and one missile in a canvas bag while his assistant carries another missile. Motorised Rifle BTR-60/70/80 (8 × 8) equipped, Soviet Naval Infantry and BMD-equipped airborne companies have an organic anti-aircraft missile squad of three SA-7 teams whereas BMP-equipped Motorised Rifle battalions have an organic anti-aircraft missile platoon with nine teams carried in the platoon's three BMPs. The gunner can either stand in the APC hatch or dismount to fire. He normally has up to four additional rounds stowed within the vehicle. The SA-7 is currently being replaced in Soviet front-line service by the SA-14 Gremlin and SA-16 shoulder-launched systems.

Despite its faults the SA-7 has achieved its design aim of forcing enemy pilots to fly above the minimum radar detection altitude of Soviet-type radars which makes them vulnerable to higher echelon air defence systems. In several conflicts it has also had the added effect of causing enemy pilots to adopt new higher altitude weapons delivery tactics and this has resulted in a significant degrading of their bombing accuracy and their capacity to aid ground forces.

Description

The system consists of the missile in its launch container canister (Soviet Factory Index number 9P54 for the Strela-2 and 9P54M for the Strela-2M), a reloadable grip-stock (Soviet Factory Index number 9P53 for the Strela-2 with a 24-pin connector and 9P58 for the Strela-2M and a 28-pin connector between it and the canister) and a can-like thermal battery.

To operate the system the gunner visually identifies and acquires his target. He then loads a missile in its disposable glass fibre container onto the grip-stock and pointing the launcher at the target he pulls the trigger back to its first stop to start the short-life battery and energise the seeker head's sealed tracker unit. This contains a folded reflective optical system that is sensitive to heat and also acts as a space-stabilised gyroscope to aid missile stability in flight. It takes between four and six seconds to do this and once the seeker is energised and uncovered a red light on the launcher's optical sight is lit. As soon as the infra-red detector cells in the seeker detect the reflection of heat energy from the optical system a green light is activated on the sight and an audible warning is sounded by a small alarm under the rear of the grip-stock near his ear. The operator then depresses the trigger fully and the missile is expelled by the first-stage solid propellant booster motor to reach a speed of 28 m/s. This burns out in 0.1 seconds, before the tail of the missile leaves the tube and protects the operator from being burned. The booster then falls away at a safe distance from the launch position and the four spring-loaded stabiliser tail fins and the two canard control fins at the front deploy as the missile coasts along. Once this operation is complete the solid propellant second-stage sustainer rocket motor cuts in about 6 m from the operator and 0.6 seconds into the flight to accelerate the weapon within 1.5 seconds to its maximum speed. The seeker head continually determines the angle of the heat it is reflecting and the onboard guidance system uses this data to resolve the difference between the direction that the head is pointing and the weapon's trajectory by moving the two variable-incidence control fins. Throughout its fuel-inefficient lag-pursuit flight the missile spins in an anti-clockwise direction for stability. The SA-7a has a maximum speed of around Mach 1.4 (470 m/s) and is capable of effectively engaging targets at a slant range of between 450 and 3600 m at altitudes between 25 and 3000 m. The improved SA-7b increased the performance envelope by using a boosted propellant charge with the same burn time to give a maximum speed of Mach 1.7 (580 m/s), slant range limits of 450 and 5600 m and altitude limits of between 15 and 4500 m. In both versions the missile warhead contains 0.37 kg of HE and is armed after 45 metres of flight. It automatically self-destructs after 15 seconds of flight, which in the case of the Strela-2 is some 6000 m down range. If this happens close to an aircraft then severe damage can still occur. The helmet-mounted Pelangator RF detection system of the Strela-2M is known to be in service with the Soviet and Polish armies. Training (coloured yellow) and exercise (coloured silver) launch tubes are also available.

Variants

The East German Army fielded its own version of a quadruple SA-7 launcher in 1979 for use on the rear of trucks. This is used to defend rear area positions such as airfields. It was originally a Soviet idea but was first seen in operation on Egyptian vehicles during the 1973 Yom Kippur War. The Soviet Navy deployed a similar system in 1974 on its small combatants, amphibious warfare vessels and auxiliaries. It was given the NATO designation SA-N-5.

In 1981 a Strela helicopter self-defence mounting was seen for the first time with the Soviet Air Force on Mil Mi-24 Hind gunship helicopters. This involved the fitting of quadruple Strela-2M launcher arrangements on the helicopter's weapon carriers. Subsequently a two-round version was seen mounted on a Polish Air Force Mil Mi-2 Hoplite variant either side of the fuselage. The Yugoslavian Air Force uses a single round Strela-2M launcher on each side of the Type NNH weapon pylons attached either side of its GAMA gunship variants of the licence-built Aerospatiale SA-342L Gazelle helicopter. Air-to-air range of the Strela-2M according to the Yugoslavs is 4200 m.

Egypt has reverse engineered the Strela-2M under the designation Sakr Eye (see entry in this section) and China has done the same under the HN-5 designation (see entry in this section). The basic HN-5 (a copy of the Strela-2) was followed by the HN-5A which is a reverse engineered version of the Strela-2M with some further improvements, including seeker cooling to enhance sensitivity.

Main components of SA-7 (Grail) surface-to-air missile

1 - LOCKING PIN
2 - TRIGGER
3 - THERMAL BATTERY
4 - GRIPSTOCK ASSEMBLY
5 - IR SEEKER HEAD
6 - STABILIZING TAIL FINS
7 - STABILIZING FINS
8 - REAR SIGHT
9 - FORE SIGHT
10 - SLING PICKUPS

SA-7 Grail manportable SAM system deployed by Afghan Mojahedin (Soviet Military Power 1988)

SPECIFICATIONS

TYPE	two-stage low altitude
LENGTH	
missile	1.34 m
launcher	1.346 m
DIAMETER	
missile	0.07 m
launcher	0.1 m
LAUNCH WEIGHTS	
Strela-2	9.2 kg
Strela-2M	9.97 kg
LAUNCHER WEIGHTS	
Strela-2	4.17 kg
Strela-2M	4.71 kg
PROPULSION	solid fuel booster and solid fuel sustainer rocket motor
GUIDANCE	infra-red passive homing
WARHEAD	1.2 kg HE-smooth fragmentation with contact and graze fuzing
MAX SPEED	
Strela-2	470 m/s
Strela-2M	580 m/s
MAX EFFECTIVE RANGE	
Strela-2	3600 m
Strela-2M	5600 m
MIN EFFECTIVE RANGE	
Strela-2	600 m
Strela-2M	500 m
MAX EFFECTIVE ALTITUDE	
Strela-2	3000 m
Strela-2M	4500 m
MIN EFFECTIVE ALTITUDE	
Strela-2	25 m
Strela-2M	15 m
LAUNCHER	manportable single-round disposable with grip-stock
RELOAD TIME	6 s

Status: In production for export. In service with Afghanistan, Algeria, Angola, Argentina, Benin, Botswana, Bulgaria, Burkina Faso, Cape Verde Islands, Chad, People's Republic of China (local version), Cuba, Cyprus, Czechoslovakia (licence-built from 1972), Egypt (and local version), Ethiopia, Finland (where it is known as the 78-Strela or SAM-78), East Germany, Ghana, Guinea, Guinea-Bissau, Guyana, Hungary, India, Iran, Iraq, Jordan, Kampuchea, North Korea, Kuwait, Laos, Libya, Mali, Mauritius, Mauritania, Morocco, Mongolia, Mozambique, Nicaragua (including SA-7c), Nigeria, Peru, Poland, Romania, Seychelles, Sierra Leone, South Africa, Soviet Union, Somalia, Sudan, Syria, Tanzania, Uganda, North Yemen, South Yemen, Yugoslavia, Zambia and Zimbabwe.

It is also in widespread service with various guerilla/terrorist groups throughout the world. These include in Europe the Provisional IRA; in Africa the South West African People's Organisation (SWAPO), Uniao Nacional para a Independencia Total de Angola (UNITA), Polisario Front, Sudanese People's Liberation Army (SPLA), Eritrean Liberation Front (ELF), Mozambique National Resistance (MNR), and Northern Armed Forces (FAN) Chad; in the Middle East the Abu Nidal Group, the Palestinian Liberation Army (PLA), the Palestinian Liberation Organisation (PLO), Popular Front for the Liberation of Palestine-General Command (PFLP-GC), Sa'iqa, Al-Fatah, Christian Militia, Druse Militia, South Lebanon Army, Hezbollah, Amal Militia, various Kurdish groups and various Afghan Mojahedin groups; in Central America the Contra guerrillas of Nicaragua; in South Asia the Liberation Tigers of Sri Lanka and in the Far East the Khmer Rouge, the Moro National Liberation Front (MNLF), the New People's Army (NPA) and the Khmer People's National Liberation Front (KPNLF).

Manufacturers: Soviet State Factories. Licence-built by Czechoslovakian State Factories. Reverse engineered copies produced by Egypt (qv) and the People's Republic of China (qv).

UNITED KINGDOM

Shorts Starstreak Close Air Defence Weapon System

Development

General Staff Requirement (GSR) 3979 was drawn up by the British MoD following requests from the British Army of the Rhine for an air defence system to supplement the tracked Rapier SAM system then in service, especially in the forward battlefield area. The Royal Armament Research and Development Establishment had already carried out a detailed study that showed that a high velocity missile system rather than a gun or a gun/missile mix was the best solution. GSR 3979 required not only a self-propelled version of the High-Velocity Missile (HVM) but also a three-round lightweight launcher and a single-round manportable launcher.

Originally 11 companies showed an interest in the project, but in the end this was narrowed down to three competitors; British Aerospace, Marconi Command and Control Systems and Shorts. Late in 1984 the British MoD awarded both British Aerospace and Shorts a one year project definition contract valued at £3 million each for the HVM, although each company invested some of its own money as well. Both companies submitted their proposals and detailed costings in October 1985.

The British Aerospace entry was called Thunderbolt and had a single warhead dependent on kinetic energy to destroy the target. The self-propelled version had 12 missiles in the ready-to-launch position with additional missiles carried below under armour protection. The Shorts solution was called Starstreak and used three individually guided darts which employ both kinetic and chemical energy to destroy the target.

In June 1986 the MoD decided to go ahead with the Shorts Starstreak and in November 1986 awarded them a £225 million contract for the development, initial production and supply of their Starstreak high-velocity missile system in all three versions. The self-propelled model will be the first to be fielded followed by the lightweight launcher and finally the single round system. Major sub-contractors to Shorts on the Starstreak programme are Royal Ordnance Westcott for the rocket motor, Alvis for the Stormer full-tracked APC and Avimo for the gunner's sighting system. Shorts had, however, already started development of an HVM under the company project number S14 following a very detailed analysis of current and future air threats which showed that the major threat of the future would be very fast attacking fixed wing aircraft and the late unmasking attack helicopter. An HVM was the only type of missile which would enable targets to be defeated before they released their weapons.

By the time they were awarded the November 1986 contract by the MoD, Shorts had already carried out over 100 test firings of the HVM since 1982 as part of a technology demonstrator programme aimed at minimising risk during the full development phase. The Starstreak HVM is complementary to the British Aerospace Rapier SAM, and the former is deployed more forward than the latter. The Shorts Starstreak HVM will be issued to 15 Air Defence Regiment, Royal Artillery, which will be reformed, and deployed to the British Army of the Rhine (BAOR). The 15 Air Defence Regiment will probably be based at Dortmund where BAOR's two Rapier Regiments (12 and 22 Air Defence) are now based. It was disbanded in 1958 and when reformed, it will have three batteries (44, 40 and 21). Manpower for the new regiment will come from within BAOR troop limits.

Description

All three versions of the Starstreak will use the same basic missile. There is a separate entry for the self-propelled version of the Starstreak HVM on the Alvis Stormer chassis in the *Self-propelled Surface-to-air Missiles* section. This version also carries a Lightweight Multiple Launcher for dismounted use.

The Starstreak missile is sealed in an environmental container that also acts as the launcher unit. It requires no field testing, as the only launch preparation required is the connection of the re-usable aiming unit.

The missile itself consists of a two-stage solid propellant rocket motor assembly with a payload separation system mounted on the front end of the second stage motor. This supports three winged darts which each have guidance and control circuitry, a small high density penetrating explosive warhead and delay action fuzing.

The aiming unit contains all the systems required for the engagement cycle and comprises two separate and detachable assemblies:

(a) a light alloy casting hermetically sealed optical head with an optics stabilisation system, aiming mark injector unit and aimer's monocular

MANPORTABLE SAM SYSTEMS / UK

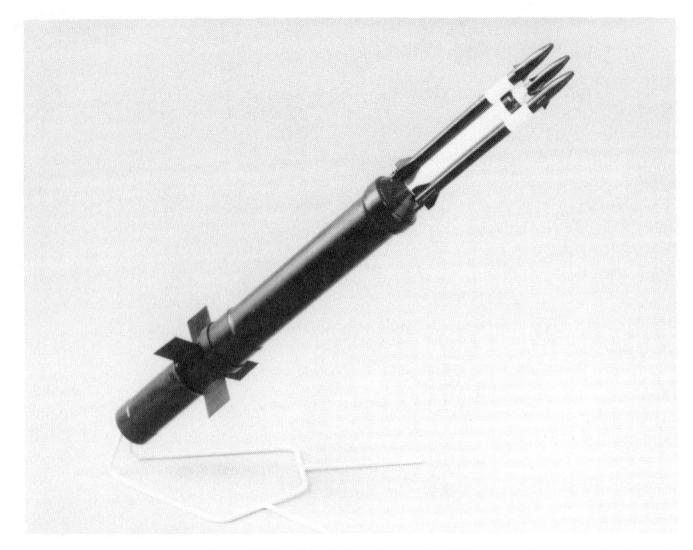

Shorts Starstreak High Velocity Missile out of its canister and showing three manoeuvrable darts each containing a high explosive warhead

Lightweight Multiple Launcher version

Manportable version of Shorts Starstreak High Velocity Missile showing detachable aiming unit

Shorts Starstreak HVM being fired for the first time in the off-the-shoulder role in mid-1988. The launch was completed with 100% success

sight. All three of these are used for acquiring and tracking the target

(b) a hermetically sealed control unit in a lightweight moulded case which contains the power supply unit (of three lightweight rechargeable batteries) and the electronics units required for processing and control. An attached control handle contains the joystick controller, trigger assembly, system switch, wind offset switch and super-elevation button.

In combat, the aimer acquires the target in his monocular sight and selects 'system-on' which energises the aiming unit battery supply. A space-stabilised aiming mark is injected into the centre of the field-of-view of the aimer who then tracks the chosen target by moving the launcher assembly so as to maintain the target in co-incidence with the aiming mark. This permits lead angles in both azimuth and elevation to be generated and ensures that the missile is brought onto the target at the end of its boost phase.

After this pre-launch tracking phase is completed, the aimer presses the firing trigger which causes a pulse of power to be transmitted from the aiming system power supply to the missile booster unit where it causes the first stage rocket motor to ignite. The Starstreak is ejected from its launch tube by this motor which completely burns out within the length of the container in order to safeguard the operator. The booster accelerates the missile to a high exit velocity while its canted exhaust nozzles impart sufficient roll on the weapon to create a centrifugal force that unfolds a set of flight stabilising fins. The first-stage motor then separates from the main missile body and falls away as the Starstreak emerges from the canister.

At a safe distance from the gunner, but within 300 m of the launch point, the main second stage rocket motor cuts in to accelerate the missile to an end-of-boost velocity which is in the region of Mach 3 to Mach 4. As the motor burns out, the attenuation in thrust triggers the automatic payload separation of the three darts which, upon clearing the missile body, are independently guided in a fixed triangular formation by their individual onboard guidance systems using the launcher's laser designator beam and a grid matrix.

The darts rely primarily on their kinetic energy for target penetration, with the impact forces generated activating the delay action fuze mechanism so that the explosive component detonates within the confines of the target for maximum effect.

All the operator has to do after the launch is to continue to track the target and maintain his sight aiming mark on it by use of the joystick. Once the engagement is over the operator discards the empty launch tube and connects a fresh one to the aiming unit.

As Starstreak does not rely on a heat source for guidance, it can engage targets from all angles including head on. A Single Shot Kill Probability (SSKP) of 0.96 has been mentioned in connection with the system.

The Lightweight Multiple Launcher version consists of three standard Starstreak rounds and a manportable aiming unit mounted on a traverse head that can be quickly slewed through a full 360°. The system can stand above ground or be sited in a trench.

The basic Starstreak HVM is a clear weather system only but target information can come from a number of other sensors such as the THORN EMI Air Defence Alerting Device (ADAD) which was ordered by the British Army in 1987.

In mid-February 1988 Shorts announced that they had signed an Intent to Team Agreement with the Boeing Aerospace Company of Seattle, USA, covering mutual promotion of the Shorts Starstreak High Velocity Missile. Boeing Aerospace has already been selected as the prime contractor for the Pedestal Mounted Stinger (covered in the *Self-Propelled SAMs* section). Under this agreement, the two companies will explore applications that can complement the Pedestal Mounted Stinger, more commonly called the Avenger.

In September 1988 Shorts revealed that it had teamed with McDonnell Douglas Helicopters for a weapon integration programme on the AH-64 Apache helicopter for close-range air-to-air engagements. Other variants being studied are a ship-borne system and the use of technology in the US DoD SDI concept.

UK / **MANPORTABLE SAM SYSTEMS** 43

SPECIFICATIONS (provisional)
TYPE	two stage high velocity missile low altitude	GUIDANCE	beam riding laser
LENGTH		WARHEAD	triple kinetic/high explosive submunitions
missile	1.397 m	MAX SPEED	Mach 4 plus
missile in canister	1.397 m	MAX EFFECTIVE RANGE	7000 m
DIAMETER		MIN EFFECTIVE RANGE	300 m
missile	0.127 m	ALTITUDE LIMITS	not available
missile in canister	0.274 m	LAUNCHER	manportable single, trainable stand mounted triple or Stormer APC mounted octuple with all using disposable containers
WEIGHT	not available		
PROPULSION	two stage booster-sustainer solid propellant rocket motor		

Status: Advanced development. Expected that first deliveries will be made to the British Army late in 1990.

Manufacturer: Short Brothers Limited, Missile Systems Division, Montgomery Road, Belfast BT6 9HN, Northern Ireland.
Telephone: (0232) 458444
Telex: 74688
Fax: (0232) 732974

Shorts Javelin Low Altitude Surface-to-air Missile System

Development

The Shorts Javelin close-range air defence weapon was developed under contract to the British MoD from 1979 as a follow-on to the Shorts Blowpipe system and was first revealed in September 1983 by which time initial firing trials had already been completed.

The Javelin has been designed to counter a wide range of low level air defence targets and it employs semi-automatic command to line-of-sight (SACLOS) guidance, rather than infra-red detection, to engage its target. Its range enables it to engage and destroy high speed attacking aircraft before they are able to release their weapon load. The Javelin can also be used against helicopters and has a secondary surface-to-surface capability.

In comparison with the earlier Blowpipe, the Javelin has a new warhead, a more powerful second stage motor for increased range and it has also benefited from recent advances in video micro-processing techniques. The updated guidance system, which has been incorporated in a new aiming unit, makes the operator's task much easier. The aiming unit of Javelin has been designed so that it is compatible with the current Blowpipe system.

Shorts stress than the Javelin does not rely on the target's infra-red signature and is therefore almost impossible to counter by decoys such as hot flares. Compared with the earlier Blowpipe, training time is much reduced with the Javelin system. First production Javelins were completed in 1984 and they have replaced Blowpipe on a one-for-one basis in regular units in the British Army and Royal Marines (the latter having one troop of three sections known as 3 Commando Brigade Air Defence Troop). During wartime in the British Army, the Javelins will normally be used in the forward area of operations under the control of brigade or higher level operations. Its three main roles are vital point (VP) defence where it is ideally sited about 500 m from the VP area, as a gap filler for the Rapier systems and for route defence where about 12 teams are required to cover a 12 km distance. The latter is the most rarely used mode of Javelin deployment.

For the rear areas four TAVR Blowpipe Regiments will be deployed and their observation posts sited well in front of their team positions in order to give as much warning as possible to the manual acquisition weapons. As both Javelin and Blowpipe are relatively slow when compared to the Rapier systems they are not suited to engaging high speed crossing targets but can be placed to engage approaching targets in a 30 to 40° arc. Normally they are engaged head-on at a range of approximately 7000 m with target interception occurring at some 3000 m after a 14 second flight time. The four TAVR Regiments are being gradually converted to Javelin.

Shorts Lightweight Multiple Launcher (LML) provides operator with multi-engagement capability for Javelin SAM system

Shorts Lightweight Multiple Launcher (LML)

MANPORTABLE SAM SYSTEMS / UK

Standard manportable Shorts Javelin SAM system deployed

Manportable Shorts Javelin SAM being launched from Royal Navy warship

In June 1984 Shorts announced a second order worth £35 million from the British MoD for production of Javelin. This increased home and exports sales to £120 million. In the middle of the same year it was announced that the Javelin had been selected by the Royal Navy to provide special protection against Kamikaze-type attacks on naval vessels, especially those operating in the Middle East. In January 1985 Shorts announced that it had received a third production contract valued at £25 million for the Javelin which brought the total Javelin order book up to over £160 million.

According to Shorts, effectiveness of the Javelin close range SAM has been demonstrated in British Army practice camps where so many Shorts Skeet targets were destroyed that one camp, at least, had to be put back due to lack of targets. One aimer of 10 (Assaye) Air Defence Battery had a 100 per cent success rate in 1985 when he destroyed eight Skeet targets in eight engagements.

During the 1986 British Army Equipment Exhibition, Shorts revealed that it was acting as Project Manager for all aspects of Close-Air Defence Weapon Systems (CADWS) on behalf of the MoD. This not only includes Blowpipe, Javelin and Starstreak, but also the system integration for enhancements to UK CADWS, the THORN EMI Air Defence Alerting Device (ADAD), the IFF equipment, the thermal imaging night sight and the Air Defence Command and Information System (ADCIS).

Description

The Javelin SAM system consists of two main components; the missile sealed within its launching canister and the aiming unit, and lightweight carrying cases are provided for both.

The canister in which the missile is factory-sealed is a lightweight environmental container designed to act as a recoilless launcher. It houses the guidance aerial, the electrical connections and the thermal battery to power the aiming unit after the missile launch.

The front cap is blown off by gas pressure when the missile gyro is fired and the laminated rear closure is ejected at launch.

The missile is a 1.4 m long slender tube with the fuzes in the tip and the warhead in the centre. The guidance equipment is in the forward part of the body and the rocket motors are in the rear. There are four delta-shaped aerofoils in the nose for aerodynamic control and four at the tail for ballistic stability. A self-destruct facility is incorporated. The nose section is free to rotate independently of the main body, to which it is attached by a low friction bearing. Twist and steer commands to the control fins guide the missile with a high response rate.

The aiming unit is a self-contained firing and control pack with a pistol grip firing handle on the right side. It contains a stabilised sighting system which provides manual target tracking and automatic missile guidance through a solid state TV camera.

Digital commands from the camera are fed to a microprocessor and the resultant guidance demands are transmitted to the missile by radio. The simple controls on the handle include the firing trigger, thumb-controlled joystick and system, fuze mode and super-elevation switches. Other controls include channel selector switches for the transmitter and an automatic cross-wind correction switch.

Marconi Avionics were awarded their first production contract, worth over £5 million, for their advanced television guidance system used in the Javelin in May 1984. The automatic gather and guidance system comprises a miniature solid state CCD (charge-couple-device), television camera and zoom lens, sophisticated signal processing electronics and a 2-axis sub-miniature gyro assembly. The camera unit and associated data extraction equipment is produced by the company's Electro-Optical Products Division, Basildon and the gyro assembly by the Gyro Division, Rochester. The complete electro-optical and gyro subsystem are contained within the operator's lightweight aiming unit. This was made possible by the use of a CCD imaging array (a light sensitive microchip) to form the TV picture, and by high-density electronic packaging involving multi-layer hybrid micro-circuits.

The Javelin is made ready for action by clipping the aiming unit onto the canister which takes less than five seconds.

Information of an imminent attack can be received over the radio net or by the team scanning the horizon visually. The aimer acquires the target in the monocular sight and switches on the system, selecting the frequency of the guidance transmitter and the mode of the fuze (proximity or impact). This activates the tracking electronics and projects an illuminated stabilised aiming mark (a red circular reticule) into his field of view. The target is tracked briefly with the aiming mark to establish a lead angle, the safety catch is released and the trigger pressed. Range is indicated stadiametrically in the aimer's eyepiece which has a magnification of ×6 compared with ×5 of a Blowpipe.

The firing trigger activates two thermal batteries, one of which supplies the power to the aiming unit while the other supplies power to the missile.

The gyro of the missile is run up by the action of the cordite burning charge, initiated by the thermal battery. The gas overpressure blows off the canister sealing cover and the missile is boosted from the canister by the first stage motor (the same type as used in the Blowpipe) which burns out in 0.2 seconds before the missile emerges from the tube. Then, at a safe distance from the aimer, the weapon is accelerated to its supersonic burn-out speed, by the second stage sustainer motor.

The Javelin's wing assembly comprises four wings mounted on a central tube and is housed at the forward end of the canister until the round is launched. The wingtips are folded in this stowed position to reduce the diameter of the canister. While the missile is being launched the main body of the missile passes through the wing assembly which is arrested by a band of tape around the rear body. When the missile is clear of the launch canister its wingtips are unfolded by the roll action that the booster motor applies to the rear body. A slight cant on the wings then rolls the missile continuously throughout flight in order to maintain aerodynamic stability. The missile is not armed until it is at a safe distance from the aimer and if guidance signals are lost it self-destructs. Javelin retains the twist and steer control method of Blowpipe with the control surfaces being mounted on the nose section which is free to rotate.

The camera detects the missile flares and, using digital techniques transmits guidance demands to the missile. The TV guidance datum-line is collimated with the aiming mark which is maintained on target by the gunner using the thumb joystick. In the event of sight failure, the integral TV camera system tracks the missile flares and sends an error signal via the command link to adjust its flight trajectory as needed.

The warhead is detonated either by the preset impact or proximity fuze.

Variants

Spartan Javelin

The Alvis Spartan APC which had a four-round missile launcher mounted on the roof will not now be entering service. The Starstreak HVM will now enter service with the Royal Artillery in the early 1990s.

Lightweight Multiple Launcher

The Lightweight Multiple Launcher (LML) has been developed by Shorts to provide the Javelin with a multi-engagement capability. All LML systems use three standard Javelin canistered missiles and a standard shoulder launched aiming unit as clip-on equipment.

In the free standing application, the support tube is held vertically by the tripod legs which pivot off an eccentric support collar. Screw jacks positioned between the top of the sleeve and the legs, are used to level the launcher.

When deployed in a trench the support collar can be slid partially down the support tube where it is clamped at the appropriate height. This means one leg hangs vertically while the other legs are used to provide lateral support to the launcher.

To deploy the LML the tripod stand is erected by unfolding the legs and sliding the leg support collar to the bottom of the support tube which is then locked in position. The LML head is then lifted onto a spigot on top of the tripod stand and the sight arm is released from its stowed position and unfolded into its operational state. After fitting the aiming unit onto the sight arm saddle and loading the three missiles in position, the LML is ready for action and the aimer now follows normal Javelin operational procedures.

Lightweight Multiple Launcher (Vehicle)

The LML(V) is suitable for mounting on many types of armoured personnel carriers and for trials purposes has already been mounted on the Shorts Shorland S53 (4 × 4) APC.

The turret ring is fitted over a hatch opening and is provided with its own integral hatch cover. The ring carries a pintle for mounting the vehicle variant of the traverse head. Turret freedom relative to the turret ring is 60°.

The ring is provided with a handgrip and frictional brake so enabling the aimer to slew it to approximate target bearing and then track the target.

Shorts Javelin SAM being launched from an LML (V) installed on a Shorts Shorland S53 mobile air defence vehicle

Lightweight Multiple Launcher (Naval)

The LML(N) has been developed for naval applications.

SPECIFICATIONS

TYPE	two stage low altitude
LENGTH	1.39 m
DIAMETER	0.076 m
WING SPAN	0.275 m
WEIGHTS	
aiming unit	8.9 kg
missile	12.7 kg
missile in canister	15.4 kg
missile in field handling container	19 kg
missile in field shipping container	43.0 kg
PROPULSION	two-stage solid propellant
GUIDANCE	semi-automatic command to line of sight (SACLOS)
FOV	
monocular	180 mils
magnification	×6
TV FOV	
wide	230 × 180 mils
narrow	36 × 36 mils
WARHEAD TYPE	2.74 kg HE fragmentation with contact and proximity fuzing
HE CONTENT OF WARHEAD	0.6 kg
MAX SPEED	about Mach 1
MAX EFFECTIVE RANGE	about 5500 m (against helicopters) about 4500 m (against jet aircraft)
MIN EFFECTIVE RANGE	about 300 m
MAX EFFECTIVE ALTITUDE	3000 m
MIN EFFECTIVE ALTITUDE	10 m
POWER SUPPLY	27.5-35.5 V DC supplied by canister thermal battery and three 12 V rechargeable batteries in aiming unit
LAUNCHER	manportable single round with grip-stock

Status: In production. In service with United Kingdom (Army, TA and Marines), Dubai, Jordan (may have ordered system in 1988), South Korea ($30 million contract placed in December 1986 with first deliveries made in April 1987, further orders involving possible local assembly of system are being negotiated), Oman and Botswana. Malaysia has an intent for 48 Javelin launchers.

Manufacturer: Short Brothers Limited, Missile Systems Division, Montgomery Road, Belfast BT6 9HN, Northern Ireland.
Telephone: (0232) 458444
Telex: 74688
Fax: (0232) 732974

Shorts Blowpipe Low Altitude Surface-to-air Missile System

Development

In the early 1960s Shorts started the private venture development of a manportable SAM system, subsequently called Blowpipe, that could provide defence against aircraft in the forward battlefield area.

By 1965 the first trial missiles had been successfully fired and the missile system was first officially revealed in September 1966 at the Farnborough Air Show.

In 1968 the British MoD started to provide funding for Blowpipe with first manned firings taking place in late 1968. By early 1972 the system had completed its research and development phases and had been accepted for final evaluation with the British Army. They placed an initial production contract for Blowpipe in 1972 and Canada was the first export customer the following year. First production Blowpipe systems were completed in 1974 and entered service with the British Army in 1975 when the first troop was formed at Kirton-in-Lindsey.

A normal British Army Blowpipe detachment consists of three men. In the UK a Land Rover (4 × 4) light vehicle is used and this also carries a small number of reserve missiles whereas the BAOR use an Alvis Spartan APC which carries a total of 10 missiles. One man normally stays with the vehicle ready to bring new missiles forward while the other two provide the firing unit.

Following its issue to British Army units in the UK and then BAOR, Blowpipe was issued to the Territorial Army where it replaced the famous Bofors 40 mm L/70 towed anti-aircraft guns.

Blowpipe was first received in 1978 by the 103 Air Defence Regiment, Royal Artillery (The Lancashire Artillery Volunteers) followed by 102 Air Defence Regiment, Royal Artillery (Ulster and Scottish) and 104 Air Defence Regiment, Royal Artillery, all part of 23 Artillery group which will deploy to BAOR in time of war. Each regiment has three batteries.

Although Blowpipe requires more training than the US Redeye — in that it uses line-of-sight guidance rather than infra-red detection to engage its target, and was designed specifically to counter on-coming attacks from high speed aircraft by destroying the target before it can release its weapon load — Shorts believe it is more effective than Redeye or the Soviet SA-7.

Although its primary role is to engage aircraft and helicopters, Blowpipe has a secondary role against surface targets out to a range in excess of 3000 m.

MANPORTABLE SAM SYSTEMS / UK

Blowpipe missile leaving launcher during trials

Two-man Blowpipe team of Canadian Armed Forces deployed in field (Canadian Armed Forces)

In mid-1981 the Canadian Department of Supply and Services placed its second contract for the Blowpipe system by which time the system had been adopted by eight armed forces and six countries (including Canada and the UK).

The Blowpipe was used by the Argentinian and British armed forces in the 1982 Falklands campaign, with the former shooting down one British BAe GR Mk 3 Harrier. The following is an extract from the British Government's Command 8758 publication *The Falklands Campaign: The Lessons*: 'Blowpipe is a point defence missile system designed to be operated, and carried limited distances, by one man. In this campaign it was used extensively against fast-crossing targets for which it was not designed, and subjected to far rougher handling than it had been designed to withstand. Despite this it brought down nine enemy aircraft and a further two probables. Experience in the campaign has confirmed the need for the series of improvements already in hand, which include enhancements to the missile warhead and motor and the introduction of an improved aiming unit and alerting device. These improvements should be completed over the next six years.'

Evaluation of the data obtained since the Falklands War indicates that the actual number of kills by Royal Marines/Army Blowpipe teams was one confirmed (a Macchi MB 339A on 28 May 1982 at Goose Green), three assists (one McDonnell Douglas A-4C Skyhawk on 24 May over San Carlos Water, two FMA IA 58A Pucara's on 28 May at Goose Green) and one severely damaged (an FMA IA 58A Pucara also on 28 May at Goose Green).

In the Spring of 1986, quantities of Blowpipes found their way to both the Afghanistan Mojahedin and the Nicaraguan Contra guerrillas. Apparently used in combat only by the former, a number have since been captured by the Soviets. They are said to be unpopular because of the high level of skill required to operate them, but despite this, it has been confirmed that they have destroyed several Soviet aircraft and helicopters.

Some sources have indicated that a number of the guerrilla weapons have been diverted to the Pakistani Army as a kind of tax.

As early as June 1979, Shorts had announced preliminary details of an advanced guidance system for Blowpipe which by then was already undergoing trials with excellent results. A multi-million pound MoD contract for further development was awarded in June 1980. This was originally known as the Blowpipe Mk 2 but eventually entered production as the Javelin system (qv). Blowpipe missiles can be used with the Javelin aiming unit if required.

In mid-1982 the Government of Thailand placed its third order for the Blowpipe missile for use by the Royal Thai Air Force for airfield defence. Late in 1982 the MoD of the Sultanate of Oman placed a multi-million pound order with Shorts for Blowpipe missiles and support equipment. In the British Army, Blowpipes were manned by the Royal Artillery and organised into batteries with each battery having two troops each of three sections with each section having four Blowpipes.

BAOR had four Blowpipe batteries (10, 21, 43 and 111) but these have now been converted to Javelin, with each battery being allocated to a division in time of war and tasked at brigade level.

By mid-1983, the Shorts Blowpipe order book, for both home and export markets, stood at over £200 million and by 1989 over 20 000 Blowpipe and 16 000 Javelin missiles had been produced. Although Javelin has now replaced Blowpipe in front line British Army and Royal Marine units, it continues in limited production for the export market.

Description

The Blowpipe system consists of two main components; the missile sealed within its launching canister and the aiming unit, with lightweight carrying cases being provided for both.

The Blowpipe missile itself is a slender tube, 1.4 m long with the warhead in the centre section and the fuzes in the tip of the nose. The forward part of the body contains the guidance equipment and the rocket motors are to the rear.

The short 0.2 second burning time of the booster stage was achieved by using thin sections of high burn rate pressurised propellant. Roll is induced in the missile by suitably angling some of the small nozzles drilled through the rear end plate.

The second stage Crake sustainer uses a conventional double base propellant to minimise smoke emission and exhausts its gases by ducting through the centre of the first spent stage booster motor via a lined blast pipe.

Premature ignition of the second stage as a result of an inadvertent ingress of hot gas from the first stage operation is prevented by a specially designed closure for the second stage nozzle. There are four delta-shaped aerofoils in the nose for aerodynamic control and four at the tail to provide ballistic stability. In each case the aerofoils are of supersonic double-wedge profile.

When a period of five seconds passes without any guidance signals being received, an in-built self-destruct facility is operated. This is initiated either by the gunner cutting off transmission or, if the missile goes off course, while in flight.

An unusual feature of the Blowpipe missile is that the nose section is free to rotate independently of the main body to which it is attached by a low-friction bearing. Twist and steer commands to the control fins guide the missile, resulting in a fast response rate. The container in which the missile is factory sealed is a lightweight environmental canister designed to act as a recoilless launcher and houses the firing sequence unit, the thermal battery to power the aiming unit and the guidance aerials and electrical connections.

The aiming unit is a self-contained firing and control pack with a pistol grip at the right side and contains a radio transmitter, an auto-gathering device, a monocular sight and optional IFF interrogator system. The simple controls include a trigger, thumb-controlled joystick and switches for fuze option, auto-gather, and guidance command frequency change. Information that an attack is imminent is either received over the radio net or by the team scanning the horizon visually.

The Blowpipe is made ready for action by clipping the aiming unit onto the canister which takes less than five seconds. The gunner then grasps the front of the canister with his left hand and clasps the hand

UK / MANPORTABLE SAM SYSTEMS

grip on the aiming unit with his right hand and supports the remainder of the launcher on his right shoulder.

He acquires the target in his monocular sight which has a magnification of ×5 and is graticulated to assist in range estimation and to allow for cross winds. He then switches on the system, selects the frequency of the guidance transmitter unit and the mode of the fuze (proximity or impact).

In addition to the monocular visual sight, the aiming unit is also fitted with a sensor which detects the position of the missile in relation to the line-of-sight. The Blowpipe missile is fitted with flares which provide outputs for both visual and automatic IR tracking. The error signals generated in the sensor are sent to the missile via a radio transmitter in the aiming unit and an aerial in the canister.

A receiver in the missile then passes these signals to the control unit and this automatically brings the weapons into the line-of-sight to the target. The effective range of the missile is limited by the available speed and lateral acceleration after the burnout of the second stage motor. The automatic system is intended for use when gathering the missile. It can do this much more quickly and consistently than the aimer and this enables targets to be intercepted at close range. For longer range targets, automatic guidance will cease after two or three seconds and after that the missile is under the control of the aimer's thumb.

To fire, the gunner releases the safety catch and squeezes the trigger to activate a generator which supplies current to thermal batteries in both the canister and the missile. The battery which powers the aiming unit is fitted in the canister. The gyro of the missile is run up by the action of the cordite burning charge, initiated by the thermal battery. The gas overpressure blows off the canister sealing cover. The missile is launched by the booster motor (which is also used in the Javelin missile), which burns out before the weapon emerges from the tube and, at a safe distance from the aimer, the missile is accelerated to supersonic speed by its sustainer motor.

After burn out, it cruises as a fully controlled dart and is automatically gathered into the centre view field of the aimer who then guides it onto the target using the thumb-controlled joystick.

The aimer keeps the missile coincident with the target until interception. When the missile is being guided by thumb control it is not necessary to track the target accurately. The aimer only needs to keep it in the field of view of the monocular.

There may be times when the automatic gathering system cannot be used and in such circumstances the aimer can switch out the automatic gathering system before missile launch and use the thumb control throughout the engagement.

The warhead of the Blowpipe is detonated either by impact or proximity fuze. The warhead is a dual blast shaped charge type and is capable of penetrating the armour plate of light armoured vehicles. Once the target has been destroyed the aiming unit is separated from the empty canister and another loaded canister attached. In peacetime the empty canister can be returned for reloading and reuse.

Variants

Blowpipe Trailer System

This consisted of a two-wheeled trailer with a power-operated one-man turret with four Blowpipe SAMs in the ready-to-launch position. It never entered service.

Blowpipe LCMADS

The Blowpipe Low Cost Mobile Air Defence System (LCMADS) was a private venture by Shorts and consisted of a 6 × 6 Land Rover or similar vehicle with a Twin Pedestal Launcher in the rear cargo area with two Blowpipe missiles in the ready-to-launch position. This never entered production.

Thai Blowpipe LCMADS

The Royal Thai Air Force has developed and deployed its own vehicle and ground pedestal mounted twin-Blowpipe launcher version of the LCMADS system with an attached optical sighting unit.

Turreted Blowpipe

This was to have a one-man four-round turret which could be mounted on AFVs such as the Spartan or M113, it never entered production and further development resulted in a four-round launcher for the Javelin. This was not adopted for service, as the Shorts Starstreak HVM on the Stormer chassis will enter service in the early 1990s in BAOR.

Air-launched Blowpipe

At one time Shorts proposed a helicopter-mounted version of the Blowpipe for use in the air-to-air role but this never progressed beyond the mock-up stage.

Naval Blowpipe

Various versions of the Blowpipe have been proposed or developed for naval applications including a twin manual system, 10-round powered operated systems, container fit systems and the submarine-launched missile system (SLAM) developed in conjunction with Vickers Shipbuilding.

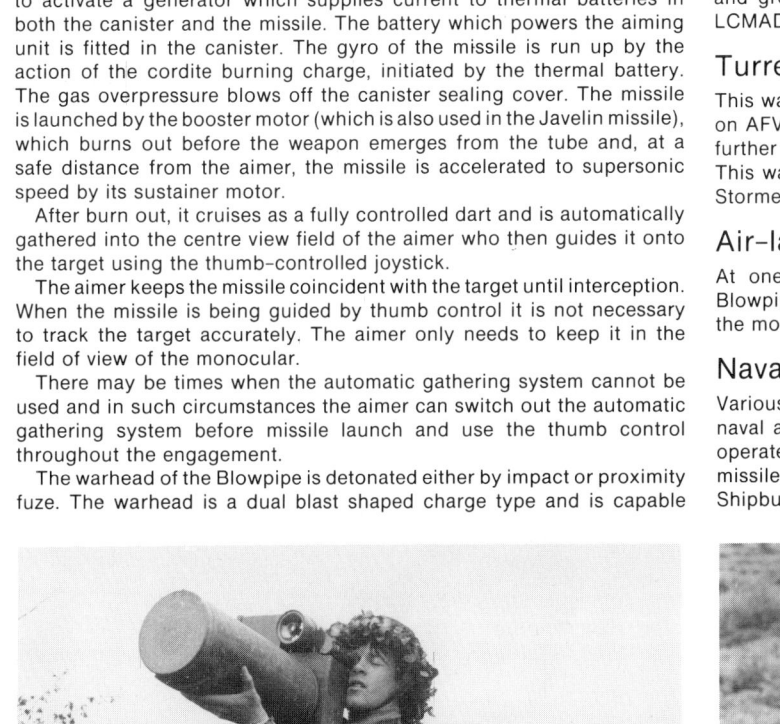

British Army Blowpipe system deployed in field

Rear view of Blowpipe deployed in field with operator using right hand for missile guidance and control

MANPORTABLE SAM SYSTEMS / UK-USA

SPECIFICATIONS

TYPE	two-stage low altitude
LENGTH OF CANISTER	1.40 m
LENGTH OF MISSILE	1.35 m
DIAMETER OF MISSILE	0.076 m
WING SPAN	0.275 m
WEIGHTS	
missile and canister	14.5 kg
missile	11 kg
aiming unit	6.2 kg
PROPULSION	dual-base solid propellant booster and sustainer rocket motors
GUIDANCE	IR auto-gathering, then command to line-of-sight (CLOS)
WARHEAD	2.2 kg HE dual fragmentation shaped charge with impact and proximity fuzing
MAX SPEED	about Mach 1
MAX EFFECTIVE RANGE	about 3500 m
MIN EFFECTIVE RANGE	about 700 m
MAX EFFECTIVE ALTITUDE	2500 m
MIN EFFECTIVE ALTITUDE	10 m
LAUNCHER	manportable single round with grip-stock

Status: In limited production. In service with Afghanistan (Mojahedin guerrillas), Argentina (Army, Special Forces and Marine Corps); Canada (Armed Forces); Chile (Air Force and Marines); Ecuador (Army); Malawi (Army); Nicaragua (Contra guerrillas); Nigeria (Army); Oman (Army); Pakistan (Army from Afghanistan guerrillas); Portugal (Army); Qatar (Army); Thailand (Air Force); United Kingdom (British Army Territorial Army units)

Manufacturer: Short Brothers Limited, Missile Systems Division, Montgomery Road, Belfast BT6 9HN, Northern Ireland.
Telephone: (0232) 458444
Telex: 74688
Fax: (0232) 732974

UNITED STATES OF AMERICA

General Dynamics FIM-92 Stinger Low Altitude Surface-to-air Missile System

Development

Even as the General Dynamics FIM-43A Redeye system achieved its initial operational capability in 1967, a joint work programme between the US Army and the General Dynamics Pomona Division was in the second year of studying new design concepts and initiating the testing of components for a Redeye II weapon system with an all-aspects target engagement capability. This Advanced Seeker Development Programme (ASDP) eventually gave rise in 1972 to the second generation manportable XFIM-92A Stinger design with a more sensitive seeker head and a better kinematic performance when compared to its predecessor and with the addition of a forward-aspect engagement capability to its flight envelope and an integral IFF system.

However, the first guided tests in 1974 at the White Sands Missile Range resulted in a number of problems being found with Stinger which caused the US Army Missile Command (MICOM) to request that the Ford Aerospace Aeronutronic Division develop what was designated the Alternate Stinger system, using a reusable laser beam device attached to the launcher assembly as the guidance system. To cure both the guidance problems and to reduce the continually rising costs of its system, General Dynamics initiated a design review which resulted in a 15 per cent reduction in the total number of electronic parts used and the introduction of a separate grip-stock assembly. These changes made a considerable improvement in the test results obtained in the 1975 firings, and by February 1976 the US Department of Defense was satisfied that the early guidance difficulties had been overcome. They were so convinced that in 1977 the funding used for the development of the Alternate Stinger was stopped. In 1978, following an Engineering Development Programme which had needed over 130 test round firings to validate the design, Stinger was finally released for production. This started in 1979 with the first production systems being delivered in 1980 and the first military units achieving initial operational capability status in February 1981 with the basic FIM-92A Stinger version.

In mid-1977 after a four-year advanced development programme, and just before the basic Stinger was released for production, General Dynamics was awarded a Full Scale Engineering Development contract for the next third generation evolutionary phase of Stinger. This involved the fitting of a microprocessor-controlled Passive Optical Seeker Technology (POST) homing head which uses a dual infra-red (IR) or ultra-violet (UV) rosette-pattern image scanning guidance technique to enhance the missile's target detection capabilities. The use of the different seeker only involves a modular change to the weapon and allows it to discriminate effectively between a target, any deployed IR decoy flares and background clutter when they lie within detectable range thus preventing a false launch.

Limited procurement of this FIM-92B Stinger-POST version began in mid-1982 alongside the earlier variant with the latter being completely superseded on the assembly line in 1985.

As a further increase to the effectiveness of Stinger, General Dynamics began development in FY85 of what is essentially a fourth generation manportable SAM system. Known as the Stinger-Reprogrammable Microprocessor (RMP) system, the change allows the onboard digital microprocessor to be periodically updated with new software to counter any new threat technology instead of having to go through a missile redesign each time. Production of this FIM-92C model began in November 1987 at the General Dynamic's Valley Systems Division Stinger plant in California. In early 1988 Valley Systems Division was awarded a $695 million multiyear Stinger production contract to produce over 20 000 rounds through 1991. For the future a night sight and ranging device is under development.

West German soldier using Stinger manportable SAM in field

USA / MANPORTABLE SAM SYSTEMS

Prior to General Dynamic's production of the Stinger-RMP on 2 September 1987, the US Army MICOM selected Raytheon Missile Systems Division as the second source contractor for production of this version. The initial $26.4 million contract was for 400 Stingers with a $54.4 million option for an additional 1500 missiles which could be exercised in 1989. Once fully qualified as a producer Raytheon will be able to compete with General Dynamics from 1990 onwards for the annual production contracts. This is being done in order to keep the overall acquisition costs down for the US armed services.

In 1983 a six nation NATO consortium headed by West Germany agreed in principle with General Dynamics to co-produce around 12 500 Stinger systems. The other five signatories were Belgium, Italy, the Netherlands, Greece and Turkey. The prime Stinger Project Group European contractor is Dornier GmbH, with a total West German production requirement of some 4500 systems, while the Turkish companies of Asalan and the Machinery and Chemicals Corporation (MKE) are taking a 40 per cent share of the production as the total Turkish requirement is believed to be 4800 systems. Low-rate production is due to start in 1992 although West Germany, the Netherlands and Turkey have already taken delivery of small batches directly from the manufacturer. The Netherlands is expecting to buy 1709 missiles (90 for the Navy/Marine Corps, 944 for the Army and 675 for the Air Force). Since signing the agreement, both Belgium and Italy have cancelled their participation in the production programme although the latter bought 150 launcher grips and 600 FIM-92A Stingers from the manufacturer to fulfill its immediate training requirements.

In West German service it is known as the Fliegerfaust-2 (FIF-2) and is being deployed with the army, navy and air force. A new palletised 8-12 round launch platform is being developed by Dornier for use on ships, wheeled and tracked vehicles. In the case of the air force the palletised launcher will be deployed on light (4 × 4) Unimog 1300L trucks with towed twin 20 mm Rh-202 cannon for airfield and Vital Point (VP) defence whereas the army will use it on tracked vehicles for battlefield air defence. All three services will also use the manportable version.

Both West Germany and the Netherlands have also undergone trials on their manportable Stinger systems with an early-warning radar system to enhance its performance. The Royal Netherlands Army used the Hollandse Signaalapparaten Radar Equipment Providing Omnidirectional Reporting of Targets at Extended Ranges (REPORTER) mobile trailer-mounted I/J-band radar system with an integral IFF system in a highly successful series of tests in late 1985. The radar provided early warning of targets up to 40 km away and flying between 15 and 4000 m altitude which were then handed over to a Stinger launch team for engagement.

Other nations which have ordered or been the recipient of varying numbers of Stinger systems include Bahrain, Chad, France, Iran, Israel, Japan, South Korea, Pakistan, Qatar, Saudia Arabia and the United Kingdom. Of these France and Chad have used limited numbers successfully against Libyan aircraft during the 1986-87 border skirmishes while the British Special Air Service (SAS) actually used a small number of FIM-92A Stingers during the 1982 Falklands War where they destroyed an Argentinian Air Force FMA IA 58A Pucara twin-propeller close-support aircraft during the 21 May San Carlos amphibious landings.

In September 1988 Switzerland chose a variant of the Stinger-RMP for its manportable air defence system. Parliamentary approval is expected in late 1989 for the purchase. A maximum of 2500 will be procured for a cost of $315 million.

In mid-1986 the first shipments of FIM-92A model Stingers were sent to the Afghan Mojahedin guerrillas for use against Soviet and Afghan Air Force aircraft. The first combat use came on 26 September when Stingers destroyed three Mil Mi-24 Hind gunship helicopters during a battle near Jalamabad. By the end of the year Stingers were apparently responsible for the destruction of at least three fixed and nine rotary-wing aircraft. As combat experience mounted, the presence of these weapons had by the end of 1987 resulted in the combat loss of 227 fixed and rotary-wing types and pressurised the Soviets into making a number of major modifications to their aircraft based there in order to reduce their vulnerability to IR guided missiles. The sucess with the Stingers continued thoughout 1988 and into 1989 as the Soviets continued their withdrawal.

Aircraft types known to have been shot down by Stinger include MiG-17 Frescoes, Sukhoi Su-7/17/20/22 series Fitters, MiG-21 Fishbeds, MiG-23 Floggers, Sukhoi Su-25 Frogfoots, Antonov An-26 Curls, Mil Mi-8/17 Hips and Mil Mi-24 Hinds. More importantly to the guerrillas they also forced the Soviets to adopt new and less accurate high level weapons delivery flight profiles thus considerably reducing the freedom of movement of the Soviet gunship and transport helicopters during operations in the hilly/mountainous areas.

The guerrillas have also introduced their own tactics for using Stingers. They used the weapon in an offensive manner by deploying a combat group armed with several launchers to the vicinity of an airfield and then for several hours interdicted the flightpath in order to try and destroy the larger logistic support and personnel transport aircraft which were needed to resupply the base.

Unfortunately, numbers of Stingers have been captured by the Soviets and the technology compromised.

Ironically it is the Stinger missiles delivered to Afghan guerrillas that have found their way to Iran where one was subsequently fired at the US Army Task Force 160 Hughes AH-6 special operations helicopters engaged in flights over the Gulf. Of the 20 launchers apparently captured by Iran only a few remain in its possession. Apart from the one used in combat another was recaptured by US forces aboard a badly damaged Iranian speedboat following an air-sea battle in the Gulf. Thirteen others were sold to Qatar in early 1988. Stinger systems were used in the region by the Royal Netherlands Marine Corps, the US Marine Corps, the US Navy and the Saudi Arabian armed forces for the close-range protection of surface-ships and shore installations.

A number of FIM-92A Stinger systems were also delivered to the Uniao Nacional para a Independencia Total de Angola (UNITA) movement in Angola during 1986-88 where they have been used successfully against the Soviet supplied Angolan Air Force destroying a number of jets and helicopters including one MiG-21, three Mil helicopters and a MiG-23 Flogger C (with a two-man Cuban crew that was captured) during the late 1987 battles in south-east Angola. In 1987 small numbers of FIM-92A Stinger launchers were given to the Contra guerrillas fighting in Nicaragua against the Sandinista government. It is believed that these were committed to battle in the latter part of the year.

Stinger manportable SAM with missile just leaving launcher

Stinger AA missile system

MANPORTABLE SAM SYSTEMS / USA

In US service all four armed services use the weapon and the US Air Force has small detachments trained to defend airfields and VPs, especially in the Far East at the four South Korean airbases used by its units. It has also been revealed that the American President's residences in Washington and elsewhere are protected by specialist Stinger teams in case of an aerial attack by terrorist organisations.

Each of the US Army's armoured, mechanised, light infantry, airborne and air assault Divisional Air Defense Artillery (ADA) Battalions have a Stinger Platoon (of four sections) with each of its four batteries. For the airborne and air assault divisions three of the sections have five two-man teams each while the fourth has only three teams to give a divisional total of four two-man section HQs and 72 firing teams. For the Division 86 mechanised and armoured units, the number of Stinger teams is reduced to 60 whereas the light infantry divisions only have 40. A team is normally equipped with a 4 × 4 Jeep or M998 series (4 × 4) HMMWV light vehicle, a GSQ-137 Target Alert Data Display (TADDS) comprising a 6 kg portable unit with a display, audio warning and VHF receiver, two AN/PPX-3 IFF interrogators and a basic load of six Stingers. Each Army Patriot, I-HAWK, Chaparral, Vulcan, and Roland fire unit and Patriot and I-HAWK fire control platoon also carry one Stinger team set (less the TADDS) as part of their normal equipment allowance. During a heavy attack both team members would shoulder a launcher providing two independent ready-to-launch weapons with four extra weapons available. A Stinger crewman is also being integrated into the M163 air defence vehicle with two rounds.

Early warning is provided by the eight M561 (6 × 6) 1¼-ton Gamma Goat-mounted 20 km range pulse Doppler MPQ-49 Forward Area Alerting Radars (FAARs), with integral AN/TPX-50 IFF systems held in the ADA headquarters radar platoon which transmit target position data to the TAADS by radio link. Increasingly, however, the FAARs are being used without TAADS and the Stinger teams are being cued onto a target by a voice communication VHF radio link direct to the radar operator. The FAARs are also used with the Chaparral and Vulcan air defence systems.

In the US Marine Corps the Stinger system is assigned to the Forward Area Air Defense (FAAD) battery of the three active force Marine Air Wing (MAW) units. These comprise five platoons each with 15 Stinger teams and are deployed with the Marine Expeditionary Unit (MEU), Marine Expeditionary Brigade (MEB) and Marine Expeditionary Force (MEF) mission orientated Marine Air-Ground Task Forces (MAGTFs) as required.

In early 1988 the Marine Corps released a request for a proposal to the US defence industry for a manportable radar system to alert and cue Stinger missile gunners to the approach of hostile aircraft. Called the Lightweight Early Warning Detection Device (LEWDD) it must have portable subsystems with a total weight of less than 90.9 kg, a range of 20 km and be able to be set up in five minutes or less. Demonstrations of off-the-shelf systems were due in late 1988.

The US Navy uses Stinger teams to supplement warship and support vessel close-range air defences in high threat areas. A team of two is normally employed with the gunner located within a circular pedestal-type open mount. The other team member acts as a target locator using information sent over the vessel's internal communications net.

Description

A Stinger system comprises the launcher assembly with a missile, a grip-stock, an IFF interrogator, an argon gas Battery Coolant Unit (BCU), and an Impulse Generator (battery energiser) unit.

The launcher assembly consists of a glass fibre launch tube with frangible end covers, a sight, desiccant, coolant line, gyro-activator coil and a carrying sling. A detachable grip-stock which has a receptacle for the BCU is fitted to the assembly, together with a connector and an Impulse Generator. The grip-stock is also fitted with a seeker head uncage bar, a weapon launch trigger, an AN/PPX-1 IFF interrogator switch and a foldable antenna and control electronics for the missile gyro.

The missile itself is a two-stage solid propellant rocket motor type and in its FIM-92A version is fitted with a second generation cooled passive IR conical scan reticle seeker head with discrete electronic components to provide signal processing. They process the IR energy received from the target in the 4.1-4.4 µm wavelength region to determine its relative angle and then, by using a proportional navigation guidance technique, continually predict an intercept point.

In the FIM-92B version the reticle seeker unit is replaced by one which uses an image scan optical processing system. This has two detector materials, one sensitive to IR and the other responsive to UV energy, together with two microprocessors which are integrated into micro-electronic circuitry for the signal processing phase. The latest Stinger-RMP takes this one stage further by introducing a microprocessor reprogramming facility into the circuitry to allow for new threat characteristics.

In all cases the seeker output is sent as steering data to the guidance assembly which converts it into guidance signal format for the control electronics. This module then commands the two fixed and two moveable forward control surfaces to manoeuvre the weapon onto the required intercept course. The control concept used is known as the single channel rolling airframe type and, as such, considerably reduces both the missile weight and manufacturing costs. As the weapon nears its target the seeker head activates its Target Adaptive Guidance (TAG) circuit within one second of impact to modify its trajectory away from the exhaust plume towards the critical area of the IR source itself. The fuzing system allows for both contact activation as well as missile self-destruction after 20 seconds of flight time following the launch. The 3 kg Picatinny Arsenal warhead carried has a smooth fragmentation casing to ensure that the desired blast-fragmentation effect is achieved.

A typical tactical engagement follows this sequence of events. Once alerted to a target the gunner shoulders the system, inserts the BCU into its grip-stock receptacle and unfolds the IFF antenna. He then removes the front protective cover of the launcher tube to reveal the IR transparent frangible disc, raises the optical sight system and connects his beltpack IFF interrogator unit via a cable to the launcher. The gunner is now ready to visually acquire the target. He does this by using the sight and then he estimates its range with the estimation facility of the system. If required he now interrogates the target using the AN/PPX-1 system. This can be done by the gunner without having to activate the weapon. The azimuth coverage of the 10 km range IFF system is essentially the same as that of the optical sight enabling the gunner to associate responses with the particular aircraft he has in view. An audio signal 0.7 seconds after the IFF challenge switch is depressed provides the gunner with the cue as to whether the target is friendly or an unknown for possible engagement.

If he decides that it is unfriendly he continues to track the aircraft and activates the weapon system by depressing the firing trigger to its first level. This causes the impulse generator to energise the BCU which then releases its pressurised argon gas coolant to the IR detector and generates a dual polarity +20V DC output for at least 45 seconds to provide all the pre-launch electrical power required for the seeker coolant system, gyro spin-up, launcher acquisition electronics, guidance electronics, activation of the missile's onboard thermal battery and ignition of the ejector motor.

The IR seeker is allowed to look at the target through the IR transparent front launcher disc and when sufficient energy is received by the detector for acquisition to have occurred an audio signal is sent to the gunner. Total time required for tracking and missile activation is about six seconds. He then depresses the seeker uncage bar and, using the open sight, inserts the superelevation and lead data.

Once this is accomplished he fully depresses the firing trigger which causes the BCU to activate the missile battery. This powers all the missile functions after launch and operates for around 19 seconds until the dual polarity +20V DC output drops below the required minimum for use. A brief time delay operates following which the umbilical connection to the grip-stock is retracted and the BCU sends a pulse to ignite the ejector motor. Total time to motor ignition from depression of the firing trigger is only 1.7 seconds. Upon ignition the initial thrust generated imparts roll to the missile airframe and starts the fuze timer system. The missile and its exhaust then breaks through the frangible discs at either end of the launcher tube.

Before the missile completely clears the end of the tube the ejector motor burns out in order to protect the gunner from the rocket blast and the two fixed and two moveable control surfaces spring out. Once it clears the tube the four fixed and folded tail fins open out and the ejector motor is jettisoned. The missile then coasts to a predetermined safe distance from the gunner where the fuze timer ignites the main sustainer rocket motor. When the correct acceleration rate is reached after one second of flight the Magnavox M934E6 fuzing circuit for the warhead is armed and the self-destruct timer started.

The seeker continues to track the target throughout the flight with the electronics processing the received signals to eliminate or reduce the line-of-sight pointing angle to the target. The weapon flies a proportional navigation path to the interception point near to which the TAG-circuit is activated and a signal is generated within the seeker head to add bias to the steering signal causing the missile airframe to guide itself into a vulnerable part of the target. Even if the target is using 8 g manoeuvres the missile is still capable of engaging it.

Once the gunner has fully depressed his trigger and the missile has left the launch tube then he is free to either assemble another weapon for a further engagement (which takes only 15 seconds), take cover or move to another location.

US Army training needs indicate that 136 hours of instruction are required on the Stinger system before weapon qualification is given. The M60 field handling and M134 tracker head training versions are used for instruction.

Variants

Air-to-air Stinger

In the late seventies General Dynamics began development of an Air-to-air Stinger (ATAS) system which completed its Full-Scale Engineering Development phase in late 1986. First production deliveries were made to the US Army in mid-1988 and the Flight Structure Division of the

USA / MANPORTABLE SAM SYSTEMS

Western Gear Corporation was the subcontractor responsible for building the launcher structural assembly.

Weighing 55.9 kg fully loaded, the lightweight two-round launcher unit is available for use on US Army Bell OH-58A/C Kiowa (one launcher), Bell AH-58D Warrior (two), Sikorsky UH-60 Black Hawk (one), Hughes AH-64 Apache (two), Hughes AH-6F/G (one) and Bell AH-1 Cobra (one) helicopters. Fixed-wing aircraft such as the Rockwell OV-10 Bronco can also be out-fitted with ATAS launchers on their underwing pylons.

Air Defence Suppression Missile

A modified Stinger incorporating a dual-mode Radio Frequency (RF)/IR seeker for use as an Air Defense Suppression Missile (ADSM) is also being studied. This uses the same launcher as the ATAS with the RF target designation system providing radar warning and initialisation of the passive guidance unit.

Tripod Mounted Stinger

General Dynamics has also privately developed the Tripod Mounted Stinger system. This has four ready-to-fire missiles mounted on two ATAS launcher shoes at 90° to the vertical and is fitted with an integrated high magnification optical sight and a Marconi Forward Looking IR (FLIR) tracking system to allow Stinger launches at night and in bad weather. The one-man system weighs less than 136.4 kg and can be mounted on the rear of a vehicle if required.

It can also be interfaced with a higher echelon command and control network using positive gunner cueing and is fitted with automatic missile sequencing and seeker uncaging. Traverse capability is a full 360° and the elevation limits are -10 to +50°.

In late 1987 the Tripod Mounted Stinger system was tested in South Korea for use in the airfield defence role. Growth potential includes the fitting of a laser rangefinder and a go/no go fire control computer.

Pedestal Mounted Stinger

This is fully described in the *Self-propelled SAMs* section of this book.

LAV-Air Defence Gun/Missile System

The competitors for this US Marine Corps requirement are described in the *Self-propelled Anti-aircraft Guns* section of this book.

Status: In production. By October 1988, General Dynamics has produced over 16 000 Stinger SAMs for the home and export markets. On order or in service with the following countries:

Country	Service	Model
Afghanistan	Mojahedin guerrillas	FIM-92A
Angola	UNITA guerrillas	FIM-92A
Bahrain	army	FIM-92A
Chad	army (limited numbers)	FIM-92A
Denmark	army	FIM-92B
France	army (limited numbers)	FIM-92A
Germany, West	army, navy and air force	FIM-92A/B
Greece	army	FIM-92B
Iran	Revolutionary Guards Corps (limited number)	FIM-92A
Israel	Army	FIM-92C
Italy	army	FIM-92A
Japan	air and ground self defence forces	FIM-92A
Korea, South	army	FIM-92A
Netherlands	army, navy and Marine Corps	FIM-92A/B
Nicaragua	Contra guerrillas	FIM-92A
Pakistan	army	FIM-92A
Qatar	army	FIM-92A
Saudi Arabia	army	FIM-92A
Switzerland	army	FIM-92C
Turkey	army	FIM-92A/B
UK	Special Air Service (limited number)	FIM-92A
USA	Special Forces, army, navy, marine corps and air force	FIM-92A/B/C

Manufacturers: General Dynamics Valley Systems Division, PO Box 50-800, Ontario, California CA 91761-1085, USA
Telephone: (714-)945 7000

Second source supplier: Raytheon Company Missile Systems Division, Bedford, Massachusetts 01730, USA
Telephone: (617) 274 222

Prime European contractor: Dornier GmbH, Postfach 1420, 7990 Friedrichshafen 1, Federal Republic of Germany

---

SPECIFICATIONS

TYPE	two-stage low altitude
LENGTH	missile 1.52 m
DIAMETER	missile 0.070 m
WING SPAN	0.091 m
WEIGHTS	
missile (launch)	10.1 kg
launcher (plus missile)	13.3 kg
launcher (complete)	15.7 kg
battery coolant unit	0.4 kg
beltpack IFF system (including connecting lead)	2.6 kg
grip-stock	2 kg
PROPULSION	solid fuel ejector and sustainer rocket motors
GUIDANCE	FIM-92A passive IR homing
	FIM-92B/C passive IR/UV homing
WARHEAD	3 kg HE-fragmentation with contact fuze
MAX SPEED	Mach 2.2
MAX RANGE	8000 m
MAX EFFECTIVE RANGE	
FIM-92A	4000 m
FIM-92B/C	4500 m
MIN EFFECTIVE RANGE	200 m
MAX ALTITUDE	
FIM-92A	3500 m
FIM-92B/C	3800 m
MIN ALTITUDE	effectively ground level
LAUNCHER	manportable single-round disposable with reusable grip-stock

---

General Dynamics FIM-43 Redeye Low Altitude Surface-to-air Missile System

Development

The development of a first generation US shoulder-launched infra-red (IR) guided fire-and-forget surface-to-air missile was started in 1956 by Convair Pomona (subsequently General Dynamics Pomona) as a private venture project.

In 1957 the firm made an unsolicited proposal to the US Army concerning a system of this type and in 1958 were awarded a one-year feasibility demonstration contract. This led in mid-1959 to the evaluation of working models and, in August of that year, the company was awarded a joint US Army/Marine Corps contract covering the research and development of what became designated the XMIM-43A Redeye system. Although initial joint production funds were requested in FY61, numerous problems were encountered that resulted in the allocation being repeatedly postponed from year to year. Finally, in 1964, sufficient funds were made available for 300 systems to be produced for extensive operational testing to take place. The subsequent trials uncovered yet more problems including the need for a longer sensor warm-up time before firing could take place. These difficulties were finally resolved in 1965 and in October that year the first contract was placed with General Dynamics for full-scale production of the definitive FIM-43A Redeye. By 1968 the first US Army and US Marine Corps units were considered to be fully operational. Production of the system continued until 1974 when the last of over 33 000 systems were delivered.

In US Army/Marine Corps service each manoeuvre battalion (depending upon its type) fielded a Redeye section with between four to six two-man firing teams. Each team comprised a commander and a gunner and was assigned a ¼-ton M151 vehicle for mobility purposes. Due to its limited engagement capabilities as a first generation tail-chase weapon the system has now been virtually replaced in US front-line service by the much more versatile FIM-92 Stinger. The systems remaining in the inventory are being kept both as back-ups for the Stinger until procurement of that system is complete and for training the low level air defence teams in live-firing and engagement techniques.

The first export customer for Redeye was the Swedish Army which started looking at the system in 1964 and eventually signed a contract

52 MANPORTABLE SAM SYSTEMS / USA

General Dynamics FIM-43 Redeye manportable surface-to-air missile being launched

General Dynamics FIM-43 Redeye manportable surface-to-air missile being launched at night

in September 1966 for a batch of 10 with several training sets for trials purposes. Following a successful evaluation, the Royal Swedish Army Material Administration adopted the Redeye under the local designation Rb-69 (Robot-69) and ordered a further 1083 systems in 1967. Subsequent purchasers through the late-sixties and seventies have included Australia (260 units), Denmark (243 improved propulsion FIM-43C units under the local designation Hamlet), West Germany (1400 units under the local designation Fliegerfaust-1, FLF-1), Greece (100 units), Israel (over 1000 units), Jordan, Saudi Arabia (500 units), Thailand and Turkey. A number of these countries are currently replacing their Redeye systems with more modern second generation manportable weapons.

In 1982 a batch of 100 Redeye firing units were delivered to Somalia as part of a military aid package given by the US Government in response to an Ethiopian attack across their common border. During 1984 a number of Redeye systems were supplied to the Sudanese government during the border crisis with Libya.

Also in the mid-eighties, small numbers of Redeyes were supplied to the Chad government as part of the emergency military aid supplied by the US Government for use against Libyan combat aircraft and helicopters in the northern provinces conflict. Subsequently, in 1986, a number of surplus Redeyes were also supplied to the US backed Contra guerrillas fighting the communist backed Sandinista government of Nicaragua. In both conflicts the weapon is known to have scored a number of kills including two Libyan MiG-23 Flogger fighter-bombers in August 1987 and at least six of the 15 Soviet Mil Mi-8 Hip, Mil Mi-17 Hip and Mil Mi-24/25 Hind combat helicopters lost in the Nicaraguan Civil War up to January 1988. Identified Contra kills by the Redeye include three Mi-8/17s and three Mi-24/25s. It was also used by the Contras to seriously damage a Douglas DC-6 cargo plane of the Nicaraguan state-run airline, Aeronica, in early 1988 as it flew over the north-eastern region of the country during a guerrilla offensive. This was the first time that the guerrillas had used a missile against a civilian aircraft in the seven years of fighting there. Examples of the weapon have been captured by the Sandinistas during combat operations, with the first falling into their hands following a CIA supply drop in July 1987.

However, like contemporary first generation weapons, the Redeye's capabilities against modern high performance combat aircraft is proving to be marginal with its best performances being shown, like the Soviet SA-7 Grail, to be against the slower moving piston-engined transports and helicopters.

Description

The missile is sealed in its launcher and is not removed in the field before firing. It is fitted with an Atlantic Research M115 two-stage solid propellant rocket motor which acts as both the ejector and sustainer. The 2 kg warhead is an HE-fragmentation type and can be detonated when the contact fuze penetrates a metal object or physically meets a solid object. However, if no physical contact is made after 15 seconds of flight, a self-destruct circuit operates.

The Redeye system comprises three components; the M46A2 molded material launcher assembly, the M41 missile and the launcher battery/coolant unit. The launcher includes an integral grip-stock fabrication, an open-sight aperture and cover and the missile launcher-container tube. The front end seal of the latter is transparent to IR radiation to allow the missile seeker to sense the target. No IFF interrogator system is fitted so target identification is undertaken by the gunner using solely visual means. Once he decides to engage he starts a sequence of actions which must not take longer than 30 seconds due to the active life of the battery unit.

The first is to insert the battery/coolant device into the launcher's receptor and then, when the target is in range, he engages the safety and actuator system which activates the battery/coolant unit and sends liberated Freon gas to the missile seeker where it expands to cool the IR detector. The 7.5× magnification open-sight with its 25° field of view is then placed on the target. The sight is designed to allow the gunner to aim the system, track the target, estimate its range and apply target

General Dynamics FIM-43 Redeye manportable surface-to-air missile system complete with grip-stock (West German Army)

elevation all in one operation. Any IR radiation received from the target is then allowed to focus through the front-end seal onto the seeker's detector cell. When sufficient energy is received to enable a lock-on to be achieved then audible and visual indicators are generated on the launcher to show the gunner that the missile has acquired its target. He then holds down the uncaging bar-switch to uncage the weapon's gyro system, which has already been spun-up to speed, and depresses the firing trigger on the grip-stock. This causes an electric squib to ignite a thermite charge that melts an electrolyte in the battery which develops a 40 V output within 0.5 seconds. The missile ejector motor fires and the exhausting gas breaks through the rear frangible end cover seal, impinges on the folded tail fins and causes the weapon to spin within the tube. Once an acceleration of 28 g is reached an inertial switch in the fuze timer closes and the fuze timer circuit becomes live. The ejector motor burns out in a fraction of a second before the missile totally emerges through the front seal cover in order to protect the gunner from blast burns. During this brief coasting phase from the launcher muzzle, the four fixed tail fins and the two movable nose fins deploy. At 1.6 seconds into the flight and approximately 6 to 7 m in front of the gunner's position the timer fuze circuit ignites the second-stage sustainer motor, arms the warhead and prepares it for detonation.

In the meantime the IR seeker is continually measuring the difference between the gyro line-of-sight and the IR source it is looking at. This data is converted into electrical tracking error signals which are then used in a tracking servo-loop to continuously reposition the seeker so that it stays aimed at the target. The use of this tail-chase proportional navigation guidance technique means that any violently manoeuvring target, especially if it is employing IR decoy systems to screen itself, has a very good chance of breaking the seeker lock and evading the weapon.

During the flight, canted nozzles impart roll to the missile which allows a single-axis control system to be used. The pair of movable 15° canted control fins near the nose are then commanded to snap in and out as required by this system, which is directed by the tracking error guidance

US soldier using General Dynamics FIM-43 Redeye manportable missile to engage ballistic aerial target (US Army)

signals already generated by the seekers IR homing package. Once in contact with the target the warhead is detonated by its fuze using either of the two contact methods described previously. If it fails to hit a target after its set flight time then the warhead automatically self destructs. Although if this happens to be near an aircraft then serious damage can still occur. After missile firing occurs the launcher and attachments are discarded and the gunner obtains a new system for the next engagement.

Training versions of the system have also been deployed.

SPECIFICATIONS

TYPE	two-stage low altitude
LENGTH	
missile	1.283 m
launcher (complete)	1.283 m
DIAMETER	
missile	0.070 m
launcher (without cover, sling or battery/ coolant unit)	0.092 m
WING SPAN	0.140 m
WIDTH	
launcher (complete)	0.119 m
HEIGHT	
launcher (complete)	0.277 m
WEIGHTS	
missile (launch)	8.2 kg
launcher (complete)	13.1 kg
launcher (without cover, sling or battery/ coolant unit)	3.9 kg
battery/coolant unit	0.5 kg

PROPULSION	solid fuel dual thrust ejector and sustainer rocket motor
GUIDANCE	infra-red passive homing
WARHEAD	2 kg HE-fragmentation with contact fuze
MAX SPEED	Mach 1.6
MAX EFFECTIVE RANGE	3300 m
MIN EFFECTIVE RANGE	600 m
MAX ALTITUDE	3000 m
MIN ALTITUDE	25 m
LAUNCHER	manportable single-round disposable

Status: Production complete. In service with Australia (army), Chad (army), Denmark (army), West Germany (army), Greece (army), Israel (army and navy), Jordan (army), Nicaraguan Contra guerrillas, Saudi Arabia (army), Somalia (army), Sudan (army), Thailand (army), Turkey (army) and the USA (second-line with army, Marine Corps, navy and air force units).

Manufacturer: General Dynamics, Pomona Division, PO Box 2507, Pomona, California 91766
Telephone: (714) 629-5111

Self-Propelled Anti-Aircraft Guns

BRAZIL

40 mm Self-propelled Anti-aircraft Gun System

Development/Description
The Brazilian Army has a requirement for a self-propelled 40 mm anti-aircraft gun system as at present, it has no mobile air defence systems apart from the four Euromissile Roland 2 systems on the West German Marder chassis.

In mid-1988 a mock-up of a new self-propelled air defence weapon call Trinity EB-3 made its first appearance. This is a joint proposal between CBV (who would be responsible for the turret) and Moto Pecas (who would be responsible for the chassis) and essentially consists of the Moto Pecas Charrua II APC with a power operated turret on top of the hull to the rear which is armed with a Bofors 40 mm L/70 air defence weapon. Mounted on the right side of the turret is the BOFI (Bofors Optronic Fire-control Instrument). The laser rangefinder is mounted to the left of the gun in the forward part of the turret.

Target surveillance is provided by the French Electronique Serge Dassault radar system with a range of over 10 km, this being mounted on the turret roof at the rear.

The turret is very similar that used on the Swedish Bofors Trinity self-propelled air defence system covered in this section under Sweden.

Although the system was first shown at the Army Technological Centre on the Moto Pecas Charrua II APC chassis, it can also be installed on other chassis such as the private venture ENGESA EE-18 Sucuri (6 × 6) tank destroyer which was unveiled earlier in 1988, although the hull would require more structural modifications.

Moto Pecas Charrua II APC fitted with full scale mock-up of Bofors Trinity EB-3 system armed with a 40 mm L/70 gun, BOFI mounted to right of weapon and ESD search radar mounted on roof

Status: Mock-up. Not in production or service.

CHINA, PEOPLE'S REPUBLIC

Type 80 Twin 57 mm Self-propelled Anti-aircraft Gun System

Development
The Type 80 self-propelled anti-aircraft gun system was developed for use by armoured and mechanised infantry units to provide defence against air attack at slant ranges of up to 5500 m by targets flying at speeds of up to 350 m/s. If required the vehicle can also be used in the ground role to support conventional anti-tank weapons. The system consists of a modified Type 69 II MBT chassis fitted with a Chinese version of the Soviet turret installed on the Soviet ZSU-57-2 twin 57 mm self-propelled anti-aircraft tank but using a twin-barrel variant of the locally produced Type 59 which is itself a copy of the Soviet single S-60 57 mm towed anti-aircraft gun. The weapons can be fired while on the move or on slopes of up to 15° but the best results are obtained when it is stationary on the ground with a slope of 3° or less.

Description
The hull of the Type 80 is divided into three compartments: driver's at the front, fighting in the centre and engine at the rear.

The driver sits at the front of the hull on the right and has a single piece hatch cover that opens to the left. An infra-red periscope is fitted for night driving together with a normal optical viewing periscope.

The open topped welded steel turret is mounted in the centre of the chassis. A wire cage mounted externally at the turret rear is provided for the empty cartridge cases and links.

The main armament consists of two Type 59 57 mm cannon with their control system used either in a semi-automatic, electro-hydraulic powered manner or manually. In the former mode the elevation is from −1 to +81°, in the latter it is −5 to +85°. Fire control is by an automatic optical vector mode sight. A crew of five is carried in the turret: commander, gunner, fuze-setter and two loaders. For internal crew communication a Type 803 intercom system is fitted. A 20-25 km range Type 889 radio is standard for external communications.

The guns are fully automatic and recoil operated with each barrel having a maximum cyclic rate of fire of 105 to 120 rds/min. The practical rate of fire is 70 rds/min. Maximum horizontal range is 12 000 m, maximum

Type 80 twin 57 mm self-propelled anti-aircraft gun system with turret traversed to front

vertical range 8800 m and effective anti-aircraft range 5500 m. The guns fire two types of fixed ammunition; a 6.47 kg high explosive tracer (HE-T) round with a percussion fuze and a 6.45 kg armour-piercing capped tracer (APC-T) round with a base fuze. A self-destruct device is incorporated into the HE-T shell to ensure automatic detonation after 6000 m of flight. A total of 300 rounds is carried.

It has torsion bar type suspension with five road wheels (the Soviet equivalent ZSU-57-2 has only four), idler at the front, drive sprocket at the rear and no track return rollers. Unlike the Soviet ZSU-57-2 the Type 80 is fitted with track skirts.

Status: Production. In service with the Chinese Army.

Manufacturer: Enquiries to China North Industries Corporation, 7A Yuetan Nanjie, Beijing, People's Republic of China.
Telephone: (86) 6898, (86) 3461, (86) 3471, (86) 7570
Telex: 22339 CNIN CN.

China, People's Republic / **SELF-PROPELLED AA GUNS**

SPECIFICATIONS

CREW	6
COMBAT WEIGHT	31 000 kg
POWER-TO-WEIGHT RATIO	18.7 hp/tonne
LENGTH	
guns forward	8.42 m
guns rear	8.24 m
hull	6.243 m
WIDTH	
with fenders	3.27 m
with side skirts	3.307 m
HEIGHT	2.748 m
FIRING HEIGHT	1.94 m
GROUND CLEARANCE	0.425 m
TRACK	2.64 m
TRACK WIDTH	580 mm
LENGTH OF TRACK ON GROUND	3.485 m
MAX ROAD SPEED	48–50 km/h
MAX ROAD RANGE	420–440 km
FORDING	1.4 m
GRADIENT	60%
SIDE SLOPE	30%
VERTICAL OBSTACLE	0.8 m
TRENCH	2.7 m
ENGINE	Model 12150 – 7BW diesel developing 580 hp at 2000 rpm
TRANSMISSION	manual with 5 forward and 1 reverse gears
STEERING	clutch and brake
SUSPENSION	torsion bar
ELECTRICAL SYSTEM	28 V
BATTERIES	4 × Type 65 12 V, 280 Ah
ARMAMENT	2 × 57 mm guns
AMMUNITION	300
GUN CONTROL EQUIPMENT	
turret power control	powered/manual
max gun elevation/depression	+85°/–5°
turret traverse	360°
ARMOUR	
hull glacis	45 mm
hull rear	30 mm
hull upper	20 mm
hull lower	20 mm
hull side	20 mm
turret (all-round)	12 mm curved

Twin 37 mm Self-propelled Anti-aircraft Gun System

Development
The existence of a new twin 37 mm self-propelled anti-aircraft gun system was first disclosed in 1986 and at that time a single prototype had been built and evaluated by the Chinese Army. As far as it is known the system has yet to enter production.

Description
It consists essentially of a modified Type 69 MBT (technical details of which are given in the previous entry) fitted with a new two-man all-welded steel turret with twin 37 mm automatic anti-aircraft guns.

The commander is seated on the left and the gunner on the right. Turret traverse is 360° and weapon elevation ranges from –7 to +87°. Maximum powered traverse speed is 60°/s with a maximum acceleration of 90°/s while maximum powered elevation speed is 50°/s with a maximum acceleration of 90°/s.

It is probable that the twin 37 mm cannon are based on those used in one of the Chinese towed air defence systems, fully described in the the Towed anti-aircraft guns section. The weapons have a muzzle velocity of 1000 m/s and a cyclic rate of fire of 380 rds/barrel/min. Whereas the towed 37 mm guns are clip fed, this system is fed by a continuous belt. This is a clear weather system only.

According to NORINCO, the 37 mm guns have a maximum range in the air defence role of 4000 m while maximum effective range while engaging air targets is 3500 m.

Twin 37 mm self-propelled anti-aircraft gun system on Type 69 series MBT chassis

Variant
During a defence exhibition held in Beijing in late 1988, another twin 37 mm self-propelled anti-aircraft gun was shown in public for the first time. It has a slightly different power operated turret and is armed with the same twin 37 mm cannon which are fitted with flash suppressors.

New Chinese twin 37 mm self-propelled anti-aircraft gun system fitted with target surveillance radar on the turret roof towards the rear (Eric Ditchfield)

Rear view of new Chinese twin 37 mm self-propelled anti-aircraft gun system fitted with target surveillance radar on the turret roof and folded down for transport (Eric Ditchfield)

56 SELF-PROPELLED AA GUNS / China, People's Republic

They have a cyclic rate of fire of 360 to 380 rds/barrel/min with a total of 500 rounds of ready use ammunition being carried. Muzzle velocity is 1000 m/s and loaded weight is 35 000 kg.

The turret is of a different design and mounted on the roof at the rear is a surveillance radar while mounted on the right forward part of the roof is an unidentified tracking system which may be of the passive type.

Status: Development complete. Ready for production.

Manufacturer: Enquiries to China North Industries Corporation, 7A Yuetan Nanjie, Beijing, People's Republic of China.
Telephone: (86) 6898, (86) 3461, (86) 3471, (86) 7570
Telex: 22339 CNIN CN

Type 63 Twin 37 mm Self-propelled Anti-aircraft Gun System

Development
Until the introduction of the Type 63 the Chinese Army had only a very limited number of Soviet ZSU-57-2s in service. The Type 63 self-propelled anti-aircraft gun was first used in action in South Vietnam where one was captured by the South Vietnamese 4th Infantry Regiment, handed over to the United States Army and eventually delivered to Aberdeen Proving Ground. The designation of the Type 63 was applied by the USA in the absence of its official Chinese designation. There is no hard evidence that it is in service with the Chinese Army in large numbers and it may well have been a local conversion carried out by the North Vietnamese.

Description
The Type 63 self-propelled anti-aircraft gun consists basically of a T-34 tank with its turret replaced by a new open-topped turret armed with twin 37 mm anti-aircraft guns.

Once the original turret was removed from the T-34/85 chassis a circular steel plate was bolted over the turret well and a support was fitted between the floor of the hull and the underside of the circular plate and welded into position. The twin Type 63 anti-aircraft guns were removed from their normal four-wheeled carriage and bolted onto the circular plate. A shield of 16 mm thick armour plate which traverses with the weapon was then bolted onto the gun mount. There is a door each side of the turret, towards the rear. When travelling the turret is normally traversed to the rear and the guns held in position by a ladder-type travelling lock which lies on top of the engine compartment when not in use.

The twin 37 mm guns have an elevation of +85°, depression of -5° and turret traverse is 360°. Both gun elevation/depression and turret traverse are manual. The guns have rising block breech-blocks, hydraulic recoil buffers and spring recuperators, and are recoil operated. Each barrel has a cyclic rate of fire of 160-180 rds/min and a practical rate of fire of 80 rds/min. Maximum horizontal range is 9500 m, maximum vertical range 6700 m and effective anti-aircraft range is 3000 m. Fixed ammunition is fed to each barrel in five-round clips and the following types of ammunition can be fired:

Ammunition type	FRAG-T	FRAG-T	AP-T*
PROJECTILE DESIGNATION	OR-167	OR-167N	BR-167
FUZE MODEL	MG-8	B-37	n/app
WEIGHT OF PROJECTILE	0.732 kg	0.708 kg	0.76 kg
WEIGHT OF BURSTING CHARGE	0.035 kg	0.036 kg	n/app
TYPE OF BURSTING CHARGE	RDX/alum	RDX/alum/wax	n/app
MUZZLE VELOCITY	880 m/s	880 m/s	880 m/s
ARMOUR PENETRATION AT 0°	n/app	n/app	37 mm at 1000 m / 46 mm at 500 m

*The HVAP projectile, which is no longer issued, would penetrate 57 mm of armour at 1000 m

A small quantity of ready-use ammunition is carried inside the turret but most of the ammunition is carried in wooden ammunition chests and stored in the large metal ammunition stowage containers which have been welded to the hull either side of the turret.

The Type 63 is not fitted with an NBC system or night vision equipment and has no amphibious capability. A new Chinese twin 37 mm self-propelled anti-aircraft system is described in the previous entry.

Type 63 twin 37 mm self-propelled anti-aircraft gun captured in Vietnam and now displayed at Aberdeen Proving Ground, Maryland (Christopher F Foss)

Status: Conversions complete. In service with China and Vietnam.

Manufacturers: Hull: Soviet state arsenals; turret: Chinese state arsenals; conversion: Chinese state arsenals.

SPECIFICATIONS (provisional)

CREW	6
COMBAT WEIGHT	30 000 kg
POWER-TO-WEIGHT RATIO	16.66 hp/tonne
LENGTH GUNS FORWARD	6.432 m
WIDTH	2.997 m
HEIGHT	
including AA sight	3.268 m
to turret top	2.995 m
GROUND CLEARANCE	0.38 m
TRACK	2.45 m
TRACK WIDTH	500 mm
LENGTH OF TRACK ON GROUND	3.85 m
MAX ROAD SPEED	55 km/h
FUEL CAPACITY	590 litres
MAX RANGE	
road	300 km
cross-country	209 km
FUEL CONSUMPTION (road)	1.9 l/km
FORDING	1.32 m
GRADIENT	60%
VERTICAL OBSTACLE	0.73 m
TRENCH	2.5 m
TURNING RADIUS	skid turns
ENGINE	Model V-2-34 or V-2-34M V-12 water-cooled diesel developing 500 hp at 1800 rpm
AUXILIARY ENGINE	none
TRANSMISSION	manual with 5 forward (some have 4) and 1 reverse gears
STEERING	clutch and brake
CLUTCH	dry multi-plate
SUSPENSION	Christie
ARMAMENT	2 × 37 mm
FIRE CONTROL SYSTEM	
turret power control	manual
traverse	360°
ELEVATION/DEPRESSION	+85°/-5°

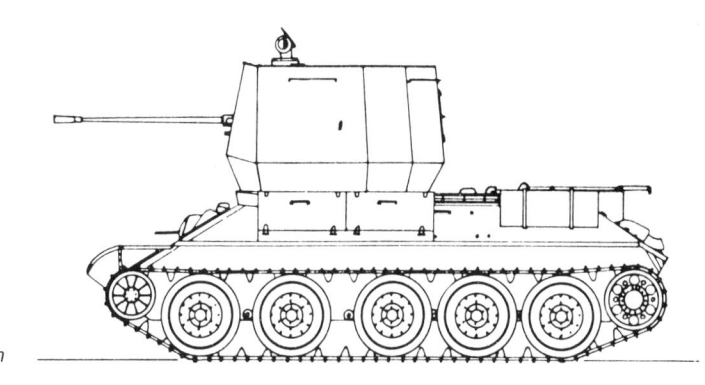

Type 63 twin 37 mm self-propelled anti-aircraft gun

CZECHOSLOVAKIA

M53/59 Twin 30 mm Self-propelled Anti-aircraft Gun System

Development
The M53/59 self-propelled anti-aircraft gun was introduced into the Czechoslovakian Army in the late 1950s and consists of an armoured version of the standard Praga V3S (6 × 6) truck with a removable modified version of the standard towed M53 twin 30 mm anti-aircraft guns mounted on the rear. The guns are often removed for ground use. The mounting has also been seen on the PTS unarmoured tracked amphibious vehicle.

Description
The M53/59 has an all-welded hull with the engine at the front, crew compartment in the centre and the armament at the rear. The hull armour is well sloped for maximum possible protection within the weight limit available. The driver is seated on the left side and the commander on the right, with a windscreen in front of them which is covered in action by an armoured cover, hinged at the top, with a vision slit. Both the driver and commander also have a door in the side of the hull, the top half of which has a vision slit and hinges downwards on the outside. The two loaders are seated one either side at the back of the crew compartment facing the rear and have a vision slit in the side, immediately behind the side door. At the rear of the crew compartment is a two-piece hatch cover which folds down into the horizontal to act as a platform for the loaders. It has a single vision slit in either side for the loaders. The commander has a hemispherical plexiglass cupola in the roof for observation.

The weapons have an elevation of +85° and a depression of -10°, except over the crew compartment, where depression is limited to +2°, and over the commander's cupola, where there is none. A steel plate at the rear of the crew compartment stops the gun barrels hitting it on the roof. The turret can be traversed through a full 360° and elevation, depression and traverse are all hydraulic with manual controls available for emergency use. The gunner is seated on the left side of the weapons and has frontal, side and rear armour protection. When originally introduced the barrels had multi-baffle muzzle brakes but more recently the weapons have been observed fitted with conical flash-hiders. The barrels can be quickly changed when they become overheated and spare barrels are kept at regimental level as part of basic equipment.

The twin 30 mm cannon are fully automatic gas-operated weapons and have a cyclic rate of fire of 450 to 500 rds/barrel/min and a practical rate of fire of 150 rds/barrel/min. Maximum horizontal range is 9700 m, maximum vertical range is 6300 m and effective anti-aircraft range is 3000 m. Each of the vertical magazines holds 50 rounds of ammunition which is fed to the magazines in clips of 10 rounds. The towed M53 twin 30 mm guns have a lower rate of fire as they have no magazines and the ammunition has to be fed to each weapon in clips of 10 rounds. The following types of fixed ammunition can be fired by the 30 mm guns: API projectile weighing 0.45 kg, with a muzzle velocity of 1000 m/s, which

M53/59 twin 30 mm self-propelled anti-aircraft gun clearly showing vertical magazines and gunner offset to left of mount

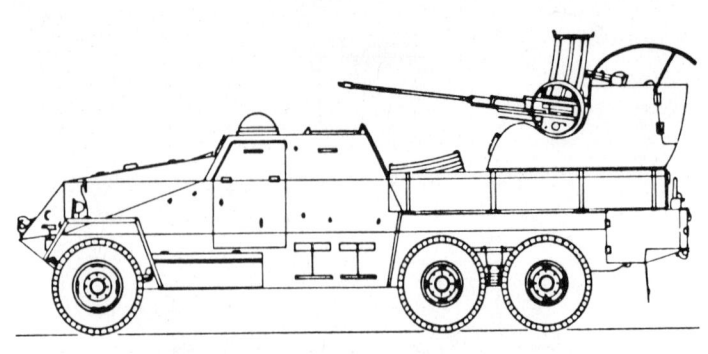

SELF-PROPELLED AA GUNS / Czechoslovakia-Egypt

M53/59 twin 30 mm self-propelled anti-aircraft gun (provisional drawing)

M53/59 twin 30 mm SPAAG in travelling configuration

will penetrate 55 mm of armour at an incidence of 0° at a range of 500 m. HEI projectile weighing 0.45 kg with a muzzle velocity of 1000 m/s.

The Yugoslav Federal Directorate of Supply and Procurement manufactures ammunition for the M53/59 twin 30 mm SPAAG system which it calls the anti-aircraft gun 30/2 mm M53, 53/59 (CS). Two types of ammunition are manufactured: HE-T, designated the M69, and cartridge, blank, designated M78. Details of these are as follows:-

DESIGNATION	M69	M78
TOTAL LENGTH	331 mm	331 mm
WEIGHT	1.14 kg	0.96 kg
MUZZLE VELOCITY	997 m/s	n/av
MAX PRESSURE	3140 bar	1760 bar
WEIGHT OF PROJECTILE	435 g	250 g
CARTRIDGE CASE	steel	steel
PROPELLING CHARGE	NC powder	NC powder

The M69 has a tracer which burns for four seconds and is fitted with an impact super-quick action fuze with mechanical self-destruct. The M78 has a maximum range of 120 m.

Filled magazines are carried in the rear of the crew compartment, fastened to the floor by quick-release catches and a further three filled magazines are carried either side of the platform.

The main drawback of this system is its lack of all-weather capability. The vehicle has no NBC system, no night vision equipment, no amphibious capability and no central tyre-pressure regulation system.

Variants
In recent years Czechoslovakia has offered an export version of the M53/59 called the M53/70, which appears to be almost identical to the earlier version but with an improved fire control system.

SPECIFICATIONS

CREW	5
CONFIGURATION	6 × 6
COMBAT WEIGHT	10 300 kg
POWER-TO-WEIGHT RATIO	11.57 hp/tonne
LENGTH	6.92 m
WIDTH	2.35 m
HEIGHT	
including magazines	2.95 m
excluding magazines	2.585 m
FIRING HEIGHT	2.41 m
GROUND CLEARANCE	0.4 m
TRACK	
front	1.87 m
rear	1.755 m
WHEELBASE	3.58 m + 1.12 m
MAX ROAD SPEED	60 km/h
FUEL CAPACITY	120 litres
MAX ROAD RANGE	500 km
FUEL CONSUMPTION	0.24 l/km
FORDING	0.8 m
GRADIENT	60%
SIDE SLOPE	30%
VERTICAL OBSTACLE	0.46 m
TRENCH	0.69 m
ENGINE	Tatra T 912-2 6-cylinder in-line air-cooled diesel developing 110 hp at 2200 rpm
TRANSMISSION	manual with 4 forward and 2 reverse gears
TRANSFER BOX	2-speed
TYRES	8.25 × 20
ARMAMENT (main)	2 × 30 mm cannon
AMMUNITION	600-800
GUN CONTROL EQUIPMENT	
turret power control	hydraulic/manual
gun elevation/depression	+85°/-10°
turret traverse	360°
ARMOUR	10 mm max (estimated)

Status: Production complete. In service with Czechoslovakia, Libya and Yugoslavia.

Manufacturers: Avia Závody, Letnany, Czechoslovakia (chassis). Czechoslovakian state arsenals (armoured body, armament and final assembly).

EGYPT

Electronique Serge Dassault Sinai 23 Twin 23 mm Self-propelled Anti-aircraft Gun

Development
In January 1984 the Egyptian Government awarded competitive contracts to the Electronic Systems Division of Thomson-CSF and Electronique Serge Dassault for the development and construction of prototypes of a twin 23 mm self-propelled anti-aircraft gun system.

Both systems were completed in 1984 and shown for the first time at the 1984 Cairo Defence Equipment Exhibition. They are based on the FMC M113A2 APC chassis and use the Soviet-designed 23 mm ZU-23 light anti-aircraft gun, now manufactured in Egypt by Abu Zaabal Engineering Industries, and fully described in the *Towed anti-aircraft guns* section.

A typical Sinai 23 platoon would consist of one leader vehicle fitted with the RA-20S radar and three or four satellite fire units each with twin 23 mm cannon. After extensive trials, the Egyptian Army adopted this system in late 1987 and production is now under way.

Description
The acquisition/surveillance vehicle has the RA-20S radar operating in the E-band which can detect aircraft and moving helicopters at a range of 12 km or helicopters hovering at a range of 5 km. Targets can be localised to one degree. This vehicle provides target information to the firing unit.

The firing unit consists of an M113A2 fitted with a TA-23E turret which is a further development of the TA-20 turret armed with twin 20 mm cannon which has been in production for some years and is also fitted on the Panhard M3 (4 × 4) air defence system and VDAA Renault covered

Egypt / SELF-PROPELLED AA GUNS

Sinai 23 firing unit showing power operated turret armed with twin 23 mm cannon, three Sakr Eye SAMs either side of turret and RA-20S radar on turret rear

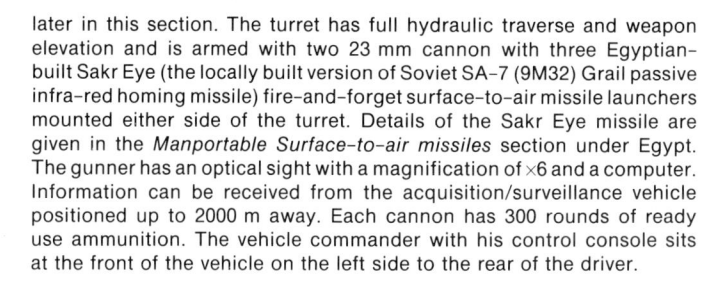

Sinai 23 firing unit showing one-man turret armed with two 23 mm cannon and six Sakr Eye SAMs

later in this section. The turret has full hydraulic traverse and weapon elevation and is armed with two 23 mm cannon with three Egyptian-built Sakr Eye (the locally built version of Soviet SA-7 (9M32) Grail passive infra-red homing missile) fire-and-forget surface-to-air missile launchers mounted either side of the turret. Details of the Sakr Eye missile are given in the *Manportable Surface-to-air missiles* section under Egypt. The gunner has an optical sight with a magnification of ×6 and a computer. Information can be received from the acquisition/surveillance vehicle positioned up to 2000 m away. Each cannon has 300 rounds of ready use ammunition. The vehicle commander with his control console sits at the front of the vehicle on the left side to the rear of the driver.

The Sinai system is of modular construction and can be coupled to thermal and infra-red night vision systems. The firing unit can also be fitted with the RA-20S radar system so enabling two targets to be engaged simultaneously by the four vehicles (one leader and three satellites).

Status: In production for Egyptian Army.

Manufacturer: Electronique Serge Dassault, 55 quai Marcel Dassault, 92214 Saint Cloud, France.
Telephone: (1) 49 11 80 00
Telex: 250787 ESD SCLOU

Thomson-CSF Nile 23 Twin 23 mm Self-propelled Anti-aircraft Gun

Development
In January 1984 the Egyptian Government awarded competitive contracts to the Electronic Systems Division of Thomson-CSF and Electronique Serge Dassault for the development and construction of prototypes of a twin 23 mm self-propelled anti-aircraft gun system.

Both systems were completed in 1984 and shown for the first time at the 1984 Cairo Defence Equipment Exhibition. They are based on an FMC M113A2 APC chassis and use the Soviet-designed 23 mm ZU-23 light anti-aircraft gun, now manufactured in Egypt by Abu Zaabal Engineering Industries, and fully described in the *Towed anti-aircraft guns* section. The Nile 23 successfully completed a series of validation test firings in mid-1986.

A typical Nile 23 battery would consist of one acquisition unit and four fire control units, each of the latter controlling four firing units. When originally announced, the Nile 23 was called the Dagger by Thomson-CSF.

Late in 1987 the Egyptian Army adopted the competing design from Electronique Serge Dassault to meet its requirements for a self-propelled twin 23 mm/Sakr Eye air defence system.

Description
The acquisition unit consists an M113A2 APC with a Thomson-CSF Crotale pulse Doppler surveillance radar operating in the E-band with a detection range of 18 km. This carries out surveillance, threat evaluation and target designation functions.

The fire control units can be fitted with various sensor combinations including a TV camera, laser rangefinder, tracking radar and an infra-red camera. It is also fitted with a digital computer, operator's console and communications equipment to transmit data to the firing units.

The fire unit consists of an M113A2 APC which has a modified version of the 23 mm ZU-23 towed anti-aircraft gun fitted with an armoured cab mounted on the roof. Either side of the turret are two Egyptian-built (Sakr Eye passive infra-red homing missile) fire-and-forget surface-to-air missile launchers. Full details of this missile are given in the *Manportable surface-to-air missiles* section.

The turret has full powered elevation and traverse, the latter to a maximum of 180° in three seconds, a local optical sight, and a computer with automatic data processing. Each 23 mm cannon has a box of 50 rounds of ready use ammunition with 1200 rounds of ammunition carried inside for reloading.

According to Thomson-CSF, Nile 23 has an effective range of 3000 m compared to the 2300 m of the standard ZU-23. The acquisition unit can be up to 500 m away from the control unit which itself is up to 500 m from the firing unit.

Nile 23 firing unit in travelling configuration

Fire control unit of Nile 23 system mounted on M113A2 chassis undergoing cross-country trials in Egypt

SELF-PROPELLED AA GUNS / Egypt-France

Variants

Nile 23 is a modular system, especially the design of the fire control unit, allowing the system to be tailored to meet specific requirements. A fire control unit could also be used to control weapons of different calibres installed on tracked or wheeled chassis or standard towed mounts. The fire control unit can also receive its target designation data from a Crotale SAM acquisition unit which can also designate targets for its own Crotale fire units.

In its back-up mode, the 23 mm firing unit can also operate by itself as it has its own simplified optical fire control system.

Status: Development complete. Ready for production.

Manufacturer: Thomson-CSF, Division Systèmes Électroniques, 1, rue des Mathurins, BP 10, 92223 Bagneux Cedex, France.
Telephone: (1) 46 57 13 65
Telex: 204780 F

FRANCE

Thomson-CSF SABRE Twin 30 mm Self-propelled Anti-aircraft Gun System

Development

The SABRE twin 30 mm air defence turret has been developed as a private venture between Thomson-CSF and SAMM and was shown for the first time at the 1981 Paris Air Show. The turret is suitable for installation on a wide range of tracked and wheeled chassis and has already been installed on the AMX-30 B2 and Chieftain MBT chassis, AMX-10 RC (6 × 6) armoured car and Steyr APC for firing trials. It can also be installed on a wide range of other chassis such as Centurion, M48, M60, Warrior, TH 400 (6 × 6), Marder/TAM and MOWAG Shark (8 × 8).

A trailer-mounted version of this turret has also been developed to the prototype stage and Creusot-Loire is responsible for the actual trailer.

This version weighs 12 tonnes, can be towed at a maximum speed of 20 km/h and takes three minutes to be brought into action.

The SABRE turret is a further development of the turret installed on the AMX-30 DCA system covered in the following entry but has an all-welded steel armour and updated electronics.

Description

The all-welded turret can be armed with twin 30 mm HSS-831A or Oerlikon-Bührle KCB-B cannon, each with 300 rounds of ready use ammunition. The fire control system includes SAGEM Vassyla gyroscopic stabilised sights for both the commander and gunner (the latest version has a single sight in the roof to the rear of the commander and gunner), digital computer, automatic tracking system, laser rangefinder, and an Oeil Vert (Green Eye) coherent D-band pulse Doppler radar which is used as a 2D surveillance radar during watch phase and precise rangefinding of the target during firing phase.

The surveillance range can be increased from 15 up to 22 km with the addition of the Oeil Vert Plus radar. This has three rather than the original two surveillance modes (22, 15 and 7 km maximum range) and three tracking modes (19.5, 12 and 6 km).

The radar can track hovering helicopters and targets crossing up to 300 m/s. The radar is linked to a TMV 850 digital computer which also allows automatic data transmission via radio and modem. The fitting of a TV or radar target angle correction system allows automatic operation. The KCB-B cannon can fire the following types of ammunition:

AMMUNITION TYPE	HEI	HEI-T	SAPHEI	TP	TP-T
WEIGHT (g)					
projectile	360	360	360	360	360
propellant	160	160	160	160	160
explosive	36	26	18	none	none
EXPLOSIVE TYPE	Hexal	Hexal	Hexal	none	none
LENGTH OF COMPLETE ROUND (mm)	285	285	285	295	295
MUZZLE VELOCITY (m/s)	1080	1080	1080	1080	1080

The gunner can select either single shots, 5- or 15-round bursts, or full automatic fire from left or right gun, or both together. Effective range of the weapons in the air defence role is 3500 m and the empty cartridges and links are ejected outside of the turret.

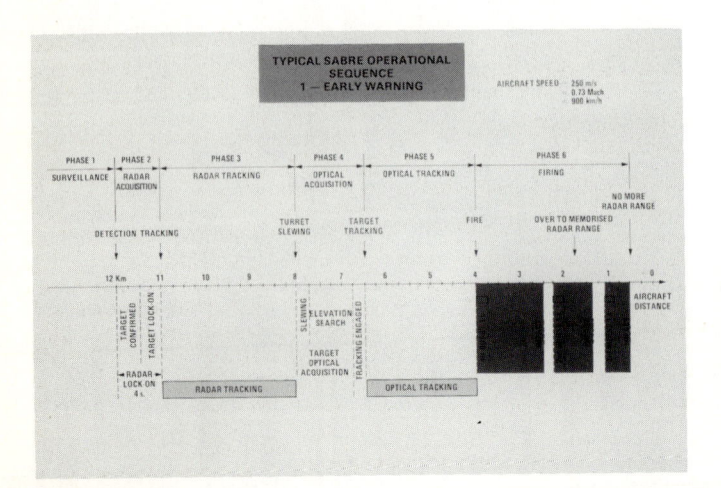

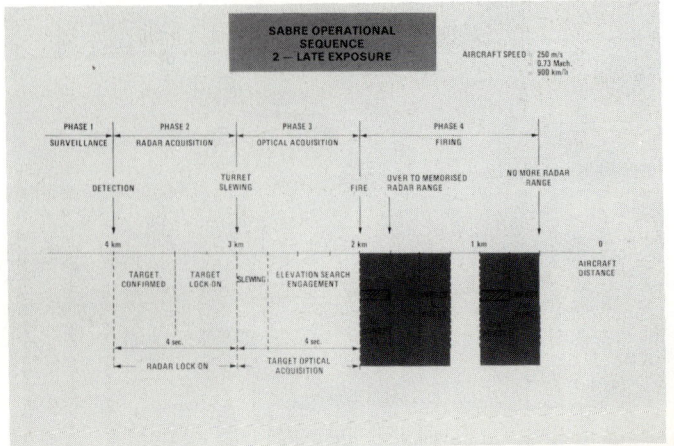

Trailer mounted version of Thomson-CSF SABRE twin 30 mm air defence system deployed in the firing position

France / **SELF-PROPELLED AA GUNS**

Thomson-CSF SABRE twin 30 mm turret on GIAT AMX-30 chassis

Status: Development complete. Ready for production on receipt of orders.

Prime contractor and systems integrator: Thomson-CSF, Division Systèmes Électroniques, 1, rue des Mathurins, BP 10, 92223 Bagneux Cedex, France.
Telephone: (1) 46 57 13 65
Telex: 204780 F

Manufacturer (turret): Société d'Applications des Machines Motrices, Chemin de Malmaison, 91570 Bièvres, France.
Telephone: (33) 69 41 80 88
Telex: 690085 F

Thomson-CSF SABRE twin 30 mm turret on GIAT AMX-10 RC (6 × 6) chassis

SPECIFICATIONS (turret)
CREW	2 (commander and gunner)	WEIGHT	6500 kg
ARMAMENT	2 × 30 mm cannon	LENGTH OVERALL (KCB-B cannon)	5.748 m
AMMUNITION (ready use)	600 × 30 mm (300 per cannon)	WIDTH	2.3 m
CONTROL TRAVERSE	360° hydraulic (180° in 5 s, 90° in 3.5 s)	HEIGHT ABOVE ROOF	
		radar up	2.29 m
ELEVATION	−8° to +85° (45° in 1.5 s)	radar down	1.5 m
OPTICS	gyro stabilised anti-aircraft sight, ground/ground sight, 2 observation periscopes		

SELF-PROPELLED AA GUNS / France

AMX-13 and AMX-30 DCA Twin 30 mm Self-propelled Anti-aircraft Gun Systems

Development

Development of a new self-propelled anti-aircraft gun based on the chassis of the AMX 105 mm self-propelled howitzer started in the late 1950s. Overall prime contractor was the Direction des Etudes et Fabrications d'Armement with the following major subcontractors: La Société d'Applications des Machines Motrices (responsible for the turret), Compagnie Générale de Télégraphie sans Fil (now Thomson-CSF, responsible for the radar system and electronics) and Hispano-Suiza of Switzerland (responsible for the armament and now part of the Oerlikon-Bührle Group).

The first prototypes of the system, called the AMX-13 Defense Contre Avions (or DCA), were completed in 1960 and were not fitted with the radar system. The first prototype with the radar system was completed in 1964 and was tested by the French Army from 1965 to 1966. These trials were satisfactory and the French Army subsequently placed an order for 60 production vehicles which were delivered between 1968 and 1969.

The French Army has two types of low level air defence regiment. The first has four batteries each with two troops, with each of these having four Euromissile Roland surface-to-air missile systems on a GIAT AMX-30 chassis. The second type has three Roland batteries plus one battery with four troops, each of which has three twin 30 mm AMX-13 DCA self-propelled anti-aircraft gun systems. In the French Army the AMX-13 DCA will be replaced by the MATRA SATCP system on the Panhard (6 × 6) armoured car chassis.

Description (AMX-13 DCA)

The DCA system consists of an AMX-13 type chassis, almost identical to that used for the 105 mm Mk 61 self-propelled howitzer, with a SAMM S 401A turret mounted at the rear carrying the optical, electrical and hydraulic systems for laying the guns onto the target and firing the two Hispano-Suiza HSS-831A 30 mm automatic cannon, and a Thomson-CSF coherent pulse Doppler DR-VC-1A (Oeil Noir 1) radar mounted on the rear.

The driver is seated at the front of the vehicle on the left and has a single piece hatch cover that opens to the rear, in front of which are three periscopes. The other two crew members are in the turret with the commander on the left and the gunner on the right. The chassis is identical to that of the 105 mm Mk 61 self-propelled howitzer.

When travelling the radar is normally retracted into its lightly armoured box on the turret rear and when raised provides omni-directional search with a high information rate, angular bearing acquisition of a target and accurate and continuous measurement of the distance of the selected target. This information is supplied by the radar, which operates in the D-band, in two modes of operation; search (omni-directional or sectorised) and rangefinding. A corrector, supplied with information coming from the radar (distance), from tele-control (target speed) and various computational terms, computes the offset to be applied between the line of fire and the line of sight to ensure that the weapons are aimed at the target. This correction is introduced automatically into the aiming chains.

A typical target is engaged as follows:

Phase 1 Omni-directional Watch: This is the responsibility of the commander who monitors the plan position indicator (PPI) inside the turret. The radar scanner rotates at 60 rpm and supplies information on the PPI tube from target echoes with radial velocities of between 50 to 300 m/s, in receiver range selection gates of 4.5 km, 7.5 km, 10.5 km and 13.5 km.

Phase 2 Bearing Acquisition: When a target, located in Phase 1, is considered a threat by the commander, he rotates the turret in its direction by means of a radial alidad which represents the turret axis on the PPI. Bearing acquisition is obtained when the alidad is brought into coincidence with the target echo. At the end of this phase the radar scanner, which is then set in the direction of the target, makes a sector scan about this position over an angle of about 30° to obtain more information. As the target changes position the commander gradually corrects the direction of the turret to hold its axis in line with the direction of the target.

Phase 3 Elevation Optical Acquisition: By the end of phase 2 the sight line is directed in bearing on the target. The gun layer then takes over control of the turret and scans in elevation, so acquiring the target.

Phase 4 Rangefinding: By the end of the three previous phases, target designation (bearing and elevation speed) has been obtained and there remains only to obtain the exact target distance which is measured by operating the radar in the rangefinding mode: a rangefinding gate locks onto the target echo enabling the target distance to be transmitted continuously to the corrector. At the same time it is displayed in luminous form in the sight of the commander who can thus check the approach of the target while identifying it.

Phase 5 Firing: During this phase the corrector is supplied with the bearing and elevation target speed and target distance data previously obtained. The gun layer introduces the correction in the sight and remote control chains. He continues to aim on the target while the guns are offset by such an angle that they are laid on the future target. The guns can be fired as soon as the target enters the optimum range of the weapons. The burst of the weapons is automatically adjusted to a number of salvoes preselected by limiters. Maximum range of this phase is 3800 m.

The two HSS-831A 30 mm guns have an elevation of +85°, depression of −5° and turret traverse is 360°. Gun elevation and turret traverse are hydraulic with manual controls provided for emergency use. The gunner can select single shots, 5- or 15-round bursts, or full automatic from either left or right gun, or both together. The weapons have a cyclic rate of fire of 600 rpm per barrel and each weapon has 300 rounds of 30 mm ammunition which is belt fed. Effective range of the weapons is 3500 m and the empty cartridges and links are ejected outside the turret.

The weapons can fire the following types of fixed 30 mm ammunition:

DESIGNATION (NATO)	SAPHEI/T	HEI/T	HEI	TP/T	TP
WEIGHT (g)					
projectile	360	360	360	360	360
explosive	18	26	36	n/app	n/app
propellant	160	160	160	160	160
complete round	870	870	870	870	870
MUZZLE VELOCITY					
(m/s)	1080	1080	1080	1080	1080

The commander and gunner both have a single piece hatch cover that opens to the outside of the turret, APX L794 observation periscopes and an APX M250 periscope for using the weapons in the ground-to-ground role. The commander and gunner have SAGEM optical sights with a magnification of ×1 and ×4 respectively for anti-aircraft use. The turret is equipped with an air-conditioning system. Two electrically-operated smoke dischargers are mounted either side of the turret.

Variants

AMX-30 DCA

In the late 1960s an AMX-30 MBT chassis was fitted with the SAMM S401A turret as fitted on the AMX-13 DCA, but was not adopted by the French Army. In 1975 Saudi Arabia placed an order with Thomson-CSF

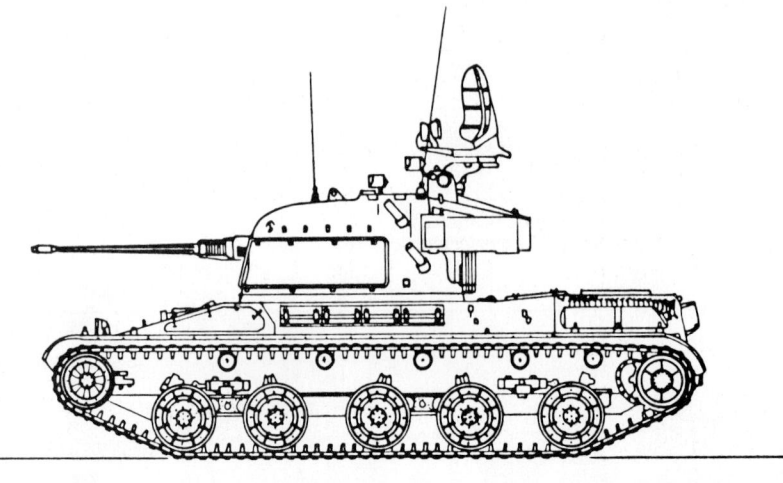

AMX-30 SA twin 30 mm self-propelled anti-aircraft gun with radar erected

France / **SELF-PROPELLED AA GUNS**

AMX-30 SA twin 30 mm self-propelled anti-aircraft gun with radar erected. This is the model in service with Saudi Arabia

AMX-13 DCA twin 30 mm self-propelled anti-aircraft gun with radar erected. This is the model in service with the French Army (ECP Armées)

SELF-PROPELLED AA GUNS / France

AMX-13 DCA twin 30 mm self-propelled anti-aircraft gun in travelling configuration with radar retracted (ECP Armées)

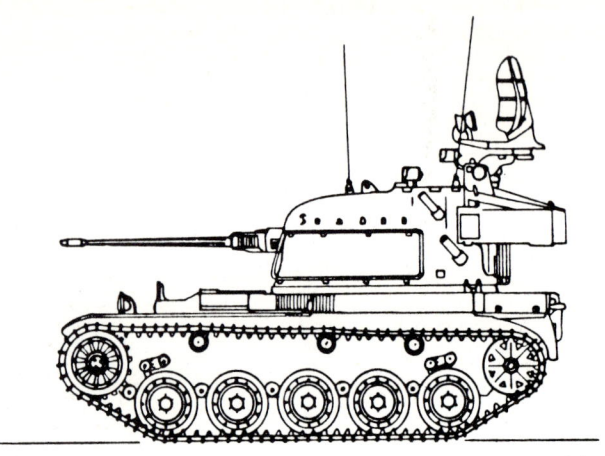

AMX-13 DCA twin 30 mm self-propelled anti-aircraft gun with radar erected

for the development of the Shahine low altitude surface-to-air missile system, a further development of the Crotale but mounted on an AMX-30 MBT chassis rather than a 4 × 4 wheeled vehicle. At the same time Saudi Arabia placed an order for 53 vehicles of an improved version of the AMX-30 DCA called the AMX-30 SA. The turret, designated the TG 230A, is a further development of the SAMM S401A and is armed with the same 30 mm weapons, each of which has 300 rounds of ammunition in the ready racks. In addition a further 900 rounds are carried inside the hull in reserve. Both the commander and gunner have a periscope for using the weapons in the ground-to-ground role and SAGEM sights with a magnification of ×1 and ×6 (12° field of view) respectively for anti-aircraft use. The SAGEM sights are used at a range of 3000 to 3500 m to identify the target.

The AMX-30 SA has the improved Thomson-CSF Oeil Vert (or Green Eye) D-band pulse Doppler radar with a maximum range of over 15 km for remote surveillance and over 7.5 km for close surveillance of pop-up targets. The radar can be used against targets between 0 and 3000 m altitudes with radial velocities from 30 to 300 m/s as well as hovering helicopters.

AMX-30 SABRE

The AMX-30S chassis has been fitted with the twin 30 mm SABRE turret developed from the TG 230A turret of the AMX-30 DCA. Details of SABRE, which as of early March 1989 had yet to enter production, were given in the previous entry.

SPECIFICATIONS (AMX-13 DCA)

CREW	3
COMBAT WEIGHT	17 200 kg
POWER-TO-WEIGHT RATIO	14.53 hp/tonne
GROUND PRESSURE	0.86 kg/cm²
LENGTH	5.4 m
WIDTH	2.5 m
HEIGHT	
with radar operating	3.8 m
with radar retracted	3 m
GROUND CLEARANCE	0.43 m
TRACK	2.159 m
TRACK WIDTH	350 mm
MAX ROAD SPEED	60 km/h
FUEL CAPACITY	415 litres
MAX ROAD RANGE	300 km
FORDING	0.6 m
GRADIENT	60%
SIDE SLOPE	30%
VERTICAL OBSTACLE	
forwards	0.65 m
reverse	0.45 m
TRENCH	1.7 m
ENGINE	SOFAM Model 8Gxb 8-cylinder water-cooled petrol developing 250 hp at 3200 rpm
TRANSMISSION	manual with 5 forward and 1 reverse gears
STEERING	Cleveland type differential
CLUTCH	Ferodo single-disc
SUSPENSION	torsion bar
ELECTRICAL SYSTEM	24 V
BATTERIES	8 × 12 V
MAIN ARMAMENT	2 × 30 mm cannon
SMOKE-LAYING EQUIPMENT	2 × 2 smoke dischargers
AMMUNITION	600
GUN CONTROL EQUIPMENT	
turret power control	hydraulic/manual
by commander	yes
by gunner	yes
max rate power traverse	80°/s (120°/s acceleration)
max rate power elevation	45°/s
gun elevation/depression	+85°/−8°
turret traverse	360°
commander's fire control override	yes
ARMOUR	
hull front	15 mm at 40°
hull sides	20 mm
hull top	10 mm
hull floor	
front	20 mm
rear	10 mm
hull rear	15 mm
turret	15 to 20 mm

Status: AMX-13 DCA, production complete. In service only with the French Army (60). AMX-30 SA, production complete. In service only with Saudi Arabia (53).

Manufacturer: Atelier de Construction Roanne (ARE).
Enquiries to Groupement Industriel Des Armements Terrestres (GIAT), 10 place G Clémenceau, 92211 Saint-Cloud, France.
Telephone: (01) 4 771 40 00
Telex: 260010 DAT-SCLOU

France / SELF-PROPELLED AA GUNS

VDAA Twin 20 mm Self-propelled Anti-aircraft Gun System

Development/Description
The VDAA (Véhicule d'Auto-Défense Antiaérienne) was developed by Renault Véhicules Industriels and Electronique Serge Dassault as a private venture specifically for the export market. It consists of either the 4 × 4 or 6 × 6 version of the VAB fitted with an ESD TA-20 twin 20 mm turret that can also be fitted with an ESD RA-20S E-band 1 to 12 km range fully coherent pulse Doppler radar system. A typical VDAA unit will comprise two vehicles: a leader vehicle with the TA-20 turret and the RA-20S radar and a satellite vehicle with the TA-20 turret only. A crew of three, comprising the driver, vehicle commander and gunner is carried. This turret is also fitted to the Panhard M3 VDA twin 20 mm self-propelled anti-aircraft gun system which is fully described in the following entry. The VAB chassis can also be fitted with the MATRA SATCP MISTRAL SAM system which is covered in the *Self-propelled surface-to-air missiles* section.

VDAA twin 20 mm self-propelled anti-aircraft gun system based on Renault VAB (6 × 6) chassis

SPECIFICATIONS (6 × 6 version)

CONFIGURATION	6 × 6
CREW	3
COMBAT WEIGHT	14 200 kg
LENGTH	5.98 m
WIDTH	2.49 m
HEIGHT (to hull top)	2.06 m
GROUND CLEARANCE	
axles	0.4 m
hull	0.5 m
TRACK	2.035 m
WHEELBASE	1.5 m + 1.5 m
MAX SPEED	
road	92 km/h
water	7.5 km/h
MAX ROAD RANGE	1000 km
FORDING	amphibious
GRADIENT	50%
SIDE SLOPE	30%
VERTICAL OBSTACLE	0.4 m
TURNING RADIUS	9 m
ENGINE	MAN D 2356 HM72 6-cylinder in-line water-cooled diesel developing 235 hp at 2200 rpm
TRANSMISSION	transfluid with 5 forward and 1 reverse gears
STEERING	recirculating ball, hydraulically-assisted
TYRES	14.00 × 20
BRAKES	disc
SUSPENSION	independent (torsion bar and telescopic shock absorbers)
ARMAMENT	2 × 20 mm cannon

Note: From 1983 the MAN engine was replaced in production vehicles by the Renault VI MIDS 06.20.45 6-cylinder, in-line, water-cooled, turbo-charged diesel developing 230 hp at 2200 rpm.

Status: Production as required. In service with Oman National Guard (total of nine systems; three with radar and six without radar).

Manufacturer: Electronique Serge Dassault, 55 quai Marcel Dassault, 92214 Saint-Cloud, France.
Telephone: (1) 49 11 80 00
Telex: 250787 ESD SCLOU

Panhard M3 VDA Twin 20 mm Self-propelled Anti-aircraft Gun System

Development
The M3 VDA (Véhicule de Défense Antiaérienne) is a joint development between Panhard and Electronique Serge Dassault (ESD) and consists of a Panhard M3 APC fitted with a new turret. Major sub-contractors are Hispano-Suiza (turret), Oerlikon (guns) and Galileo (sight).

Design work on the M3 VDA began in 1972 and the first prototype was completed in December 1973. Manufacturers' trials took place between January and March 1974 and qualification trials in May 1974. Production began in April 1975 and the vehicle is now in service with three countries.

Description
The hull of the M3 VDA is almost identical to that of the M3 APC and is of all welded steel armour construction which provides the crew with protection from small arms fire and shell splinters. The driver is seated at the very front and has a single piece hatch that opens to the left with three integral periscopes. The engine is to his immediate rear. In either side of the hull is a door that opens to the front and there are also two doors in the hull rear that open outwards. The only difference is that the M3 VDA has four hydraulically-operated outriggers which are lowered to the ground before firing to provide a more stable firing platform. In an emergency the weapons can be fired without the outriggers in position at the lower rate of fire of 200 rds/min per gun.

The gunner is seated in the turret and the commander in the hull to the rear of the turret. The gunner has a single piece hatch cover, six periscopes and the Galileo P56T sight which has a magnification of ×5

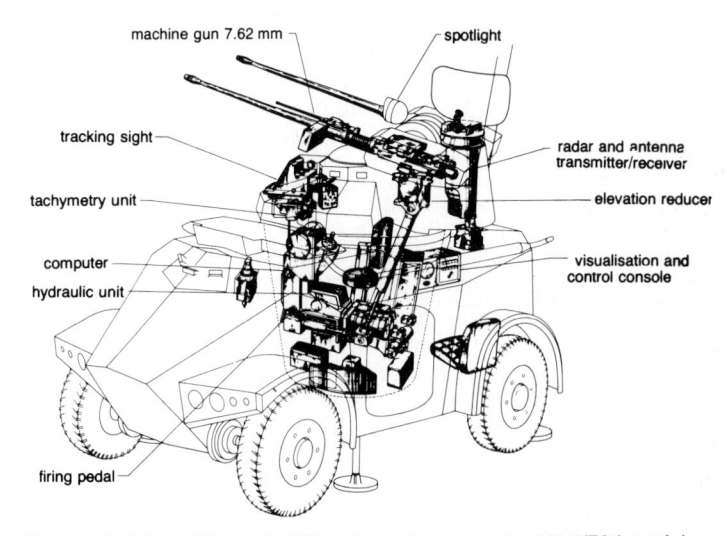

Panhard M3 VDA fitted with ESD radar on turret rear (not to 1/76th scale)

and a 12° field of view for engaging aircraft, a sight for engaging ground targets, and a wiper and washer.

Main armament consists of two Hispano-Suiza 820 SL 20 mm cannon mounted externally on the rear of the turret. Reloading and cocking are carried out from inside the turret, and the empty cartridge cases and links are ejected externally. French M621 or M693 cannons can be fitted in place of the Hispano-Suiza 820 SL weapons if required. The gunner

SELF-PROPELLED AA GUNS / France

Panhard M3 twin 20 mm VDA in firing position with outriggers deployed

Panhard M3 VDA twin 20 mm SPAAG in travelling configuration

Close-up of turret of Panhard M3 VDA twin 20 mm SPAAG with driver's hatch open

can select single shots, bursts or full automatic, and the weapons have two cyclic rates of fire; 200 or 1000 rds/barrel/min. The gunner can select either left or right weapons, or both together. Each barrel is provided with 300 rounds of ready use ammunition.

The weapons have an elevation of +85°, depression of −5° and turret traverse of 360°. Gun elevation and turret traverse are hydraulic with an electric back-up system and manual controls for emergency use. Maximum effective altitude of the 20 mm cannon is 1500 m and maximum horizontal range is 2500 m. The full range of 20 mm ammunition can be fired including HE-I, HEI-T, APHE-I, APIC-T and practice.

A 7.5 mm or 7.62 mm machine gun with 200 rounds is provided for local protection and two electrically-operated smoke dischargers are mounted either side of the lower part of the turret and fire forwards.

Mounted on the rear of the turret is an ESD RA-20 1 to 8 km range fully coherent pulse Doppler radar which operates in the E-band and rotates at 40 rpm, carries out both surveillance and target acquisition (track while scan) and can track four targets simultaneously. The commander is provided with a radar implementation control, PPI, target assignment and acquisition controls, sound alarm that warns when a target has entered the surveillance area and a warning light that indicates the presence of a jammer. Once the commander has decided that the target is to be engaged the radar feeds the target bearing to the optical sight and the range and target speed to the computer. The gunner keeps the optical sight on the target with the aid of a joystick, the computer calculates the lead angle and when the target is in range firing begins.

Optional equipment for the M3 VDA includes an IFF system, laser rangefinder and a TV tracking system. The manufacturer considers that it is possible to replace the guns with short-range anti-aircraft missiles.

The M3 VDA can provide target information by radio to up to four other vehicles without radar. Radar-less vehicles can also be fitted with a satellisation device on the commander's console which allows the M3 VDA with radar to pass data directly to the vehicle. Vehicles without the radar system are delivered with all the mountings and cabling to enable the radar to be retrofitted.

The vehicles without the radar system have two POSs (Postes Optiques de Surveillance), one for the driver and one for the commander, each with a magnification of ×1.5 and a 40° field of view and covering an arc of 190°. When the vehicle is stationary both the commander and driver search for targets and as soon as one of them detects a target he lines up the sight with it and transfers the target to the turret, which automatically swings in azimuth onto it and the guns are simultaneously elevated onto the target. When the target is within range firing begins.

Variants
There are no variants other than those mentioned in the description. This turret has also been fitted on other chassis including the AMX VCI, VAB (6 × 6), ERC (6 × 6), SIBMAS (6 × 6), Urutu (6 × 6) and Steyr APC. Algeria has bought a quantity, known as TA-23, which uses Soviet 23 mm cannon in place of the 20 mm guns. It is not known on which vehicle Algeria has mounted the turrets.

Status: Production complete. In service with the Ivory Coast (6), the United Arab Emirates (Abu Dhabi 42) and one unidentified country.

Note: Future production versions of the M3 VDA would be based on the chassis of the new Panhard Buffalo. The latter has additional external stowage space, slightly longer wheelbase and the choice of a V-6 petrol engine developing 145 hp or a 98 hp diesel engine. The Buffalo is already in service in its basic APC version with Benin, Colombia and Rwanda.

Manufacturer (chassis): Société de Constructions Mécaniques Panhard et Levassor, 18 avenue d'Ivry, 75621 Paris, Cedex 13, France.
Telephone: (33) (1) 49 11 80 00
Telex: 270 276 F

Manufacturer (turret integration): Electronique Serge Dassault, 55 quai Marcel Dassault, 92214 Saint-Cloud, France.
Telephone: (1) 46 02 50 00
Telex: 250787 ESD SCLOU

France / **SELF-PROPELLED AA GUNS** 67

Close-up of turret of Panhard M3 VDA

Belgian SIBMAS (6 × 6) APC fitted with twin 20 mm turret for trials purposes

SPECIFICATIONS			
CREW	3	SUSPENSION	independent, coil spring and hydro-pneumatic shock absorbers acting on suspension trailing arms of wheel mechanism
CONFIGURATION	4 × 4		
COMBAT WEIGHT	7200 kg		
POWER-TO-WEIGHT RATIO	12.5 hp/tonne	TYRES	11.00 × 16
LENGTH	4.45 m	BRAKES	
WIDTH	2.4 m	main	hydraulic, dual circuit
HEIGHT (without radar)	2.995 m	parking	handbrake operating on gearbox output shaft
GROUND CLEARANCE	0.35 m		
TRACK	2.05 m	ELECTRICAL SYSTEM	24 V
WHEELBASE	2.7 m	BATTERIES	2 × 12 V
MAX ROAD SPEED	90 km/h	ARMAMENT	
FUEL CAPACITY	165 litres	main	2 × 20 mm cannon
MAX ROAD RANGE	1000 km	secondary	1 × 7.62 mm MG
FORDING	amphibious	SMOKE-LAYING EQUIPMENT	2 × 2 smoke dischargers
GRADIENT	60%	AMMUNITION	
SIDE SLOPE	30%	main	600
VERTICAL OBSTACLE	0.3 m	secondary	200
TRENCH		GUN CONTROL EQUIPMENT	
with 1 channel	0.8 m	turret power control	hydraulic/electric/manual
with 4 channels	3.1 m	by commander	no
TURNING RADIUS	5.25 m	by gunner	yes
ENGINE	Panhard Model 4 HD 4-cylinder air-cooled petrol developing 90 hp at 4700 rpm	max rate power traverse	60°/s
		max rate power elevation	90°/s
		gun elevation/depression	+85°/−5°
TRANSMISSION	manual with 6 forward and 1 reverse gears	turret traverse	360°
		ARMOUR	
CLUTCH	centrifugal with electromagnetic control	hull	8–12 mm
		turret	8–10 mm

Panhard AML S530 twin 20 mm Self-propelled Anti-aircraft Gun

Development
This system was developed specifically for the export market and consists of a Panhard AML (4 × 4) light armoured car chassis fitted with the SAMM S530 twin 20 mm powered anti-aircraft turret. It was first shown at the Satory exhibition of military equipment in 1971.

A total of 12 systems were delivered to Venezuela in 1973 and these remain in service today.

Description
The basic chassis is virtually identical to the standard AML, over 4800 of which have been built in France and under licence in South Africa by Sandock Austral.

The all welded steel hull of the AML is divided into three compartments: driver's at the front; fighting in the centre and engine at the rear. The driver is seated at the front of the hull and is provided with a single piece hatch cover that opens to the right with three integral periscopes. The centre periscope can be replaced by an infra-red or image intensification periscope for night driving.

The all welded steel armour turret is mounted in the centre of the hull and was designed and built by SAMM. The commander, who also operates the roof-mounted white light searchlight, sits on the left and

Panhard AML S530 twin 20 mm SPAAG from front with hatches closed and showing sand channels on front of hull

SELF-PROPELLED AA GUNS / France

Panhard AML S530 twin 20 mm SPAAG from rear

Panhard AML S530 twin 20 mm SPAAG with turret traversed partly left and showing space for spare wheel and tyre on side door

Panhard ERC Sagaie (6 × 6) Kriss, a further development of the S530 with slightly different front and sides

the gunner on right. The commander has a single piece hatch cover that opens to the rear while the gunner has a single piece hatch cover that opens to the right.

Observation equipment consists of seven L794B periscopes; three for the gunner and four for the commander. Each of these has a vertical field of view of 27° and a horizontal field of view of 55° while the gunner has a roof mounted M411 periscopic sight.

The M411 has a ×6 sight for engaging ground targets with a 10° field of view, an observation periscope with ×1 magnification, vertical field of view of 12° and a horizontal field of view of 55° and a collimator. The latter has an adjustable light intensity reticle with image set to infinity, display lead for slow (100 m/s) and fast (200 m/s) dive down and horizontal flights and fire range estimation (1300 m).

The turret was also offered with another sighting system, type M251 for observation and engaging ground targets and with the L834-13 for anti-aircraft use.

Turret traverse and weapon elevation is under full power control with manual controls provided for emergency use. Turret traverse is 360° at a maximum speed of 80°/s while elevation is from -10 to +75° at a maximum speed of 40°/s.

Main armament comprises two GIAT M621 20 mm cannon, each of which has 300 rounds of ammunition. The gunner can select either single shots, short bursts or full automatic with the cyclic rate of fire being 740 rds/barrel/min.

The firing switch is on the gunner's control handle although there is also an emergency foot pedal. Effective range in the anti-aircraft role is between 1500 and 2000 m.

French and US M56 types are included in the types of 20 mm ammunition fired. Among the French types used are the following: an HE tracer (muzzle velocity 990 m/s); an armour piercing tracer which can penetrate 23 mm of armour at 0° at a range of 1000 m muzzle velocity (1000 m/s); an HE (muzzle velocity 1026 m/s) and an incendiary (muzzle velocity 1026 m/s).

The gunner can also select either the left or right cannon and both weapons are normally used for air defence purposes. The empty cartridge cases and links are ejected from turret.

The system is clear weather only with no provision for off carriage fire control, although general target information such as range, altitude and bearing can be provided over the radio net.

Two electricity operated smoke dischargers are mounted either side of the turret towards the rear. Either side of the hull below the turret ring is a door. The left door, on which a spare wheel and tyre is mounted, opens to the rear while the right door opens to the front. The engine compartment which is at the rear of the hull has two access panels. The gearbox is crosswise and consists of two gearboxes in one (high and low), coupled on both sides of the bevel pinion.

The low-range box is for cross-country use and comprises two low gears, a top gear and one reverse gear. When the low-range box is in normal drive the four ratios of the high-range box command the four upper gears of the range: sixth, fifth, fourth and third. The high-range box is for normal road use and has three low gears and one overdrive. There are Panhard-type ball differentials in the gearbox and in each rear transfer box which automatically prevent gear slip. Drive is transmitted from the gearbox to two lateral transfer boxes via pinions to the rear wheels and via drive shafts that run along the inside of the hull to the front wheels.

The independent suspension at each wheel station consists of coil springs and hydro-pneumatic shock absorbers acting on the trailing arms of the wheel mechanism. The tyres are fitted with puncture-proof Hutchinson inner tubes.

The basic vehicle has no NBC system or night fighting aids, but these could be fitted as optional extras as could an air-conditioning system. Sand channels are carried across the hull front and when in position these enable the vehicle to cross ditches and other obstacles.

Variants

The SAMM S530 turret was also offered for installation on many other tracked and wheeled armoured vehicles but the only other known installation, for trials purposes, was on the AMX-13 light tank.

The S530 A has an M411 sight with a magnification of ×1 for engaging aircraft, retractable sun filter and a ×6 magnification sight with a 10° field of view for engaging ground targets. The S530 F is the latest version and is also known as the TAB 220. Four of these have been sold to Gabon and installed on the Panhard ERC Sagaie (6 × 6) chassis and full details of this are given in the entry for the French SANTAL self-propelled surface-to-air missile system. The S530 F has the M411 sight and a moving prism episcopic channel for observation with an elevation from -10 to +70°, a magnification of ×1, a horizontal field of view of 77°, and a vertical field of view of 32° plus seven observation periscopes. This turret can also be fitted with a Ferranti Mk 3 self-contained gyroscopic sight and receive target information from a vehicle with a radar system. Typically one DARD radar vehicle would control six twin 20 mm systems. When fitted onto the Sagaie (6 × 6) armoured car the system is known as the Kriss.

The S531 is similar to S530 A but has smaller dimensions; the S532 has thinner armour and an open roof and the S533 is the same as S530 A but has twin HSS 820 20 mm cannon in place of the GIAT M621 20 mm cannon.

France-International / **SELF-PROPELLED AA GUNS**

SPECIFICATIONS

CREW	3
CONFIGURATION	4 × 4
COMBAT WEIGHT	5500 kg
POWER-TO-WEIGHT RATIO	16.36 hp/tonne
LENGTH GUNS FORWARD	3.90 m
LENGTH HULL	3.79 m
WIDTH	
overall	1.97 m
over hubs	1.925 m
HEIGHT	
overall	2.24 m
hull top	1.385 m
GROUND CLEARANCE	0.33 m
TRACK	1.62 m
WHEELBASE	2.5 m
MAX ROAD SPEED	
6th gear, high range	90 km/h
5th gear, high range	61 km/h
4th gear, high range	35 km/h
3rd gear, high range	18.8 km/h
3rd gear, low range	18.8 km/h
2nd gear, low range	9.3 km/h
1st gear, low range	4.5 km/h
reverse	5.5 km/h
FUEL CAPACITY	156 litres
MAX ROAD RANGE	600 km (at 60 km/h)
FORDING	1.1 m
GRADIENT	60%
SIDE SLOPE	30%
VERTICAL OBSTACLE	0.3 m
TRENCH	
with one channel	0.8 m
with four channels	3.1 m
TURNING RADIUS	6 m
ENGINE	Panhard Model 4HD 4-cylinder air-cooled diesel developing 90 hp at 4700 rpm (see note)
TRANSMISSION	manual with 6 forward and 1 reverse gears
CLUTCH	centrifugal with electro-magnetic automatic control
SUSPENSION	independent spring and hydro-pneumatic shock absorbers acting on suspension trailing arms of wheel mechanism
TYRES	11.00 × 16
BRAKES	
main	hydraulic, dual circuit
parking	handbrake operating on gearbox output shaft
ELECTRICAL SYSTEM	24 V
BATTERIES	2 × 12 V
ARMAMENT	2 × 20 mm cannon
SMOKE DISCHARGERS	2 × 2
AMMUNITION	600 × 20 mm
GUN CONTROL EQUIPMENT	
turret power control	electro-hydraulic/manual
turret traverse	360°
gun elevation/depression	+75°/−10°
GUN STABILISER	no
ARMOUR	
hull	8 mm (max)
turret	7 to 14 mm

Note: New production vehicles would be powered by the Peugeot XD 3T diesel developing 98 hp coupled to the standard Panhard manual transmission. This more fuel-efficient engine increases the operational range of the vehicle to 700/800 km.

Status: Production as required. In service with Venezuela (12). The Panhard ERC Sagaie (6 × 6) Kriss is in service with Gabon (4).

Manufacturer (chassis): Société de Constructions Mécaniques Panhard et Levassor, 18 avenue d'Ivry, 75621 Paris, Cedex 13, France.
Telephone: (33) (1) 40 77 40 00
Telex: 270 276 F

Manufacturer (turret): Société d'Applications des Machines Motrices, Chemin de Malmaison, 91570 Bièvres, France.
Telephone: (33) 69 41 80 88
Telex: 690 085 F

INTERNATIONAL

Gepard and CA 1 Twin 35 mm Self-propelled Anti-aircraft Gun Systems

Development

In 1965 a decision was taken to develop a new self-propelled anti-aircraft gun for the West German Army as a replacement for the clear weather M42, which would have an all-weather fire control system and be based on the chassis of the Leopard 1 MBT. In June 1966 a contract was placed for the development of a twin 30 mm vehicle which later became known as the Matador. Prime contractors for this were Rheinmetall (armament and turret), AEG-Telefunken (target tracking radar and computer), Siemens (search radar and IFF) and Krauss-Maffei/Porsche (chassis and power supply system).

At the same time a contract for two vehicles armed with twin 35 mm cannon was awarded to a consortium consisting of Oerlikon (armament and turret), Contraves (computer and systems integration), Siemens-Albis (tracking radar), Hollandse Signaalapparaten (search radar) and Krauss-Maffei/Porsche (chassis and power supply system). These two prototypes were called the 5PFZ-A and were delivered in 1968.

Following comparative trials with the Matador and the 5PFZ-A a decision was taken in 1970 to concentrate further development on the twin 35 mm version developed in Switzerland. Before this decision an order had been placed for a further four twin 35 mm vehicles called the 5PFZ-B, which were delivered in 1971 and had their original Dutch search radar replaced by a West German Siemens MPDR-12 radar with a Siemens MSR-400 IFF system. A pre-production batch of 12 vehicles was subsequently ordered and delivered by 1973. In September 1973 an order for 420 Gepards was placed for the West German Army and the first production vehicles were delivered late in 1976; production was finally completed late in 1980. The first 195 vehicles were delivered as B2 versions

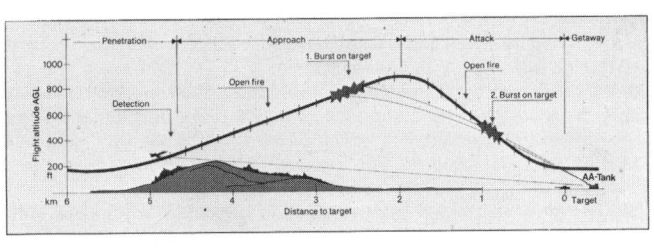

Typical dive attack profile assuming target flying at constant speed of approx 200 m/s

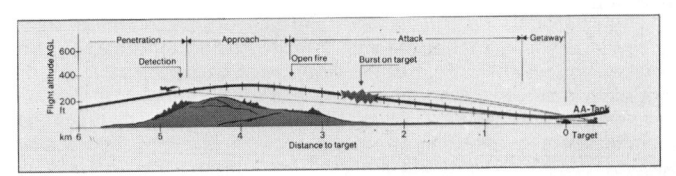

Typical low level attack profile assuming target flying at constant speed of approx 200 m/s

and the remaining 225 as B2L which are fitted with a laser rangefinder of Siemens design and manufacture. Belgium ordered 55 vehicles which were delivered between 1977 and 1980.

In 1969 the Dutch ordered a version with the same chassis and turret as the 5PFZ-B but fitted with Hollandse Signaalapparaten integrated Ka-band monopulse Doppler surveillance and tracking radar with moving target indication and a peak emission power output of 160 kW. This model was called the 5PFZ-C and was followed by five pre-production vehicles

SELF-PROPELLED AA GUNS / International

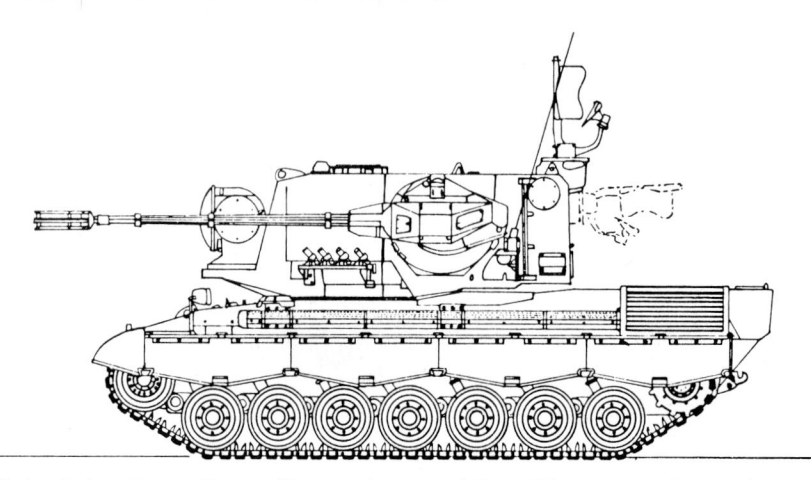

Gepard twin 35 mm self-propelled anti-aircraft gun with surveillance radar erected. Dotted lines to rear of turret show radar's position when retracted

which were delivered in 1971/72. The Dutch subsequently ordered 95 production vehicles under the designation CA 1 which were delivered between 1977 and 1979. The Dutch Army designation for the vehicle is the Pantser Rups Tegen Luchtdoelen (PRTL).

In order for the Gepard to remain effective into the 1990s it will need a mid-life update and in 1984 prototypes were evaluated by the West German Army. AEG Telefunken, Siemens and SIGNAAL/Oerlikon-Bührle have each provided one prototype with the last mentioned being one of the original Dutch vehicles. Wherever possible the new components will be straight substitutes for the current ones. One prototype will be selected for final development, with the West German Army fleet being refitted to the new standard in the future.

The definition stage for the upgrade, which will be implemented by both West Germany and the Netherlands, was carried out in 1987/88.

The development phase commenced in 1988 and is scheduled to continue until 1992, with procurement from 1993 through to 1999. The programme covers two key areas: first, the fire control system (which will be digitised, modified tracking radar and a passive optronic sensor) and second, the turret and weapons subsystem (mainly by the use of more effective 35 mm ammunition).

Acting in its capacity as contractor with responsibility for the fire control system in collaboration with consortium partners Contraves and Krupp Atlas Elektronic, and sub-contractors Zeiss and AEG, Siemens designed a concept employing advanced microprocessor technology to provide greater system effectiveness, combined with improved availability/logistics support at the unit level.

The definition included a new control unit (digital processor), modifications to the controls and display, detailed modifications to the tracking radar and an optronic sensor to which the tracker is assigned.

Prime contractor for the chassis subsystem is Krauss-Maffei while Wegmann will be responsible for the turret/weapons subsystem.

Description

The all-welded steel hull of the Gepard is slightly longer than the Leopard 1 MBT's and has slightly thinner armour.

The driver is seated at the front of the hull on the right side and has a single piece hatch cover that opens to the left of his position and three periscopes in front of him. To the left of the driver is the Daimler-Benz OM314 95 hp auxiliary power unit, for which the exhaust pipe runs along the left side of the hull to the rear.

The two-man all-welded steel turret is in the centre of the hull with the commander seated on the left and the gunner on the right. Over their position is a single piece hatch cover that opens to the rear and periscopes arranged around it give all-round observation with the hatch closed.

In front of both the commander's and gunner's position is a fully-stabilised panoramic telescope with a magnification of ×1.5 (50° field of view) and ×6 (12.5° field of the view), each of which has a swing-in sun filter, screen washer and wiper, and a de-icing and de-misting heater. The sights can be automatically slaved to the tracking radar and therefore have an elevation of +85°, a depression of -10° and a total traverse of 360°. The sights are used for optical target acquisition, battlefield surveillance and the laying of the guns against ground targets. An optical target indicator mounted on the commander's panoramic telescope is operated by the commander standing in his open hatch.

The Gepard has a vehicle navigation system and the screen of the radar is always north oriented. Information from the radar system can be transmitted by radio in digital form and displayed on a similar monitor at headquarters. The vehicle is also provided with an NBC system and four smoke dischargers are mounted on either side of the turret.

Mounted on the rear of the turret is the fully coherent pulse Doppler search radar, which operates in the E/F-bands and has a range of 15 km. It rotates at 60 rpm and provides continuous air space surveillance with

Gepard twin 35 mm self-propelled anti-aircraft gun system with tracking and surveillance radars in operating positions

an IFF capability. The radar can be operated when the vehicle is moving and when not required, it can be folded down behind the rear of the turret to reduce overall height. As soon as an aircraft appears on the scope the crew is alerted. The target is displayed in terms of azimuth, angle and range and is identified as friend or foe. If the aircraft is hostile, information is passed to the coherent Siemens-Albis pulse Doppler tracking radar mounted on the front of the turret which has a range of 15 km, operates in the Ku-band and when not in use can be traversed through 180° so that the antenna is facing the front of the turret. The tracking radar tracks the target automatically in terms of azimuth, elevation and range. At the same time the search radar is still maintaining a search for other targets. The acquisition range of the tracking radar allows target acquisitions within an angle of about 200° without rotating the turret.

The analogue computer calculates the lead angles taking into account weather, continuously measured muzzle velocity and the cant of the vehicle. Wind speed and direction, ballistic air pressure and ballistic air temperatures are fed in manually once a day. The guns normally open fire when the aircraft is between 3000 and 4000 m away, with the rounds reaching the target at a range of 2000 to 3000 m. The duration of the burst is a function of the range with a normal burst consisting of 20 to 40 rounds.

Main armament consists of two Oerlikon 35 mm KDA cannon with a cyclic rate of fire of 550 rds/barrel/min. The guns are mounted externally, one either side of the turret and the anti-aircraft ammunition is fed via fixed and moving chutes, which are hermetically sealed from the fighting compartment. Each cannon is provided with 310 rounds of anti-aircraft and 20 rounds of armour-piercing ammunition. The following types of ammunition can be fired:

AMMUNITION TYPE	HEI	HEI-T	SAPHEI-T	APDS-T	TP/TP-T
WEIGHT OF PROJECTILE	0.55 kg	0.535 kg	0.55 kg	0.294 kg	0.55 kg
WEIGHT OF PROPELLANT	0.33 kg	0.33 kg	0.33 kg	0.33 kg	0.33 kg
WEIGHT OF EXPLOSIVE	0.112 kg	0.098 kg	0.012 kg	n/app	n/app
WEIGHT OF COMPLETE ROUND	1.58 kg	1.565 kg	1.552 kg	1.46 kg	1.58 kg
MUZZLE VELOCITY	1175 m/s	1175 m/s	1175 m/s	1390 m/s	1175 m/s

Dutch version of Gepard, called CA 1, with tracking and surveillance radars by Hollandse Signaalapparaten, and six smoke dischargers each side of turret rather than four as on West German and Belgian Army vehicles

The computer is provided with an automatic unit which can check the total serviceability of the complete fire control system. If the main computer fails the crew can switch to an independent stand-by computer.

Variants
The Dutch Ministry of Defence awarded Hollandse Signaalapparaten a contract for the feasibility study of a self-propelled anti-aircraft missile system based on the chassis of the Leopard 1 MBT which was to be fitted with American Chapparal, British Rapier or Euromissile Roland SAMs and a Dutch radar system. However, the project was subsequently dropped.

Further developments have included the mounting of the turret on the Palmaria, Pz 68 MBT chassis (tested by the Swiss Army but not adopted).

This turret can also be installed on the Leopard 2.

At present there is a combat effectiveness improvement programme underway which has just switched from the concept phase into the project definition phase. To meet the new Soviet combat aircraft and ECM threats the trilateral programme is planning to introduce new higher velocity ammunition, integrate the system with an external search unit (to be known as the HFlaAFüSyS), replace the present fire control, internal control and monitoring computer by a new digital one and fit a passive optronic sensor with a thermal imaging and tracking device to allow minimum active radar transmissions from the vehicle itself.

Note: The Contraves AG twin 35 mm ATAK self-propelled anti-aircraft gun system is no longer being marketed.

SPECIFICATIONS

CREW	3	TRENCH	3 m
COMBAT WEIGHT	47 300 kg	ENGINE	MTU MB 838 Ca M500, 10-cylinder multi-fuel developing 830 hp at 2200 rpm
UNLOADED WEIGHT	44 800 kg		
POWER-TO-WEIGHT RATIO	17.54 hp/tonne		
GROUND PRESSURE	0.95 kg/cm^2	TRANSMISSION	ZF 4 HP 250 planetary gear shift with hydraulic torque converter, 4 forward and 2 reverse gears
LENGTH GUNS FORWARD	7.73 m		
LENGTH HULL	6.85 m		
WIDTH	3.37 m	STEERING	regenerative double differential
over tracks	3.25 m	SUSPENSION	torsion bar
HEIGHT		ELECTRICAL SYSTEM	24 V
radar up	4.03 m [3.7 m Dutch model]	ARMAMENT (main)	2 × 35 mm cannon
to top of periscopes	3.01 m	SMOKE-LAYING EQUIPMENT	2 × 4 smoke dischargers [2 × 6 Dutch model]
FIRING HEIGHT	2.37 m		
GROUND CLEARANCE	0.44 m	AMMUNITION	
TRACK	2.7 m	AA	620
TRACK WIDTH	550 mm	AP	40
MAX ROAD SPEED	65 km/h	GUN CONTROL EQUIPMENT	
FUEL CAPACITY	985 litres	turret power control	hydraulic/manual
MAX RANGE		by commander	yes
road	550 km	by gunner	yes
cross-country	400 km	turret traverse	360°
FORDING	2.5 m	gun elevation/depression	+85°/−10°
GRADIENT	60%	max rate power traverse	90°/s
VERTICAL OBSTACLE	1.15 m	max rate power elevation	45°/s

72 SELF-PROPELLED AA GUNS / International

West German Army Gepard twin 35 mm self-propelled anti-aircraft gun system with tracking and surveillance radars in travelling positions (Pierre Touzin)

West German Army Gepard 35 mm self-propelled anti-aircraft gun with search radar antenna erected (Pierre Touzin)

Gepard twin 35 mm self-propelled anti-aircraft gun system of the Belgian Army with both radars in travelling position (C R Zwart)

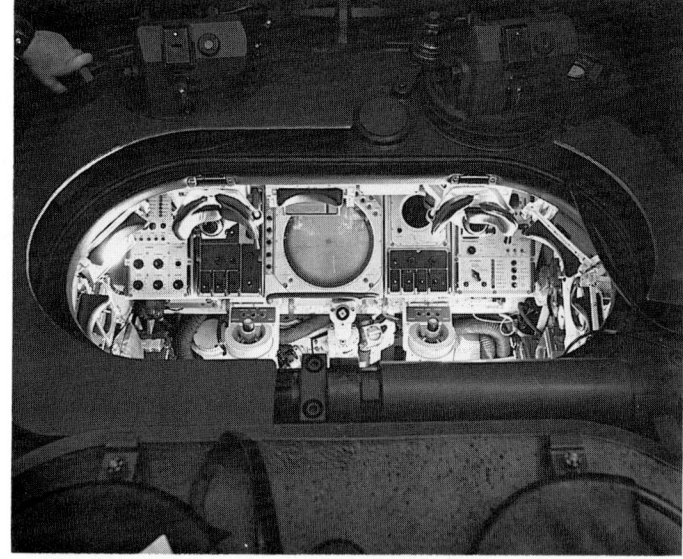

Commander's and gunner's turret position in the Dutch version of the Gepard twin 35 mm self-propelled anti-aircraft gun system

Status: Production complete. In service with:-

Country	Quantity	User	Comment
Belgium	55	army	delivered 1977/1980
Germany, West	420	army	delivered 1976/1980
Netherlands	95	army	delivered 1977/1979

Manufacturer: Krauss-Maffei, Wehrtechnik GmbH, Krauss-Maffei Strasse 2, 8000 Munich 50, Federal Republic of Germany assembled the complete Gepard and CA 1. Prime contractor is Contraves AG, Schaffhauserstrasse 580, CH-8052, Zürich, Switzerland.
Telephone: 01 306 2211
Telex: 823 402

Hotspur/Rheinmetall Twin 20 mm Mobile Gun Platform

Development
The twin 20 mm mobile gun platform was developed as a private venture between Hotspur Armoured Products of the United Kingdom and Rheinmetall GmbH of West Germany.

It essentially consists of a modified version of the Hotspur One-Fifty 6 × 6 drive conversion of the well known Land Rover chassis, with the Rheinmetall twin 20 mm air defence system mounted on the rear. The latter is normally towed behind a truck but by installing it on the 6 × 6 chassis it has greater cross-country mobility and can be brought into action much more quickly.

Description
The layout of the Hotspur mobile gun-platform is conventional, with the engine at the front, driver and gunner in the centre and the platform with the twin 20 mm cannon at the rear. The base chassis incorporates a driver's cab which is manufactured from aluminium and hinged so that it can be folded down and protect the driver's compartment, instrument panel, seats when the system is deployed in the firing position. Attached to the driver's cab is an 'in-transit' muzzle protection and branch deflection bar which is hinged and folded down with the vehicle cab when in the firing position.

The gun platform is fitted with a four pod automatic self-levelling hydraulic stabilising system which is operated automatically from the driver's position. The automatic system can be overridden by manual operation from the controls fitted at the rear of the gun platform, if required.

Additional features of the mobile gun platform include the capacity for carrying extra ammunition with locker and tool kit space being provided. A collapsible frame can be fitted to a canvas cover or camouflage net.

Status: Development complete. Ready for production.

Manufacturers: Hotspur Armoured Products, Division of Penman Engineering Limited, Heathhall, Dumfries DG1 3NY, UK.
Telephone: (0387) 52784
Telex: 779771
Fax: (0387) 52784

Rheinmetall GmbH, Ulmenstrasse 125, D-4000 Dusseldorf, Federal Republic of Germany.
Telephone: (0211) 4471
Telex: 8584963

International-Italy / **SELF-PROPELLED AA GUNS** 73

Hotspur/Rheinmetall twin 20 mm mobile gun platform in firing position with outriggers deployed and cab in travelling configuration

Hotspur/Rheinmetall twin 20 mm mobile gun platform with outriggers raised and cab folded forward on bonnet

SPECIFICATIONS

CREW	2
CONFIGURATION	6 × 6
GROSS WEIGHT	5350 kg
POWER-TO-WEIGHT RATIO	25 bhp/tonne
LENGTH	5.86 m
WIDTH	1.84 m
HEIGHT (travelling position)	2.5 m
GROUND CLEARANCE	0.21 m
TRACK	1.486 m
WHEELBASE	3.81 m
ANGLE OF APPROACH/DEPARTURE	35°/29°
MAX ROAD SPEED	95 km/h
FUEL CAPACITY	85 + 68 litres
MAX RANGE	300 km + 230 km
TURNING RADIUS	8.6 m
ENGINE	V8, petrol 3.5 litre, water-cooled, developing 134 bhp at 4000 rpm
TRANSMISSION	manual, 5 forward, 1 reverse
TRANSFER BOX	2 speed
CLUTCH	single dry plate, hydraulic
STEERING	power assisted, worm and roller
SUSPENSION	
front	dual rate coil springs, worm and roller dual rate coil springs, live beam axle double acting hydraulic dampers
mid and rear	A - dual frame live rear axle, dual rate coil springs, double acting hydraulic dampers
BRAKES	dual circuit
front	hydraulic servo-assisted disc
mid and rear	hydraulic servo-assisted drum
TYRES	7.50 × 16
NUMBER OF TYRES	6 + 1
ELECTRICAL SYSTEM	12 V split charge
BATTERIES	2 × 50 Ah

ITALY

OTO Melara Quad 25 mm Self-propelled Anti-aircraft Gun System (SIDAM 25)

Development

The Quad 25 mm self-propelled anti-aircraft gun system, also known as the SIDAM 25, is a joint development between the Italian Army and OTO Melara with the assistance of a number of other Italian manufacturers, to meet an Italian Army requirement for a self-propelled anti-aircraft gun system.

Technical and operational evaluations of the two prototype systems commenced in 1983 with the final tests being carried out in 1986. Production of the turret systems commenced at OTO Melara's La Spezia facility in 1988 with first production systems due to be completed in 1989. The total Italian Army requirement is for 340 systems, although the initial order is for a much smaller quantity.

The Italian Army will install the system on existing Italian built M113 series APCs which have been upgraded to the M113A2 standard in Italy. OTO Melara is offering the turret system for installation on a wide range of other chassis, tracked and wheeled, including the Brazilian ENGESA EE-11 Urutu (6 × 6) APC, the OTO Melara C13 APC and the VCC 80 IFV which is being developed by OTO Melara under contract to the Italian Army.

Other major sub-contractors to OTO Melara include Officine Galileo, Military Systems Division for the MADIS primary stabilised sighting system and Oerlikon-Italiana for the four Oerlikon-Bührle 25 mm KBA cannons.

The M113 chassis is being modified by Astra with the internal fuel tank being removed and replaced by two fuel tanks mounted one either

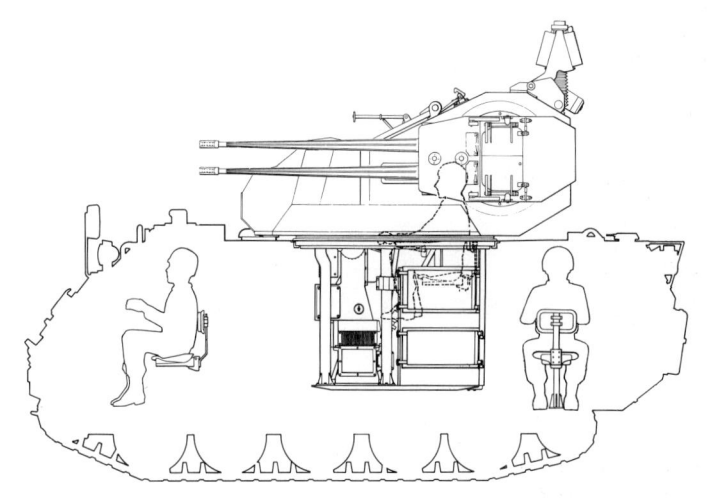

M113A2 armoured personnel carrier with SIDAM 25 turret, showing crew positions (not to 1/76th scale)

side of the rear power operated ramp, installation of the more powerful Detroit Diesel 6V-53T engine developing 265 hp coupled to the existing TX-100 fully automatic transmission, fitting a reverse flow cooling system and modifying the suspension to allow for a gross vehicle weight of 15 tonnes.

SELF-PROPELLED AA GUNS / Italy

OTO Melara Quad 25 mm SPAAG system SIDAM 25 with rear ramp lowered and turret traversed left

Close up of gunner's position in rear of SIDAM 25 SPAAG

Prototype of OTO Melara Quad 25 mm SPAAG on M113A2 APC chassis

OTO Melara Quad 25 mm SPAAG system SIDAM 25 (not to 1/76th scale)

Description
The overall layout of the chassis is almost identical to the basic M113 series armoured personnel carrier with the driver being seated at the front left and provided with a single piece hatch cover and the powerpack to his right. The turret is mounted on the roof just to the centre of the vehicle with the power operated ramp being retained at the rear. The suspension either side consists of five rubber tyred road wheels, drive sprocket at the front and idler at the rear. There are no track return rollers and the upper part of the suspension is covered by a rubber skirt.

To the rear of the driver on the left side of the hull is the auxiliary power unit while on the right side of the hull are the fire control computer, TV tracer electronics, stable element, power supply unit, radio sets and finally the gunner's console.

The one-man all-welded aluminium alloy turret has four externally-mounted Oerlikon-Italiana 25 mm KBA-B cannon. The turret is fitted with a day clear weather and low light level TV camera sighting system capable of tracking targets automatically. The fire control system utilises the Officine Galileo sighting equipment and gun electro-hydraulic servo-system, a Selenia laser rangefinder, FIAR TV components and displays and an ITALTEL IFF system. A laser rangefinder, connected to a digital computer, provides the fire control data. The system has, however, no all-weather capability. The fire control system is controlled by two operators, with the commander being seated in the turret and the gunner in the vehicle. An IFF subsystem is also installed. An electronic tracking unit connected to the optronic sight performs the angular tracking of the target. Direct target detection and acquisition can be carried out

Italy / **SELF-PROPELLED AA GUNS** 75

by the commander in the turret by sight or via an optical sight. From the commander's acquisition, the target is assigned to the gunner who performs automatic tracking or manual tracking using a joystick. As an accurate stabilisation device is installed, all of the operations, with the exception of firing, can be carried out while the vehicle is moving. Target designation from an external source can also be accepted through a Target Alert Display Data Set (TADDS).

For all-weather and night operations a video-compatible thermal imager unit can be connected to the optronic sight for use in haze and smoke conditions together with a passive IR night and day sight. An inertial navigation system for improved attitude sensing may also be fitted. The crew consists of three: driver, commander and gunner and the combat weight is estimated to be about 12 500 kg. The practical rate of fire of the four guns is 2400 rpm, with the 600 HEI-T ready use rounds carried providing sufficient ammunition for eight two-second bursts or full automatic fire. A further 30 APDS-T ready use rounds are carried for ground defence. The maximum range of the guns is 2500 metres although their effective range is 2000 metres. The maximum traverse rate of the turret is 120° a second, and the maximum elevation rate 90° a second. The guns can be elevated to +87° and depressed to -5°. The mode of fire is either single shot, 15- or 25-round bursts or full automatic fire. Two of the guns have a dual feed arrangement for firing both the APDS-T and HEI-T rounds. Other round types that can be fired are SAPHEI-T, TP-T, and APP-T (the last two for practice).

M113 with SHORAR

Late in 1988 the Italian Army took delivery of an M113 series APC fitted with a Contraves SHORAR (SHOrt-Range-Acquisition Radar) which will be used for extensive trials with the OTO Melara SIDAM 25.

The Contraves SHORAR is a family of radars which has been developed as a private venture to meet a range of different applications which include the towed Pagoda, vehicle mounted as part of the ADATS system (covered in the *Self-propelled surface-to-air missiles* section) and the SHORAR/ACV ordered by the Italian Army (ACV means armoured command vehicle).

SHORAR is a fully coherent dual-beam I/J-band pulse Doppler radar which has been optimised for the detection of aircraft, RPVs and hovering helicopters flying at medium, low and very low altitudes with a range of about 25 km. It has a track-while-scan (TWS) facility for up to 10 targets while threat evaluations are automatic. It also has a good performance in heavy clutter and a high ECM resistance.

Up to 10 targets can be evaluated with target information being provided for up to six air defence systems with the information being transmitted via a Contraves DRU (data receiver unit). In addition it has the ability to be integrated with a higher level air surveillance system.

The SHORAR/ACV has a number of enhancements to enable it to be used as a command and control system so enabling it to assign emerging threats to the weapon system, gun or missile that is best positioned to deal with a particular target.

The operator is seated in the rear of the vehicle and is provided with a console on which the tactical and air situations are displayed on a PPI. Only one operator is required as there is a high degree of automation of all weather functions and there is an interactive dialogue with the computer.

Contraves SHORAR/ACV with rear ramp lowered to show interior details

The Italian Army will evaluate the Contraves SHORAR/ACV with both the SIDAM 25 and manportable SAMs to determine the best numbers of SHORAR/ACVs required and the best tactical mix.

Status: In production for Italian Army with first vehicles to be delivered in 1989. The turret can also be mounted on other APCs such as OTO Melara C13, VCC 80 or the Engesa EE-11 Urutu.

Manufacturer: OTO Melara SpA, via Valdilocchi 15, 19100 La Spezia, Italy.
Telephone: (39 187) 530 111
Telex: 270368 211101 OTO I
Fax: (39 187) 430 669

OTO Melara 76 mm Self-propelled OTOMATIC Air Defence Tank

Development

The OTOMATIC 76 mm AA tank has been developed by OTO Melara as a mobile armoured anti-aircraft system for operation in forward areas to provide protection against attacks from helicopters and low-flying aircraft and by lightly armoured mobile ground forces. It will be capable of engaging helicopters at 6000 m before they release their ATGWs, aircraft at 4000 m and AFVs at 1500 m. Normally a five-round burst would be used against a helicopter.

The other operational requirements issued for the OTO 76 mm AA tank are the all-weather operational capability, data link interface for external target acquisition and/or designation and the autonomous search capability. The prototype was shown publicly for the first time at the 1987 Paris Air Show.

The second prototype was shown and operated (less the laser rangefinder for safety reasons) during the 1988 Farnborough Air Show.

By September 1988 the first prototype had had its search radar installed and carried out search and tracking tests against helicopters through to late 1988. It then went to an Italian Air Force base where it was able to carry out tracking trials against both aircraft and helicopters. In the spring 1989 the OTOMATIC went to Sardinia for final tests including firing against aerial targets.

Late in 1988 negotiations were underway between OTO Melara and the Italian Army for the purchase of one prototype of the OTOMATIC for extensive user trials, as at the present time the Italian Army does not have a self-propelled air defence system that can operate in the forward area. The new SIDAM 25 (4 × 25 mm) will be deployed more to the rear.

Description

The chassis is basically that of the Palmaria 155 mm self-propelled howitzer, although the turret can be installed on a variety of other chassis. The driver is seated front right with the APU to his left, the turret is in the centre and the engine and transmission at the rear. The all-welded steel turret has the loader on the left and the commander and gunner on the right. There is an entry door in either side of the turret while there is also a circular hatch cover above the commander's and gunner's positions.

The turret is traversable through 360° and is made of all-welded steel armour that is sloped for maximum ballistic protection. It is controlled in traverse and elevation by an electro-hydraulic servo system that provides a high turret slew rate and stability. The main armament is a 76 mm 62-calibre automatic gun with a vertical sliding breech-block and mechanical firing. The 62-calibre gun is derived from the 76 mm OTO Compact naval gun with the maximum cyclic rate of fire per minute increased to 120 rounds. The gun has a maximum range of 16 km and is effective in the anti-aircraft mode out to 6000 m. The ammunition used

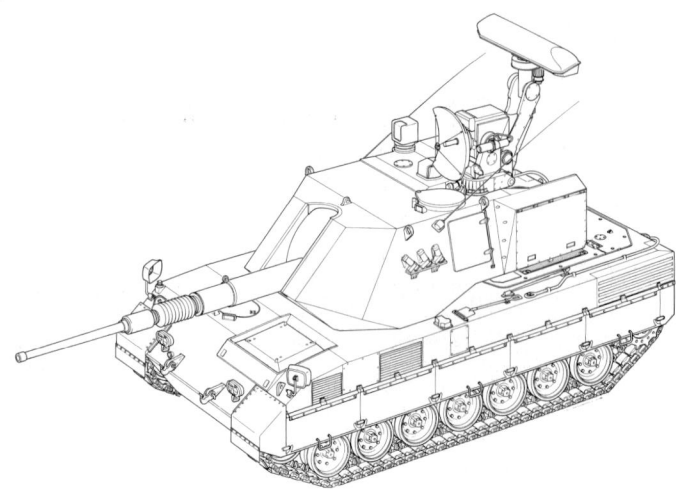

SELF-PROPELLED AA GUNS / Italy

OTO Melara 76 mm OTOMATIC air defence tank (not to 1/76th scale)

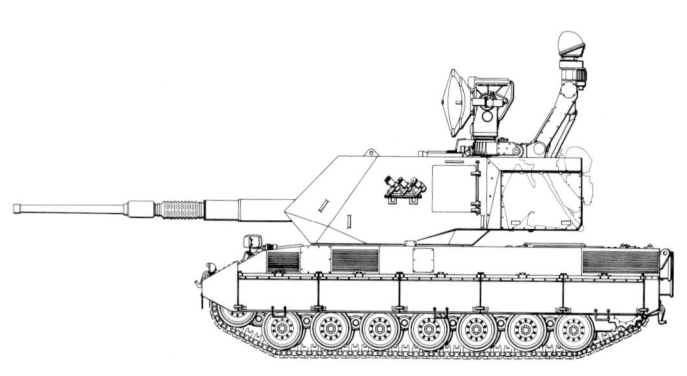

OTO Melara 76 mm OTOMATIC air defence tank showing position of main components (not to 1/76th scale)

OTO Melara 76 mm OTOMATIC air defence tank with radars erected, showing travelling position of radars (not to 1/76th scale)

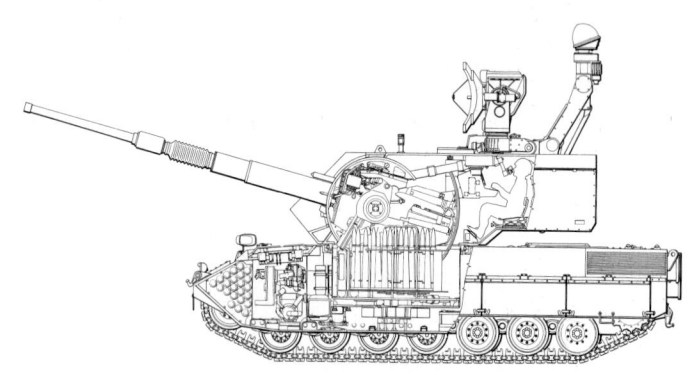

includes the PFF prefragmented 12.2 kg anti-aircraft round with proximity fuze and the MOM multirole 12.25 kg round with VT, PD and time delay fuzing. A 9.1 kg total weight APFSDS round is under development for use against armoured ground targets. This will penetrate 200 mm of armour at 60° incidence at 1500 m range. For the future OTO Melara will integrate the 76 mm course-correction shell that it is developing with British Aerospace into the system.

Ninety rounds of ammunition are carried, 64 in the turret, 29 of which are in the gun's feeding and loading systems. A further 26 are carried in the hull. The hydraulically-operated gun feeding and loading mechanisms allow ammunition loading at all gun elevations from −5 to +60°. Bursts of five to six rounds are normally fired. The gun is also independently stabilised to counter vehicle movement. The fire control equipment includes an optical sight system utilising a low light level TV camera, a TV tracker and a neodymium-YAG laser rangefinder for use in both air and ground defence. A new fire control system has been developed. The new system includes a 15-20 km range S-band search radar, an IFF system, a 10 km range K-band tracking radar with coaxial TV camera and a secondary optical fire control unit for engaging ground targets. The tracking antenna has a maximum elevation of +84° and a depression of −6° 30 minutes. The maximum detection and tracking ranges of the two radars are around 15 km and 14 km respectively. At least eight targets may be tracked simultaneously. The target is detected and acquired by the vehicle commander and target tracking is automatic, although manual control is also possible. The firing solution computer is inside the vehicle hull together with a gyro-stabilised navigation system to provide vehicle position data.

The system has a back-up configuration that increases the overall survivability of failures of the computer system and other subsystems. The command console is fully computer controlled and operated to simplify the operator's action. Built-in test equipment simplifies maintenance.

There are three smoke dischargers either side of the turret. An NBC overpressure air-conditioning protection system is also fitted, together with an automatic fire extinguisher unit and a gas turbine auxiliary power unit to generate hydraulic and electrical power.

The computerised fire control system of the OTOMATIC enables it to provide real time target information to other OTOMATIC systems with their radars switched off, or to other air defence systems, gun or missile, that do not have their own surveillance system installed.

The suspension system is of the torsion bar type with each side having seven dual rubber tyred road wheels, idler at the front and drive sprocket at the rear. The track return rollers and upper part of the track are covered by a skirt. The steel tracks have rubber bushed pins and removable pads.

Variants
The OTOMATIC turret may be mounted on any vehicle that can take a weight of 15 000 kg such as the medium MBT chassis from the Leopard 1 to the M1 or a self-propelled gun chassis such as the Palmeria. In the case of the Leopard 1 the vehicle is known as the HEFAS76-L1 self-propelled gun and is a joint venture between Krupp MaK and OTO Melara.

OTO Melara 76 mm OTOMATIC air defence tank in operating configuration with turret right and both radars erected

OTO 76 mm OTOMATIC self-propelled air defence gun showing all-welded turret

Italy-Japan / **SELF-PROPELLED AA GUNS** 77

OTO Melara 76 mm OTOMATIC air defence tank in travelling configuration with radars retracted under cover

OTO Melara OTOMATIC air defence tank with radar antennas erected during high speed trials

SPECIFICATIONS

CREW	4
COMBAT WEIGHT	46 000 kg
POWER-TO-WEIGHT RATIO	22 hp/tonne
GROUND PRESSURE	0.82 kg/cm²
LENGTH	
gun forward	9.736 m
hull	7.274 m
WIDTH	3.51 m
HEIGHT	
to turret top	3.013 m
with radar up	4.925 m
to hull top	1.707 m
GROUND CLEARANCE	0.4 m
TRACK WIDTH	584 mm
LENGTH OF TRACK ON GROUND	4.25 m
MAX ROAD SPEED	
forward	65 km/h
reverse	25 km/h
FUEL CAPACITY	1000 litres
MAX ROAD RANGE	500 km
FORDING (without preparation)	1.2 m
GRADIENT	60%
SIDE SLOPE	30%
VERTICAL OBSTACLE	1.15 m
TRENCH	3 m
ENGINE	turbo-charged intercooled 4-stroke water-cooled multi-fuel diesel developing 1000 hp at 2400 rpm
TRANSMISSION	power shifting 6-speed planetary type (4 forward and 2 reverse) with hydraulic torque converter
STEERING	2 radius regenerative
CLUTCH	lock-up
FINAL REDUCTION RATIOS	1:4.2
SUSPENSION	torsion bar
ELECTRICAL SYSTEM	24 V
BATTERIES	6 × 24 V, 100 Ah
ARMAMENT	
main	1 × 76 mm 62-calibre gun
SMOKE-LAYING EQUIPMENT	3 smoke dischargers either side turret
AMMUNITION	
main	90 rounds
GUN CONTROL EQUIPMENT	
gun elevation/depression	+60°/-5° (at 45° s)
turret traverse	360° (at 70° s)

Status: The first two prototypes were completed in 1987 and it is anticipated that production could commence in 1990/1991 on receipt of firm orders.

Manufacturer: OTO Melara SpA, via Valdilocchi 15, 19100 La Spezia, Italy.
Telephone: (39 187) 530 111
Telex: 270368 2111010 OTO I
Fax: (39 187) 430 669

JAPAN

AW-X Twin 35 mm Self-propelled Anti-aircraft Gun System

Development/Description

The Japanese Ground Self-Defence Force has a requirement for a new self-propelled anti-aircraft gun system to replace its old American-supplied M42 self-propelled anti-aircraft guns which are limited to clear weather use. The new system has the provisional designation of AW-X and consists of the modified chassis of the Type 74 MBT fitted with a new turret armed with twin 35 mm Oerlikon-Bührle KDA cannon and all-weather surveillance and tracking radars mounted on the roof at the turret rear.

For the AW-X application the sides of the Type 74 MBT have been raised slightly and are now vertical to accommodate the new turret with its deeper basket. There is an access hatch to the right of the driver in the nose of the AW-X and this is almost certainly where the auxiliary power unit is located.

Mounted externally on the left side of the tracking radar is a flat box which is believed to contain a laser rangefinder, optical tracker and possibly an LLLTV. The commander and gunner sit in the forward part of the turret and have a joint single piece hatch cover that opens to

Prototype of the AW-X twin 35 mm self-propelled anti-aircraft gun system

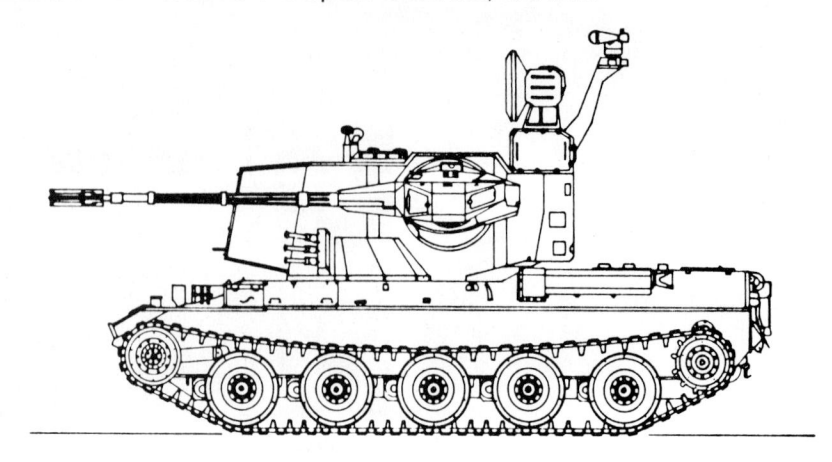

SELF-PROPELLED AA GUNS / Japan-Korea, South

Provisional drawing of AW-X SPAAG prototype on type 74 MBT chassis

the rear with gunnery sights to the front and two fixed observation periscopes either side.

The prime contractor for the fire control system is believed to be Mitsubishi-Denki with the Nippon Seiko-Jyo Company responsible for the armament. The first fire control system was delivered in 1980 with modified 35 mm KDA cannon delivered initially in late 1979. Prototype turret, turret stabilisation and drive systems were produced in 1981 and full scale engineering of the total gun system began in 1982. The first complete prototype AW-X was assembled at the Sagamihara works of Mitsubishi Heavy Industries in early 1984. Testing started later in the year. It is expected that this system will enter service with the Japanese Ground Self Defence Force in the early 1990s.

Status: Prototype trials.

Close up of AW-X twin 35 mm SPAAG radar (via Kensuke Ebata)

KOREA, NORTH

14.5 mm Self-propelled Anti-aircraft Gun M1983

United States sources have stated that the North Korean Army has taken into service a self-propelled anti-aircraft gun system which has been designated the M1983. This is understood to consist of a full tracked armoured chassis fitted with the North Korean built, Soviet designed, 14.5 mm ZPU-4 (quad) anti-aircraft gun system which has been provided with a fire control radar system to offer an increased first round hit probability. No further details of this system are available.

KOREA, SOUTH

Twin 30 mm Self-propelled Anti-aircraft Gun System

Currently under development is a tracked twin 30 mm self-propelled anti-aircraft gun system which uses a local derivative of the Emerlec twin 30 mm gun mount used aboard South Korean warships. Daewoo Heavy Industries is the prime contractor, manufacturing both the turret and chassis, Samsung Precision Instruments is responsible for the optronic tracker and Goldstar Electrical Co/Siemens AG for producing a search radar based on the West German Siemens MPDR 18X model. The Tong Il Industry Company will produce the cannon under licence. The chassis is a stretched variant of the KIFV APC.

Status: Prototype.

M55 Quad 12.7 mm Self-propelled Anti-aircraft Gun System

The South Koreans have manufactured 12.7 mm Quadruple M55 anti-aircraft machine gun mountings and fitted them on the rear platform of M35 series trucks for low altitude air defence and ground operations.

Status: Production complete. In service with the South Korean Army.

South Korean M55 self-propelled anti-aircraft gun system on M35 (6 × 6) truck (Kensuke Ebata)

SOUTH AFRICA

Ystervark 20 mm Self-propelled Anti-aircraft Gun System

Development
The Ystervark was developed to meet an urgent South African requirement for an armoured self-propelled anti-aircraft gun system which could also be used for escorting convoys. It was first deployed in the Operational Area (Namibia) in the mid-1980s and during fighting in 1988 successfully engaged and shot down a number of high performance jet aircraft of the Angolan Air Force.

Prior to the introduction of the Ystervark, the South African Army used a Buffel (4 × 4) tractor fitted with a similar weapon, but these lacked armour protection when compared to the Ystervark.

Description
The Ystervark 20 mm self-propelled anti-aircraft gun system essentially consists of a SAMIL 20 (4 × 4) 2 tonne truck chassis which is provided with full length protection for mines, armoured engine compartment at the front, armoured driver's cab to the right and the 20 mm Oerlikon-Bührle GAI-C01 cannon, fully described in the *Towed anti-aircraft guns* section, mounted on top at the rear. An armoured cabin is provided to protect the gun detachment from shell splinters and small arms fire. The position of the 20 mm cannon is such that its field of fire is about 200° through the rear arc.

Ystervark 20 mm SPAAG on SAMIL 20 truck chassis

The Ystervark has a combat weight of 7.7 tonnes and is powered by a diesel engine giving a maximum road speed of 93 km. The 200 litre fuel tank gives an operating range of 950 km.

Status: Production complete. In service with the South African Army.

SWEDEN

Bofors Trinity 40 mm Self-propelled Air Defence System

Development
In 1982 Bofors started private venture development of the Trinity air defence weapon system for both naval and land applications, and the first announcement of this was made in September 1984. The following year trials of a module installed on a MOWAG Shark (8 × 8) chassis were successfully carried out.

By late 1988 two prototypes of the naval Sea Trinity had been built and one prototype of the land system which was demonstrated on a MOWAG Shark (8 × 8) weapons carrier.

Trinity team members include Ericsson (laser rangefinder), Litef (heading and attitude reference system), Intertechnique (muzzle velocity radar) and Rosemount (meteorological sensors). Raychem were responsible for the complete interconnection system while Canadian Marconi developed the operator console.

The Trinity turret is also referred to as the EB-3 and in mid-1988 a mock-up of the turret was installed on a Brazilian Moto Pecas Charrua II APC (qv).

Description
The Trinity two man power operated turret has been designed for installation on a wide range of tracked and wheeled vehicles with the former including the Austrian Steyr-Daimler-Puch 7FA G127 APC.

The turret is of all welded steel construction that provides the crew with protection from small arms fire and shell splinters. The commander and gunner are seated one on either side of the weapon, with each being provided with a roof-mounted hatch and periscopes.

The 40 mm L/70 gun has been designed to engage a wide range of battlefield targets including high performance aircraft, helicopters, RPVs, low flying missiles, and ground targets. Once the air target has been designated by the Trinity's radar or early warning sensor, the engagement sequence is completely automatic.

The 40 mm L/70 gun fires the new Bofors 3P round under the exact control of the onboard fire control system which is of modular design

SELF-PROPELLED AA GUNS / Sweden

Prototype of the self-propelled Bofors 40 mm L/70 Trinity air defence system on a Swiss MOWAG Shark (8 × 8) weapons carrier chassis

with a digital computer. Either a 2D or 3D tracking radar can be fitted and the system demonstrated in 1988 was fitted with the French Electronique Serge Dassault RA-20S system which is in quantity production for a number of applications. An Ericsson Eagle tracking radar is due to be fitted for trials in 1989.

To these can be added further remote sensors such as an optronic sight or infra-red tracker with a laser rangefinder, or external fire control directors such as a central search radar or an IFF system as required.

Aircraft and helicopter sized targets can be detected up to 12 000 m away and engaged up to 6000 m away, while for missiles the range drops to 3000 m.

The 3P round weighs 2.8 kg and is individually aimed to maximise the proximity-fuzed ammunition effect. Using a typical 10 round burst pattern it is possible to 'ring' a target to ensure destruction, while low flying missiles can be engaged by a 'half-moon' pattern.

A total of 100 rounds of ammunition are carried, one in the feed system and nine vertical rows each of nine rounds, 45 to the left of the gun and 54 to the right of the gun. Barrel life is 5000 rounds and all functions of the gun and magazine are remotely controlled and automatically tested and supervised by the computer system. The basic Trinity gun module is already in production for the West German Navy.

The actual 3P PFHE (pre-fragmented high explosive) projectile weighs 0.975 kg and is of the multi-function type that can be programmed while the round is in the feed system just prior to firing. Each projectile contains 0.14 kg Octol HE charge with some 1100 three mm tungsten alloy pellets to ensure that the explosion covers 180 m^2 of sky. Muzzle velocity is 1012 m^2. It matches the external ballistics of the conventional HE-T projectile out to a range of about 3000 m.

Each round is individually programmed before firing by means of a proximity fuze programmer (PFP) which acts as the interface between the fire control system and the actual round. The PFP activates the fuze electronics and sets the basic mode by means of a DC voltage fed via two contacts in the automatic loading device.

Futher information is supplied to the round just before ramming in the form of an HF message relayed through antennas in the ammunition hopper.

Six modes are available:-
Auto mode 1
Range gated proximity function with impact function and self-destruction at the end of the gate
Auto mode 2
Range gated proximity function with impact priority and self-destruction at the end of the gate
Time mode
Highly accurate time function
Impact mode
Impact function with post impact delay and self-destruction after about 15 seconds
Armour mode
Armour piercing function
Proximity mode
Normal proximity function with impact function and self-destruction.

Any of the above can be chosen for the engagement of aerial targets. In the auto modes, range to the predicted future point of the target is transmitted to the fuze and the fuze ignores all signals until reaching the gate. Thereby, total immunity to all kinds of electronic countermeasure and natural disturbances outside the absolute proximity of the target is achieved. In auto mode 2, the proximity function is held back to give priority to a possible impact function.

Due to the fact that the fuze ignores all signals outside the range gate, the sensitivity of the proximity fuze has been increased to 8-9 m against aircraft and helicopters, and 5 m against missiles without affecting reliability. The increased sensitivity together with the powerful shell greatly increase the kill effect against all kinds of aerial targets.

According to Bofors, against an aircraft or helicopter, the single round kill probability of the 3P rounds will be in the order of 0.5 to 0.6.

Time function causes the fuze to act as a normal fuze, using the predicted time of flight information from the fire control instrument as input. This mode is most effective for the engagement of soft ground targets or aerial targets concealed behind a mask. The accuracy of the time setting is designed to be about 0.5 per cent of the time of flight, or minimum 8 ms.

The impact mode is selected for the engagement of lightly armoured ground targets or extremely hard helicopters and in this mode the S/A device is prevented from arming and the shell, on impact with a hard target, will shock-ignite with a delayed low order detonation as a result.

When no mode selection is made or the actual range to target is unknown, the fuze will impact function and self-destruct after 15 seconds time of flight.

The full designation of the 3P is the PFPPX-HV, but this is normally shortened to the 3P-HV.

In addition to the new Bofors 3P PFHE round, Trinity fires all existing Bofors 40 mm rounds including PFHE Mk 2, the MPT (developed with Raufoss of Norway) and a new APFSDS developed for the Swedish Army's new Combat Vehicle 90.

According to Bofors, the single round kill probability of Trinity is nearly double that of other 40 mm systems, mainly as a result of the improved weapon accuracy, shorter time of flight and the lethality of the projectile itself, in combination with the extended triggering distance of the proximity fuze.

SPECIFICATIONS (turret)
CALIBRE	40 mm
CYCLIC RATE OF FIRE	330 rpm
FIRING DISPERSION	0.7 mrad
ELEVATION/DEPRESSION	+80°/-10°
TRAVERSE	360°
MAGAZINE CAPACITY	54 + 45 rounds
WEIGHT OF TURRET	5000 kg
POWER CONSUMPTION	
peak	30 kW
average	15 kW
TARGET TRACKING RANGE	200 to 20 000 m
TARGET SPEED	0 to 1000 m/s

Status: Development. Not yet in production or service.

Manufacturer: Bofors AB, Box 500, S-69 180 Bofors, Sweden.
Telephone: (46) 586 81000
Telex: 73210
Fax: (46) 586 58145

SWITZERLAND

GDF-D03 Escorter 35 Twin 35 mm Self-propelled Anti-aircraft Gun System

Development
The GDF-D03 self-propelled anti-aircraft Escorter 35 was developed as a private venture by Oerlikon-Bührle to fill the gap between the 35 mm towed anti-aircraft gun, the 35 mm anti-aircraft tank and the ADATS missile system. The GDF-D03 is designed to protect rear area mechanised combat support units during deployment and in action, motorised units on the march and in action, and time sensitive important rear area positions. By late 1986 the Escorter 35 had undergone trials in the Middle East, West Germany and Switzerland. Long lead items for vehicle numbers 2 and 3 had been ordered for use as trials and company development vehicles. These will be to production standard, but as of Spring 1989 no firm orders had been received and production had yet to commence.

A full tracked version of the Escorter 35 twin 35 mm system was built on a lengthened M548 tracked chassis but development of this model has now ceased.

Description
The Escorter is based on the 120 km/h four-wheel drive giant-tyred HYKA with an extremely small turning circle.

The twin 35 mm KDF gun arrangement has a rate of fire of 1200 rds/min which is said to guarantee a high hit probability with small round dispersion and a heavy concentration of fire. The drum magazines used each carry 215 rounds that can be of two different types. Automatic selection is available to the gunner so that targets can be engaged with the appropriate ammunition type. The magazines can be reloaded easily, each drum taking three minutes. The 35 mm guns have an effective range of 100 to 4000 m and can fire all of the current Oerlikon 35 mm ammunition family including two new types that form the new generation of ammunition under development by the company. These have increased performance to enhance their lethality and are known as the APFIDS, Armour-Piercing Fragmentation Incendiary Discarding-Sabot with a muzzle velocity of 1395 m/s and an extremely short flight time, and the HEI, High Explosive Incendiary round with a muzzle velocity of 1175 m/s which is optimised for its destructive effect.

The Contraves 3D sight fitted to the system is an all-weather unit with a 10 micron wavelength, 10 km range (in normal visibility), FLIR tracker for passive automatic target following, a 10 km range (in normal visibility) 10 micron laser rangefinder and a periscope for use in the manual joystick mode. The 20 km range pulse Doppler fully-coherent I/J-band surveillance radar with track-while-scan facilities for two targets is also produced by Contraves, using state of the art technology to provide high reliability. Its sub-assemblies are also employed in the ADATS system with simple modifications and a redesign of the unit having been made to make it compatible with the requirements of the Escorter 35.

The vehicle has a crew of three: commander, gunner and driver. The commander (located in the driver's cabin) operates the search radar from the PPI console, performs the threat analysis and target assignment for the system. The gunner (located in the cabin of the mount) operates the fire control system, monitors the automatic lock-on and tracking and fires the weapons while the driver, as well as operating the vehicle, also surveys the air space and ground during the engagement and acts as a reloader with the gunner when the system needs replenishing. The system has a five second reaction time between target unmasking and opening fire.

Loading clip of 35 mm ammunition into Escorter 35 self-propelled anti-aircraft gun system magazine

Escorter 35 in travelling configuration

Escorter 35 with twin 35 mm cannon horizontal to engage ground targets

Escorter 35 carrying out firing trials with turret traversed to right

82 SELF-PROPELLED AA GUNS / Switzerland-USSR

Status: Development complete. Ready for production.
Production will be carried out in Italy by Oerlikon Italiana at its Milan plant.

Manufacturer: Enquiries to Military Products Division, Machine Tool Works, Oerlikon-Bührle Limited, CH-8050 Zürich, Switzerland.
Telephone: (01) 316 22 11
Telex: 823 205 WOB CH

Interior view of Oerlikon-Bührle GDF-D03 Escorter 35 twin 35 mm SPAAG with driver's position on left and commander's console on right

SPECIFICATIONS

CREW	3	MAX RANGE	600 km
COMBAT WEIGHT	24 000 kg	FORDING	1 m
POWER-TO-WEIGHT RATIO	18.75 hp/tonne	ENGINE	450 hp diesel
LENGTH	8.745 m	ARMAMENT	2 × 35 mm cannon
WIDTH	2.98 m	AMMUNITION	430
HEIGHT (radar up)	3.943 m	GUN CONTROL EQUIPMENT	
GROUND CLEARANCE (axles)	0.475 m	turret power control	powered/manual
WHEELBASE	4.74 m	gun elevation/depression	+85°/-5°
ANGLE OF APPROACH/DEPARTURE	38°/37°	turret traverse	360°
MAX ROAD SPEED	120 km/h		

UNION OF SOVIET SOCIALIST REPUBLICS

ZSU-57-2 Twin 57 mm Self-propelled Anti-aircraft Gun System

Development

The ZSU-57-2 was developed in early 1951 and was first seen in public during a parade in Moscow in November 1957. ZSU is the Soviet designation for self-propelled anti-aircraft gun, 57 is for the calibre of the guns (57 mm) and 2 is for the number of guns. The system consists of a chassis based on T-54 components but with much thinner armour, four rather than five road wheels and a large open-topped turret armed with twin 57 mm S-68 guns which have the same performance and use the same ammunition as the towed single S-60 anti-aircraft gun which is fully described in the *Towed anti-aircraft guns* section. ZSU stands for Zenitnaia Samokhodnaia Ustanovka (self-propelled anti-aircraft mount).

The weapon was originally deployed in Soviet tank and motorised rifle divisions but has now been replaced in first-line service by the much more effective ZSU-23-4 system. The ZSU-57-2 is, however, still used by some Soviet second-line units, members of the Warsaw Pact and other countries that have received Soviet aid.

Description

The all-welded hull of the ZSU-57-2 is divided into three compartments: driver's at the front, fighting in the centre and engine at the rear.

The driver is seated at the front of the hull on the left and has a single piece hatch cover that opens to the left, in front of which are two periscopes, one replaceable by an infra-red periscope which is used in conjunction with the infra-red headlamp mounted on the right side of the glacis plate. Mounted at right angles to the glacis plate is a narrow board to stop water rushing up the glacis plate when the vehicle is fording shallow rivers.

The large turret has slightly sloping sides, well curved corners and is fitted with external grab rails on either side. The engine, mounted transversely at the rear of the hull, is provided with a compressed-air system for cold weather starting; for normal use there is an electric starter. The air-inlet and air-outlet louvres are in the roof of the engine compartment at the rear with the exhaust outlet on the left track guard.

The torsion bar suspension consists of four dual rubber-tyred road wheels with the drive sprocket at the rear, idler at the front but no return

ZSU-57-2 with turret traversed to right

rollers. The first and last road wheel stations are provided with a hydraulic shock absorber. The all-steel track has steel pins that are not secured at the outer end and are free to travel towards the hull. A raised piece of metal welded to the hull just forward of the drive sprocket drives the track pins into position each time they pass.

The ZSU-57-2 has no NBC system and no amphibious capability. It is believed that the vehicle is not fitted with a smoke-laying system similar to that on T-54/T-55 and T-62 tanks. Long-range fuel drums can be fitted to the rear of the hull to increase the operational range of the ZSU-57-2.

Main armament of the ZSU-57-2 consists of twin 57 mm S-68 cannon with 24 lands and grooves, an elevation of +85°, depression of -5°, and 360° turret traverse. Elevation, depression and turret traverse are powered,

Polish Army ZSU-57-2s

with manual controls available for emergency use. The ammunition, in clips of four rounds, is fed to the magazines each side of the weapon by a loader seated in the forward part of each side of the turret. The right-hand gun is modified to be loaded from the right so as to avoid loading problems. The gunner is seated on the left side of the turret towards the rear and the commander on the other side almost opposite him. The fuze setter is seated to the right rear of the gunner at the rear of the turret.

The guns are fully automatic, recoil-operated, and each gun has a cyclic rate of fire of 105 to 120 rounds per minute with a practical rate of fire of 70 rounds per gun per minute. Maximum horizontal range is 12 000 metres, maximum vertical range 8800 metres, although effective ranges are less than this. Effective slant range is 3993 metres, effective altitude limit with weapons elevated at 45° is 2835 metres and effective altitude limit with weapons elevated at 65° is 4237 metres. The weapon does not have the same effective anti-aircraft range as the towed S-60, as the latter can be used in conjunction with off-carriage fire control equipment. Fire control for the ZSU-57-2 is achieved by an optical mechanical computing reflex sight. The maximum traverse rate is 30° a second and the maximum elevation rate 20° a second. The weapons can fire the following types of fixed ammunition:

AMMUNITION TYPE	FRAG-T	FRAG-T	APC-T
PROJECTILE DESIGNATION	OR-281	OR-281U	BR-281*
FUZE MODEL	MG-57	MG-57	MD-10
FUZE TYPE	PD SD	PD SD	BD
WEIGHT OF PROJECTILE	2.81 kg	2.85 kg	2.82 kg
BURSTING CHARGE			
weight	0.168 kg	0.154 kg	0.018 kg
type	RDX/Alum	RDX/Alum	RDX/Alum
MUZZLE VELOCITY	1000 m/s	1000 m/s	1000 m/s
ARMOUR PENETRATION AT			
0° OBLIQUITY	n/app	n/app	96 mm/ 1000 m

* also very similar BR-281U

The Yugoslav Federal Directorate of Supply and Procurement produce an HE-T round for the ZSU-57-2 and the towed S-68 and details of this are as follows:

AMMUNITION TYPE	HE-T
DESIGNATION	M66
FUZE	impact, super quick action with pyrotechnical self-destruction
COMPLETE ROUND	
weight	6.386 kg
length	536 mm
PROJECTILE	
weight	2.85 kg
length	258 mm
FUZE MATERIAL	steel
PROJECTILE BODY MATERIAL	steel
TYPE OF BURSTING CHARGE	RDX/Alum
CARTRIDGE CASE	brass
PROPELLING CHARGE	NC powder
GUN PRIMER	fulminate
MUZZLE VELOCITY	1000 m/s

Of 316 rounds of 57 mm ammunition carried, 264 are for ready use and the rest are stowed below the turret. The ammunition is not interchangeable with that used in the 57 mm ASU-57 airportable self-propelled anti-tank gun or towed anti-tank guns. The empty cartridge cases and clips are deposited on a conveyor belt which runs under the weapons. This takes the cases and clips to the rear of the turret where they are deposited in the wire cage mounted externally on the turret rear.

The main drawback of the ZSU-57-2 is its lack of an all-weather fire control system but it is highly effective in the ground role and is capable of destroying most AFVs on the battlefield with the exception of MBTs, and even those would be very vulnerable to penetration by the 57 mm APHE projectile on their sides and rear.

Late production ZSU-57-2 SPAAGs were fitted with a more sophisticated sighting system. This model is identified by two small ports in the forward upper portion of the turret front.

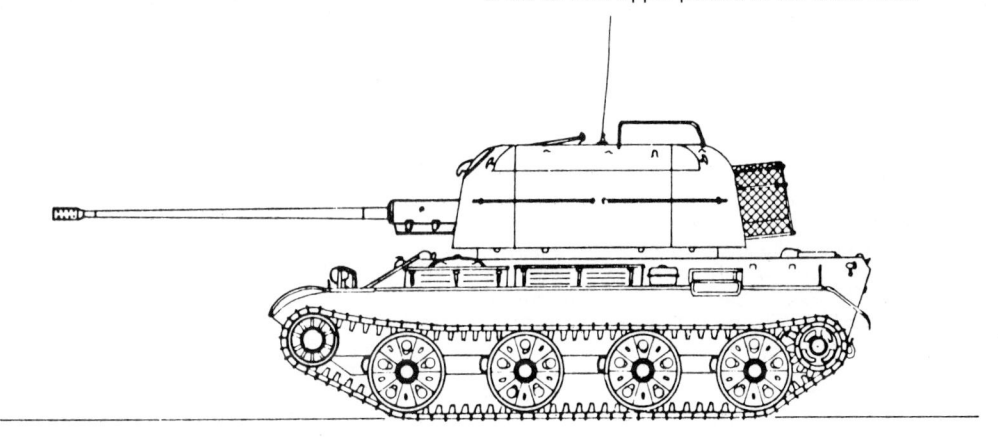

ZSU-57-2 twin 57 mm self-propelled anti-aircraft gun

84 SELF-PROPELLED AA GUNS / USSR

Variants
The East German Army has rebuilt some of its ZSU-57-2s as driving training vehicles designated FAP-500U. The turret has been replaced by an observation cabin with seats for the instructor and trainees.

China is producing the Type 80 self-propelled anti-aircraft tank which uses a Type 69 II MBT chassis fitted with a Chinese built copy of the turret of the ZSU-57-2. Additional details of this are given in this section under China.

Status: Production complete. In service with the following countries:

Country	Quantity	User	Comment
Algeria	100	army	approximate number
Angola	40	army	
Bulgaria	60	army	held in reserve
China, People's Republic	50–100	army	more of locally built model called Type 80
Cuba	25+	army	
Egypt	110	army	could be as low as 40
Ethiopia	40	army	approximate number
Finland	12	army	to be replaced
Germany, East	50+	army	held in reserve
Hungary	30+	army	held in reserve
Iran	80	army	status uncertain
Iraq	100+	army	
Kampuchea	10+	army	
Korea, North	250+	army	
Mozambique	20+	army	
Poland	50+	army	held in reserve
Romania	60	army	unconfirmed
Syria	100+	army	
USSR	750	army	held in reserve
Vietnam	100+	army	
Yugoslavia	100+	army	

Manufacturer: Soviet state factories.

SPECIFICATIONS

CREW	6
COMBAT WEIGHT	28 100 kg
POWER-TO-WEIGHT RATIO	18.56 hp/tonne
GROUND PRESSURE	0.63 kg/cm²
LENGTH	
guns forward	8.48 m
guns rear	7.43 m
hull	6.22 m
WIDTH	3.27 m
HEIGHT	2.75 m
FIRING HEIGHT	2.05 m
GROUND CLEARANCE	0.425 m
TRACK	2.64 m
TRACK WIDTH	580 mm
LENGTH OF TRACK ON GROUND	3.84 m
MAX ROAD SPEED	50 km/h
FUEL CAPACITY	812 litres (+ 400 litres auxiliary)
MAX ROAD RANGE	420 km (595 km with auxiliary fuel)
FUEL CONSUMPTION	1.9 litres/km
FORDING	1.4 m
GRADIENT	60%
SIDE SLOPE	30%
VERTICAL OBSTACLE	0.8 m
TRENCH	2.7 m
ENGINE	model V-54, V-12 water-cooled diesel developing 520 hp at 2000 rpm
TRANSMISSION	manual with 5 forward and 1 reverse gears
STEERING	clutch and brake
CLUTCH	multi-plate
SUSPENSION	torsion bar
ELECTRICAL SYSTEM	28 V
BATTERIES	4 × 12 V, 280 Ah
ARMAMENT	2 × 57 mm guns
AMMUNITION	316
GUN CONTROL EQUIPMENT	
turret power control	powered/manual
gun elevation/depression	+85°/−5°
turret traverse	360°
ARMOUR	
hull glacis	13.5 mm at 58.8°
hull rear	10.6 mm at 45°
hull upper	15 mm at 0°
hull lower	13.5 mm at 0°
turret (all round)	13.5 mm curved

2S6 TWIN 30 mm Self-propelled Anti-aircraft Gun System

Development
The M1986 self-propelled air defence gun system was first identified in 1986 and entered widespread operational service with the Group of Soviet Forces Germany (GSFG) in 1988.

The M1986 (its US Army designation) has also been referred to as the ZSU-30-2 and ZSU-X. It is the replacement for the ZSU-23-4 self-propelled air defence system in the air defence gun and missile batteries organic to Soviet motor rifle and tank regiments and as it is armed with SAMs, it may well be replacing both the ZSU-23-4 and the SA-13 (Gopher) SAM.

Description
In overall layout the M1986 is very similar to the West German Gepard twin 35 mm self-propelled air defence system on a modified Leopard 1 chassis which is in service with the Belgian, West German and Netherlands armies.

Initial reports, including the US Government publication, *Soviet Military Power*, indicated that the M1986 was mounted on a T-72 MBT chassis, but it is now clear that it is based on a new medium armoured transporter family that evolved from the MT-S armoured transporter. The same chassis is also used with the SA-11 (Gadfly), SA-15 (SA-8 follow-on) and SA-X-17 (SA-11 follow on), as well as their associated support vehicles.

The layout of the vehicle is conventional, with the driver seated at front left, the turret in the centre and the engine and transmission at the rear. The driver has a single piece hatch cover over his position and to the immediate front of this are three periscopes. To his immediate

Model of 2S6 twin 30 mm self-propelled anti-aircraft gun system with guns and missiles in horizontal position (3AD via USAREUR)

front is a hatch cover in the glacis plate which is raised when driving in a non-combat area for improved forward visibility.

The turret has vertical sides with the commander's cupola being well forward on the right side. This has a single piece hatch cover that opens to the rear and three periscopes that give observation to the front. On the forward part of his hatch is an infra-red searchlight. There is another hatch cover, opening to the rear, in the centre of the turret.

USSR / SELF-PROPELLED AA GUNS

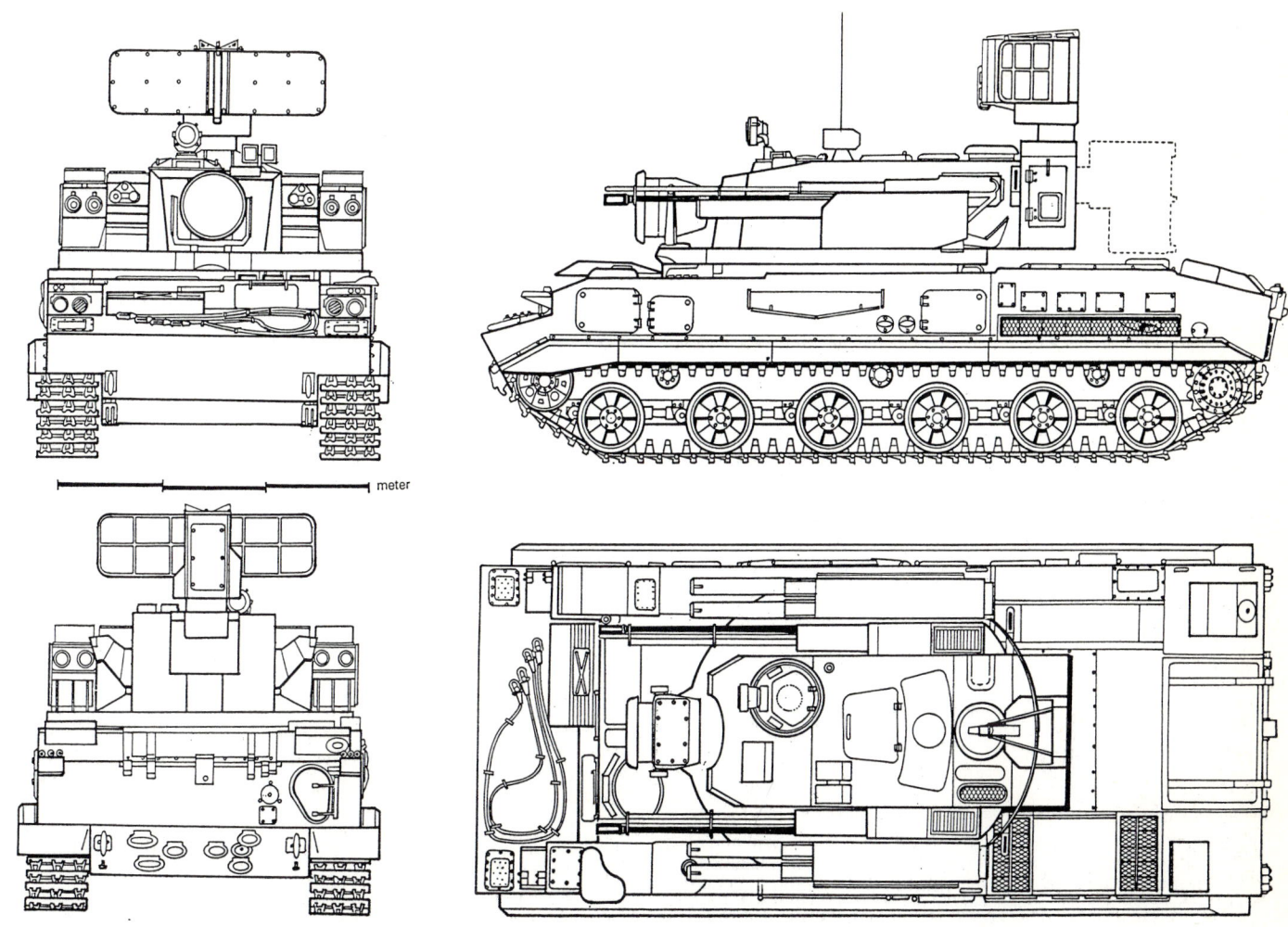

2S6 twin 30 mm self-propelled anti-aircraft gun system (provisional drawing) (not to 1/76th scale) (Steven Zaloga)

Suspension is of the hydro-pneumatic type with six equally spaced road wheels, drive sprocket at the rear, idler at the front and three track return rollers. The wheel pattern of the M1986 resembles the earlier 2S3/2P24/GMZ medium chassis but is wider. When travelling, the suspension is lowered to provide maximum possible ground clearance, but when in the firing position it is raised and locked out to provide a more stable firing platform. It is estimated that the vehicle height is changed by 250 to 200 mm when the suspension is locked out.

The M1986 is probably powered by a derivative of the V-59 diesel engine used on the 2S3/2P24/GMZ chassis although in this application the engine is supplemented by a 50 kW turbine system to allow the system to operate with the main engine switched off. The air inlet and air outlet for the main engine are located in the left rear side of the hull.

The power operated turret is armed with twin 30 mm cannon which are mounted externally on either side. The guns probably share the same ammunition as the 2A42 gun on the BMP-2 IFV and the 30 mm guns on the Mi-24G Hind F, MiG-29 and Su-25K Frogfoot C. However, in the M1986 application they have longer barrels, increased range and higher initial muzzle velocity. The gun tube is fitted with a muzzle reference system and a muzzle velocity measurement device.

The two tubes beside the barrel are probably cabling for the muzzle velocity measurement system and a liquid cooling tube. The extensive parallel tubing near the gun tube has led to some speculation that the weapons on board were multi-barrel Gatling guns, but this has now been shown to be incorrect. As the guns are externally mounted, fumes are prevented from entering the turret.

Ammunition feed appears to come primarily from containers on both sides of the guns although it is unclear if any additional ammunition is stowed inside the vehicle. Total ammunition capacity is probably around 500 to 700 rounds per gun. Mounted to the right of each 30 mm cannon is a box of two SA-19 surface-to-air missiles which can be elevated independently of the 30 mm cannon. No hard details of the missiles' guidance system are available although they could be radar, infra-red or laser. If laser guided, the laser designator is presumably located in the double headed electro-optical sensor package mounted on the turret roof. It is possible that this sensor can be slaved to the radar, providing automated guidance in some circumstances.

The M1986 has both radar and electro-optical aiming systems. The radar system, which is named Hot Shot by NATO, has two separate radars. At the front of the turret is the fire control radar used to track the target and direct the twin 30 mm cannon. This radar can be independently slewed about 220° for target tracking. At the rear of the turret is a surveillance and target acquisition radar which sweeps through a full 360° and can be folded down over the rear of the turret to reduce the overall height of the system and any damage to the antenna.

The use of two separate radars, compared to the single Gun Dish radar used on the older Shilka, offers a number of tactical advantages. It permits the vehicle to continue target surveillance during engagements, thereby reducing the vulnerability of the vehicle to multiple attacks. In contrast, the Gun Dish radar can be operated either in a surveillance or fire control mode. No firm information on radar performance is available, but the range of the surveillance radar is estimated to be about 15 km and that of the fire control radar about 5 km.

The Hot Shot radar system is supplemented by an electro-optical system which may include a thermal imaging sight as well as a daylight electro-optical package which is mounted on the turret roof opposite the commander's hatch and consists of two sensor containers which elevate and traverse in unison with the front tracking radar. A laser rangefinder is probably incorporated as well, as the system presumably includes an IFF interrogator which interacts with the usual Khrom-Nikel (Odd Rods) IFF system found on Warsaw Pact combat aircraft. The turret has seats for three crew members.

Until recently each Soviet motor rifle and tank regiment had an air defence battery with a platoon of four missile vehicles (SA-9 or more recently the SA-13) and four ZSU-23-4 self-propelled anti-aircraft guns. It would appear that the unit is being expanded into a battalion.

This consists of a surveillance platoon with a mobile Dog Ear forward alerting radar, six 2S6 twin 30 mm self-propelled air defence guns and six BMP-2s which also have a single 30 mm cannon. The BMP-2s appear to be used to transport regimental SA-14/SA-16 manportable teams. It would appear that the Soviets are withdrawing the SA-14 and SA-16 teams from the motor rifle companies and consolidating them at regimental level to give better overall control.

86 SELF-PROPELLED AA GUNS / USSR

Status: In production. In service with USSR.

Manufacturer: Soviet state factories.

Model of 2S6 twin 30 mm self-propelled anti-aircraft gun system with four SA-19 missiles elevated (3AD via USAREUR)

SPECIFICATIONS (provisional)

CREW	4	TRACK WIDTH	600 mm
LENGTH	7.84 m	ENGINE	V-59 diesel derivative developing 520 hp
WIDTH	3.47 m		
HEIGHT		APU	50 kW turbine
radar up	3.89 m	ARMAMENT	2 × 30 mm cannon
radar down	3.08 m		2 × SA-19 SAM
MAX TURRET DIAMETER	1.42 m	AMMUNITION	500 per gun

ZSU-23-4 Quad 23 mm Self-propelled Anti-aircraft Gun System

Development

The main drawback of the twin 57 mm ZSU-57-2 (qv) self-propelled anti-aircraft gun was its slow rate of fire and lack of any radar or fire control system. In the late 1950s the Astrov KB design bureau started work on the new system which consisted of a chassis based on that used for the ASU-85 85 mm self-propelled anti-tank gun fitted with a new turret with four water-cooled AZP-23 guns which was already being developed as a twin towed air-defence system which was to enter service as the ZU-23 (qv). The turret was also fitted with an acquisition and tracking radar which supplied information to the fire control computer.

ZSU is the Soviet designation Zenitnaia Samokhodnaia Ustanovka (self-propelled anti-aircraft mount), 23 is the calibre of the weapons (23 mm) and 4 is for the number of weapons in the system. The common Soviet name for the ZSU-23-4 is the Shilka (Awl).

The first prototypes were completed in the early 1960s with troop trials being carried out in 1963/64. It was first seen in public during a parade held in Red Square, Moscow, in November 1965. Production commenced in 1965 with first units becoming operational in 1966 and production continued until 1983. In addition to being produced in the USSR, production was also undertaken under licence in Czechoslovakia. Total production was between 6000 and 7000 units.

The ZSU-23-4 was first used operationally by Egypt and Syria during the 1973 Middle East conflict where it accounted for about 30 per cent of the aircraft lost by the Israeli Air Force. On its own the ZSU-23-4 can be overcome but used in conjunction with other Soviet air defence systems such as the SA-6, it is highly effective.

It has replaced the clear weather ZSU-57-2 self-propelled anti-aircraft gun in front-line units and is issued on the scale of four ZSU-23-4s per Soviet Motorised Rifle and Tank Regiment anti-aircraft battery (with four SA-9 or SA-13 vehicles) to give a total of 16 ZSUs per Motorised Rifle and Tank Division. They usually operate in pairs with about 150 to 200 m between the individual vehicles. In the Soviet Army the ZSU-23-4 is now being supplemented by the new twin 30 mm 2S6 air defence gun/missile system.

Description

The all-welded steel hull of the ZSU-23-4 is divided into three compartments: driver's at the front, fighting in the centre and the engine at the rear.

The driver is seated at the front of the vehicle on the left and has a single piece hatch cover to his front that opens upwards on the outside. When it is raised a windscreen and wiper can be positioned in front of the driver. When the driver's hatch is closed, forward observation is maintained by a BM-130 periscope which can be replaced by an infra-red TVN-2 periscope for night driving. Either side of the driver's position is a vision block.

Column of East German Army ZSU-23-4V1 model 1972s from rear with radar scanners erected

ZSU-23-4 SPAAG with turret traversed right and driver's hatch closed

USSR / **SELF-PROPELLED AA GUNS**

ZSU-23-4V1 model 1972 self-propelled anti-aircraft gun with driver's hatch locked open and radar traversed to rear (US Army)

Mounted on the lower part of the glacis plate is a splash board to stop water rushing up the front of the vehicle when it is fording a stream.

The other three crew members, commander, search radar operator/gunner and range operator, are all seated in the large square turret. The guns and ammunition are in the forward part of the turret and separated from the crew by a gas-tight and armoured bulkhead. Access to the guns and ammunition is by two large hatches, one either side of the turret roof, which are hinged in the centre and open vertically. The commander is seated on the left side of the turret and has a cupola which can be traversed through a full 360°. The cupola has a single piece hatch cover that opens to the rear and, in the forward part, three periscopes, the centre one a TPKU-2 which can be replaced by a TKN-1T infra-red periscope for night use. This has a range of 200 to 250 m. The commander also has an infra-red searchlight mounted on the forward part of the cupola.

To the right of the commander is a large single piece hatch cover that opens to the rear in front of which are two BM-190 periscopes.

The engine and transmission are at the rear of the hull as is the DG4M-1 gas turbine. The torsion bar suspension system consists of six single rubber-tyred road wheels with the idler at the front and the drive sprocket at the rear. There are no track return rollers. Hydraulic shock absorbers are provided for the first and last road wheel stations.

Standard equipment on all vehicles includes an air filtration and overpressure NBC system, FG-125 infra-red driving lights and a vehicle navigation system for both the driver and commander which allows them to plot their exact position at any given time. An R-123 radio is used for communications.

Main armament comprises four AZP-23 23 mm cannon (basically the same guns used on the towed ZU-23) with an elevation of +85°, depression of -4°, and 360° turret traverse. The 23 mm cannon is gas operated with a vertically moving breech-block locking system which drops to unlock, and has a cyclic rate of fire of 800 to 1000 rds/barrel/min. The ZSU-23-4 can engage targets using only one or two of the four cannon. Normally bursts of three to five, five to ten or a maximum of 30 rounds per barrel are fired. The barrels are water-cooled and are provided with flash-hiders. The weapons have a maximum effective anti-aircraft range

ZSU-23-4M model 1977 clearly showing modifications to turret compared to early production models (US Army)

of 2500 m and a maximum effective ground range of 2500 m. A total of 2000 rounds of 23 mm ammunition is carried in 40 box magazines containing 50 belted rounds each. The following types of fixed ammunition are fired:

API-T with the projectile weighing 0.189 kg and a muzzle velocity of

SELF-PROPELLED AA GUNS / USSR

970 m/s, which will penetrate 25 mm of armour at a range of 500 m and 19.3 mm at 1000 m;
HEI-T with the projectile weighing 0.19 kg and a muzzle velocity of 970 m/s.

Each ammunition belt of 500 rounds contains one API-T and three HEI-T rounds in sequence. Supply trucks which follow the ZSUs at a distance of 1.5 to 2.5 km carry an additional 3000 rounds for each of the vehicles.

The fire control system consists of the radar, sighting device, computer, line-of-sight and line-of-elevation stabilisation units.

The radar, which has the NATO designation Gun Dish, operates in the J-band, is mounted at the rear of the turret and the 1 m diameter antenna can be folded down to the turret rear to reduce the overall height of the vehicle for air transport. The radar performs search, detection, automatic tracking, range to target and angular position. Range of the radar in a panoramic search mode is said to be up to 20 km and in the target-tracking mode up to 8000 m. An optical sight enables the weapons to be used in an ECM environment. The ZSU-23-4 can fire while stationary or on the move at speeds up to 25 km/h, or on slopes with inclinations up to 10°. However, gunfire accuracy is reduced by up to half when firing on the move. The onboard fire control radar is subject to ground clutter interference when employed against targets flying below 200 m or so.

A typical target engagement is believed to take place as follows: the search operator/gunner and range operator first observe the target on their scope when the radar is being used for surveillance or sector scan. If required the target data can also be accepted from other target acquisition or tracking radars of the division. If the target is confirmed as hostile the radar is switched to automatic tracking and target data is fed into the computer for determining the gun lead angle. When the target is in effective range of the weapons the computer advises the commander or scan-operator and the guns are fired. The weapons can be aimed when the vehicle is travelling across country and can also be laid without the use of the radar, computer or stabilisation system. Acquisition, lock-on and firing takes 20-30 seconds. The ZSU-23-4 is credited with being 50 per cent more accurate than the American Vulcan anti-aircraft system and having a 66 per cent greater effective range than the same system.

Variants

At least nine identifiable separate versions of the ZSU-23-4 have been seen. These include the ZSU-23-4 model 1965 (pre-series version), the ZSU-23-4 model 1965 (initial production version), the ZSU-23-4V model 1968, the ZSU-23-4V1 model 1972, and the ZSU-23-4M model 1977. Most differ only in stowage, external fittings or cooling vents. Large ammunition panniers, mounted on the turret sides, were introduced in an intermediate production model. The latest variant, the ZSU-23-4M features these panniers, three (instead of two) access ports on each side of the hull and an armoured cover for the guns. It also has a digital computer, an improved Gun Dish radar and can be linked to off-carriage radar and fire control equipment if required. The Gun Dish radar on the ZSU-23-4M is capable of being used independently in the search mode whereas on previous versions it had been slaved to the gun tubes.

In 1985 a modified ZSU-23-4M was seen with protrusions on the right and left sides of the Gun Dish radar dome and vanes down its centre. The vanes are side-lobe clutter-reducing devices and the protrusions are IFF receivers.

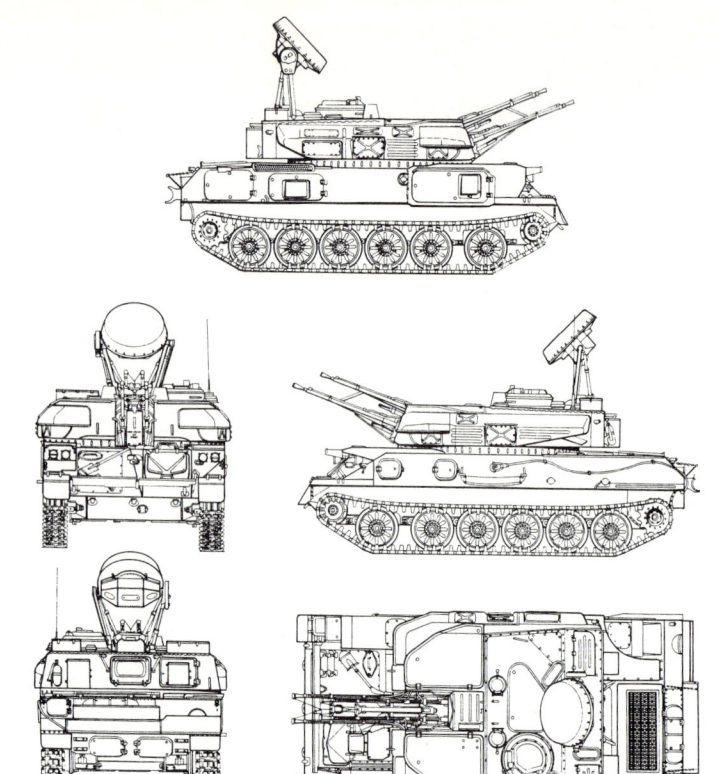

ZSU-23-4V1 Model 1972 (not to 1/76th scale) (Steven Zaloga)

ZSU-23-4 model 1977 clearly showing modifications to turret compared to early production models and splash board fitted across lower glacis plate

SPECIFICATIONS

CREW	4
COMBAT WEIGHT	20 500 kg
POWER-TO-WEIGHT RATIO	20 hp/tonne
GROUND PRESSURE	0.69 kg/cm²
LENGTH	6.54 m
WIDTH	2.95 m
HEIGHT	
with radar	3.8 m
without radar	2.25 m
FIRING HEIGHT	
(lower guns)	1.83 m
GROUND CLEARANCE	0.4 m
TRACK	2.67 m
TRACK WIDTH	360 mm
LENGTH OF TRACK ON GROUND	3.8 m
MAX ROAD SPEED	44 km/h
FUEL CAPACITY	250 litres
MAX RANGE	450 km
FUEL CONSUMPTION	0.96 litre/km
FORDING	1.07 m
GRADIENT	60%
SIDE SLOPE	30%
VERTICAL OBSTACLE	1.1 m
TRENCH	2.8 m
ENGINE	model V-6R, 6-cylinder in-line water-cooled diesel developing 280 hp
TRANSMISSION	manual with 5 forward and 1 reverse gears
SUSPENSION	torsion bar
ELECTRICAL SYSTEM	24 V
ARMAMENT	4 × 23 mm cannon
SMOKE-LAYING EQUIPMENT	none
AMMUNITION	2000
UNIT OF FIRE	2000 rounds
GUN CONTROL EQUIPMENT	
turret power control	powered/manual
by commander	yes
by gunner	yes
gun elevation/depression	+85°/-4°
turret traverse	360°
ARMOUR	
glacis plate	15 mm at 55°
hull sides	15 mm
turret front	9.2 mm at 15°
turret sides	9.2 mm
turret rear	9.2 mm

USSR / SELF-PROPELLED AA GUNS

Status: Production complete. In service with the following countries:

Country	Quantity	User	Comment
Afghanistan	20	army	
Algeria	110	army	
Angola	20+	army	
Bulgaria	35	army	
Congo	8	army	
Cuba	36	army	
Czechoslovakia	100	army	licence built
Egypt	150	army	
Ethiopia	60	army	
Germany, East	100	army	
Hungary	50	army	
India	75	army	
Iran	100+	army	
Iraq	200+	army	
Jordan	36	air force	
Korea, North	100+	army	
Laos	10+	army	
Libya	250	army	
Mozambique	25	army	approximate number
Nigeria	30	army	
Peru	35	army	
Poland	150	army	
Somalia	4	army	
Syria	100+	army	
USSR	n/av	army	also naval infantry
Vietnam	100+	army	
Yemen, North	20+	army	
Yemen, South	30+	army	
Yugoslavia	n/av	army	unconfirmed user

Manufacturer: Czechoslovakian and Soviet state factories.

BTR-40A and BTR-152A twin 14.5 mm Self-propelled Anti-aircraft Gun Systems

Development

The BTR-40A and BTR-152A twin self-propelled weapons were developed in the late 1940s and were originally designed to provide long-range fire support to motor rifle battalions with a secondary air defence capability. Within the Warsaw Pact they have long since been replaced by new systems although some remain in service in the Third World as they are simple to operate and maintain and can also be used in an urban/counter-insurgency role.

The BTR-40A entered service in 1950 and is essentially a BTR-40 (4 × 4) APC with a ZTPU-2 mount in the rear whilst the BTR-152A, which entered operational service in 1952, is a BTR-152 (6 × 6) APC with a similar arrangement.

Description

Both vehicles have an all-welded steel hull with the engine at the front, commander and driver in the centre and the twin 14.5 mm turret mounted at the rear. The driver sits on the left of the vehicle with the vehicle commander to his right, and it has a windscreen which can be covered by an armoured shutter hinged at its upper part. The shutter has a vision block for observation when it is lowered. Both the commander and driver have a door in the side of the hull, in the upper part of which is a vision flap that hinges open on the outside and has a vision slit.

A spare wheel is carried on the rear of the hull in the centre and a saw is often carried on the left side of the hull.

Neither vehicle has an NBC system, or night vision equipment and they are not amphibious. The BTR-40A is not fitted with a central tyre pressure regulation system although the later models of the BTR-152A do have such a system.

The turret is fitted with twin 14.5 mm KPV heavy machine guns that have manual traverse through 360° and manual elevation from −5 to +80°.

The 14.5 mm machine guns have a maximum horizontal range of 8000 m and a maximum vertical range of 5000 m but effective anti-aircraft range is 1400 m and effective range in the ground role is 2000 m.

The KPV machine gun has a cyclic rate of fire of 600 rounds per minute per barrel but its practical rate of fire is 150 rds/barrel/min, and it is air cooled.

The API (BS 41) projectile weighs 64.4 g and has a muzzle velocity of 1000 m/s penetrating 32 mm of armour at a range of 500 m. The API-T (BZT) projectile weights 59.6 g and the I-T (ZP) projectile weighs 59.68 g. Approximately 2400 rounds of boxed ammunition are carried for ready use.

Both the BTR-40A and BTR-152A are clear weather systems with no provision for off carriage fire control although target information such as speed, range and altitude can be provided over the radio net.

The 14.5 mm KPV machine gun is also used in the ZPU-1 (single barrel), ZPU-2 (twin barrel) and ZPU-4 (quad barrel) covered in the *Towed anti-aircraft guns* section.

Variants

BTR-152D with Twin 14.5 mm ZPU-2 Mount

The BTR-152D is essentially the same as the BTR-152A vehicle but has the chassis of the BTR-152V APC that entered service in 1955 and which is fitted with a central tyre pressure regulation system.

BTR-152 fitted with 23 mm ZU-23 mm automatic anti-aircraft gun mounted in rear (Israel Defence Forces)

BTR-152A twin 14.5 mm SPAAG crossing pontoon bridge

BTR-152A twin 14.5 mm SPAAG, late production vehicle with central tyre pressure regulation system

90 SELF-PROPELLED AA GUNS / USSR

BTR-152E with Quad 14.5 mm ZPU-4 Mount
This is the BTR-152V chassis fitted with the quadruple ZPU-4 mount. Only a small number were produced and as far as is known, none now remain in service.

BTR-152 with Twin 23 mm ZU-23
During the fighting in the Lebanon in the summer of 1982 the Israeli Army captured a number of BTR-152 APCs from the PLO which were fitted with the towed automatic anti-aircraft gun ZU-23 in the rear of the troop compartment. The twin 23 mm ZU-23 has a maximum range of 2500 m in the anti-aircraft role. Full details are given in the *Towed anti-aircraft guns* section.

BTR-152 with M53 MGs
Many years ago the Egyptians fitted a number of their BTR-152s with the Czechoslovakian quad 12.7 mm M53 anti-aircraft gun system which consists of four Soviet designed 12.7 mm DShK machine guns on a Czechoslovakian designed two-wheeled mount. Full details of the M53 are given in the *Towed anti-aircraft guns* section. It is unlikely that this vehicle is still in service.

BTR-40A twin 14·5 mm SPAAG

SPECIFICATIONS

MODEL	BTR-40A	BTR-152A
CREW	4-5	4-5
CONFIGURATION	4 × 4	6 × 6
COMBAT WEIGHT	5800 kg	9600 kg
POWER-TO-WEIGHT RATIO	13.7 hp/tonne	11.45 hp/tonne
LENGTH	5 m	6.83 m
WIDTH	1.9 m	2.32 m
HEIGHT		
overall	2.5 m	2.8 m
hull top	1.75 m	2.05 m
FIRING HEIGHT	2.05 m	2.35 m
GROUND CLEARANCE	0.275 m	0.295 m
TRACK		
front	1.588 m	1.742 m
rear	1.6 m	1.742 m
WHEELBASE	2.7 m	3.3 m + 1.13 m
MAX ROAD SPEED	80 km/h	65 km/h
FUEL CAPACITY	120 litre	300 litres
MAX ROAD RANGE	285 km	780 km
FUEL CONSUMPTION (road)	0.42 litre/km	0.46 litres/km

MODEL	BTR-40A	BTR-152A
FORDING	0.8 m	0.8 m
GRADIENT	60%	55%
SIDE SLOPE	30%	30%
VERTICAL OBSTACLE	0.47 m	0.6 m
TRENCH	0.7 m	0.69 m
ENGINE MODEL	GAZ-40	ZIL-123
TYPE	6 cylinder	6 cylinder
COOLING	water	water
OUTPUT/RPM	80 hp/3400 rpm	110 hp/3000 rpm
TRANSMISSION TYPE	manual	manual
GEARS	4F/1R	5F/1R
TRANSFER BOX	none	2-speed
CLUTCH	single dry plate	twin dry plate
TYRES	9.75 × 18	12.00 × 18
BRAKES	hydraulic drum on all wheels	
ELECTRICAL SYSTEM	12 V	12 V
ARMOUR	8 mm	13.5 mm

Status: Production complete. A full list of users of the BTR-40 and BTR-152 is given below, although in many cases these are used by second line units or held in reserve, some of these are known to use the BTR-40A or BTR-152A anti-aircraft vehicles:

Country	BTR-40	BTR-152
Afghanistan	yes	yes
Albania	yes	yes
Algeria	no	yes
Angola	no	yes
Bulgaria	yes (R)	yes (R)
Burundi	yes	no
Central African Republic	no	yes
China, People's Republic	yes	yes
Congo	no	yes
Cuba	yes	yes
Egypt	yes	yes
Equatorial Guinea	yes	no
Ethiopia	yes	yes
Germany, East	yes (R)	yes (R)
Guinea	yes	yes
Guinea-Bissau	yes	yes
Hungary	no	yes (R)
Indonesia	yes	yes
Iran	yes	yes
Iraq	no	yes
Kampuchea	yes	yes
Korea, North	yes	yes
Laos	yes	yes
Mali	no	yes
Mongolia	no	yes
Mozambique	yes	yes
Nicaragua	yes	yes
Poland	no	yes (R)
Romania	no	yes (R)
Somalia	yes	yes
Sri Lanka	no	yes
Sudan	no	yes
Syria	yes	yes
Tanzania	yes	yes
Uganda	yes	yes
USSR	yes (R)	yes (R)
Vietnam	yes	yes
Yemen, North	yes	yes
Yemen, South	yes	yes
Yugoslavia	yes	yes
Zaire	yes	no
Zimbabwe	no	yes

UNITED KINGDOM

Marconi Marksman Twin 35 mm Anti-aircraft Turret

Development

Following a worldwide market survey into the type of air defence system required to protect armoured and mechanised formations and units from the low level fighter ground attack aircraft and pop-up helicopter threat, Marconi Command and Control Systems commenced development in 1983 of a prototype of the Marksman twin 35 mm anti-aircraft turret. This was in response to identified requirements for a system which could be rapidly fitted to an existing chassis, had fast reaction and high lethality with the maximum possible range and which would operate in all weather by day and night.

The principal feature of the Marksman gun turret is that it is a completely self-contained turret which can be fitted to any main battle tank hull without modification. The 35 mm guns are considered by Marconi to provide the optimum balance of the requirements of range, lethality and accuracy and the combined surveillance and tracking radar gives fast reaction with an all-weather day and night capability.

Marconi Command and Control Systems has three partners in the project: Vickers Defence Systems of Newcastle who manufacture the armoured turret, Oerlikon-Bührle who supply the 35 mm cannon and the new ammunition transfer system and Société de Fabrication d'Instruments de Mesure (SFIM) of France who supply the gyro-stabilised sights and inertial reference system. Integration of Marksman is carried out by Marconi at its Leicester works.

The first prototype was complete in 1984 with a turret of mild steel, while the second, fully armoured and equipped to production standard, was completed in 1985. The two turrets have allowed Marconi to retain one for trials and development work while the other is used for demonstrations at home and abroad. Trials have been successfully conducted both in the UK and overseas in conditions varying from hot desert to arctic winter and in temperatures ranging from -36° to +42° Celsius. The turret has undergone trials and tests on a number of different tank hulls, including T-55, Type 59, M48, Centurion, Challenger, Chieftain and Vickers Mk 3. The average time to fit the turret to a tank hull is about two hours.

In December 1988 the Finnish Ministry of Defence placed an order worth FM 75 million (£10 million) for an initial quantity of Marksman twin 35 mm anti-aircraft turrets, training, spares, test equipment and on site support.

The initial contract is a straight buy, but it also includes an option for a further quantity in 1992 which will probably include a substantial offset package. Marconi Command and Control Systems will ship the turrets direct to Finland where they will be installed on T-54/T-55 tank chassis. They will be used to provide protection for the armoured brigade.

Description

The Marksman anti-aircraft gun turret consists of a self-contained armoured turret fitted with twin rapid-firing 35 mm Oerlikon KDA cannon together with an automatic highly ECM resistant surveillance and tracking radar, fixed or gyrostabilised optical sights and a modern digital fire control system.

The radar used with the system is the Marconi 400 series combined surveillance and tracking radar which utilises a single antenna. The decision to fit just one radar was taken for various reasons, including quicker reaction time, reliability, cost and weight. The radar is therefore smaller and lighter than previous short range air defence radars and the radar equipment, mounted in the turret hull, is of modular design. The radar rotates at 60 rpm, operates in the X/J-band and has a range of 12 km in the surveillance mode. Tracking range is 10 km. It provides fully automatic operation, has a particularly good ECCM capability because of its very wide bandwidth and frequency agility, and has been designed to minimise the effects of rain attenuation and to overcome the problem of secondary ground reflection (multipath) effects. The radar is mounted on the turret roof, and is stabilised to enable it to operate in surveillance on the move. The director can be swung backwards through 180° for stowage in a travelling position if required, thus reducing the overall height of the vehicle.

Two SFIM roof-mounted sights are provided together with a high PRF laser rangefinder. These may be either fixed sights slaved to the gun boresight or independent gyrostabilised fully panoramic optical sights. The sights not only provide an alternative mode of operation if for any tactical or operational reason the radar cannot be used, but also visual identification and verification of radar engagements. The two gyrostabilised sights when used in conjunction with the radar give the crew three independent means of surveillance and tracking. This allows the crew considerable flexibility particularly against multiple targets, permitting extremely rapid switches from one target to another. The gunner's sight includes a fixed aiming graticule for the engagement of surface targets.

Target data from the radar or optical sights is passed in digital form to a modern digital fire control system which is based on a modified version of Marconi designs currently in service in main battle tanks. The fire control system produces accurate output signals which are used by the electric turret drives to track the target and correctly aim the guns. It also indicates when the weapon system is ready and able to engage the target.

The Marksman turret is fitted with two Oerlikon 35 mm KDA cannon mounted externally on each side of the turret on large diameter bearings. The cannon was selected by Marconi as the optimum gun solution due to its combination of range, lethality, excellent terminal effects, high muzzle velocity, rate of fire and proven performance. The KDA cannon

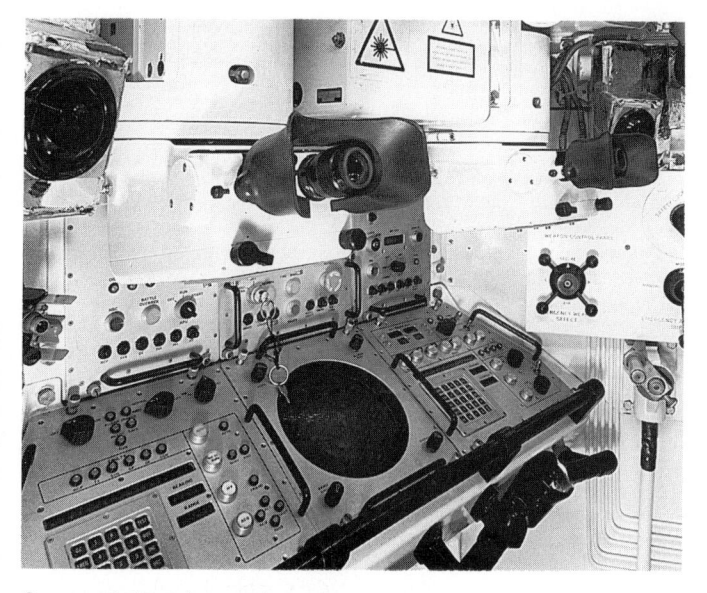

Commander's and gunner's position in Marconi Command and Control Systems Marksman anti-aircraft turret

Marconi Command and Control Systems Marksman twin 35 mm anti-aircraft turret on T-55 MBT chassis

Marconi Command and Control Systems Marksman twin 35 mm anti-aircraft turret on Type 59 MBT chassis

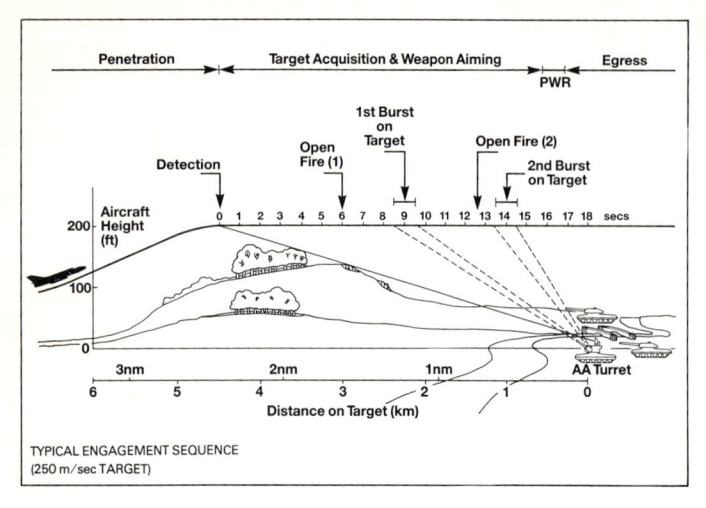

92 SELF-PROPELLED AA GUNS / UK

Typical Marksman anti-aircraft turret target engagement sequence

Removal of Marksman turret from a Type 59 MBT hull and fitting to an M48 hull in September 1986

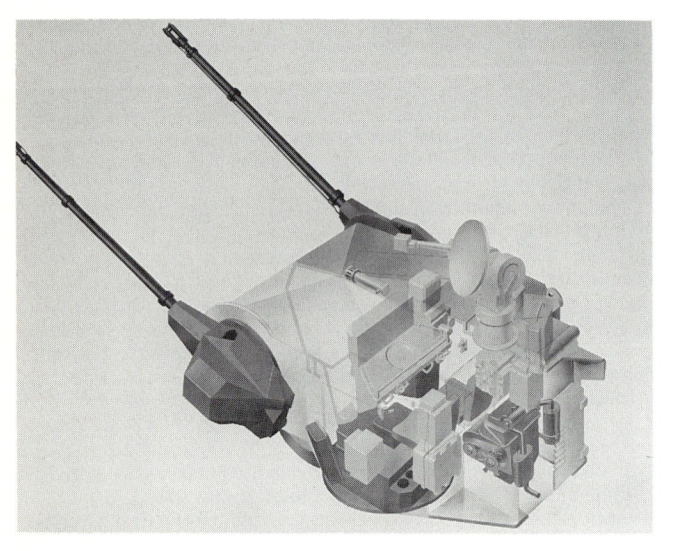

Cutaway drawing of Marconi Command and Control Systems Marksman anti-aircraft turret showing position of electronics

Marconi Command and Control Systems Marksman twin 35 mm anti-aircraft turret on Chieftain MBT chassis with weapons firing

and mount are identical to those installed on the Gepard twin 35 mm self-propelled anti-aircraft gun system in service with West Germany (420), Belgium (55) and the Netherlands (95). They are, however, of the latest standard with an improved lubrication system.

Each cannon has 230 rounds of anti-aircraft and 20 rounds of armour-piercing ammunition for engaging ground targets. A major feature of Marksman is that a total ammunition reload, so critical on the battlefield, takes well under 10 seconds. Each cannon is provided with an ammunition container mounted inside the turret which feeds ammunition through the ammunition transfer system via the elevation bearings to the cannon. The ammunition containers are readily replaced using a small davit on the side of the turret. Alternatively a separate vehicle equipped with a crane could be used. Each cannon has a cyclic rate of fire of 550 rds/min and a maximum effective range of 4000 m. Sufficient ammunition is carried for between 15 and 20 engagements before ammunition resupply is necessary. The KDA cannon fires the following types of fixed ammunition:

AMMUNITION TYPE	APDS-T	HEI	HEI-T	SAPHEI-T	TP	TP-T
WEIGHT						
projectile	294 g	550 g	535 g	550 g	550 g	550 g
propellant	330 g	330 g	330 g	330 g	330 g	330 g
explosive	none	80 g+ 20 g	98g	22g	none	none
complete round	1460 g	1580 g	1565 g	1552 g	1580 g	1580 g
EXPLOSIVE TYPE	none	Hexal	Hexal	Hexal	none	none
LENGTH						
complete round	370 mm	387 mm	387 mm	387 mm	387 mm	387 mm
MUZZLE VELOCITY	1385m/s	1175m/s	1175m/s	1175m/s	1175m/s	1175m/s
FLIGHT TIME						
to 1100 m	0.75 s	0.96 s	0.96 s	0.96 s	0.96 s	0.96 s
to 2000 m	1.58 s	2.18 s	2.18 s	2.18 s	2.18 s	2.18 s
to 3000 m	2.51 s	3.78 s	3.78 s	3.78 s	3.78 s	3.78 s

Under development by Oerlikon-Bührle is a new range of 35 mm ammunition with increased muzzle velocities and therefore reduced flight times to target as well as major advances in fuzing.

The cannon are located externally to the turret shell so no fumes can affect the crew and to allow the empty cartridge cases and links to be ejected outside the turret. To compensate for the effect of barrel wear on muzzle velocity, which in turn affects time of flight and hence aim-off distances, each barrel is fitted with measuring equipment which measures the muzzle velocity of every projectile fired and feeds the information into the fire control system.

The cannon can be elevated from -10° to +85° at a maximum speed of 60°/s with turret traverse through a full 360° at up to 90°/s.

Marksman is fitted with the latest solid state stabilised turret drive system with electronics, servo controls, solid state power amplifiers and batteries being positioned on the floor of the turret basket, below which is a rotary base junction. The turret batteries have a combined capacity of 300 Ah and provide sufficient power to run the complete turret for some time without recharge, thus allowing the turret to operate in a silent watch mode at a moment's readiness. The batteries are recharged by an auxiliary diesel generator mounted on the rear of the turret. The tank engine can also be used for this purpose in an emergency.

The Marksman turret is of all-welded steel construction and over its frontal arc provides complete protection from 14.5 mm API ammunition fired by the Soviet KPVT heavy machine gun, with protection being provided against 7.62 mm armour-piercing ammunition over the remainder. Protection is also provided against 155 mm airburst artillery projectiles. As an option the turret can be fitted with an NBC system, as space for this is provided each side of the generator. Other equipment, such as radio installations, would be to the requirements of the user.

The Marksman turret is normally operated by a crew of two: commander and gunner, although one man operation is possible. The commander and gunner sit side by side in front of an ergonomically designed console which allows either crew member full access to the fire control system as well as to an independent optical sight. The console includes a centrally located radar display and incorporates all the operator interfaces required for the radar, gun control equipment and power distribution within the turret. The comprehensive built-in test equipment (BITE) facility is controlled and monitored at the console. An optional IFF panel is fitted above the console.

Marksman is designed to operate fully automatically from the initial acquisition of a target by the radar to a 'ready to fire' indication to the crew. This is achieved by a variable guard zone which is set up on the radar display using the commander's keypad on the central console. With the radar in surveillance in the automatic mode, any target entering the airspace covered by the guard zone will be automatically interrogated by the IFF, if fitted, and if hostile, acquired and tracked. The only action required by the crew is to press the fire button. The system reaction time in the automatic mode is well under six seconds (4.6 seconds average on trials). Targets that appear outside the guard zone can be manually designated using a marker on the radar display, after which the sequence will proceed as for a target acquired automatically. Targets can also be designated to the radar using the optical sights.

In the optical mode, the target is acquired and tracked using the sights which provide target data to the fire control system to calculate aim-off, together with a built in laser rangefinder.

The turret can be mounted on any main battle tank hull without modification to either the turret or the hull. It is designed to fit directly to a T-tank hull; for other tank chassis a simple adaptor ring is required. A simple electrical connection is made to enable the turret crew to communicate with the driver. Connection of the turret to the electrical system of the tank is not required as the turret has its own power supply; however an interface is provided to allow the use of the tank engine in an emergency.

SPECIFICATIONS (turret)
RADAR
TYPE	Marconi Series 400 surveillance and tracking radar – X/J-band coherent frequency agile
RANGE	
surveillance	12 km
tracking	10 km
TARGET SPEED	up to 400 m/s
ANTENNA	offset front fed parabolic dish
RECEIVER	monopulse MTI and digital signal processing

OPTICAL SIGHT
GYRO-STABILISED or	dual FOV 5° × 10 and 18° × 3
FIXED TRAVERSE	dual FOV 7° × 8 and 40° × 1
Each with Integral Laser Rangefinder	

CANNON
TYPE	twin Oerlikon KDA stabilised in 2 axes
CALIBRE	35 mm
MAX EFFECTIVE RANGE	4000 m
MUZZLE VELOCITY	1175–1385 m/s ammunition type dependent
RATE OF FIRE	550 rds/min/barrel
ELEVATION	+85° to −10°
AMMUNITION	HEI, HEI-T, TP, TP-T, SAPHEI-T, APDS-T 230 AA per barrel (containerised) 20 APDS per barrel

SYSTEM
CREW	2 (commander and gunner)
REACTION TIME	alarm to ready to fire under 6 s (automatic)
POWER DRIVES	28 V from turret batteries recharged by the turret APU electric solid state
FIRE CONTROL	automatic digital
TRAVERSE	360° at up to 60°/s
ELEVATION	+85° to −10° at 60°/s
WEIGHT OF TURRET	11 000 kg
OVERALL LENGTH WITH GUNS	
radar up	7.12 m
radar stowed	7.585 m
OVERALL WIDTH	3.45 m
HEIGHT	
radar up	2.705 m
radar down	1.910 m
TURRET RING DIAMETER	1.99 m

Status: Entered production late in 1988 following order placed by Finland. Tested on seven MBT chassis types.

Manufacturer: Marconi Command and Control Systems Limited, New Parks, Leicester LE3 1UK, UK.
Telephone: (0533) 871481. Telex: 34551. Fax: (0533) 871746

UNITED STATES OF AMERICA

M42 Twin 40 mm Self-propelled Anti-aircraft Gun System

Development
At the end of the Second World War the standard tracked self-propelled anti-aircraft gun of the United States Army was the twin 40 mm M19. It was a member of the Light Combat Team, all of which shared the same basic chassis and included the M24 light tank, M37 105 mm howitzer motor carriage and the M41 155 mm howitzer motor carriage.

In August 1951 authorisation was given to design, develop and build prototypes of a twin 40 mm self-propelled anti-aircraft gun (designated the T141 interim vehicle), twin 40 mm self-propelled anti-aircraft gun (designated the T141E1 ultimate vehicle) and a carrier fire control vehicle (designated the T53). In May 1952 the T141E1 and its associated T53 fire control vehicle were cancelled 'for reasons of complexity, time required for development and cost'. The T141 was designed by the Cadillac Motor Car Division of the General Motors Corporation with the first prototype being completed late in 1951. The T141 had a very short development period as it was based on components of the M41 light tank which was also being produced by the Cadillac Motor Car Division of the General Motors Corporation at the Cleveland Tank Plant and used the same turret with twin 40 mm guns as the earlier M19A1.

The T141 was standardised as the Gun, Twin 40 mm, Self-propelled, M42, in October 1953, after the vehicle had already been in production for more than a year. At the same time the M19 was classified as a limited standard type. The M19 has the same turret as the M42 but it was mounted

M42 twin 40 mm self-propelled anti-aircraft gun system used by Taiwan with locally produced 32-round magazine above 40 mm weapon (DTM)

at the rear rather than in the centre of the hull as in the case of the M42.

The M42 was in production at Cleveland Tank Plant from late 1951 to June 1956 and at ACF Industries Incorporated of Berwick, Pennsylvania, from early 1952 to December 1953. Production of the M42 amounted to 3700 units. To improve the fuel economy and increase

94 SELF-PROPELLED AA GUNS / USA

Austrian Army M42 twin 40 mm self-propelled anti-aircraft gun (Austrian Ministry of Defence)

operational range a fuel injection system was designed for the AOS-895-3 engine. The fuel injection model became known as the AOSI-895-5 and trials showed fuel savings of 20 per cent. In February 1956 the basic M42 was reclassified as limited standard and the M42A1 as standard. Most M42s were subsequently brought up to M42A1 standard.

The M42 was replaced in front-line service with the United States Army by the 20 mm Vulcan Air Defense System from 1969, but today M42s remain in service with the National Guard. Eight battalions, each with 36 M42s were active in 1982. Four of the battalions were based in New Mexico, and one each in Ohio, Virginia, South Carolina and Florida. One of the New Mexico battalions has since been re-equipped with the Roland SAM, while the other seven are to transition to a mixture of guns and missile systems and by early 1989 about four battalions remained equipped with the M42 in the National Guard. During the Vietnam War the M42 was widely used in the ground role where it proved highly effective. The system's main drawbacks are its relatively slow rate of fire and lack of an all-weather fire control system.

Description
The all-welded hull of the M42 is divided into three compartments: driver's and commander's at the front, turret in the centre and the engine at the rear.

The driver is seated at the front of the hull on the left with the commander/radio operator to his right. Both have a single piece hatch cover that opens to the outside of the vehicle, with a single M13 periscope which can be traversed through 360°. The other four crew members are seated in the open-topped turret in the centre of the vehicle.

The engine compartment at the rear of the hull is separated from the fighting compartment by a fireproof bulkhead and has a fire extinguisher operated by the driver. The engine is mounted towards the front of the engine compartment and the transmission at the rear.

The torsion bar suspension consists of five dual rubber-tyred road wheels with the idler at the front, drive sprocket at the rear and three track return rollers. The first, second and fifth road wheel stations have a hydraulic shock absorber. The steel tracks have replaceable rubber pads.

The M42 has no amphibious capability or NBC system but most vehicles were fitted with infra-red driving lights.

Main armament comprises twin 40 mm cannon M2A1 in mount M2A1 in a turret with a traverse of 360°. The weapons have hydraulic elevation from −3 to +85° and manual operation from −5 to +85°. The weapons are recoil operated and have vertical sliding breech-blocks and the gunner can select either single shots or full automatic. Early vehicles had flash-hiders but they were replaced on later production vehicles by flash suppressors which were subsequently retrofitted to the earlier vehicles. Practical rate of fire is 120 rds/barrel/min, maximum anti-aircraft range is 5000 m and maximum ground-to-ground range is 9475 m. The following types of fixed ammunition can be fired:
AP-T (M81 series) with the complete round weighing 2.077 kg, muzzle velocity of 872 m/s;
HE-T with the complete round weighing 2.15 kg, muzzle velocity of 880 m/s;
TP-T (M91) with the complete round weighing 2.14 kg, muzzle velocity of 872 m/s.

Of 480 rounds of 40 mm ammunition carried, most is stored in the ammunition containers along the tops of the track guard either side of the turret. Three sighting devices are incorporated into the fire control system of the M42: computing sight M38, reflex sight M24C and the speed ring sight. The computing sight M38 is designed to provide an effective means of controlling fire of the 40 mm cannon against both air and ground targets. The reflex sight M24C is designed to superimpose a graticule pattern in the gunner's line of sight and is used in conjunction with the

USA / SELF-PROPELLED AA GUNS

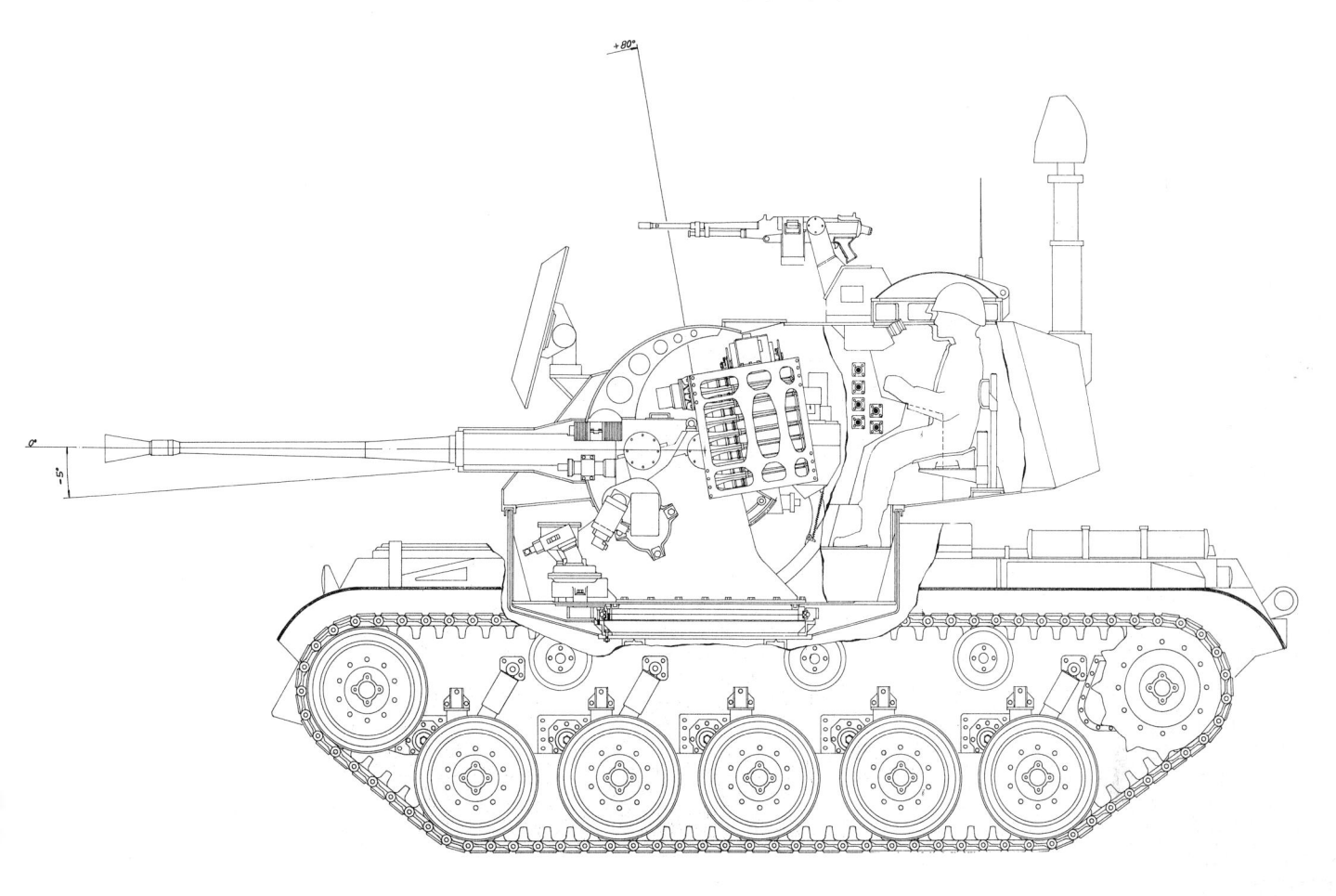

Cutaway drawing of an M42 fitted with a new turret by Breda armed with a single 40 mm L/70 gun

computing sight M38 during power operation. The speed ring sight is used during manual operation if a power failure or local control system malfunction occurs.

Mounted on the left rear of the turret is a 7.62 mm (0.30) M1919A4 machine gun, which has been replaced by an M60 MG in the United States Army. The machine gun has a traverse of 360°, elevation of +76° to the front and an elevation of +60° at the rear.

Breda M42 Upgrade

The Italian company of Breda Meccanica Bresciana is now offering a new fully enclosed armoured turret armed with a single 40 mm L/70 gun for installation on the current M42 chassis with little modification.

The turret is of all-welded steel armour construction which varies in thickness from 9 to 16 mm and this provides the same degree of protection as the hull. Both the commander and gunner are provided with a cupola with observation devices for all round observation and the gunner, seated on the left, has a roof-mounted periscopic sight.

The 40 mm L/70 gun has a dual feed ammunition system and can be used to engage aircraft, helicopters and ground targets.

The gunner controls the turret functions when operated through the optical sight and the tracking radar. The second crewman, the commander, is seated on the right and operates the 7.62 mm roof-mounted machine gun. Both turret crew members carry out loading and reloading of the magazine.

Ammunition can be loaded via a hatch in each side of the turret towards the rear and the empty 40 mm cartridge cases are ejected from the turret automatically. In addition to the ready rounds stowed in the on-gun magazine and in the existing external racks on either side of the hull, over 60 additional rounds are also stowed inside the turret. These will be stowed forward of the commander's and gunner's seats.

The 40 mm L/70 gun has a cyclic rate of fire of 450 rds/min and in addition to firing the existing types of 40 mm L/70 ammunition it will also fire a new SNIA APFSDS round.

The rate of fire is 50 per cent more than the standard L/70 weapon and this has been achieved by a private venture research and development programme carried out by Breda. The modifications have included the use of stronger materials, reducing recoil length and installation of a new ramming system.

The ready use magazine holds a total of 90 rounds of fixed ammunition including a quantity for engaging ground targets.

Turret traverse and weapon elevation is hydraulic with turret traverse through a full 360° and weapon elevation from -3 to +80°.

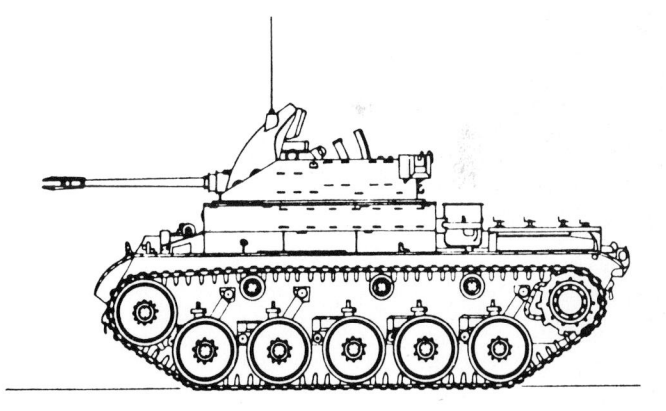

M42 self-propelled anti-aircraft gun

M42 twin 40 mm self-propelled anti-aircraft guns showing ready use ammunition stowed on turret rear (US Army)

96 SELF-PROPELLED AA GUNS / USA

A number of fire control options are available including one with a surveillance radar mounted on the turret rear and the tracking radar mounted to the right of the 40 mm weapon.

Variants
In 1982 an M42 was fitted with the same NAPCO powerpack as the M41 light tank but with a modified cooling system. The vehicle was also fitted with a Cadillac Gage weapon control system to improve target tracking. Firing trials were undertaken at the US Army Air Defense School at Fort Bliss, Texas. During these the upgraded vehicle successfully shot down one of the target drones engaging it. As of early 1989 this improvement package had not been adopted by any country.

Taiwan is known to have refitted several of the M42A2s in service with its army as TOW ATGW vehicles.

SPECIFICATIONS

CREW	6
COMBAT WEIGHT	22 452 kg
UNLOADED WEIGHT	20 094 kg
POWER-TO-WEIGHT RATIO	22.26 hp/tonne
GROUND PRESSURE	0.65 kg/cm^2
LENGTH GUNS FORWARD	6.356 m
LENGTH HULL	5.819 m
WIDTH	3.225 m
HEIGHT	2.847 m
GROUND CLEARANCE	0.438 m
TRACK	2.602 m
TRACK WIDTH	533 mm
MAX ROAD SPEED	72.4 km/h
FUEL CAPACITY	530 litres
MAX ROAD RANGE	161 km
FUEL CONSUMPTION	3.29 litres/km
FORDING	1.016 m
GRADIENT	60%
SIDE SLOPE	30%
VERTICAL OBSTACLE	0.711 m
TRENCH	1.828 m
ENGINE	Continental or Lycoming AOS-895-3, 6-cylinder air-cooled super-charged petrol developing 500 bhp at 2800 rpm (M42A1 has AOSI-895-5 with fuel injection which develops the same bhp)
AUXILIARY ENGINE	GMC A41-1 or A41-2
TRANSMISSION	General Motors Allison Division cross-drive model CD-500-3 with one forward and one reverse range
SUSPENSION	torsion bar
ELECTRICAL SYSTEM	24 V
BATTERIES	4 × 12 V, 6TN
ARMAMENT	
main, anti-aircraft	2 × 40 mm MG
secondary, anti-aircraft	1 × 7.62 mm MG
AMMUNITION	
main, anti-aircraft	480
secondary, anti-aircraft	1750
GUN CONTROL EQUIPMENT	
turret power control	hydraulic/manual
by commander	no
by gunner	yes
max rate power traverse	40°/s
max rate power elevation	25°/s
gun elevation/depression	+85°/(powered) -3° (manual) -5°
turret traverse	360°
ARMOUR	
hull front lower	25.4 mm at 45°
hull front upper	12.7 mm at 33°
hull sides	12.7 mm
hull top	12.7 mm
hull floor	9.05 - 31 mm
hull rear	12.7 mm
turret	9.52 - 15.87 mm

Status: Production complete. In service with the following countries:

Country	Quantity	User	Comment
Austria	38	army	
Greece	101	army	from West Germany
Guatemala	n/av	army	small number
Jordan	222	army	not all operational
Lebanon	n/av	army	small number
Taiwan	295	army	
Thailand	16	army	
Tunisia	16	army	
Turkey	153	army	from West Germany
USA	400+	National Guard	declining numbers
Venezuela	30	Marine Corps	
Vietnam	135	army	probably non-operational

Manufacturers: Cadillac Motor Car Division of General Motors Corporation, Cleveland Tank Plant.
ACF Industries Incorporated of Berwick, Pennsylvania.

Eagle Twin 35 mm Mobile Air Defence System

Development
The Eagle Air Defence System is the result of a four year advanced development programme by ARES Inc on behalf of the then Imperial Iranian Army to find a cost effective mobile air defence system to protect rear area targets such as bridges, factories and refineries. The system is now at the production engineering phase after the evaluation of prototypes, the first of which was complete in 1979.

Description
The Eagle system is composed of a modular turret unit mounted on a modified M548 tracked vehicle chassis. The turret can be adapted to fit many other types of vehicles. The turret has cradles either side for two 270 kg externally-mounted 35 mm TALON automatic cannon which have a nominal cyclic rate of fire of 575 rds/min per gun, an effective anti-aircraft engagement range of 4000 m and can fire the following types of 35 mm Oerlikon-Bührle ammunition in fully automatic or semi-automatic modes:

NATO DESIGNATION	APDS-T	HEI	HEI-T	SAPHEI-T	TP	TP-T
WEIGHT						
projectile	294 g	550 g	535 g	550 g	550 g	550 g
propellant	330 g	330 g	330 g	330 g	330 g	330 g
explosive	none	80 g + 20 g	98 g	22 g	none	none
complete round	1460 g	1580 g	1565 g	1552 g	1580 g	1580 g
EXPLOSIVE TYPE	none	Hexal P 30	Hexal P 30	Hexal P 30	none	none
LENGTH (complete round)	370 mm	387 mm	387 mm	387 mm	387 mm	387 mm
MUZZLE VELOCITY	1385m/s	1175m/s	1175m/s	1175m/s	1175m/s	1175m/s
FLIGHT TIME						
to 1000 m	0.75 s	0.96 s	0.96 s	0.96 s	0.96 s	0.96 s
to 2000 m	1.58 s	2.18 s	2.18 s	2.18 s	2.18 s	2.18 s
to 3000 m	2.51 s	3.78 s	3.78 s	3.78 s	3.78 s	3.78 s

USA / SELF-PROPELLED AA GUNS

Eagle Air Defence system in static defence with hydraulic levelling jacks lowered and remote tracking sight mounting deployed

APDS-T will penetrate 40 mm of armour at 60° NATO at 1000 m range
SAPHEI-T projectile will penetrate 15 mm of armour at 60° NATO at 1000 m
Weight of complete APDS-T projectile is 380 g with penetrator weighing 294 g.

The System has a digital fire control system and is fitted with an optical tracking sight that has a direct ×1 optical system for target acquisition, a ×4 telescopic sight for tracking and an infra-red laser rangefinder. The laser has minimum and maximum ranges of 200 and 5300 m respectively. The sight unit can either be mounted on the vehicle for use by the gunner inside the vehicle or on a single-man ground mount at distances up to 100 m from the vehicle for remote tracking, in which case the unit can be used to operate several turrets simultaneously. Alternative fire control directors such as radar, TV or IR can easily be interfaced with the high speed solid-state fire control electronics of the system. Stability in the static firing role can be ensured by lowering three hydraulic levelling jacks. Reloading of the system takes up to 12 minutes. The system is ready to fire instantaneously when on a tracked vehicle, otherwise from travelling configuration to ready to fire takes one minute for the hydraulic jacks to be lowered and 15 minutes for the jacks to be lowered and the remote sight to be deployed.

SPECIFICATIONS (M548 chassis)

CREW	2-3
COMBAT WEIGHT	14 500 kg
UNLOADED WEIGHT	13 600 kg
GROUND PRESSURE	0.39 kg/cm^2
LENGTH (travelling)	6.705 m
WIDTH (travelling)	2.69 m
HEIGHT	
travelling with sight	3.175 m
travelling without sight	2.67-2.44 m
GROUND CLEARANCE	0.355 m
TRACK	2.159 m
TRACK WIDTH	381 mm
LENGTH OF TRACK ON GROUND	2.82 m
MAX ROAD SPEED	48 km/h
FUEL CAPACITY	397 litres
MAX RANGE (cross-country)	265 km
TURNING RADIUS	4.3 m
MAX GRADIENT	60%
MAX SIDE SLOPE	30%
VERTICAL OBSTACLE	0.609 m
TRENCH	1.68 m
SUSPENSION	torsion bar
ENGINE	GMC Model 6V-53 Detroit Diesel, 6-cylinder, liquid cooled, developing 215 hp at 3800 rpm
ARMAMENT	2 × 35 mm cannon
AMMUNITION	560 rounds
GUN ELEVATION/DEPRESSION	+80°/-8°
TURRET TRAVERSE	360°

Status: Prototype, ready for production engineering.

Manufacturer: ARES Inc, Building 818, Erie Industrial Park, Port Clinton, Ohio 43451, USA.

SELF-PROPELLED AA GUNS / USA

General Electric Blazer Air Defence Turrets

Development
As a private venture, the Armament Systems Department of GE Aerospace has developed the Blazer family of air defence turrets. The basic air defence turret is the Blazer 25. It consists of a 25 mm GAU-12/U Gatling Gun and four Stinger or Mistral fire and forget surface-to-air missiles on a two-man turret.

This power operated turret has been installed on the M2 Bradley chassis, the MOWAG Piranha (8 × 8) and Alvis Stormer, and can be fitted on the M113, the Cadillac Gage V-300 (6 × 6) and V-150 S (4 × 4) vehicles.

Two derivatives for Blazer 25 have also been developed; Blazer 30: a 30 mm GAU-13/Gatling Gun with four Stinger, Mistral or Javelin missiles, on a one-man turret. This variant has been installed on a MOWAG Piranha (8 × 8) but can be readily fitted to the above APCs; LAV/AD: A 25 mm GAU-12/U Gatling gun with four Stinger missiles configured specifically for the US Marine Corps Light Armored Vehicle (LAV), GE is currently under contract for full scale development of the USMC LAV/AD system in competition with FMC. There is a separate entry for the LAV/AD system in this section.

All systems have a digital fire control system, eye-safe laser rangefinder, FLIR/TV stabilised sight and a 2D search radar. The systems have been fitted with the ESD RA-20S radar and are currently offered with the Thomson-CSF Gerfault digital radar. (The Blazer 25 for the USMC does not have radar.)

Description
The Blazer turret is power operated and of all welded construction with light armour. It can be mounted on any tracked or wheeled vehicle that could accommodate a 1.625 m diameter turret ring. The two-man turret houses both gunner and commander, each capable of full system operation including acquisition, tracking, weapon selection and firing. Vision is through armoured windows on the front and sides.

Main armament comprises either the 25 mm GAU-12 gun which fires the Bushmaster family of ammunition at 1800 rds/min, or the GAU-13/U mm cannon which fires the GAU-8 family of ammunition at up to 2400 rds/min. In addition, four infra-red seeker missiles are mounted above the gun cradle and integrated into the Blazer's fire control system. Command guided missiles (Blowpipe, Javelin or RBS 70) can also be fitted effectively due to the system's pointing accuracy.

Sensors comprise the 2D Gerfault Radar or the RA-20S, and a FLIR/TV sight for viewing and auto tracking. The system has demonstrated day/night capability and the ability to track and fire while the vehicle is moving at up to 50 km/h over uneven terrain. In 1985 US testing, both gun and missile kills were recorded under such conditions.

The radar has a range of 12 km, IFF, automatic track-while-scan and data exchange for netting capability. The latter feature allows one system to act as a command unit for several units without operating acquisition sensors. The 25 mm cannon can engage targets at up to 2500 m and the 30 mm at ranges up to 3000 m. The missiles can engage targets up to 6000 m. Up to 400 ready rounds are in the magazine, with up to 600 stowed rounds in the vehicle. Internal loading of the 25 mm gun could be accomplished in 15 minutes. Depending on the chassis, additional missiles can be stored internally. Electronically operated smoke dischargers are located in banks of four on either side of the turret.

SPECIFICATIONS
CREW	2 (commander/gunner)
ARMAMENT	25 mm 5 barrel GAU-12/U
	4 fire and forget SAM (Stinger, Mistral)
TRAVERSE	360°
ELEVATION/DEPRESSION	+65°/8°
HEIGHT	
above ring, radar up	1.989 m
TRANSPORT HEIGHT	1.59 m
DEPTH	
below turret ring	1.06 m
WEIGHT	
loaded	2936 kg

Status: Pre-production prototype.

Manufacture: GE Aerospace, Armament Systems Department, Lakeside Avenue, Burlington, Vermont 05401-4935, USA.
Telephone: (802) 657 6000
Telex: 510 2990 028
Fax: (802) 657 6969/6921

M2 Bradley IFV with Blazer 30 turret armed with Stinger SAM

LAV (8 × 8) fitted with Blazer 30 turret with Electronique Serge Dassault RA-20S radar erected and carrying Javelin SAM

Light Armored Vehicle (LAV) Air Defence

Development
At the present time the US Marine Corps has no mobile battlefield air defence weapons and relies on the manportable General Dynamics Stinger and towed Raytheon Improved HAWK SAMs to meet its air defence requirements, although it is expected to procure the Pedestal Mounted Stinger (PMS) system from Boeing which won the US Army competition as part of the FAADS programme in 1987.

Before deciding on a gun/missile/rocket hybrid system, the Marine Corps evaluated five possible solutions to meet the LAV (AD) requirements. These were:
(1) a baseline system consisting of a standard LAV-25 equipped with the McDonnell Douglas Helicopters 25 mm Chain Gun and carrying two 2-man Stinger SAM teams.
(2) basic LAV-25 modified to carry Stinger SAM pods and equipped with a narrow field of view FLIR system
(3) LAV with new turret mounting for British Aerospace Rapier SAMs and a millimetre wave radar
(4) LAV with Oerlikon-Bührle ADATS which at that time had not been adopted by the US Army

USA / SELF-PROPELLED AA GUNS

(5) LAV with General Electric GAU-12/U 25 mm Gatling gun, Stingers and HYDRA-70 rockets with growth potential.

In May 1987 the US Army Tank Automotive Command (TACOM) solicited bids from 75 companies for an air defence version of the Light Armored Vehicle (LAV), but only two bids were received, one from FMC Corporation and one from the General Electric Company.

In December 1987 the FMC Corporation was awarded an initial contract worth $8.916 million while General Electric was awarded a contract worth $6.718 million. Total cost of building the four prototypes is expected to be $31.32 million.

Each company will build two prototypes based on the Light Armored Vehicle (8 × 8) chassis which will be provided by the Marine Corps and these will be evaluated from the third quarter of FY 1988 in Development Test II (DT/II) which is expected to be completed in early FY 1989. Operational Test II will be completed in the fourth quarter of FY 1989.

One of the two competing designs is expected to be selected for production with the production award due in the first quarter of FY 1990 with an IOC (Initial Operational Capability) in the first quarter of FY 1993. The weapon system selected will be capable of being upgraded with future air defence missiles using command-to-line-of-sight guidance.

The main role of the LAV AD is to engage fixed-wing aircraft and helicopters with a secondary role to engage ground targets using its cannon and HYDRA-70 rockets which are already fired by US Marine Corps helicopters.

Typically the Stingers would be used to engage targets out to 5000 m with the cannon engaging targets out to 2000/2500 m. The HYDRA-70 rockets can be used both in ground/ground and ground/air role and have a range of up to 7000 metres. In the ground/air role they would be used to engage hovering helicopters.

The US Marine Corps Requirement is for a total of 125 vehicles with the original intention being to utilise chassis already built for other applications. Total cost of the 125 production LAV AD has been estimated at $507 million. Each of the three active Marine Amphibious Forces will have 24 vehicles with a further 12 vehicles being allocated to the Marine Corps 4th Marine Division.

The US Marine Corps has already ordered 758 LAVs in six configurations from the Diesel Division, General Motors of Canada, with final deliveries made in 1988.

It is however possible that additional chassis will be built for both the LAV air defence and projected Assault Gun (AG).

The LAV AD will be fully airportable being slung under the Sikorsky CH-53E heavy-lift helicopter and like other members of the LAV family will be fully amphibious as it is propelled in the water by two propellers mounted at the rear of the hull. It will also be air transportable in a Lockheed C-130 and large-size transport aircraft.

Description

Both versions will use a modified LAV (8 × 8) chassis in which the driver is seated at the front left with engine compartment to his right and the remainder of the hull free for the turret and ammunition stowage. The commander and gunner can enter the vehicle through the turret and via the twin doors at the rear of the hull.

FMC LAV (AD)

The FMC version of the LAV will have a two-man power operated turret armed with a pod of four General Dynamics Stinger SAMs in the ready to launch position at left rear; a McDonnell Douglas Helicopters M242 25 mm Chain Gun with a high rate of fire in the centre of the turret and above this will be two pods of HYDRA-70 (2.75 in) rockets, each with seven rockets in the ready to launch position. The rockets can be fitted with a wide range of warheads.

Cadillac Gage will provide the electric turret controls with turret traverse a full 360° and weapon elevation from -8 to +65°.

The M252 25 mm Chain Gun is already in service with the US Marine Corps and is installed on LAV-25 (8 × 8) vehicles.

Mounted on the turret rear is the fire control system which includes a primary sight with two fields of view, FLIR and TV, multi-mode auto-tracker, eye safe laser rangefinder and two video displays. Backup sights will also be fitted.

The four round Stinger launcher, 25 mm Chain Gun and two pods of HYDRA rockets will all be mounted on a common rotor. Total ammunition supply will consist of 12 Stinger missiles, 990 rounds of 25 mm, 14 HYDRA rockets and 16 smoke grenades.

The FLIR magnification is ×8 and ×2.67 while the day TV is ×12 and ×4. In addition there are two backup sights boresighted to the weapons. Sensors include wind, pressure and temperature. The vehicle is also fitted with a land navigation system. Total weight of the LAV turret is projected to be 2840 kg complete with ammunition and two man crew.

General Electric LAV AD

The General Electric system is based on the company's private venture Blazer two man power operated turret covered in the previous entry and will be armed with the GA-12/U 25 mm Gatling Gun, four Stinger surface-to-air missiles and HYDRA-70 rockets. The 25 mm GAU-12/U is already used by the Marine Corps McDonnell Douglas AV-8B ground attack aircraft.

This will be armed with a 25 mm GAU-12 Gatling cannon, Stinger surface-to-air missiles and HYDRA-70 (2.75 in) rockets.

In addition to the four missiles in the ready to launch position, each version carries a further eight missiles in reserve which are loaded manually. A standard Stinger gripstock is also carried so that missiles can be deployed away from the vehicle if required by the tactical situation. Each version will also have a 7.62 mm machine gun for local protection and two banks of four electrically operated smoke dischargers.

Combat weight of the LAV AD, complete with crew and ammunition is estimated to be 13 154 kg. Turret traverse is powered through a full 360° with powered weapon elevation from -8° to +65°. It will have a fire on the move capability with sensors including temperature, pressure, wind and vehicle tilt.

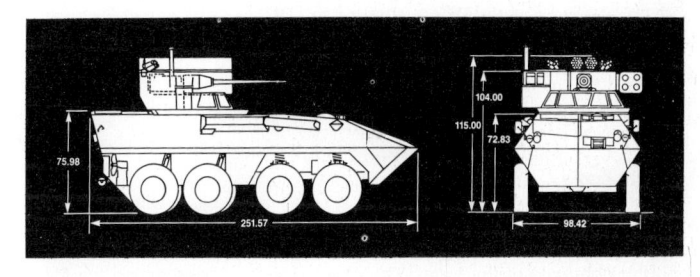

Side drawing of FMC Corporation's air defence version of Light Armored Vehicle (not to 1/76th scale)

Mock-up of the Light Armored Vehicle/Air Defense turret currently under development for US Marine Corps by General Electric

Scale model of FMC Corporation's air defence version of Light Armored Vehicle showing two pods of HYDRA-70 rockets mounted above 25 mm cannon (Christopher F Foss)

SELF-PROPELLED AA GUNS / USA

Status: Prototypes under construction for US Marine Corps trials.

Manufacturers: FMC Corporation, Land Systems Division, 1105 Coleman Avenue, San Jose, California 95108, USA.
Telephone: (408) 289 3960
Telex: 34 6462
General Electric Company, Armament Systems Department, Lakeside Avenue, Burlington, Vermont 05401-4985, USA.
Telephone: (802) 657 6000
Telex: (510) 299 0028

M163 20 mm Vulcan Self-propelled Anti-aircraft Gun System

Development

Development of the Vulcan air defence system began under the direction of the United States Army Weapons Command at Rock Island Arsenal, Illinois, in 1964. Two versions of the Vulcan were subsequently developed, a self-propelled model called the M163 (development designation XM163) and a towed model called the M167 (development designation XM167). Prime contractor for both models is the Armament Systems Department of the General Electric Company of Burlington, Vermont.

After trials carried out by the United States Army Air Defense Board at Fort Bliss, Texas, and at Aberdeen Proving Ground, Maryland, in 1965, the system was accepted for service in that year as the replacement for the twin 40 mm M42 self-propelled anti-aircraft gun. First production M163s were delivered to the United States Army in August 1968 and final deliveries were made in 1970. Since then the system has been placed back in production for export during 1975-79 and briefly again in 1982 before finally closing down. Israel used the system during the 1982 invasion of Lebanon when it destroyed several Syrian aircraft, including one Sukhoi Su-7 fighter-bomber and several Gazelle ATGW helicopters. The Israelis have also developed the M163 for use in the ground defence role in support of the Infantry.

The M163 is deployed with the United States Army in composite battalions with the Chaparral low altitude surface-to-air missile system. This battalion has 24 Chaparral systems (two batteries each with 12 launchers) and 24 M163s (two batteries with 12 each). Early warning for the M163 batteries is provided by the Sanders Associates Forward Area Alerting Radar model AN/MPQ-49. By early 1987 a total of 671 M163 systems had been built, of which 601 were for the US Army and 70 for export. However, a considerable number of US Army vehicles have been diverted to foreign users since a total of 292 vehicles (including the 70 export) have been sold under the FMS programme. This leaves 389 in US Army service which is close to the 1981 inventory total of 379 M163A1s.

Description

The M163 basically consists of an M113A1 APC fitted with a one-man electrically-driven turret which has an M61A1 Vulcan cannon, Navy Mk 20 Mod 0 gyro lead-computing sight and an EMTECH range-only radar mounted on the right side of the turret. The chassis, which is designated the M741, differs from the M113A1's in minor details only, including the provision of a suspension lock-out system to provide a more stable firing platform when the weapon is being fired, the installation of buoyant pods on either side of the hull and a buoyant trim vane at the front of the hull to improve its amphibious characteristics, and an additional circular hatch cover in the hull roof on the right side. The 20 mm six-barrelled M61A1 cannon is a development of the weapon originally developed for aircraft such as the Lockheed F-104 Starfighter and has two rates of fire; 1000 and 3000 rds/min. The original version fired up to 6000 rds/min. The 1000 rds/min rate is normally used in the ground role and the 3000 rds/min rate in anti-aircraft defence. Maximum effective anti-aircraft range is 1600 m, maximum ground range 3000 m and maximum indirect fire range 4500 m. The kill probability per engagement of the basic system is quoted as 0.35 against targets with velocities between 0 and 450 knots.

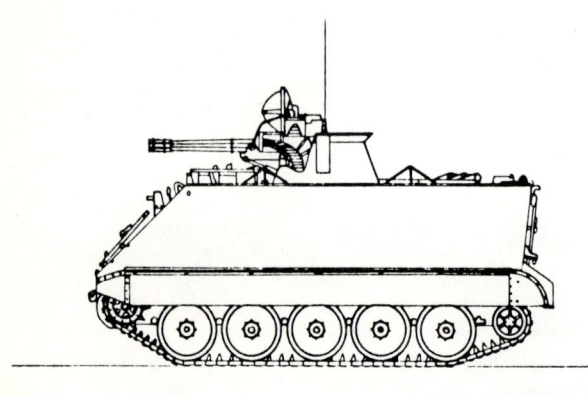

The weapon has an elevation of +80°, depression of -5° and 360° turret traverse. The gunner can select either 10-, 30-, 60- or 100-round bursts. The dispersion pattern can be increased by fitting a special muzzle adaptor, which causes the pattern to be spread, resulting in an increased hit probability. The linkless ammunition feed system in the M163 carries 1100 rounds ready to fire and an additional 1000 rounds in reserve inside the hull. Rows of ammunition are held in the feed drum in lateral tracks. A helix mounted in the centre of the drum moves ammunition along the tracks to the exit-port of the drum. The ammunition is carried from the feed drum to the gun feeder through conveyor chuting. The turret drive is controlled by solid-state, rate servo-amplifiers, one for elevation and two for azimuth. These servo-amplifiers are interchangeable in function, as are the drive motors they control. Power for the system is provided by three 24-volt nickel-cadmium batteries, two of which drive the Vulcan cannon and the third the drives of the turret. The batteries are charged either by the vehicle generator or an APU. Fire control for the system consists of a gyro lead-computing gunsight, a sight current generator and an EMTECH AN/VPS-2 fully coherent I-band pulse Doppler range-only radar that can track targets at up to 5000 m distance. The gunner visually acquires and tracks the target with the gyro lead-computing gunsight. The antenna axis of the radar is servoed to the optical line-of-sight. The radar supplies target range and range-rate data to the sight generator. With range, range-rate, and angular tracking of the optical line-of-sight (measured by a freely gimballed gyro), the sight automatically computes the future target position and adds the required super-elevation to hit the target. The lead angle is equal to the angular rate of the target multiplied by the time of flight of the projectile to the future target position. Turret fire control is a disturbed line-of-sight system. The sight case and gun bore are physically fixed in alignment. The sight graticule, which defines the optical line-of-sight, is positioned by the gyro and is displaced from the gun bore as the gunner tracks the target, thereby establishing the proper lead angle. The amount of optical line-of-sight displacement is dependent on the range and range rate inputs to the sight. The required tracking time to establish the lead angle is about one second. A green light appears in the sight optics signalling that the radar has acquired the target and that the target is within the effective range of the turret system. In the manual mode the gunner must estimate target range and speed and set the estimates on indicator dials on the control panel. The gyro lead-computing gunsight then computes the lead angle based on these estimates.

The 20 mm M61A1 cannon can fire the following types of fixed ammunition:
M53 (APT) with the projectile weighing 0.1 kg and a muzzle velocity of 1030 m/s
M54 (HPT) with the projectile weighing 0.127 kg
M55A2 (TP) with the projectile weighing 0.098 kg and a muzzle velocity of 1030 m/s

M163 Vulcan self-propelled anti-aircraft gun

M163A1 Vulcan self-propelled air defence system fitted with Lockheed Electronics Company Product Improved Vulcan Air Defense System (PIVADS)

USA / SELF-PROPELLED AA GUNS

US Army M163A1 20 mm self-propelled anti-aircraft gun system in West Germany (Pierre Touzin)

M56A3 (HEI) with the projectile weighing 0.103 kg and a muzzle velocity of 1030 m/s
M220 (TPT) with the projectile weighing 0.097 kg and a muzzle velocity of 1030 m/s
M242 (HEIT) with the projectile weighing 0.094 kg and a muzzle velocity of 1030 m/s.

Variants

Stinger in M163A1

In 1988 it was stated that a Stinger gunner would be the fourth member of Vulcan SPAAG crew replacing the crew member who had observer duties. A total of two Stinger SAMs will be carried inside the vehicle.

Product Improved Vulcan Air Defense System (PIVADS)

General Electric has modified the fire control system of the current Vulcan Air Defense System family and incorporated the ability to fire a new Mk 149 APDS round which increases the effective range of the system to 2600 metres. The fire control improvements include replacing the disturbed line of sight currently used with a director sight to give a rate-aided tracking capability and linking a digital fire control computer to the range-only radar for more accurate lead and superelevation commands to the cannon. The net result of the programme is to increase effectiveness while greatly simplifying the operation. The PIVADS programme is available in the form of modification kits for both the towed and self-propelled Vulcan air defence systems. In September 1982 the US Army awarded Lockheed Electronics a contract for 285 kits for both the towed and self-propelled versions of the 20 mm Vulcan air defence systems with first deliveries made in June 1984. These are being installed on towed and self-propelled Vulcan air defence systems with final deliveries in 1988.

US Army 20 mm M163A1 Vulcan air defence system crossing ribbon bridge in West Germany (US Army)

Improved Fire Control System for Vulcan Air Defense System

The Lockheed Electronics Company has developed an improved fire control system for the Vulcan Air Defense System which includes a new optical sight, a digital processor, and harmonic drives for both azimuth and elevation. A new director type optical sight is provided as the angle tracking device which permits rapid acquisition and accurate tracking when turret disturbances are present. The sight contains integrated rate gyros for azimuth and elevation tracking, in conjunction with proportional hand-grip controls. A new digital processor replaces the existing analogue computer to improve weapon tracking and operational capabilities. The system also includes built-in test equipment and permits multiple ballistics selection via the operator control panel. System response and pointing accuracies are also improved with the new Lockheed Electronics system. Harmonic drives replace the older azimuth and elevation gear trains to improve stiffness, backlash and power consumption characteristics. This version has yet to enter production.

SPECIFICATIONS

CREW	4
COMBAT WEIGHT	12 310 kg
POWER-TO-WEIGHT RATIO	17.46 bhp/tonne
GROUND PRESSURE	0.61 kg/cm^2
LENGTH	4.86 m
WIDTH	
overall	2.85 m
reduced	2.54 m
HEIGHT	
including turret	2.736 m
to top of driver's hatch periscope	2.07 m
to hull top	1.83 m
GROUND CLEARANCE	0.406 m
TRACK	2.159 m
TRACK WIDTH	381 mm
LENGTH OF TRACK ON GROUND	2.667 m
MAX SPEED	
road	67.59 km/h
road, on 10% gradient	18.7 km/h
water	5.6 km/h
FUEL CAPACITY	360 litres
MAX RANGE	483 km
FORDING	amphibious
GRADIENT	60%
SIDE SLOPE	30%
VERTICAL OBSTACLE	0.61 m
TRENCH	1.68 m
ENGINE	Detroit Diesel model 6V-53 6-cylinder water-cooled diesel developing 215 bhp at 2800 rpm
TRANSMISSION	Allison TX-100 consisting of 3-speed gearbox and 2-stage torque converter giving 6 forward and 2 reverse gears
SUSPENSION	torsion bar
ELECTRICAL SYSTEM	24 V
ARMAMENT (main)	1 × 6-barrel 20 mm cannon
SMOKE-LAYING EQUIPMENT	none
AMMUNITION	2100
GUN CONTROL EQUIPMENT	
turret power control	electric/manual
by commander	no
by gunner	yes
max rate power traverse	60°/s
max rate power elevation	45°/s
gun elevation/depression	+80°/-5°
turret traverse	360°
ARMOUR	12-38 mm

SELF-PROPELLED AA GUNS / USA

Status: Production complete. In service with the following countries:

Country	Quantity	User	Comment
Israel	46	air force	delivered in 1970s
Jordan	100	army	delivered 1976 to 1978
Morocco	60	army	
Portugal	10	army	
Saudi Arabia	60 to 104	army	ordered may include 20 turrets on Commando V-150 (4 × 4) chassis used by National Guard
Sudan	8	army	delivered 1982
Thailand	24	army	
USA	360	army	some being upgraded to PIVADS
Yemen, North	20	army	

Manufacturer: General Electric Company, Armament Systems Department, Lakeside Avenue, Burlington, Vermont 05401-4985, USA.
Telephone: (802) 657 6000
Telex: (510) 299 0028
(Carrier provided by FMC Corporation and radar by Lockheed Electronics.)

Vulcan-Commando 20 mm Self-propelled Air Defense System

Development
The Vulcan-Commando air defence system is an outgrowth of a requirement generated by Saudi Arabia. The 20 mm Vulcan turret used is designed as a 'drop-in' installation, requiring only correct location of mounting holes in the vehicle hull, while remaining operationally independent of the vehicle. The basic Vulcan air defence system turret (without radar) can be used as an alternative installation. Future production systems would be based on the new Commando V-150 S (4 × 4) chassis.

Description
The Vulcan-Commando system uses the same turret, weapon and associated feed, power and radar equipment as the M163 Vulcan air defence system. The vehicle used is the Cadillac Gage Commando V-150 fitted with three hydraulic stabilising jacks controlled from inside the vehicle. The system has four operational modes: Radar, which is the most accurate of the three anti-aircraft engagement modes. The radar supplies continuous range and range rate information to the system's analogue computer so that computations for the gyro lead sight can be made. Manual, in which the gunner estimates the engagement range and target speed and then manually enters them on the control panel. External, in which a second person off-mount estimates the target's range and enters the data on a hand-held potentiometer connected to the fire control system by a cable. Ground, in which the gyro sight is not operated and the lead angle not computed. The sight is mechanically caged at zero lead angle and 7 mils of superelevation.

The vehicle has a crew of four; driver, gunner, commander and radio operator.

Vulcan-Commando in travelling configuration with outriggers raised and locked in position

Vulcan-Commando self-propelled anti-aircraft system with turret traversed to left and 20 mm cannon firing

SPECIFICATIONS
CREW	4
CONFIGURATION	4 × 4
COMBAT WEIGHT	10 206 kg
LENGTH	5.689 m
WIDTH	2.26 m
HEIGHT (to hull top)	1.981 m
WHEELBASE	2.667 m
MAX SPEED	
road	88.54 km/h
water	4.828 km/h
FORDING	amphibious
GRADIENT	60%
SIDE SLOPE	30%
VERTICAL OBSTACLE	0.914 m
TURNING RADIUS	8.382 m
ENGINE	V-8 diesel developing 202 bhp at 3300 rpm
TRANSMISSION	automatic
ARMAMENT	1 × 6-barrel 20 mm cannon
AMMUNITION	1300

Status: Production as required. A total of 20 systems were delivered to the Saudi Arabian National Guard.

Manufacturer: General Electric Company, Armament Systems Department, Lakeside Avenue, Burlington, Vermont 05401-4985, USA.
Telephone: (802) 657 6000
Telex: (510) 299 0028
(Chassis provided by Cadillac Gage Textron, Warren, Michigan).

USA / **SELF-PROPELLED AA GUNS** 103

High Mobility 20 mm Vulcan Wheeled Carrier (VWC) Anti-aircraft Gun System

Development/Description
Privately developed by the Standard Manufacturing Company Inc, the High Mobility 20 mm Vulcan Wheeled Carrier (VWC) Anti-aircraft Gun System uses a modified M167A1 20 mm Vulcan towed system on the company's trailing-arm-drive (TAD) eight-wheeled high-speed all-terrain hydrostatically driven carrier that can attain speeds of up to 72 km/h and is capable of pivot steering, independent raising and lowering of wheels, silhouette reduction and central tyre inflation. The VWC carries the turret, fire control system and mount of the M167A1 with the added bonus of more ammunition. A total of 550 rounds is carried in the ready use magazine with another 2000 rounds on the vehicle as a reserve. The US Army's 9th Infantry Division successfully tested a prototype in 1983-84 and the company provided a further four for platoon-sized trials during 1985 with the Division.

Status: Development complete. Ready for production. Has been evaluated by US Army.

Manufacturer: Standard Manufacturing Company Inc, 4012 W Illinois Ave, PO Box 210300, Dallas, Texas 75211, USA.
Telephone: (214) 337 8911
Telex: 73326

High Mobility 20 mm Vulcan Wheeled carrier (VWC) anti-aircraft gun system during US Army trials

High Value Site Defense System

Development
The Pomona Division of General Dynamics has proposed development of the US Navy Phalanx 20 mm Close In Weapon System (CIWS) to provide High Value Site Defense (HVSD) of the Patriot surface-to-air missile system and other high value targets on the battlefield.

It has proposed to mount the HVSD system on a portable platform suitable for attachment to common use flat bed vehicles and adaptable to aircraft transportation.

The system would have four stabilisers lowered to the ground before firing so as to provide a more stable firing platform.

Since 1979, General Dynamics' Pomona Division has built well over 500 Phalanx CIWS for installation on a wide range of surface warships ranging from frigates to battleships, with large numbers being exported.

The HVSD would be used to knock out anti-radiation missiles aimed at High Value Sites, as well as cruise missiles, glide bombs and low flying aircraft, using its 20 mm cannon.

Each HVSD would be a complete self-contained unit with its own power supply and would automatically carry out search, target threat evaluation, tracking and firing.

Description
The system consists of a radar-servo unit, 20 mm gun assembly, mount and train drive platform, barbette equipment, electronics enclosure and a pair of control panels.

The fire control system, supported by a high-speed digital computer, carries out target search, detection and declaration, target acquisition, target track and measurement of range, velocity and angle, projectile tracking and measurement of projectile velocity and angle.

Situated on the top of the gun mount is the pulse Doppler radar which shares a single transmitter to carry out target search, acquisition, tracking and electronic spotting functions. Phalanx uses the closed loop electronic spotting technique. Aim correction is based on the ability to track both an incoming target and the outgoing projectile and eliminate any error as they near one another. The 20 mm Gatling gun, built by General Electric, has a cyclic rate of fire of 3000 rds/min.

When firing, the ammunition feed system removes rounds from the front of the magazine drum which is located under the gun and feeds them through the chute conveyor system to the gun breech bolt assembly.

After each round is fired, the empty cartridge case is extracted from the breech and conveyed back to the rear of the magazine.

The APDS round has a heavy metal penetrator with a high mass-to-diameter ratio to penetrate the incoming target. An improved version of Navy Phalanx has been authorised designated Mk 16 Mod 1. This has a number of significant improvements including increased search area coverage and detection, increased ammunition magazine capacity and dual gunfire rate for maximum engagement flexibility.

Status: Private venture proposal.

Manufacturer: General Dynamics, Pomona Division, PO Box 2507, Pomona, California 91769-2507, USA.
Telephone: (714) 868-4400

Artist's impression of General Dynamics, Pomona Division, HVSD system in self-propelled configuration protecting an air base against anti-radiation missiles

SELF-PROPELLED AA GUNS / Yugoslavia

YUGOSLAVIA

BOV-3 Triple 20 mm Self-propelled Anti-aircraft Gun System

Development
The BOV-3 self-propelled anti-aircraft gun system is part of an indigenously-designed family of wheeled armoured vehicles and was shown officially for the first time at the 1984 Cairo Defence Exhibition.

Description
The hull of the BOV-3 is of all-welded steel construction. The driver sits at the front left and the commander to his right, both with a rear-opening single piece hatch cover. The driver has three periscopes for forward observation and a single vision block and firing port in the left side of the hull; the commander has a single forward-facing periscope. There is a crew entry hatch in the left side of the hull and a single roof hatch to the rear of the driver. The other two crew members, the gunner and loader, normally sit inside the vehicle when not manning the anti-aircraft weapons.

The engine compartment is at the rear of the hull with air-inlet and air-outlet louvres on the top and an engine access door at the rear. It also contains the air filters, heating device, fuel piping and control mechanism. The vehicle is powered by a West German Deutz type F 6L 413 F six-cylinder diesel developing 148 hp at 2650 rpm. This is coupled to a manual gearbox with five forward and one reverse gears and a two-speed transfer case. Two hatches in the roof and the rear access door allow access for servicing of the engine and other systems. Steering is power assisted to reduce driver fatigue and a central tyre-pressure system is fitted as standard, pressure can be adjusted from 0.7 to 3.5 bars to suit the ground being crossed. The main brakes are air-hydraulic dual circuit with a hand-operated parking brake. Suspension consists of leaf type springs with telescopic shock absorbers with 1300 - 18 PR10 cross-country tyres fitted as standard. The differential locks are controlled electro-pneumatically.

Standard equipment includes a Jugo-Webasto 7.5 kW heater, day and infra-red night vision equipment, intercom and radios.

Mounted in the centre of the roof is the open-topped turret with an external turret basket at the rear. Access to the turret is only from outside of the vehicle with extension pieces provided on the hull top either side of the turret for reloading.

The turret is based on the standard towed 20/3 mm gun M55 A4 B1 which has been in service with the Yugoslavian Army for some years. The turret has full 360° hydraulic traverse at a speed of 80°/s with an acceleration of 120°/s². Weapon elevation is from -4.5° to +83° at 50° with an acceleration of 60°/s².

Each of the three 20 mm barrels has a drum-type magazine holding 60 rounds of ammunition with an external indicator showing how many rounds are available (10, 30, 40, 50, 60). The weapons have a cyclic rate of fire of 750 rds/barrel/min and the gunner, seated at the turret rear, can select either single shots, bursts of 10 rounds, bursts of 10 to 20 rounds or sustained fire. A total of 1500 rounds of ammunition is carried, which, apart from the three ready use drums in the turret, is stowed internally on special racks for quick access. Ammunition types that can be fired include:-

BOV-3 20 mm self-propelled anti-aircraft gun system with turret traversed to front

BOV-3 20 mm self-propelled anti-aircraft gun system showing climbing capability

TYPE	HEI-T	HE-T	HEI	HE	API	API-T	AP-T
DESIGNATION	M57	M57	M57	M57	M60	M60	M60
WEIGHT OF PROJECTILE	137 g	137 g	132 g	132 g	142 g	142 g	142 g
TYPE OF BURSTING CHARGE	TNT or RDX/Alum	TNT or RDX/Alum	TNT o Inc	TNT or RDX/Alum	nil	nil	nil
TOTAL WEIGHT OF ROUND	261 g	261 g	257 g	257 g	274 g	274 g	274 g
MUZZLE VELOCITY	850 m/s	850 m/s	850 m/s	850 m/s	840 m/s	840 m/s	840 m/s

Additional rounds include TP-T (M57), TP (M57), Blank (M77) and drill.

All of the above have brass cartridge cases 110 mm long with propellant being NC powder.

Maximum anti-aircraft engagement altitude is quoted as 2000 m although effective anti-aircraft range is between 1000 and 1500 m. The weapons can also be used in the direct fire support role against ground targets when the maximum range is about 2000 m.

The triple 20 mm cannon are aimed via a J-171 sight mounted to the rear of the gun shield. The gunner has a joystick to control elevation and traverse and a foot pedal for firing the cannon. The BOV-3 is a clear weather system only with no provision for external fire control, although general warning of targets approaching could be given over the radio net.

Variants
The BOV-3 20 mm self-propelled anti-aircraft gun system is a member of the BOV 4 × 4 series of wheeled light armoured vehicles. These include the BOV-1 anti-tank vehicle armed with the Sagger ATGW and the BOV-M armoured personnel carrier. In 1985 the BOV-30 self-propelled anti-aircraft gun system was revealed. This uses the chassis of the BOV-3 but with a smaller, upright turret with the gunner seated in a raised cupola at the rear and is armed with two externally-mounted 30 mm cannon. The turret has a rate of fire of 1200 rds/min. Three grenade launchers are attached to each side of the turret for smoke rounds.

Yugoslavia / SELF-PROPELLED AA GUNS

Status: In production. In service with the Yugoslavian Army.

Manufacturer: Enquiries to Federal Directorate of Supply and Procurement, PO Box 308, 9 Nemanjina Street, Belgrade, Yugoslavia.
Telephone: 621 522
Telex: 11360

BOV-30 twin 30 mm self-propelled anti-aircraft gun in travelling configuration with hatches open

SPECIFICATIONS

CREW	4
CONFIGURATION	4 × 4
COMBAT WEIGHT	9400 kg
POWER-TO-WEIGHT RATIO	15.74 hp/tonne
LENGTH	5.791 m
WIDTH	2.525 m
HEIGHT	3.21 m
GROUND CLEARANCE	0.325 m
TRACK	1.9 m
WHEELBASE	2.75 m
MAX ROAD SPEED	93.4 km/h
RANGE	500 km
FORDING	1.1 m
GRADIENT	55%
SIDE SLOPE	30%
VERTICAL OBSTACLE	0.54 m
TRENCH	0.64 m
TURNING RADIUS	7.75 m
ENGINE	Deutz type F 6L 413 F 6-cylinder diesel developing 148 hp at 2650 rpm
TRANSMISSION	manual, 5 forward and 1 reverse gears
SUSPENSION	leaf springs and hydraulic shock absorbers
ELECTRICAL SYSTEM	24 V
BATTERIES	2 × 12 V, 143 Ah
ARMAMENT	3 × 20 mm cannon
TURRET TRAVERSE	360°, powered/manual
ELEVATION/DEPRESSION	+83°/−4.5°
AMMUNITION	1500 × 20 mm
SMOKE DISCHARGERS	yes

Self-Propelled Surface-to-Air Missiles

FRANCE

Thomson-CSF Mygale Air Defence System

Development/Description
The Mygale low level short-range co-ordinated air defence system has been developed by the Electronic Systems Division of Thomson-CSF and consists of two key components. The first of these is the Mygale warning and fire control station (C^2) normally installed on a Panhard VBL (4 × 4) light armoured vehicle in production for the French Army and export market. This carries out the main functions of air space watch and surveillance using its pulse Doppler radar system while the vehicle is stationary or travelling, IFF, threat assessment, firing stations co-ordination, target designation for the Aspic firing stations and integration into tactical command stations (C^2 and C^3).

The solid state 2D radar is mounted on a hydraulic arm which is raised above the vehicle when stationary; it has a range of 18 km against aircraft and 7.5 km against hovering helicopters. Data processing includes IFF, automatic threat assessment and a simultaneous target designation capability. The maximum distance betwen the Mygale warning and fire control station and the Aspic firing station is 3 to 5 km.

The Aspic firing station can be mounted on a variety of chassis including the VBL armoured car or a 4 × 4 light vehicle such as the Peugeot P4. Turret traverse is 360° with the operator positioned up to 30 m away from the vehicle with his remote firing console. The other crew member has a DALDO helmet pointing system. As an option, an IFF, FLIR and laser rangefinder can be incorporated into the system.

Aspic receives its target information from Mygale which controls up to eight gun or missile systems or a combination of these. The latter include Stinger, Mistral, RBS 70 and the Soviet SA-7.

Status: Production as required. In service with Gabon (one Mygale vehicle plus five Aspic/Mistral vehicles).

Manufacturer: Thomson-CSF, Division Systèmes Électroniques, 1 rue des Mathurins, BP 10, 92223 Bagneux Cedex, France.
Telephone: (1) 46 57 13 65
Telex: 204780 F

Peugeot P4 (4 × 4) light vehicle used as Aspic firing unit

Mygale warning and fire control station on Panhard VBL (4 × 4) light vehicle

Aspic firing unit on Panhard VBL (4 × 4) light vehicle

France / **SELF-PROPELLED SAMS** 107

ACMAT (4 × 4) cross-country truck fitted with Thomson-CSF Aspic firing unit

Shahine Low Altitude Surface-to-air Missile System

Development

In 1975 Thomson-CSF was awarded a contract from Saudi Arabia for the design, development and production of a mobile all-weather low level self-propelled anti-aircraft missile system called Shahine. The initial contract covered the supply of a battery comprising two acquisition units and four firing units. The second component of the system is the Air-Transportable Towed System (ATTS) which is the Shahine-S shelter version based on a three-axle trailer. Both can take either a Shahine firing unit or an acquisition unit since the installation rings are common to both.

The Electronic Systems Division of Thomson-CSF is the prime contractor for the complete system including the radars and electronics and Engins Matra is responsible for the missile.

Description

In concept Shahine is based on the AMX-30 MBT chassis which has improved cross-country mobility compared to the 4 × 4 vehicles used on the basic Crotale system. An added advantage is that Saudi Arabia already operates the AMX-30 MBT.

The 32 700 kg acquisition unit has a pulse Doppler E-band surveillance radar with an 18.5 km detection range and a digital receiver for the MTI function. The SN1050 automatic information processing and threat evaluation system allows up to 40 targets to be registered on the computer and 18 targets to be handled simultaneously. A TV system featuring a TV turret concentric with and independent of the radar turret provides ground monitoring of moving fire units and optical target reconnaissance.

The 38 800 kg firing unit comprises a monopulse J-band 17 km range fire control radar which can simultaneously track the target and, on a transponder basis, guide one or two missiles. This radar has a digital receiver and a circularly polarised antenna that tracks the missile and sends out the guidance commands. The missile is acquired during the initial part of the flight via an infra-red receiver sensitive to the wavelength of the booster's exhaust. A TV system integrated into the firing turret assumes the target tracking and missile tracking functions and assures a full back-up mode in case of jamming. The firing unit has six ready to launch missiles rather than four as with the basic Crotale system. Once the six missiles have been launched new missiles are brought up and loaded with the aid of a light crane.

The R460 missile used in the Shahine system is a development of the R440 Crotale weapon. It is 3.12 m long, has a diameter of 0.156 m and a wing span of 0.59 m. Total weight is 100 kg with a 15 kg focalised splinter warhead triggered by a contact or infra-red (IR) proximity fuze. The warhead's lethal radius is about 8 m.

Behind the missile nose cone, which contains the fuzing circuitry, is a fairing that houses the canard flight control fins and actuator mechanism. The next section accommodates the battery, autopilot, support instrumentation, warhead and weapon safety/arming units. Immediately behind this is the 4.5 second burn SNPE Lens double-stage extruded double-base solid propellant rocket motor that boosts the missile to its maximum speed of Mach 2.8.

Around the exhaust area are the guidance data link and transponder units, the roll control servomotor (for the ailerons mounted on the rear of the larger cruciform tail fins) and the wingtip mounted transponder transmitter and guidance data receiver antennas.

At ranges up to 6000 m, the missile can manoeuvre at up to 35 g which reduces at 10 000 m range to 15 g and at 14 000 m range to 2.5 g. Minimum and maximum engagement ranges for a target flying at 250 m/s at heights between 15 and 6800 m are 500 to 11 500 m. The maximum range for engagements against slower moving targets such as helicopters is the full 14 000 m.

The acquisition unit and firing units can manoeuvre and deploy as they are fitted with an automatic 500 to 4000 m range J-band data transmission and reciprocal location microwave system known as Inter-Vehicle Positioning and Data Link (IVPDL). Between acquisition units the maximum data link range is increased to 7000 m. The IVPDL also allows the complete Shahine system to deploy over a much larger area, and, coupled with the improved radar and missiles, makes it a much more efficient system. A data link can also be provided to connect the acquisition unit with a higher command, enabling the system to be integrated into an overall air defence system.

In March 1979 Thomson-CSF announced that prototypes of the Shahine system had begun the second phase of their trials late in 1978 at the

Shahine-S acquisition unit deployed in field with APU on right and operator's cabin on left

Shahine-S firing unit with six missiles in ready to launch position and four stabilisers lowered to ground

108 SELF-PROPELLED SAMS / France

Shahine firing unit (left) compared with the acquisition unit (right) both of which are based on an AMX-30 MBT chassis

Integral turret/electronics package of the Shahine firing unit removed from vehicle

Renault TRM 10 000 (6 × 6) cross-country truck used as missile resupply vehicle for Saudi Arabian Shahine air defence systems. Hydraulic crane at rear can lift new pack of three missiles

Centre d'Essais des Landes in south-west France. These trials, which were completed late in 1979, had been preceded by the initial test phase of the acquisition unit. System integration of the tracked vehicles and the shelter systems also took place in 1979. First production Shahine systems were delivered to Saudi Arabia in January 1980 with final deliveries of that order made in 1982.

Saudi Arabia has also ordered the AMX-30 twin 30 mm DCA self-propelled anti-aircraft gun system to operate with the Shahine system. Details of the AMX-30 DCA are given earlier in the *Self-propelled anti-aircraft guns* section of this book.

In January 1984, Saudi Arabia announced the 'Al Thakeb' arms contract with France. This mainly involves the supply of a new Shahine 2 improved version mounted on the AMX-30 chassis and shelters. Twelve Shahine batteries have been purchased in addition to the four already used. These in turn will be brought up to the new system's standard using retrofit kits. The main difference is an increase in the acquisition radar's range to 19.6 km and altitude capability to 6000 m, the incorporation of the Shahine Data Link (SHDL) to allow the Shahine batteries to accept data from a Litton TSQ-73 command and control centre and the option of an electromagnetic proximity fuze on the missile warhead to replace the current IR fuze circuitry.

Variant
To meet the requirements of the US Army for a FAADS-LOS-RH system, Thomson-CSF teamed with LTV of the USA and offered the Liberty, a growth of the current Shahine air defence system.

An interim Liberty system was one of the four systems evaluated by the US Army in the Autumn of 1987, but the competition was won by the Martin Marietta/Oerlikon-Bührle ADATS system.

The interim system tested in the USA was based on the standard AMX-30 chassis but had it entered production it would have been based on the General Dynamics, Land Systems Division, M1A1 MBT tank chassis. This would have been fitted with a new powered turret armed with twin 25 mm McDonnell Douglas Helicopters 25 mm Chain Guns and two pods each of six LTV developed VT-1 missiles in the ready to launch position and a new optronic guidance system with both FLIR and TV sensors.

Although Liberty lost the US Army FAADS-LOS-FH competition, its development continued as a private venture and the first VT-1 missiles were test fired in the USA early in 1988. Subsequently, in July 1988, Finland selected the VT-1 system mounted on Sisu XA-180 (6 × 6) armoured vehicles to meet a requirement for a mobile air defence weapon (see International part of this section for details).

Status: Shahine is in production and in service with the Saudi Arabian Army which has placed orders for a total of 4000 missiles, 16 Shahine acquisition and 40 firing units on the AMX-30 tracked chassis, 16 acquisition, and 32 firing units in shelter-mounted configuration.

Manufacturers: Thomson-CSF, Division Systèmes Électroniques, 1 rue des Mathurins, BP 10, 92223 Bagneux Cedex, France.
Telephone: (1) 46 57 13 65
Telex: 204780 F

MATRA, 37 avenue Louis Breguet, BP 1, 78146 Vélizy-Villacoublay, France.
Telephone: (1) 39 46 96 00
Telex: 968007 F

France / **SELF-PROPELLED SAMS** 109

Firing unit of Shahine with missile leaving upper container

Shelter-mounted Shahine-S acquisition unit with antenna lowered being loaded into a Hercules C-130 transport aircraft

Crotale Low Altitude Surface-to-air Missile System

Development
Following the British Government's refusal to supply South Africa with surface-to-air missiles, in 1964 South Africa placed a development contract with the French company, Thomson-Houston (later Thomson-CSF) for a mobile, all-weather, low altitude surface-to-air missile system. The Electronic Systems Division of Thomson-CSF was prime contractor for the complete system including the radar and electronics, and Engins Matra was responsible for the missile.

The South African Government paid 85 per cent of the development costs of the system, which it calls the Cactus, and the remaining 15 per cent was paid by France. After trials the first of seven platoons was delivered to South Africa in 1971 with the final one delivered in 1973.

In February 1971 the French Air Force placed an order for one acquisition vehicle and two firing units which were delivered in 1972. After extensive trials with these units the French Air Force ordered the Crotale system for airfield defence and by late 1978, 20 batteries had been delivered.

Lebanon ordered Crotale in the late 1960s but the order was cancelled before the systems were delivered. In 1975 Saudi Arabia ordered a new version of the Crotale mounted on the chassis of the AMX-30 MBT, known as the Shahine, for which there is a separate entry as the system has a number of improvements over the standard Crotale. The Saudis also ordered the standard Crotale in late 1978 for their Air Force. The Crotale has also been adopted by the French, People's Republic of China and Saudi Arabian navies in various forms.

As produced at present Crotale is mounted on a P4R (4 × 4) vehicle, and can also be mounted on a tracked chassis for increased cross-country mobility, or shelter-mounted for use in static defence (the latter is known as the Crotale-S system). The first Crotale, produced in 1969, was called the 1000 series. This was followed by the 2000 series in 1973, the 3000 series in 1975, the 4000 series in 1983 and the 5000 series in 1985. Crotale 3000 fire and acquisition units are not ready for action as soon as they come to the halt but have to be connected together by cables at a maximum distance of 800 m apart. The 4000 series have the LIVH (Liaison InterVéhicule Hertzienne) radio link and mast which not only allows them to come into action faster but also to be up to 10 000 m apart to cover more area. The 5000 series have further improvements such as the possibility of mounting two MATRA SATCP missiles either side of two of the Crotale container-launcher canisters to help meet saturation air attacks.

It is known that by early 1987 a total of 182 launcher and 85 acquisition units had been sold to eight countries. In September 1988 it was revealed that a total of 6200 Crotale/Shahine missiles had been ordered by France and the export countries. Greece is also believed to have ordered the system.

Early in 1988 it was stated by a consortium of Aerospatiale, Matra and MBB that an advanced surface-to-air missile system was under development to replace Crotale and that this would have a Mach 4.0 hypervelocity operating speed, longer range and also incorporate increased hardening against countermeasures. The system is currently known as MISSAT (Munition Interoperable Sol/Surface-air Téléguide).

In November 1988, at the 2nd ASIANDEX exhibition in Beijing, the China Precision Machinery Import and Export Corporation (CPMIEC) revealed the FM-80 land mobile shelter-mounted surface-to-air missile system on two-axle trailers. Examination of available evidence has shown this system to be a direct copy of the Crotale-S in practically all details,

Shelter-mounted version of Crotale-S firing unit in travelling configuration

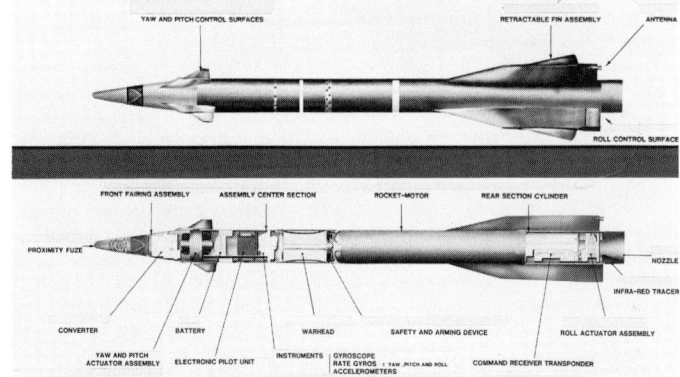

Main components of Crotale R440 missile

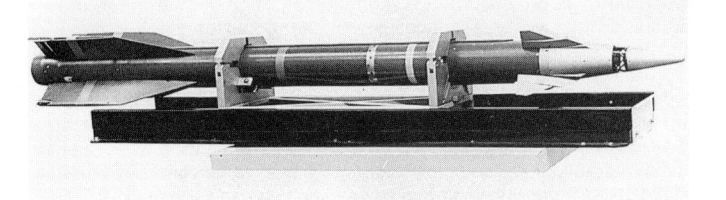

Crotale missile, which is made by MATRA, out of its transport/launch container

SELF-PROPELLED SAMS / France

Crotale Series 4000 PAR firing unit with three hydraulic jacks lowered to provide more stable launching platform, showing radio link system mast extended

bar a difference in the acquisition radar construction. Performance figures are also believed to be lower than those quoted for Crotale. The FM-80 is being procured by the Chinese Armed Forces as well as being offered for export.

Description
The basic Crotale has an all-weather capability and a typical platoon consists of one acquisition unit and two to three firing units with a battery having two platoons. All the operators, except Libya and Abu Dhabi (UAE), have one radar acquisition vehicle to two firing units. The two exceptions have one radar vehicle to three firing units. The system cannot operate on the move and takes less than five minutes to become operational once it has stopped. Once the target has been detected the missile can be launched within about 6.5 seconds. The system has been designed to combat targets flying at a speed of Mach 1.2 at an altitude of 50 to 3000 m and an equivalent radar area of 1 m^2 fluctuating. Data is transmitted from the acquisition unit to the firing units via a cable that allows operations up to 400 m (Crotale 3000 and later versions 800 m) away or via a radio link up to 50-5000 m away. Between the fire/acquisition units of the Crotale 4000 and later versions the maximum radio link range is increased to 10 000 m.

Both vehicles have an all-welded steel hull with the driver at the front, electronics and operators in the centre and the thermal motor at the rear. There is a door in the right side of the hull which opens to the rear. Energy is provided by the thermal motor and an alternator, driven by the thermal motor, produces power, the output of which is rectified and then fed to a series of DC motors which in turn drive each of the four road wheels by epicyclic reduction gears. Sufficient electric power is provided for all the vehicle's electrical systems including the electronics, air-conditioning system and the hydraulic circuit which operates the three levelling jacks, steering, suspension and brakes. Each road wheel station has a hydraulic and pneumatic suspension system designed by Messier. This acts as a pneumatic spring, suspension spring and shock absorber simultaneously. The position of each jack is controlled by a selector valve connected to a differential gear and the driver has a lever which enables him to select one of five positions.

The acquisition unit carries out target surveillance, identification and designation. Mounted on the top of the vehicle is a Thomson-CSF E-band Mirador IV pulse Doppler radar which rotates at 60 rpm and has a maximum detection range of 18.5 km against low level targets with speeds of between 35-440 m/s and altitudes limits of zero to 800 m, and 15 km against high level targets with the same speed range and altitude limits between 1800 and 4500 m. The system also has an IFF interrogator-decoder, a non-saturable extractor, real-time digital computer, display console and a digital data link for transmitting information to the firing units. The computer, which is the same as that installed in the firing unit, is used to generate accurate data for confirmation of threat evaluation. Thirty targets can be processed per antenna revolution with up to 12 targets simultaneously tracked by the system.

Once the target has been detected the computer triggers the IFF interrogator and the final threat information is displayed. The target is then allocated to one of the firing units and target designation data and operational orders are transmitted by the data link which also supplies information from the firing unit on operational status, for example, the number of missiles available.

The firing unit has a J-band monopulse 17 km range single target tracking radar mounted concentrically with the launcher turret, which carries four ready to launch missiles, two each side. The system also has an I-band 10° antenna beamwidth command transmitter, infra-red gathering system with a ±5° wide field of view (and in French Air Force systems a further narrow field of view mode for passive operations), an integrated TV tracking mode as a low elevation back-up, an optical designation tripod mounted binocular device (which is controlled manually by a handlebar arrangement and used primarily in a heavy ECM environment or whenever passive operation is required), digital computer, operating console and a digital data link. All the vehicles are fitted with an inter-vehicle link network to transmit data and orders by cable and for radio communication by a VHF radio-link.

The radar can track one target and guide two missiles simultaneously. The missiles, fired 2.5 seconds apart, are acquired immediately after launch by the 1.1° tracking beam of the radar with the help of infra-red detection and radar transponders during the gathering phase. There

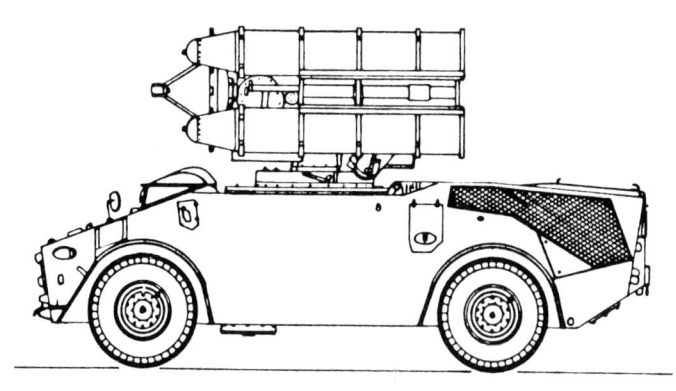

France / **SELF-PROPELLED SAMS** 111

Crotale P4R firing unit with four ready to launch missiles

Shelter-mounted Crotale-S air defence system being carried on rear of RVI (6 × 6) cross-country trucks with acquisition unit in foreground and firing unit in background. In both cases the upper part is in travelling configuration

Crotale P4R firing unit launching missile with launcher traversed to rear

Shelter-mounted Crotale-S acquisition unit showing dolly wheels raised

is also an optronic system. Guidance signals are transmitted to the missiles by radio.

No spare missiles are carried on the vehicle and fresh missiles are brought up by a truck and loaded with a light crane. A well-trained crew of three can load four missiles in about two minutes.

The missile is designated the R440 and weighs 84 kg, has an overall length of 2.89 m, span of 0.54 m and a diameter of 0.15 m. The missile complete with its transport/launch container weighs 100 kg. The HE directed burst fragmentation warhead in the centre of the missile weighs 15 kg, has a lethal radius of 8 m and is activated by an infra-red proximity fuze (the fuze is commanded to activate 350 m before interception) or contact fuze. The missile has a SNPE Lens III rocket motor with 25.45 kg of solid propellant powder. The missile reaches a maximum speed of 930 m/s in 2.8 seconds. Minimum and maximum guided ranges of the R440 are 800 to 10 000 m between altitude limits of 15 to 4000 m. Against slow moving targets the range can be increased to about 13 000 m. Minimum flight time is 2.2 seconds (the time required to arm warhead section) and the maximum 19 seconds (extending to 20 seconds plus for the slower targets).

In early 1987 Thomson-Brandt Armement (TBA) tested a new HE-fragmentation warhead for Crotale. This uses a time-space convergence technique to ensure that the warhead fragments arrive coincidentally within a 40 cm band at a distance of 5 to 8 m irrespective of the missile/target miss distance. The fragments are capable of penetrating up to 10 mm of steel plate within this range or severing the aluminium alloy body of a missile.

Variants

For the Canadian Armed Forces Low Level Air Defence (LLAD) competition Thomson-CSF teamed with the Diesel Division, General Motors of Canada Limited (which would have provided the licence-built 8 × 8 MOWAG Piranha chassis), General Electric Corporation of the USA and its subsidiary Canadian General Electric, and Litton Systems Canada to provide Piranha vehicles equipped with the Crotale SAM system and the General Electric four-barrel 30 mm GAU-13/A cannon. This system was not however shortlisted by Canada and in April 1986 the competition was won by Oerlikon-Bührle.

In September 1988 Thomson-CSF and Hollandse Signaalapparaten concluded an agreement for the development by the Dutch company of a VARIBEAM multibeam surveillance radar for the Crotale family of Thomson air defence missile systems, should the French weapon (believed to be in the VT-1 format) be chosen by the Royal Netherlands Air Force to meet its Low Level Air Defence system requirement.

SPECIFICATIONS

Type	Acquisition vehicle	Launch vehicle
CREW	2	2
COMBAT WEIGHT	12 620 kg	14 950 kg
LENGTH	6.22 m	6.22 m
WIDTH	2.72 m	2.72 m
HEIGHT		
(reduced for air transport)	3.05 m (max)	3.41 m (max)
GROUND CLEARANCE		
travelling	0.45 m	0.45 m
action	0.156–0.656 m	0.156–0.656 m

Type	Acquisition vehicle	Launch vehicle
WHEELBASE	3.6 m	3.6 m
MAX ROAD SPEED	70 km/h	70 km/h
MAX RANGE	600 km	600 km
FORDING	0.68 m	0.68 m
GRADIENT	40% at 2 km/h	40% at 2 km/h
	10% at 25 km/h	10% at 25 km/h
VERTICAL OBSTACLE	0.3 m	0.3 m
ARMOUR	3–5 mm	3–5 mm

SELF-PROPELLED SAMS / France

Status: In production. In service with the following countries:

Country	Quantity acquisition units	Quantity fire units	User
Chile	2	4	air force
Egypt	12	24	air defence command
France	24	48	air force
Greece	n/av	n/av	possible local production/assembly for army or air force
Libya	9	27	air defence command
Pakistan	12	24	air force
Saudi Arabia	16	48	air force
South Africa	7	14	air force
UAE	3	9	army

In late 1986 it is believed that Thomson-CSF signed a co-production agreement with Hellenic Arms Industry to produce the fire unit and missile under the local name Apollo. This is to be integrated into an air defence system with the Artemis 30 mm cannon.

Manufacturers: Thomson-CSF, Division Systèmes Électroniques, 1 rue des Mathurins, BP 10, 92223 Bagneux Cedex, France.
Telephone: (1) 46 57 13 65
Telex: 204780 F

MATRA, 37 avenue Louis Breguet, BP 1, 78146, Vélizy-Villacoublay, France.
Telephone: (1) 39 46 96 00
Telex: 968007 F

Crotale P4R series 4000 acquisition unit with radio link system mast raised and radar rotating

MATRA SANTAL Low Altitude Surface-to-air Self-propelled Missile System

Development/Description

The MATRA SATCP Mistral (Système Antiaérien à Très Courte Porté) portable surface-to-air missile system can also be integrated in a turret-mounted version on a variety of different light armoured vehicle chassis. After studies of the VAB and Panhard ERC (6 × 6) vehicles, the latter was accepted for service with the French Army.

The SANTAL (Système Antiaérien Autonomme Léger) turret has been designed by Hispano-Suiza and is fitted with three missiles either side of the turret in the ready to launch position with a further six missiles carried within the vehicle's hull. Mounted on the turret rear is a surveillance unit, the ESD RODEO 2 pulse Doppler radar (selected by the French Army).

The first prototype turret (PO1) was completed by Hispano-Suiza in May 1987 with the second prototype turret (PO2) following later the same year.

MATRA is the prime contractor for the complete system including the turret and following delivery from Hispano-Suiza integrate the TRT Castor thermal camera, RODEO 2 radar system, fire control system and two three-round launchers. A further six reserve missiles are carried, three either side of the hull above the two rear road wheels and ready for manual reloading.

The turret weighs 1800 kg complete with six missiles and its two-man crew consists of a radio operator/vehicle commander and a missile operator. A 7.62 mm machine gun can be installed on the roof of the turret for local protection and mounted on the forward part of the turret are four electrically operated smoke dischargers.

The system will have a crew of three: the driver, missile operator and radar operator/commander. The last two will sit in the turret with the radar console and fire control equipment.

The turret has full electric power traverse through 360° at 50°/s and the missiles in their launch boxes can be elevated from -10 to +60° at a speed of 50°/s; manual controls are provided for emergency use. The gunner has periscopes for all-round observation plus a Sopelem periscopic sight in the forward part of the turret roof with magnifications of ×1 and ×6 and a TRT Castor thermal camera mounted on the left-hand side of the turret. The turret has a single piece hatch cover that opens to the rear, two electrically operated smoke dischargers either side and can be fitted with a spotlight.

A typical target engagement takes place as follows. The search radar first detects the target and if it is confirmed as hostile the turret is traversed onto the target bearing. The gunner then searches for the target in elevation using the thermal camera or periscopic sight and once he finds the target he keeps tracking it. When the target is within range a missile is launched and no further action is required by the gunner.

The missile itself has a launch weight of 17 kg and is 1.8 m long and 90 mm in diameter. The 3 kg high explosive warhead contains a large number of tungsten balls and has a laser proximity fuze with a precise distance cut-off feature to reduce the chances of premature triggering by ground or sea clutter, and an impact fuze. The pyramid-shaped infra-red homing head can engage any aircraft or helicopter from any angle. Maximum speed of the missile is Mach 2.5 and the minimum and maximum ranges are less than 500 and 6000 m respectively with an engagement altitude against Mach 1.2 targets of up to 3050 m. Against a lightweight manoeuvring helicopter the maximum range is reduced to around 4000 m.

Panhard ERC (6 × 6) chassis fitted with mock-up of SANTAL turret

Close up of SANTAL turret installed on Panhard ERC Sagaie (6 × 6) armoured car chassis showing radar and six Mistral missiles in ready to launch position

Status: It is anticipated that the French Army will place its first production order for the SANTAL system in early 1989 with first turrets being delivered to MATRA for integration in 1990. First production systems for a total requirement of 90 vehicles are due to be delivered in 1990 for use by the 6th Light Armoured Division and 9th Marine Infantry Division of France's Rapid Intervention Force.

Manufacturer: Prime contractor for the missile and systems based on the SATCP MISTRAL missile is MATRA, 37 avenue Louis Breguet, BP 1, 78146 Vélizy-Villacoublay, France.
Telephone: (1) 39 46 96 00
Telex: 968007 F

GERMANY, WEST

High Energy Laser Air Defence Armoured Vehicle

Development/Description
The West German companies of Diehl and MBB Aerospace have joined together to develop a short-range High Energy Laser (HEL) system for use at the divisional level against low-flying, high performance battlefield aircraft, missiles and helicopters.

The project incorporates a 10.6 μm wavelength HEL generator, sights and passive tracking and target acquisition sensors on a tracked vehicle. As the laser used is a dynamic carbon dioxide gas type the vehicle will carry commercial hydrocarbon fuel and the nitrogenous oxidator needed to generate the energy required for the tactical laser air defence role. The vehicle will thus be able to be refuelled with these materials as well as with its own diesel fuel. Combustion of the two components forms the carbon dioxide which is then passed through a line of Laval nozzles which cause it to expand until it reaches supersonic speeds and is directed through an optical resonator to stimulate emission. The laser beam produced is directed upwards to a 1 m diameter focussing mirror on an extendable arm to be fired at a target. The hot fumes resulting from the gas formation are vented rearwards from the laser generator system.

The destructive effect of the HEL is achieved by focussing the beam onto a small spot to give very high energy density in a very short space of time that will cause a material to become successively heated, melted and vapourised. Combat range is expected to be around 8000 m.

Status: Study phase. Small scale version has been successfully tested in trials, West German MoD funding provided.

Main components of conceptual High Energy Laser system installed on tracked vehicle chassis

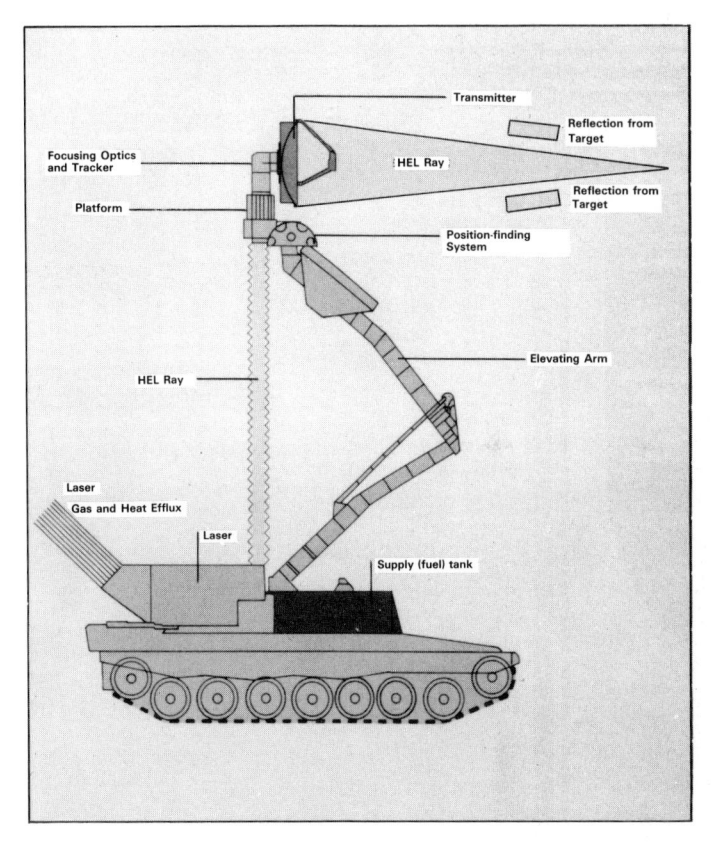

INTERNATIONAL

Euromissile Roland Low Altitude Surface-to-air Missile System

Development
In 1964 Aerospatiale of France and Messerschmitt-Bölkow-Blohm of West Germany began design work on a low altitude surface-to-air missile system which eventually became known as the Roland. Aerospatiale had overall responsibility for the clear-weather version, called the Roland 1, and MBB overall responsibility for the Roland 2 all-weather version. At a later stage a joint company called Euromissile was established to market this and other missiles produced by the two companies. Currently the all-weather version (formerly called Roland 2) is offered together with the latest variant known as Roland 3.

The French Army had a requirement for 200 firing units based on the AMX-30 MBT chassis, designated for this purpose the AMX-30R. Of these, 181 have been funded to date, with all 98 Roland 2 and 83 Roland 3 vehicles now delivered. They are organised to provide the 51st, 53rd, 57th and 58th Roland regiments at Corps level, each of four batteries with two troops of four fire units apiece, and the hybrid 54th Roland/AMX-13 DCA regiment with three Roland batteries each of two troops of four fire units and a battery of four troops with three 30 mm AMX-13 DCA guns apiece. The latter are due to be replaced in the near future by Matra SATCP Mistral low altitude SAM systems. Each Roland fire unit is accompanied in the field by a VAB (4 × 4) armoured personnel carrier mounting a 20 mm cannon in a GIAT T20-2 turret for ground and anti-helicopter overwatch defence within the close-range dead zone of the Roland's engagement envelope.

Brazilian Army Roland 2 system on Marder chassis (Ronaldo S Olive)

France plans to update its Roland fire units by the addition of an infra-red camera-based passive acquisition and tracking channel with a 15-20° field of view. Selection of a system is not expected until 1991 with the modified vehicles due to be fielded in 1995. The first Roland fire units were delivered to the French Army in December 1977.

The first Roland firing trials unit was delivered to the West German Army in 1978 as the replacement for the towed 40 mm L/70 Bofors guns.

SELF-PROPELLED SAMS / International

West German Army Roland 2 system on Marder chassis

In June 1981 the West German Army officially took delivery of the first of 140 Roland SAM systems. The first operational units were in fact delivered to the anti-aircraft school at Rendsburg in 1980. In July 1981 the 100th anti-aircraft rocket regiment of the West German Army began re-equipment, followed by the 200th regiment in July 1982 and the 300th in July 1983. Each regiment has one HQ battery, three firing batteries (each with 12 fire units) and one support battery. In the West German Army the system is based on the chassis of the Marder manufactured by Thyssen Henschel.

Brazil took delivery of four Roland 2 Marder fire units from West Germany together with 50 missiles.

In 1984 the Spanish Defence Ministry selected the Roland for its mobile battlefield low level air defence system. The Pts 29 000 million contract placed was for integration and co-production of the weapon system (nine Roland clear-weather and nine Roland all-weather fire units on the AMX-30 MBT chassis with 414 missiles) in Spain.

Six Spanish companies were chosen to participate in the programme. INISEL is responsible for the electronic components (including the surveillance radars), fire units and production of the complete missile rounds, Santa Barbara is responsible for building the AMX-30 chassis, producing most of the missile components and total system integration whilst CESELSA has designed and built an indigenous IFF subsystem to meet national requirements.

Industrial offsets set against the programme represent nearly 50 per cent of its total cost and include the manufacture of 100 fire units (including the 18 for the Spanish Army) and 2000 missile rounds exportable to third world countries.

To accommodate the system the Spanish Army has established the Roland Group within the auspices of the 71st Independent Air Defence Regiment. This comprises an HQ, an HQ battery, a services battery and two fire batteries each of two platoons with four fire units apiece.

Each platoon is expected to deploy two clear-weather and two all-weather systems. Of the remaining two vehicles one is to go for use in crew and maintainer training at the Artillery School while the other is to be used by the Artillery Missile Weapons Maintenance Centre.

In reality the Roland Group is an administrative device for centralising personnel training and equipment maintenance to reduce overall costs and optimise use of available resources.

The fire batteries will be attached operationally as de facto autonomous units to the 1st (Brunete) Armoured Division and the 2nd (Guzman el Bueno) Mechanised Division of the Immediate Intervention Forces.

The Roland Group is due to be fully operational by the end of 1990.

A shelter version of Roland has also been developed and Argentina used a single example during the Falklands War of 1982 to defend Port Stanley against airstrikes from the Royal Navy Task Force. The system fired 8 out of the 10 missiles it carried and is known only to have shot down one Sea Harrier and two 454 kg bombs. The system was captured intact. Iraq has used its Roland systems in combat against Iran.

A paired launcher ramp installation has been developed to meet saturation attacks by flights of 8 to 16 aircraft. Successfully tested in 1982 the new launcher unit for the Roland 3 has two additional ramps fitted outboard of the existing ones and can take Stinger, Mistral or other fire-and-forget missile systems if required. This raises the number of Roland missiles carried to 12 including four in the ready to fire position. The outboard ramps can be manually reloaded either in the field or more usually during a resupply operation. The new installation is designed for the truck and shelter versions, but it can be installed on an armoured vehicle chassis. Another recent development is the Roland system on the Leopard 1 MBT chassis, a proposal put forward by Euromissile, MaK, IBH and Blohm and Voss for countries with the Leopard 1 MBT.

In December 1983 the Roland shelter variant was selected to protect the NATO US and West German air bases in West Germany. A further

International / SELF-PROPELLED SAMS

Roland SAM being launched from a West German Army Roland 2 system based on the Marder chassis

Euromissile Roland FlaRakRad (8 × 8) in operating configuration with both tracking and surveillance antenna erected (Christopher F Foss)

Marder chassis is used to mount the Siemens 30 km range radar system, shown here in elevated configuration

option for 95 firing units has been taken up, 27 to defend three US bases, 60 for twelve German bases (six for each of six Tornado and four for each of six Phantom bases) and the remaining eight units for training. All 95 units will be manned by West German Air Force personnel. The agreement for the 27 Roland units for USAF bases was signed in June 1984. Besides this agreement, a further 20 Roland fire units are being procured by the West German Navy to protect three of its air bases. Delivery of the 115 units is to be in:

	1986	1987	1988	1989	1990
USAF	—	8	16	3	—
West German Air Force	3	2	14	33	16
West German Navy	—	—	6	8	6

During mid-1984 more discussions were held between West Germany and the USA to deploy an additional 30 Roland fire units manned by West German personnel from the early 1990s onwards at US and German main operating and co-located operating bases. If taken up these would follow the 115 units already mentioned on the production line. The first production Euromissile Roland FlaRakRad was officially handed over to the West German Air Force and Navy in September 1987, although three pre-production systems were delivered early in 1986 to enable training to commence.

The system is installed on the latest production MAN (8 × 8) high-mobility cross-country truck which has a number of minor improvements including a new three-man cab. The Luftwaffe Roland systems will be supported by a MAN (8 × 8) 10-tonne truck fitted with a hydraulic crane and carrying replacement missiles. Adoption of the Roland 3 missile is underway.

In February 1988 AEG delivered the first Roland air defence fire control and co-ordination command post (known as Flugagwehr Gefechtsstand Roland: FGR) to the Luftwaffe for use in protecting its own USAF Europe airbases. Installed as a three-man operated NBC-protected shelter unit on a MAN (8 × 8) 10-tonne truck a total of 21 are due to be delivered by the end of October 1990.

The 2D radar used is the TRM-L D-band frequency-agile model with integrated IFF system. This can distinguish between moving fixed-wing aircraft and helicopters as well as being capable of detecting anti-radiation missiles (ARMs) and hovering helicopters. Maximum elevation coverage is 60° within altitude limits of very low level to 6000 m. Detection range against a 1 m^2 target in high intensity ECM and clutter is said to be 46 km with a maximum radar range of 60 km claimed.

The antenna is mounted on a hydraulically raised 12 m high mast assembly. The whole system can be set up and made ready for operation within 15 minutes.

Two work stations are provided in the operator's section of the shelter, one for air situation processing and the other for operations control. The other two sections are the electronics bay and the protective systems bay with transmitter-cooling, air-conditioning and NBC units.

The FGR detects the targets (thus allowing the Roland fire units to shut down their surveillance radars so as to improve their own survivability against ARMs), processes the target information and displays it on an air situation display with an indication of the nature of the threat. The FGR commander decides on the most suitable air defence system, from up to 40 gun or missile systems he can control, to use for the engagement. The extensive on-board radio and cable-based communications suite is then used to inform the chosen weapon system of the target's parameters so that it can commence target acquisition and tracking. Data transfer to and from the weapons systems is carried out by radio or wire links whilst the voice links use either SEL SEM 80 and SEM 90 radios or field telephones. The system data renewal rate is two seconds.

For use with its Roland and Gepard anti-aircraft systems the West German army has the HFlaAFüSys low level air defence warning network. As part of this, Siemens AG produced the Radarpanzer TÜR (Tiefflieger-Überwachungs-Radar) vehicle based on a modified raised hull Marder ICV chassis with the turret replaced by a hydraulically operated foldable 'cherry-picker' arm topped with a rotating radar antenna for looking over tree lines and extending the radar horizon.

The vehicle has a crew of four and contains the display and electronics for the E-band 30 km range MPDR 3002-S 2D radar, the electronic units of the integrated DII 211 (formerly MSR400/9) IFF subsystem, two operator work stations, an air situation processing system for the vehicle commander, a comprehensive communications suite and all the ancillary power supplies, cooling systems and hydraulic equipment required for their operational use. There is also a vehicle navigation system to ensure accurate vehicle positioning data.

Trials of the production standard (EPM C) radar on the TÜR vehicle were completed by the end of 1988 with the original TÜR prototype testing starting in late 1981.

SELF-PROPELLED SAMS / International

The full contract list of French and German orders to date is as follows:-

	Roland I fire units	Roland I missiles	Roland II fire units	Roland II missiles
Option 1A				
France	34	1244	—	—
West Germany	—	—	39	790
Option 1B				
France	46	1440	—	—
West Germany	—	—	50	1684
Option 2				
France	—	680	36	1010
West Germany	—	—	51	6520
Option 3				
France	—	—	40	2045
West Germany	—	—	—	—
Option 4				
France	—	—	20	836
West Germany	—	—	—	—
Option 5				
France	—	—	—	—
West Germany	—	—	115	4900*

* of which 2940 are for the West German Air Force, 800 for the Navy, 200 for Army and 900 for the US Air Force.

In November 1986 the Qatari Army placed an order for three batteries of three fire units each. One battery uses the AMX-30 chassis version whilst the other two use the shelter type. Deliveries and equipment training were completed in 1989.

Description

The current Roland 2 SAM system has been designed to engage enemy aircraft flying at Mach 1.2 or less between a minimum altitude of 10 m and a maximum altitude of 5500 m and between a minimum effective range of 700 m and a maximum range of 6300 m. The system has two modes of operation; optical and radar with possible switching from one to the other during an engagement. In both cases the target is first detected by the pulse Doppler Siemens MPDR-16 D-band surveillance radar which rotates at 60 rpm and automatically suppresses fixed echoes. The radar scanner, which can be operated while the vehicle is travelling, has an acquisition range of 1.5 to 16.5 km for a 1 m² target operating between speeds of 50-450 m/s and can be folded down behind the turret rear for transport. The radar is capable of detecting hovering helicopters. Once the target has been detected it is interrogated by either a Siemens MSR-400/5 (German vehicles) or an LMT NRAI-6A (French vehicles) IFF system, acquired and then either tracked by the tracking radar (in the radar mode) or by the operator using the optical sight (optical mode).

In the optical mode the missile is slaved to the line-of-sight of the operator in the following manner. The sight measures the angular velocity of the target and the infra-red localiser determines the deviation of the missile in relation to the line-of-sight. Using this data the computer calculates the required guidance commands which are then transmitted to the missile by a radio command link. The signals received by the missile are then converted into jet-deflection orders.

In the radar mode at the tracking stage the radar beam is slaved to follow the target by misalignment, voltage signals originating from the radar target tracking channel. The tracking radar, mounted on the front of the turret, is a two-channel, monopulse Doppler microwave Thomson-CSF Domino 30 system: one channel tracks the target and the second locks in on a microwave source on the missile.

After launch an infra-red localiser on the antenna on the tracking radar is used to capture the missile within a distance of 500 to 700 m, at which range the missile has entered the pencil beam of the tracking radar. A second tracking channel follows the missile by means of a transponder carried on it. Missile deviation is calculated from the angular deviation between target/antenna and antenna/missile. The deviation information is supplied to the computer and from then on the operation of the guidance loop is the same as that of the optical mode.

It is possible to switch from optical to radar guidance mode, or vice versa, in both the target pursuit and firing modes. This facility significantly increases the resistance of the Rolands to jamming in either mode.

The two-stage solid-propellant powered missile itself has a launch weight of 66.5 kg, of which the hollow-charge warhead weighs 6.5 kg, including 3.5 kg of explosive which is detonated either by impact or a TRT electro-magnetic continuous-wave radar type proximity fuze. Maximum lethal radius of the warhead's 65 projectile charges is approximately 6 m plus from the detonation point. The missile has a cruising speed of Mach 1.6, an overall length of 2.4 m, wing span of 0.5 m and a body diameter of 0.16 m. It is delivered in its container

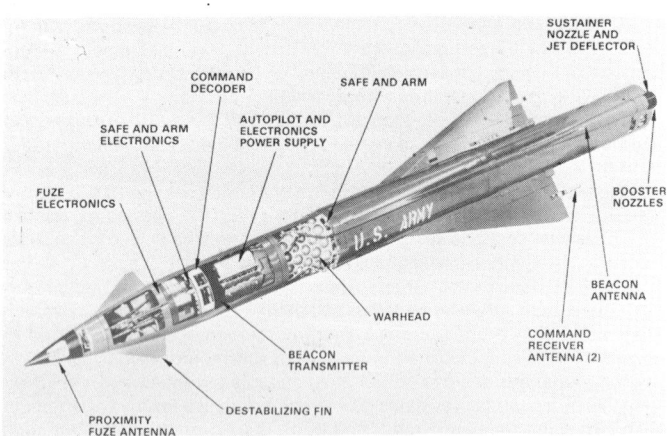

Roland missile common to all firing unit systems

French Roland 2 system on AMX-30R tracked chassis

Model of Roland 2 system on Leopard 1 chassis with radars in operating mode

Shelter version of Roland 3 SAM system on MAN (8 × 8) truck chassis

American Roland

After evaluating the Thomson-CSF Crotale, Euromissile Roland and the British Aerospace Rapier, the US Army chose the Roland in January 1975 as its short-range all-weather air defence system (SHORADS). Roland is managed in the USA by the Army Missile Command at Redstone Arsenal, Alabama, with the Hughes Aircraft Company and Boeing Aerospace as associate prime contractors.

The first contract, to demonstrate technology transfer, was for four fire units and just over 100 missiles. The first group of four missiles was delivered in October 1977 and the first fire unit was delivered in November 1977. In February 1978 the first firing of an American missile from an American fire unit took place and by September 1978 major testing had been completed. The first production delivery of a Roland system to the US Army took place in October 1981.

The US Department of the Army decided in 1983 to field and sustain a viable US Roland battalion in the Army National Guard through the year 2000. This battalion, in the New Mexico National Guard, has been assigned a high priority mission under the US Central Command (USCENTCOM). Twenty-seven additional fire units organised in three batteries of nine units each have been procured, together with a total of 595 missiles.

The US Roland module can be carried on a variety of tracked or wheeled vehicles, such as the modified chassis of the M109 155 mm self-propelled howitzer, designated the XM975, or the M812A1 truck. The USCENTCOM Roland configuration consists of a palletised fire unit module which can be operated on a truck or emplaced, independent of the carrier vehicle. The palletised fire unit can be transported by a truck with a tilt load/unload feature or by helicopters such as the CH-47D.

The following strategic and tactical deployment capabilities have been demonstrated:

Lockheed C-141B Starlifter: load/unload times of approximately five minutes. Targets can be engaged in under one minute after unloading;
Lockheed C-130H Hercules: load/unload times of approximately five to eight minutes. Targets can be engaged in under one minute after unloading;
Boeing Vertol CH-47D Chinook: palletised fire unit can be airlifted by helicopter. Targets can be engaged in under two minutes after unloading.

The USCENTCOM configuration has a 24-hour crew of four consisting of the commander, gunner, driver and assistant gunner. One or two crew member(s) can operate the system if required. The fire unit module has a height of 2.5 m, width of 3 m, length of 5 m, weighs 10 400 kg fully loaded, contains 250 litres of fuel for 37 hours of continuous operation, and carries 10 missiles weighing 860 kg in total. The fire unit module has no NBC system but this can be installed. From a shutdown condition to a fully operational mode takes less than four minutes. In any mode, the fire unit module can operate individually and autonomously or under control through command netting, if required.

Hughes provided the electro-optical sight and acquisition and tracking radars, built the missile electronics and assembled the complete missile.

Boeing provided the warhead and aft section of the missile and built the missile launcher/fire unit module, command transmitter, and controls and displays. It also procured the prime power unit and environmental unit and integrated all these elements into the complete fire unit which is mounted on a steel pallet for truck installation or ground emplacement by truck or helicopter. The IFF unit is built by Hazeltine and is a licence-built version of the Siemens MSR-400/5 system.

A high degree of interchangeability has been maintained between the United States and European Roland systems with all missiles and 85 per cent of the field replaceable parts interchangeable between the systems.

Early in 1988 it was indicated that the US Army's only Roland air defence unit, 5th Battalion, 200th Air Defence Artillery, New Mexico National Guard, was to be deactivated to cut costs. The battalion is currently being re-equipped with Chaparral missile systems.

US Roland autonomous fire unit module, mounted on modified M812A1 (6 × 6) truck, launching Roland missile

which also serves as a launcher tube. The complete container (including the missile) weighs 85 kg, is 2.6 m long and has a diameter of 0.27 m.

The 1.7 second burn 1600 kg thrust SNPE Roubaix boost rocket motor is of the extruded double-base solid propellant type and accelerates the missile to 500 m/s. The 200 kg thrust 13.2 seconds burn SNPE Lampyre sustainer rocket motor, located in front of the boost motor, then cuts in 0.3 seconds after booster burn out with its cast double-base solid propellant fuel to maintain the speed until main motor burn out. Minimum flight time required by the weapon to arm itself is 2.2 seconds with the maximum flight time around the 13-15 second mark.

Two missiles are carried ready to launch and another eight are carried in two revolver type magazines each of which holds four rounds.

An improved missile, Roland 3, with increased speed (620 m/s compared to 500 m/s) and range (8 km compared to 6.3 km) entered service in 1989. The new missile has a 9.1 kg warhead with 84 projectile charges to increase its lethality without any change in its dimensions.

An improved proximity fuze coupled with a new 5000 m/s maximum velocity fragmentation pattern (over 2.5 times the Roland 2 warhead fragment pattern maximum velocity) increases the lethal radius of the warhead to around 8 m. Maximum flight time is now approximately 16 seconds, missile weight 75 kg, and complete container (including missile) 95 kg.

The uprated booster motor retains the missile's minimum effective engagement range of 700 m but allows an increase of 500 m in the maximum interception altitude limit to 6000 m. It also allows targets taking evasive action at up to 9 g to be engaged out to the maximum limit of the missile's range.

For both the Roland 2 and Roland 3 the maximum effective engagement altitude is said to be 3000 m. Response time for the first missile launch is six to eight seconds and for the second missile two to six seconds depending on the target. Reloading the launcher from the magazines takes less than 10 seconds. A fresh batch of missiles can be reloaded in two to five minutes.

If required for defence of an air base or other high value target, up to eight Roland fire units can be integrated in the CORAD (Co-ordinated Roland Air Defence) system which includes a surveillance radar, a Roland Co-ordination Centre (RCC) and up to eight guns.

SPECIFICATIONS (Marder chassis)

CREW	3	MAX ROAD RANGE	520 km
COMBAT WEIGHT	32 500 kg	FORDING (with preparation)	1.5 m
POWER-TO-WEIGHT RATIO	18.5 hp/tonne	GRADIENT	60%
GROUND PRESSURE	0.93 kg/cm²	VERTICAL OBSTACLE	1.15 m
LENGTH	6.915 m	TRENCH	2.5 m
WIDTH	3.24 m	ELECTRICAL SYSTEM	24 V
HEIGHT (antenna retracted)	2.92 m	ARMAMENT	
GROUND CLEARANCE	0.44 m	main	1 × twin rail Roland launcher
LENGTH OF TRACK ON GROUND	3.9 m	AA	typically 1 × 7.62 mm MG
MAX ROAD SPEED (forward)	70 km/h	AMMUNITION	10 Roland missiles
FUEL CAPACITY	652 litres		

SELF-PROPELLED SAMS / International

Status: In production. In service with countries shown in table below. In August 1988 Euromissile stated that the Roland order book stood at 644 firing posts (231 AMX-30, 148 Marder, 234 Shelter and 31 US Army) and 25 500 missiles. By late 1986 over 1000 missiles, including Roland 3, had been fired in trials, training and combat.

Country	Quantity	User	Comment
Argentina	4	army	shelter version
Brazil	4	army	Roland 2, Marder chassis
France	181	army	Roland 2, AMX-30 chassis
Germany, West	20	navy	Roland 2 on 8 × 8 chassis, still being delivered
	144	army	Roland 2, Marder chassis, all delivered
	68	air force	Roland 2, 8 × 8 chassis, still being delivered
Iraq	13	army	Roland 2, AMX-30 chassis
	100	air force/army	Roland 2 shelter
Nigeria	16	army	Roland 2, AMX-30 chassis
Qatar	3 + 6	army	3 Roland 2 on AMX-30 chassis, 6 Roland 2 on MAN 8 × 8 chassis
Spain	18	army	Roland co-production, AMX-30 chassis, first delivery November 1988
USA	31	army	Roland 2, on 6 × 6 truck, National Guard
	27	air force	Roland 2, 8 × 8 chassis, still being delivered; West German manned
Venezuela	6	army	Roland 2, shelter mounted

US Roland fire control unit module dismounted for use in stand alone configuration

Manufacturers: Aerospatiale, France and MBB, West Germany.
Marketing and sales are handled by Euromissile, 12 rue de la Redoute, 92260 Fontenay-Aux-Roses, France.
Telephone: (1) 46 61 73 11
Telex: EUROM 204691 F

Associate Contractors in the USA are Hughes Aircraft Company, Missile Systems Group, 8433 Fallbrook Avenue, Canoga Park, California 91304 and Boeing Aerospace, Seattle, Washington, USA.

Associated contractors in Spain are INISEL, Mar Egeo, s/n, Poligono Industrial No 1, San Fernado de Henares; Empresa Nacional Santa Barbara SA, Manuel Cortina 2,28010 Madrid; and CESEL SA, Paseo de la Castellana 143-60, PO Box 36189, 28046 Madrid.

VT-1 Low Altitude Surface-to-air Missile System

Development
The VT-1 hypervelocity missile development programme was begun by LTV Missiles and Electronics Group for Thomson-CSF before its inclusion in their Liberty air defence system entry for the US Army's FAAD-LOS-FH programme.

Although unsuccessful in the trials, the VT-1 project continued and in 1988 the Finnish Army chose the system for its medium-range mobile low level air defence weapon to fill the gap between the SA-7/14/16 manportable and SA-3 static systems which it operates. Operational deployment is scheduled for the early nineties.

Following a mid-1987 general agreement concluded with Fokker, Thomson-CSF signed a second agreement in December 1988 for the Dutch company to undertake the final development and production of a major subsystem for the VT-1 missile and of the shelters. Fokker will also be responsible for the production of Thomson-CSF developed electronic and mechanical subsystems. The co-operation relates to the Crotale systems proposed to the Dutch Government and other countries and is in addition to the agreement previously signed between Thomson-CSF and Signaal described in the Crotale entry in this section.

Description
In Finnish service the VT-1 system will be mounted on the indigenous SISU XA-180 (6 × 6) Pasi wheeled APC. Each vehicle will carry Thomson-CSF all-weather radars and electronics plus eight ready to fire missile rounds.

The missile itself is 2.29 m long, has a diameter of 0.165 m and is fitted with four folding steel fins. A 13 kg HE focussed fragmentation warhead is carried which is detonated by an RF proximity fuzing system. Guidance is by radar and electro-optical command-to-line-of-sight systems. Maximum speed is Mach 3.5 with a flight time of 10 seconds to a range of 8000 m where the missile can still manoeuvre at up to 35 g if required.

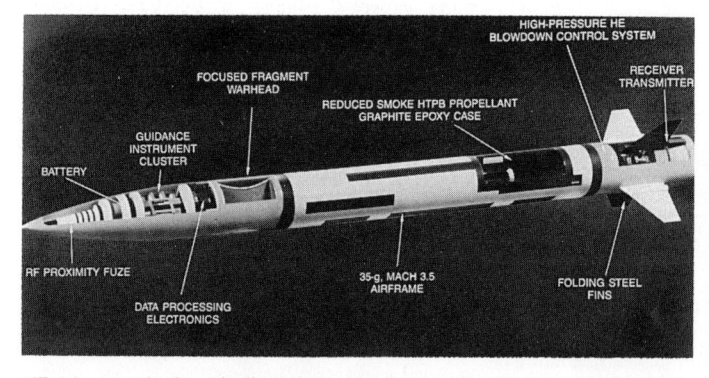

VT-1 hypervelocity missile cutaway to show main components of system

Status: Production. On order for the Finnish Army.

Manufacturers: Prime contractor and system integrator: Thomson-CSF, Division Systèmes Électroniques, 1 rue des Mathurins, BP 10, 92223 Bagneux Cedex, France.
Telephone: (1) 39 46 96 00
Telex: 968007 F

VT-1 missile: LTV, Missile and Electronics Group, Missile Division, PO Box 650003, Dallas, Texas 75265-0003, USA.
Telephone: (214) 266 1824

ISRAEL

Rafael ADAMS Vertical Launch Low Altitude Surface-to-air Missile System

Development/Description
The ADAMS (Air Defence Advanced Mobile System) vertical launch surface-to-air missile system is a lightweight launcher unit about 1.25 m² in area, designed for fitting on armoured vehicles such as the LAV-25, M2 Bradley IFV or as a Shelter system or simple ground launcher. The vertical launch configuration allows for an immediate 360° coverage around the launcher without the need for time consuming mechanical aiming required by more traditional launch methods. A pulse Doppler search radar is fitted to the larger launchers to provide all the necessary data for the missile's guidance radar. The search radar can track up to 20 targets while still scanning for new contacts and has the ability to track targets operating within the speed range of Mach 0.3 to 3. These are interrogated by an IFF system and handed over to the guidance radar if hostile. The guidance radar is actually of the search-track-guidance type but has been optimised for use in the last two modes. Operating in the I/J and K-bands it provides target position and command to line-of-sight data for the Barak missile used in the system. Alternatively in a heavy ECM environment electro-optical guidance can be used, although both can be used at the same time to guide missiles at two separate targets. The Barak is stored in the launcher tube with its wings folded and is practically maintenance free. It weighs 94 kg and has an HE warhead weighing 22 kg with a sophisticated proximity fuze system. The minimum engagement range is in the order of 300-400 m, the maximum is over 10 000 m. A key feature of the missile is its ability to vector over quickly from its vertical launch attitude to as low as 25° below the horizon or as much as 85° above the horizon to engage an incoming target. The fire control system can operate totally automatically if required.

In 1987 it was announced that trials had confirmed the missiles vertical launch facility and achieved a direct hit during the intercept of a TOW ATGW. The interception test was conducted with the TOW ATGW emulating an incoming skimmer missile.

Status: Advanced development.

Manufacturer: Enquiries to Rafael, PO Box 2082, Haifa, Israel.
Telephone: (04) 706965
Telex: 471508 VERED IL
Fax: (04) 794657

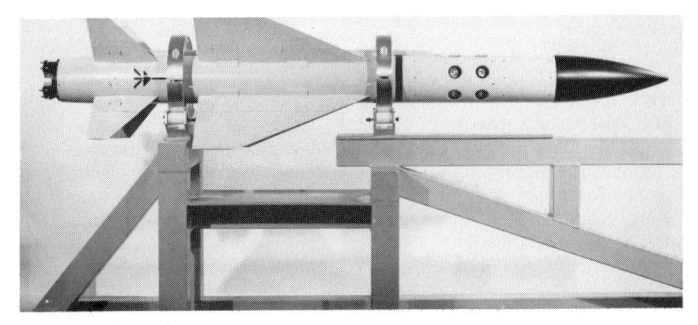

Barak missile as used in ADAMS vertical launch low altitude surface-to-air missile system

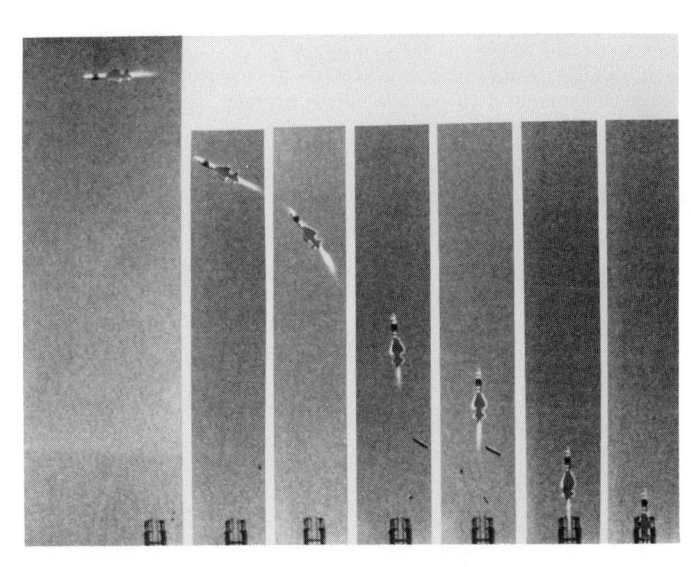

Sequence of photographs taken during Barak trials showing vertical launch and leanover manoeuvre

Model of MOWAG Piranha (8 × 8) vehicle fitted with vertical launcher for Barak missiles at rear of hull (T J Gander)

SOUTH AFRICA

Cactus Low Altitude Surface-to-air Missile System

Development/Description
The Cactus is the South African name for the French Thomson-CSF/Matra Crotale low altitude surface-to-air missile system. It was developed to meet the requirements of South Africa following the British Government's refusal to supply South Africa with surface-to-air missiles in 1964. Full details of the system are given in the Crotale entry in the French section. South Africa took delivery of seven acquisition and 14 fire units and these are used by the South African Air Force for air base defence.

SWEDEN

Bofors RBS 70/M113 Low Altitude Surface-to-air Missile System

Development

In March 1988 Bofors announced that it had test fired its latest vehicle-mounted application of the RBS 70 missile system, the RBS 70/M113 combination.

Designed to meet a Pakistan Army requirement for a mobile SAM system to protect mechanised units in the field the conversion has now gone into production at a Parkistan Ordnance Factory facility.

The missile system is transported in a folded down state to present the M113 as a 'normal' APC and conceal its air defence role from overhead observers. Once in a combat situation and assigned a fire mission the system is raised to its operating position as described below.

Description

The M113 variant chosen by Pakistan for the conversion is the M113A2. The operating crew consists of four; the fire (and vehicle) commander, missile operator, loader/radio operator and vehicle driver.

The latter sits at the front of the all-welded aluminium hull on the left side and has a single piece hatch cover that opens to the rear. To his right is the engine compartment with the fire commander seated to his rear in the centre front of the troop compartment. Above him is a cupola that can traverse through 360° and mount a 12.7 mm calibre heavy machine gun.

To his immediate left on the crew compartment wall and above a bank of two radio transceiver sets is the Target Data Receiver (TDR). This is connected to one of the radios and provides the combat control information and target data from an external surveillance radar required for an engagement.

The loader/radio operator sits adjacent to these electronic units on a foldable seat with the missile operator alongside him. Both face inwards and look directly at the RBS 70 missile platform which is hinged to the compartment roof on its right side and held upright in the travelling position by two torsion springs. Behind this and on the vehicle's right wall overhanging the track is the missile store for six RBS 70 standard container-launcher tubes.

In normal mobile combat situations the fire commander receives a radio alert from his parent unit's Tactical Control Officer. This causes him to order both the vehicle driver to stop on a level piece of ground and the other crew members to assume their battle positions. The loader releases the crew compartment's rectangular two-piece foldable roof hatch and moves it to the open left position. He then releases the springs on the missile platform and, together with the missile operator, swings the unit upwards to act as the compartment's roof. The platform is automatically locked and secured in position.

The fire commander enters the vehicle's co-ordinates and reference North into the TDR if they have not already been set before deployment. The missile operator leaves the vehicle via the rear power-operated ramp and climbs onto the missile platform where he releases the lock of the missile hatch located over the top of the missile store and assembles the RBS 70 launcher stand from its components.

In the meantime the driver moves from the front of the vehicle to assist the loader who is preparing the first two missile containers inside the store for use. He removes the front end cap of the immediate ready-to-use round and the missile operator lifts this container up through the missile hatch, fits it onto the launcher stand and removes the rear end cap. The operator then closes the missile hatch and positions himself on the stand's seat where he connects up his intra-vehicle headphone communications unit and makes the system ready for firing. Inside the vehicle the loader prepares and positions the next missile container-launcher for use under the hatch cover.

The fire commander and missile operator orientate the RBS 70 fire unit to the TDR and the former reports the fire unit ready for combat. When a target is assigned over the TDR the missile operator slews the stand to the actual target bearing and starts a target engagement of the type described in the *Manportable surface-to-air missile* section RBS 70 entry. Final permission to fire is given by the fire commander when the target is in effective range.

Once the engagement is concluded, the commander can order the missile operator and loader to reload the system. The operator locks the RBS 70 sight in elevation, discards the empty missile tube and repeats the loading sequence described above but without disconnecting his headphone. If disengagement or redeployment is required then the reverse of the operating sequence is followed to secure the vehicle for travelling.

The vehicle also carries a standard RBS 70 field stand for deploying the fire unit independently. For close-to-the-vehicle operations this must be within a 40 m radius and the fire commander decides upon the site to be used. The missile platform is deployed as for the mobile engagement mode in order for the missile operator to remove the sighting unit. The loader simultaneously removes the field stand from the vehicle and positions it at the designated site. The complete assembly is erected and a missile container attached. A signal cable is run from the vehicle to the field stand and the transceivers in the vehicle are connected to the TDR by twin cable. The fire commander then connects the field stand cable to his TDR and checks with the missile operator that the cable link is functioning. If correct the missile operator reports that he is in the ready to fire state.

In the case of operations which are further than 40 m from the vehicle because it has had to be abandoned, or it cannot be located in or near to the commander's designated site, then all the portable RBS 70 equipment is unloaded, namely the sight unit, field stand, the six missile containers, two radio transceivers, TDR with its signal cables and the systems accessories box. The deployment sequence then becomes the same as for the manportable RBS 70.

Bofors RBS 70/M113 SAM system ready to engage target

RBS 70 SAM leaving its launching tube

Sweden / **SELF-PROPELLED SAMS** 121

SPECIFICATIONS

CREW	4	GRADIENT	60%
COMBAT WEIGHT	11 600 kg	TRENCH	1.68 m
LENGTH	4.863 m	ENGINE	GMC Detroit Diesel Model 6V-53T 6-cylinder water-cooled diesel developing 275 bhp at 2800 rpm
WIDTH	2.686 m		
HEIGHT			
transport mode	2.04 m	TRANSMISSION	GMC, Allison TX-100-1 with 3 forward and 1 reverse ranges
deployed mode	3.44 m		
MAX SPEED		SUSPENSION	torsion bar
cross-country	23 km/h	ELECTRICAL SYSTEM	24 V
road	67 km/h	ARMAMENT	1 × RBS 70 missile launcher
FORDING	amphibious	AMMUNITION	6 × RBS 70 missiles
VERTICAL OBSTACLE	0.61 m	ARMOUR	12–44 mm

Status: Production. In service with the Pakistan Army (locally produced conversion on M113A2 APC).

Manufacturers: RBS 70/M113 conversion package: AB Bofors, Box 500-S69180, Bofors, Sweden.
Telephone: 46 586 81000
Telex: 73210 bofors s
Fax: 46 586 581 45

M113 APC: FMC Corporation, Ground Systems Division, 881 Martin Avenue, Santa Clara, California 95052, USA.
Telephone: (408) 289 0111
Telex: 6714210
Fax: (408) 289 2150

Lvrbv 701 RBS 70 Low Altitude Surface-to-air Missile System

Development

In February 1983, following the successful trials with a prototype vehicle, the Swedish Defense Material Administration awarded a contract to Hägglund and Söner (now Hägglunds Vehicle AB) for the conversion of a number of obsolete Ikv-102 and Ikv-103 self-propelled infantry cannon, which were withdrawn from the service some years ago, into Lvrbv 701 RBS 70 surface-to-air missile carriers. At the same time the company was awarded a contract to convert Ikv-103 chassis into Hughes TOW ATGW carriers.

First vehicles were delivered to the Swedish Army in 1984 and production continued to 1986.

The modifications have been extensive and include the replacement of the engine and transmission, extending the crew compartment, improving protection and fitting new communications equipment and observation devices.

The vehicles are organised into companies and deployed with both armoured and mechanised brigades. Radar warning is provided by vehicles equipped with the LM Ericsson Giraffe radar system, designated the PS-701/R.

Description

The gun has been removed from the glacis plate and the position plated over. The driver sits at the front of the hull on the left side and has a single piece hatch cover and fixed periscopes for observation to the front and sides. The commander sits to the right of the driver and has a single piece hatch cover that opens to the right rear and observation periscopes. The commander's position is raised above the driver to give improved observation.

Bofors RBS 70 SAM just after it has left the launcher during trials in Sweden

Lvrbv 701 anti-aircraft vehicle with Bofors RBS 70 surface-to-air missile system in operating position (FMV)

Lvrbv 701 anti-aircraft vehicle with magazine for RBS 70 surface-to-air missiles raised, showing IFF system above RBS 70 launcher (FMV)

122 SELF-PROPELLED SAMS / Sweden-Switzerland

In the centre of the hull roof is a large circular opening with a two-piece hatch cover that opens to either side. The Bofors RBS 70 surface-to-air missile system is carried inside the hull and raised up when required for action. The IFF system is mounted on the stand above the missile launcher tube. Reserve missiles are stowed in the hull rear above the engine and transmission compartment with access via the front edge of the magazine, which folds upwards.

The suspension, which is identical to that on the Ikv-102 and Ikv-103, consists of six rubber-tyred road wheels with the drive sprocket at the rear, idler at the front and two rack return rollers. The original engine has been replaced by a Ford V-6 petrol engine which is also installed in the Bv 206 all-terrain vehicle which is already in service with the Swedish Army.

The crew of four of the Type 701 consists of the commander, gunner, loader and driver.

SPECIFICATIONS

CREW	4
COMBAT WEIGHT	9700 kg
POWER-TO-WEIGHT RATIO	14 hp/tonne
GROUND PRESSURE	0.4 kg/cm^2
LENGTH	4.81 m
WIDTH	2.54 m
WIDTH OVER TRACKS	2.23 m
HEIGHT	
missile system extended	2.89 m (inc IFF)
missile system extended	2.46 m (top of launcher)
system lowered into vehicle	2.07 m
GROUND CLEARANCE	0.33 m
TRACK	1.83 m
TRACK WIDTH	400 mm
LENGTH OF TRACK ON GROUND	3 m
MAX ROAD SPEED	
high range forwards	41 km/h
low range forwards	21 km/h
reverse	7 km/h
FUEL CAPACITY	240 litres
MAX ROAD RANGE	300 km
FORDING	0.9 m
GRADIENT	60%
TRENCH	1.5 m
ENGINE	Ford Model 2658E V-6 petrol developing 136 hp at 5200 rpm
TRANSMISSION	Mercedes W 4A-018, 4 forward and 1 reverse gears
ARMAMENT	1 × RBS 70 SAM launcher
ELECTRICAL SYSTEM	24 V
BATTERIES	4 × 12 V, 57 Ah

Status: Production complete. In service with the Swedish Army.

Manufacturer: Hägglund Vehicles, S-891 01 Örnsköldsvik, Sweden.
Telephone: 0660 800 00
Telex: 6051 HAEGG S
Fax: 0660 826 49

SWITZERLAND

ADATS Missile System

Development

Based on an analysis of threat projections, Oerlikon-Bührle began studies on a cost effective modular missile system that has a high lethality against both air and ground targets. In 1979 Oerlikon began developing such a system under the trade name ADATS, after selecting Martin Marietta as prime sub-contractor. In June 1981 the first firings of the missile took place at the White Sands Missile Range, New Mexico. Trials of the complete system started in 1982 and development was completed in August 1984. Two prototypes were built on the M113A2 APC chassis and have been fully tested.

Worldwide (USA excluded), ADATS is marketed by Oerlikon-Bührle, whereas Martin Marietta markets it in the USA. The system integration programme is under the leadership of Oerlikon-Aerospace Inc, with the following partners: Litton Systems Canada (electronics), Martin Marietta (EO module), Spar Aerospace (FLIR system) and Contraves Italiana (radar). Oerlikon-Bührle has the overall responsibility for the ADATS missile system as well as for production of the missiles.

The Swiss Army has tested ADATS in 1984, 1985 and 1986 as has the US Army in May 1985. In June 1986 the Canadian Armed Forces selected ADATS as part of the system to meet its requirement for a Low Level Air Defence (LLAD) system.

The order comprised 36 ADATS systems, 20 Oerlikon-Bührle GDF-005 twin 35 mm cannon and 10 Skyguard fire control systems with the first units being delivered in 1988.

The first four ADATS units (nicknamed 'Pathfinder' by the Canadian Armed Forces (CAF) and mounted on modified M113A2 APC chassis) were delivered to the CAF Low Level Air Defence School at Chatham, New Brunswick in October 1988.

Control of the CAF's battlefield low level air defence assets in Europe has been assigned to the newly raised 4th Air Defence Regiment. This has command of the following sub-units:-
(a) 127th Air Defence battery at Baden with four Skyguards, eight GDF-005 guns and four ADATS to protect the McDonnell Douglas CF-18 Hornet equipped airbase there
(b) 128th Air Defence Battery at Lahr with similar equipment to the 127th battery to protect the CF-18 airbase there
(c) 129th Air Defence Battery at Baden with 12 ADATS with 15 Blowpipe

ADATS on FMC M3 Bradley chassis launching missile

ADATS on FMC M3 Bradley chassis with missiles elevated ready to engage target

Switzerland / SELF-PROPELLED SAMS

ADATS system on M113A2 APC chassis with eight missiles ready to fire

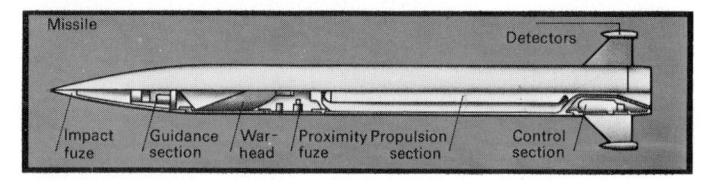

ADATS launcher on MOWAG Shark (8 × 8) chassis

launchers for deployment with units of the 1st Canadian Division in the field.

In addition there is the 119th (Independent) Air Defence Battery at Chatham with 12 ADATS and 15 Blowpipe launchers available in the reinforcement role. The remaining GDF-005 guns and Skyguard fire control systems are for training use.

The whole Canadian LLAD network is due to be operational by the end of 1991.

Martin Marietta/Oerlikon-Bührle supplied two ADATS systems for trials in the USA in the Autumn of 1987 to meet the US Army requirement for the FAAD-LOS-FH system. The British Aerospace Tracked Rapier, Thomson-CSF Shahine and the Euromissile Roland were all modified in a number of areas and supported by a US partner.

In November 1987 the US Army announced that Martin Marietta, under contract with the Oerlikon-Bührle of Switzerland, had been selected as the winner of the FAAD-LOS-FH system. Four ADATS units were purchased with FY88 funds for use in extensive operational tests in 1988-89 before a final decision is made to go into full production.

Assuming that approval is given for production, then only 140 systems are to be funded instead of the 166 originally planned. The first modified M3 Bradley vehicles will be deployed with the 3rd Armoured Cavalry Regiment at Ft Bliss, Texas then with the 1st Cavalry Division Ft Hood, Texas and finally with the V and VII Corps in Europe. The latter will not be fully equipped until FY 1996.

The 140 ADATS will not now mount a 25 mm Bushmaster cannon. Such a weapon integration is expected to be part of a future new-build and retrofit ADATS product improvement programme.

Total procurement of ADATS by the US Army is projected at 562 systems. Oerlikon will provide the first 60 fire units and 1000 missiles while Martin Marietta will build the remaining fire units and missiles as well as the electro-optics for all fire units. The electro-optical units will be built at Martin's facility in Orlando, Florida, while the missiles will be built at a facility in Ocala, Florida.

Description

The ADATS consists of a 360° traversable turret fitted with a surveillance radar, 8-12 μm wavelength forward looking infra-red (FLIR) and TV trackers, a neodymium-YAG laser rangefinder and a carbon dioxide (CO_2) missile guidance laser. Four missile launcher-containers are carried either side of the turret. The turret can be installed on a variety of tracked or wheeled vehicles such as the M113 APC, the M2 IFV and the MOWAG Shark 8 × 8 or in shelters. Two control consoles, one for the radar operator and the other for the electro-optics (gunner) operator are placed inside the carrier vehicle.

Airborne targets are detected by a fully coherent I/J-band pulse Doppler frequency-agile dual-beam SHORAR surveillance and acquisition radar supplied by Contraves Italiana, the antenna of which rotates through 360° and is capable of detecting targets from very low levels up to 6000 m altitude at ranges of over 24 km. An integral IFF set (US vehicles Mark XII/AN/MPX-2) is associated with the radar which is also capable of displaying track information on up to 20 targets on the radar operator's PPI display. Output of the FLIR and/or TV sensor systems appears on the display which is operated by the electro-optics operator. Once a target is designated as hostile by the radar operator the turret is automatically slewed round to its bearing and a search is initiated to bring it into the field of view of the FLIR (9° wide field of view, 3.2° narrow field of view) or TV camera (4° wide field of view, 0.9° narrow field of view) which are installed in a bin on the front of the turret. The electro-optics operator then selects either the FLIR or TV for tracking depending on the light level and prevailing weather conditions. The selected sensor then 'locks-on' to the target and begins automatic tracking. The range is measured either by the neodymium-YAG laser rangefinder or is provided by the track-while-scan facility of the surveillance radar to ensure that the target is within engagement range. A missile is then launched and guided by a 10.6 μm wavelength coded CO_2 laser to the target.

The Mach 3 plus smokeless propellant missile itself is 2.057 m long, 0.152 m in diameter and weighs 51.4 kg. The hollow charge warhead carried weighs 12.5 kg with the casing providing a fragmentation effect against aircraft. The missile warhead can penetrate around 100 cm of steel armour. The minimum and maximum ranges for air targets up to 6000 m altitude are 1 km and 10 km respectively and against armour targets the minimum and maximum ranges are 500 m and 8 km. The missile is fitted with an impact fuze and an electro-optical laser proximity fuze for air targets. Depending on the carrying chassis type, up to eight additional missile launcher-containers can be carried as manual reloads. The launcher-containers are 2.2 m long, 0.24 m in diameter and weigh about 65 kg loaded and 13 kg empty. The containers can be elevated from -9 to +85° for missile launch; intercept is guaranteed up to 90°.

Ground targets are acquired electro-optically and the range determined by the laser rangefinder. The remainder of the engagement sequence is as for the air target.

Variants

In addition to being installed on an M113A2/M113A3 or M3 Bradley chassis, ADATS could also be installed on other tracked and wheeled chassis, including the MOWAG Shark (8 × 8) and the Italian IVECO (8 × 8) developed for the Italian Army.

Longer term applications include helicopter mounted, elevated platform and shelter versions. For the elevated platform, Oerlikon-Bührle is working with Diehl of West Germany. This version would have its own separate surveillance system or search radar.

For the shelter version Oerlikon-Bührle is working with Fokker who have considerable experience in this field. This version will have eight missiles ready to launch, can be carried on the rear of a seven tonne truck or equipped with mobilisers to convert it into a trailer. The basic version would not have a surveillance radar as it would be netted in

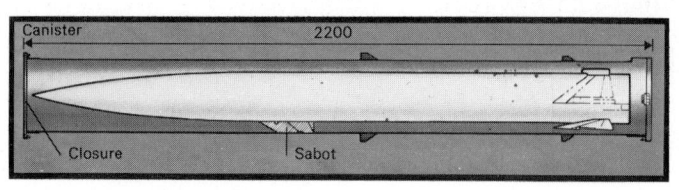

ADATS missile

ADATS missile in its container-launcher

124 SELF-PROPELLED SAMS / Switzerland

Launching of ADATS missile

Trailer-mounted ADATS system with stabilisers lowered

Model of shelter-mounted ADATS system on rear of MAN (4 × 4) seven-tonne truck

ADATS missile out of its transport/launch container

Leopard 2 MBT chassis fitted with elevated arm on which ADATS system is mounted

to the existing radar fire control system, such as Skyguard or Flycatcher. The company is also proposing a combined gun/missile battery which would have one Skyguard trailer-mounted fire control system, two twin 35 mm Oerlikon-Bührle towed anti-aircraft guns and a shelter-mounted ADATS system without its surveillance radar.

Status: In production. First deliveries made to Canadian Armed Forces late in 1988. The complete Canadian LLAD order comprises 36 ADATS systems, 20 GDF-005 guns and 10 Skyguard fire control systems at a total cost of C$1 billion. Selected by the US Army in 1987. They have a requirement for 562 fire units, four of which have so far been purchased, which will be used for extensive trials prior to becoming fully operational.

Manufacturer: Machine Tool Works, Oerlikon-Bührle Ltd, CH-8050 Zurich, Switzerland.
Telephone: (01) 316 22 11
Telex: 823 205 WOB CH

UNION OF SOVIET SOCIALIST REPUBLICS

Soviet Laser Air Defence Weapons

According to the 1987 edition of *Soviet Military Power*, published by the US Department of Defense, the Soviet tactical laser programme has progressed to the point where battlefield weapons could soon be deployed. No further details are available but both ground- and ship-based versions are understood to be involved. In the late 1970s a tactical laser weapon testbed was spotted near Golovino.

SA-4 Ganef Medium to High Altitude Surface-to-air Missile System

Development

The SA-4 Ganef (its US/NATO designations) medium to high altitude surface-to-air missile system's development began in the mid-1950s and it was first seen in public during a parade in Moscow in May 1964. Limited operational deployment began in 1967 but due to a number of major faults being found it was not fully deployed until 1969. The initial production variant was designated the 3M8, the later versions had the designations 9M8, 9M8M, 9M8M1 and 9M8M2. The system, known in the Soviet Army as the ZRD-SD (Zenitniy Raketniy Kompleks — Srednoye Deistvie: Anti-aircraft missile system — medium range) Krug (Russian for Circle) is now used by a number of armies. The system is airportable in the An-22 Cock aircraft.

The air defence elements for front, tank and combined arms armies includes several SA-4 brigades (two for a Front, one for an Army). The Ganef brigade consists of a brigade headquarters, three SAM battalions (each with nine ZU-23 towed anti-aircraft gun systems) an SSRT (Samokodnaya Stanitsaya Razvedki seleyukazanya: mobile detection and designation radar nicknamed Long Track by NATO) and three Ganef batteries and a technical battalion with one Long Track and one height-finding Thin Skin radar. Each Ganef battery in peacetime has one SSNR (Samokhodnaya Stantsiya Navendeniya Raket: mobile missile guidance station) radar nicknamed Pat Hand, three SA-4 SPU (Samokhodnaya Puskovaya Ustanovka: mobile launcher unit) launchers and four Ural-375 TZM (Transportna-zaryazhyushcha Mashina: transporter-loader vehicle) reload vehicles each with an integral cradle crane to lift the single missile carried onto the SPU. Additional resupply missiles are carried by the missile technical battery singly on double-axle semi-trailers towed by ZIL-157V or ZIL-131V articulated tractors. On mobilisation for war a fourth launcher might be added to each battery. The Ganef system is normally deployed between 10 and 25 km behind the FEBA, and forms part of an overall air defence system incorporating SA-2, SA-6, SA-7, SA-8, SA-9, SA-11, SA-12a, SA-13, SA-14, SA-15, SA-16 and SA-19 missiles and 23 mm, 30 mm and 57 mm anti-aircraft guns. The Ganef is gradually being replaced in Soviet service by a mix of SA-11 Gadfly and SA-12a Gladiator brigades.

Reload Ural-375 TZM (6 × 6) truck with integral crane carrying 9M8M1 variant Ganef missile

SA-4 Ganef launcher with missiles in travelling configuration

Pat Hand radar used with Ganef system

SA-4a Ganef system with 9M8M2 missiles and launcher elevated

SELF-PROPELLED SAMS / USSR

SA-4 Ganef launchers deployed in the field and ready to launch missiles

Long Track E-band surveillance radar on AT-T tracked chassis being prepared for rail transport. Note unditching beam carried at rear of hull

Description

Each SPU consists of a tracked armoured chassis on top of which is mounted a hydraulically operated turntable carrying the two missiles. The chassis is a new design, not based on an existing vehicle. The driver is seated at the front of the vehicle on the left and has a single hatch cover in front of which are two periscopes. At the front of the glacis plate is a splash board to stop water rushing up the glacis plate when the vehicle is fording. The engine is to the right of the driver with the remainder of the space in the vehicle taken up by the crew and electronics. There are hatches for the other crew members either side of the missile turntable.

The torsion bar suspension consists of seven dual rubber-tyred road wheels with the drive sprocket at the front and the idler at the rear, and four track return rollers. Hydraulic shock absorbers are provided for the first and last road wheel stations. The vehicle has an air filtration and overpressure NBC system and an IR night vision system for the commander and driver but no amphibious capability.

The chassis has since been adopted for a number of other roles including the 152 mm M-1973 self-propelled howitzer and minelaying. The latter model is called the GMZ and has the mines and minelaying equipment at the rear.

The launcher can be traversed through 360° with the missiles being elevated up to an angle of 45° on their launcher arms for launching. Before the missiles can be launched the rear vertical fins are replaced, the protective coverings of the ramjet airscoop and the various unit nozzles removed, the calliper clamps that hold each missile in the travelling position released manually and the calliper frame folded forwards. The left missile is carried about 0.25 m above the right one. (Note: for transit purposes the rear vertical fins are removed).

The missile is launched by four solid booster rockets mounted externally on the body, in a similar manner to those mounted on the British Bloodhound SAM. After launch the boosters fall away when the fuelled ramjet kerosene sustainer motor ignition speed is attained. The four fins are fixed and the four wings, in two pairs, are hydraulically operated.

A typical target engagement is believed to take place as follows. The target is first detected at long range by a 150 km range and 30 000 m maximum altitude Long Track early warning radar which is mounted on a lengthened version of the AT-T heavy artillery tractor with a large van body added and is also used for the SA-6 SAM. Long Track operates in the E-band and passes data to the SA-4 Ganef battery where the H-band Pat Hand continuous wave fire control and command-guidance radar takes over. Height information is also provided by the 240 km range Thin Skin truck- or trailer-mounted height finder radar which operates in the H-band. The 2.44 m diameter Pat Hand radar is mounted on essentially the same chassis as the Ganef launcher with the whole assembly collapsed flat and a grill raised in front of the radar for road transit. This radar acquires the target and when it is within range a single missile is launched and guided to the target by the guidance beam with a semi-active terminal homing phase for the final stage. The missile is tracked in flight by a continuous-wave radar transponder beacon attached to one of the tail fins. The antennas fitted to the edge of the four forward wings are the semi-active guidance receivers for the terminal homing system. The reserve missiles are carried on Ural-375 (6 × 6) trucks. Reloading the SPU takes between 10 and 15 minutes.

It is known that there have been as many as four sub-variants of the missile, designated 9M8, 9M8M, 9M8M1 and 9M8M2. External differences between them were minimal as any improvements were internal. The last two sub-variants are the predominant types in service. The 9M8M1 is the 1967 8.8 m long-nosed version (the SA-4a) with range limits of 9.3 to 72 km and a maximum effective altitude of 27 000 m. The 9M8M2, introduced in 1973, is the short-nosed 8.3 m version (SA-4b or Ganef Mod 1). This has an improved close range performance to reduce the dead zone above the SPU at the expense of losing some 3000 m in altitude and 22 km in maximum range capabilities. The minimum engagement range is reduced to 1.1 km. Both versions have a fuselage diameter of 0.9 m, a wing span of 2.3 m and a tail span of 2.6 m. The HE warhead weighs 135 kg and is detonated by a proximity fuze. The missile is armed 300 m from the launcher. The launch weight is estimated to be in the region of 2500 kg. A battery is likely to have one SPU fitted with the 9M8M2 and two SPUs with the 9M8M1 missile, although some SPUs have been seen carrying one missile of each type. An electro-optical fire control system is believed to be fitted for use in a heavy ECM environment.

SPECIFICATIONS (provisional)

CREW	5
WEIGHT	30 000 kg
LENGTH	
with missiles	9.46 m
vehicle	7.3 m
WIDTH (of vehicle)	3.2 m
HEIGHT (with missiles)	4.472 m
GROUND CLEARANCE	0.44 m
TRACK	2.66 m
TRACK WIDTH	540 mm
LENGTH OF TRACK ON GROUND	5 m
MAX SPEED	50 km/h
FUEL CAPACITY	850 litres
MAX RANGE	450 km
FORDING	1.5 m
GRADIENT	30%
VERTICAL OBSTACLE	1 m
TRENCH	2.5 m
ENGINE	V-12 water-cooled diesel developing 600 hp
MAX ARMOUR PROTECTION	15 mm
UNIT OF FIRE	2 missiles

USSR / SELF-PROPELLED SAMS

ZRK-SD (Krug) SA-4a Ganef surface-to-air missile system with two-round launcher traversed to front (not to 1/76th scale) (Steven Zaloga)

Other key components of the SA-4 Ganef air defence system (from top to bottom) include the Pat Hand missile guidance radar, Long Track surveillance radar and the TZM missile resupply vehicle on a Ural-375D (6 × 6) truck chassis. For rail transport the antenna of both of the radar systems is removed (not to 1/76th scale) (Steven Zaloga)

Status: Production probably complete. In service with the following countries:

Country	Quantity	User
Bulgaria	27	army
Czechoslovakia	27	army
Germany, East	27	army
Hungary	27	army
USSR	n/av	army

Manufacturer: Soviet state factories.

SA-6 Gainful Low to Medium Altitude Surface-to-air Missile System

Development

Development of the SA-6 Gainful (its US/NATO designations) low altitude surface-to-air missile system was begun by I I Toropov's OKB-134 design bureau at Tushino in 1959 but it was not seen in public until the 1967 Moscow Parade. The system, known as the ZRK-SD Kub (Russian for Cube) in the Soviet Army and ZRK-SD Kvadrat for export, entered full operational service in 1970 after a prolonged and troubled development and trials period. It is airportable in the An-22 and Il-76 aircraft. The missile industrial index number is 9M9 for the basic version.

The first known use in action was during the 1973 Middle East war by Syria and Egypt when it proved highly effective against Israeli aircraft during the first few days of the war. The SA-6 forced aircraft to fly very low where they would encounter the ZSU-23-4 self-propelled anti-aircraft gun. It has been widely deployed, not only with the Warsaw Pact, but with many other countries that have received Soviet aid. Subsequent use of the SA-6 in combat has included the war between Iraq and Iran, the Syrian-Israeli missile crisis in Lebanon during 1981 and the Israeli invasion of Lebanon in 1982. It has been used by both the Polasario Front and Algeria in border skirmishes with Morocco, destroying at least five aircraft, and by both Egypt and Libya during their 1977 seven-day border war. It was used by Libya during the 15 April 1986 bombing attack by the USA and against French aircraft in the battles in northern Chad during 1986 and 1987.

Previously in Army level air defence units, the SA-6 is now found mostly at Divisional level in the anti-aircraft Regiment. Each SA-6 Regiment consists of a Regimental headquarters (with one Thin Skin-B and two Long Track radars) and five SA-6 batteries. Each battery in peacetime consists of one SSNR Straight Flush radar vehicle, four SA-6 SPU launcher vehicles and two ZIL-131 TZM reload vehicles each with a large hydraulic crane centrally located on the tailboard and three reserve missiles. There are a further five TZMs and 15 ZIL-131V or ZIL-157V articulated tractors towing double-axle semi-trailers carrying six resupply rounds each in the missile technical battery of the Regiment. On mobilisation for war each battery would receive two further launchers,

128 SELF-PROPELLED SAMS / USSR

SA-6 Gainful SAM launch in travelling configuration from above (US Army)

SA-6 Gainful missile being launched

Long Track E-band surveillance radar on AT-T tracked chassis

normally kept in storage. Other Warsaw Pact members have only four launchers per battery.

Description
Developed by the Astrovo KB design bureau, the SA-6 is related to the ZSU-23-4 self-propelled air defence system and the ASU-85 self-propelled anti-tank gun. It is all-welded with the crew compartment at the front, missiles on the turntable immediately behind the crew compartment and the engine at the rear. The driver is seated at the front of the hull on the left side with the vehicle commander to his right. Both have a large windscreen to their front which can be covered by a single piece hatch cover hinged at the top which opens on the outside. When these hatches are closed, forward observation is via periscopes mounted in the forward part of the crew compartment. On the glacis plate is a splash plate to stop water rushing up the front of the vehicle when fording.

The engine and transmission are at the rear of the hull. The torsion bar suspension system consists of six rubber-tyred road wheels with the drive sprocket at the rear and the idler at the front. There are no track return rollers. Hydraulic shock absorbers are provided for the first and last road wheel stations. The SA-6 vehicle has an air filtration and overpressure NBC system and infra-red night vision equipment fitted as standard but the vehicle has no amphibious capability.

Three SA-6 missiles are carried on a turntable which can be traversed through a full 360° with the missiles elevated on their launchers to a maximum of +85°. When travelling the turntable is normally traversed to the rear and the missiles are horizontal to reduce the overall height of the vehicle.

It is estimated that the SA-6a (NATO designation Gainful Mod 0) missile has a length of 5.8 m, body diameter of 0.335 m, span (wing) of 1.245 m, span (tail) of 1.524 m and has a launch weight of 580 kg with an 80 kg HE-fragmentation warhead (40 kg of which is the explosive). The fuzes are armed after some 50 m of flight.

The missile has an integral ram/rocket propulsion system. The latter accelerates the missile after launch to a speed of about Mach 1.8 when the solid-propellant booster rocket nozzle at the rear is jettisoned and the missile is then propelled by a solid-fuel ramjet with a much larger nozzle. It is fed with ram air from the four ducts just in front of the centrebody wings, maximum speed then reaches Mach 2.5. The missile is controlled by cruciform centrebody wings with ailerons for roll control. Tail fins carry I-band mid course command link receiver antennas and G/H-band beacon transmitter antennas. These antennas were not observed on the first versions of the SA-6 seen in the 1960s. Terminal homing has been confirmed as a semi-active radar type.

There appear to be several versions of the SA-6. The basic SA-6a has a maximum effective range of 24 000 m and a minimum effective range of 3700 m, the minimum engagement height is 100 m when using the Straight Flush fire control radar and 80 m when in the optical tracking mode, the maximum effective altitude is about 12 000 m. Reload missiles are carried on modified ZIL-131 (6 × 6) trucks and are loaded onto the launcher by a crane carried on the rear of the loader vehicle. Reloading an SPU takes approximately 10 minutes.

A typical engagement is believed to take place as follows: the target is first detected at long-range by the Long Track tracked AT-T vehicle-mounted early-warning radar which operates in the E-band and passes bearing, altitude and range to the SA-6 battery where Straight Flush takes over. Additional height information is provided by the Thin Skin truck or trailer-mounted height finder radar which operates in the H-band.

Straight Flush has a similar chassis to that of the SA-6 with a range of 60 to 90 km and a 10 000 m altitude capability depending upon conditions and target size, and performs limited search, low altitude detection/acquisition, target tracking and illumination, missile radar command guidance and secondary radar missile tracking functions. The vehicle also carries the fire control computers for the missile battery. Some modified Straight Flush vehicles have been observed with a TV camera of 30 km range to enable the battery to remain in action even if the vehicle's radars are jammed or forced to shut down because of the threat of anti-radiation missiles. Straight Flush can also be linked to the launch vehicles by either a radio data link or a 10 m long cable for direct data input to the launcher's systems. The data link antenna is carried on the right forward hull corner of the SPU.

The upper foldable Straight Flush dish antenna is of the conical scanning type and is used for low altitude G/H-band sector search scans, target tracking and target illumination. The lower parabolic antenna is of the G-band medium altitude target acquisition and early warning radar type, with the lower feed for medium to high altitude coverage and the upper feed for low altitude coverage. A Straight Flush SSNR can guide

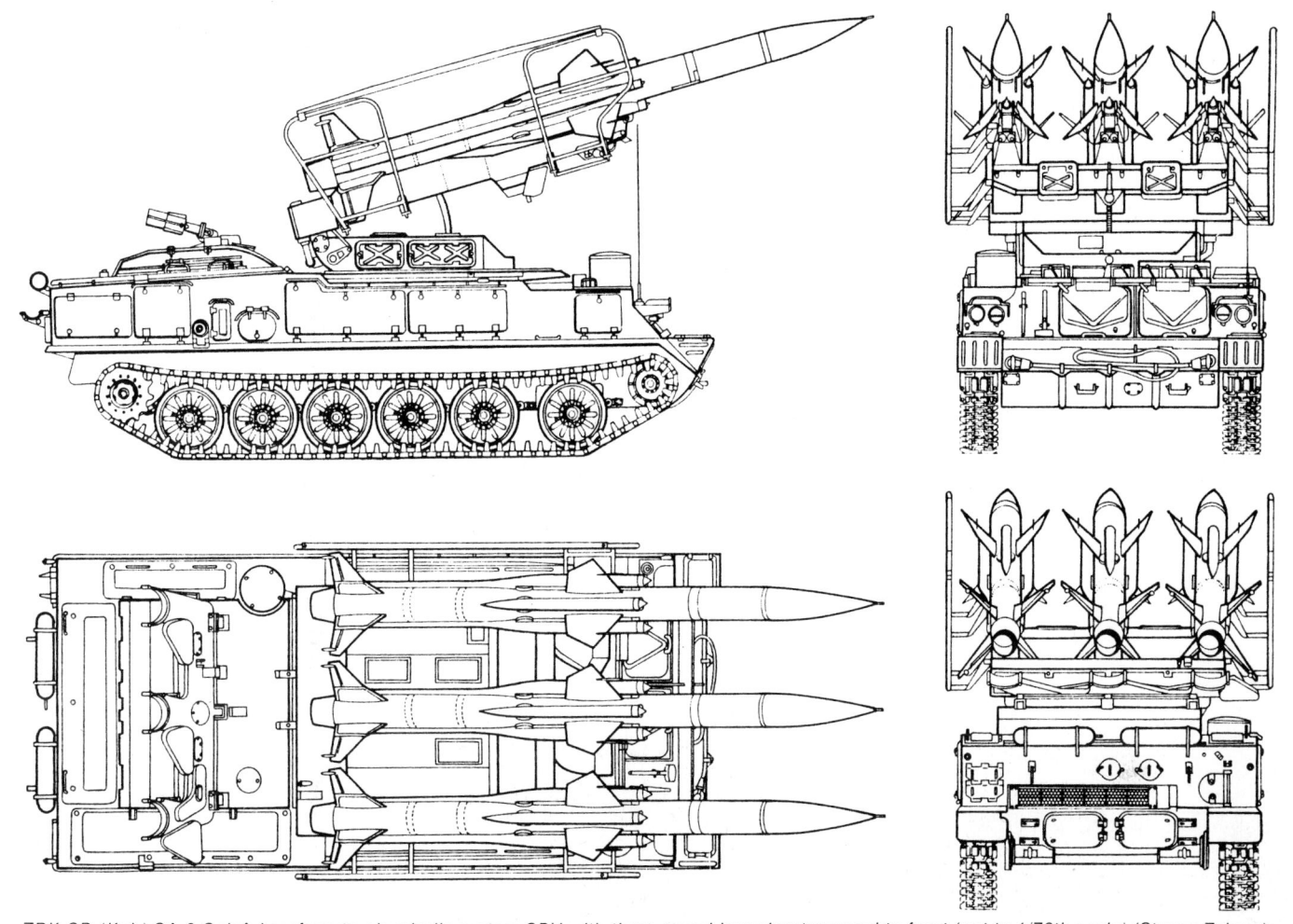

USSR / SELF-PROPELLED SAMS

ZRK-SD (Kub) SA-6 Gainful surface-to-air missile system SPU with three round launcher traversed to front (not to 1/76th scale) (Steven Zaloga)

up to three missiles at a time against a target to ensure its destruction.

When a target track has been initiated, the SSNR will order the launch of up to three missiles from one or more SPUs using their G/H-band tail fin tracking beacons to monitor the trajectories. The fire control computer uses these signals to generate course corrections and each missile is then guided on an intercept course via transmission commands sent to a reference antenna on the lower left tail fin. The missile's terminal phase is flown in a semi-active homing mode with the seeker homing in on reflected energy from the target which is being illuminated by the SSNR's radar operating in a continuous wave setting. The course flown in both phases is of the lead pursuit type. The warhead is detonated either by a contact fuze or a Doppler radar proximity fuze. The warhead has a lethal radius of 5 m against an F-4 Phantom-sized target at low altitude.

With radars up, reaction time from a dormant condition through the target acquisition, IFF interrogation and lock-on phases to missile launch is about three minutes. If the radar vehicle is already active then the time taken for the sequence is reduced to between 15 to 30 seconds. A battery is able to become mobile and relocate to an alternate firing position in approximately 15 minutes from systems being shutdown.

Egyptian SA-6 systems have had their Russian auxiliary power unit turbines replaced by Garrett Turbine Engine Company GTP-30-150 APU that supply up to 75 kW for system operations on the Straight Flush SSNR (25 kW required) and SPU (35 kW required). The missiles themselves have also been renovated with Chinese and US assistance.

SA-6 Gainful in travelling configuration with missiles traversed to rear (Soviet Military Power 1988)

Czechoslovakian SSNR Straight Flush radar vehicle in travelling configuration

East German SA-6 Gainful low altitude surface-to-air missile launcher in firing position

130 SELF-PROPELLED SAMS / USSR

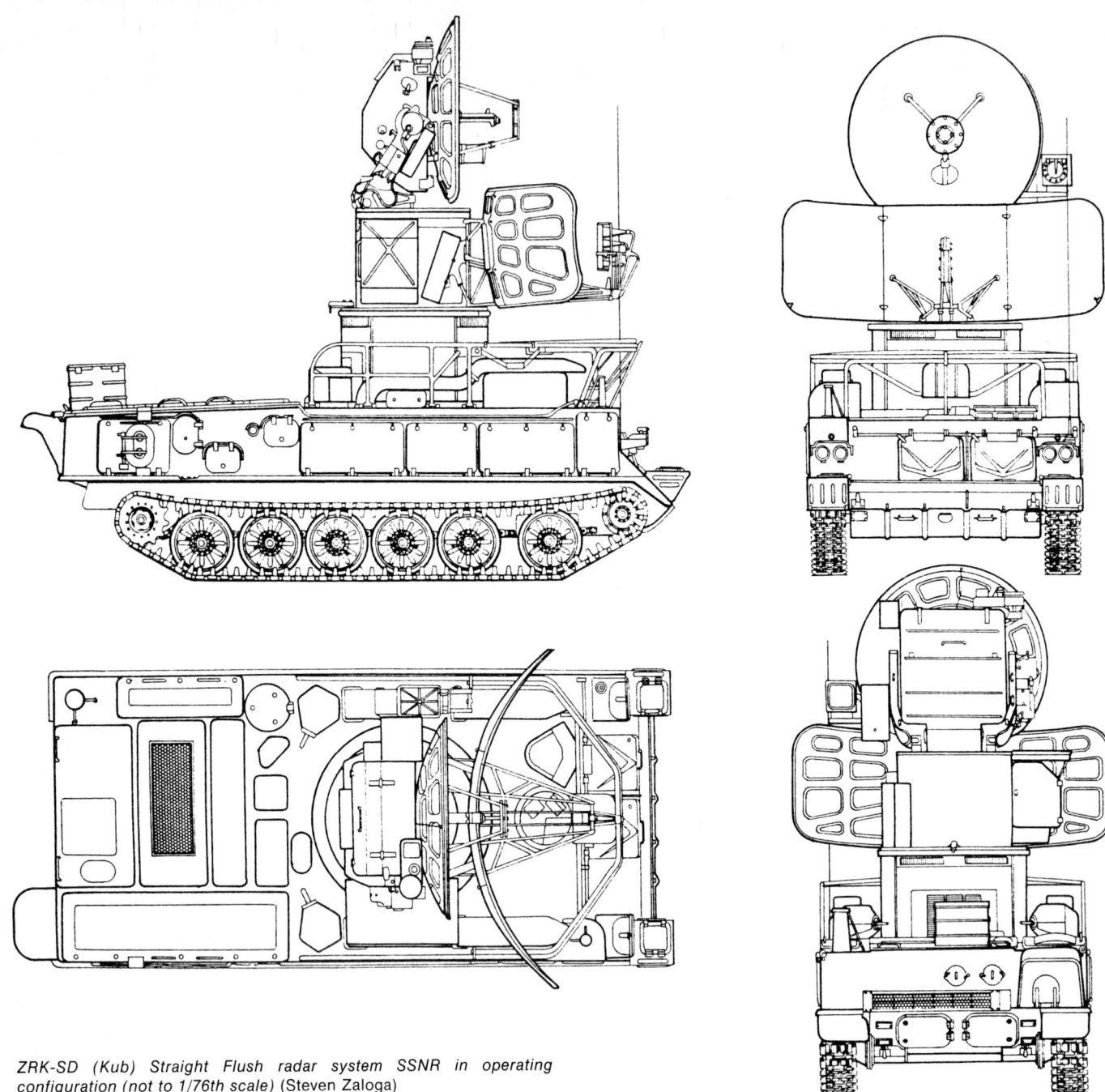

ZRK-SD (Kub) Straight Flush radar system SSNR in operating configuration (not to 1/76th scale) (Steven Zaloga)

Variants

In 1977 the SA-6b (NATO designation Gainful Mod 1) entered service. Mounted on a new SPU that is believed to be derived from the MT-S medium tracked transporter chassis the launcher has, in addition to the three missiles, its own guidance radar. The SA-6b was initially deployed on the basis of one SPU per SA-6a battery, possibly as an interim system until the SA-11 Gadfly was fielded. The Syrians were also given the system following the débâcle in the Bekaa Valley during the 1982 Peace for Galilee War with Israel. The Chadian Army captured a number of Libyan SA-6a launchers fitted to fire the SA-6b missile when they overran the Libyan airbase at Ouadi Doum in early 1987.

SPECIFICATIONS

CREW	3
COMBAT WEIGHT	14 000 kg
POWER-TO-WEIGHT RATIO	17.14 hp/tonne
GROUND PRESSURE	0.48 kg/cm^2
LENGTH OVERALL	
including missiles	7.389 m
hull	6.79 m
WIDTH	3.18 m
HEIGHT	
including missiles	3.45 m
hull top	1.8 m
GROUND CLEARANCE	0.4 m
TRACK	2.67 m
TRACK WIDTH	360 mm
LENGTH OF TRACK ON GROUND	3.8 m
MAX ROAD SPEED	44 km/h
FUEL CAPACITY	250 litres
MAX RANGE	260 km
FUEL CONSUMPTION	0.96 litre/km
FORDING	1.1 m
GRADIENT	60%
SIDE SLOPE	30%
VERTICAL OBSTACLE	1 m
TRENCH	2.5 m
ENGINE	model V-6R, 6-cylinder, in-line, water-cooled diesel developing 240 hp at 1800 rpm
TRANSMISSION	manual with 5 forward and 1 reverse gears
STEERING	clutch and brake
SUSPENSION	torsion bar
ELECTRICAL SYSTEM	24 V
BATTERIES	2 × 12 V, 100 Ah (for vehicle)
ARMAMENT	3 × SA-6 missiles
SMOKE-LAYING EQUIPMENT	none
ARMOUR	9.4 mm max

Status: In production. In service with the following countries:

Manufacturer: Soviet state factories.

Country	Quantity	User	Country	Quantity	User
Algeria	40	army	Iraq	180	army
Angola	24	Air Defence Force	Libya	160	army
Bulgaria	30	army	Mozambique	12	army
Cuba	12	army	Poland	120	army
Czechoslovakia	120	army	Polasario Front	4+	guerilla force
Egypt	60	Air Defence Command	Romania	60	army
Ethiopia	20+	army	Somalia	12	Air Defence Force
Germany, East	120	army	Syria	108	army
Guinea	4	army		108	Air Defence Command
Guinea-Bissau	8	army	Tanzania	12	army
	8	Air Defence Command	USSR	n/av	army
Hungary	80	army	Vietnam	80	army
India	185	army	Yemen, North	12	army
			Yugoslavia	80	army

SA-8 Gecko Low Altitude Surface-to-air Missile System

Development

The SA-8 Gecko (its US/NATO designations) all-weather low altitude surface-to-air missile system entered service in 1974 and was first seen in public during a parade in Moscow in November 1975. The system, known as ZRK-SD Romb (Russian for Diamond) in the Soviet Army, has been designed to fill the gap between the SA-7/SA-9 and the SA-6 and was developed in conjunction with the SA-N-4 point defence system used by the Soviet Navy. The Soviets have designated it a ZRK (Zentniy Raketniy Komplex) system to indicate it as a complete and integral SAM system. The SA-8 Gecko is issued on the scale of 20 fire units per Soviet Divisional anti-aircraft regiment in place of the S-60 57 mm towed anti-aircraft gun. The organisation of an SA-8 regiment is a regimental headquarters, a target acquisition and early warning battery with one Long Track, one Flat Face and a Thin Skin-B radar, a missile support battery, a transport company, a maintenance company and five SA-8 batteries. Each battery in peacetime has four SA-8 SPU launcher vehicles and two TZM reload vehicles. The TZMs are supported by 24 ZIL-131 (6 × 6) cargo trucks used as missile transporters by the Regimental transport company. On mobilisation a further two launchers are added to each battery. It has also replaced the SA-6 system in some units because of its greater mobility. It is airportable in the An-22 and Il-76 transport aircraft. First recorded combat use was in the Bekaa Valley region of Lebanon, in late July 1982, when Israeli aircraft destroyed three of these systems belonging to the Syrians. Angola subsequently used it during the December 1983 South African cross-border raid code-named Askari. It was also used by Libya during the 15 April 1986 American bombing attack without success. In the 1987 fighting in Southern Angola a number of SA-8b Gecko systems were captured by UNITA and the South African Defence Forces.

Description

The SA-8 vehicle is a new six-wheeled design designated BAZ-5937. It is based on a number of earlier six-wheeled all-terrain vehicles developed by V A Grachev's design team at the Likhachev Automobile Plant (ZIL) in Moscow. The driver's compartment at the front of the vehicle has accommodation for two, the driver and commander, with access to it via a hatch in the roof. There are no other entrance/exit hatches apparent on the vehicle. The engine is at the very rear. The vehicle is thought to have torsion bar suspension with steering on the front and rear axles and a central tyre-pressure regulation system. Blast shields can be folded down over the windscreens to prevent damage when the missiles are launched. The vehicle is fully amphibious, being propelled in the water by two water jets at the rear of the hull. Before entering the water, a trim vane which is folded back onto the glacis plate when not in use is erected at the front of the hull. The vehicle is fitted with an air filtration and overpressure NBC system together with IR systems for the commander and driver. Four command-guided missiles are carried ready to launch, two either side.

The main fire control radar is at the rear of a one-man gunner-radar operator position and folds back through 90° to reduce the overall height of the vehicle for air transport and during high speed road travel. It is known that the radar operates in the H-band with a 360° traverse and has a maximum range of about 30 km. The complete conical-scan radar installation of the Gecko has been assigned the NATO code name Land Role.

SA-8a Gecko in travelling configuration with surveillance radar lowered to rear (US Army)

132 SELF-PROPELLED SAMS / USSR

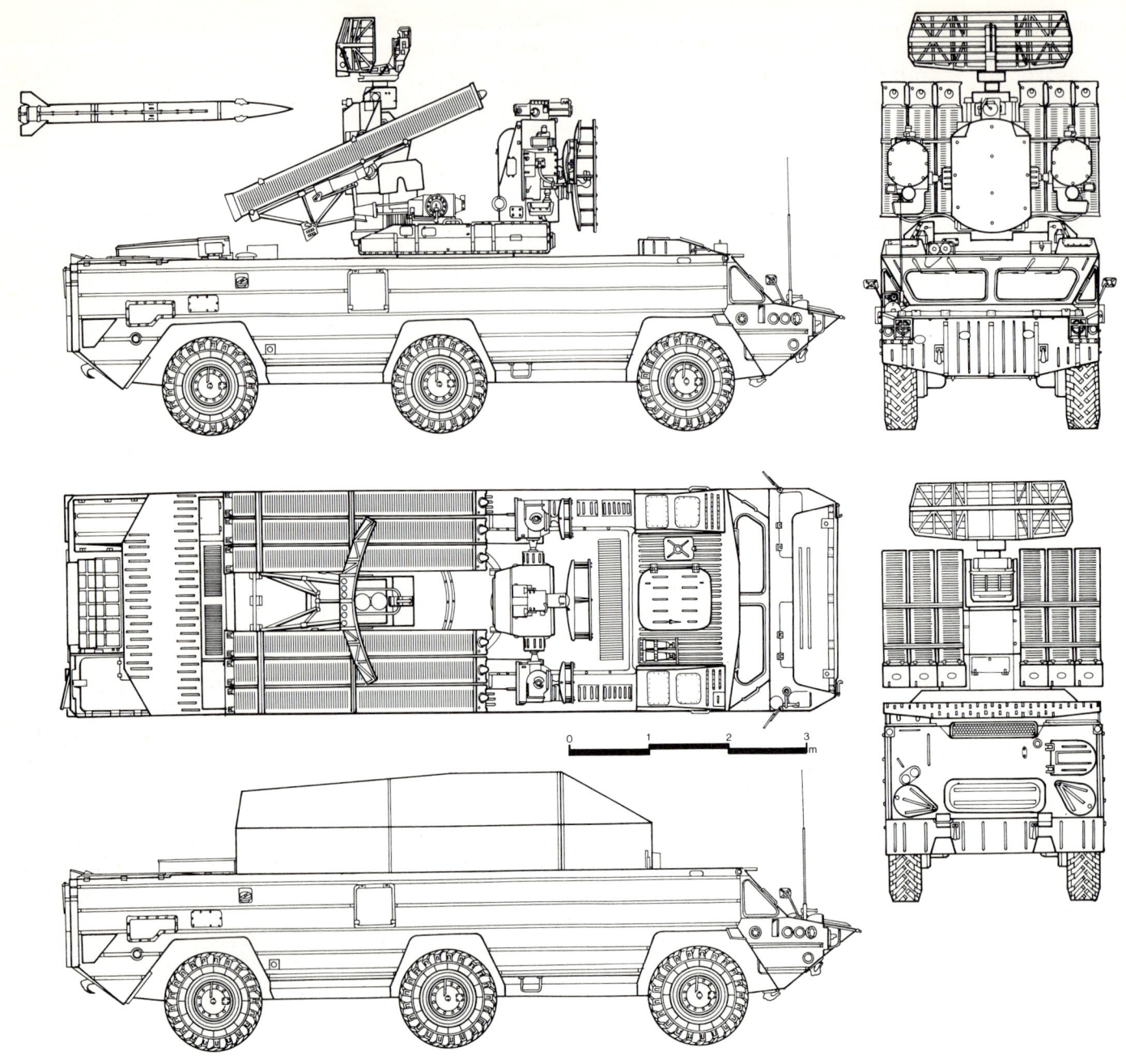

ZRK-SD Romb (SA-8b Gecko Mod 1) and its supporting TZM resupply vehicle (not to 1/76th scale) (Steven Zaloga)

In front of the radar is the guidance group comprising a central monopulse target tracking radar with truncated sides, which operates in the J-band and has a range of 25 km, two monopulse missile guidance radar up-link transmitters, one either side of the tracking radar, which have truncated sides and limited traverse and operate in the I-band; two command-link horns for missile gathering, one either side and below the missile guidance radars, which operate in the I-band and two rectangular devices which are believed to assist in tracking in an ECM environment to the left and right of the missile guidance radars. Mounted on top of each missile guidance radar is an LLLTV/optical assist system for target tracking in low visibility and heavy ECM. Mounted on the top of the tracking radar is what is thought to be a feed and below the tracking radar is a periscope, the exact role of which is uncertain. Land Role is also known to have a short-range target acquisition capability.

It is known that the two missile guidance radars operate on different frequencies, each controlling one missile in flight, which would enable the system to engage a single target with a staggered two-missile salvo operating on different frequencies to avoid guidance problems and degrade the target's ECM capabilities.

The SA-8a (Gecko Mod 0) high acceleration missile is powered by a single-stage rocket motor burning solid propellant, has a launch weight of about 170 kg, is 3.1 m long, 0.21 m in diameter and has a span of 0.64 m. Maximum speed is Mach 2, minimum altitude is 10 m, maximum altitude 13 000 m. The minimum range is 1600 m and the maximum range 12 000 m. Against an F-4 Phantom target the warhead's lethal radius at low altitude is 5 m. In 1980 a newer missile, the SA-8b or Gecko Mod 1, was introduced into service. Contained in a rectangular launch box it has improved guidance and speed characteristics to give an increased maximum range of 15 000 m. The warhead weight of both missiles is 40 kg. The reloading time is five minutes. Each battery also has two missile transloaders based on the same chassis with a long coffin-like blunt pointed tarp roofed structure covering the cargo space and crane. When operating, the blunt point area is raised and the tarped structure is slid to the rear. A total of 12 reloads in boxed sets of three are transferred to the SPUs by the hydraulic crane mounted centrally behind the vehicle cab. In the Regiments Maintenance battery there is a single radar collimation vehicle using the same chassis. This has a collimation antenna which lies on both sides of the vehicle and overhangs the rear during transit. In operation it is raised and mounted on each side of the hull directly behind the cab.

Variants
There are at least three major families of SA-8 launch vehicles. The first has a very blunt nose, and may be a pre-series prototype. The standard production type for the SA-8a has a sharper nose, and there appear to be sub-variants of this vehicle with minor changes in the detail of hull fittings. The SA-8b vehicle is basically similar to the SA-8a vehicle mentioned above aside from the launcher details to accommodate six missile canisters. There are also indications that a distinctly different SA-8b launcher may exist, with a reconfigured rear end.

USSR / SELF-PROPELLED SAMS

Close-up of rear of SA-8a Gecko showing four missiles and surveillance radar lowered

SA-8b Gecko system from rear with surveillance radar lowered over launch canisters

TZM resupply vehicle in travelling configuration. This is provided with a hydraulic crane to resupply the SA-8 Gecko system in the field

East German SA-8b Gecko system in operating configuration with surveillance radar erected

---

SPECIFICATIONS (SA-8b)

CREW	3
COMBAT WEIGHT	18 600 kg
LENGTH	9.14 m
WIDTH	2.9 m
HEIGHT	
surveillance radar lowered	4.2 m
to hull top	1.845 m
GROUND CLEARANCE	0.4 m
WHEELBASE	3.075 m + 2.788 m
MAX SPEED	
road	60 km/h
water	5 km/h
CRUISING RANGE (road)	500 km
FUEL CAPACITY	350 litres
VERTICAL OBSTACLE	0.5 m
TRENCH	1.2 m
FORDING	amphibious
ENGINE	UTD-20 diesel developing 175 hp at 2000 rpm
ARMOUR	none
UNIT OF FIRE	6 × SA-8 missiles

Status: In production. In service with the following countries:

Manufacturer: Soviet state factories.

Country	Quantity	User
Algeria	30	army
Angola	30	army
Czechoslovakia	40	army
Germany, East	40	army
Guinea	4	army
Guinea-Bissau	8	army
Hungary	20	army
India	100	army
Iraq	50	army

Country	Quantity	User
Jordan	20+	Air Force
Kuwait	20	army
Libya	40	army
	50	Air Defence Command
Poland	60	army
Syria	160	army
USSR	n/av	army
Yugoslavia	20+	army

SELF-PROPELLED SAMS / USSR

SA-9 Gaskin Low Altitude Surface-to-air Missile System

Development
Apparently developed in parallel with the ZSU-23-4 and attaining operational status in 1968, the SA-9 Gaskin (US/NATO designations) low altitude clear-weather surface-to-air missile system's first recorded combat use waš in May 1981 when a Libyan SA-9 battery engaged Israeli aircraft flying over Lebanon; no hits were made and the battery was destroyed in a retaliatory airstrike. Israel subsequently captured a complete SA-9 battery in Lebanon for which the search radar coverage was provided by a J-band Gun Dish radar system mounted on a ZIL-157 truck chassis. A large number of SA-9 systems were also destroyed by the Israelis in their destruction of the Bekaa Valley Syrian missile belt during the 1982 Lebanon invasion. Iraq used SA-9s against Iran in the Gulf War. At least 16 complete SA-9 vehicles were captured together with missiles by South Africa following operation Askari in Angola during 1983 after several missiles had been fired at its aircraft on bombing and reconnaissance missions.

The SA-9 Gaskin is issued to the anti-aircraft batteries of Soviet motorised and tank regiments on the basis of four systems per battery to give a total of 16 per division. Replacement by the SA-13 Gopher system is well underway. Recently higher readiness Tank and Motorised Rifle Divisions have begun to field enlarged Regimental level air defence battalions of six ZSU-23-4 and six SA-13 Gopher vehicles. It is possible that the same structure is being adopted for the lower readiness Divisions still equipped with SA-9 vehicles. Some of the forward deployed Category 1 Divisions have had their air defence battalions of SA-13/ZSU-23-4 vehicles replaced by battalions fielding six 2S6 and six BMP-2, the latter apparently being used to transport regimental level SA-14/SA-16 manportable SAM teams. The surveillance unit equipped with a Dog Ear radar vehicle remains the same.

Description
The system consists of a BRDM-2 transporter-erector-launcher (TEL) with the normal turret and chain-driven belly wheels removed and replaced by one with four ready to launch SA-9 container-launcher boxes. These are normally lowered to the horizontal when travelling to reduce the overall height of the vehicle. The original version of the Strela 1 was known as the 9M31 (US designation SA-9a, NATO codename Gaskin Mod 0) and used an uncooled first-generation IR seeker. This was supplemented by the 9M31M variant (US designation SA-9b, NATO codename Gaskin Mod 1) which has an improved cooled seeker to provide greater target sensitivity and lock on ability. The 43 kg Mach 1.5 missile is 1.8 m long, 0.12 m in diameter and has a wing span of 0.38 m. The

SA-9 Gaskin low altitude SAM system showing Hat Box passive radar detectors either side of hull front

Close up of SA-9 Gaskin from above showing four missiles in ready to launch position (US Army)

SA-9 Gaskin SAM system based on BRDM-2 (4 × 4) amphibious chassis with four missiles ready to launch (US Army)

USSR / **SELF-PROPELLED SAMS** 135

minimum range of the 9M31 is 800 m and the maximum range 6500 m within altitude limits of 20 to 5000 m. The minimum range of the 9M31M is 560 m and the maximum range 8000 m (increasing to a possible 11 000 m when used in a tail-chase engagement) within altitude limits of 15 to 6100 m. Both missile types have an effective upper altitude limit of 1900 m. The SA-9 is fitted with a 7 kg (2.6 kg explosive) warhead and proximity fuze which detonates within 1.5 m of a target. One SA-9 TEL in each battery has been fitted with Hat Box passive radar detection antenna, one either side of the hull above the front wheel housings, one under the left launch canisters pointing forward and one mounted on a small frame above the rear engine deck plate pointing rearwards to give 360° coverage. The vehicle crew of three consists of the commander, driver and gunner and there is an IR system for the first two to use at night. An air-filtration and overpressure NBC system is fitted as standard.

Using an optical-mechanical sighting system to acquire the target, the SA-9s are salvo fired (usually two missiles per target) sequentially with the SA-9b missile infra-red seekers set to operate against different target intensities to defeat any flare counter-measures. Time between missiles is said to be five seconds, the reloading time is believed to be five minutes. The SA-9 is known as ZRK-BD Strela-1 in the Soviet Army. Strela-2 is the shoulder-launched 9M32/SA-7a, Strela-2M the 9M32M/SA-7b and Strela-3 is the SA-14 Gremlin.

SA-9 Gaskin SAM system of the East German Army in travelling configuration with missiles folded down

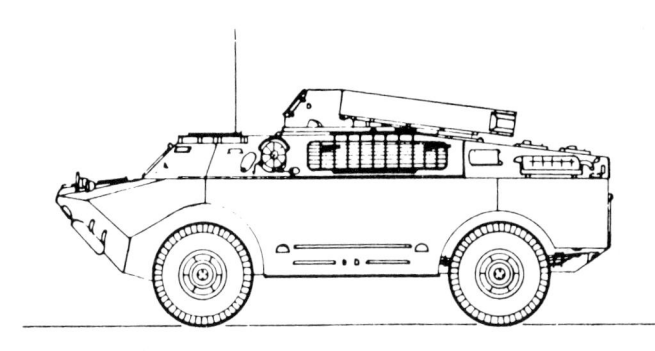

SA-9 Gaskin SAM system based on BRDM-2 chassis, with launching arms and missiles in travelling position

SPECIFICATIONS

CREW	3
CONFIGURATION	4 × 4
COMBAT WEIGHT	7000 kg
LENGTH	5.8 m
WIDTH	2.4 m
HEIGHT (travelling)	2.3 m
GROUND CLEARANCE	0.43 m
TRACK	1.84 m
WHEELBASE	3.1 m
MAX SPEED	
road	100 km/h
water	10 km/h
ROAD RANGE	750 km
FUEL CAPACITY	290 litres
FORDING	amphibious
GRADIENT	60%
VERTICAL OBSTACLE	0.4 m
TRENCH	1.2 m
ENGINE	GAZ 41 V-8 water-cooled petrol developing 140 hp at 3400 rpm
ARMAMENT	4 × SA-9 missiles
AMMUNITION	4 + 2 SA-9s
ARMOUR	5-14 mm

Status: Production probably complete. In service with the following countries:

Country	Quantity	User
Algeria	36	army
Angola	30	army
Benin	4	army
Bulgaria	60+	army
Cuba	60	army
Czechoslovakia	80+	army
Egypt	20	army
Germany, East	60+	army
Guinea	16	army
Guinea-Bissau	32	army
Hungary	50	army
India	200	army
Iraq	100+	army
Libya	60	army
Madagascar	4	army
Mali	8	army
Mauritania	4	army
Mozambique	32	army
Nicaragua	8-12	army
PLO	few	guerrilla force
Poland	160+	army
SWAPO	few	guerrilla force
Syria	150	army
Tanzania	40	army
USSR	n/a	army, naval infantry
Vietnam	100+	army
Yemen, South	20+	army
Yugoslavia	100+	army

Note: They are also used by Israel, South Africa and the USA for training purposes

Manufacturer: Soviet state factories.

SA-10 Grumble Low to High Altitude Surface-to-air Missile System

Development/Description
Developed during the 1970s the SA-10a Grumble entered service with the V PVO (Voyska Protivovozdushnoy Oborony: Troops of Air Defence) as a static system in 1980. Used for both strategic and theatre roles, it is a high speed high performance land-based version of the Soviet Navy's SA-N-6 air defence missile which also entered service during 1980 as the main anti-aircraft/missile armament of the nuclear-powered battle-cruiser Kirov.

Apart from engaging aircraft, the SA-10a Grumble Mod 0 (US/NATO designations) is also capable of being fired against both air and ground launched cruise missiles as well as tactical ballistic missiles such as the US Pershing Ia/II series. By 1987 nearly 1200 four-rail launchers had been deployed at around 100 SA-10a complexes throughout the Soviet Union as replacements for the elderly R-113 (SA-1 Guild) and S-75 (SA-2 Guideline) weapons.

The single-stage solid-propellant powered missile is 7 m long, 0.45 m

136 SELF-PROPELLED SAMS / USSR

in diameter and has a 1 m wing-span. Launch weight is 1500 kg and the warhead can either be a conventional 90-130 kg HE-fragmentation one or a low yield (probably around 5 kt) nuclear type. Maximum speed is Mach 6.0 with minimum and maximum engagement ranges of 3 to 100 km between altitude limits of 300 to 30 400 m. System guidance is similar to the American MIM-104 Patriot in that it is of the Track-via-Missile (TVM) type with an active radar terminal seeker, hence several weapons from the battery can be in the air at any one time being guided to different targets.

The US Department of Defense has indicated that a mobile version, the SA-10b Grumble Mod 1 (US/NATO designations), will support Soviet Army theatre forces and act as a mobile territorial defence system to defend high value targets against strike aircraft and theatre nuclear weapons. The SA-10b Grumble SPU (Samokhodnaya Pusskovaya Ustanovka: mobile launcher unit) used is derived from the MAZ-7910 (8 × 8) wheeled tractor with four cylindrical missile launcher-containers on the rear decking that elevate vertically in a group for firing. Missile reloads and a Flap Lid B I/J-band SSRT (Samokhodnaya Stanitsiya Razvedki i Tselyukazaniya: mobile detection and designation radar station) combined 2.75 m square phased planar array target tracking and fire control radar with a 24.4 m extendable tower mounted antenna are carried on separate variants of the same chassis as that used for the SPU. A battalion of SA-10b Grumble vehicles is thought to comprise three SPUs, an SSRT and perhaps two TZM (Transportna Zaryyazyushcha Mashina: transporter-loader vehicle) transloaders with a Regiment comprising three battalions and a radar unit with a large Clamshell pulse

Artist's impression of mobile version of SA-10 Grumble low to high altitude surface-to-air missile system battalion deployments. Vehicle on right has elevated launchers. Flap Lid radar vehicle is on centre background (Soviet Military Power 1986)

Doppler continuous wave I-band target acquisition radar and a Big Bird F-band long-range 4 m high antenna-mounted and target tracking radar. When a battery is used as a stand alone unit the low level engagement range is said to be 32 000 m which increases to 43 200 m if the Flap Lid B radar is extended to its full height.

SPECIFICATIONS (SA-10b Provisional)

CREW	4	MAX SPEED	85 km/h
COMBAT WEIGHT	20 000 kg	MAX ROAD RANGE	650 km
LENGTH	9.4 m	ENGINE	D12A diesel developing 525 hp
WIDTH	3.1 m	ARMOUR	none
HEIGHT	3.7 m		

Status: SA-10a and SA-10b in production and service with the Soviet Army.

Manufacturer: Soviet state factories.

SA-11 Gadfly Low to Medium Altitude Surface-to-air Missile System

Development/Description
The SA-11 Gadfly (US/NATO designations) mobile missile system was developed in the early 1970s and entered service in 1983 to complement the SA-4 Ganef and SA-6 Gainful mobile SAM systems. The launcher vehicle, which is based on the MT-S tractor chassis, carries four ready to fire missiles on a turntable that can be traversed through a full 360° and a Fire Dome monopulse guidance and tracking radar. The associated tracked SSNR vehicle carries the early warning and acquisition radars (NATO codename Tube Arm) and provides the target's height, bearing and range data. Once a target is identified then it is turned over to an SPU via a data link for tracking and attack. The Mach 3 semi-active homing missile closely resembles the US Navy's Standard MR1 RIM-66 weapon with a maximum slant range of 28 km and has a minimum range of 3 km. It is capable of engaging targets between the altitude limits of 30 and 14 000 m. The missile length is 5.6 m, diameter is 0.4 m and the wing span is 1.2 m. Launch weight is 650 kg with a 90 kg HE warhead. Propulsion is by a solid fuel rocket motor.

An SA-11 regiment comprises five batteries each with four SPUs and one SSNR radar vehicle. There is also a new long-range early warning radar in the regiments replacing the Long Track system. The SA-11 can also be integrated into the SA-6 air defence network using that system's Straight Flush radar vehicle to provide all the necessary target acquisition data in place of its own radar vehicle.

Status: In production. In service with the Soviet Army, also deployed with India (army), Syria (army, about 20 launchers), Poland (army, about 20 launchers) and Yugoslavia (army manned Protiv- Vazdušna Obrana—literally Protective Air Defence units).

Manufacturer: Soviet state factories.

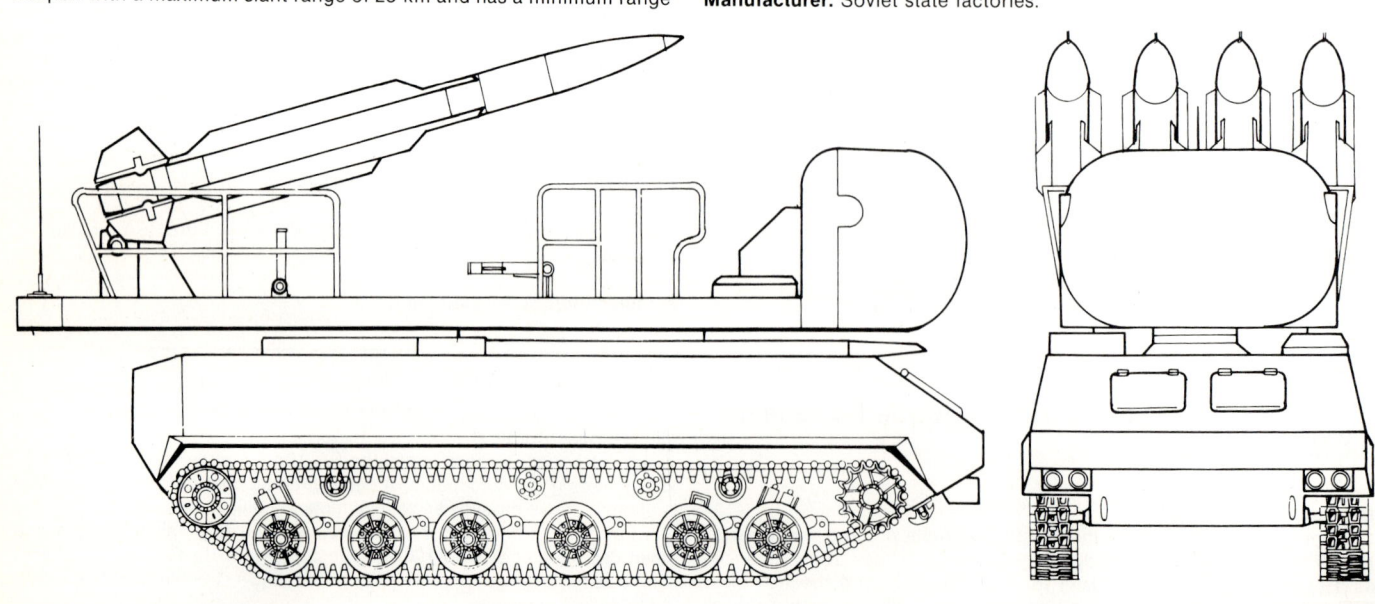

Provisional drawing of SA-11 Gadfly air defence missile launch vehicle (not to 1/76th scale) (Steven Zaloga)

USSR / **SELF-PROPELLED SAMS** 137

SPECIFICATIONS (provisional)
CREW	4	HEIGHT	3.7 m
COMBAT WEIGHT	16 000 kg	MAX SPEED	50 km/h
LENGTH	9.4 m	MAX ROAD RANGE	300 km
WIDTH	3.1 m	ARMOUR	9 mm (max)

SA-12a Gladiator/SA-X-12b Giant Low to High Altitude Missile Systems

Development/Description

The SA-12a Gladiator missile system was developed initially to augment and then eventually to replace the SA-4 Ganef in the SAM brigades at the Front and Army level. The system entered operational service in 1984 and is apparently deployed in the southern and western USSR Military Districts in two slightly different versions, one for the conventional engagement of aircraft and the other for the anti-tactical ballistic missile (ATBM) role to engage weapons such as the Lance or Pluton.

The conventional version of the Mach 3.0 two-stage SA-12a missile is 7.5 m long, 0.5 m in diameter and has a wing span of 1.5 m. Both the booster and sustainer rocket motors use solid fuel propellants. Launch weight is said to be around 2000 kg with a 150 kg HE-fragmentation warhead as the payload. Guidance is of the command type with semi-active radar homing for the terminal phase.

The Gladiator SPU (Samokhodnaya Pusskovaya Ustanovka: mobile launcher unit) is based on the tracked MT-T tractor chassis which is derived from the T-64 MBT design and carries two cylindrical missile container-launchers that can be raised independently to the vertical for firing. The SPU also has a hydraulically operated telescopic missile guidance radar on the rear decking.

Within the battery there are three other vehicles based on the same chassis. At the battery HQ there is a single KShM (Komando-Shtabnaya Mashina: command-staff vehicle), an SSNR (Samodokhodnaya Stanitsiya Navedeniya Raket: mobile missile guidance station) engagement radar (NATO codename Grill Pan) vehicle and a TZM (Transportna Zaryyazyushcha Mashina: transporter-loader vehicle) transloader.

The combined phased array multiple tracking and fire control SSNR radar can be used to control the three SPUs of the battery but is more likely to be used to track targets handed over by the battalion and brigade level search radar systems. When in range these would then be passed on to the individual SPU guidance radars for engagement. The single TZM serves all three SPUs and carries four SA-12a reload rounds on its rear decking. It is probable that one of the three SPUs is configured slightly differently to the other two in order to carry the SA-12a ATBM variant.

A battalion appears to have three of these batteries and an HQ unit. The latter has two KShM vehicles and a single unit of the fourth vehicle type based on this chassis, the SSRT (Samokhodnaya Stanitsiya Razvedki i Tselyukanzaniya: mobile detection and designation radar station) long-range target search and acquisition radar vehicle (NATO codename Bill Board). Additional TZMs are also likely to be found at the battalion level.

A brigade has three of these battalions and an HQ unit with two SSRTs and three KShM vehicles. The minimum and maximum engagement limits for the SA-12a system are 5.5 to 80 km respectively for targets between 90 and 30 000 m.

In the 1987 edition of *Soviet Military Power* it was revealed that the SA-X-12b Giant variant was at the flight testing stage and is to be used by the ZRV (Zenitnyye Raketnyye Voyska: Zenith Rocket Troops) on behalf of the PRO (anti-rocket defence) component of the V PVO (Voyska Protivovozdushnoy Oborony: Troops of Air Defence). The weapon is similar in appearance to the SA-12a but has a higher altitude interception capability and a 100 km maximum range. The SPU carries two ready to fire SA-12b missiles and is heavier at 22 400 kg when fully loaded.

Artist's impression of the various vehicles of the SA-12 low to high altitude surface-to-air missile family mounted on tracked chassis. In the background are the Bill Board warning and acquisition radar vehicle (on left) command vehicle and Grill Pan fire control radar vehicle (on right). The vehicle left foreground is the SA-12b launcher vehicle, the vehicle centre foreground is the reload carrier and the vehicle right foreground is the SA-12a launcher. (Soviet Military Power 1986)

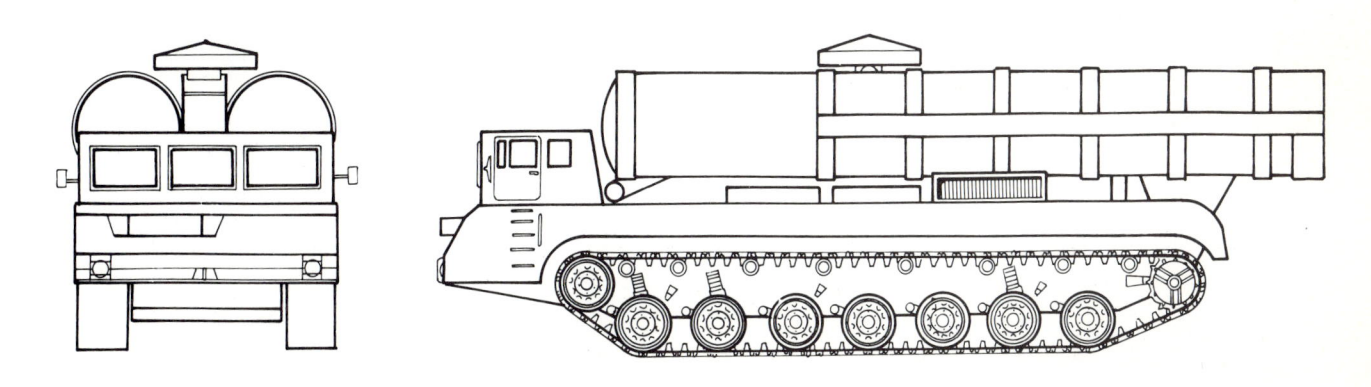

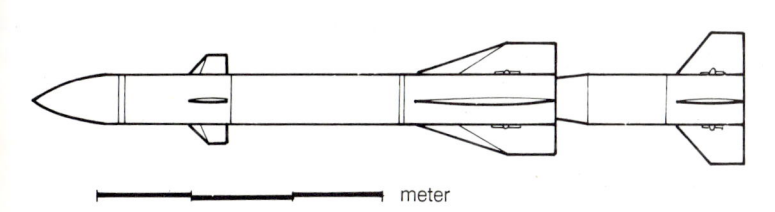

SA-12b Giant transporter-erector launcher vehicles (not to 1/76th scale) (Steven Zaloga)

138 SELF-PROPELLED SAMS / USSR

One of the roles assigned to this system is to be carried on low-loader rail-cars as part of the rail-mobile SS-24 Scalpel ICBM system. When an ICBM train is moved out of its tunnel-hide and into its launch area the attached Giant battalion or battery unit will unload itself and disperse into the surrounding country-side to provide a point defence ABM shield to intercept any incoming strategic missile re-entry vehicles which threaten the Scalpel systems.

Deployment of the SA-12b may be different to the SA-12a system with three or four batteries per battalion and up to four battalions in a brigade. Each battery will have two or more SPUs with one or two TZMs, a KShM and an SSNR at the battery HQ. At battalion level there is a different SSRT radar system to that used by the SA-12a, another KShM vehicle and several more TZMs. The brigade HQ unit is believed to be similar in composition to that of the SA-12a brigade.

SA-X-12b Giant SPU in firing position (US Department of Defense)

SPECIFICATIONS (SA-12a provisional)

CREW	4	MAX SPEED	50 km/h
COMBAT WEIGHT	20 364 kg	MAX RANGE	300 km
LENGTH	12.5 m	ENGINE	D12A diesel developing 525 hp
WIDTH	3.5 m	ARMOUR	9 mm (max)
HEIGHT	3.8 m		

Status: The SA-12a, is in production and service with the Soviet Army. The SA-X-12b is in development phase.

Manufacturer: Soviet state factories.

SA-13 Gopher Low Altitude Surface-to-air Missile System

Development/Description

The fully amphibious NBC-equipped SA-13 Gopher mobile SAM system with a range-only radar entered operational service in 1977. It is replacing the far less capable SA-9 Gaskin/BRDM-2 system on a one-for-one basis to improve the mobility of the anti-aircraft batteries in the Motorised Rifle and Tank divisions. The SA-13 was introduced into the Group of Soviet Forces Germany in the spring of 1980 and has since been seen in a number of other countries. The SA-13 Gopher has seen combat use in Chad (with Libyan forces) and in Angola with the MPLA and Cuban forces. In both areas examples have been captured by pro-western adversary forces. Recently high readiness Tank and Motorised Rifle Divisions have begun to field enlarged Regimental level air defence battalions of six ZSU-23-4 and six SA-13 Gopher vehicles. The totals for a Division then become 24 ZSU-23-4 and 24 SA-13 systems. In addition some of the forward deployed Category 1 Divisions have had their air defence battalions of SA-13/ZS-23-4 vehicles replaced by battalions fielding six 2S6 and six BMP-2, the latter apparently being used to transport regimental level SA-14/SA-16 manportable SAM teams. The surveillance unit equipped with a Dog Ear radar vehicle remains the same.

There are at least two versions of the SA-13 transporter-erector-launcher-and-radar (TELAR) variant of the MT-LBu vehicle in service, designated TELAR 1 and TELAR 2. Appraisal of both does not show any significant structural differences but it is known that the TELAR-1 carries four Hat Box passive radar detection antenna units, one on either corner of the vehicle's rear deck, one facing aft and one between the driver's vision ports at the front, whereas the TELAR-2 has none.

Known as the ZRK-BD Strela 10 system in Soviet service the 55 kg SA-13 missile (9M37M) is 2.2 m long, 0.12 m in diameter with a 0.4 m wingspan and has a maximum speed of Mach 1.5. It carries a 4 kg HE warhead and is fitted with a cryogenically cooled passive all-aspects infra-red seeker unit which operates in two frequency bands to give high

Czechoslovakian Army SA-13 Gopher SAM system from rear showing two hull doors

Czechoslovakian Army SA-13 Gopher SAM system in travelling configuration clearly showing Hat Box passive antenna between two front hatches

SA-13 Gopher SAM system with 7·62 mm MG over front of vehicle and missile resupply racks on side of hull

USSR / SELF-PROPELLED SAMS

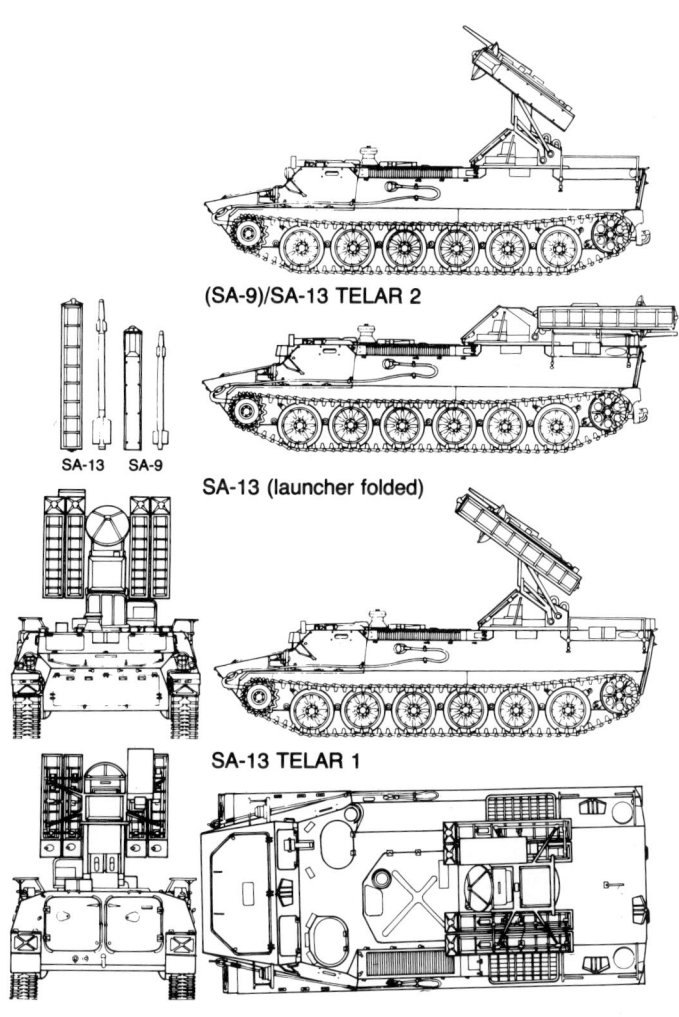

SA-13 Gopher Mobile SAM system (not to 1/76th scale) (Steven Zaloga)

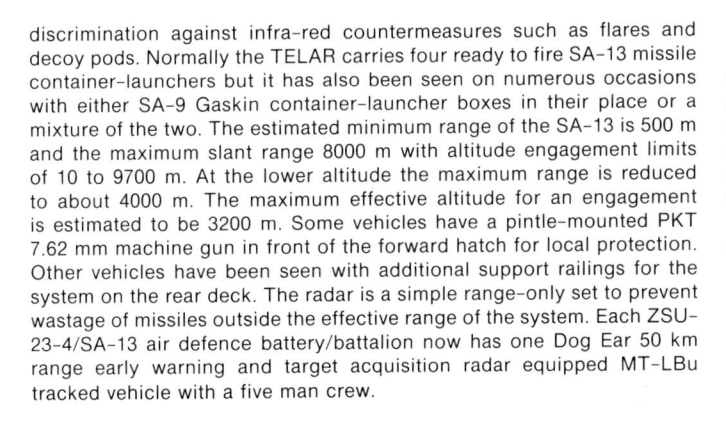

SA-13 Gopher SAM system of the Soviet Army with launcher arms elevated

Dog Ear surveillance radar vehicle which is used by SA-9 and SA-13 SAM units to provide target information

discrimination against infra-red countermeasures such as flares and decoy pods. Normally the TELAR carries four ready to fire SA-13 missile container-launchers but it has also been seen on numerous occasions with either SA-9 Gaskin container-launcher boxes in their place or a mixture of the two. The estimated minimum range of the SA-13 is 500 m and the maximum slant range 8000 m with altitude engagement limits of 10 to 9700 m. At the lower altitude the maximum range is reduced to about 4000 m. The maximum effective altitude for an engagement is estimated to be 3200 m. Some vehicles have a pintle-mounted PKT 7.62 mm machine gun in front of the forward hatch for local protection. Other vehicles have been seen with additional support railings for the system on the rear deck. The radar is a simple range-only set to prevent wastage of missiles outside the effective range of the system. Each ZSU-23-4/SA-13 air defence battery/battalion now has one Dog Ear 50 km range early warning and target acquisition radar equipped MT-LBu tracked vehicle with a five man crew.

Status: In production. In service with the following countries:

Country	Quantity	User
Algeria	32+	army
Angola	30+	army
Cuba	40	army
Czechoslovakia	100+	army
Germany, East	40+	army
Iraq	60+	army
Jordan	20	air force
Libya	60+	army
Poland	60+	army
Syria	60+	army
USSR	n/av	army, naval infantry

Manufacturer: Soviet state factories

SPECIFICATIONS
CREW	3
COMBAT WEIGHT	13 000 kg
LENGTH	6.6 m
WIDTH	2.9 m
HEIGHT	
firing position	3.8 m
travelling	2.3 m
MAX SPEED	55 km/h
RANGE	450 km
ENGINE	YaMZ-238V diesel developing 240 hp
ARMAMENT	4 × SA-13 missiles
UNIT OF FIRE	16 missiles
ARMOUR	14 mm (max)

SA-X-15 Low to Medium Altitude Self-propelled Surface-to-air Missile System

Development/Description
The Soviet Union is currently developing a new mobile SAM system designated SA-X-15 in the US designation series to replace the SA-8 Gecko. Limited details are available at present. The missile is believed to be 3.5 m long and 0.6 m in diameter. Minimum and maximum ranges are some 1000 to 16 000 m respectively between altitude limits of 18 to 18 000 m. It is possible that the SA-X-17 is similar to the Soviet Navy's SA-N-9 missile.

Status: Development phase. Believed to be undergoing troop trials. Not yet in quantity production.

140 SELF-PROPELLED SAMS / USSR-UK

SA-X-17 Low to Medium Altitude Surface-to-air Missile System

Development/Description
The Soviet Union is currently developing a new mobile SAM system designated SA-X-17 in the US designation series to augment and eventually replace the SA-11 Gadfly. No other details are available at present, except that it may use the same launch vehicle chassis.

Status: Development phase. Initial work believed to have started in the early eighties with the first Western intelligence reports concerning the system emerging in 1986-87.

SA-19 Low to Medium Altitude Surface-to-air Missile System

Development/Description
The Soviet Union has developed a tube-launched hypersonic low altitude SAM for use on its 2S6 (NATO/STANAG codename SPAAG M1986) (qv) hybrid tracked air defence gun/missile vehicle. The missile is mounted in elevatable launcher tube pairs on either side of the turret and is designed primarily for use against NATO anti-tank helicopters. Guidance is thought to be via a passive infra-red homing seeker. No other details are available at present.

Status: Production. In service with the Soviet Army (on 2S6 anti-aircraft vehicles).

Manufacturer: Soviet state factories.

UNITED KINGDOM

British Aerospace Tracked Rapier Low Altitude Surface-to-air Missile System

Development
Development of the Tracked Rapier began early in 1974 by the Guided Weapons Division of the British Aircraft Corporation, now British Aerospace (Dynamics). After study of the tracked vehicles on the world market the FMC M548 tracked cargo carrier was chosen. It is a member of the M113 family of APCs which is in service with over 40 countries and has been built in larger numbers than any other military vehicle in the West. In September 1974 it was announced that the Imperial Iranian Ground Forces had placed an order worth $400 million for 72 Tracked Rapier systems.

By late 1978 development of the Tracked Rapier was advanced in preparation for production. Early in 1979 the new Iranian Government cancelled a large number of defence contracts including that for the Tracked Rapier. Following evaluation by the British Army, the MoD placed an order for 50 Tracked Rapiers in June 1981. The first Tracked Rapier was accepted into service in January 1983. A further 20 were ordered in the post-Falklands defence review. Current army planning is for three Light Air Defence Regiments, the 12th, 16th and 22nd, to be equipped with both Tracked and Towed Rapier. A regiment will have two batteries of each system with 12 firing units per battery. The basic towed Rapier is in service with Australia, Brunei, Indonesia, Iran (army and air force), Oman, Qatar, Singapore, Switzerland, Turkey, United Arab Emirates (Abu Dhabi), United Kingdom (army and air force), United States (air force) and Zambia. Of these, Indonesia and Zambia have Optical Rapier, the others have Blindfire Rapier. By 1988 signed orders for Rapier and Tracked Rapier had exceeded 700 fire units, 27 000 missiles and 350 Blindfire radars.

The missile with Towed Rapier has seen combat use in the 1982 Falkland Islands War and, it is believed, with Iran against Iraq during the border skirmishes of the 1970s and the Gulf War.

Tracked Rapier with a number of modifications, including the installation of 12.7 mm M2 HB machine guns, was one of the four contenders for the US Army FAADS-LOS-FH competition which was won by the ADATS system late in 1987.

Description
The Tracked Rapier Launch Vehicle (TRLV) is based on the M548 chassis which for this role is designated the RCM 748. The crew of three is seated in the aluminium armoured cab which protects them from small arms fire and shell splinters. The driver is seated on the left, commander in the centre and the tracker operator on the right. There is a door in each side of the cab and bullet-proof windows in the front and sides of the cab. Both the driver and commander can be provided with night vision equipment and smoke dischargers are mounted front and rear.

A hatch is provided for the commander. When surveillance radar data is not available the commander can acquire and engage a target visually

Tracked Rapier Launch Vehicle with launcher traversed right and command link antenna lowered (BAOR)

UK / **SELF-PROPELLED SAMS** 141

Tracked Rapier Launch Vehicles in travelling configuration (left) and in action configuration (right) with commander using Helmet Pointing System

Forward Area Support Team (FAST) vehicle

Tracked Rapier vehicle commander using Ferranti Helmet Pointing System

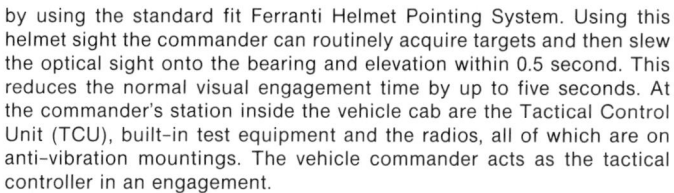

Tracked Rapier Launch Vehicle (right) being resupplied with Rapier missiles by M548 Tracked Rapier Support Vehicle (left) that carries 20 missiles

by using the standard fit Ferranti Helmet Pointing System. Using this helmet sight the commander can routinely acquire targets and then slew the optical sight onto the bearing and elevation within 0.5 second. This reduces the normal visual engagement time by up to five seconds. At the commander's station inside the vehicle cab are the Tactical Control Unit (TCU), built-in test equipment and the radios, all of which are on anti-vibration mountings. The vehicle commander acts as the tactical controller in an engagement.

The TCU provides tactical control facilities and is connected to the launcher and the optical tracker. The TCU is divided into 32 sectors in azimuth, each sector thus covering 11.25°. By operating sector switches, blind areas can be established to provide safe channels and heights for friendly aircraft or to set in priority arcs of fire for the fire unit, should this be required.

A day and night capability is provided by the addition of a class 2 common module based 10 km range thermal imager with associated electronics and a compressed air cooling unit mounted on the Tracker rotary head. The operator can select optical or thermo-optical as required. The tracker, designated as TOTE (Tracker Optical Thermally Enhanced), can be programmed for an automatic passive search programme in addition to its day and night tracking role. TOTE is mounted on anti-vibration mounts in the roof of the cab on the right side in place of the optical tracker. When deployed the tracker is raised into the operating position and when not required can be retracted into the cab and covered by an armoured hatch. The operator tracks the target either using the optical channel or TOTE by means of a joystick control to establish a sightline to the target. A TV system collimated with the target tracking system is used to gather the missile onto the sightline and then to measure the displacement of the missile from the sightline during flight so that correcting commands can be generated and sent to the missile automatically. The operator is provided with a biocular sight for target tracking and has the few simple controls required to operate the system at the control station. A monocular sight at the rear of the tracker allows either an instructor to monitor students' performances during training in the field or the fitting of a CCTV camera.

Immediately behind the cab there is an air-cooling unit and the cab also has a heater. The diesel generator set is to the rear of the engine bay and uses an HD 30 diesel engine identical to that in the Chieftain MBT. To the rear of the cab is the shield which protects the forward part of the vehicle from blast when a missile is launched.

Installed on anti-vibration mounts at the rear is the launcher which has four missiles on each side with 25 mm armour protection. The turntable and base of the launcher are also protected to APC standards by armour plate. The J-band command antenna is mounted on an elevating mechanism which, when raised, allows missiles to be launched and guided at low altitudes over the cab. Under a radome, on the armoured turntable, are the pulse Doppler F-band all-weather 11.43 km range surveillance radar antenna that rotates once every second, and the IFF antennas and interrogator. The radar transmitter/receiver is mounted in the base of the launcher unit. The turntable can rotate through 360°.

The Rapier Mk 1 missile is identical to that used in the towed Rapier system and is manufactured as a round of ammunition and requires no maintenance, testing or servicing once it has left the ordnance depot except for routine changing of desiccators. The missile has a shelf life of at least 10 years when stored in controlled conditions.

The missile consists of four main sections: warhead, guidance, propulsion motor and control. The warhead section contains the 1.4 kg warhead, safety and arming unit and crush fuze. The guidance section is in two parts, the electronics pack and the instrument pack. The propulsion unit is an integral two-stage booster motor and gives the missile a maximum speed of over Mach 2. The rear control section contains the hot gas-driven control surface actuation mechanism which controls the missile in flight and flares to facilitate TV gathering and tracking. The two-stage, solid fuel motor missile is 2.24 m long, has a body diameter of 0.133 m, wingspan of 0.381 m and weighs 42.6 kg. The missile has an effective range of 247 to 7000 m and can operate from very low levels to over 3000 m. The warhead is of the semi-armour-piercing type with a 0.5 kg HE charge and a contact fuze. The missile has proved to be extremely agile and to be able to pull high *g* turns out to its maximum range against both manoeuvring and fast crossing targets. Once the eight missiles have been fired the launcher can be reloaded by hand in under five minutes. The average Single Shot Kill Probability of the system is over 70 per cent which has been demonstrated in MoD practice range firings.

From a tactical move the launcher can be put into action and begin an engagement within 15 seconds of coming to a halt; reaction time for the first missile is five seconds, the second two seconds with the time out of action 20 seconds.

A typical engagement takes place as follows. The surveillance radar aerial mounted on top of the launcher is continuously rotating through

142 SELF-PROPELLED SAMS / UK

Tracked Rapier launcher at BAe Bristol with surveillance antenna uncovered

360° looking for aircraft which come within its range. When detected an aircraft is automatically interrogated by the IFF system. If no friendly reply is received the operator is alerted by an audible signal in his headphones. At the same time the rotating head on the optical tracker automatically lines up with the target in azimuth followed by the launcher turntable with the missiles at the rear of the vehicle. If necessary the operator then undertakes an elevation search to acquire the target. Once the operator has acquired the target he switches to the track mode and begins to track the target using a joystick. He can then identify the target aircraft visually. Information from the optical tracker and the surveillance radar are fed into the system computer in the launcher. This information is used to calculate whether or not the aircraft is within the range of the system. When the aircraft comes within firing range a lamp signal appears in the operator's field-of-view and he immediately presses the firing button to launch a missile. The computer also calculates and sets the launcher towards the optical line-of-sight. The missile is automatically gathered and guided along the sight line by the TV system until impact. During missile flight the operator's only task is to keep track of the target. When the engagement is finished the operator may switch back to search so that another engagement sequence can begin immediately if required. Or, a second missile may be fired at the same target or another target in the operator's field-of-view.

To give the system all-weather capability a Marconi Command and Control Systems Blindfire radar can be added. In operation the Blindfire monopulse radar employs differential tracking of both the missile and the target using a very narrow pencil beam to achieve the accuracy required. Frequency agility is used to reduce the effect of target glint and ECM. Each TRLV is also accompanied by an M548 Tracked Rapier Support Vehicle (TRSV) with a crew of two and 20 reload Rapier missiles in their travelling containers.

A Forward Area Support Team (FAST) vehicle, which is a modified M548, has also been developed. This has a crew of two, VHF radio, front-mounted crane, test equipment and spare line replacement units in order to provide the maintenance and support requirements of Tracked Rapier in the field. Twelve FAST vehicles have been ordered to date.

Modifications to give Tracked Rapier a night capability are already under way. The incorporation of a thermal imager in addition to the optical target tracking channel allows completely passive night operations up

Tracked Rapier Launch Vehicle during British Army trials in the Hebrides. In this firing, the Mk 1 missile was launched over the cab with microwave command link antenna raised to obtain unobstructed view

British Army Tracked Rapier launching a missile over the rear during trials

to the moment of missile launch. The tracker, optical, thermally-enhanced (TOTE) programme involves additional equipment being mounted on the rotary head of the optical tracker. The Class 2 common module based thermal imager is on an elevating mount on one side of the tracker with a compressed-air cooling bottle on the other side, and electronic units mounted front and rear. The operating sequence for night engagements remains essentially as described earlier. The current optical only Tracked Rapier vehicle is designated the SP Mk 1A by the British Army and those retrofitted with TOTE become the SP Mk 1B.

Tracked Rapier retains the cross-country performance and amphibious capability of the vehicle in the original role. It is easily airportable, one tracked fire unit being carried combat ready in a C-130 aircraft. Particular attention has been given to the system's ability to survive in battle. With its low profile and rotating aerial hidden by a radome the fire unit is easy to conceal, has a low IR signature, and is capable of passive surveillance when required. The system is designed to be operated in NBC clothing.

The system will also be compatible with the Rapier Mk 2 missile that is being developed for the Rapier 2000 programme which was initiated in late 1986 for deployment in Towed form during the mid-1990s. The missile will be available in two versions: the Mk 2A semi-armour-piercing round and the Mk 2B with a fragmentation warhead and proximity fuze. To exploit the weapon's full capabilities, Tracked Rapier will probably be upgraded in the same period as the missile's introduction.

SPECIFICATIONS

CREW	3
COMBAT WEIGHT	14 010 kg
POWER-TO-WEIGHT RATIO	14.89 hp/tonne
GROUND PRESSURE	0.63 kg/cm^2
LENGTH	6.4 m
WIDTH	2.8 m
HEIGHT	
optical tracker raised	2.78 m
airportable	2.5 m
GROUND CLEARANCE	0.41 m
TRACK	2.159 m
TRACK WIDTH	381 mm
LENGTH OF TRACK ON GROUND	2.819 m
MAX SPEED	
road	48 km/h
water	5.6 km/h
FUEL CAPACITY	398 litres
CRUISING RANGE	300 km
FORDING (with screen)	amphibious
GRADIENT	60%
SIDE SLOPE	30%
VERTICAL OBSTACLE	0.609 m
TRENCH	1.676 m
TURNING RADIUS	4.3 m
ENGINE	GMC model 6V-53 6-cylinder liquid-cooled diesel developing 210 hp at 2800 rpm
TRANSMISSION	Allison TX-100 3-speed, torque converter
SUSPENSION	torsion bar
ELECTRICAL SYSTEM	24 V
ARMAMENT	8-round launcher for Rapier SAM
SMOKE DISCHARGERS	yes (front and rear)

Status: Production complete. A total of 72 Tracked Rapiers have been delivered to the British Army. Production can be resumed if additional orders are placed.

Manufacturer: British Aerospace (Dynamics) Limited, Six Hills Way, Stevenage, Hertfordshire, SG1 2DA, UK.
Telephone: (0438) 312422
Telex: 825125, 825126

British Aerospace Rapier Laserfire Low Altitude Surface-to-air Missile System

Development

Feasibility studies carried out in 1984 resulted in the proposal to fit British Aerospace's pallet-mounted low level air defence system Rapier Laserfire on an Alvis Stormer APC chassis to provide a mobile system to defend forces in battle. Stormer's characteristics remain unaffected and no changes are required to the Rapier Laserfire weapon system. Other vehicle types that could be used include the LAV, M113, TADS, Hummer, Bedford (now AWD) 4-tonne and US M939 truck. For static defence the pallet can be mounted on the ground.

In February 1988, British Aerospace announced that the Rapier Laserfire low level air defence system had fully met its performance targets during recent phases in its development programme. The system achieved automatic acquisition and automatic laser tracking of an aircraft and a small Hayes towed target. Firing trials have resulted in target hits on the Hayes target and on a simulated hovering helicopter. Both firings were conducted in the fully automatic mode. In addition, a representative operational system undertook a five-week programme of trundling and mobility trials across country and over a variety of simulated potentially damaging terrain such as 5 cm concrete blocks. These tests exceeded standard defence specifications (DEF-STAN 07-55) and the system continued to operate throughout these trials with no functional failures.

Description

The Stormer base, fitted with a flat rear deck developed for the Alvis Streaker which carries the pallet-mounted Laserfire allowing 360° cover, can come into action, if necessary, on sloping ground. There is no need to cross level the equipment as sensors in Laserfire will allow the computer to compensate for slopes of up to 5°. Power for the system is supplied from the vehicle main engine PTO.

The Rapier Laserfire is a self contained fire unit, consisting of an M-band 10 km range coherent continuous-wave Doppler very narrow beam Surveillance Radar, an automatic Laser Tracker, four ready to fire Rapier missiles and a cabin for the crew of two. It has a day and night capability to engage attacking aircraft or helicopters. The Rapier Mk 1 missile, common to other Rapier variants, weighs 42.6 kg and can be reloaded by the crew quickly and easily without cranes or special handling equipment. The missile has a range of 247 to 7000 m to give a high lethality (averaged over 70 per cent Single Shot Kill Probability) over an area of approximately 140 sq km, against directly approaching and fast crossing targets.

When targets are detected by the millimetric Surveillance Radar, the pallet automatically slews in azimuth to the bearing, and the gyro-stabilised pulsed Ferranti Type 629 neodymium-YAG Laser Tracker unit, automatically put on in elevation, acquires and tracks the target. When the computer instructs the operator to fire, he presses the fire button to launch the missile. A TV camera in the laser tracker displays the scene within the cabin on a screen at up to ×13 magnification and automatically tracks the missile flares and measures any divergence of the missile from the laser sight line. These measurements are converted into commands to return the missile to the Sight Line, and sent to the missile by the command aerial mounted on the cab. The whole engagement from detection to target impact is automatic, although the operator can override the computer at any time, for instance by rejecting a target selected by the computer in favour of another of the seven possible shown on his visual display unit. In periods of radar silence targets can be engaged by the detachment commander acting as air sentry putting the Laser Tracker onto the target with an Auxiliary Sight or Pointing Stick mounted on the cab.

System reaction time is fast enough to cope with either high speed low flying aircraft or helicopters which may use terrain screening until they are exposed at short-range. Built-in test facilities in the weapon system monitor performance and can diagnose faults to line replaceable units, allowing these to be changed by the operator when required, thus reducing the need for technicians to operate in the forward area of the battlefield.

SELF-PROPELLED SAMS / UK

Model of Stormer Rapier Laserfire low altitude surface-to-air missile system with launcher traversed to right

Rapier Laserfire System mounted on Bedford (now AWD) 4-tonne (4 × 4) truck chassis firing a missile during trials at British MoD test range at Aberporth, Wales

Pallet-mounted Rapier Laserfire which can also be removed from its carrier chassis and deployed as stand alone unit as shown

Rapier Laserfire mounted on Bedford (now AWD) 4 tonne (4 × 4) truck chassis with cab folded down for firing

Status: Feasibility study (Stormer version). Development of the pallet-mounted Rapier Laserfire is virtually complete.

Manufacturers: Rapier missile system: British Aerospace (Dynamics) Limited, Six Hills Way, Stevenage, Hertfordshire, SG1 2DA, UK.
Telephone: (0438) 312422
Telex: 825125 825126

STORMER RAPIER SPECIFICATIONS (provisional)

CREW	3
MAX COMBAT WEIGHT	10 000 kg
LENGTH	5.69 m
WIDTH (over tracks)	2.311 m
HEIGHT	2.408 m
TRACK	1.888 m
TRACK WIDTH	432 mm
LENGTH OF TRACK ON GROUND	3.112 m
MAX ROAD SPEED	80 km/h
MAX ROAD RANGE	655 km
FORDING	1 m
GRADIENT	60%
VERTICAL OBSTACLE	0.46 m
ARMAMENT	4 × Rapier missiles
PALLET	
length	3.3 m
width	2.4 m
height	1.9 m
weight	2000 kg

Shorts Starstreak Low Altitude Self-propelled High Velocity Missile System

Development

In order to fulfil the British Army's General Staff Requirement (GSR) 3979 supplementing Rapier in the battlefield role of engaging late-unmasking close support aircraft and ATGW-equipped hovering helicopters, the Ministry of Defence originally approached 11 different companies to provide a new High Velocity Missile (HVM) design. Of these, British Aerospace and Short Brothers were each awarded a 12-month project definition contract in 1984. In late 1986 the latter was awarded a £225 million fixed price contract to cover the development, initial production and supply of the Starstreak HVM weapon.

In the self-propelled form the system will be mounted on the Alvis Stormer AFV chassis and issued to the 21st, 40th and 44th batteries of the reformed 15th Air Defence Regiment, Royal Artillery, in the early 1990s as part of the BAOR contingent's future air defence network. A total procurement of 151 vehicles is envisaged with the first due to start trials in 1989.

UK-USA / SELF-PROPELLED SAMS

Shorts Starstreak HVM system on Alvis Stormer APC

Shorts Starstreak HVM system on Alvis Stormer APC

Description
The Stormer in the Starstreak launcher configuration carries a crew of three, driver, gunner and commander, with eight ready to fire rounds in two armour-protected servo-controlled containers on the vehicle roof. Collocated with these is the gunner's surveillance, firing and target tracking turret which is fitted with an Avimo panoramic servo-controlled target acquisition and tracking sight and the THORN-EMI passive infra-red Air Defence Alerting Device (ADAD). A guidance beam transmitter is also housed in the sight unit and this is collimated to the target sight line. A total of 12 reload rounds are carried within the hull and these can be used to reload the missile containers or to provide a shoulder-launch or lightweight multiple launcher capability off vehicle. For these roles an additional aiming unit is carried.

A full description of the missile and method of operation is given in the *Manportable Surface-to-air missiles* section.

Shorts has offered the Starstreak HVM system to the US Army as a candidate for inclusion in the FAADS network at some future date.

Status: Under development for British Army.

Manufacturers: Prime contractor: Short Brothers plc, Missile Systems Division, Castlereagh, Belfast BT6 9HN, Northern Ireland.
Telephone: (0232) 458444
Telex: 74688
Fax: (0232) 732974
Vehicle: Alvis Limited, Holyhead Road, Coventry CV5 8JH.

UNITED STATES OF AMERICA

Boeing Avenger Pedestal-Mounted Stinger Self-Propelled Air Defence System

Development
In the early 1980s the Defense Systems Division of the Boeing Aerospace Company developed the Avenger air defence system as a private venture. Total time from concept through to delivery to the US Army for trials was only 10 months.

The Avenger consisted of a 4 × 4 High Mobility Multi-Purpose Wheeled Vehicle (HMMWV) with a turret mounted in the rear with eight missiles in the ready to launch position. The turret was also designed to operate military vehicles but the HMMWV was used during virtually all of the trials and the proof-of-principle testing. It can also be deployed as a fixed stand-alone unit.

Target acquisition was either by direct vision using the optical sight or through the use of a Forward Looking Infra-red System (FLIR). Mounted either side of the turret are four General Dynamics Stinger SAMs which are identical to those used in the manportable version.

During tests carried out in May 1984 by the US Army at the Yakima Washington Firing Center, three live Stinger rounds were fired at ballistic aerial targets. The first shot was fired from the vehicle moving along an unapproved road about 32 km/h and scored a direct hit. The second shot was at night with the unit stationary and scored a direct hit while for the third shot the vehicle was on the move, in the rain, and narrowly missed the target but was scored as a tactical kill as the missile passed within kill range of what would have been an attacking aircraft. The three missiles were fired by different gunners who had never fired a missile before.

In August 1984 the Avenger system was evaluated by the US Army Air Defense Board and during this evaluation 171 of the 178 fixed and rotary wing aircraft targets were successfully engaged by the system during the day and night operations.

In 1985 the General Electrical GECAL-50 .50 calibre Gatling Gun was fitted on the Avenger and test fired at the Ethan Allen range in Vermont. The three-barrel GECAL-50 was fired from the Avenger at different burst durations and showed that the turret's gyro-stabilised drive maintains a shot pattern of only 1 to 3.5 mils. These trials proved that the gyro-stabilisation system can track targets as easily as when installed on the HMMWV.

In 1986 the US Army issued a request for proposals (RFP) for a Pedestal Mounted Stinger (PMS), or Line of Sight - Rear (LOS-R) as one of the five key parts of the Forward Area Air Defense System, an overview of which is given under United States of America in the *Inventory* section. Three teams were subsequently shortlisted and each awarded a $100 000 contract to supply a single prototype system for US Army trials installed on a HMMWV chassis. The three teams were Boeing Aerospace with the Avenger, General Dynamics/Thomson-CSF/Hughes Electro-Optical Data Systems Group and LVT Aerospace with Crossbow. Extensive trials began early in 1987 at Oragrande Range, New Mexico, after which the Boeing Aerospace Avenger was selected. The extensive trial series included firing, target acquisition and tracking and environmental tests.

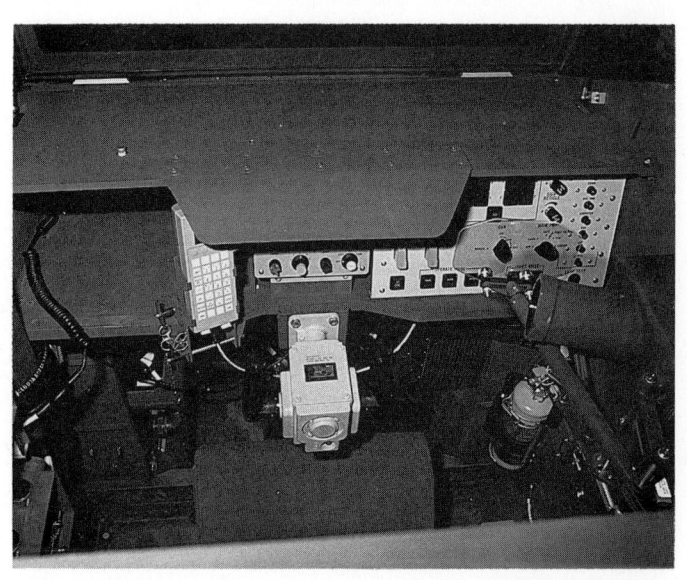

Close-up of gunner's position on production Avenger system. Both visual and forward looking infra-red sights are used to detect and track pop-up helicopters, remotely-piloted vehicles and low altitude aircraft

SELF-PROPELLED SAMS / USA

Production Boeing Aerospace Avenger/Pedestal Mounted Stinger (PMS) system on High Mobility Multi-Purpose Wheeled Vehcile (HMMWV) (4 × 4) chassis

In August 1987 the Defense Systems Division of Boeing Aerospace Company, was awarded a contract by the United States Army Missile Command to commence production of the PMS air defence system. The initial contract was for $16.2 million for the first option buy of 20 systems. The contract has a potential value of $189 million for 273 fire units over a five year period together with associated logistic support. The second option covering 39 systems was exercised in 1988 (with deliveries to run from July 1989 through to June 1990), the third for 70 firing units in 1989, the fourth 72 firing units in March 1990 and the fifth for 72 firing units in May 1991.

First production PMS systems were delivered in November 1988, the system becoming operational with the US Army in 1989, initially with the US Army 3rd Armored Cavalry Regiment at Ft Bliss. A total of 394 are due to be in service by the mid-nineties instead of the 462 originally planned.

The Avenger will be the first shoot-on-the-move air defence weapon to enter production for the US Army. With the award of the production contract, the Avenger programme moved to Huntsville, Alabama, where the system is assembled, tested and delivered to the Army Missile Command at nearby Redstone Arsenal. Boeing's manufacturing facility at Oak Ridge, Tennessee, makes the turret assembly, launcher mechanism and the base assembly that mounts the turret on the HMMWV.

According to Boeing Aerospace, the US Army's total requirement could reach 2300 systems with the US Marine Corps also looking for around 278 systems. As the Stinger has been sold to a number of foreign customers, Boeing believe that foreign military sales could eventually double the original US requirement. In addition to firing the original Stinger missile it will also be able to launch follow-on models including the Stinger POST (Passive Optical Seeker Technology). Typically the Stingers would be used at close range as well as for engaging ground targets.

Main sub-contractors to Boeing Aerospace are:
General Electric Armament Systems, computer and remote control unit
General Electric Ordnance Systems, electric turret drive as used in M2 Bradley Infantry Fighting Vehicle
CAI, CA-562 optical sight
DBA, autotracker
FN, 12.7 mm machine gun
KECO, heater and ventilator
Magnavox, forward looking infra-red system
Texstar, canopy
Texas Instruments, laser rangefinder.

Magnavox will supply the IR-18 FLIR system to enable Stinger to acquire targets at night and in bad weather. The PMS FLIR is a derivative of the IR-18 sensor developed by Barr & Stroud, UK. The IR-18 FLIR will be produced by Magnavox's Electro-Optical Division at Mahwah, New Jersey.

The system can be installed on other types of chassis, tracked and wheeled and is also fully airportable. During a demonstration at McChord Air Force Base, Washington, it was shown that three systems and their crews could be carried in a C-130 Hercules transport aircraft while six could be transported in a C-141B Starlifter. The turret module can be carried by a UH-60 while a CH-47 Chinook can carry a complete PMS system.

For the US Army PMS system, Stinger missiles are standard, but according to the company its design is such that it can accommodate other sensors and other missile systems including laser directed, wire guided or infra-red seeking.

An example would be the Short Brothers Starstreak High Velocity Missile selected by the British Army for fielding on the Stormer APC chassis. Boeing Aerospace and Shorts have signed a formal agreement under which they will work together on the integration of Starstreak into the Avenger. In addition, a mock-up installation of a pod of 36 Hypervelocity Rockets, a current US Army Missile Command (MICOM) project, was installed on the Avenger system.

In addition to the HMMWV and Bv 206 chassis, other potential chassis include the Commercial Utility Cargo Vehicle (CUCV) 2½-ton truck, M548 tracked cargo carrier and M113A3 APC.

Description

The driver is seated on the left and in addition to having all of the controls required to drive and operate the HMMWV he also has complete intercommunications with the gunner in the turret. All voice (intercom and radio) and system tones (IFF and missile) are provided.

Production Avengers are fitted with AN/PRC77 and AN/VRC47 radios and can accommodate the AN/VRC91 SINCGARS radio system when this is fielded. FAAD C²I equipment will also be incorporated as it is fielded with the gunner and driver communicating with each other via the AN/VIC1 intercom system. IFF is provided by the Stinger AN/PPX3B interrogator.

In addition the driver has access to the Remote Control Unit (RCU) for a redundant control of the turret if required. This is fitted with the same system controls and displays as the turret and enables the Avenger crew to dismount and conduct engagements from remote positions up to 50 m from the fire unit. The RCU can be rotated through 180° to allow a crewman in the passenger seat to operate it and is fitted with training facilities.

Target engagement from the RCU is identical to engagement from within the turret because of hand control switches and indicators on the gunner's console. Components connecting the RCU to the Avenger are control console with FLIR display, drivers combat vehicle crewman helmet, cable connecting CVC helmet and built-in test terminal.

The design of Avenger is modular so that it can accept advances in technology such as the replacement of Stinger by a laser beam rider missile, new sensors, advanced fire control system, Enhanced Position Locator, Reporting System, User System and Handheld Computer, HVRs or a larger calibre weapon.

The gunner is seated in the electrically powered turret which is traversed through a full 360°. If required the complete fire unit can be removed from the HMMWV and used as a stand-alone system. The batteries in the base of the fire unit are interconnected in parallel to the HMMWV's 24 V DC system to provide turret power. The Stinger pods can be elevated from −10 to +70°. The gunner has a large transparent canopy for all-round observation and to aim the missiles he looks through a sight glass on which he sees the projection of a driven graticule display. The graticule indicates the aiming point of the missile seeker, confirming to the gunner that the missile seeker is locked on the same target he is tracking and planning to engage.

Sensor package mount includes a CAI optical sight, Magnavox FLIR, DBA automatic video tracker (AVT) and a Texas Instrument's CO_2 eyesafe laser rangefinder, thus enabling the system to acquire and track targets under a wide range of operational conditions.

The FLIR is mounted on the left launch arm beneath the missile pod. This is a self-contained system operating in the 8-12 μm wavelength region. It has dual field capability and the gunner's foot pedal is used to select the field required. Production systems will have an electrically operated optics cover. The gunner tracks the target either by direct vision using the optical sight or through the use of the FLIR system for night and poor weather operation.

The AVT provides an automatic tracking mode. The FLIR video target-to-bore error signals determine the azimuth and elevation repositioning required by the turret drive system in order to maintain turret positioning on the target.

The laser rangefinder is mounted on the left hand launch arm behind the FLIR with target range being displayed on a hand held display in the turret. Target range is processed by the Avenger control electronics for use in the automated fire permit and fire control algorithms. The Avenger's FCS processes data from the LRF and displays an advisory fire permit symbol in the sight and FLIR display. The fire permit function maximises use of the Stinger's engagement boundaries. The electric turret driver is gyrostabilised so as to automatically maintain the missile pod aiming direction regardless of the vehicle's movement.

The gunner has a hand controller on which the missile and gun controls are located. In addition, he can transfer tracking control to the automatic tracking systems, one of which uses signals from the uncaged missile seeker and the other data from the FLIR video autotracker, to track the target until the gunner is ready to fire. This allows the gunner to concentrate on target identification. The firing sequence is fully automated and the gunner has only to pull the fire trigger to initiate the launch sequence and immediately select and prepare the next missile for firing.

For self-protection and for coverage of the Stinger dead zone, an M3P 12.7 mm MG is attached to the right hand launch beam as supplementary armament. The M3P is an improved AN-M3 MG with a cyclic rate of fire of 1100 rds/min, 5000 mean rounds between failure, an IR/muzzle blast reducing flash hider and a five mil dispersion. Three hundred rounds of ammunition are carried for ready use with additional rounds in reserve. Mounted either side of the turret is a pod of four Stinger low altitude surface-to-air missiles. Full details of the Stinger missile are given in the *Manportable Surface-to-air missiles* section.

In addition, to the eight missiles in the ready to launch position, an additional eight Stingers are carried in reserve and a standard Stinger gripstock is also carried for use in the dismounted role. Reloading takes less than four minutes.

SPECIFICATIONS

CREW	2
CONFIGURATION	4 × 4
COMBAT WEIGHT	3900 kg
WEIGHT OF TURRET MODULE	1134 kg
SYSTEM	
length	4.953 m
width	2.184 m
height	2.59 m
TURRET MODULE	
length	2.13 m
width	2.159 m
height	1.778 m
GROUND CLEARANCE	0.406 m
TRACK	1.81 m
WHEELBASE	3.3 m
ANGLE OF APPROACH/DEPARTURE	69°/45°
MAX SPEED	105 km/h
RANGE	563 km
FUEL CAPACITY	94 litres
MAX GRADIENT	60%
SIDE SLOPE	40%
VERTICAL OBSTACLE	0.56 m
FORDING	0.76 m
ENGINE	V-8 6.2 litre, air-cooled diesel
TRANSMISSION	automatic, 3 forward and 1 reverse gears
TRANSFER BOX	2-speed
SUSPENSION (front and rear)	independent, double A-arm, coil spring
STEERING	power assisted
TURNING CIRCLE	14.63 m
BRAKES	
front	hydraulic
rear	disc
TYRES	36 × 12.5 − 16.5
ELECTRIC SYSTEM	24 V
ARMAMENT	2 × 4 Stinger SAMs
	1 × 12.7 mm MG
TURRET TRAVERSE	360°
WEAPON ELEVATION	−10 to +70°

Status: In production for US Army, first systems delivered in October 1988 with system becoming operational in 1989.

Manufacturer: Boeing Aerospace, Defense Systems Division, PO Box 1470, Huntsville, Alabama, 35807, USA.
Telephone: 205 461 2803

LTV Crossbow Pedestal Mounted Weapons System

Development

The Crossbow PMWS was designed as a lightweight pedestal-mounted platform and drive system with on-the-move target acquisition and engagement capabilities.

It is based on a modified 4 × 4 High Mobility Multi-purpose Wheeled Vehicle (HMMWV) with a pedestal weapon/sensor package mounted in the rear. This can be fitted with a wide variety of anti-air/anti-armour weapons in single or combination type configuration according to the user's stated requirements.

The target acquisition and tracking sensor are carried in a compartment located directly above the pedestal post upright on top of the weapons carrier beam. They feed their information directly into the Gunner's Fire Control Console (GFCC) which contains all the elements of the Fire Control System and is used to control the engagement.

148 SELF-PROPELLED SAMS / USA

LTV Crossbow Pedestal Mounted Weapons system on HMMWV chassis and showing 12.7 mm MG on right side

LTV Crossbow Pedestal Mounted Weapons system on HMMWV chassis

LTV Crossbow Pedestal Mounted Weapons system on HMMWV chassis with rocket pod on left side

Close-up of LTV Crossbow Pedestal Mounted Weapons system showing optics mounted in centre

Prototype testing of the system has already taken place with firing of 25 mm M242 cannon, 12.7 mm heavy machine guns, Spike rockets and Basic Stinger and Stinger POST surface-to-air missile system configurations.

Future growth potential built into the PMWS includes the possible mechanical or electrical integration of radio frequency interferometers (RFI) and infra-red search sets (IRSS) into the system.

Description
In the redesigned crew compartment of the HMMWV, the driver remains seated at his normal left hand position but the gunner takes over the passenger's station on the right. In front of him is the GFCC which is stowed for travel into the space left by relocating the compartment's heater unit to the left wheel well.

In combat the GFCC is extended 279.4 mm into the compartment to a position just in front of the gunner. The unit's integrated video screen displays the target cues, weapon status and firing and aiming reticle symbology data while the gripstick (positioned on the right hand side of the GFCC) is used to control the weapons platform azimuth and elevation, choose either the TV or FLIR field-of-view scene and select and fire the weapons.

If required the GFCC can be removed from the vehicle for operation at a remote location. The gunner retains full control of all functions independent of the actual pedestal location.

All the gunner has to do wherever he is located is to acquire the target, as an automatic tracking facility maintains the track. This allows him to concentrate on target identification, ranging, weapon selection and optimum firing time. Once he decides these then the superelevation and azimuth lead angles are automatically commanded based on the target range, angular rates and whether a missile, rocket or a gun is being fired.

The sensor compartment contains a FLIR with three fields of view, a militarised TV camera (which provides much higher daytime resolution than the FLIR and increases the probability of detecting and identifying targets in high humidity conditions) and a neodymium-yttrium-aluminium-garnet (Nd-YAG) laser rangefinder with a 5 m resolution capability.

The weapons pedestal has a special 'kneeling' stow feature to meet air transport and air drop requirements while still achieving the depressed firing angle required. It is able to traverse a full 360° at up to 60°/s and has elevation/depression limits of +75°/-10°.

The normal weapons configuration is two standard four round ready to fire missile launcher pods for use with either Basic Stinger or Stinger Post surface-to-air systems. These may be replaced by the Matra Mistral, Bofors RBS 70 or Shorts Starstreak weapons.

If the vehicle is used in the anti-armour role then either a member of the Hughes TOW family or the Rockwell International Hellfire modular missile is used in the missile pods. Only minor modifications to the FCS are required in order to be able to fire any of these missiles. Two spare rounds are stowed within the vehicle hull itself.

Between the electro-optics and the left side missile pod is mounted a 26.4 kg lightweight SACO 12.7 mm calibre machine gun which can fire saboted light armour piercing ammunition to penetrate armoured helicopter airframes. This can be replaced by a 7.62 mm FN GPMG if required.

Other armament configurations available include the use of two Oerlikon 20 mm KAA cannon with 250 rpg in place of the missile pod/machine combination, the replacement of the 20 mm guns by 25 mm Mauser or M242 Bushmaster cannon, the replacement of one of the missile pods by a seven round unguided Spike rocket pod, or the fitting of up to 10 nine round clips of unguided rockets. In the latter case the sensor compartment is fitted with closable blast doors.

Status: Ready for production.

Manufacturer: LTV, Missiles and Electronics Group, Missiles Division, PO Box 650003, Dallas, Texas 75265-0003, USA.
Telephone: (214) 266-1824

Fibre Optic Guided Missile (FOG-M) System

Development/Description

In December 1988 the US industrial team of Boeing Military Airplane Company, Military Systems Division (58 per cent of designated work) and Hughes Aircraft Company Missile Systems Group (42 per cent of designated work) were awarded the first increment of a $131.3 million cost-plus-incentive-fee contract by the US Army Missile Command (MICOM) for the full-scale development of the Non-Line-of-Sight (NLOS) FOG-M component of the US Army's FAADS network.

Previous development details are give in *Jane's Battlefield Air Defence 1988/89* pages 25-26.

Overall programme costs are expected to exceed $2 billion if the US Army follows the expected procurement of 285 heavy fire units (probably based on the US Army/FMC tracked Fighting Vehicle Systems Carrier with up to 24 missiles aboard for use by Heavy Divisions), 118 light fire units (based on the AM General 4 × 4 High Mobility Multi-purpose Wheeled Vehicle—HMMWV—with six missiles aboard for use by Light Divisions) and 16 550 missile rounds based on the MICOM developed FOG-M weapon.

The initial 43 month contract will be completed in June 1992 with the team having had to deliver four heavy and five light fire units and 40 missiles. Contractor engineering development and government operational assessments will take place during Fiscal Year (FY) 1990 and 1991.

A low-rate initial production decision is expected during FY1991 with early user test and evaluation trials in late FY1991 followed by force development test and experimentation through to early FY1992.

Initial unit operational test and evaluation is scheduled for mid-FY1993 with current US Army plans calling for one platoon of NLOS weapons being deployed with three platoons of LOS-F-H ADATS per air defence battery and three batteries per battalion.

The role of the FOG-M is primarily to engage and destroy hostile helicopters masked behind battlefield terrain features but it has some secondary anti-armour/ground target capability.

When engaging a helicopter it is launched vertically, flips over 90° and levels off to fly in the general direction of the pre-programmed target position. If it is being used against an enemy ground target the only differences are that it follows a 200 m constant altitude mid-flight course and terminally dives onto the target. In both cases the Hughes day/night/adverse weather mercury: cadmium: telluride (HgCdTe) nose-mounted passive seeker unit transmits target imagery back over the rear-mounted spool wound and employs fibre-optics data link cable to be computer processed for display on the gunner's video console. The two-way link also transmits the guidance commands to the missile.

Once the operator has attained a visual lock-on he simply centres the cross-hairs on his tactical display onto the target and automatically guides the missile to its destination. If necessary, during the flight he can reject the chosen target and acquire and lock on to another higher priority one.

The system will also generate a full-colour digital terrain map from a stored data base to help the gunner choose the best routes for the initial phase of a missile flight as well as to determine a location for the fire unit. During the mid-course flight phase the missile seeker 'compares' the terrain features it is measuring to the information stored in the data base by a system similar in concept to the one fitted to the Pershing II ballistic missile.

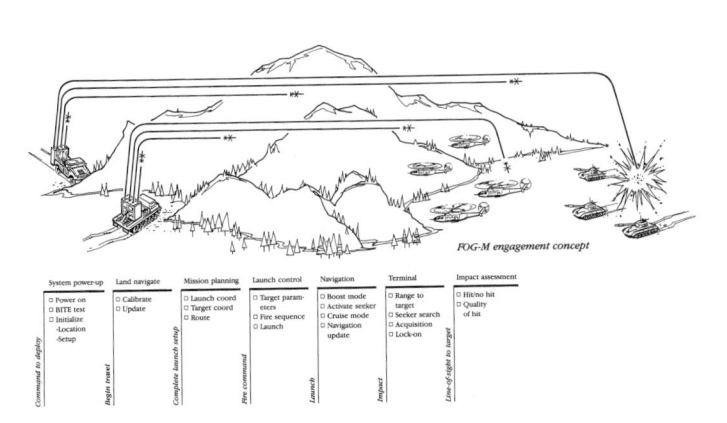

The objective system or Block I missile is about 2 m in length and weighs some 43-45 kg. It features wings and control fins in cruciform configuration, a booster motor for launching and a small throttleable turbojet sustainer motor. The warhead is of two-part type separated by a cryogenic bottle/blast shield. The forward shaped-charge is taken from an I-TOW ATGW and is used initially to create a hole in an armoured helicopter airframe or detonate any explosive reactive armour present on an armoured fighting vehicle. This allows the follow-on TOW-2 ATGW shaped charge to penetrate into the target's interior and destroy it.

Maximum range is between 15-20 000 m for the missile's speed range of 200-400 kts.

As currently configured, FOG-M is mounted in six-round ready to fire container-launcher modules. The launch vehicle contains the bulk of the guidance and control micro-electronics as an integral part of its gunner's station.

Status: Full-scale development for the US Army.

Manufacturers: Gunner station and system integration: Boeing Aerospace, Defence Systems Division, PO Box 1470, Huntsville, Alabama 35807, USA.
Telephone: (205) 859 8357

Missile: Hughes Aircraft Company, Missile Systems Group, 8433 Fallbrook Ave, Canoga Park, California 91304, USA.
Telephone: (213) 883 2400
Telex: 910 4944 997

Mock-up of light fire unit version of FOG-M on a HMMWV with launch container in vertical position and FOG-M leaving launcher box

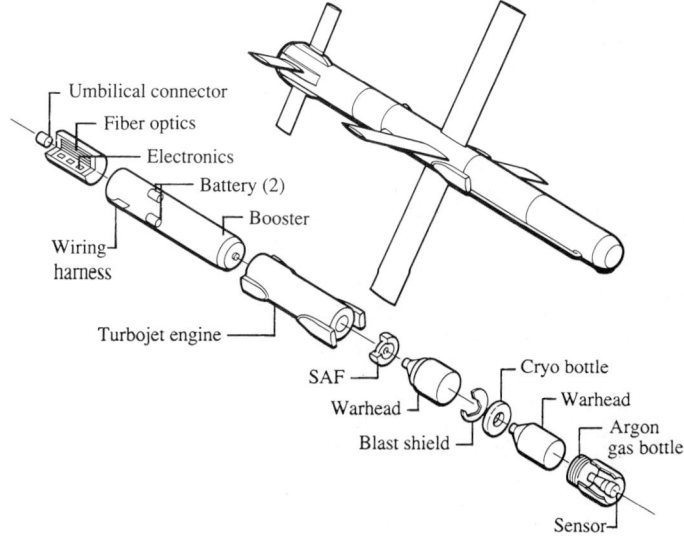

Mission phases of the Boeing/Hughes FOG-M system

Major components of the FOG-M system

SELF-PROPELLED SAMS / USA

Ford Aerospace M48A1 Chaparral/M48A2 Improved Chaparral Low Altitude Self-propelled Surface-to-air Missile Systems

Development

The Chaparral low altitude surface-to-air missile system was initiated with the US Navy Sidewinder 1C (AIM-9D) air-to-air proportional navigation guidance infra-red homing missile modified for ground-to-air launch. Study and evaluation of the Chaparral began in 1964 at the Naval Weapons Center, China Lake, California. The following year a development contract was awarded to the Aeronutronic Division of Ford Aerospace & Communications Corporation (formerly Philco-Ford Corporation), Newport Beach, California. Development and testing were undertaken by Aeronutronic, the Naval Weapons Center and at the White Sands Missile Range in New Mexico and first production missile systems were delivered to the US Army in 1969. Aeronutronic produces the launch and control station, and test equipment as well as being responsible for overall system integration including the development and production of the improved missiles. In the past, the original MIM-72A missiles had been supplied by Raytheon and General Electric.

The M48A2 Chaparral is deployed with the US Army in composite battalions with the M163 Vulcan self-propelled anti-aircraft gun. Each battalion has 24 Chaparral systems (two batteries each with 12 launchers) and 24 M163s (two batteries each with 12 guns). Early warning for the battalion is provided by the Sanders Associates Forward Area Alerting Radar model AN/MPQ-49.

A ground emplaced system, designated M54, uses the same launch and control system as the self-propelled M48. Chaparral saw combat use with the Israeli Army on the Golan Heights when it shot down a MiG-17 in the latter stages of the 1973 war and in the 1982 Israeli invasion of Lebanon against Syrian aircraft.

By early 1985 677 Chaparral systems had been built, of which 544 had been purchased by the US Army which has a total procurement objective of 632 systems.

The Chaparral low altitude surface-to-air missile system is still in production for the United States Army and for export.

In 1983 the Pentagon announced a letter of offer to Egypt for the sale of 26 M730A1/M48A2 Improved Chaparral self-propelled air defence systems, MIM-72F missiles, seven FLIR systems and seven modified M577A2 command post vehicles at a total cost of $112 million. This offer was accepted the following year and first deliveries were made early in 1988.

As part of the Egyptian contract, Saunders Associates provided seven of its TRACKSTAR (Tracked Search and Target Acquisition Radar Systems) mounted on top of modified FMC M577A2 tracked command post vehicle chassis.

In 1986 Portugal ordered five Chaparral systems, 28 MIM-72F missiles, two AN/MPQ-54 Forward Area Alerting Radars (FAARS), spares and support equipment with a total value of $45 million. These have now been delivered.

In 1986 Taiwan ordered 52 Chaparral fire units and associated spare parts valued at $29 million with final deliveries made during 1989.

Description

A Chaparral fire unit consists of two main elements, a tracked carrier and a missile launch station. The carrier is designated the M730 and is based on the M548 tracked cargo carrier which in turn uses components of the M113A1 armoured personnel carrier.

The crew of five comprises a squad leader (who makes the target selections, identifications and issues the fire orders), senior gunner (who operates the launch and control station and is vehicle second-in-command), vehicle driver (who can also function as an observer and/or radio operator) and two gunners (who primarily act as target observers).

The M730 has the engine and crew compartment at the front of the vehicle and the missile launch station at the rear. The crew compartment is equipped with front, sides, rear and top, which are removed before the missiles can be launched. The torsion bar suspension consists of five dual rubber-tyred road wheels with the drive sprocket at the front and idler at the rear. There are no track return rollers. The vehicle has no NBC system but is fitted with infra-red driving lights. When the flotation screen is erected around the rear of the hull the vehicle is fully amphibious, being propelled in the water by its tracks.

The launch and control station (designated the M54), consists of the base structure and turret. The base structure provides mechanical support and contains essential auxiliary equipment (including the electrical power source), storage for missiles, crew equipment and tools. The senior gunner's compartment, which is inside the turret, has filtered and conditioned air and an adjustable seat. The missile control electronics operate in conjunction with the control panel switches and indicators to control the activation of the system, missile selection and sequencing, missile launch sequencing and test functions. Each missile launch station contains an IFF subsystem.

The system uses a hydraulic turret drive that responds to rate commands from the gunner's hand control. The drive subsystem allows unrestricted movement in azimuth, but in elevation, movement is from -10 to +90°. The air compressor is part of the missile air supply subsystem which supplies air for the infra-red detector. The subsystem accepts outside air, compresses, filters and purifies it, and distributes it to each launcher assembly.

The main power unit, with associated power supply, provides the regulated power needed for all functions and if the power unit

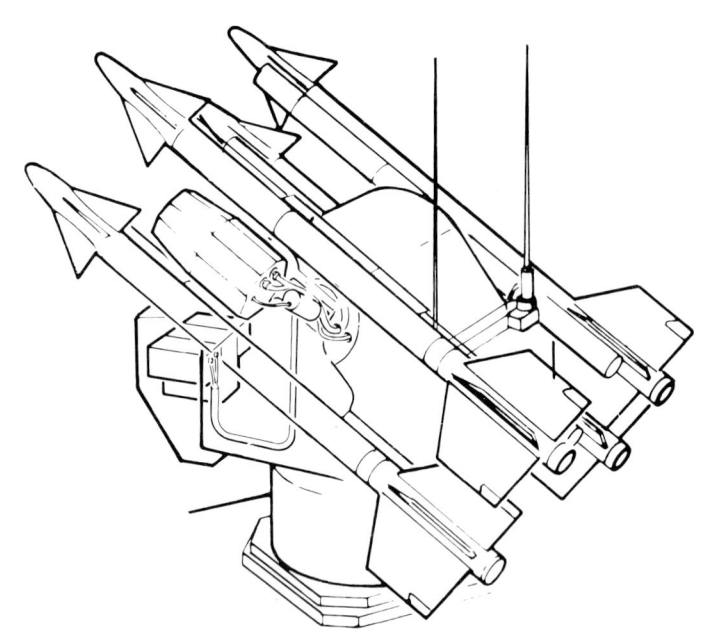

FLIR installed on senior Chaparral launcher

Chaparral surface-to-air missile system showing main components, bows stowed at front of vehicle and anti-blast shield positioned over cab

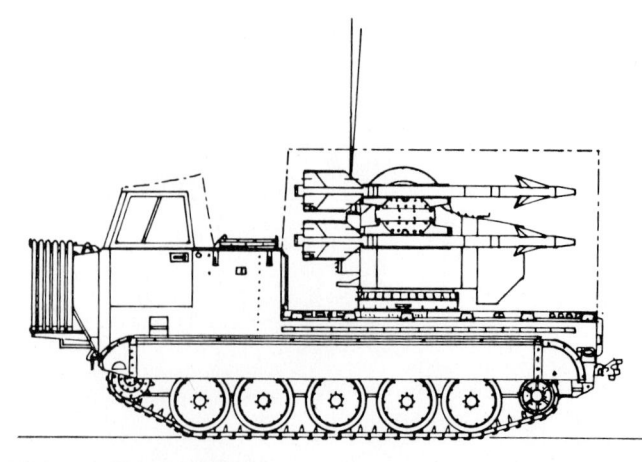

Chaparral surface-to-air missile system in travelling order without bows or tarpaulin cover in position

USA / SELF-PROPELLED SAMS

M48 Chaparral low altitude self-propelled SAM system showing FLIR pod on left side of mount and four missiles in ready to launch position

malfunctions the operator can continue for a limited period using the on-board storage batteries.

The missile itself is an in-line cruciform with two pairs of canard control surfaces at the forward end and two pairs of fixed wings at the rear. One pair of the rear wings is provided with rollerons to reduce roll rate. The missile is attached to the launch rail by hangers fixed to the rocket motor case. Four missiles are carried ready to launch and a further eight are carried in reserve.

The original missile was designated the MIM-72A, has a launch weight of 85 kg, is 2.604 m long and has a diameter of 127 mm, a wingspan of 0.631 m and is fitted with an 11.2 kg high explosive warhead. Between 1970 and 1974 an improved all aspect missile called the MIM-72C was developed, which entered service in July 1978. It weighs 86.2 kg, the other dimensions remain the same, and includes an M817 radar proximity fuze developed by Harry Diamond Laboratories, a 12.6 kg M250 HE blast-fragmentation warhead developed by Picatinny Arsenal and an AN/DAW-1 all-aspect IR seeker developed by Ford Aerospace. Effective launch range is increased to over 9000 m. Later versions of this missile are designated the MIM-72E and MIM-72F. All versions are powered by a single-stage solid propellant rocket motor.

The battlefield signature of the system has been reduced by the adoption of a smokeless motor for the later missiles. The US Army has started to retrofit launchers with a 130 detector element lead selenide 3.5 µm wavelength, 40 × 20° wide field-of-view, 10 × 5° narrow field-of-view, forward-looking infra-red (FLIR) thermal-imaging device, with autotrack features to provide a night and bad-weather capability and to improve daylight performance in smoke and haze. It is able to operate in either a wide or narrow field-of-view to optimise the infra-red detection capability of the receiver and improve the thermal image for the gunner. The optics on the receiver magnify the image and the infra-red target video obtained is presented on the video display located on the mount. Target range is established by a 6 km range boresighted laser rangefinder and identification by a lightweight Mk XII IFF system. The returns from these are evaluated in the fire control computer and a visual launch 'OK' signal is lit on the gunner's control panel. At the moment of missile launch a small protective cover will briefly close over the FLIR to protect the sensitive optics. To replace the existing 10 hp petrol engine used in the power unit a new 30 hp diesel engine is being retrofitted. This will both increase the power available and introduce fuel commonality with the M730. With all the improvements the designation changes to M48A2 Improved Chaparral.

Before the system can be used the crew leaves the cab, folds down the windscreen, removes the cab cover and folds a six-piece hinged blast-shield over the cab and engine compartment. An additional fixed blast-shield protects the back of the engine compartment. The six bows and tarpaulin cover are then removed from the launcher area and the bows are stowed on the front of the hull. The launcher is then mechanically raised into the firing position.

A typical daylight target engagement takes place as follows. Early warning is provided either by the AN/MPQ-49 Forward Area Alerting Radar or by a visual sighting. Once the gunner detects the target he moves the turret to acquire and maintain the aircraft within his sight. The turret can be traversed through 360° and the launch rails have an elevation of +90° and a depression of -9°. As the gunner tracks the target, an audio tone in his headset notifies him when the target is within infra-red sensing range.

The gunner then launches a missile which operates under its own internal power. Proportional navigation guidance commands are generated from seeker tracking rates and used to control the missile flight path. Proximity fuzing assures that the warhead will detonate even without a direct hit. The fire-and-forget capability allows the gunner to begin to search for and attack another target immediately. The rate of fire of the basic system is four missiles per minute with a full reload time of five minutes. The single shot kill probability was assessed at 0.5 against targets with velocities between 0 to 550 knots but this has been improved.

The basic MIM-72A Chaparral surface-to-air missile has maximum effective range limits from 500 to 6000 m and effective altitude limits of 15 to 3000 m. Maximum missile range is 9300 m with a total flight time of 22 seconds. The new Rosette Scan Seeker (RSS) for the Chaparral missile was developed from 1982 under contract to Missile Command by the Ford Aerospace and Communications Corporation and was type classified in August 1987. Modified missiles from the MIM-72C standard will be known as MIM-72G weapons. In November 1988 Hughes Aircraft

152 SELF-PROPELLED SAMS / USA

Towed Chaparral SAM system – US Army has taken delivery of 13

US Army Chaparral surface-to-air missile system in travelling configuration (US Army)

Chaparral missile being launched during trials at White Sands Missile Range (US Army)

Chaparral launch and control station, designated the M54, being used in stand alone configuration (US Army)

Company Tuscon was awarded a $39.1 million contract as a second source producer of 749 RSS guidance and control sections for delivery between 1990-92. This second source production contract contains options for an additional 422 sections.

The RSS is based on software that can be reprogrammed to take into account evolving threats such as different heat signatures, flares and other infra-red countermeasures. It is electronically reprogrammed by means of an external wire.

According to the manufacturer, Chaparral achieve virtual immunity to all types of infra-red countermeasures. Increased engagements and earlier launches are achieved by Chaparral with the Rosette Scan Seeker. Target acquisitions at 50 per cent longer range than the current guidance have been demonstrated, including a contact hit on a helicopter target beyond 8 km launch range.

TRACKSTAR

The TRACKSTAR is a self-contained 360° D-band 60 km range AN/MPQ-49 derivative integration radar/command and control C^2 system. It is used by the Egyptian army with its Chaparral fire units and automatically broadcasts cueing, fire distribution and IFF data via its VHF radio or hard-wire data links to Integrated Weapon Display (IWD) operator control and processor units (total weight 8.2 kg) that are mounted in or near the Chaparral vehicles.

The target cueing information is transmitted in terms of UTM coordinates and converted and orientated to each fire unit by the IWD processor. This has a target/display capacity for up to 32 targets and permits the input of operational parameters and selection of tactical modes.

Command messages from the TRACKSTAR commander can also be added to the target information flow over the data link and may be addressed to any or all the fire units as required.

The IWD also superimposes the radar and C^2 information on the integrated display of the fire unit in a B-scan format.

If optical target acquisition is used the IWD presents the radar data and C^2 information on a dedicated electroluminescent panel in a PPI format.

With either format, the senior gunner of the fire unit simply positions the boresight symbol over the designated target symbol, thereby prepositioning the missile launch station to ensure that the target will appear in his field-of-view.

This flexibility allows fire distribution tasks to be centrally controlled or delegated to gunners according to standard operating procedures whilst automatic netting of multiple radar data uncovers terrain masked targets.

Variants

A version known as Sea Chaparral is in use with the Taiwanese Navy aboard its larger warships. With reduced procurement of the Roland, Ford Aerospace is looking at advanced Chaparral systems to meet the short-range air defence requirements. One such system is based on an FMC FVS chassis for improved mobility, a reduced crew in an armoured cab, improved vehicle protection and eight ready to fire missiles in two armoured quadruple box launchers on a turntable at the vehicle rear. Ford Aerospace has also developed a 525 kg empty weight, four-wheeled trailer mounted version of Chaparral, with four ready to fire missiles, for the Rapid Deployment Force. In early 1984 a $10.6 million contract was placed for 13 systems of this type for use by the 9th Infantry Division on rapid deployment-style exercises.

A further study by the Aeronutronic Division would incorporate multi-mode guidance systems and tail controls in the Chaparral missile to increase the range and firepower whilst retaining the passive characteristics. The Sidewinder variant would be fitted with an infra-red search and track set, an acoustic sensor, a passive radio-frequency sensor and a low probability of intercept range-only radar in a new reduced-drag configuration with tail controls rather than forward fin ones as on the current missile. The missile is known as Chaparral II and it will have a range in excess of 10 000 m. Integration of the improved Chaparral or Chaparral II launcher with the MLRS carrier vehicle reduces the crew to two. In addition a Chaparral II system with 10 ready to fire container-launchers on a derivative of the Standard Manufacturing Company's hydrostatic vehicle with a mast-mounted surveillance radar and interferometer (to detect electronic emissions from aircraft) is being suggested for the US Army's new Light Infantry Divisions as it would only weigh about 6818 kg and be air-transportable.

In 1982 a Product Improvement Program was approved to modify the M730 missile carrier for use with the RISE power train developed for the M113A1E1 APC to give the M730A1E1 RISE vehicle. The M730 is

USA / SELF-PROPELLED SAMS

in particular need of improvement to its drive train reliability and performance because of its combat weight. The first conversions to this standard took place in 1987 with the whole fleet of 495 to be completed by 1989. The vehicle is then known as the M730A2.

Status: In production in both basic and Improved Chaparral configurations. In service with the following countries:

Country	Quantity	User	Comment
Egypt	26	army	M48A2 delivered 1988
Israel	52	air force	
Morocco	37	army	delivered 1987
Portugal	5	army	
Taiwan	52	army	
Tunisia	26	army	
USA	600+	army	deliveries still under way

Manufacturers: Aeronutronic Division, Ford Aerospace & Communications Corporation, Newport Beach, California 92660, USA (chassis is supplied by FMC Corporation of San Jose, California).
Telephone: (714) 720 4512
Telex: 67-8470
TRACKSTAR and Integrated Weapon Display (IWD): Sanders Associates Inc (a Lockheed company), Defence and Information Systems Division, Nashua, New Hampshire, NH 03061-2035, USA.
Telephone: (603) 9522
Telex: 94-3430

Egypt is the only user of the Sanders Associates TRACKSTAR integrated radar/command and control system based on an FMC M577A2 tracked chassis

SPECIFICATIONS

CREW	5
COMBAT WEIGHT	11 500 kg
UNLOADED WEIGHT	
(without launcher and missiles)	6611 kg
POWER-TO-WEIGHT RATIO	18 bhp/tonne
GROUND PRESSURE	0.53 kg/cm^2
LENGTH	6.06 m
WIDTH	2.69 m
reduced	2.54 m
HEIGHT (with bows and tarpaulin cover)	2.68 m
GROUND CLEARANCE	0.4 m
TRACK	2.159 m
TRACK WIDTH	381 mm
LENGTH OF TRACK ON GROUND	2.82 m
MAX SPEED	
road, forwards	61.2 km/h
on 10% gradient	20.1 km/h
water	5.5 km/h
FUEL CAPACITY	401 litres
MAX RANGE	504 km
FORDING (with preparation)	amphibious
GRADIENT	60%
SIDE SLOPE	30%
VERTICAL OBSTACLE	0.62 m
TRENCH	1.68 m
ENGINE	Detroit Diesel model 6V-53 6-cylinder water-cooled diesel developing 202 bhp at 2800 rpm
TRANSMISSION	Allison TX-100 consisting of 3-speed gearbox and 2-stage torque converter giving 6 forward and 2 reverse gears
SUSPENSION	torsion bar
ELECTRICAL SYSTEM	28 V
ARMAMENT	launcher with 4 Chaparral missiles (8 reserve missiles carried)
ARMOUR	none

Note: Current production systems weigh 13 024 kg complete with ready-use and reserve missiles.

Towed Anti-Aircraft Guns

BELGIUM

FN HERSTAL (S.A.) Bofors 40 mm L/60 Upgrade Kit

Development
The FN HERSTAL (S.A.) Bofors 40 mm L/60 upgrade kit has been developed as a private venture by FN HERSTAL (S.A.) specifically for the export market and was announced for the first time early in 1988. It replaces the earlier Gather modernisation kit which is no longer being offered.

The main drawbacks of the Bofors 40 mm L/60 anti-aircraft gun, which was developed before the Second World War, include limited magazine capacity of eight rounds, effectiveness of ammunition against new targets, simple iron sights, slow rate of fire, poor gun control equipment and the general overall condition of the weapons, most of which are over 45 years old.

Description
The private venture 40 mm L/60 upgrade package from FN HERSTAL (S.A.) consists of the following key elements: overhaul and improvements to the actual weapon, new ammunition and a new fire control system.

FN HERSTAL (S.A.) has technicians who can visit the customer and carry out a complete on-site inspection of the existing 40 mm L/60 weapons before submitting a detailed tender. They can also supply the parts which can be fitted by the customer's own armourers.

A four or five round burst limiter can be installed which helps to conserve ammunition, as it has been shown that with this type of weapon it is

Close up of Galileo Vanth sight on retrofitted Bofors 40 mm L/60 anti-aircraft gun from FN HERSTAL (S.A.)

FN HERSTAL (S.A.) upgraded 40 mm L/60 anti-aircraft gun system deployed in firing position

FN HERSTAL (S.A.) upgraded 40 mm L/60 anti-aircraft gun showing 12 round magazine

FN HERSTAL (S.A.) upgraded 40 mm L/60 anti-aircraft gun showing eight round ready use magazine on rear of carriage

Belgium-Brazil / **TOWED AA GUNS** 155

FN HERSTAL (S.A.) upgraded 40 mm L/60 anti-aircraft gun system deployed with gunner using Galileo sight

the first shots of a burst which have the greatest hit probability. The burst limiter is mounted on the left side of the weapon.

The 40 mm L/60 has a cyclic rate of fire of 120 rds/min which can be increased to 180 rds/min. A cylindrical magazine, mounted over the breech, holds a further 12 rounds and these, together with the eight ready rounds, give the gunner a total of 20 rounds which is sufficient for four 5 round bursts. Two further magazines each holding eight rounds can be fitted on the rear of the mount.

Mechanical improvements have also been carried out on the wheels and tyres, braking system and towing arms.

The 40 mm L/60 weapon fires 40 mm PF/HE-PrF rounds developed by FN HERSTAL (S.A.) under the designation of the FN 108. This is a short proximity fuzed round and is fed to the weapon in clips of four rounds. It gives a significantly increased kill probability over existing ammunition, also developed by FN HERSTAL (S.A.).

Two key parts of FN 108 round are the highly effective electro-magnetic proximity fuze, which detects the target within a 3 m radius, and its high fragmentation effect. The projectile body is treated to obtain the maximum fragmentation with the high explosive containing HMX. The training equivalent of the FN 108 is the FN 109 Spotter.

SPECIFICATIONS (ammunition)

DESIGNATION	**FN 108**	**FN 109**
TYPE	PF/HE-PrF	PF/Spotter
CARTRIDGE LENGTH	447 mm	447 mm
CARTRIDGE WEIGHT	2.19 kg	2.19 kg
PROJECTILE WEIGHT	900 g	900 g
MUZZLE VELOCITY	875 m/s	875 m/s
CHAMBER PRESSURE	3138 bar	3138 bar

It is also recommended that the Italian Officine Galileo Vanth optronic fire control system is installed. The basic Vanth sight features fully automatic target computation based on laser ranging, local control with remote designation (radar or optical) and integrated autotest. The

FN HERSTAL (S.A.) 40 mm L/60 ammunition, on left FN 108 and on right FN 109

operator controls the weapon using a two degree of freedom joystick with a manual backup mode also provided.

The Vanth sight is of modular design and growth potential includes an integrated training system. Full details of the Galileo sight are given later in this book in the *Towed anti-aircraft gun sights* section.

Status: Development complete. Ready for production on receipt of orders.

Manufacturer: FN HERSTAL (S.A.), B 4400 Herstal, Belgium.
Telephone: (32 - 41) 64 84 00
Telex: 41223 Fabna
Fax: (32 - 41) 64 54 52

BRAZIL

Modernised 12.7 mm Anti-aircraft Machine Gun M55

Development/Description

Brazil was one of many countries to receive 12.7 mm Quad M55 machine gun mounts from the USA during the Military Assistance Program of the 1950s and 1960s. The Brazilian armed forces still use these mounts, but for some time they have had difficulty in obtaining spares and various attempts have been made to modernise it. During the early 1970s the Istituto de Pesquina e Desenvolvimento (IPD — Research and Development) in Rio de Janeiro carried out a development programme to produce spares locally, but this did not prove feasible, nor did a 1979 project to substitute a hydraulic-powered drive. In mid-1980 it was decided to produce an entirely new electro-mechanical drive system using some existing parts, but replacing the electrical components with a commercially available petrol engine and accessories.

Operational testing of the new system took place at the Campo de Provas da Marambaia (CPrM — Marambaia Proving Grounds) between September 1980 and July 1981 when production certification was granted. The trials were carried out under the auspices of the Centro Tecnólogico do Exército (CTEx — Army Technological Centre) in Rio de Janeiro. Production of the modernised mounts is now under way in Rio de Janeiro by LYSAM, Indústria e Comércio de Máquinas e Equipamentos Limitade.

This modernisation involves the overhaul of all mechanical and electrical components and the new items added include a five or six hp Montgomery M-226 or M-252 petrol engine with a five-litre fuel tank (fuel consumption is 2.33 l/hr), a standard 12 V 36 A battery, a 14 V 36 A Wapsa alternator, a 12 V 36 A Wapsa power regulator, a 12 V Bosch starter motor, a Fiat 147 ring gear and a V-belt transmission. The modernised mount can now be powered permanently and the traverse and elevation velocities are now over 90°/s (originally they were at best 60°/s). In the case of a petrol engine failure, the mount can be operated using the starter motor for three minutes.

Variants

LYSAM is now producing the mount to meet Brazilian Army requirements and for export. A version armed with two 20 mm Hispano-Suiza HS 404 cannon was completed in 1984.

Early in 1984 the prototype of a self-propelled anti-aircraft gun system was tested in Brazil. This consists of an X1A light tank chassis fitted with the modernised M55 12.7 mm anti-aircraft machine gun. As of early 1989 this version had not entered production for the Brazilian Army.

Status: Production for Brazilian Army and export.

Manufacturer: LYSAM — Indústria e Comércio de Máquinas e Equipamentos Limitade, Rua Marques de Oliveira, 53 — Ramos — 21031 Rio de Janeiro, RJ — Brazil.

Prototype LYSAM twin 20 mm anti-aircraft gun mounting two Hispano-Suiza HS 404 cannon (Ronaldo S Olive)

CANADA

40 mm L40/60 Boffin Automatic Anti-aircraft Gun

Development/Description

The Bofors L40/60, mounted on an Oerlikon twin 20 mm Mark V(C) mount, was originally used by the Royal Canadian Navy during the Second World War. In 1972/73 the weapons were refurbished and permanently emplaced around Canadian airfields at Baden and Lahr in West Germany.

The gun is called the Boffin and is manned by a detachment of three. The gunner uses an optical speed-ring sight and controls elevation, traverse and firing by hydraulically-assisted hand controls. The ammunition handler loads ammunition of the standard 40 mm fixed type (eg HE-T SD) into the automatic loader in four round clips. The detachment commander controls the engagement from the rear.

The Boffin has a 120 rpm cyclic rate of fire and a 60 rpm practical rate. Elevation is +66°, depression -3° and traverse 360°. Maximum rate of elevation is 34°/s and maximum rate of traverse 56°/s. The weight of the complete gun and mount is 1770 kg.

40 mm L40/60 Boffin automatic anti-aircraft gun which is deployed in static role in West Germany (Canadian Armed Forces)

These 40 mm L40/60 Boffin automatic anti-aircraft guns are soon to be replaced by a new Low Level Air Defence System (LLADS). After studying detailed proposals by Bofors of Sweden, Contraves of Switzerland and Oerlikon-Bührle of Switzerland, the latter was selected in spring 1985. Further details are given in the inventory section under Canada.

Status: Production complete. In service only with Canada.

CHILE

FAMIL FAM-2M Twin 20 mm Light Anti-aircraft Gun

Development/Description
The first 20 mm anti-aircraft guns in the FAMIL series were produced under the name Sogeco; FAMIL is now a subsidiary of Sogeco. The first guns in the series used Hispano-Suiza HSS 820 cannon taken from redundant Vampire T.11 aircraft, but the latest guns in the series use Oerlikon KAD B16 and B17 cannon with a muzzle velocity of 1040 m/s. These guns are mainly used for airfield defence, but they can also be used against ground targets.

The carriages on all the guns produced so far are similar and are supported in the firing position on four folding outriggers. For transport, the gun is carried on a removable twin-wheeled yoke carriage. Power for the mounting is supplied by a small petrol engine on the right-hand side of the carriage. The engine drives a hydraulic system which is controlled by the gunner using a single joystick control. The latest models also have a 24 V electrical system supplied from two 12 V batteries for the sight electrics. A shield is fitted.

Early models use a simple cartwheel sight, but the latest models have a Ferranti gyroscopic reflector sight that can be used together with a Ferranti target injection training system. Now in service is a central control system that controls up to four guns from a single control box mounting a single joystick to act as a fire director system for a battery. A version using centralised radar control is under development.

The Hispano-Suiza 820 cannon versions use drum magazines each holding 120 rounds of ready use ammunition. The Oerlikon KAD cannon have box magazines each holding belts of 200 rounds.

SPECIFICATIONS (Oerlikon KAD cannon version)

CALIBRE	20 mm
OPERATION	gas, automatic
CARRIAGE	2-wheel with 4 outriggers
SHIELD	yes
WEIGHT	
in action	approx 1700 kg
in firing position	1250 kg
of transport carriage	350 kg
of ammunition	68 kg
one cannon	68 kg
RATE OF FIRE (cyclic)	2100 rpm
FEED	2 × 200 round belts in boxes
EFFECTIVE RANGE	1500 m

Status: In production. In service with the Chilean Air Force.

Manufacturer: FAMIL SA, Mac-Iver 125 - 6° Piso, Santiago, Chile.

FAMIL FAM-2M twin Oerlikon-Bührle KAD 20 mm anti-aircraft gun with Hispano-Suiza 820 cannon (T J Gander)

FAMIL FAM-2M twin Oerlikon-Bührle KAD 20 mm anti-aircraft gun with side covers removed to show petrol engine, hydraulic system and Ferranti reflector sight (T J Gander)

Twin 12.7 mm Anti-aircraft Gun

Development/Description
This twin 12.7 mm (0.50) Browning M2 anti-aircraft gun uses water-cooled barrels converted from the normal air-cooled barrels. The water-cooling barrel liners are contained in perforated jackets around each barrel and the barrels are fitted with new multi-baffle muzzle brakes. Water is circulated via flexible hoses through the barrel liners by a single water pump, powered by two 12 V batteries. The complete system is mounted on a modified M63 pedestal mounting. A cartwheel sight is provided.

The water-cooled Browning M2 machine guns are converted from aircraft guns and the receiver, mechanism and ammunition feed remain unchanged.

Indications are that the modifications have been introduced by the Chilean Air Force.

Status: Production complete. In service with the Chilean Air Force.

158 TOWED AA GUNS / Chile-China

Chilean twin 12.7 mm water-cooled anti-aircraft gun showing water pump for circulating water through barrel cooling liners; two 12-volt batteries used to power water pump can be seen either side of central pedestal tube (T J Gander)

CHINA, PEOPLE'S REPUBLIC

Chinese Towed Anti-aircraft Guns

China produces and uses a number of different anti-aircraft guns, ranging in calibre from 12.7 mm (see following entries) to 100 mm. Most of these weapons are copies or derivatives of existing Soviet designs, for instance the Type 56 is a copy of the Soviet 85 mm M1939 and the Type 59 is a copy of the Soviet 100 mm KS-19. It is believed that neither of these two large calibre guns is still in production, but they are available for export with stocks taken from the strategic reserve for this purpose. Weapons still in production are being actively promoted for export and it is expected that many of these weapons have been provided to nations that have accepted Chinese military or other aid, such as Pakistan.

NORINCO 12.7 mm Anti-aircraft Machine Gun Type 54

Development
The NORINCO 12.7 mm anti-aircraft machine gun Type 54 is essentially the Soviet 12.7 mm Degtyarev Model 38/46 (DShKM) heavy machine gun made in China under the designation of the Type 54.

It has been designed to engage both air and ground targets. In the first application the tripod is almost vertical, while in the second application it is almost horizontal. The Type 54 is also used on a number of Chinese armoured fighting vehicles as an air defence weapon.

Description
Ammunition is fed from the left in boxes of 70 rounds and two types of 12.7 mm × 108 ammunition can be fired; armour piercing incendiary and armour piercing incendiary-tracer, both with a muzzle velocity of 820 m/s. The round will penetrate 10 mm of armour at a range of 800 m.

The foresight is a pillar which slides up and down, while the rear sight has twin vertical pillars with a U-backsight between them. In addition there is a special anti-aircraft sight which requires two men to use to its best advantage.

Variants
The Type 54-1 is an improved version of the Type 54 weapon and weighs 45 kg, with elevation in the air defence role being from -26° to +72°.

NORINCO Type 54 anti-aircraft machine gun being used in air defence role

China / **TOWED AA GUNS** 159

SPECIFICATIONS
CALIBRE	12.7 mm
PRACTICAL RATE OF FIRE	80 rpm
OPERATION	gas, automatic
METHOD OF LOCKING	projecting lugs
FEED	belt
WEIGHT OF GUN	35.7 kg
WEIGHT OF BARREL	12.7 kg
EFFECTIVE RANGE AGAINST AIR TARGETS	1600 m
EFFECTIVE RANGE AGAINST GROUND TARGETS	1500 m
ELEVATION IN AIR DEFENCE ROLE	-34° to +78°
TRAVERSE IN AIR DEFENCE ROLE	360°
TRAVERSE IN GROUND DEFENCE ROLE	120°

Status: In production. In service with Chinese Army and other countries.

Manufacturer: China North Industries Corporation, 7A Yuetan Nanjie, PO Box 2137 Beijing, Beijing, People's Republic of China.
Telephone: (86) 6898, (86) 3461, (86) 3471, (86) 7570
Telex: 22339 CNIN CN

NORINCO Type 54 anti-aircraft machine gun being used in ground defence role

NORINCO 12.7 mm Type 77 Anti-aircraft Machine Gun

Development
The NORINCO 12.7 mm Type 77 anti-aircraft machine gun has been designed to engage both air and ground targets. In the first application the tripod is almost vertical, while in the second application it is almost horizontal.

Description
The weapon appears to be recoil operated and has both ground and anti-aircraft sights. A distinctive pepperpot muzzle brake is provided.

Ammunition is fed from the left in boxes of 60 rounds and two basic types of 12.7 mm × 107 ammunition can be fired; armour piercing incendiary and armour piercing incendiary-tracer, both with a muzzle velocity of 800 m/s.

Type 77 anti-aircraft machine gun in air defence role

Type 77 anti-aircraft machine gun in ground defence role

SPECIFICATIONS
CALIBRE	12.7 mm
RATE OF FIRE (cyclic)	650 to 750 rpm
WEIGHT (with empty ammunition box)	56.1 kg
LENGTH IN GROUND ROLE	2.15 m
WIDTH IN GROUND ROLE	1.3 m
AXIS OF FIRE	
ground role	0.36 m
air defence role	1.3 m
EFFECTIVE RANGE	
air targets	1600 m
ground targets	1500 m
ELEVATION IN AIR DEFENCE ROLE	-15° to +80°
TRAVERSE	
air defence role	360°
ground role	120°

Status: In production. In service with Chinese Army and other countries.

Manufacturer: China North Industries Corporation, 7A Yuetan Nanjie, PO Box 2137 Beijing, Beijing, People's Republic of China.
Telephone: (86) 6898, (86) 3461, (86) 3471, (86) 7570
Telex: 22339 CNIN CN

160 TOWED AA GUNS / China

NORINCO 12.7 mm Type W-85 Anti-aircraft Machine Gun

Development

The NORINCO 12.7 mm Type W-85 anti-aircraft machine gun has been developed as a multi-purpose weapon for use at the battalion level to engage both air and ground targets. In the first application the tripod is almost vertical, while in the second it is almost horizontal. Compared with the older Type 54 12.7 mm anti-aircraft machine gun, it is some 58 per cent lighter and can be easily disassembled into three parts, the heaviest of which does not exceed 20·kg; these are the weapon, mount and ammunition box.

Description

The 12.7 mm Type W-85 machine gun can be quickly stripped and reassembled without tools and the barrel can be quickly changed in the field. According to NORINCO, the machine gun mechanism has a malfunction rate not exceeding 0.2 per cent. The barrel is certified for 3500 rounds while the remainder of the weapon exceeds 7000 rounds.

The manufacturer also claims that dispersion of the Type W-85 is good, with 70 per cent of the rounds fired impacting an area 31 × 31 cm at a range of 100 m.

The Type W-85 machine gun is fitted with an optical telescope enabling it to engage a wide range of battlefield targets under both day and night conditions. This can be replaced quickly by a special anti-aircraft sight.

The weapon can fire the following types of 12.7 mm × 107 ammunition, all with a muzzle velocity of 800 m/s: Type 54 armour piercing, Type 54 armour piercing with tracer and Type 54 armour piercing incendiary. It can also fire the Type 54 tungsten alloy cored bullet with a muzzle velocity of 1150 m/s. Ammunition feed is from the left, with each metal box holding 60 rounds.

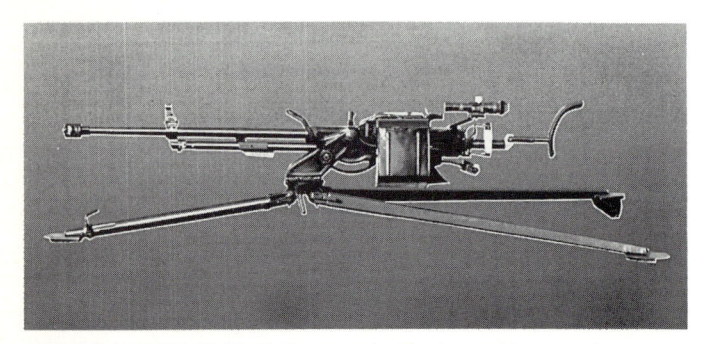

NORINCO TYPE W-85 12.7 mm anti-aircraft machine gun in ground defence role and showing muzzle brake

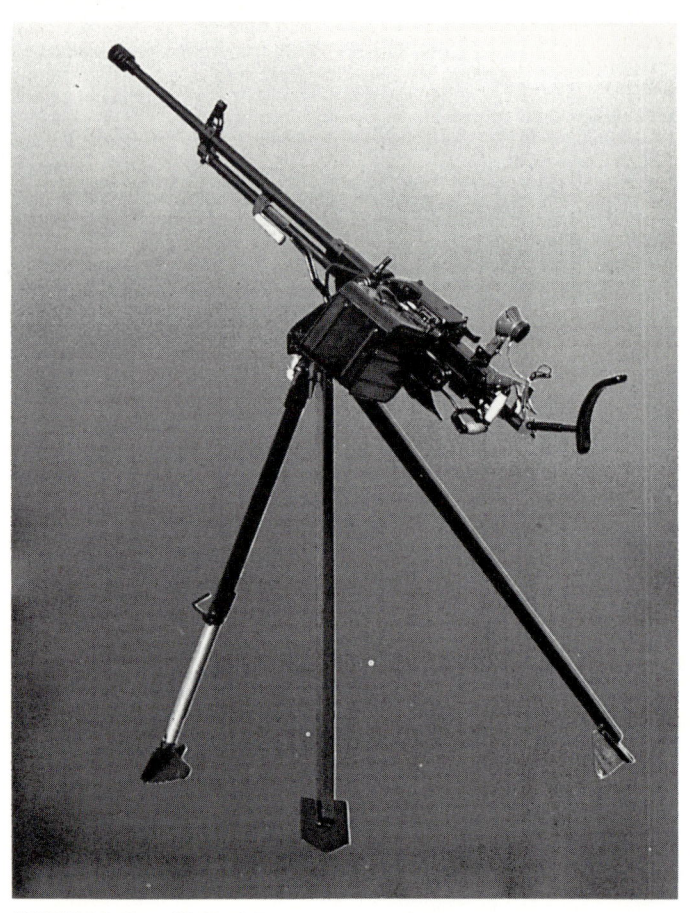

NORINCO Type W-85 12.7 mm anti-aircraft machine gun in air defence configuration

SPECIFICATIONS

CALIBRE	12.7 mm
PRACTICAL RATE OF FIRE	80 to 100 rpm
WEIGHT OF SYSTEM	39 kg
WEIGHT OF GUN ONLY	18.5 kg
WEIGHT OF GUN MOUNT	15.5 kg
LENGTH IN HORIZONTAL FIRING POSITION	1.995 m
EFFECTIVE RANGE	
air targets	1600 m
ground targets	1500 m
TRAVERSE	
horizontal position	120°
air defence role	360°
ELEVATION IN HORIZONTAL POSITION	−15° to +25°
MAX ELEVATION	+80°

Status: In production. In service with Chinese Army.

Manufacturer: China North Industries Corporation, 7A Yuetan Nanjie, PO Box 2137 Beijing, Beijing, People's Republic of China.
Telephone: (86) 6898, (86) 3461, (86) 3471, (86) 7570
Telex: 22339 CNIN CN

57 mm Type 59 Anti-aircraft Gun

Development/Description

The Chinese 57 mm Type 59 anti-aircraft gun is a close copy of the Soviet 57 mm S-60 and differs in few details from the original. The Type 59 fires only one type of ammunition, HE-T. This HE-T round has a complete weight of 6.31 kg and a projectile weight of 2.8 kg. It has a muzzle velocity of 1000 m/s and is fitted with a Liu-2 nose fuze. The explosive charge is 0.153 kg of aluminised RDX. Chinese sources state that the Type 80 twin 57 mm self-propelled anti-aircraft gun system fires two types of ammunition; HET-PF (high-explosive tracer with percussion fuze) and APCT-BF (armour-piercing capped tracer with base fuze). It is probable that the Type 59 57 mm towed anti-aircraft gun can also fire this improved ammunition.

Time into action of the Type 59 is stated to be one minute and time

57 mm Type 59 anti-aircraft gun towed by Type 59 artillery tractor

China / **TOWED AA GUNS** 161

Battery of Chinese Type 59 anti-aircraft guns deployed in firing position with radar and anti-aircraft fire director in foreground

57 mm Type 59 anti-aircraft gun in firing position

to prepare for travelling is two minutes. A twin-barrel naval version known as the Type 66 is known to be in production. This utilises a water cooling system for the barrels and a chain-type hoist system for the ammunition. All the towed 57 mm systems use the Type GW-03 anti-aircraft fire control director. This four-wheel trailer mounted system utilises a 3 m range finder with on-board computation facilities to control a complete battery of guns firing against either airborne or surface targets. The GW-03 can engage targets between 780 and 31 600 m. It can be coupled to a fire control radar if required. The Type 80 twin 57 mm self-propelled anti-aircraft gun system, fully described in the *Self-propelled anti-aircraft guns* section, uses the same gun and ammunition as the 57 mm Type 59 anti-aircraft gun.

The data provided in the Specifications is taken from Chinese sources.

Type GW-03 anti-aircraft fire director in travelling configuration

SPECIFICATIONS

CALIBRE	57 mm
BARREL LENGTH (overall)	4.39 m
MUZZLE BRAKE	multi-perforated
OPERATION	recoil full automatic
CARRIAGE	4-wheel
SHIELD	optional
WEIGHT (total)	4780 kg
LENGTH (travelling)	8.6 m
WIDTH (travelling)	2.07 m
HEIGHT (travelling)	2.46 m
MAX TOWING SPEED	35 km/h
ELEVATION/DEPRESSION	+85°/-5°
TRAVERSE	360°
LAYING SPEED (electrical)	
traverse	up to 24°/s
elevation	up to 15°/s
RATE OF FIRE (cyclic)	100-120 rpm
FEED	4 round clip
MAX RANGE (effective)	6000 m
CREW	7 or 8
TOWING VEHICLES	Type 59 artillery tractor, 6 × 6 heavy truck

Status: Production. In service with the Chinese armed forces and offered for export.

Manufacturer: China North Industries Corporation, 7A Yuetan Nanjie, PO Box 2137 Beijing, Beijing, People's Republic of China.
Telephone: (86) 6898, (86) 3461, (86) 3471, (86) 7570
Telex: 22339 CNIN CN

Chinese 37 mm Anti-aircraft Guns

Development/Description

37 mm Type 55

The most commonly encountered model of Chinese 37 mm anti-aircraft gun is the Type 55, a direct copy of the Soviet 37 mm M1939 from which it differs in few details. The ammunition used with the Type 55 is of two types, HE and HE-T. Both types of round weigh 1.416 kg, with the projectile weighing 0.732 kg. When fired from the Type 55, both have a muzzle velocity of 866 m/s and are fitted with the Liu-1 nose fuze.

37 mm Type 65

The 37 mm Type 65 is a direct copy of the Soviet twin-barrelled version of the M1939 while the Type 74 is a model with revised detail engineering to suit Chinese manufacturing methods and can operate with radar fire control at a slightly increased rate of fire compared to the Type 65. The Type 65 and Type 74 use the same ammunition as the Type 55.

37 mm Type P793

The Type P793 is a twin-barrelled anti-aircraft gun based on the Type 74 but with many new features. The twin guns themselves have a higher rate of fire and are available with two types of barrel and rate of fire. The Type A gun has a muzzle velocity of 880 m/s while the Type B has a muzzle velocity of 1000 m/s. The rate of fire of a single P793 Type A barrel is 220 to 240 rds/min, while that of a Type B barrel is 270 to 300 rds/min. Both types of barrel continue to use Type 55 ammunition. The effective slant range for a Type A is 3500 m while for the Type B it is 4000 m.

The P793 carriage has its own generator powered by an engine developing 7 hp at 3750 rpm. The generator powers the carriage electrical controls and also the electro-optical sight system. The sight is known as the C335 and appears to be of the Officine Galileo pattern having a ×5 magnification and a 12° field of view. The C335 is stated to be a self-powered electro-optical aiming sight which takes three to four seconds to be ready for firing once a target has been detected. The sight can cope with target velocities of 60 to 350 m/s. Maximum lead

TOWED AA GUNS / China

Twin 37 mm anti-aircraft gun Type 65 in firing position

37 mm Type P793 in firing position with outriggers extended

China National Electronics Import & Export Corporation Type 311A fire control radar system

Close up of sight of 37 mm Type P793 anti-aircraft gun in firing position

angle is 25°. Target ranges are between 100 and 1500 m, while ground target maximum range is 3000 m. Maximum barrel angular acceleration for traverse is 95°/s², while that for elevation is 80°/s².

The P793 has 182 rounds stored on the carriage and has a crew of five or six. It can be towed at speeds of up to 60 km/h on roads or 25 km/h on dirt roads. Weight of the P793 is 3100 kg.

Fire Control Systems

All the 37 mm towed systems can be coupled to a fire control radar. Known as the Type 311A, this uses a four-wheel trailer van with an I/J-band search, acquisition and tracking radar antenna on a roof-mounted pedestal. The set operates on three preselected frequencies which can be manually switched without any adjustments. Minimum and maximum ranges are 500 and 30 000 m respectively, against low radar cross-section fighter sized targets with speeds of less than 550 m/s. An 8 ton truck is needed to tow the 4 ton trailer and this carries the ancillary equipment and the power supply generator. The radar is also used with the 57 mm towed systems. Further development of the Type 311 has led to the Type 311B and Type 311C models. The Type 311B introduces an integral IFF system, increased frequency coverage and a maximum detection range of 35 000 m using a new antenna design. The Type 311C goes one stage further and has a frequency agile capability radar with a maximum range of 40 000 m. The minimum range stays the same in both cases.

SPECIFICATIONS

DESIGNATION	Type 65	Type 74
CALIBRE	37 mm	37 mm
BARREL LENGTH (approx)	2.73 m	2.73 m
OPERATION	recoil	recoil
RECOIL	hydraulic recoil buffer and spring recuperator	
BREECH MECHANISM	rising block	rising block
CARRIAGE	4-wheel	4-wheel
SHIELD	no	no
WEIGHT (total)	2700 kg	2835 kg
LENGTH (travelling)	6.36 m	6.205 m
WIDTH (travelling)	1.80 m	1.816 m
HEIGHT (travelling)	2.25 m	2.28 m
MAX TOWING SPEED	35 to 60 km/h	35 km/h
ELEVATION/DEPRESSION		
manual drive	+85°/−10°	+87°/−5°
electric drive	n/app	+81.5°/0°

DESIGNATION	Type 65	Type 74
TRAVERSE	360°	360°
TRAVERSE LAYING SPEED		
manual, rate 1	n/av	15.33°/turn
manual, rate 2	n/av	25.26°/turn
automatic	n/app	up to 50°/s
ELEVATION LAYING SPEED		
manual	n/av	9.08°/turn
automatic	n/app	up to 30°/s
RATE OF FIRE		
(both barrels)	320–360 rpm	440–480 rpm
FEED	5 round clip	5 round clip
EFFECTIVE SLANT RANGE	3500 m	3500 m
MAX RANGE		
vertical	6700 m	6700 m
horizontal	8500 m	8500 m

China / **TOWED AA GUNS** 163

Status: All are in production and service with the Chinese armed forces. Chinese 37 mm anti-aircraft guns have been exported in some numbers but as they are almost identical to the Soviet weapons, the following list of users should be taken as provisional:
Type 55 - Gabon, Guinea, Korea (North), Mozambique, Pakistan, Sudan, Tanzania, Tunisia and Zambia
Type 63 - Cameroon, Iraq and Zaire
Type 68 - Mozambique
Type 74 - 60 Thailand, an additional 18 systems were ordered for the Royal Thai Air Force in 1988.

Manufacturer: China North Industries Corporation, 7A Yuetan Nanjie, PO Box 2137 Beijing, Beijing, People's Republic of China.
Telephone: (86) 6898, (86) 3461, (86) 3471, (86) 7570
Telex: 22339 CNIN CN

37 mm Type 74 anti-aircraft gun in firing position

Chinese 25 mm Light Anti-aircraft Gun

Development/Description
For some time now, China has been producing a copy of the Soviet twin 23 mm ZU-23 light anti-aircraft gun, but at Asiandex 86 a new twin 25 mm calibre towed low altitude defence anti-aircraft gun was unveiled, which is believed to have the designation WA709. Other sources have stated that this is designated the WA309, with the Chinese Army designation being Type 85.

This is very similar to the ZU-23 with distinctive parallel flash eliminators and a handle on each barrel to facilitate a quick change.

It has a crew of three with the elevation operator on the left, the commander in the centre and the traverse operator on the right. The elevation and traverse controls are manual and the cannon has a muzzle velocity of 1050 m/s. The fixed ammunition types used are HE-T, AP-T and HEAP-T.

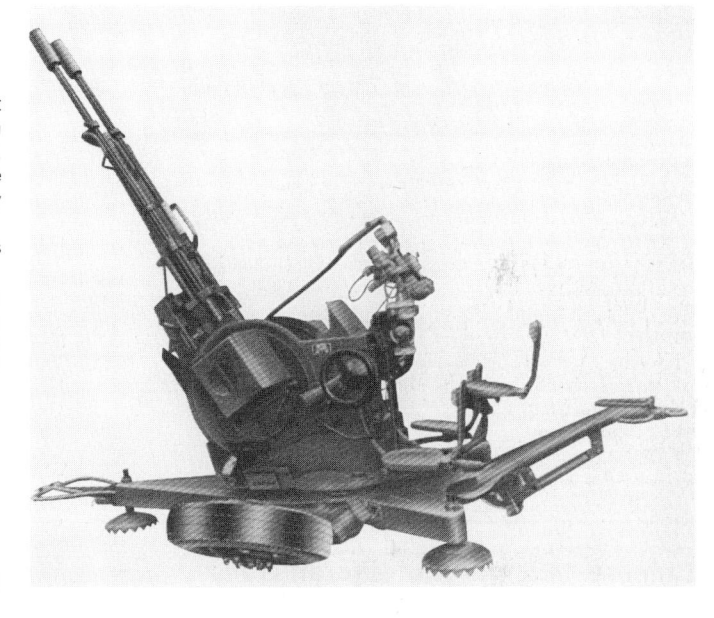

Chinese twin 25 mm light anti-aircraft gun in firing position

SPECIFICATIONS
CALIBRE	25 mm
OPERATION	gas, full automatic
CARRIAGE	2-wheeled
SHIELD	no
WEIGHT (travelling)	
with ammunition	1500 kg
LENGTH (travelling)	4.68 m
WIDTH (travelling)	2.04 m
HEIGHT (travelling)	2.08 m

ELEVATION/DEPRESSION	+90°/-10°
TRAVERSE	360°
RATE OF FIRE PER BARREL (cyclic)	600-700 rpm
MAX RANGE (vertical)	5000 m
EFFECTIVE VERTICAL RANGE	3200 m
CREW	3 plus off mount loaders
TOWING VEHICLE	4 × 4 vehicle

Status: Believed to be in production and in service with the Chinese Army.

Manufacturer: China North Industries Corporation, 7A Yuetan Nanjie, PO Box 2137 Beijing, Beijing, People's Republic of China.
Telephone: (86) 6898, (86) 3461, (86) 3741, (86) 7570
Telex: 22339 CNIN CN

Chinese 23 mm Light Anti-aircraft Gun

Development/Description
The Chinese 23 mm light anti-aircraft gun has been in production for many years and is a reverse engineered copy of the Soviet ZU-23 with several minor differences to suit Chinese manufacturing processes.

The gun is operated by a crew of two on the mount and three off who serve as ammunition carriers and loaders for the two metallic linked 50 round ammunition belts in the box magazines.

In all operational respects, the gun is similar to the Soviet weapon and it is effective against low flying targets at ranges up to 2500 m and an altitude of 1500 m. It can also be used to engage ground targets out to 2000 m effective range.

The cannon fire two types of 0.236 m long 0.45 kg fixed ammunition.

Chinese twin 23 mm light anti-aircraft gun in travelling configuration

TOWED AA GUNS / China

Both are copies of the standard Soviet ammunition used with the ZU-23. The HEI-T round has a 0.1885 kg projectile fitted with a nose delay fuze whilst the API-T round has a 0.19 kg weight projectile. The rounds are incorporated into the ammunition belts in the ratio of three HEI-T to one API-T.

Status: In production. In service with the Chinese armed forces.

Manufacturer: China North Industries Corporation, 7A Yuetan Nanjie, PO Box 2137 Beijing, Beijing, People's Republic of China.
Telephone: (86) 6898, (86) 3461, (86) 3471, (86) 7570
Telex: 22339 CNIN CN

Chinese twin 23 mm light anti-aircraft gun in firing position

SPECIFICATIONS

CALIBRE	23 mm
BARREL LENGTH (overall)	2.01 m
OPERATION	gas, full automatic
BREECH MECHANISM	vertical sliding wedge
CARRIAGE	2-wheeled
SHIELD	none
WEIGHT	
(travelling order with ammunition)	950 kg
(firing position with ammunition)	950 kg
LENGTH (travelling)	4.57 m
WIDTH (travelling)	1.83 m
HEIGHT (travelling)	1.87 m
ELEVATION/DEPRESSION	+90°/-10°
TRAVERSE	360°
RATE OF FIRE PER BARREL	
cyclic	800-1000 rpm
practical	200 rpm
FEED	50 round belt
MAX RANGE	
horizontal	7000 m
vertical	5100 m
EFFECTIVE RANGE	
horizontal	2000 m
vertical	2500 m
CREW	5
TOWING VEHICLE	4 × 4 vehicle

Chinese 14.5 mm Anti-aircraft Guns

Development/Description

Type 56 LAAG

The Chinese 14.5 mm anti-aircraft guns all use the Chinese version of the Soviet KPV heavy machine gun. The 'base' model as far as Chinese production is concerned is the Type 56, a direct copy of the Soviet ZPU-4. The Type 56 fires three types of ammunition, API, API-T, and Incendiary, all identical to their Soviet counterparts. The Type 56 has been exported widely and is also produced in North Korea.

Type 58 LAAG

The Type 58 is a direct copy of the Soviet ZPU-2 and resembles the late production version of the Soviet original.

Type 75 LAAG

The Type 75 is the Chinese version of the ZPU-1 and is designed to be pack transported if necessary. The Type 75-1 has a more complex optical sight which may have image intensification characteristics.

Type 80 LAAG

The Type 80 is a version of the ZPU-1, re-engineered to Chinese standards and with a redesigned carriage that enables it to be fired from the prone position against ground targets. It has a more robust carriage than either of the Type 75s and may be towed behind a light 4 × 4 vehicle.

The Types 58, 75, 75-1 and 80 all fire the same ammunition as the Type 56.

14.5 mm Type 58 anti-aircraft machine gun in travelling configuration

Close-up of computing sight Type 58 used on Chinese 14.5 mm LAAGs

China / **TOWED AA GUNS** 165

14.5 mm Type 58 anti-aircraft machine gun in firing position

14.5 mm Type 75-1 anti-aircraft machine gun in firing position

14.5 mm Type 56 anti-aircraft machine gun in firing position

14.5 mm Type 80 anti-aircraft machine gun in firing position

SPECIFICATIONS

DESIGNATION	**Type 56**	**Type 58**	**Type 75**	**Type 75-1**	**Type 80**
CALIBRE	14.5 mm	14.5 mm	14.5 mm	14.5 mm	14.5 mm
NUMBER OF BARRELS	4	2	1	1	1
BARREL LENGTH	1.348 m	1.348 m	1.348 m	1.348 m	1.348 m
CARRIAGE	4-wheel	2-wheel	tripod	2-wheel	2-wheel
WEIGHT	2100 kg	660 kg	140 kg	165 kg	214 kg
LENGTH	4.54 m	3.9 m	2.93 m	2.93 m	2.5 m
WIDTH	1.86 m	1.66 m	1.62 m	1.62 m	1.8 m
HEIGHT	2.34 m	1.1 m	1.07 m	1.27 m	2.2 m
ELEVATION/DEPRESSION	+90°/-10°	+90°/-15°	+85°/-10°	+85°/-10°	+85°/-15°
TRAVERSE	360°	360°	360°	360°	360°
RATE OF FIRE (all barrels)	2200 rpm	1100 rpm	550 rpm	550 rpm	550-600 rpm
MAX EFFECTIVE RANGE					
air target	2000 m	2000 m	2000 m	2000 m	2000 m
ground target	1000 m	1000 m	1000 m	1000 m	1000 m
AMMUNITION BOX CAPACITY	150 rounds	150 rounds	80 rounds	80 rounds	80 rounds
MUZZLE VELOCITY	995 m/s	995 m/s	995 m/s	995 m/s	995 m/s

Status: Production. In service with the Chinese armed forces and other armed forces including Cameroon (18). Offered for export.

Manufacturer: China North Industries Corporation, 7A Yuetan Nanjie, PO Box 2137 Beijing, Beijing, People's Republic of China.
Telephone: (86) 6898, (86) 3461, (86) 3471, (86) 7570
Telex: 22339 CNIN CN

166 TOWED AA GUNS / China-Czechoslovakia

CZECHOSLOVAKIA

30 mm Automatic Anti-aircraft Gun M53

Development/Description
The 30 mm automatic anti-aircraft gun M53 is used by Czechoslovakia in place of the Soviet 23 mm ZU-23 anti-aircraft gun and entered service in the late 1950s. The Czechoslovakian weapon is heavier than the Soviet ZU-23 and has a slower rate of fire, but its effective anti-aircraft range is 3000 m compared with the ZU-23's 2500 m.

In action, the four wheels are raised off the ground and the carriage is supported on four jacks, one at the front, one at the rear and one each side on outriggers. The guns are gas operated, fully automatic and are fitted with quick-change barrels. Ammunition is fed horizontally in clips of 10 rounds. The following types of fixed ammunition can be fired: API with the projectile weighing 0.54 kg and a muzzle velocity of 1000 m/s, which will penetrate 55 mm of armour at an incidence of 0° at a range of 500 m, and HEI with the projectile weighing 0.45 kg and a muzzle velocity of 1000 m/s. The M53 is a clear-weather system only with no provision for radar control.

There is also a self-propelled model of the M53 called the M53/59 based on an armoured Praga V3S (6 × 6) truck which is described in the *Self-propelled anti-aircraft guns* section. The guns of the M53/59 have a higher rate of fire as the vertical magazines each hold 50 rounds of ammunition in clips of 10 rounds.

Variant
The Cuban Army has modified a number of BTR-60P (8 × 8) armoured personnel carriers to carry the Czechoslovakian twin 30 mm automatic anti-aircraft gun system M53.

Status: Production complete. In service with the following countries:

Country	Quantity	User	Comment
Czechoslovakia	n/av	army	some in reserve
Cuba	100	army	status uncertain
Guinea	n/av	army	unconfirmed user
Romania	300	army	
Vietnam	150	army	probably in reserve
Yugoslavia	n/av	army	status uncertain

Manufacturer: Czechoslovakian state factories.

30 mm automatic anti-aircraft guns M53 in travelling order

30 mm automatic anti-aircraft gun M53 defending Bar Lock radar installation

SPECIFICATIONS
CALIBRE	30 mm
BARREL LENGTH (overall)	2.429 m
MUZZLE BRAKE	multi-baffle
CARRIAGE	4-wheel with outriggers
SHIELD	no
WEIGHT	
travelling order	2100 kg
firing position	1750 kg
LENGTH (travelling)	7.587 m
WIDTH (travelling)	1.758 m
HEIGHT (travelling)	1.575 m
AXIS OF BORE (firing)	0.86 m
GROUND CLEARANCE (travelling)	0.3 m
TRACK	1.575 m
ELEVATION/DEPRESSION	+85°/-10°
TRAVERSE	360°
RATE OF FIRE PER BARREL	
cyclic	450-500 rpm
practical	100 rpm
FEED	10 round clip
MAX RANGE	
horizontal	9700 m
vertical	6300 m
EFFECTIVE VERTICAL RANGE	3000 m
CREW	4
TOWING VEHICLE	Praga V3S (6 × 6) truck

Quad 12.7 mm M53 Anti-aircraft Machine Gun

Development/Description
This anti-aircraft gun was developed in Czechoslovakia in the 1950s and is essentially a two-wheeled carriage fitted with four Soviet 12.7 mm M1938/46 DShKM machine guns. The single 12.7 mm DShKM is the standard tank-mounted anti-aircraft machine gun of the Warsaw Pact and is also installed on a number of armoured personnel carriers.

In the firing position the two rubber-tyred road wheels are removed and the weapon is supported on three outriggers. The M53 fires an API projectile weighing 49.5 g with a muzzle velocity of 840 m/s, which will penetrate 20 mm of armour at an incidence of 0° at a range of 500 m.

The M53 is no longer in front-line service with Czechoslovakia. It is reported that the Egyptian Army had a number of Quad 12.7 mm M53 anti-aircraft machine guns mounted on the rear of a BTR-152 (6 × 6) armoured personnel carrier. There is also a Czechoslovakian twin-barrelled version mounted on a Soviet UAZ-469 (4 × 4) light vehicle, but its exact status is uncertain.

The 12.7 mm anti-aircraft machine gun has an effective slant range of 1006 m. Effective altitude limit with an elevation of +45° is 671 m, while effective altitude limit with an elevation of +65° is 914 m.

Czechoslovakia / **TOWED AA GUNS** 167

Quad 12.7 mm M53 anti-aircraft machine gun captured by US forces in Grenada showing two stabilisers lowered on forward part of two-wheeled carriage (US Army)

Quad 12.7 mm M53 anti-aircraft machine gun captured by US forces in Grenada with stabilisers raised in travelling configuration and showing drums each holding 50 rounds (US Army)

SPECIFICATIONS

CALIBRE	12.7 mm	TYRES	5.00 × 16
BARREL LENGTH		ELEVATION/DEPRESSION	+90°/−7°
without muzzle brake	0.967 m	TRAVERSE	360°
with muzzle brake	1.588 m	RATE OF FIRE PER BARREL	
MUZZLE BRAKE	yes	cyclic	540–600 rpm
OPERATION	gas, automatic	practical	80 rpm
CARRIAGE	2-wheeled with outriggers	FEED	50 round belt in drum
SHIELD	no	MAX RANGE	
WEIGHT		horizontal	6500 m
travelling order	2830 kg	vertical	5600 m
firing position	628 kg	EFFECTIVE VERTICAL RANGE	1000 m
LENGTH (travelling)	2.9 m	UNIT OF FIRE	2000 rounds
WIDTH (travelling)	1.57 m	CREW	6
HEIGHT (travelling)	1.78 m	TOWING VEHICLE	GAZ-69 (4 × 4) truck
TRACK	1.5 m		

Status: Production complete. In service with Cuba (Army, reserve), Egypt (Army, reserve), Vietnam (Army, reserve) and other countries in the Middle and Far East.

Manufacturer: Czechoslovakian state factories.

EGYPT

ZU-23M Twin 23 mm Automatic Anti-aircraft Gun

Development/Description
The ZU-23M is essentially the Soviet 23 mm ZU-23 (see entry later in this section) produced under licence at Heliopolis in Egypt by Abu Zaabal Engineering Industries (Factory 100) and differs only slightly from the Soviet original and fires the same ammunition. It has also been referred to as the SH-23M.

The ZU-23M has a five-man detachment, two of whom are on the weapon, one on either side of the mount and the other three off the carriage with two of these acting as ammunition members. Each barrel is fed from a 50 round belt of ammunition in a steel magazine, a new magazine can be loaded in 10 seconds. The ammunition feeding system has been designed to prevent the firing of the last round and the moving parts stay to the rear ready to receive the first round of the new belt so that firing can start immediately.

All specifications are identical to those of the original Soviet weapon but the Egyptians provide the following additional information:

CREW	5 men
MAX TOWING SPEED	70 km/h
TIME TAKEN TO BRING INTO ACTION	15–20 s
TIME TAKEN TO COME OUT OF ACTION	35–40 s

Variants

Ramadan 23

In 1987 Factory 100 and Contraves of Italy fitted two ZU-23Ms with the Contraves Gun King laser/computer sighting system, which is already in volume production for a number of other applications including the Oerlikon-Bührle twin 35 mm GDF towed anti-aircraft gun system.

The Egyptians call the ZU-23M/Gun King combination the Ramadan and firing trials were completed in late 1987.

Ramadan 23 has just one man on the mount, with full power control by an on-board electric motor powered by an off-carriage generator. One man can control two ZU-23Ms with not only greater response but with a greatly enhanced kill probability.

If and when Gun King is formally adopted by Egypt, it is envisaged that a co-production plan would form part of the contract. Full details of the Contraves Gun King sight are given in the *Towed anti-aircraft gun sights* section.

Egyptian-built 23 mm ZU-23M in firing position (Christopher F Foss)

Self-propelled twin 23 mm System

This uses the basic 23 mm ZU-23 cannon and is covered in the *Self-propelled anti-aircraft guns* section under Egypt.

Status: In production. In service with the Egyptian and Sudanese armed forces and is offered for export.

Manufacturer: Abu Zaabal Engineering Industries Company, PO Box 5888, Heliopolis West, Cairo, Arab Republic of Egypt.
Telephone: 2917305/2917033
Telex: 21487 HVRT UN

FRANCE

53T4 Twin 20 mm Automatic Anti-aircraft Gun

Development/Description
First shown publicly at the 1983 Satory Exhibition, the GIAT 53T4 is an anti-aircraft weapon intended for the defence of local areas, or of convoys with the guns and mounting removed from the carriage and placed on a truck.

The 53T4 is a twin-barrelled weapon mounting two 20 mm cannon side by side. The guns and carriage can be towed across country and brought into action by moving the two road wheels towards the towbar and laying them flat. The carriage is then supported on a pad under the towbar and two further pads on jacks carried by short outrigger arms. If required, the mounting can be lifted from the carriage and carried on a truck flat-bed. The carriage may then be used as an ammunition limber, towed behind the truck. In action the gun may be hydraulically powered or manually traversed and elevated. Maximum speed of hydraulic aiming is 80°/s in azimuth and 50°/s in elevation. In the manual mode, one turn of the traverse handwheel elevates the barrels 10.5° and a turn of the elevation handwheel elevates the barrels 6.5°. The gunner sits to the left of the barrels and moves with them and the gun sight to align himself and the barrels rapidly with a target. Firing is electrical and cut-out switches can be set to prevent firing over selected arcs. The anti-aircraft sight has a magnification of ×1 and has an off-set graticule to compensate for target speeds. For use against ground targets, a ×5.2 magnification telescope is provided. Hydraulic re-cocking of the guns is available.

Prototype of 53T4 with twin 20 mm cannon replaced by single GIAT 25 mm model 811 cannon

53T4 20 mm twin anti-aircraft gun ready for towing (Terry J Gander)

France / **TOWED AA GUNS** 169

The 53T4 uses two 20 mm CN-MIT 20 M693 ACA cannon with a combined rate of fire of 1800 rds/min. Ammunition is fed into the guns from two 150 round boxes loaded with HE rounds in belts, but a further 50 AP rounds are held in readiness on the gun. Each belt has an end-stop device to assist reloading.

If required the 53T4 can be fired direct from the carriage wheels.

Variant
The prototype of the 53T4 was shown for the first time in mid-1987, with its twin 20 mm cannon replaced by a single GIAT 25 mm Model 811 cannon.

Status: Development complete. Not yet in production or service.

Manufacturer: Groupement Industriel des Armements Terrestres (GIAT), 10 place G Clémenceau, 92211 Saint-Cloud, France.
Telephone: (1) 4 771 40 00
Telex: 260010 DAT-SCLOU

53T4 20 mm twin anti-aircraft gun showing method of wheel stowage when emplaced and spare ammunition box stowage

SPECIFICATIONS
CALIBRE	20 mm
WEIGHT (with ammunition and gunner)	2000 kg
ELEVATION/DEPRESSION	+83°/-8°
TRAVERSE	360°
MAX LAYING SPEED (hydraulic)	
traverse	80°/s
elevation	50°/s
RATE OF FIRE (per barrel, cyclic)	900 rpm
FEED	2 × 150 round belts in boxes, 50 AP rounds on carriage
CREW (on gun)	1

Cerbere 76T2 Twin 20 mm Automatic Anti-aircraft Gun

Development/Description
The Cerbere twin 20 mm automatic anti-aircraft gun is essentially the West German Rheinmetall twin 20 mm system, with the original Rh 202 cannon replaced by the French M693(F2). A full description of the mount is given in the entry for the original West German system in this section.

The French designation for the Cerbere is the 76T2. It has been adopted by the French Air Force for close-range protection of airfields with Crotale SAM batteries. A total of 299 systems were delivered to the French Air Force between 1980 and 1985. Somalia ordered a total of 40 systems.

In a more advanced version the mounting can be integrated in a defence system and directed automatically at the target, either by a surveillance radar, or a director equipped with a DALDO target indicator helmet.

Cerbere 76T2 twin 20 mm automatic anti-aircraft gun in firing position

SPECIFICATIONS
CALIBRE	20 mm
OPERATION	delayed blowback with locked breech
CARRIAGE	2-wheeled with outriggers
SHIELD	yes
WEIGHT	
in travelling order without ammunition	2150 kg
in firing position with ammunition	1600 kg
LENGTH	
travelling	5.05 m
firing	4.02 m
WIDTH	
travelling	2.39 m
firing	2.06 m
SWEPT RADIUS (at 0° elevation)	2.48 m
HEIGHT	
travelling	2.075 m
firing	1.67 m
AXIS OF BORE (firing)	0.765 m
ELEVATION/DEPRESSION	
powered	+81.5°/-3.5°
manual	+83°/-5°
TRAVERSE	360°
RATE OF FIRE (cyclic)	900 rpm, per barrel
FEED	dual selectable belt feed with disintegrating links, 270 rounds per barrel
EFFECTIVE AA RANGE	2000 m
CREW	3 (1 on mount)
TOWING VEHICLE	4 × 4 truck

Status: Production complete but can be resumed if further orders are placed. In service with the Somalian Army (40) and the French Air Force.

Manufacturer: Groupement Industriel des Armements Terrestres (GIAT), 10 place G Clémenceau, 92211 Saint-Cloud, France.
Telephone: (1) 4 771 40 00
Telex: 260010 DAT-SCLOU

170 TOWED AA GUNS / France

Tarasque 53T2 20 mm Automatic Anti-aircraft Gun

Development
The Tarasque 20 mm automatic anti-aircraft gun, official designation 53T2, has been selected as the standard weapon in its class for the French Army, and first production weapons were delivered in 1982. The system is armed with a single 20 mm French M693(F2) cannon which is also installed in the Cerbere twin 20 mm automatic anti-aircraft gun, certain versions of the AMX-30 MBT, AMX-32 MBT (still at prototype stage), AMX-40 MBT (still at prototype stage), the AMX-10P IFV and the South African Ratel 20 IFV.

Description
Although designed primarily for anti-aircraft use, Tarasque can also be used against personnel and light armoured vehicles. Its low weight makes it easily transportable across rough country and it can also be carried slung under a helicopter.

A heat motor-driven rotary pump charges an oil receiver supplying the traversing and elevation hydraulic motors and the hydraulic recocking mechanism. If the motor is unserviceable the receiver can be charged by a hand-operated pump. Maximum powered traverse speed is 40°/s. Handwheels are also fitted for emergency use; one turn of one handwheel gives 10° of traverse and one turn of the other gives 6.5° in elevation.

The gunner can select either single shots or full automatic, with the hydraulic firing mechanism actuated by the gunner depressing his right foot. Safety controls, ammunition selector and hydraulic reloading controls are to the right of the gunner's position. On the forward part of the mount on the left side, are two discs adjustable to within 25 mils, to prevent the gun being fired in predetermined zones.

The M348 sight includes an anti-aircraft sight with a magnification of ×1 and a ground sight with a magnification of ×5.

The M693(F2) cannon has dual feed, with the weapon provided with 100 rounds of HE/HEI ammunition and 40 rounds of APDS ammunition. Standard HSS 820 ammunition can be fired, including APDS (French designation OPT-SOC) with a muzzle velocity of 1293 m/s, HEI (French designation OEI) with a muzzle velocity of 1050 m/s, HEI-T (French designation OEIT) with a muzzle velocity of 1050 m/s, Practice Tracer (French designation OXT) and Practice Inert (French designation OX). The APDS projectile will penetrate 20 mm of armour at an incidence of 0° at a range of 1000 m.

The Tarasque is carried on a two-wheeled carriage that can be towed by a 4 × 4 light vehicle and takes only 15 seconds to bring into action. A normal crew would consist of three, one on the gun and two ammunition numbers.

SPECIFICATIONS
CALIBRE	20 mm
BARREL LENGTH	2.065 m
MUZZLE BRAKE	yes
OPERATION	delayed blowback
CARRIAGE	2-wheeled
SHIELD	no
WEIGHT	
travelling order with ammunition	840 kg
firing position with ammunition	660 kg
SWEPT RADIUS (at 0° elevation)	2.4 m
WIDTH (travelling)	1.9 m
TRACK	1.72 m
ELEVATION/DEPRESSION	+83°/-8°
TRAVERSE	360°
RATE OF FIRE	
cyclic	740 rpm
practical	200 rpm
CREW	3 (1 on gun)
TOWING VEHICLE	Jeep type (4 × 4) truck

GIAT Tarasque 53T2 20 mm automatic anti-aircraft gun in firing position

GIAT Tarasque 53T2 20 mm automatic cannon mounted in rear of TRM 2000 (4 × 4) truck

Status: In production. In service with France, Djibouti and Senegambia.

Manufacturer: Groupement Industriel des Armements Terrestres (GIAT), 10 place G Clémenceau, 92211 Saint-Cloud, France.
Telephone: (1) 4 771 40 00
Telex: 260010 DAT-SCLOU

53T1 Single 20 mm Light Anti-aircraft Gun

Development/Description
Although produced in the sixties, the 20 mm single-barrel 53T1 mount has been included because it has been seen with the French forces in Chad, in both the local air and ground defence roles.

The gun consists of four main parts: a three-trail carriage supporting a swivel and a laying ring; a pivoting section with the gunner's seat, manual laying controls and the box magazine; an oscillating section with the gun cradle, ammunition supply chute and optical sight system; and the hydraulically operated laying assembly with its motor.

The gun is normally used to defend infantry units and is drawn by a light vehicle or, if required, mounted on the rear of one.

Renault TRM 2000 (4 × 4) light truck towing GIAT 53T1 single 20 mm light anti-aircraft gun system (Pierre Touzin)

53T1 single 20 mm light anti-aircraft gun deployed in Chad by French forces (ECP Armées)

SPECIFICATIONS
CALIBRE	20 mm
CARRIAGE	2-wheeled with three outriggers
WEIGHT	
(in travelling order with ammunition)	635 kg
(in firing position with ammunition)	480 kg
LENGTH (travelling)	3.25 m
WIDTH (travelling)	1.76 m
HEIGHT (travelling)	1.60 m
ELEVATION/DEPRESSION	+83°/−3°
TRAVERSE	360°
FEED	200 round belt with disintegrating links
BASIC LOAD	400 rounds
CREW	2 (one on mount)
TOWING VEHICLE	4 × 4 vehicle

Status: Production complete. In service with the French Army.

53T1 single 20 mm light anti-aircraft gun mounted on rear of ACMAT (4 × 4) truck (ECP Armées)

GERMANY, WEST

30 mm Arrow Anti-aircraft Gun

Development
The twin 30 mm Arrow air defence system has been developed by a West German consortium to meet the requirements of the Royal Thai Air Force (RTAF). First production systems were delivered to Thailand in late 1988 and production is still underway.

The system is of modular construction to enable it to be tailored to meet the specific requirements of the user. The RTAF uses a single Contraves Skyguard-M trailer-mounted fire control system to control two twin 30 mm Arrow systems.

According to the manufacturer, the main advantages of the twin 30 mm Arrow air defence system can be summarised as short reaction time, good mobility, high fire power with cyclic rate of fire of 1600 rds/min, reduced manning and maintenance requirements.

Description
In appearance, the twin 30 mm Arrow air defence system is similar to the Greek Artemis system which was developed by the same consortium (qv), but it does incorporate nine detailed improvements:
(a) Automatic levelling system
(b) Modified reload ammunition boxes
(c) Double support for the optical aiming device
(d) Integrated data unit
(e) Ability to wheel the cannon aside without removing the barrel
(f) Modified barrel guide bearing
(g) Twin tyres on the rear axle
(h) Spare parts stowed on the mount
(i) Improved performance of drive units.

A total of 500 rounds are carried for ready use. Traverse is electric through 360°, with elevation also electric from −5° to +85°. Horizontal levelling is accomplished automatically with a hydraulic device in combination with an electronic sensor package.

Three modes of operation are possible; fully automatic with input from fire control system, autonomous by the gunner using the joystick and optical sight, and manual with elevation and traverse using handcranks. There are also three firing modes; electric from the fire control system, electric by actuating the fire trigger on the joystick and manual by mechanical foot pedal operation.

When used with a fire control system such as the Skyguard, a typical target engagement takes place as follows. The target is detected at a range of around 20 km and once acquired is tracked by the fire control sensor. A digital computer continuously calculates the lead values relative

Twin 30 mm Arrow anti-aircraft gun system deployed in firing position and showing stabilisers extended

TOWED AA GUNS / Germany, West

Twin 30 mm Arrow anti-aircraft gun system deployed in firing position

to the gun position, including meteorological data. Target information is relayed via a data transmission link to the guns.

Should there be a fault or if there is a threat of anti-radiation missiles, each mount is provided with an auxiliary sight to enable targets to be engaged visually.

Status: In production. First deliveries to the Royal Thai Air Force were made in 1988.

Manufacturers: Mount: KUKA Wehrtechnik GmbH, Zugspitzstrasse 140, PO Box 43 12 80, 8900 Augsburg 43, Federal Republic of Germany.
Telephone: (0821) 797 228
Telex: 5383840

Cannon: Mauser-Werke GmbH, Werk Schramberg-Sulgen, Postfach 562, D-7230 Schramberg, Federal Republic of Germany.
Telephone: (0743) 701
Telex: 760307

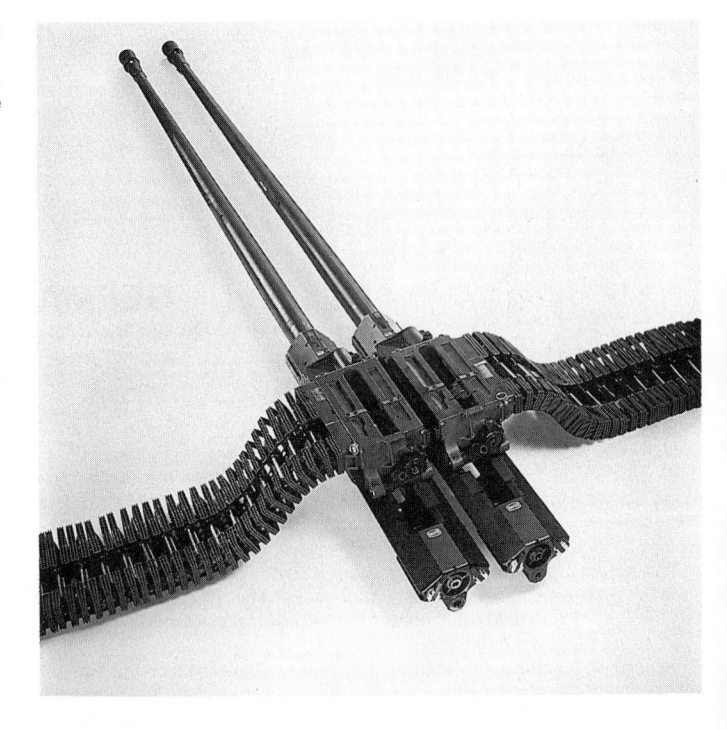

Close up of Mauser Mk 30 × 137 Model F twin 30 mm cannon used in Arrow air defence system

SPECIFICATIONS

CALIBRE	30 mm
BARREL LENGTH (with muzzle brake)	3.35 m
OPERATION	gas, automatic
CARRIAGE	4-wheel, cruciform
SHIELD	no
WEIGHT	6800 kg
LENGTH (travelling)	7.884 m
WIDTH (travelling)	2.38 m
WIDTH (firing)	3.464 m
GROUND CLEARANCE	0.40 m
WHEELBASE	4.71 m
ELEVATION/DEPRESSION	+85°/-5°
TRAVERSE	360°
LAYING RATE (traverse)	
remote	95°/s
autonomous	60°/s
LAYING RATE (elevation)	
remote	75°/s
autonomous	60°/s
RATE OF FIRE (cyclic)	1600 rpm
NUMBER OF ROUNDS (ready use)	500
TOWING SPEED	
road	80 km/h (max)
cross-country	30 km/h (max)

20 mm AA Twin Gun Air Defence System

Development

This anti-aircraft gun system has been developed by Rheinmetall under contract to the West German Department for Ordnance Technology and Procurement. By early 1989 over 1800 twin 20 mm systems have so far been delivered to West German and other forces. The main advantages of the system are a high rate of fire, accurate laying of the guns by the computerised optical fire control system, large ammunition supply, rapid elevation and traverse due to hydraulic servo-drive, no requirement for an external power source, suitability for operations under a wide range of climates and a very short training time for operators.

Description

The 20 mm AA twin gun air defence system consists of the following main components; two MK 20 Rh 202 cannon, ammunition supply, fire control equipment, laying mechanism, cradle, upper carriage, lower carriage and the two-wheeled trailer.

The 20 mm Rheinmetall MK 20 Rh 202 gas-operated and fully automatic cannon is also installed in the Marder IFV, Luchs 8 × 8 reconnaissance vehicle, FIAT/OTO Melara Type 6616 armoured car and the Norwegian 20 mm automatic anti-aircraft gun FK 20-2 which is described in this section. The weapon has a low recoil force and can be stripped into the main assemblies without any tools. By means of the belt feeder Type 3, the cartridges can be fed selectively from two sides, the left gun from the left and above and the right gun from the right and above.

The ammunition feed comprises two ammunition boxes, two flexible belt clips and two belt-centring mechanisms. The two ammunition boxes are fixed to the upper carriage, one right and one left of the twin guns. Each box contains 270 rounds of ammunition and there are another 10 rounds in the feed mechanism. Flexible cartridge belt guide channels connect the ammunition boxes to the belt-centring devices, which centre the cartridges in the links of disintegrating belts and introduce belted ammunition to the feed mechanism.

The laying mechanism is mounted over the rear bearings of the upper carriage and carries the laying system. Maximum powered traverse speed is 80°/s and maximum powered elevation speed is 48°/s.

The weapons are fired by a foot-operated mechanism fitted with a safety device. An interlock, which can be overridden, stops the gun before the last round is fired. A selector lever enables the gunner to choose either single shots or sustained fire, with either electric or mechanical firing from one or both barrels. The following types of fixed (20 mm × 139) ammunition can be fired:

AMMUNITION TYPE	APDS-T	API-T	HEI	HEI-T	TP/TP-T	Break Up
GERMAN DESIGNATION	DM63	DM43A1	n/app	DM51A2/ DM81	DM48 DM48A1	DM78A1
WEIGHT OF PROJECTILE	108 g	111 g	120 g	120 g	120 g	120 g
MUZZLE VELOCITY	1250 m/s	1100 m/s	1050 m/s	1050 m/s	1050 m/s	1050 m/s

The Italian Galileo P56 computing sight (to be replaced by the P75 fire control system with a laser rangefinder) has the following main components: monocular optical sight with a magnification of ×5 and a 12° field of view with a swivelling objective prism for laying the gun against air and ground targets; electronic analogue computer for calculating lead values; joystick with two degrees of freedom for the speed control of the line of sight; input panel for target speed and crossing point distance of air targets and target distance of ground targets.

The cradle is made of light alloy and its trunnions engage in the trunnion bearings of the upper carriage and rotate the cradle in elevation. During firing the cradle acts as the recoil bed of the guns. At the forward end of the cradle are two hinged covers to enable the weapons to be removed and at the top it is closed by two lockable hinged frames which also hold the belt feed mechanisms and the ejectors. The trigger mechanism and the cocking device are also housed on the cradle.

The upper carriage is also made of light metal with the laying mechanism fitted to the sidewalls. It also carries the gunner's seat and at the top of the upper carriage are the trunnion bearings in which the cradle fits. The centre of gravity of the cradle system, when fitted with the cannon, is off-centre, with static weight equilibrium achieved by two balancers. Two multi-stage elevating gears are flanged to the cheeks of the upper carriage. On the left side of the upper carriage is the firing pedal and the hand lever for locking the guns is on the right.

The lower carriage has three outriggers, two of which are adjustable for levelling. On the lower carriage is a brake lever for locking the upper carriage and at the end of each outrigger is a socket for securing the mounting on the trailer.

The two-wheeled trailer is used to transport the mounting with the lower carriage secured to the trailer by a swivel ring at the front and two lockable devices at the rear. The towing bracket of the trailer is adjustable to fit the height of the coupling of the vehicle and couplings and wiring for 12 or 24 V lighting are standard. When the mounting is

Rheinmetall 20 mm AA twin gun air defence system in firing position

Rheinmetall 20 mm AA twin gun air defence system deployed in firing position

20 mm twin Rheinmetall anti-aircraft gun in travelling order

TOWED AA GUNS / Germany, West-Greece

put on or taken off the trailer, the wheels are secured by wedges, this being the only task which requires three men.

Optional equipment includes a Taboo facility which can be programmed by the gunner to prevent the guns firing at specific objects, laying exercise kit S11 for the simulation of programmed flight paths with the sight for training purposes, video training system and radio equipment to link the gun with the battery commander or command post.

The French Air Force uses an identical mount fitted with French 20 mm M693(F2) cannon under the designation 76T2, or Cerbere. A description of this model is given in the French section.

Variants
There is a separate entry under International in the *Self-propelled anti-aircraft guns* section for this system on a British Hotspur 6 × 6 modified Land Rover chassis.

Status: Production as required. In service with the following countries:

Country	Quantity	User	Comment
Argentina	30+	air force	used with Elta early warning radar. Army may also use 30+ systems
Belgium	56	army	
Chile	40	army and air force	
El Salvador	n/av	army	
Germany, West	1670	air force	
Greece	30+	army	
Indonesia	10	army?	
Portugal	36	army	
Turkey	100+	army	

Manufacturer: Rheinmetall GmbH, Ulmenstrasse 125, D-4000 Düsseldorf, Federal Republic of Germany.
Telephone: (0211) 4471
Telex: 8584963

Rheinmetall 20 mm AA gun air defence systems on the production line at Düsseldorf

SPECIFICATIONS

CALIBRE	20 mm
BARREL LENGTH (including muzzle brake)	2.61 m
OPERATION	gas, automatic
CARRIAGE	2-wheeled with outriggers
SHIELD	yes
WEIGHT	
in travelling order without ammunition	2160 kg
in firing position with ammunition	1640 kg
SWEPT RADIUS (at 0° elevation)	2.62 m
LENGTH	
travelling	5.035 m
firing	4.05 m
WIDTH	
travelling	2.36 m
firing	2.3 m
HEIGHT	
travelling	2.075 m
firing	1.67 m
AXIS OF BORE (firing)	0.735 m
ELEVATION/DEPRESSION	
powered	+81.6°/-3.5°
manual	+83.5°/-5.5°
TRAVERSE	360°
RATE OF FIRE PER BARREL (cyclic)	1000 rpm
EFFECTIVE ANTI-AIRCRAFT RANGE	2000 m
CREW	3 or 4 (1 on mount)
TOWING VEHICLE	4 × 4 truck

GREECE

Artemis 30 mm Light Anti-aircraft Gun System

Development
The Artemis twin 30 mm air defence system has been designed by the Hellenic Arms Industry SA to meet the requirements of the Greek Army and was shown in public for the first time during the Defendory Exposition held in Athens in October 1982.

The carriage was designed in collaboration with the West German company of KUKA GmbH while the twin 30 mm cannon and its associated ammunition come from Mauser, also of West Germany. The fire control system has been designed by Philips of Sweden and the battery co-ordination and acquisition radar system by Siemens AG.

In June 1983 it was announced that negotiations on a production contract for deliveries over a five year period were being conducted with the Greek Ministry of Defence and the contract was signed in October 1984. The first two Artemis 30 mm light anti-aircraft guns were completed in early 1988, but by October the same year they still had to be handed over to the Greek Ministry of Defence for quality testing. Under the original plan, first production weapons should have been in service with the Greek armed forces in 1988 with production continuing through to 1990-91.

Description
The Artemis 30 fire unit is a twin 30 mm cannon system towed on a twin-axled split-type carriage. The axle nearest to the towing arm carries the generator which powers the cannon system in action. When deployed this axle/generator assembly is removed and placed some distance away from the mount. The deployed mount is lowered and levelled by means of three hydraulically-operated pads, two on outrigger arms, while the rear axle is power-retracted upwards.

The weapons are mounted on each side of a horizontal drum assembly which elevates the cannon. This assembly is placed on a central support

Greece / TOWED AA GUNS

Artemis 30 in travelling configuration

Close-up of gunner's position on Artemis 30 LAAG

Interior view of Artemis fire control system

on a turntable effecting the weapon traverse movement. The circular ammunition hoppers holding 500 linked rounds (250 for each cannon) are also on the central support. Each cannon receiver has a protective housing that covers the cannon to the base of the barrel. Each of these boxes can be opened to reveal the mechanism to clear jams or for routine servicing. By removing the gun barrel, the entire receivers can be swung outwards for more involved repairs and maintenance. The linked ammunition is fed from the hoppers upward through the central drum and into the feeders from the inside. Spent links and cases are ejected through slots in the cannon housings.

The weapons are the Mauser 30 mm Model F cannon, with EBO-produced cold-forged barrels with a constant rifling pitch. The twin cannon upper mount assembly has an unlimited 360° arc in traverse, while the elevation arc is from -5° to +85°.

The mount has three distinct modes of operation:
(1) Operation via a remote fire control system
(2) Operation via a gunner seated directly behind the central mount support. In this mode the gunner is supplied with all necessary controls including a periscope for ground targets and a gyroscopic angle predicting sight for air target engagement
(3) Emergency operation via the gunner (no power supplied to the mount).

Weapon aiming is accomplished via hand wheels, firing via a foot trigger. The weapons use the well-known 30 mm × 173 GAU-8/A family of ammunition including HEI-SD, TP, TP-T, HEI-SD-T, and Break-up.

It was established early on that Artemis 30 would not be fully dependent on radar fire control. However, it was decided that any fire control method would be of modular form to encompass radar when required.

Philips Elekronikindustrier AB of Sweden have developed the Trackfire modular fire control system, the first production application of which is for the Greek Artemis twin 30 mm system. Philips delivered the first production Trackfire systems in early 1988 with deliveries expected to continue through to late 1989.

The complete Trackfire system consists of the sight, target designator, meteorological sensors, computer control and display console and the gun adaptors.

The Greek version is mounted on a two wheeled trailer that can be towed by a light truck. The standard system consists of a frequency agility radar, TV tracker and a laser rangefinder, but an infra-red camera can be added to give a night capability if required.

The fire control centre, or battery co-ordination post and acquisition radar system was developed by Siemens of West Germany who handed over the first system to Greece in July 1988. This system is shelter-mounted and consists of a roof-mounted pulse Doppler radar system for surveillance and target acquisition, secondary radar for IFF, command and control computer display, and communications equipment.

It processes all incoming data and transmits gun-laying data and firing commands to the weapons via land lines. It can provide information to up to 12 weapon systems and is also capable of tracking up to 20 targets simultaneously.

A fire control centre usually controls three or four guns spread over an area about the size of an airfield with each gun operating over a range of 2000 to 3500 m with a maximum engagement range of 5000 m.

Being modular the Artemis 30 fire control system can be expanded and adapted to suit the operational requirement. For use at night an infra-red sensor can be added and for all-weather use an amplitude monopulse tracking radar can be installed on the director. An example of such an arrangement was shown at the Defendory 1982 Exhibition. The system can also be adapted to handle up to four twin 30 mm cannon carriages or for use with guided missile systems.

Variants
The company has proposed that this system could be mounted on the chassis of the Steyr 4K 7FA armoured personnel carrier which is already being manufactured under licence in Greece for the Greek Army, and negotiations are currently taking place with ELVO as to the implementation of this project.

176 TOWED AA GUNS / Greece

Artemis 30 with guns firing

Philips Trackfire fire control system mounted on a two-wheeled trailer and deployed in the operating position

Artemis fire control centre, or battery co-ordination post and acquisition radar system deployed in the field and showing roof-mounted radar antenna

The fire control centre is also shelter-mounted and can be carried on the rear of a cross country truck

SPECIFICATIONS

CALIBRE	30 mm
BARREL LENGTH (with muzzle brake)	3.35 m
OPERATION	gas, automatic
CARRIAGE	4-wheel, cruciform
SHIELD	no
WEIGHT	
travelling (without ammunition)	6900 kg
travelling (with ammunition)	7400 kg
firing (with ammunition)	5900 kg
LENGTH (travelling)	8.02 m
WIDTH (travelling)	2.38 m
HEIGHT (travelling)	2.48 m
TRACK	1.8 m
WHEELBASE	4.35 m
GROUND CLEARANCE	0.30 m
ELEVATION/DEPRESSION	+85°/−5° at 75°/s
ELEVATION ACCELERATION	166°/s^2
TRAVERSE	360° at 100°/s
TRAVERSE ACCELERATION	200°/s^2
RATE OF FIRE (both guns)	1600 rpm
NUMBER OF ROUNDS (ready use)	500
OVERALL CARRIAGE ACCURACY	less than 1.5 mrad
MAX TOWING SPEED	80 km/h

Status: In production for Greek Army, Navy and Air Force.

Manufacturer: Hellenic Arms Industry SA, 160 Kifissias Avenue, Athens, Greece.
Telephone: 6472611 16
Telex: 21 8562 EBO GR

ISRAEL

Spider II

Development/Description

The Spider II Air Defence Artillery System was introduced at the 1981 Paris Air Show. It consists of up to six twin 30 mm TCM-30G cannon turrets controlled from a central fire control system. The fire control system features radar and optronic target acquisition and tracking and can provide automatic ballistic prediction for anti-aircraft guns of calibres from 30 to 57 mm. The radar can detect small radar cross-section targets at ranges of up to 19 km.

The TCM-30G is an Israel Aircraft Industries development of its naval TCM-30 twin 30 mm mounting and is stated to have a high rate of fire, low shell dispersion, elevation from -20 to +85°, a rapid slewing rate and precise servo control. When used in conjunction with the Spider II System the number of men on the gun mountings can be kept to a minimum. The gun is suitable for use against high and low flying aircraft, helicopters and missiles. Five types of 30 mm ammunition can be used to provide flexibility against the various targets to be engaged.

Status: Development complete. Ready for production.

Manufacturer: Israel Aircraft Industries Limited, Ben-Gurion International Airport 70100, Israel.
Telephone: (03) 971311
Telex: ISRAVIA 371133/371114
Fax: 9712290/9713131

Spider II twin 30 mm towed anti-aircraft gun in travelling configuration

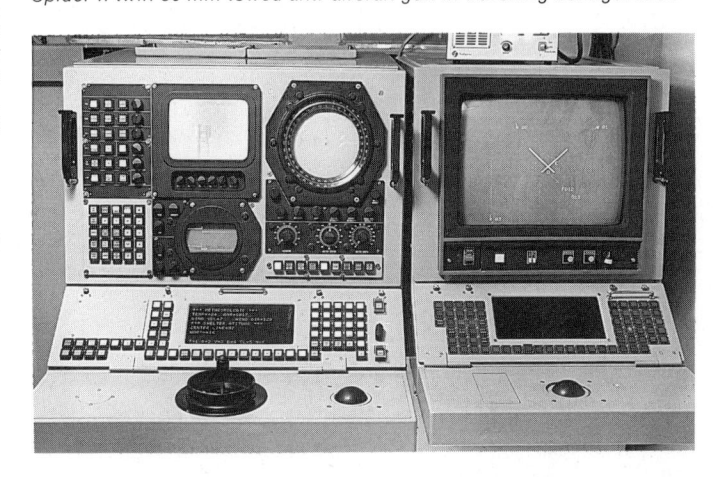

Spider fire control console showing two operator consoles

TCM Mk 3 Light Air Defence Artillery System

Development

Based on its experience in the design, development and production of the TCM-20 twin 20 mm anti-aircraft system (fully described in the following entry), RAMTA Structures and Systems has now developed the TCM Mk 3 light air defence artillery system. It was first announced in 1983 and was said to be in production and service in 1984.

Description

The mount is similar to the earlier TCM-20's but has been fitted with advanced systems and sub-assemblies, such as new drives, and has a more modern sight. The system can also be integrated with a fire control system manufactured by the MBT Electronics division of Israel Aircraft Industries which is based on a computerised sight and system integrated laser rangefinder. Using suitable adaptors the TCM Mk 3 can accept most 20 to 25 mm light guns, the self-propelled models shown in the photographs being fitted with the Soviet 23 mm ZU-23 cannon. In addition the system can be installed on naval craft as main and secondary armament.

Command and control of the TCM Mk 3 mount is through a variable speed joystick system. Mechanical movement of the joystick by the gunner at the rear of the mount is converted to an electrical signal which passes to servo-amplifiers which convert it through acceleration cards into a command for the motors. The firing lock is on the joystick so the gunner does not have to move his hand to release the lock and open fire.

The new drive system consists of two separate and similar units, traverse and elevation. Each unit includes a 24 V servo-motor, servo-amplifier, torque limiter, gear and feedback system. The drive system is very sensitive to joystick commands so the gunner can track fast and slow targets.

The bearing system consists of three sealed, maintenance free bearings, two for elevation and one for traverse. Their crosswire structure minimises backlash and increases firing accuracy. The elevation bearings have gear selectors and the traverse bearing has a ring gear.

Status: In production. In service with the Israel Defence Force Air Force.

Manufacturer: RAMTA Structures and Systems, PO Box 323, Beer Sheba, Israel (a Division of Israel Aircraft Industries Limited).
Telephone: (057) 74851/3
Telex: 5298 IAIBS IL

TCM Mk 3 system fitted with 23 mm ZU-23 cannon

TCM Mk 3 system on half-track chassis

TOWED AA GUNS / Israel

SPECIFICATIONS

CALIBRE	20 to 25 mm (eg 20 mm HS 404, HS 804, HS 820, Rh 202 and F623)
CARRIAGE	towed or self-propelled
SHIELD	yes
WEIGHT	1350 kg (towed model with HS 404 guns)
ELEVATION/DEPRESSION	
mechanical	+90°/-10°
electrical	+85°/-6°
TRAVERSE	360° (0.25²/s to 75-0°/s max)
ELECTRICAL POWER	24 V DC
MAIN POWER SOURCE	2 × 12 V, 80 Ah batteries
AUXILIARY POWER SOURCE	28 V DC, 3.75 hp petrol engine generator
SIGHTS	
standard	M18 optical
optional	×4 Starlight system for night operation, MBT fire control system including computerised sight and system integrated laser rangefinder

TCM-20 Twin 20 mm Anti-aircraft Gun System

Development
The TCM-20 twin 20 mm anti-aircraft gun system was developed by the MBT Division of Israel Aircraft Industries from 1969 to meet the requirements of the Israeli Defence Air Force. It was first used in 1970 during the War of Attrition when it was credited with shooting down 10 aircraft in 10 engagements. During the Yom Kippur War it is credited with shooting down 60 per cent of the aircraft downed by ground air defences.

By March 1983 the company had built a total of 700 TCM-20 twin 20 mm anti-aircraft systems which had been delivered to Israel and seven other countries.

In the 1982 Lebanon campaign the TCM-20 was used in three roles, against ground forces in urban areas, against aircraft and helicopters and against ground forces in the field as a close support weapon. In the anti-aircraft role it shot down a Syrian MiG-23 Flogger.

Israel uses the TCM-20 in two models, towed and self-propelled. The latter is basically the standard towed model mounted on the rear of a half-track; it crossed the Suez Canal with the Israeli spearhead. It was used to defend convoys and bridgeheads and also proved effective in urban fighting.

The TCM-20 can also be used in conjunction with the EL/M 2106 point defence alert radar.

Description
The TCM-20 is essentially a modernised version of the American M55 trailer-mounted anti-aircraft gun system with the original four Browning 12.7 mm (0.50) M2 HB machine guns replaced by two Hispano-Suiza HS 404 20 mm cannon modified to fire HS 804 ammunition which includes HEIT-SD, HEI, APT and TP-T.

Main components of the TCM-20 are the carriage, mount, APU, two 12 V batteries with a capacity of 80 Ah, two 20 mm cannon and an M18 reflex sight.

The gunner has front and side armour protection. If required elevation and traverse limiters can be installed. No external power source is required as all the drive and firing systems are electric and the APU maintains the charge levels of each of the standard 12 V batteries. Turret traverse and gun elevation speeds are 60 to 72°/s in azimuth and 60 to 67°/s in elevation.

TCM-20 twin 20 mm anti-aircraft gun system with EL/M 2106 point defence alert radar in background

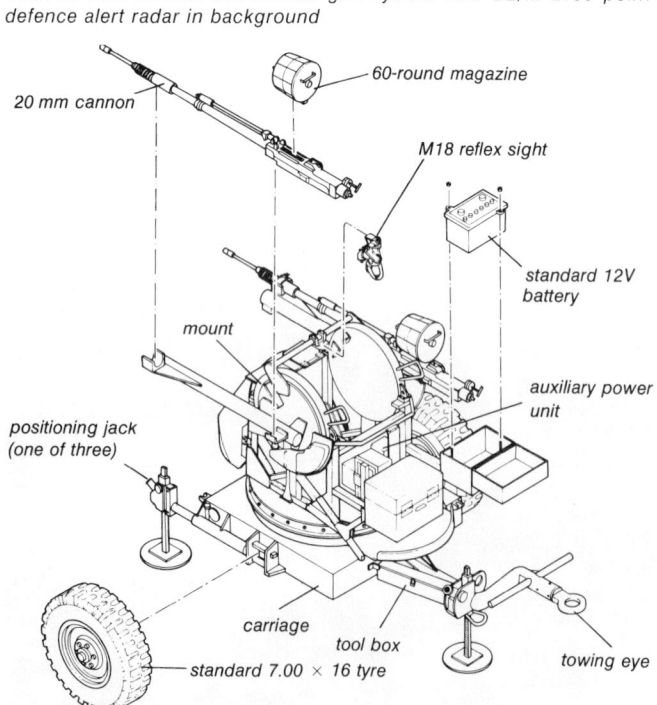

TCM-20 twin 20 mm anti-aircraft gun system installed on Israeli half-track

Main components of TCM-20 twin 20 mm anti-aircraft gun system

TCM-20 twin 20 mm anti-aircraft gun system in firing position with jacks lowered

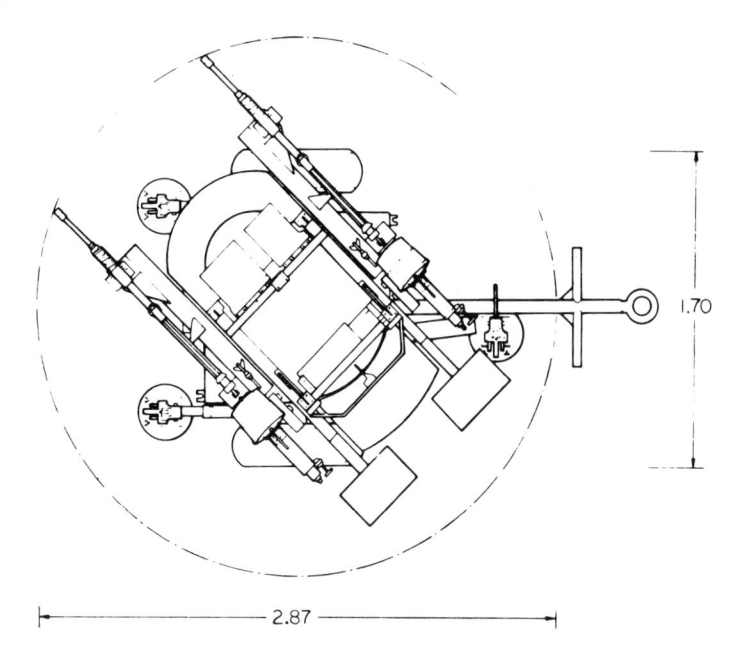

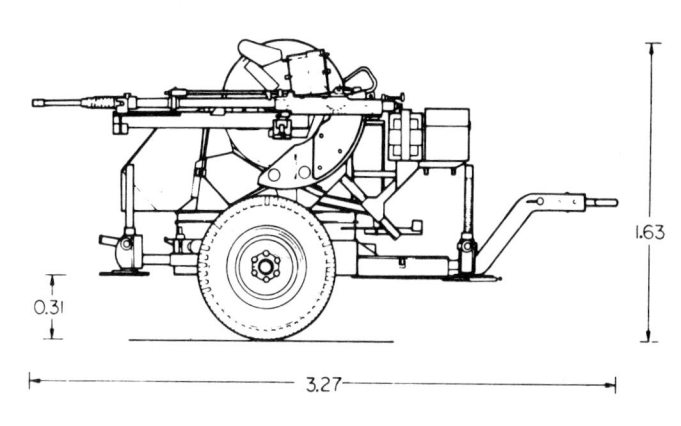

Israel / TOWED AA GUNS

Top and side drawing of TCM-20 twin 20 mm anti-aircraft gun system (not to 1/76th scale, dimensions in metres)

The cannon are cocked manually and fired by an electrically driven solenoid controlled by redundant triggers in the gunner's control handle. Each of the 20 mm cannon has a 60 round drum type magazine which weighs 12 kg empty and 28 kg loaded.

The towed version can be carried slung under a Bell 205 helicopter while a CH-53 helicopter can carry a Jeep and a TCM-20. The TCM-20 can be uncoupled from its towing vehicle and be ready for action in less than 40 seconds. In the firing position the carriage is supported on three jacks, one at the front of the carriage to the rear of the towing eye and the other two at the rear of the carriage.

RAMTA Structures and Systems RAM (4 × 4) light armoured vehicle fitted with TCM-20 twin 20 mm air defence system

SPECIFICATIONS

CALIBRE	20 mm
OPERATION	blowback with positive breech locking
CARRIAGE	2-wheeled
SHIELD	yes
WEIGHT (travelling order)	1350 kg (with two loaded magazines)
LENGTH (travelling)	3.27 m
WIDTH (travelling)	1.7 m
HEIGHT (travelling)	1.63 m
GROUND CLEARANCE (travelling)	0.31 m
TYRES	7.00 × 16
ELEVATION/DEPRESSION	+90°/−10°
TRAVERSE	360°
RATE OF FIRE PER BARREL	
cyclic	600/700 rpm
practical	150 rpm
MAX RANGE	
horizontal	5700 m
vertical	4500 m
EFFECTIVE RANGE	
aircraft targets	1200 m
ground targets	1500 m
TOWING VEHICLE	Jeep type (4 × 4) truck

Status: In production. In service with at least seven countries including:

Country	Quantity	User	Comment
Argentina	24+	air force	uses Elta radar, towed version only
Haiti	6	army	towed version only
Israel	370	air force	uses Elta radar, both towed and self-propelled systems used, total is for both types
Kenya	50	army	towed version only

Manufacturer: RAMTA Structures and Systems, PO Box 323, Beer Sheba, Israel. (A division of Israel Aircraft Industries Limited.)
Telephone: (057) 74851/3
Telex: 5298 IAIBS IL

ITALY

Breda Twin 40L70 Field Mounting

Development

Breda Meccanica Bresciana has produced a field mounting version of its well-established twin 40 mm naval anti-aircraft gun for use against low-flying aircraft and missile targets. The gun is fully automatic and no-one needs to be on the mounting when the gun is in action. It can be used in conjunction with a wide range of fire control systems such as the Hollandse Signaalapparaten 'Flycatcher'. The combination of two Breda Twin 40L70s and a Signaalapparaten 'Flycatcher' is marketed as a low level air defence system known as Guardian. A total of 36 mounts were acquired by Venezuela in the early 1980s as part of a Guardian system. These are operated by the Army.

Description

The guns used with the Breda Twin 40L70 are two Bofors 40 mm L/70 guns joined together to form a twin elevating mass by a specially designed twin cradle. The barrels are set 30 cm apart to reduce the elevating mass recoil forces and to reduce weight. Each gun is a standard Bofors 40 mm L/70, which is already in widespread production.

The field mounting consists of a 360° traverse training platform supported on a wire race bearing. The platform has parallel vertical lightweight aluminium alloy trunnion supports. The platform also supports the servo and ammunition feed motors, together with the upper ammunition feed mechanism, firing mechanism and system junction box. The upper section of the mounting is completely enclosed in a watertight reinforced glass fibre cupola fitted with three servicing hatches, one at the rear and one on each side.

Under the mounting platform is the magazine inside the mounting carriage. The carriage is normally carried on four wheels on two axles. To get the gun into action the carriage is emplaced in the firing position and levelled using six outrigger jacks: one each at the front and rear and the other four on outrigger arms that are swivelled outwards. Once emplaced pickets are driven into the ground from the outrigger feet and the connections to the gun from the external generator and the fire control system are made via junction boxes. The external generator supplies 440 volts ac at a frequency of 60 Hz. Hatches on each side of the lower carriage give access to the ammunition magazine.

Rounds are fed into the magazine from four round clips. The magazine consists of four horizontal layers equipped with a system of inner moving bands and ratchets that propel the rounds towards the ammunition hoisting chains. The system is divided into two independent sections, each of which delivers ammunition to one of the guns. The magazine trains with the mounting, and the supply system is arranged so that if one gun is out of action the other can continue to fire. The forward section of the magazine supplies the left-hand gun and the rear section supplies the right-hand gun. The system is driven by a 400 V, 60 Hz motor which supplies either fast or slow drive. The slow drive operates the magazine conveyors and the scuttle transferring the rounds to the lower chain hoist. The fast drive operates at speeds in excess of 300 rpm to drive the ammunition chain hoists and the scuttle at the top of the hoist. From this top scuttle the fast drive also feeds the rounds into fan-shaped shifters which move the rounds through 90° into the gun feeders. Empty cases are ejected from a chute that feeds to the front of the gun. The chain hoists take four rounds from the magazine every 0.7 seconds. A series of brakes and slipping clutches detect any misfeeds. Rounds

Twin 40L70 Field Mounting in travelling configuration with outriggers and stabilisers retracted

Twin 40L70 Field Mounting ready for action with outriggers and stabilisers in position

Breda Twin 40L70 Field Mounting deployed in firing position with Flycatcher fire control system in right background

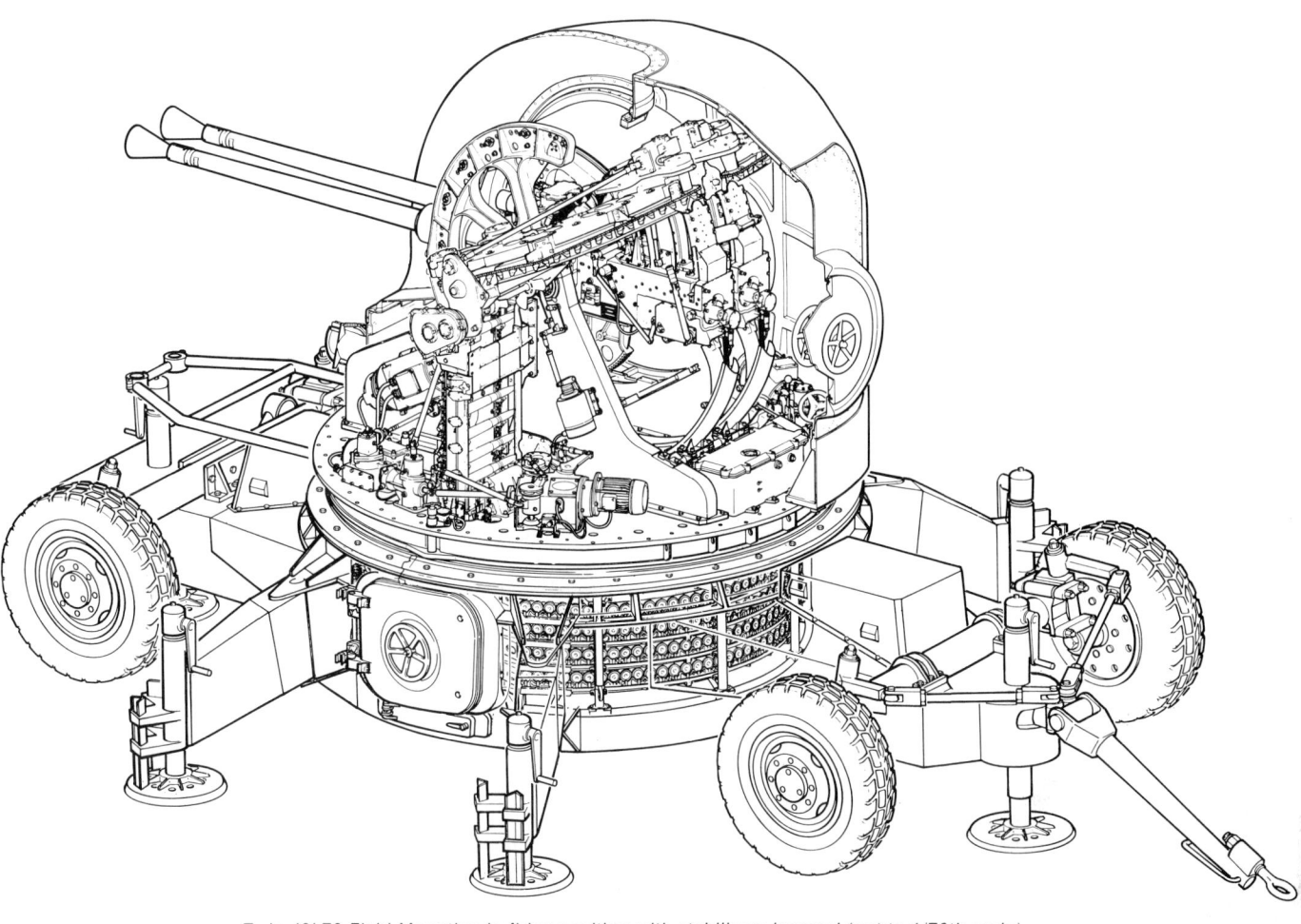

Twin 40L70 Field Mounting in firing position with stabilisers lowered (not to 1/76th scale)

are fed into the lower magazine manually via the side hatches and when fully loaded each mounting can hold 444 rounds.

The gun is trained by electrical dc motors driving epicyclic gearboxes. The gearboxes have a coarse synchro ratio of 1:1 and a fine rate of 1:36 but this fine rate may be varied to suit individual systems.

The interior of the watertight cupola is supplied with forced ventilation. The Breda Twin 40L70 Field Mounting can accommodate all the many forms of Bofors 40 mm ammunition, including proximity fuzed rounds.

The twin mounting can supply a rate of fire of 600 rds/min, but variations may occur depending on the type of ammunition used.

Variant

Future Breda Twin 40L70 Field Guns will be fitted with a new Breda recoiling mass called the Fast Forty which enables the system to have a cyclic rate of fire of 450 rounds per barrel per minute.

The dramatic increase in performance has been aided by wide adoption of materials such as titanium which is characterised by high resistance. The new design entailed a sweeping reduction of the distance run by moving components with a consequent saving in time. Valuable milliseconds have been gained, for example, by greatly reducing the recoil length and in addition a new conception ramming device has been introduced which allows the transfer of the round direct from the feeding position to the breech block closing position, taking a shorter route analogous to the hypotenuse of a triangle instead of following the two sides as in the current 40L70 weapon.

Energy made available in firing, accumulated in hydropneumatic linear motors in the return in battery phase, affords faster and better controlled breech operation allowing optimisation of the requisite acceleration and deceleration. These devices are employed, for example, for return in battery of the recoiling mass, for moving the ramming device and to decelerate the round immediately before breech block closing, accumulating energy employed to render faster the upward movement of the block.

Digital control is also fitted which allows (1) easy and fast introduction of prohibited zones by means of a key board (2) rapid alignment of the gun and fire control system (3) automatic correction of line of fire in relation to platform inclination (4) visualisation of diagnostic messages on the local control panel (5) control of the gun by means of serial transmission of gun orders through a two wire cable.

SPECIFICATIONS

CALIBRE	40 mm
BARREL LENGTH	2.8 m
RECOIL MECHANISM	hydro-spring
BREECH MECHANISM	vertical sliding
CARRIAGE	4-wheeled with 6 out-riggers
SHIELD	glass fibre cupola
WEIGHT OF TRAINING MASS (without ammunition)	5350 kg
TOTAL WEIGHT (without ammunition)	9900 kg
WEIGHT OF AMMUNITION	1100 kg
LENGTH (travelling)	8.05 m
WIDTH (travelling)	3.2 m
HEIGHT (travelling)	3.65 m approx
GROUND CLEARANCE (travelling)	0.3 m approx
TRACK	2.5 m
WHEELBASE	5 m
RECOIL FORCE (average per barrel)	2700 kg
TRAINING VELOCITY	90°/s
TRAINING ACCELERATION	120°/s^2
TRAVERSE	360°
ELEVATION VELOCITY	60°/s
ELEVATION ACCELERATION	120°/s^2
MAGAZINE CAPACITY	444 rounds
RATE OF FIRE (both barrels)	600 rpm approx
MAX RANGE	
vertical	8700 m
horizontal	12 500 m
AMMUNITION FEED RATE	330 rounds per barrel per minute
TOWING VEHICLE (typical)	FIAT 6605 (6 × 6) truck

182 TOWED AA GUNS / Italy

Status: Production as required. In service with Venezuela (36 Army).

Manufacturer: Breda Meccanica Bresciana SpA, 2 Via Lunga, 25128 Brescia, Italy.
Telephone: (030) 31911
Telex: 300056 BREDAR I

Breda 40 mm Anti-aircraft Gun

Development/Description

Breda Meccanica Bresciana has manufactured the Swedish Bofors 40 mm L/70 anti-aircraft gun under licence as well as a number of naval mounts of both its own and Swedish Bofors design. The first Breda 40 mm guns were produced for the Italian Army in 1969.

Breda has also developed an Automatic Feeding Device (AFD) which can be fitted to single versions of the 40 mm L/70 anti-aircraft gun, as well as naval weapons of this calibre. The AFD can be provided by Breda in kit form, installed on new production guns or fitted when the guns are returned to Breda for overhaul.

The conversion consists of substituting parts of the elevating mass to increase the cyclic rate of fire from 240 to 300 rds/min, where this has not already been done, and installing the ammunition feeding complex on the platform. The performance of the gun is not affected by the modification and loading and firing rates remain constant through all the elevation range. All types of ammunition can be fired including proximity fuzed ammunition. Main advantages of the system are the higher rates of fire and the reduced manning requirements as only two men are required on the mount when the optical fire control system is being used.

Loading is simple and quick and only one loader is required. The magazine, which comprises three layers, rests on the traversing platform and four round clips of 40 mm ammunition are fed into the magazines via prepared ramps. The magazine holds 144 rounds of ammunition.

When firing the rounds are automatically fed along the layer and taken up in threes by the elevation chain to a fan-shaped shifter at trunnion axis level, which through differentials adjusts to barrel elevation and conveys the rounds to the feeder. The power to carry out this operation is provided by an electric motor. A 32 round feeder called the AL-100 is also available from Breda.

Breda-built 40 mm L/70 anti-aircraft gun in firing position with automatic feeding device on rear part of traversing platform

Breda 40 mm L/70 anti-aircraft gun with automatic feeding device in travelling order

SPECIFICATIONS
(where different from Swedish 40 mm Bofors L/70)

WEIGHT (travelling order)	5300 kg
LENGTH (travelling)	7.28 m
WIDTH (travelling)	2.289 m
HEIGHT (travelling)	2.655 m
AXIS OF BORE (travelling)	1.735 m
TRACK	
front	1.77 m
rear	1.796 m
WHEELBASE	4.025 m
ELEVATION/DEPRESSION	+85°/-5°
TRAVERSE	360°
TRAVERSE SPEED	85°/s
ELEVATION SPEED	45°/s
RATE OF FIRE (cyclic)	300 rpm
CREW	2 (on mount)

Italy / **TOWED AA GUNS** 183

Status: Production as required. It is understood that 200 40 mm L/70 guns were built for the Italian Army and 50 for the Greek Army.

Manufacturer: Breda Meccanica Bresciana SpA, 2 Via Lunga, 25128 Brescia, Italy.
Telephone: (030) 31911
Telex: 300056 BREDAR I

Breda Sentinel Twin 30 mm Anti-aircraft Gun

Development/Description
First shown publicly at the 1983 Paris Air Show the Breda Twin 30 mm anti-aircraft gun uses two 30 mm Mauser Model F guns mounted side by side on a mobile field mounting. The Twin 30 mm is intended to operate as an independent unit and has its own power source and optronic fire control unit.

On tow the Twin 30 mm has its barrels pointing to the rear and is carried on two, two-wheeled axles. To bring the weapon into action the wheels are raised on swivels until they are clear of the ground, the gun is then supported on four levelling jacks, one each at the front and rear and the two side jacks on outward-folding outrigger arms. The guns traverse with the mounting on a turntable with the aimer, who is provided with a shield, seated to the left of the barrels. The second prototype has hydraulic wheel-drives for limited self-propulsion, an automatic outrigger extension and levelling and optronic improvements. Other improvements include a new gunner's position, new type shield and a different generator at carriage rear.

The aimer is provided with an Officine Galileo model P75D optronic fire control system. This system comprises a control panel, a laser rangefinder, an optical aiming device and a computer combined in one unit. To track a target the target line of sight is held by operating the system joystick to enable the lead angle to be automatically applied to the guns while at the same time the laser rangefinder also provides fire data. Passive infra-red night aiming equipment is optional and at all times target acquisition data from external sources such as radar may be fed into the system.

Power for the mounting and the fire control system is provided by a power supply unit carried over the rear axle. The main power source is a HATZ 3L 40C four-stroke diesel engine. This air-cooled engine has three cylinders and a capacity of 2.5 litres. Using a direct injection system the engine has a maximum speed of 3000 rpm. Electrical power is supplied by SACCARDO GS 132 M/16 three phase brushless alternators.

Second prototype of the Breda Sentinel twin 30 mm anti-aircraft gun system which has hydraulic road wheel drive system

The two 30 mm Mauser Model F guns are mounted side by side and are provided with 500 rounds of ammunition. Each barrel has a rate of fire of 800 rds/min (cyclic) and the ammunition feed uses belt guides to move the rounds to the guns. The ammunition used is of the GAU-8/A type and includes HEI, API, HEI-SD and TP with a maximum muzzle velocity of 1040 m/s.

Prototype Breda Sentinel Twin 30 mm anti-aircraft gun in firing position with outriggers lowered

184 TOWED AA GUNS / Italy-Norway

Second prototype Breda Sentinel twin 30 mm anti-aircraft gun with stabilisers being deployed

Second prototype Breda Sentinel twin 30 mm anti-aircraft gun in travelling configuration and showing APU on rear of carriage

SPECIFICATIONS

CALIBRE	30 mm
BARREL LENGTH	2.458 m
CARRIAGE	4-wheeled with two outriggers
SHIELD	yes
WEIGHT (with ammunition)	5000 kg
LENGTH (travelling)	6.46 m
WIDTH (travelling)	1.76 m
HEIGHT (travelling)	1.94 m
GROUND CLEARANCE	0.43 m
TRACK	1.76 m
WHEELBASE	3.5 m
ELEVATION/DEPRESSION	+85°/-5°
ELEVATION SPEED	80°/s
ELEVATION ACCELERATION	120°/s^2
TRAVERSE	360° at 120°/s
TRAVERSE ACCELERATION	150°/s^2
FLIGHT TIME TO 3000 m	5.2 s
RATE OF FIRE (combined)	1600 rpm
MUZZLE VELOCITY	1040 m/s
AMMUNITION CAPACITY	500 rounds

Status: Development complete. Ready for production.

Manufacturer: Breda Meccanica Bresciana SpA, 2 Via Lunga, 25128 Brescia, Italy.
Telephone: (030) 31911
Telex: 300056 BREDAR I

NORWAY

20 mm Automatic Anti-aircraft Gun FK 20-2

Development/Description

The 20 mm automatic anti-aircraft gun FK 20-2 is a joint development between Hispano-Suiza of Switzerland (now part of the Oerlikon-Bührle group), Norsk Forsvarsteknologi AS (previously A/S Kongsberg Våpenfabrikk) of Norway, Rheinmetall GmbH of West Germany and Kern and Company AG. The system, which was developed in the late 1960s, basically consists of a modified HSS 669 mount fitted with a Rheinmetall 20 mm automatic cannon (as installed in the Marder IFV, Luchs 8 × 8 reconnaissance vehicle, FIAT/OTO Melara Type 6616 armoured car and the twin 20 mm automatic anti-aircraft gun), with the cradle, ammunition cases and flexible feed channels designed by Kongsberg and the optical sight designed by Kern.

The FK 20-2 can be used against both ground and air targets and can be quickly dismantled without special tools into loads suitable for carrying over short distances. The FK 20-2 weighs only 620 kg in travelling order compared with the twin 20 mm MK 20 Rh 202 automatic anti-aircraft gun which weighs 2160 kg in travelling order.

The FK 20-2 consists of five main components, the cannon, cradle, upper mounting with seat, lower mount and carriage. The Rheinmetall 20 mm MK 20 Rh 202 cannon are gas operated and fully automatic. Of 160 rounds of ammunition carried, 75 are in each of the side magazines and 10 rounds (normally APDS-T or API-T) in the magazine on top of the cannon. The following types of fixed ammunition (20 mm × 139) can be fired:

20 mm automatic anti-aircraft gun FK 20-2 in travelling order

Norway / TOWED AA GUNS

20 mm automatic anti-aircraft gun FK 20-2 in firing position

Kraka (4 × 2) light vehicle of the West German Army fitted with 20 mm automatic anti-aircraft gun FK 20-2 (Peter Siebert)

TYPE	APDS-T	API-T	HEI
GERMAN DESIGNATION	DM63	DM43A1	n/app
WEIGHT OF PROJECTILE	108 g	111 g	120 g
MUZZLE VELOCITY	1150 m/s	1100 m/s	1045 m/s

TYPE	HEI-T	TP/TP-T	Break Up
GERMAN DESIGNATION	DM51A2/ DM81	DM48/ DM48A1	DM78A1
WEIGHT OF PROJECTILE	120 g	120 g	120 g
MUZZLE VELOCITY	1045 m/s	1045 m/s	1045 m/s

More recently Raufoss has developed the new 20 mm NM75 multi-purpose round to meet the requirements of the West German and Norwegian armies. This multi-purpose round does not detonate until it is inside of the vehicle and also has an improved incendiary effect.

The lower mount is of the tripod type and the two shorter trails may be disconnected for transport. The two-wheeled carriage is horseshoe shaped and the tow bar may be set at different positions to compensate for different towing vehicles.

The cradle, which carries the gun and guides its recoil, is made of cast aluminium alloy and pivots on the upper mounting. It contains the recoil brakes, components forming part of the fire selector and trigger mechanism and a hinged frame assembly which contains the feeder mechanism and belt guides. The frame assembly can be latched semi-raised for quick inspection of the gun during action, and fully raised to remove the top feeder mechanism. The cocking crank is on top of the cradle.

The upper mounting holds the cradle and contains the elevation and traverse mechanisms which include adjustable twin gears to prevent play in the transmission. Operation of the quick-release locking device enables the upper mounting to be removed from the lower mounting. Fire selection, triggering and main locking controls are on the elevation and traverse handwheels. The optical sight is mounted between the handwheels. The gunner's seat can be folded forward to provide the gunner with a prone support position when the gun is being used against ground targets. The mount has a one-piece shield which can be removed.

The optical sight has a magnification of ×5 for use against ground targets and ×1.5 for use against air targets. The partially combined light paths for the air target sight give individual sighting images and optical values for both targets. Lead angle curves in the sight simplify firing against air targets at various speeds. The sighting image of the ground target sight comprises a simple cross-hair and range prediction lines for firing at targets at ranges of 500, 1000 and 1500 m.

Variants
The West German Army has fitted a number of its Kraka (4 × 4) light cross-country vehicles with the 20 mm automatic anti-aircraft gun FK 20-2 for use in both the air defence and ground fire support roles.

25 mm Mount

Trials of an FK 20-2 with the Rheinmetall 20 mm cannon replaced by the more recent Mauser automatic machine gun MK 25 mm × 137 Model E have now been completed. The 25 mm cannon has a cyclic rate of fire of 900 rds/min with a muzzle velocity of 1100 m/s with a total of 90 rounds of ready use ammunition being provided in two magazines on either side of the cannon, each holding 45 rounds.

Basic specifications are as follows:

LENGTH	4.6 m
WIDTH	1.86 m
WEIGHT	650 kg
ELEVATION/DEPRESSION	+80°/−8°
TRAVERSE	360°

SPECIFICATIONS

CALIBRE	20 mm
BARREL LENGTH (including muzzle brake)	2.61 m
OPERATION	gas, automatic
CARRIAGE	2-wheeled with outriggers
SHIELD	yes
WEIGHT	
travelling order	620 kg
firing position	440 kg
LENGTH	
travelling	4 m
firing	3.72 m
WIDTH	
travelling	1.86 m
firing	1.8 m
HEIGHT	
travelling	2.2 m
firing	1.2 m
AXIS OF BORE (firing)	0.58 m
GROUND CLEARANCE	0.38 m
TRACK	1.62 m
ELEVATION/DEPRESSION	+83°/−8°
TRAVERSE	360°
RATE OF FIRE (cyclic)	1000 rpm
EFFECTIVE VERTICAL RANGE	1500–2000 m
CREW	3 (1 on gun)
TOWING VEHICLE	light (4 × 4) truck

Status: Production complete. In service with West Germany (Army) and Norway (Army). Production can be resumed if further orders are received.

Manufacturer: Norsk Forsvarsteknologi AS, Manufacturing Division, PO Box 1003, N-3601 Kongsberg, Norway.
Telephone: (473) 738250
Telex: 11491
Fax: (473) 738586

TOWED AA GUNS / Spain

SPAIN

SA Placencia de las Armas Bofors 40 mm L/70 Anti-aircraft Guns

Development/Description
The Sociedad Anonima de Placencia de las Armas has been licensed by AB Bofors for over 20 years for production of the 40 mm L/70 anti-aircraft gun. The company has produced 274 40 mm L/70 guns for the Spanish Army and more for the Spanish Navy and for export. The company also produces the BOFI system for the 40 mm L/70 gun and carries out upgrading programmes for the Bofors 40 mm L/60 anti-aircraft gun.

Specifications for the 40 mm L/70 guns are identical to those of the Swedish model (see entry in this section).

Status: Production complete but can be resumed if further orders are placed. In service with the Spanish Army and Navy and with some other countries.

Manufacturer: SA Placencia de las Armas. Head office: Apartardo de Correos no 8, Andoain — (Guipuzca) — Spain.
Madrid office: Nunex de Balboa 49, 28001 Madrid, Spain.

Type A version of Bofors 40 mm L/70 anti-aircraft gun produced by SA Placencia de las Armas in travelling configuration

Meroka 20 mm Multi-barrel Anti-aircraft Gun System

Development
The Meroka 20 mm multi-barrel anti-aircraft gun system has been designed and developed by the Compañia de Estudios Técnicos de Materiales Espaciales (CETME) and is produced in land and sea versions. The naval version is in production and has been installed on Spanish Navy warships. The land version is still under development. The naval version uses a fully-automatic fire control system developed by Lockheed Electronics but the towed land version uses a CETME optronic system.

Description
The Meroka has 12 barrels to fire projectiles in salvos and each salvo has a virtual cyclic rate of fire of 24 rds/s or 9000 rpm; two salvos a second can be fired. The weapon operations (loading, feeding and unlocking) are carried out by compressed air from reservoirs mounted in the frame of the lower carriage that are recharged by a compressor during pauses in combat.

The 12 barrels are arranged in two superimposed rows and use a common breech-block. An adjustable clamp towards the ends of the barrels is used to optimise fire dispersion to suit the fire control system limitations. Feed is carried out using two munition belts, the ammunition is contained in a cylindrical drum containing 720 rounds, enough for 60 salvos. When loaded, fire can be opened almost immediately, the first salvo being fired within 0.08 seconds.

When ready for action the breech-block is at the rear and the ammunition is ready for feeding. The firer can then turn on the combat switch, the ammunition feed is made and the breech-block locks. When the trigger is depressed the 12 rounds will be fired in four groups of three shots in about 0.08 seconds. When the fourth group has been fired a contact automatically activates the unlocking cycle and the breech-block moves to the rear, extracting the empty cases (along with any misfires). When the breech-block reaches its rear position, compressed air powers the transport cycle to draw the ammunition belts six steps to align 12 fresh rounds with the barrels. The feed cycle then starts to load the fresh rounds and lock the breech-block again for firing. These cycles are automatically repeated for as long as the trigger is kept depressed.

In action Meroka is controlled by one man who sits to the rear of the barrels under a clear housing. For fire control he has a laser rangefinder, a video tracking device, a prediction calculator, servo-electronic controls, a control panel and a generator. The laser rangefinder has a wavelength of 1.06 µm and a repetition rate of 10 pulses per second; pulse energy is 65 mJ. The video system uses a camera with an automatic zoom feature with a focal length of between 30 and 300 mm. The camera is mounted over the barrels in a common housing with the laser rangefinder and the operator has a monitor in his control cab. The fire control system uses an analogue prediction calculator and power for the servo-electronic system is hydraulic. The operator has a control panel inside the cab which apart from the usual system controls has a built-in test system for first line maintenance. The generator is powered by a one-cylinder internal combustion engine that also powers the hydraulic system.

The ammunition fired is Oerlikon HE-I with a muzzle velocity of 1200 m/s. CETME has also developed a 20 mm APDS-T round with a projectile weight of 98 g and a penetrator weight of 72 g. Muzzle velocity is 1260 m/s with a velocity loss of 25 m/s every 100 m. The penetrator can pierce 40 mm of 100 kg/m^2 plate at 500 m and 30 mm at 1500 m. The projectile has an aluminium alloy shell body with a plastic protective ogive and the penetrator has a tracer element that lasts 2.5 seconds.

Meroka 20 mm multi-barrel anti-aircraft gun system in travelling configuration

Status: Prototypes completed. Not yet in production or service.

Manufacturer: Compañia de Estudios Técnicos de Materiales Espaciales, (SA) (CETME), Julian Camarillo 32, Madrid-17, Spain.

SWEDEN

Bofors 40 mm L/70 Automatic Anti-aircraft Gun

Development
The Bofors 40 mm L/70 automatic anti-aircraft gun entered service with the Swedish Army in 1951 as the successor to the 40 mm L/60 and is also manufactured under licence in India, Italy (see separate entry in this section) and Spain (production complete but can be resumed) and has been made under licence in West Germany, the Netherlands and the United Kingdom.

Description
There were two basic models of the L/70, Types A and B. Type B has a 3-phase 220 V 50 Hz APU mounted on the rear of the carriage whereas Type A is fed from an external power source.

The high rate of fire of 300 rds/min is obtained by ramming the rounds during the run-out, with the empty cartridge cases being ejected towards the end of recoil. The empty cartridge cases are deflected into a chute at the front of the mounting.

Ammunition is fed in four round clips to the feed guides by the automatic loading device by two loaders positioned one either side of the gun. Waist-high supports protect the loaders against falling during the high training acceleration of the mounting. An ammunition stay can be placed on top of the automatic loading device to serve as a magazine, thus permitting 26 rounds to be fired from the unmanned gun. Two ready use ammunition racks, holding 96 rounds, are fitted at the rear end of the gun platform. These racks are fed from the outside by an ammunition supply party and are emptied from the inside by the two loaders.

The monobloc barrel is provided with a flash suppressor. The recuperator spring encircles the rear part of the barrel and this, together with the recuperator spring, forms an easily exchangeable unit. The recoil buffer is hydraulic and the breech mechanism has a vertically sliding breech-block which opens and closes automatically.

There are two close-range sights, model NIFE SRS 5, fitted on a sight bracket on the breech casing of the gun, one for the elevation layer and one for the traversing layer. Elevation and traverse are electro-hydraulic with maximum elevation speed 45°/s and maximum traverse speed 85°/s. There are manual controls for emergency use.

In the remote-control mode the power operation devices for elevating and traversing are controlled by the input signals received from a fire control system connected to the gun by a cable. The Bofors precision remote-control system with transistorised amplifiers is used. In remote-control the data from the fire control equipment is transmitted with one cable and with Type B there is also a cable for connecting the gun with the power supply unit.

In local control the gun is operated by one man on the left side of the platform. This joystick is used in combination with the close-range sight if a central fire control equipment is not being used or is out of order, or if the gun is being operated as an independent unit.

A firing limiting gear for the electrical firing is provided and is set by pushing stop bolts, one for every 10° of traverse, and setting the highest limited elevation for any of the zones limited in traverse.

The following types of 40 mm ammunition are now produced by Bofors:

AMMUNITION TYPE	PFHE	HCHE	HE-T	APC-T	P-T
WEIGHT OF COMPLETE ROUND	2.4 kg	2.4 kg	2.5 kg	2.5 kg	2.5 kg
WEIGHT OF SHELL	0.88 kg	0.87 kg	0.96 kg	0.92 kg	0.96 kg
WEIGHT OF EXPLOSIVE	0.12 kg	0.165 kg	0.103 kg	none	none
TYPE OF EXPLOSIVE	octal	octal	hexotonal	n/app	n/app
ROUND LENGTH	534 mm	534 mm	534 mm	534 mm	534 mm
MUZZLE VELOCITY	1025 m/s	1030 m/s	1005 m/s	1010 m/s	1005 m/s

The PFHE pre-fragmented round has a proximity fuze with an effective range of up to 6.5 m against aircraft and 4.5 m against missiles. A new

TOWED AA GUNS / Sweden

Bofors 40 mm L/70 automatic anti-aircraft gun Type A fitted with muzzle velocity measuring equipment (West German Army)

Bofors 40 mm L/70 automatic anti-aircraft gun Type B in firing position

Mark 2 round with an improved proximity fuze can effectively double these figures. Flight time to 1000 m is 1.1 seconds, to 2000 m 2.44 seconds and to 3000 m 4.44 seconds. The PFHE projectile is made up of high-grade steel which, together with the explosive charge, gives a large number of fragments. To increase the projectile's effectiveness 650 tungsten carbide pellets, with a penetration capability of about 14 mm of duraluminium, are contained in the walls of the forward section. Large fragment dispersion is improved by the 'boat tail' of the projectile.

The new High Capacity High Explosive (HCHE) shell is a multi-purpose projectile designed for use against all types of target from light aircraft to vessels and armoured personnel carriers. It can, to a certain extent, replace conventional types of HE and AP ammunition. The casing of the HCHE shell is manufactured from a special steel which is sufficiently strong to allow penetration of armour plate without breaking up. The shell also protects the post-impact delay fuze, which means that the shell will explode only when inside the armoured target. The shell has a filling of 165 g of octonal, a powerful high explosive.

More recently Bofors have developed two new rounds for 40 mm L/70 guns, these are the Pre-fragmented Programmable Proximity-Fuzed 3P (PFPPX) and the Armour Piercing Fin Stabilised Discarding Sabot (APFSDS), neither of which are yet in volume production.

The Bofors 40 mm L/70 anti-aircraft gun is normally used in conjunction with central fire control systems such as the 'Flycatcher' designed by Hollandse Signaalapparaten and used by India and the Netherlands (Army and Air Force) and the Swiss Skyguard and Super-Fledermaus system. During 1980 the L M Ericsson Giraffe search radar, designed for use with the RBS 70 surface-to-air missile, was successfully used in conjunction wih the 40 mm BOFI gun to shoot down an attacking missile.

Bofors 40 mm L/70 automatic anti-aircraft gun system from rear with BOFI equipment, empty cartridge cases being ejected forward (T J Gander)

BOFI Fair-weather Gun System

The Bofors 40 mm BOFI (Bofors Optronic Fire control Instrument) gun system consists of a modified version of the basic 40 mm L/70 Type B, BOFI optronic fire control system and proximity fuzed ammunition. The FCE is integrated with the gun and is based on a computer which calculates the angles of aim-off to the target. The range to the target

Bofors 40 mm L/70 automatic anti-aircraft gun Type B with APU mounted on rear of carriage, outriggers in position and ammunition stay on top of loading device holding 26 rounds of ammunition

Bofors 40 mm L/70 automatic anti-aircraft gun with fair-weather BOFI equipment

is continuously provided by a laser rangefinder. The movements of the target are measured by the operator continuously keeping the gun aimed at the target. Once tracking has been established the computer automatically takes over the aiming of the gun and all the operator has to do is to make minor corrections to obtain accurate tracking. The operator observes the target through a sighting device consisting of a combination day and night sight with a light amplifier.

Target designation is made by an optical target indicator or a central search radar linked to the BOFI gun via a target data receiver (TDR) located beside the gun. Target data is transmitted to the TDR by wire or radio. By 1983 about 200 fair-weather BOFI guns had been delivered for service in Europe and Asia and Yugoslavia is known to have taken delivery of a quantity of systems.

BOFI All-weather Gun System

The all-weather BOFI gun system is in production with over 100 sold to date, with Malaysia being the first customer. This version has a multi-sensor fire control using a J-band pulse Doppler radar as the main sensor. The radar gives the system an all-weather operation and automatic acquisition and tracking capabilities. The radar operates on the MTI mode at target acquisition and switches automatically over to frequency agility in the tracking mode, which radically improves tracking accuracy. The radar sensor can be backed up by the optronics for tracking supervision or noise tracking using radar for angular tracking and laser for ranging. All of the sensors can be used in different combinations for maximum flexibility and jam resistance. A total of 22 ready use and 96 reload rounds are carried on each BOFI mount with the gun normally firing two-second bursts of 10 rounds against a target using the PFHE Mk 2 ammunition that was introduced in 1982 to a maximum range of over 4000 m.

Netherlands 40 mm L/70 Upgrade

Late in 1987 Bofors was awarded a contract from the Royal Netherlands Army for the modernisation of 60 Bofors 40 mm L/70 anti-aircraft guns which were originally built in the Netherlands under licence in the 1950s. Bofors was awarded the contract, worth 220 MSEK, after the Royal Netherlands Army considered modernising the 40 mm L/70 weapons or purchasing new Oerlikon-Bührle twin 35 mm systems.

The contract covers the production of the modernisation kits and delivery of proximity fuzed ammunition. Dutch industry will be involved

Bofors 40 mm L/70 automatic anti-aircraft gun with all-weather BOFI equipment, tracking radar and showing optical target indicator to left of carriage

TOWED AA GUNS / Sweden

SPECIFICATIONS (Types A and B)

CALIBRE	40 mm	GROUND CLEARANCE	
BARREL LENGTH	2.8 m	(travelling)	0.39 m
RECOIL MECHANISM	hydro-spring	TRACK	1.8 m
BREECH MECHANISM	vertically sliding	WHEELBASE	4.025 m
CARRIAGE	4-wheeled with outriggers	ELEVATION/DEPRESSION	+90°/-4°
SHIELD	yes	TRAVERSE	360°
WEIGHT IN TRAVELLING ORDER		RATE OF FIRE	300 rpm
		FEED	4 round clip
BOFI all-weather	5700 kg	NUMBER OF ROUNDS	
BOFI fair-weather	5500 kg	in ammunition stay	26
Type A	4800 kg	in racks	96
Type B	5150 kg	EFFECTIVE ANTI-AIRCRAFT RANGE	3000-4000 m
LENGTH (travelling)	7.29 m	CREW	4-6
WIDTH (travelling)	2.225 m	TOWING VEHICLE	3 ton (4 × 4 or 6 × 6) truck
HEIGHT (travelling)	2.349 m		
AXIS OF BORE			
travelling	1.735 m		
firing	1.335 m		

in the programme as the first six weapons will be modernised at Bofors in Sweden and the remaining 54 weapons will be modernised at the RDM facility in Rotterdam. First deliveries are due to be made to the Netherlands Army in August 1989.

The modernisation includes the installation of a new servo system, new amplifiers, increased rate of fire kit (now to be 300 rds/min), ammunition racks and a diesel power unit.

Spanish Bofors Upgrade

In 1987 the Spanish Army took delivery of its first Felis optronic automatic tracking system for its Bofors 40 mm L/70 anti-aircraft guns.

Felis consists of a high definition TV set with automatic tracking coupled to a telemetry laser, portable target designator and a radar interface. Spain uses the Contraves LPD-20 radar although other types can be used.

The system has three modes of operation: the first of these, radar acquisition, sends initial information to start the automatic tracking optical sequence; the second mode uses the portable autonomous visual designator which starts the same sequence while the third option uses a pre-determined TV scanning pattern until acquisition is achieved.

Inisel is the prime contractor for the system which was previously called Linca and was developed by CETME.

By the end of 1987 one tracking system plus eight 40 mm L/70 weapons fitted with the kits were being used for trials purposes with a total of 100 systems due to be delivered to the Spanish Army from 1988 to 1993.

Status: In production and in service with the following countries:

Country	Quantity	User	Comment
Argentina	n/av	army	
Austria	60	army	with Super Fledermaus/Skyguard FCS
Brazil	36+	army	Some are BOFI, also used with FILA FCS
Chile	n/av	army	L/70 use unconfirmed
Denmark	n/av	air force	Super Fledermaus FCS upgraded from 1986
Ecuador	24	army	
Finland	60+	army	
Germany, West	251	army	with Super Fledermaus FCS
Greece	100	army	of which 50 came from Breda of Italy
India	800+	army	local production, Super Fledermaus is used but these will be supplemented by the Signaal Flycatcher system. The first order is for 40 systems (2 + 38) with an option being held on a further 212 systems which will include local production
Indonesia	40	army	some may also be used by Marines
Iran	n/av	army	also used by Air Force
Ireland	2	army	
Israel	n/av	air force	with Super Fledermaus FCS which is being upgraded locally
Italy	230	army	local production by Breda, used with Fledermaus FCS modified to CT/40-G, upgraded by Contraves with LPD-20 surveillance radar
Korea, South	n/av	army	
Libya	n/av	army	present status uncertain
Malaysia	30	army	some are BOFI
Malta	6	armed forces	
Netherlands	60	army	with Flycatcher FCS
	72	air force	with Flycatcher FCS
Norway	64	air force	with Super Fledermaus FCS, upgraded by SATT from 1984
Peru	40	army	
Singapore	16	air force	originally used Super Fledermaus for both 40 mm L/70 and twin 35 mm Oerlikon-Bührle cannon, but these are being upgraded with the Swedish SATT package with first conversion being carried out in Sweden and remainder in Singapore
Spain	243	army	local production, getting Felis FCS
Sweden	600	army	
Taiwan	n/av	army	L/70 use unconfirmed from UK in 1987
Thailand	48	army	also Air Force
Turkey	n/av	army	
Venezuela	18	army	
Yugoslavia	n/av	army	

Manufacturer: AB Bofors, S-691 80 Bofors, Sweden. It is, or has been, produced under licence in Italy (see separate entry), Spain (by SA Placenia de las Armas, see separate entry), UK (Royal Ordnance Nottingham), and India.
Telephone: (0586) 81000
Telex: 73210
Fax: (0586) 58145

Sweden / **TOWED AA GUNS**

Bofors 40 mm m/36 L/60 Automatic Anti-aircraft Gun

Development
In 1928 AB Bofors started development of a 40 mm automatic anti-aircraft gun for both army and navy use. The first prototype of the army version was completed in 1931 and within a few years it had been adopted by almost 20 countries world-wide. Licenced manufacture of the 40 mm anti-aircraft gun was undertaken in a number of countries including Austria, Belgium, Brazil, Finland, France, Greece, Hungary, Italy, Norway, Poland and the United Kingdom. Some of these countries produced weapons both for their own use and for export; for example, the United Kingdom bought guns from Sweden and Poland until it could set up its own production facilities. There is a separate entry in this section for the British Mk 1 anti-aircraft gun and the American M1 which was manufactured in the USA during the Second World War.

There are at least three different Swedish carriages for the m/36: the m/38 (total weight of system 2150 kg), m/39 (total weight of system 2400 kg) and m/49e (total weight of system 2050 kg). The m/36 was succeeded in production after the end of the Second World War by the m/48 for which there is a separate entry. The list of user countries should be treated with caution as it is difficult to determine which particular model of the 40 mm Bofors gun (Swedish, British or US) some countries have in service.

Description
In the firing position the weight of the carriage is supported on four screw jacks, one at either end of the carriage and one either side on outriggers. Ammunition is fed to the breech vertically in four round clips with the empty cartridge cases being ejected under the forward part of the mount. The following types of fixed ammunition can be fired:
AP with the projectile weighing 0.89 kg and a muzzle velocity of 850 m/s, which will penetrate 52 mm of armour at an incidence of 0° at a range of 914 m.
HE projectile weighing 0.955 kg with a muzzle velocity of 850 m/s.

In August 1984 Bofors Ordnance announced that LIAB (Lindesbergs Industri AB), a subsidiary, had collaborated with the company in the development of a 40 mm L/60 pre-fragmented proximity round based on the same principles as used successfully in the L/70 Mk 2 round.

A special double-walled shell body containing hundreds of heavy metal pellets is charged with 100 g of the highly potent explosive octol to give a high penetration velocity to the pellets and shell fragments.

The effective initiation distance of the L/60 PFHE round is 6.5 m against aircraft and up to 4.5 m against missiles. The fuze incorporates a high-sensitive impact function, self-destruction and circuits to reduce initiation distance at very low altitudes. Muzzle velocity is 860 m/s.

LIAB has also developed a 40 mm L/60 APHC-T which has a 40 per cent increase in penetration compared to the original AP-T round. Ballistics of the APHC-T are the same as for the HET round.

Variants
In early 1986 AB Bofors announced a modification and renovation package for existing 40 mm L/60 guns that involves power laying, an increased rate of fire, an enlarged magazine capacity and ammunition-related improvements.

The increased rate of fire involves a kit that will provide a new fire rate of 190, plus or minus 10, rds/min. Changes to the carriage include hydraulic power laying machinery allowing one man to operate a single joystick for all movements in traverse and elevation, a new gyroscopic sight, a slip ring unit (SLU) for use with an external power unit, on-carriage ammunition racks for 24 rounds and a support unit for the single loader. The magazine capacity is increased to 20 rounds. A proximity fuze disconnector (PFD) may be fitted to disconnect PFHE round fuzes when required. The latter is used in conjunction with the LIAB PFHE ammunition. A generator is provided to supply all units of the gun system with power. It can also be fitted with the new Bofors Aerotronics U-sight and fire control system which is covered in the *Towed Anti-aircraft gun sights* section.

The new gun laying rates are as follows:

TRAVERSING SPEED	85°/s
TRAVERSING ACCELERATION	90°/s^2
ELEVATING SPEED	50°/s
ELEVATING ACCELERATION	115°/s^2
DISPERSION	<4 mrad

The above modifications may be carried out in local military workshops using a Bofors-supplied kit or in a special containerised workshop also supplied by AB Bofors.

There are separate entries in this section for the Belgian FN and Swedish Weibull 40 mm L/60 upgrade kits.

SPECIFICATIONS
(m/39 carriage)

CALIBRE	40 mm
BARREL LENGTH	
56-calibre	2.24 m
60-calibre	2.4 m
OPERATION	recoil
RECOIL	hydro-spring
BREECH MECHANISM	vertical sliding block
CARRIAGE	4-wheeled with outriggers
SHIELD	optional
WEIGHT	
travelling order	2400 kg
firing position	2400 kg
LENGTH (travelling)	6.38 m
WIDTH	
travelling	1.72 m
firing	3.92 m
HEIGHT (travelling)	2 m
ELEVATION/DEPRESSION	+90°/-5°
TRAVERSE	360°
RATE OF FIRE (cyclic)	120 rpm
FEED	4 round clip
MAX RANGE	
horizontal	4750 m
vertical	4660 m
EFFECTIVE VERTICAL RANGE	2560 m
CREW	4-6
TOWING VEHICLE	2½ ton (6 × 6) truck

Bofors 40 mm L/60 anti-aircraft gun fitted with full AB Bofors upgrading kit

Irish Army Bofors 40 mm m/36 L/60 automatic anti-aircraft gun in firing position (Raymond Molony)

192 TOWED AA GUNS / Sweden-Switzerland

Status: Production complete. In service with the following countries:

Country	Quantity	User	Comment
Argentina	n/av	army	may have been replaced by 40 mm L/70
Brazil	n/av	army	may have been replaced by 40 mm L/70
Denmark	36	army and air force	used with Super Fledermaus FCS
El Salvador	n/av	army	small number may be in service
Finland	n/av	army	some have been upgraded with Gather kit
Ireland	24	army	no fire control systems used
Nepal	2	army	no fire control systems used
Norway	32	air force	used with Super Fledermaus FCS, being upgraded
	n/av	army	

Country	Quantity	User	Comment
Peru	40	army	
Portugal	20	army	
Senegambia	n/av	army	small number may be in service
South Africa	n/av	army	now in reserve
Sudan	60	army	status uncertain
Sweden	n/av	army	
Uruguay	2	army	
Venezuela	60	army	some may be Bofors 40 mm L/70
Zaire	n/av	army	status uncertain

Manufacturer: AB Bofors, S-691 80 Bofors, Sweden.
Telephone: (0586) 81000
Telex: 73210
Fax: (0586) 58145

40 mm Anti-aircraft Gun Update

Development
The Swedish company of J L Weibull AB is known for its extensive range of training systems which are widely used by the Swedish armed forces and several other countries.

J L Weibull started to develop sighting systems in 1970 by which time it already had some experience in power laying systems. In 1984 the company started to develop a gun update concept and the first prototype was complete in 1985 with first live firings in 1986.

The update can be done in steps with the first step, the Mk I consisting of a reflex sight with sight arm, the Mk II adds a power aiming system (all electric, aiming device, electric firing, power unit with backup and a new aimer's seat) while the Mk III adds a centre aimed sight system (sight arm, rotating table, sight, computer/calculating unit and a rangefinder). The latter can be a laser or a radar system.

Although the prototype systems are fitted to Bofors 40 mm L/60 weapons they are applicable to other air defence guns.

For the Bofors 40 mm L/60 weapon Weibull has collaborated with the LIAB ammunition company while for the Bofors 40 mm L/70 it has worked with the Swedish Defence Material Administration. According to Weibull this updating kit is applicable to many other types of anti-aircraft gun.

Description
The power laying system comprises a control system using modern DC technology, DC motors connected to the gun via toothed belts, an aiming device with automatic lock-up when firing and electric firing replacing manual firing.

The fire control system comprises a sight arm attached to the gun using the existing screw holes, a rotating table which turns the optical sight laterally and vertically and carries the sensors which measure the movement in both axes, a Racal I/J-band ranging radar positioned on the right side of the mount, or an Ericsson laser rangefinder, and a computing unit with advanced filter technology and the possibility of ammunition selection.

Both the power laying system and the fire control system are run from an on-mount 28 V DC power supply with battery back-up.

Bofors 40 mm L/60 anti-aircraft gun fitted with updated package from J L Weibull showing ranging radar mounted on right of mount

As the gunner tracks the target, the on-board computer processes the sensor data to calculate the required lead angle and drive the rotating table continuously to the correct aim-off point. The gunner then places his cross hairs back over the target and fires.

So far Weibull has built four prototype systems for extensive trials which have demonstrated that in the speed range of 100 m/s, 30 per cent of the rounds are within 4 m of target centre and at least 80 per cent are within 8 m. Using proximity-fuzed pre-fragmented ammunition the target would be destroyed.

Status: Development complete. Ready for production. First production systems could be delivered within 12 months of receipt of order.

Manufacturer: J L Weibull AB, PO Box 43, S-232 02 Akarp, Sweden.
Telephone: (46) 40 465080
Telex: 33159
Fax: (46) 40 461677

SWITZERLAND

Machine Tool Works Oerlikon-Bührle Limited

Machine Tool Works Oerlikon-Bührle Limited is in Zürich, Switzerland. In 1972 the company took over Hispano-Suiza of Switzerland and integrated some of its extensive range of automatic weapons into the Oerlikon-Bührle range to form the most comprehensive range of 20 to 35 mm calibre automatic weapons in the world. In Oerlikon gun designations the second letter denotes the calibre i.e. A = 20 mm, B = 25 mm, C = 30 mm and D = 35 mm. Machine Tool Works Oerlikon-Bührle Limited has two other companies. For convenience, all Oerlikon-Bührle weapons are listed under Switzerland, although some are manufactured in Italy. The overseas companies are:
Oerlikon Aerospace Inc, 225 blvd. du Séminaire sud, Saint-Jean-sur-Richelieu, Quebec, J3B 8E9, Canada
Oerlikon-Italiana, 20161 Milan, 14 Via Scarsellini, Italy.

Note: The British subsidiary of Oerlikon-Bührle, British Manufacture and Research Company, was sold to Astra Holdings in 1988, although it still manufactures Oerlikon-Bührle products.

Switzerland / **TOWED AA GUNS**

Oerlikon Twin 35 mm GDF-002 and GDF-005 Automatic Anti-aircraft Guns

Development

In the late 1950s Oerlikon-Bührle started the development of a twin 35 mm automatic anti-aircraft gun. The first prototype of this was completed in 1959 under the designation 1 ZLA/353 MK. This entered production as the 2 ZLA/353 MK but was subsequently re-designated the GDF-001. This model was also manufactured under licence in Japan for the Japanese Ground Self Defence Force.

In 1980 the GDF-002 model was introduced. This advanced version has a Ferranti instead of a Xaba sight, and digital data transmission. By 1989 well over 1700 GDF twin 35 mm systems had been produced with sales made to around 25 countries.

The Oerlikon twin 35 mm GDF-002 automatic anti-aircraft gun is used primarily as an anti-aircraft weapon but can also be used against ground targets. It can be used on its own with its onboard optical sight but is normally used in conjunction with an off-carriage fire control system. A typical battery would consist of two GDF series anti-aircraft guns, each with a power supply unit, and a fire control unit. The fire control unit was originally the Contraves Super Fledermaus, now replaced in production in Switzerland by the Contraves Skyguard fire control system which is much more effective. The 35 mm cannon type KDB used in the GDF-002 are also used as a modified version (the KDC) in the GDM-A twin 35 mm naval gun system.

In May 1985 the GDF-005 was introduced. This is an overall improvement of the GDF-001/2/3 and the earlier models can be modified to the GDF-005 standard by the use of combat improvement kits supplied by Oerlikon. The GDF-005 features a new autonomous gun sighting system, an onboard power supply system, an automatic reloader and other improvements. The GDF-001 can be upgraded to any of the other gun standards by using kits. The NDF-B is particularly useful as it introduces an automatic ammunition replenishment from auxiliary magazines to the main magazines.

Description

The Oerlikon twin 35 mm GDF-002 automatic anti-aircraft gun consists of the following main components; two KDB (former designation 353 MK) cannon, cradle, two automatic ammunition feed mechanisms, upper mount, lower mount and the sighting system.

The Oerlikon KDB cannon is a positively locked gas-operated weapon. The weapon housing, together with the barrel, slides in the cradle during recoil. The cannon cover contains the ammunition feed mechanism and does not move during recoil. The manual cocking device is also mounted on the cannon cover. The barrels have progressive twist rifling, are fitted with muzzle brakes and if required can also be fitted with muzzle velocity measuring equipment.

The cradle is designed to carry both guns and is on the elevation axis. It contains the hydro-mechanical recoil mechanism which absorbs the recoil forces. The ammunition containers are on each side of the cradle and rotate with it. Each fully-loaded ammunition container holds 56 rounds. The ammunition is reloaded in seven round clips from the reloading container passed through the upper mount trunnions to the cannon. The drive for the feed is independent of the cannons and uses electric spring motors. Rewinding the spring motors, which is normally automatic, can also be done manually.

Traverse of the guns is determined by the upper mount which is in the pivot bearing of the lower mount. The upper mount platform supports the auxiliary aiming equipment, the seats for the crew and both 63 round reloading containers. The guns have a maximum elevation speed of 56°/s and a maximum traverse speed of 112°/s.

The lower mount forms the stable base of the gun. It comprises the two-axle chassis and the outriggers with the levelling spindles for three-point support in the firing positions. Raising and lowering the levelling spindles and raising the wheels are done electro-hydraulically, or manually in case of power failure. The weapon can be brought into the firing position in 1½ minutes by a crew of three or in 2½ minutes by one. A hand pump is also fitted and when it is used the weapon can be brought into action in five minutes.

The sighting equipment consists of a Ferranti sight Type GSA Mark 3,

Oerlikon twin 35 mm GDF anti-aircraft gun with NDF-C modification package showing generator mounted at end of carriage

Oerlikon twin 35 mm GDF-001 automatic anti-aircraft gun of Japanese Ground Self Defence Force in travelling position (Kensuke Ebata)

Oerlikon twin 35 mm GDF-002 automatic anti-aircraft gun in firing position with Contraves Skyguard fire-control system in background

Oerlikon twin 35 mm GDF-001 automatic anti-aircraft gun in firing position (Austrian Army)

TOWED AA GUNS / Switzerland

Oerlikon-Bührle twin 35 mm GDF-005 complete with camouflage kit

Replenishing the automatic loading unit of the Oerlikon-Bührle twin 35 mm GDF-005 air defence system with clips of ammunition

Oerlikon-Bührle twin 35 mm GDF-005 deployed and showing generator mounted on rear of carriage

Contraves Skyguard fire control system deployed in the field

a ground target sight mounted on the Ferranti sight housing and an optical alignment sight. The target range is the only parameter to be adjusted in action on the Ferranti sight.

The following types of fixed ammunition can be fired:

OERLIKON DESIGNATION	MLD	MSD	SSD
NATO DESIGNATION	HEI-T	HEI	HEI
WEIGHT OF PROJECTILE	0.535 kg	0.55 kg	0.55 kg
EXPLOSIVE	0.098 kg	0.112 kg	0.07 kg
PROPELLANT	0.33 kg	0.33 kg	0.33 kg
COMPLETE ROUND	1.565 kg	1.58 kg	1.58 kg
MUZZLE VELOCITY	1175 m/s	1175 m/s	1175 m/s

OERLIKON DESIGNATION	PLD	ULD	UGD
NATO DESIGNATION	SAPHEI-T	TP-T	TP
WEIGHT OF PROJECTILE	0.55 kg	0.55 kg	0.55 kg
EXPLOSIVE	0.022 kg	n/app	n/app
PROPELLANT	0.33 kg	0.33 kg	0.33 kg
COMPLETE ROUND	1.552 kg	1.58 kg	1.58 kg
MUZZLE VELOCITY	1175 m/s	1175 m/s	1175 m/s

Modification Packages

Oerlikon-Bührle is now offering a number of modification packages for the twin 35 mm GDF series of towed anti-aircraft guns and brief details of these follow:

COMBAT IMPROVEMENT KIT	NDF-A	NDF-C
FERRANTI SIGHT	yes	no
WEAPON OPTIMISATION	yes	yes
WEAPON LUBRICATION	yes	yes
CAMOUFLAGE	yes	yes
AUTOMATIC RELOADERS	no	yes
CAB FOR GUNNERS	no	no
INTEGRATED POWER SUPPLY	no	yes

The NDF-A kit comprises several changes, notably the addition of the Ferranti GSA Mk 3 sight for engaging air and ground targets, a quick-erect camouflage assembly, a transistorised power supply unit and the KDC-02 gun modification package. The NDF-C kit is used to bring any of the GDF-001/2/3 series up to the GDF-005 standard. In this version the gunner does not have a completely enclosed cab and the power unit is mounted on the rear of the trailer and lowered to the ground while firing so as not to impede the guns. A Gun King sight system is fitted.

GDF-005

Introduced in May 1985 the 35 mm Oerlikon GDF-005 has several overall improvements that can be retrofitted to existing GDF versions using modification kits.

One of the main improvements is the fitting of the Gun King 'three-dimensional' autonomous computer-controlled optronic sighting system which eliminates the need for the gunner to estimate target parameters. A built-in micro-computer processes all target data such as target range obtained via a laser rangefinder, muzzle velocity and meteorological data, to generate lead data for the gun control system. The Gun King system allows engagements out to a possible range of 4000 m. The addition of a fully-automatic reloader reduces the number of crew on the gun from three to one (the layer) and at the same time the number of rounds on each gun has been increased to 280 rounds, enough for 10 combat bursts. The reloaders are powered by a hydraulic system which also supplies power for the automatic weapon and breech-block lubrication system (under a new gun cover) and power for the hydraulic emergency trigger systems. The cannon used are the type KDC with a breech recoil brake, rate of fire attenuation and a firing pin lock. A new on-board integrated power supply unit supplies not only the gun control systems but also provides power for emplacing the gun. When on site an electro-hydraulic circuit is used to extend the outriggers, operate the jacks and pivot the carriage wheels to their inclined position. The power supply unit is also lowered to the ground. Levelling is carried out using a push-button control and for use in an emergency a hand-operated pump is provided. Permanently attached camouflage material is optional.

The GDF-005 has been field tested in Switzerland, Finland and Austria. Modification kits have been sold to a Near East nation and by late 1988 over 200 GDF-005 upgrade packages had been delivered to unspecified customers.

The weight of a fully loaded GDF-005 is 7700 kg, unloaded weight is 7250 kg.

Skyguard Gun Missile System

Each battery will consist of one Contraves Skyguard fire control system, two missile launchers each with four Sparrow missiles in the ready to launch position and two twin Oerlikon 35 mm GDF-002/003 or 005 cannon. Details of this system are given in the *Static and towed surface-to-air missiles* section.

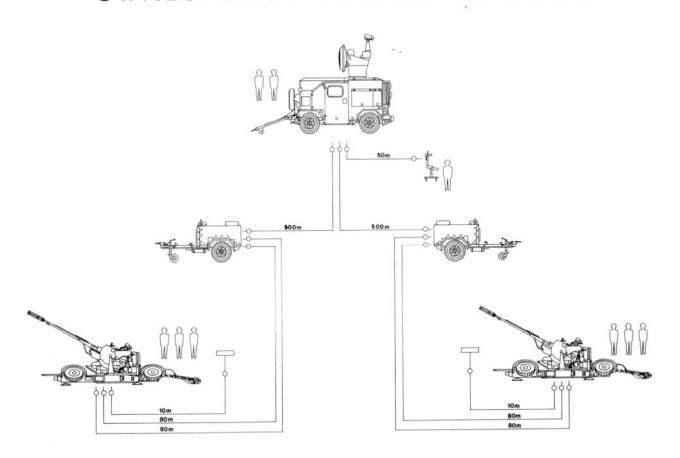

Typical Oerlikon Twin 35 mm GDF-002 anti-aircraft gun battery comprising two guns, each with generator and Contraves Skyguard fire control system

SPECIFICATIONS (GDF-001)

CALIBRE	35 mm
BARREL LENGTH	3.15 m
CARRIAGE	4-wheeled with outriggers
WEIGHT	
travelling order with ammunition and accessories	6700 kg
travelling order without ammunition and accessories	6300 kg
SWEPT RADIUS (at 0° elevation)	4.63 m
LENGTH	
travelling	7.8 m
firing	8.83 m
WIDTH	
travelling	2.26 m
firing	4.49 m
HEIGHT	
travelling	2.6 m
firing	1.72 m
AXIS OF BORE (firing)	1.28 m
GROUND CLEARANCE	0.33 m
TRACK	1.9 m
WHEELBASE	3.8 m
ELEVATION/DEPRESSION	+92°/-5°
TRAVERSE	360°
RATE OF FIRE PER BARREL (cyclic)	550 rpm
FEED	
ready use	112
reserve	126
total on gun	238
MAX EFFECTIVE RANGE (vertical)	4000 m
CREW	3 (local mode)
TOWING VEHICLE	5 ton (6 × 6) truck

Status: GDF-001, 003 and 005 in production. In service with:

Country	Quantity	User	Comment
Argentina	100	army	GDF-002 with Skyguard fire control system
	n/av	air force	with Super Fledermaus FCS
		marines	small number
Austria	74	army	delivered as GDF-002 (and called 3,5 cm Zwillings FIAMK 75 bzw.79) but now upgraded to GDF-005 standard, used with Skyguard FCS (called Feuerleitgerät 75 bzw.79)
	18	air force	GDF-002, Super Fledermaus FCS
Brazil	38	army	GDF-001, Super Fledermaus FCS
Cameroon	6	army	Super Fledermaus FCS
Canada	20	army	GDF-005, Skyguard FCS, first deliveries 1988
Chile	24	army/air force	
Cyprus	n/av	army	GDF-005, Skyguard FCS, first deliveries 1988
Ecuador	24	air force	GDF-003
Egypt	36	air defence command	final deliveries in 1987, GDF-003 used with Skyguard FCS and Sparrow SAM, system is called Amoun
Finland	n/av	army	GDF-002, upgraded to GDF-005 standard with kit
Greece	40	air force	with Skyguard FCS delivered in 1980s
Iran	100	army	with Skyguard FCS
Japan	56	army	licenced production in 1970s, with Super Fledermaus FCS
Korea, South	18+	army	GDF-003
Pakistan	n/av	army	also used for airfield defence
Saudi Arabia	200	army/air force	with Skyguard FCS, upgraded with GDF-005 kit
Singapore	34	air force	GDF-002, used with Super Fledermaus FCS which are being upgraded with a SATT designed kit
South Africa	150	army	GDF-002, with Super Fledermaus FCS, also uses LPD-20 surveillance radar
Spain	96	army	with Super Fledermaus and Skyguard FCS
Switzerland	260	army/air force	with Super Fledermaus and Skyguard FCS
Taiwan	?	army?	with Skyguard FCS
Turkey	n/av	army	local production now under way
UAE	30	army	with Skyguard FCS, replaced twin 30 mm Oerlikon cannon
UK	12	air force	GDF-002 with Skyguard FCS, ex Argentinian

TOWED AA GUNS / Switzerland

Manufacturer: Machine Tool Works Oerlikon-Bührle Limited, CH-8050 Zürich, Switzerland.
Telephone: (01) 316 2211
Telex: 823 205 WOB CH

Oerlikon GBF-BOB Diana 25 mm LAAG

Development
The GBF-BOB Diana is Oerlikon-Bührle's solution for a lightweight mobile system for combatting low flying aircraft and helicopters of today's battlefield. Although primarily designed for anti-aircraft use it has a secondary ground capability.

Description
The weapon is mounted on a two-wheeled carriage that can be towed by a light vehicle and the overall weight of the system is such that it can be slung under helicopters such as the Sea King and Puma.

When in the firing position the side outriggers are extended and the platform is levelled by a three point support system.

The gunner's cab is in the centre of the rotating structure between the externally-mounted cannons. This has enabled the length and height of the system to be kept compact and reduces the rotational effects on the crew. The cab protects the gunner from the weather and shell fragments.

The system has two positively-locked gas-operated Oerlikon 25 mm KBB automatic cannon, each with a cyclic rate of fire of 800 rpm and 250 rounds of ready use ammunition. The cannon barrel and receiver body recoil. The ammunition feed mechanism is fixed to the mounting cradle and does not recoil. The feed mechanism is such that a round cannot be fed into the chamber when the selector control is set at neutral.

The dual belt feeds allow the gunner to select one of two types of ammunition. The 25 mm KBB cannon fires the 25 mm × 127 round of which the following types are currently available:

NATO DESIGNATION	HEI-T	APDS-T	AMDS	TP-T	APP-T
WEIGHT OF COMPLETE ROUND	615 g	615 g	615 g	625 g	615 g
LENGTH OF ROUND	288 mm	288 mm	288 mm	288 mm	288 mm

The Oerlikon-Bührle GBF-BOB is fitted with the Contraves developed Gun King sight (details given in *Towed anti-aircraft gun sights* section).

This system provides highly automated three-dimensional target tracking. Precise fire control data is automatically determined and updated by means of a modern high speed computer which also controls the combat sequence of the entire weapon system. A collimator allows for rapid, autonomous acquisition of both airborne and ground targets.

The Diana mount has an integrated power supply. With hub motors fitted the operator can, with the aid of a remote control cable, manoeuvre the Diana mount into the exact firing position required.

Oerlikon-Bührle GBF-BOB Diana twin 25 mm LAAG deployed in firing position

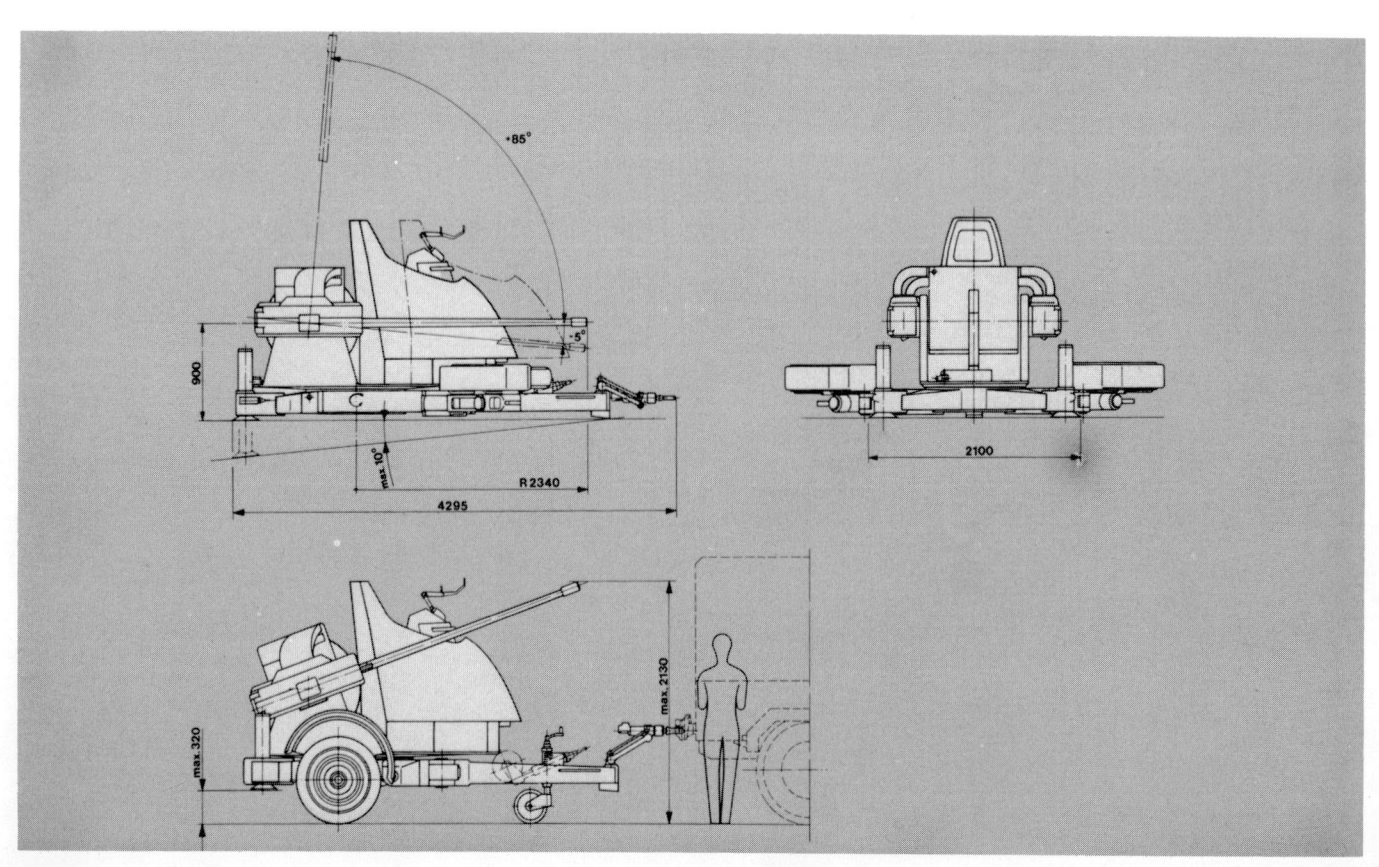

Scale drawings of Diana twin 25 mm light anti-aircraft gun in travelling and firing configurations (not to 1/76th scale) (dimensions in mm)

Switzerland / **TOWED AA GUNS** 197

Oerlikon GBF-BOB Diana twin 25 mm light anti-aircraft gun in travelling configuration being moved under remote control

Oerlikon GBF-BOB Diana twin 25 mm light anti-aircraft gun from rear in firing position

Status: In production.

Manufacturer: Military Products Division, Machine Tool Works, Oerlikon-Bührle Limited, CH-8050 Zurich, Switzerland.
Telephone: (01) 316 22 11
Telex: 823 205 WOB CH

Oerlikon-Bührle GBF-BOB Diana twin 25 mm LAAG deployed in firing position

SPECIFICATIONS (GBF-BOB)

CALIBRE	25 mm
BARREL LENGTH	92 calibres
CARRIAGE	2 wheels with outriggers
WEIGHT	
without ammunition	3600 kg
with ammunition, ready for firing	4000 kg
SWEPT RADIUS	2.30 m
LENGTH (travelling)	4.295 m
WIDTH (travelling)	2.1 m
HEIGHT (travelling)	2.13 m
AXIS OF FIRE (firing position)	0.9 m
GROUND CLEARANCE (travelling, under jacks)	0.32 m
ELEVATION/DEPRESSION	+85°/-5°
TRAVERSE	360°
TRAVERSE SPEED	max 1.4 rad/s
ELEVATION SPEED	max 0.85 rad/s
TRAVERSE ACCELERATION	max 1 rad/s^2
ELEVATION ACCELERATION	max 1.3 rad/s^2
RATE OF FIRE (per gun)	800 rpm
EFFECTIVE RANGE (vertical)	3000 m
AMMUNITION SUPPLY (per weapon)	250 rounds (200 HEI, 50 APDS-T)
CREW (on weapon)	1

Oerlikon 25 mm Infantry Gun Iltis

Development
The 25 mm infantry gun Iltis has been developed as a private venture by Oerlikon-Bührle to give light units the capability of rapidly engaging aerial targets such as helicopters as well as ground targets including armoured personnel carriers, to a range of 2000 m. The existence of the Iltis was announced late in 1986.

Description
The Iltis can be mounted in the rear of light 4 × 4 cross-country vehicles such as the Land Rover or dismantled without tools into sub-assemblies for transportation over rough terrain. With exception of the cannon, each Iltis assembly can be carried by one person.

The Iltis uses the Oerlikon-Bührle 25 mm KBB cannon which is already in production for a number of other applications. These include the Sea Zenith naval anti-missile system, Diana twin light anti-aircraft gun system, and the GBD-BOB turret for installation on armoured vehicles.

The 25 mm KBB has been designed for belt feed and has a cyclic rate of fire of 800 rds/min. For the Iltis application snap-in magazines of 10 or 15 rounds are also available, with two magazines for ready use each filled with a different type of ammunition for engaging different targets. For example, one with APDS-T (Armour Piercing Discarding Sabot-Tracer) for engaging armoured targets and the other with HEI (High Explosive Incendiary) for engaging non-armoured and lightly armoured targets.

The standard sight is of the notch and bead type which can also be used in combination with other sights. As an intermediate step a parallax-free reflex sight is available between the notch and bead sight and the main sight. The main sight brings the target image, which is adjustable in size, to the gunner's position well below the axis of the weapon, via a fibre optic cable. Other options include night vision devices and laser rangefinders.

The weight of the Iltis has been kept as low as possible by the use of composite materials. When in action the mount is supported on three adjustable outriggers. It can also be mounted on a two-wheeled carriage that can be towed behind light cross-country vehicles.

TOWED AA GUNS / Switzerland

Oerlikon 25 mm Infantry Gun Iltis in firing position, gunner is safely below axis of weapon with sighting accomplished using fibre-optic cable

Oerlikon 25 mm Infantry Gun Iltis from front showing sight mounted above KBB cannon in front of gunner

SPECIFICATIONS

CALIBRE	25 mm
CYCLIC RATE OF FIRE	800 rpm
MUZZLE VELOCITY	1160/1355 m/s
READY USE AMMUNITION	2 × 15 rounds
WEIGHT OF CANNON WITHOUT BARREL	69 kg
WEIGHT OF BARREL	48 kg
WEIGHT OF COMPLETE SYSTEM	240 kg
ELEVATION	−10° to +45°
TRAVERSE	60° (left and right)
	360° (total)

Status: Prototype. Not yet in production or service.

Manufacturer: Military Products Division, Machine Tool Works Oerlikon-Bührle Limited, CH-8050, Switzerland.
Telephone: (01) 316 22 11
Telex: 823 205 WOB CH

Oerlikon 25 mm GBI-A01 Automatic Anti-aircraft Gun

Development/Description
The Oerlikon 25 mm GBI-A01 automatic anti-aircraft gun is fitted with a gas-operated Oerlikon KBA-C cannon and can also be used to engage light AFVs and other battlefield targets. The weapon is normally manned by a crew of three, one on the mount and the other two acting as ammunition handlers.

The weapon has three firing positions:
Normal firing position mounted on its tripod with an elevation of +70°, depression of −10° and a traverse of 360°
Mounted on its travelling carriage with the rear supported by the towing eye, with an elevation of +70°, no depression and a traverse of 360°
Emergency mode with the carriage still coupled to the towing vehicle, with an elevation of +70°, depression of −10° and a traverse of 45° left and 45° right.

Elevation and traverse are manual with one revolution of the elevation handwheel giving 4° of elevation and one revolution of the traversing handwheel giving 10° of traverse. The gunner can declutch the traverse mechanism if required to give free traverse. The mount and travelling gear can be dismantled into individual loads.

The gunner can select either single-shot fire or full automatic and has a binocular sight for engaging ground targets and a delta sight for air targets. Mounted either side of the dual feed KBA-C cannon is a 40 round box magazine each of which weighs 33 kg when loaded. The following types of fixed ammunition can be fired:

OERLIKON DESIGNATION	TLB	SLB/SBB	PLB/PSB	ULB/UGB
NATO DESIGNATION	APDS-T	HEI-T/HEI	SAPHEI-T/ SAPHEI	TP-T/TP
WEIGHT OF PROJECTILE	150 g	180 g	180 g	180 g
WEIGHT OF FILLING	105 g	91 g	91 g	91 g
WEIGHT OF COMPLETE ROUND	480 g	500 g	500 g	500 g
MUZZLE VELOCITY	1335 m/s	1100 m/s	1100 m/s	1100 m/s

SPECIFICATIONS

CALIBRE	25 mm
BARREL LENGTH	2.182 m
MUZZLE BRAKE	multi-baffle
OPERATION	gas, automatic
CARRIAGE	2-wheeled
SHIELD	no
WEIGHT	
travelling order with ammunition	666 kg
travelling order without ammunition	600 kg
firing position without ammunition	440 kg
SWEPT RADIUS (at 0° elevation)	2.915 m
LENGTH	
travelling	4.72 m
firing	4.17 m
WIDTH	
travelling	1.8 m
firing	1.79 m
HEIGHT	
travelling	1.65 m
firing	1.45 m
AXIS OF BORE	
travelling	0.975 m
firing	0.5 m
GROUND CLEARANCE (travelling)	0.4 m
ELEVATION/DEPRESSION	+70°/−10°
TRAVERSE	360°
RATE OF FIRE	
cyclic	570 rpm
practical	160 rpm
EFFECTIVE VERTICAL RANGE	2000-2500 m
CREW	3 (1 on gun)
TOWING VEHICLE	light (4 × 4) truck

Switzerland / **TOWED AA GUNS** 199

Oerlikon-Bührle 25 mm GBI-A01 automatic anti-aircraft gun in firing position

Status: Production complete. This weapon is no longer offered.

Oerlikon-Bührle 25 mm GBI-A01 automatic anti-aircraft gun in travelling configuration

Manufacturer: Machine Tool Works Oerlikon-Bührle Limited, CH-8050 Zürich, Switzerland.
Telephone: (01) 316 22 11
Telex: 823 205 WOB CH

Oerlikon Twin 20 mm GAI-D01 Automatic Anti-aircraft Gun

(former designation HSS 666A)

Development/Description

The Oerlikon twin 20 mm GAI-D01 automatic anti-aircraft gun was designed to fill the gap between single manual 20 mm anti-aircraft guns such as the GAI-C01, GAI-C03 and the GAI-C04 and the sophisticated and effective Oerlikon twin 35 mm anti-aircraft gun Type GDF-002. It can be used as both an anti-aircraft and ground weapon and is normally operated by a detachment of five, with only one on the mount. The prototype was produced during 1976 and the first production example appeared in 1978.

The GAI-D01 is fitted with two 20 mm KAD cannon and is available in a left-feed model designated the KAD-B16 and a right-feed model designated the KAD-B17. The gunner can select either single shot, rapid single shot, automatic fire limited and automatic fire unlimited. Each cannon is provided with 120 rounds of ready use ammunition, with each full magazine weighing 68 kg. The following types of linked ammunition can be fired:

Oerlikon twin 20 mm GAI-D01 automatic anti-aircraft gun in firing position clearly showing Wankel engine under gunner's seat

OERLIKON DESIGNATION	HLA	MLA	MSA	PLA	PSA	ULA	UGA
NATO DESIGNATION	AP-T	HEI-T	HEI	SAPHEI-T	SAPHEI	TP	TP-T
WEIGHT OF PROJECTILE	110 g	125 g	125 g	125 g	125 g	125 g	125 g
WEIGHT OF EXPLOSIVE	nil	5.6 g	10 g	4.7 g	4.7 g	nil	nil
WEIGHT OF PROPELLANT	53 g	53 g	53 g	53 g	53 g	53 g	53 g
WEIGHT OF COMPLETE ROUND	322 g	337 g	337 g	337 g	337 g	337 g	337 g
MUZZLE VELOCITY	1150 m/s	1100 m/s	1100 m/s	1100 m/s	1100 m/s	1100 m/s	1100 m/s

The upper mounting consists of the cradle with belt damper unit, counterweight for the elevating assemblies, Galileo P56 sighting and aiming unit, Wankel engine and an adjustable gunner's seat. Two compressed air containers on each side of the mounting provide compressed air for the electro-pneumatic operation of the trigger mechanism. The lower mounting consists of the tripod support and attachment points for the travelling carriage. The carriage is a tubular construction and has a towing-eye which is adjustable for height, independently sprung wheels and a hydraulically-operated over-running brake which can also be operated by hand. The GAI-D01 can be brought into action from the travelling position with a team of five in 60 seconds.

Elevation and traverse are hydraulic, with maximum traverse speed of 80°/s and maximum elevation speed of 48°/s. Manual controls are provided for emergency use.

The Italian Galileo P56 sight is used to engage low-flying aircraft up to a range of 1500 m and surface targets to 2000 m. The target is initially engaged using the mechanical auxiliary sight and then located and tracked using the optical sight, which has a magnification of ×5 and a 12° field-of-view. In the 'air-target' mode (automatic/hydraulic) the unit calculates the overall lead on a continuous basis. Surface targets may also be engaged using this mode or a manual/mechanical mode.

The P56 sight consists of an optical sight, an electro-mechanically operated servo drive-unit for the view prism and a computer, plus a gun-laying system consisting of a control-stick assembly, hydraulic unit, mechanical transfer gearboxes and manual controls.

Facilities are provided for integrating the GAI-D01 automatic anti-aircraft gun with an early warning radar such as the Contraves LPD-20, and connecting the gun to a remote input equipment specifying target speed, crossover point range, fire release and also incorporating a two-way intercom. An alternative sight with a radar data decoder is also available.

Status: Production complete, no longer offered. In service with Guatemala and other undisclosed countries.

Manufacturer: Machine Tool Works Oerlikon-Bührle Limited, CH-8050 Zürich, Switzerland.
Telephone: (01) 316 22 11
Telex: 823 205 WOB CH

Note: Licenced production of this weapon is now being undertaken in Turkey (qv this section).

TOWED AA GUNS / Switzerland

SPECIFICATIONS

CALIBRE	20 mm
BARREL LENGTH (overall)	1.906 m
OPERATION	gas, automatic
CARRIAGE	2-wheeled
SHIELD	yes
WEIGHT	
travelling order with ammunition	1800 kg
firing position with ammunition	1330 kg
SWEPT RADIUS (at 0° elevation)	3 m
LENGTH	
travelling	4.59 m
firing	4.555 m
WIDTH	
travelling	1.86 m
firing	1.81 m
HEIGHT	
travelling	2.34 m
firing 0° elevation	1.3 m
AXIS OF BORE (firing)	0.6 m
TRACK	1.86 m
ELEVATION/DEPRESSION	+81°/-3°
TRAVERSE	360°
RATE OF FIRE PER BARREL (cyclic)	1000 rpm
EFFECTIVE RANGE	1500-2000 m
CREW	5 (1 on gun)
TOWING VEHICLE	light (4 × 4) truck

Oerlikon twin 20 mm GAI-D01 automatic anti-aircraft gun in firing position showing ammunition boxes either side

Oerlikon 20 mm GAI-C01 and GAI-C04 Automatic Anti-aircraft Guns

(former designations HS 693-B 3.1 and HSS 639-B5)

Development/Description

Both are fitted with a gas-operated weapon, the GAI-C01 with an Oerlikon cannon type KAD-B13-3 (former designation HS 820-SL7° A3-3) with single feed from the right, and the GAI-C04 with an Oerlikon cannon type KAD-B14 (former designation HS 820-SL7° A4) with dual feed. They can be used as both anti-aircraft and ground weapons and are normally manned by a crew of three, one on the mount and the other two acting as ammunition handlers. The mount is normally carried on a two-wheeled carriage that can be towed by most light vehicles and if required, the mount and carriage can be dismantled into individual loads.

Elevation and traverse are manual with one revolution of the handwheel giving 8° of elevation. Traverse is by using a pedal and the gunner can also declutch the traverse mechanism to give free traverse.

The gunner can select either single shots or full automatic and has a Delta IV reflector sight with a magnification of ×1 for engaging aerial targets plus a telescopic sight with a magnification of ×2.5 that can be swung into position for engaging ground targets. The aircraft sight has two graticules, one for aircraft flying at high speed (up to 900 km/h) and the other for slower flying aircraft or helicopters (up to 200 km/h). The graticules can be illuminated by two 4.5 V batteries.

Mounted on the right side of the GAI-C01 is a 75 round box magazine that weighs 44 kg when loaded, while the GAI-C04 has two 75 round box magazines, one each side of the mount. Ammunition details are as in the earlier entry for the Oerlikon 20 mm GAI-D01 anti-aircraft gun.

Oerlikon 20 mm GAI-C01 automatic anti-aircraft gun in firing position

Oerlikon 20 mm GAI-C04 automatic anti-aircraft gun in firing position

Switzerland / **TOWED AA GUNS**

Variant
The South African Army has a self-propelled version of this weapon on a 4 × 4 truck. Details are given in the *Self-propelled anti-aircraft guns* section under South Africa.

Status: Production complete, no longer offered. In service with Chile (GAI-C01), Indonesia (10), Nicaragua, South Africa (GAI-C01) and other undisclosed countries.

Manufacturer: Machine Tool Works Oerlikon-Bührle Limited, CH-8050 Zürich, Switzerland.
Telephone: (01) 316 22 11
Telex: 823 205 WOB CH

SPECIFICATIONS
(data in square brackets relates to GAI-C04 where different from GAI-C01)

CALIBRE	20 mm
BARREL LENGTH	1.84 [1.906] m
OPERATION	gas, automatic
CARRIAGE	2-wheeled
SHIELD	no
WEIGHT	
travelling order with ammunition	534 [589] kg
travelling order without ammunition	512 [535] kg
firing position with ammunition	370 [435] kg
SWEPT RADIUS (at 0° elevation)	2.65 m
LENGTH (firing)	3.87 m
WIDTH (firing)	1.7 m
HEIGHT (firing)	1.45 m
AXIS OF BORE (firing)	0.5 m
ELEVATION/DEPRESSION	+83°/-7°
TRAVERSE	360°
RATE OF FIRE (cyclic)	1050 rpm
EFFECTIVE VERTICAL RANGE	1500-2000 m
CREW	3 (1 on gun)
TOWING VEHICLE	light (4 × 4) truck

Oerlikon 20 mm GAI-B01 Automatic Anti-aircraft Gun
(former designation 10 ILa/5TG)

Development/Description
The Oerlikon 20 mm GAI-B01 automatic anti-aircraft gun is fitted with an Oerlikon 20 mm cannon model KAB-001 (former designation 5TG) and is the lightest of the extensive Oerlikon range of anti-aircraft weapons. It can be used in both anti-aircraft and ground defence and is normally operated by a detachment of three with one on the mount and the other two acting as ammunition handlers. The mount is normally carried on a two-wheeled carriage that can be towed by most light vehicles but it can also be mounted on the rear of a 4 × 4 or a 6 × 6 truck chassis. If required the mount and carriage can be dismantled into individual loads.

The 20 mm GAI-B01 automatic anti-aircraft gun consists of four main components; the cannon, mount, aiming equipment and the carriage.

The Oerlikon 20 mm automatic cannon KAB-001 is a positively locked gas-operated cannon with mechanical ignition and can fire single shots or automatic. The breech is cocked using the manual cocking device and is held open automatically after firing the last round. The lower part of the weapon recoils in the cradle together with the barrel, whereas the trigger housing is locked firmly with the cradle. Ammunition is fed from a magazine which can be changed in three seconds. Three types of magazine are available: 50 round drum weighing 41.5 kg loaded and 24.5 kg empty, 20 round drum weighing 23.5 kg loaded and 17 kg empty and eight round box weighing 8 kg loaded and 4.5 kg empty.

Ammunition details are given in the entry for the Oerlikon 20 mm GAI-D01 anti-aircraft gun.

The mount is the standard base for the cannon and consists of the cradle with weight compensator and trunnions, pivot with elevation drive and trigger to support the cradle and allow elevation and traverse movement of the cannon, sight bracket to support the sight, tripod as a firm base when firing without the wheels in position and the chassis with slide plate for transport and rapid change of position. The gunner controls elevation with the upper handwheel, one revolution of which gives 10° of elevation. Traverse is free with the gunner's feet.

For engaging air targets an ellipse sight or a Delta IV sight can be fitted. The former can be used against aircraft and also ground targets after fitting a diopter. It has a glass fibre or metal graticule with the appropriate lead marks. The Delta IV sight can be used against aircraft and ground targets with the lead ellipse being controlled by a mechanical attachment. For engaging ground targets a telescope with a magnification of ×3.7 is secured to the cradle on a separate bracket. Effective range against a low flying aircraft is 1500 m whilst against helicopters it is 2000 m.

The two-wheeled carriage has a ground clearance of 0.34 m which can be reduced to 0.2 m by repositioning the wheels. A slide plate allows the gun to slide over obstacles.

When being used as an anti-aircraft gun the tripod legs are horizontal and the gunner is seated at the rear of the mount, the gun has an elevation of +85°, a depression of -5° and a total traverse of 360°.

When being used against ground targets the tripod legs remain horizontal but the gunner lies prone and uses the lower elevating gearing and the lower trigger, the gun has an elevation of +25°, a depression of -5° and a total traverse of 60°.

Oerlikon 20 mm GAI-B01 automatic anti-aircraft gun in firing position with 50-round drum magazine and optical sight

The mount can also be set up in a higher position for engaging ground targets. The side spades are folded downwards and packing pieces are inserted. The towing hook which is used as a trail spade is pivoted downwards until the cannon is horizontal. When being used in this mode the gun has an elevation of +35°, a depression of -5° and a total traverse of 80°. In addition the gun can also be fired with the wheels in position.

The gun can be brought into action from the travelling position by two men in about 20 seconds. The chassis is pulled to the rear and the gun is placed on its tripod support.

SPECIFICATIONS
CALIBRE	20 mm
BARREL LENGTH	2.4 m
OPERATION	gas, automatic
SHIELD	no
WEIGHT	
travelling order	547 kg
firing position	405 kg
SWEPT RADIUS (at 0° elevation)	2.99 m
LENGTH	
travelling	3.85 m
firing	4.71 m
WIDTH	
travelling	1.55 m
firing	1.55 m
HEIGHT	
travelling	2.5 m
firing	1.2 m
AXIS OF BORE (firing)	0.425 m
GROUND CLEARANCE	0.2 or 0.34 m
ELEVATION/DEPRESSION	+85°/-5°
TRAVERSE	360°
RATE OF FIRE (cyclic)	1000 rpm
EFFECTIVE VERTICAL RANGE	1500-2000 m
CREW	3 (1 on mount)
TOWING VEHICLE	light (4 × 4) truck

TOWED AA GUNS / Switzerland

Status: Production complete. In service with many countries including Austria (1000), Singapore, South Africa, Spain and Switzerland (250). Around forty 20 mm Oerlikons of unspecified type have been given to the Mojahedin guerrillas in Afghanistan. They are broken down into loads for carriage by animals or porters and have been used successfully against both Soviet fixed and rotary-wing aircraft.

Manufacturer: Machine Tool Works Oerlikon-Bührle Limited, CH-8050 Zürich, Switzerland.
Telephone: (01) 316 22 11
Telex: 823 205 WOB CH

Oerlikon 20 mm GAI-C03 Automatic Anti-aircraft Gun

(former designation HS 639-B 4.1)

Development/Description

The Oerlikon 20 mm GAI-C03 automatic anti-aircraft gun is fitted with an Oerlikon gas-operated 20 mm cannon model KAD-A01 (former designation HS 820 SAA1). The carriage and mount are identical to those used for the 20 mm GAI-C01 and GAI-C04 automatic anti-aircraft guns. The weapon can be used as both an anti-aircraft and ground gun and is normally crewed by a detachment of three, one on the mount and the other two acting as ammunition handlers. The mount is normally carried on a two-wheeled carriage that can be towed by most light vehicles and if required the mount and carriage can be dismantled into individual loads.

Elevation and traverse are manual with one revolution of the handwheel giving 8° of elevation. Traverse is controlled by a pedal and the gunner can also declutch the mechanism to give free traverse.

The gunner can select either single shots or full automatic and has a Delta IV reflector sight with a magnification of ×1 for engaging aerial targets plus a telescopic sight with a magnification of ×2.5 that can be swung into position for engaging ground targets. The anti-aircraft sight has two graticules, one for aircraft flying at high speed (up to 900 km/h) and the other for slower flying aircraft and helicopters (up to 200 km/h). The graticules can be illuminated by two 4.5 V batteries.

Mounted over the cradle of the KAD-A01 cannon is a drum type magazine that holds 50 rounds of ammunition and weighs 36 kg loaded and 20 kg empty. Ammunition details were given in the earlier entry for the Oerlikon 20 mm GAI-D01 anti-aircraft gun.

Oerlikon 20 mm GAI-C03 automatic anti-aircraft gun in firing position

Status: Production complete, no longer offered. In service with undisclosed countries.

Manufacturer: Machine Tool Works Oerlikon-Bührle Limited, CH-8050 Zürich, Switzerland.
Telephone: (01) 316 22 11
Telex: 823 205 WOB CH

SPECIFICATIONS

CALIBRE	20 mm
BARREL LENGTH	2.24 m
OPERATION	gas, automatic
CARRIAGE	2-wheeled
SHIELD	no
WEIGHT	
travelling order with ammunition	510 kg
travelling order without ammunition	495 kg
firing position with ammunition	342 kg
SWEPT RADIUS (at 0° elevation)	2.65 m
LENGTH (firing)	4.27 m
WIDTH (firing)	1.7 m
AXIS OF BORE (firing)	0.5 m
ELEVATION/DEPRESSION	+83°/-7°
TRAVERSE	360°
RATE OF FIRE (cyclic)	1050 rpm
EFFECTIVE VERTICAL RANGE	1500-2000 m
CREW	3 (1 on gun)
TOWING VEHICLE	light (4 × 4) truck

Hispano-Suiza Anti-aircraft Guns

Hispano-Suiza was taken over by the Machine Tool Works Oerlikon-Bührle Limited in 1972. Some of its weapons were integrated into the Oerlikon-Bührle range and others phased out of production. Listed below is a résumé of the Hispano-Suiza anti-aircraft guns:

HS 630	This mount with three HSS-804 20 mm cannon is manufactured under licence in Yugoslavia as the 20 mm M55 and M75 anti-aircraft guns, details of which are given under Yugoslavia.
HS 639-B 3.1	Became Oerlikon GAI-C01 for which there is a separate entry
HS 639-B 4.1	Became Oerlikon GAI-C03 for which there is a separate entry
HS 639-B5	Became Oerlikon GAI-C04 for which there is a separate entry
HS 661	Armed with single HS 831 30 mm cannon

HS 661 30 mm anti-aircraft gun in firing position (ECP Armées)

HS 665	Armed with three 20 mm cannon
HS 666	Became Oerlikon GAI-D01 for which there is a separate entry
HS 669	Armed with single 20 mm cannon
HS 673	Armed with single 20 mm cannon

SPECIFICATIONS (HS 661)

CALIBRE	30 mm
SHIELD	yes
WEIGHT	
travelling order	1540 kg
firing position	1150 kg
SWEPT RADIUS	
(at 0° elevation)	3.595 m
LENGTH (travelling)	5.4 m
WIDTH (travelling)	1.86 m
HEIGHT (travelling)	2.4 m
AXIS OF BORE (firing)	0.575 m
ELEVATION/DEPRESSION	
manual	+83°/−5°
hydraulic	+81°/−3°
TRAVERSE	360°
CREW	3 (1 on gun)

THAILAND

Royal Thai Air Force Anti-aircraft Guns

Development/Description

The Royal Thai Air Force (RTAF), Research and Development Office, has adapted some of their surplus M39 aircraft cannon for the anti-aircraft defence of airfields. Two different mountings are in use, one is a twin gun modification of the US supplied M55 quad 0.50/12.7 mm machine gun mount while the other is a hitherto unknown triple power mounting.

The 20 mm M39 cannon is a US design and is normally installed in the Northrop F-5A and F-5E/F fighter aircraft in service with the RTAF. Operating on the Mauser revolver principle, the M39 fires electrically primed 20 mm × 102 ammunition at a cyclic rate of fire of 1200 to 1500 rpm. At 162 kg (2 × 81 kg), two M39s represent only a slight increase in weight over the four 0.50/12.7 mm machine guns (162 kg) which they replace in the M55 modification. In contrast, the HS 404 20 mm cannon fitted in the Israeli TCM-20 system modification weigh only 45 kg each.

The great increase in rate of fire and recoil impulse means that the M39s mounted on the M55 mounts have to have muzzle brakes installed. The modified M55 mount retains the M18 reflex sight as in the case of the Israeli TCM-20 modification of the M55. The triple power mounting appears to be of a local design but mounted on surplus four-wheeled Bofors 40 mm carriages. When in the firing position the wheels are raised from the ground and the carriage is supported on four screw-type jacks, one at the front and rear and one either side on outriggers.

Being more robust than the M55, this mounting does not require the use of muzzle brakes as on the M39s. The sighting system on this mount appears to be an AN/ASG-29 lead computing (disturbed line-of-sight) system removed from the F-5s.

At the combined rate-of-fire of some 3600 to 4200 rpm, this mounting provides impressive firepower with the added advantage of commonality, in both gun and ammunition, with the aircraft that it is protecting. This system may have entered service in 1981.

The Royal Thai Air Force also has a requirement to upgrade their large stock of M55 mountings and in 1987 ISC Technologies presented a package called the Light Air Defense System (LADS) to meet this requirement. This involves upgrading the turrets electric and mechanical components, replacing the four 0.50/12.7 mm machine guns with two GIAT M621 20 mm cannon and replacing the M18 reflex sight with a new dual-image lead estimating gunsight from Fraser Volpe. The GIAT M621 cannon fires the same 20 mm × 102 ammunition as the M39. It has roughly half the rate-of-fire of the M39, 750 visa 1500 rds/min, but is much lighter (58 kg visa 81 kg) and the lower recoil forces of the French gun probably give lower dispersion which compensates for its lower rate of fire.

The Royal Thai Air Force also operates Short Blowpipe SAMs, twin 30 mm Arrow air defence guns used in conjunction with Contraves Skyguard fire control systems and other towed anti-aircraft guns, (see *Inventory* section). More recently the Thai Air Force has taken delivery of Chinese twin 37 mm towed anti-aircraft guns.

Status: The triple 20 mm mount may be in front line service with the Royal Thai Air Force while the 2 × 20 mm on M55 mount is believed to be still at the prototype stage.

TURKEY

Turkish Anti-aircraft Gun Production

The Machinery and Chemicals Industry Establishment at Cankiri is now producing the twin 20 mm GAI-D01 anti-aircraft gun system under licence from Oerlikon-Bührle of Switzerland. Full details of this weapon are given under Switzerland. By late 1988 a total of eight weapons had been completed with 80 per cent of the system being made in Turkey, the sight and the engine being imported. It is believed that Turkey is also making the twin 35 mm Oerlikon-Bührle GDF series of towed anti-aircraft gun under licence.

UNION OF SOVIET SOCIALIST REPUBLICS

130 mm Anti-aircraft Gun KS-30

Development

The 130 mm anti-aircraft gun KS-30 was introduced into service in the early 1950s and is the Soviet equivalent of the American 120 mm anti-aircraft gun M1 which is no longer in service. It is possible that the ordnance of the KS-30 was developed from a naval weapon of this calibre.

Development of the 130 mm KS-30 anti-aircraft gun commenced at Zavod No 9 at Kalinin in 1946 under M N Loginov and this has a 25 per cent increase in altitude over the 100 mm KS19 anti-aircraft gun. Development of the KS-30 was initially slow as it was decided to concentrate on surface-to-air missile systems for air defence. When it became apparent that it would take time to develop and deploy sufficient SAMs, development of the KS-30 and its associated fire control system was pushed ahead again.

The 130 mm KS-30 was deployed in 1955 and this, together with the 100 mm KS-19, was the backbone of Soviet anti-aircraft gun defences well into the 1960s although their effectiveness against high flying aircraft was limited.

US intelligence sources estimated that in 1952 the Soviets had 25 air defence divisions rising to 70 in 1956 and 80 in 1957, in addition there were over 120 separate anti-aircraft brigades.

The 130 mm KS-30 was the largest calibre anti-aircraft gun used by the North Vietnamese and some have been deployed by Iraq in its conflict with Iran.

There were also plans for a 152 mm anti-aircraft gun with a maximum altitude of over 20 000 m, but this was never deployed. The KS-30 has now been replaced in the Warsaw Pact by surface-to-air missiles but KS-30s are still held in reserve.

TOWED AA GUNS / USSR

130 mm anti-aircraft gun KS-30 being towed by AT-T heavy tracked artillery tractor

130 mm anti-aircraft gun KS-30 in static position with ammunition members to left

Description
When travelling the KS-30 is carried on a two-axle, eight-wheel carriage and in the firing position the axles are removed and the four outriggers are swung from their folded vertical position into the horizontal position. To the rear of the mount is a firing platform which, when travelling, is folded up at an angle of 45°. The KS-30 is fitted with a power rammer and an automatic fuze setter.

The KS-30 is provided with on-carriage fire control equipment but is normally used in conjuction with the PUAZO-30 director and the SON-30 (NATO designation Fire Wheel) fire control radar.

The ammunition fired by the KS-30 is of the fixed charge, separate loading type which is not interchangeable with that fired by the 130 mm Field Gun M-46 or the 130 mm Coastal Gun SM-4-1. Ammunition is fed from the left and both the APHE and HE projectiles weigh 33.4 kg and have a muzzle velocity of 970 m/s. The APHE projectile will penetrate 250 mm of armour at an incidence of 0° at a range of 1000 m.

Status: Production complete. The only known front line users of the KS-30 today are Iraq (200) and Vietnam.

Manufacturer: Soviet state factories.

130 mm anti-aircraft gun KS-30 in firing position with axles removed

SPECIFICATIONS

CALIBRE	130 mm
BARREL LENGTH (overall)	8.412 m
MUZZLE BRAKE	none
BREECH MECHANISM	semi-automatic horizontal sliding wedge
CARRIAGE	2 axles, each with 4 wheels
SHIELD	none
WEIGHT	
travelling order	29 500 kg
firing position	24 900 kg
LENGTH (travelling)	11.521 m
WIDTH (travelling)	3.033 m
HEIGHT (travelling)	3.048 m
AXIS OF BORE	2.576 m
GROUND CLEARANCE (travelling)	0.408 m
TRACK	2.388 m
WHEELBASE	4.953 m
ELEVATION/DEPRESSION	+80°/-5°
TRAVERSE	360°
RATE OF FIRE	10-12 rpm
MAX RANGE	
horizontal	27 000 m
vertical	20 000 m
EFFECTIVE VERTICAL RANGE	13 720 m
CREW	15-20
TOWING VEHICLE	AT-T heavy tracked artillery tractor

USSR / **TOWED AA GUNS** 205

100 mm Anti-aircraft Gun KS-19

Development
The 100 mm anti-aircraft gun KS-19 was introduced in the late 1940s as the replacement for the 85 mm M1939 and M1944 anti-aircraft guns. It is no longer in service with the Soviet Union having been replaced by surface-to-air missiles, but it is still used by some members of the Warsaw Pact and many other countries. The KS-19 has been manufactured in China as the Type 59.

Deployed 100 mm KS-19M anti-aircraft guns

Description
When travelling the mount is traversed to the rear and the ordnance is held in position by a travelling lock at the rear of the carriage. In the firing position the wheels are raised off the ground and the carriage is supported on four screw jacks, one at each end of the carriage and one either side on outriggers. The KS-19 has a power rammer, automatic fuze setter and a single round loading tray. The KS-19 has on-carriage fire control equipment but is normally used in conjunction with the PUAZO-6/19 director and the SON-9/SON-9A (NATO codename Fire Can and operated in the E-band) fire control radar. It is also reported that the KS-19 is used in conjunction with the PUAZO-7 director and the SON-4 (NATO code name Whiff) fire control radar.

Ammunition is of the fixed type and is fed from the left. The following types can be fired:

Ammunition type	AP-T*	APC-T
PROJECTILE DESIGNATION	BR-412B	BR-412D
FUZE MODEL	MD-8	DBR-2
WEIGHT OF PROJECTILE	15.89 kg	16 kg
WEIGHT OF BURSTING CHARGE	0.56 kg	0.63 kg
TYPE OF BURSTING CHARGE	RDX/aluminium	RDX/aluminium
MUZZLE VELOCITY	1000 m/s	900 m/s

* will penetrate 185 mm of armour at incidence of 0° at range of 1000 m

Ammunition type	HE	HE-FRAG	FRAG
PROJECTILE DESIGNATION	F-412	OF-412	O-415
FUZE MODEL	RGM	V-429	VM-30/VL-30L
WEIGHT OF PROJECTILE	15.91 kg	15.61 kg	15.44 kg
WEIGHT OF BURSTING CHARGE	2.159 kg	1.46 kg	1.58 kg
TYPE OF BURSTING CHARGE	TNT	TNT	n/app
MUZZLE VELOCITY	900 m/s	900 m/s	900 m/s

SPECIFICATIONS
CALIBRE	100 mm
BARREL LENGTH (overall)	5.742 m
MUZZLE BRAKE	multi-baffle
BREECH MECHANISM	semi-automatic horizontal sliding wedge
CARRIAGE	4-wheeled
SHIELD	yes
WEIGHT (travelling)	9550 kg
LENGTH (travelling)	9.45 m
WIDTH (travelling)	2.35 m
HEIGHT (travelling)	2.201 m
AXIS OF BORE	1.682 m
GROUND CLEARANCE	0.33 m
TRACK	2.165 m
WHEELBASE	4.65 m
ELEVATION/DEPRESSION	+85°/-3°
TRAVERSE	360°
RATE OF FIRE	15 rpm
MAX RANGE	
horizontal	21 000 m
vertical, proximity fuze	15 000 m
vertical, time fuze	12 700 m
EFFECTIVE VERTICAL RANGE (proximity fuze)	13 700 m
UNIT OF FIRE	100 rounds
CREW	15
TOWING VEHICLES	AT-S medium tracked artillery tractor AT-T heavy tracked artillery tractor

Status: Production complete. In service with the following countries:

Country	Quantity	User	Comment
Afghanistan	n/av	army	
Albania	n/av	army	unconfirmed
Algeria	50	army	also used by Air Force
Bulgaria	n/av	army	
China	n/av	army/air force	built in China as Type 59
Cuba	75	army	
Egypt	300	air defence command	
Germany, East	n/av	n/app	held in reserve
Guinea	4	army	
Hungary	n/av	army	held in reserve
Iraq	200	army	
Kampuchea	n/av	army	believed no longer operational
Korea, North	500	army	
Morocco	10	army	believed no longer operational
Nicaragua	18	army	
Poland	90	army	believed no longer operational
Romania	30	army	
Somalia	45	army	
Sudan	n/av	army	
Syria	n/av	army	
Vietnam	n/av	air defence force	

Manufacturer: Soviet state factories.

206 TOWED AA GUNS / USSR

Late production model of KS-19, designated KS-19M2, in travelling order with outriggers retracted and ordnance in travelling lock

85 mm Anti-aircraft Guns M1939 and M1944

Development
The 85 mm anti-aircraft gun M1939 (KS-12) was designed by M N Loginov at Artillery Plant No 8, Kaliningrad near Moscow and was introduced into the Soviet Army shortly before the start of the Second World War as the replacement for the 76.2 mm M1938. The ordnance of the M1939 was later adopted for use in the SU-85 assault gun and later still the T-34/85 tank.

Description
When travelling the mount is traversed to the rear and the ordnance is held in position by a travelling lock at the rear of the carriage. In the firing position the carriage is supported on four screw jacks, one at either end of the carriage and one either side on outriggers. The M1939 is often seen without the shield. The original KS-12 had a built-up ordnance whereas the later KS-12A had a monobloc ordnance.

The M1939 is provided with on-carriage fire control equipment but is normally used in conjunction with the PUAZO-6/12 director and the SON-9/SON-9A (NATO designation Fire Can) E-band fire control radar.

The ammunition fired by the M1939 is of the fixed type, some of which is interchangeable with that fired by 85 mm assault guns, field and tank guns. In addition to firing all the rounds of the Soviet 85 mm field guns, the M1939 85 mm anti-aircraft gun has special cartridges with time-fuzed projectiles for firing at aircraft:

Ammunition type	FRAG	FRAG
PROJECTILE DESIGNATION	O-365*	O-365M
FUZE MODEL	T-5†	VM-2‡
WEIGHT OF PROJECTILE	9.2 kg	9.24 kg
WEIGHT OF BURSTING CHARGE	0.64 kg	0.776 kg
TYPE OF BURSTING CHARGE	TNT	TNT
MUZZLE VELOCITY	792 m/s	792 m/s

* there are variants in O-365 projectiles giving different bursting charge weights as well as projectile weights
† powder train time fuze can be set from 1.6-32 s
‡ mechanical clockwork fuze can be set from 0.8-30 s

85 mm anti-aircraft gun M1939 showing shape of shield (Franz Kosar)

Other projectiles include: AP-T BR-365 (fitted with MD-5 fuze), AP-T BR-365K (fitted with MD-8 fuze), HVAP-T BR-365P (no fuze), HVAP BR-365-PK (no fuze).

Effective slant range of the 85 mm M1939 is 8382 m, effective altitude limit with an elevation of +45° is 5944 m, effective altitude limit with an elevation of +65° is 7620 m while self-destruct range is 10 516 m.

The M1939 has been replaced in most members of the Warsaw Pact by the 100 mm KS-19, but is still widely used by other countries and quantities are held in reserve in the Soviet Union. The M1939 is known as the Type 56 in China.

The M1939 was succeeded in production in 1944 by the M1944, which was designed by G D Dorokhin, had a number of modifications including a longer ordnance with a T-shaped muzzle brake and fired the same ammunition as the M1939 except that the HE round had a more powerful charge that increased its muzzle velocity to 900 m/s compared with the 792 m/s of the basic round. The complete HE round weighed 15.9 kg compared with the 15.1 kg of the standard round. The M1944 was not used by the Soviet Army in large numbers as it was soon replaced by the 100 mm KS-19. Production of the M1944 was undertaken in Czechoslovakia in the post-Second World War period.

85 mm anti-aircraft gun M1939 in travelling order with outriggers retracted and ordnance in travelling lock

USSR / TOWED AA GUNS

SPECIFICATIONS
(data in square brackets relates to M1944 where different from M1939)

CALIBRE	85 mm
BARREL LENGTH (overall)	4.693 [5.743] m
MUZZLE BRAKE	multi-baffle [T-shaped]
RECOIL	hydraulic buffer and hydro-pneumatic recuperator
BREECH MECHANISM	semi-automatic vertical sliding wedge
CARRIAGE	2-axle, 4-wheeled
SHIELD	yes
WEIGHT	
travelling order	4300 [5000] kg
firing position	4300 [5000] kg
LENGTH (travelling)	7.049 [8.2] m
WIDTH (travelling)	2.15 m
HEIGHT (travelling)	2.25 m
AXIS OF BORE	1.55 m
GROUND CLEARANCE (travelling)	0.4 m
TRACK	1.8 m
TYRES	34.00 × 7
ELEVATION/DEPRESSION	+82°/−3°
TRAVERSE	360°
RATE OF FIRE	15-20 rpm
MAX RANGE	
horizontal	15 650 [18 000] m
vertical	10 500 [11 600] m
EFFECTIVE VERTICAL RANGE	8382 [10 000] m
UNIT OF FIRE	150 rounds
CREW	7
TOWING VEHICLE	ZIL-157 (6 × 6) truck

Status: Production complete. In service with the following countries:

Country	Quantity	User	Comment
Afghanistan	n/av	army, air force	with Fire Can radar
Albania	n/av	army	unconfirmed user
Algeria	20+	army	with Fire Can radar
	30+	air force	with Fire Can radar
Bulgaria	n/av	army	with Fire Can radar
China	n/av	army	with Chinese radar
	n/av	air defence force	with Chinese radar
Cuba	100	army	with Fire Can radar
Egypt	400	air defence command	with Fire Can radar
Iran	n/av	army	unconfirmed user
Iraq	200	army	with Fire Can radar
Korea, North	400	army	with Fire Can radar
Romania	75	army	with Fire Can radar
Sudan	n/av	army	with Fire Can radar
Syria	n/av	army	with Fire Can radar
Vietnam	n/av	air defence command	with Fire Can radar
South Yemen	n/av	army	with Fire Can radar
Yugoslavia	260	army	with Fire Can radar
Zambia	16	army	with Fire Can radar

NB: Most Warsaw Pack countries, including the Soviet Union, hold quantities of these weapons in reserve

85 mm anti-aircraft guns M1944 deployed in the firing position and showing different muzzle brake to earlier M1939

Manufacturers: Czechoslovakian and Soviet state factories (Artillery Plant No 8, Kaliningrad, near Moscow and evacuation site in Sverdlovsk).

57 mm Automatic Anti-aircraft Gun S-60

Development
The 57 mm automatic anti-aircraft gun S-60 was designed by L V Loktev and introduced in 1950 as the replacement for the older 37 mm M1939 anti-aircraft gun. Main improvements over the latter include greater range and the facility to use an off-carriage fire control system.

In the Soviet Army it is issued on the scale of 24 per Tank Division and 24 per Motorised Rifle Division. Each of them has an anti-aircraft regiment which has four batteries each of six guns, with each battery having two three-gun platoons. The HQ battery has two Flat Face target acquisition radars and each of four gun batteries has a single Fire Can fire control radar. The S-60 has now been replaced in front line units by the SA-8 Gecko mobile SAM system.

Description
In the firing position its wheels are raised off the ground and the carriage is supported on four screw jacks, one at the front and one at the rear of the carriage, and one either side of the carriage on outriggers. The gun can be fired from its wheels in an emergency. Fire control equipment consists of a reflex sight for anti-aircraft use and a telescope sight for ground use. There are four modes of operation: manual with the handwheels operated by the crew; assisted, with the handwheels operated by the crew assisted by a servo motor; automatic, remotely controlled by a director and zero indicator, remotely controlled by radar.

When originally introduced it was used in conjunction with the PUAZO-5 director and the SON-9 radar but today it is used in conjunction with the PUAZO-6/60 director and the SON-9 or SON-9A (NATO name Fire Can) E-band radar, but in recent years improved director and radar combinations have entered service. Photographs of Soviet-built Flap Wheel anti-aircraft radars associated with the 57 mm S-60 anti-aircraft gun in Iraqi service show that the radar has been modernised. A low light television camera, similar to that seen on the Land Roll radar on SA-8 vehicles and some Low Blow radars associated with the SA-3 system, has been mounted on top of the Flap Wheel antenna. Flap Wheels with long cables have also been observed, enabling them to be placed 200 m away from the firing position. These modifications will increase the effectiveness of the S-60, especially when confronted by chaff or jamming.

The top of each side of the shield folds forwards through 180°. The ammunition, which is fed to the gun in four round clips, is not interchangeable with that used by the 57 mm ASU-57 self-propelled anti-tank gun or the 57 mm towed anti-tank guns due to a different configuration. A horizontal feed tray on the left side of the mounting holds one clip of four rounds and a second clip can be placed on an upright stand that rotates with the mounting.

The following types of fixed ammunition can be fired by the S-60:

Ammunition type	FRAG-T	FRAG-T	APCT-T
PROJECTILE DESIGNATION	OR-281	OR-281U	BR-281*
FUZE MODEL	MG-57	MG-57	MD-10
WEIGHT OF PROJECTILE	2.81 kg	2.85 kg	2.82 kg
WEIGHT OF BURSTING CHARGE	0.168 kg	0.154 kg	0.018 kg
TYPE OF BURSTING CHARGE	RDX/aluminium	RDX/aluminium	RDX/aluminium
MUZZLE VELOCITY	1000 m/s	1000 m/s	1000 m/s
ARMOUR PENETRATION AT 0° OBLIQUITY	n/app	n/app	96 mm/1000 m
			106 mm/500 m

* also very similar BR-281U

TOWED AA GUNS / USSR

Egyptian Army 57 mm automatic anti-aircraft gun S-60 in travelling configuration (DIA)

Effective slant range using on-board optical sights is 3993 m which increases to 6005 m with radar, effective altitude limit with an elevation of +45° is 2835 m with on board optical sights and 3627 m with radar, effective altitude limit with an elevation of +65° is 4237 m with on-board optical sights and 5425 m with radar. Self-destruct range is 7224 m.

The S-60 is also manufactured in China as the Type 59. The ZSU-57-2 twin 57 mm self-propelled anti-aircraft gun has the same ballistic performance as the S-60 and uses the same ammunition. Details of this clear weather anti-aircraft gun system are given in the *Self-propelled Anti-aircraft Guns* section. The Chinese equivalent of the ZSU-57-2 is the Type 80 SPAAG, details of which will be found in the relevant section. The 57 mm gun is also used in a number of naval applications.

57 mm automatic anti-aircraft gun S-60 captured in Angola by South African Army in 1983 (South African Defence Forces)

SPECIFICATIONS

CALIBRE	57 mm
BARREL LENGTH (overall)	4.39 m
MUZZLE BRAKE	multi-perforated
OPERATION	recoil, full automatic
CARRIAGE	4-wheel
SHIELD	no
WEIGHT	
travelling order	4660 kg
firing position	4500 kg
LENGTH (travelling)	8.5 m
WIDTH (travelling)	2.054 m
HEIGHT (travelling)	2.37 m
AXIS OF BORE (firing)	1.3 m
GROUND CLEARANCE	
(travelling)	0.38 m
TRACK	1.935 m
TYRES	34.00 × 7
ELEVATION/DEPRESSION	+85°/−4°
TRAVERSE	360°
RATE OF FIRE	
cyclic	105–120 rpm
practical	70 rpm
FEED	4 round clip
MAX RANGE	
horizontal	12 000 m
vertical	8800 m
EFFECTIVE VERTICAL RANGE	
with off-carriage fire control	6000 m
with on-carriage fire control	4000 m
UNIT OF FIRE	200 rounds
CREW	7
TOWING VEHICLES	ZIL-151 (6 × 6) truck
	Ural-375D (6 × 6) truck
	AT-L light tracked artillery tractor

USSR / **TOWED AA GUNS** 209

Three 57 mm automatic anti-aircraft gun S-60s in firing position with PUAZO-6/60 director in background. Loading tray for ammunition can be seen on first S-60 (Novosti)

Status: Production complete. In service with the following countries:

Country	Quantity	User	Comment	Country	Quantity	User	Comment
Afghanistan	n/av	army	also used by Air Force	Laos	n/av	army	
Albania	n/av	army	unconfirmed	Libya	150	army	
Algeria	60	army		Mali	6	army	
Angola	100	army		Mongolia	n/av	army	
Bulgaria	n/av	army		Morocco	60	army	
China	n/av	army	also used by Air Force, built as Type 59	Mozambique	70	army	
				Nicaragua	n/av	army	
Cuba	200	army		Pakistan	n/av	army	from China
Czechoslovakia	600	army		Poland	200	army	
Egypt	600	army	also used by Air Defence Command	Romania	150	army	
				Somalia	50	army	
Finland	n/av	army		Syria	n/av	army	
Germany, East	n/av	army	now held in reserve	USSR	n/av	army	
Guinea	12	army		Vietnam	n/av	army	
Guinea Bissau	10	army		Yemen, North	n/av	army	
Hungary	100	army		Yemen, South	n/av	army	
Indonesia	200	army	also used by Air Force, not all operational	Yugoslavia	n/av	army	
				Zambia	55	army	
Iraq	500	army					
Iran	200	army					
Kampuchea	n/av	army					
Korea, North	600	army					

Manufacturer: Soviet state factories.

37 mm Automatic Anti-aircraft Gun M1939

Development
The 37 mm automatic anti-aircraft gun M1939 entered service with the Soviet Army shortly before the start of the Second World War and is based on the Swedish Bofors 40 mm design used by the UK and USA in the same period. The design was a joint task by L A Loktev and M N Loginov in the Design Bureau of Artillery Plant No 8 at Kaliningrad near Moscow. It is no longer in front-line service with any member of the Warsaw Pact as it has been replaced by the 57 mm S-60, but is still used by second-line and militia units of the Warsaw Pact and large numbers have been exported to Africa, the Middle East and the Far East.

The M1939 is built in China as the Type 55. A twin version built for export is known to be in service with Algeria and Egypt and is manufactured in China as the Type 65. The 37 mm gun has also been used by the Soviet Navy in both single (70-K) and twin liquid-cooled mounts (V-11M).

Description
In the firing position its wheels are raised off the ground and it is supported by four screw jacks, one at the front and one at the rear of the carriage, and one either side on outriggers. When travelling the barrel is pointed to the rear and is held in position by a lock hinged at the rear of the carriage. The shield, which weighs about 100 kg, has been removed by many countries. The M1939 is a clear-weather system only with no provision for radar fire control.

The M1939 can fire the following types of fixed ammunition which is fed in clips of five rounds:

210 TOWED AA GUNS / USSR

Twin version of 37 mm automatic anti-aircraft gun M1939 in service with Egyptian Army (Egyptian Army)

37 mm automatic anti-aircraft gun M1939 fitted with shield and with outriggers in position (Franz Kosar)

Ammunition type	FRAG-T	FRAG-T	AP-T*
PROJECTILE DESIGNATION	OR-167	OR-167N	BR-167
FUZE MODEL	MG-8	B-37	n/app
WEIGHT OF PROJECTILE	0.732 kg	0.708 kg	0.77 kg
WEIGHT OF BURSTING CHARGE	0.035 kg	0.036 kg	n/app
TYPE OF BURSTING CHARGE	RDX/aluminium	RDX/aluminium/wax	n/app
MUZZLE VELOCITY	880 m/s	880 m/s	880 m/s
ARMOUR PENETRATION AT 0° OBLIQUITY	n/app	n/app	37 mm/1000 m 47 mm/500 m

* HVAP no longer used, it penetrated 57 mm of armour at 1000 m

37 mm automatic anti-aircraft gun M1939 without shield in travelling order (US Army)

The 37 mm M1939 anti-aircraft gun has an effective slant range of 2499 m. Effective altitude limit with an elevation of +45° is 1768 m while effective altitude limit with an elevation of +65° is 2865 m. Self-destruct range is 4389 m.

SPECIFICATIONS

CALIBRE	37 mm
BARREL LENGTH (overall)	2.729 m
OPERATION	recoil
RECOIL	hydraulic recoil buffer and spring recuperator
BREECH MECHANISM	rising block
CARRIAGE	4-wheel
SHIELD	optional
WEIGHT (firing position without shield)	2100 kg
LENGTH (travelling)	6.036 m
WIDTH (travelling without shield)	1.937 m
HEIGHT (travelling without shield)	2.105 m
AXIS OF BORE (firing)	1.1 m
GROUND CLEARANCE (travelling)	0.36 m
TRACK	1.545 m
TYRES	6.50 × 20
ELEVATION/DEPRESSION	+85°/-5°
TRAVERSE	360°
RATE OF FIRE	
cyclic	160–180 rpm
practical	80 rpm
FEED	5 round clip
MAX RANGE	
horizontal	9500 m
vertical	6700 m
EFFECTIVE VERTICAL RANGE	3000 m
UNIT OF FIRE	200 rounds
CREW	8
TOWING VEHICLE	GAZ-63 (4 × 4) truck

USSR / TOWED AA GUNS

Status: Production complete. In service with the following countries:

Country	Quantity	User	Comment
Afghanistan	n/av	army	
Albania	50	army	
Algeria	190	army	
Angola	n/av	army	
Bulgaria	n/av	army	held in reserve
Cameroon	18	army	from China
China	n/av	army	
Congo	28	army	
Cuba	300	army	
Egypt	400	air defence command	
Ethiopia	n/av	army	
Germany, East	n/av	army	held in reserve
Gabon	10	army	
Guinea	8	army	
Guinea-Bissau	6	army	
Iran	300	army	
Iraq	250	army	
Kampuchea	n/av	army	
Korea, North	1000	army	
Laos	n/av	army	
Mali	6	army	
Mauritania	6	army	
Mongolia	n/av	army	
Morocco	n/av	army	
Mozambique	n/av	army	
Nicaragua	56	army	
Pakistan	n/av	army	from China, Type 55 and Type 65
Romania	100	army	
Somalia	120	army	
Sudan	100	army	including some from China
Syria	n/av	army	
Tanzania	120	army	from China, Type 55
Thailand	50	army	from China in 1987, also used by Air Force for airfield defence
Togo	6	army	
Tunisia	18	army	from China, Type 55
Uganda	20	army	
Vietnam	n/av	army	including some from China
Yemen, North	n/av	army	
Yemen, South	n/av	army	
Yugoslavia	400	army	not all operational
USSR	n/av	army	not in front line use, also used by Reserves and Militia
Zaire	n/av	army	
Zambia	40	army	
Zimbabwe	n/av	army	

There is a separate entry for the Chinese weapons in this section.

Manufacturers: Artillery Plant No 8, Kaliningrad, No 4, Krasnoyarsk, No 586, Kolomna. Also Chinese and Polish state factories.

Twin 23 mm Automatic Anti-aircraft Gun ZU-23

Development
The twin 23 mm automatic anti-aircraft gun ZU-23 was introduced into the Soviet Army in the 1960s as the replacement for the 14.5 mm ZPU-2 and ZPU-4 anti-aircraft guns. In the Soviet Army it was issued on the scale of 24 per Airborne Division, 12 in the divisional artillery element and 4 in each of the 3 airborne rifle regiments. The Airborne Divisions have now been restructured as Airborne Rifle Divisions and recent TOEs show that they no longer have ZU-23 towed guns as part of their equipment. Instead they have 48 SA-9 Gaskin SAM systems, 12 in each of the three airborne rifle regiments and 12 in the divisional artillery element.

Description
In the firing position the wheels are raised off the ground and the weapon is supported on its triangular platform which has three screw-type levelling jacks. The quick-change barrels have flash suppressors. The guns used in the ZU-23 are also used in the quad ZSU-23-4 self-propelled anti-aircraft gun system, but in this case the barrels are water cooled.

The ZU-23 mm fires fixed ammunition with the same cartridge case dimension as the obsolete 23 mm automatic aircraft gun model VYa ammunition. The ZU-23 fires two types of ammunition, API-T (BZT) and HEI-T (MG25). The API-T projectile weighs 0.189 kg, has a muzzle velocity of 970 m/s and will penetrate 25 mm of armour at an incidence of 0° at a range of 500 m. The HEI-T projectile weighs 0.19 kg and has a muzzle velocity of 970 m/s. The ZU-23 has an effective slant range of 2012 m with ammunition having a self-destruct range of 3780 m.

The ZU-23 is a clear-weather system only with no provision for radar fire control. Care must be taken not to confuse the 14.5 mm ZPU-2 (late model) with the ZU-23, which has different flash suppressors and horizontal rather than vertical ammunition boxes on either side.

There are separate entries for the Chinese and Egyptian built models of the ZU-23 light anti-aircraft gun systems.

Twin 23 mm automatic anti-aircraft gun ZU-23 in firing position (US Army)

212 TOWED AA GUNS / USSR

Angolan ZU-23 23 mm automatic anti-aircraft gun captured by South African Defence Forces

Twin 23 mm automatic anti-aircraft gun ZU-23 in travelling configuration (Israeli Ministry of Defence)

Variants
A single-barrel version also exists. During the fighting in the Lebanon in the summer of 1982 Israel captured a number of Soviet built BTR-152 (6 × 6) APCs with a ZU-23 anti-aircraft system mounted in the rear. It is believed that this was a local modification by the PLO. In Afghanistan the Soviets mounted the ZU-23 on the rear of ZIL-135 trucks for convoy escort.

BTR-152 (6 × 6) armoured personnel carrier with ZU-23 23 mm automatic anti-aircraft gun mounted in rear (Israeli Defence Forces)

SPECIFICATIONS

CALIBRE	23 mm
BARREL LENGTH (overall)	2.01 m
OPERATION	gas, full automatic
BREECH MECHANISM	vertical sliding wedge
CARRIAGE	2-wheeled
SHIELD	no
WEIGHT	
travelling order with ammunition	950 kg
firing position with ammunition	950 kg
LENGTH (travelling)	4.57 m
WIDTH (travelling)	1.83 m
HEIGHT (travelling)	1.87 m
AXIS OF BORE (firing)	0.62 m
GROUND CLEARANCE	0.36 m
TRACK	1.67 m
TYRES	6.00 × 16
ELEVATION/DEPRESSION	+90°/−10°
TRAVERSE	360°
RATE OF FIRE PER BARREL	
cyclic	800–1000 rpm
practical	200 rpm
FEED	50 round belt
MAX RANGE	
horizontal	7000 m
vertical	5100 m
EFFECTIVE VERTICAL RANGE	2500 m
UNIT OF FIRE	2400 rounds
CREW	5
TOWING VEHICLE	GAZ-69 (4 × 4) truck, MT-LB, BMD-2

USSR / TOWED AA GUNS

Status: Production complete. In service with the following countries:

Country	Quantity	User	Comment
Afghanistan	n/av	army	also truck mounted
Albania	n/av	army	from China
Algeria	50–60	army	
Angola	n/av	army	and Air Defence Force
Bulgaria	300	army	
Chad	n/av	army	
China	n/av	army	locally built, also Marines, Air Force and Militia
Cuba	400	army	
Czechoslovakia	n/av	army	and Air Defence Command
Djibouti	24	army	
Egypt	n/av	army	locally built, also Air Defence Command
Ethiopia	n/av	army	
Finland	n/av	army	
Germany, East	n/av	army	also Air Defence Command, Militia and Frontier Troops and Ministry for State Security
Guinea-Bissau	18	army	
Hungary	n/av	army	and Air Defence Command
India	n/av	army	
Iran	300	army	and Air Force, Revolutionary Guard Corps
Iraq	750	army	and Air Defence Troops
Israel	n/av	air force	including self-propelled
Korea, North	1500	army	
Laos	n/av	army	
Lebanon	n/av	army	and various Militias
Libya	100	army	and Air Defence Force
Mauritania	n/av	army	
Mongolia	n/av	army	
Morocco	35	army	
Mozambique	120	army	
Nicaragua	30	army	
Oman	n/av	army	
Pakistan	n/av	army	from China
Peru	n/av	army	
Poland	450	army	also Air Defence Command and Troops of Territorial Defence
Somalia	n/av	army	
Sudan	n/av	army	from Egypt
Syria	n/av	army	also Air Defence Command
Tanzania	40	army	
USSR	n/av	army	also Air Defence Troops, KGB, MVD and Militia
Uganda	20+	army	
Vietnam	900	army	
Yemen, North	n/av	army	
Yemen, South	n/av	army	
Zimbabwe	n/av	army	

Note: In Air Defence Command, they provide close in defence to SAM batteries and radar stations

To meet Egyptian requirements ESD and Thomson-CSF of France have each developed a self-propelled model of the ZU-23 based on an M113A2 chassis. Details of these are given in the *Self-propelled anti-aircraft guns* section. Following extensive trials the ESD version was selected for service. The ZU-23 cannon are also used in the Israeli TCM Mk 3 light air defence artillery system described earlier in this section.

Manufacturer: Soviet state factories. Also licence-produced in China and Egypt; see entry in this section.

14.5 mm ZPU Series of Anti-aircraft Machine Guns (ZPU-1, ZPU-2 and ZPU-4)

ZPU-1

The ZPU-1 was introduced into the Soviet Army in the immediate post-Second World War period and, like the ZPU-2 and ZPU-4, uses the 14.5 mm Vladimirov KPV heavy machine gun which has a quick-change barrel and is also fitted to a number of AFVs including the T-10M tank, BRDM-2 reconnaissance vehicle, BTR-60PB (8 × 8) APC, BTR-70 (8 × 8) APC, Czechoslovak OT-64 (8 × 8) APCs models OT-64C(1) and OT-64C(2) and the OT-62C tracked APC. The ZPU-1 is no longer in service with any member of the Warsaw Pact but is still found in Africa, the Middle and Far East.

The two-wheeled carriage of the ZPU-1 was designed by Vodop'yanov and Rachinskiy and for transport in rough terrain can be dismantled into units weighing about 80 kg each. The quick-change barrel is air-cooled, with the ammunition box on the right side. All weapons in this series fire the following fixed ammunition: API (BS 41) projectile weighing 64.4 g with a muzzle velocity of 1000 m/s which will penetrate 32 mm of armour at an incidence of 0° at a range of 500 m, API-T (BZT) projectile weighing 59.56 g and I-T (ZP) projectile weighing 59.68 g. The 14.5 mm ZPU series of anti-aircraft machine guns have an effective slant range of 1402 m, effective limit at +45° elevation is 975 m while effective altitude limit at +65° is 1280 m.

ZPU-2

The first model of the ZPU-2 entered service in 1949 and had larger mudguards and a double tubular tow bar. In the firing position the wheels are removed and the weapon rests on a three-point platform, each point having a screw jack for levelling.

The late production model is lighter and lower and has narrower mudguards and a lighter single tow bar. In the firing position the wheels are raised clear of the ground but not removed.

The ZPU-2 is no longer in front-line service with Soviet units as it has been replaced by the similar 23 mm ZU-23 which is distinguishable by its ammunition boxes which are horizontal rather than vertical and its parallel flash hiders. The ZPU-2 is manufactured in China as the Type 58. Two self-propelled models in service are based on the BTR-40 (4 × 4) and the BTR-152 (6 × 6) APC and designated the BTR-40A and BTR-152A. Both use the ZPTU-2 mount. Details are given in the *Self-propelled Anti-aircraft Guns* section.

14.5 mm ZPU-1 anti-aircraft gun in firing position in Zimbabwe (UK Land Forces)

ZPU-4

The ZPU-4 entered service with the Soviet Army in 1949 and although no longer in front-line service with the Soviet Army, like the ZPU-2 may be found in second-line units defending airfields and other high-priority targets. The ZPU-4 has a four-wheel carriage designed by Leshchinskiy. In the firing position the wheels are raised off the ground and the carriage is supported at four points, screw jacks at each end of the carriage and

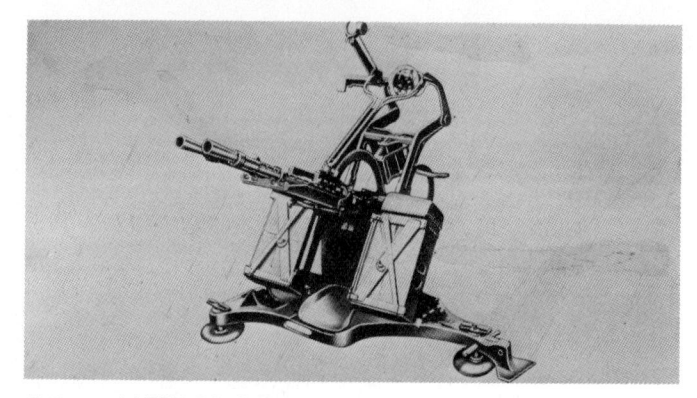

214 TOWED AA GUNS / USSR

Early model ZPU-2 in firing position

Early model ZPU-2 in travelling order (US Marine Corps)

ZPU-4 in travelling order

on outriggers on each side of the carriage that are also provided with screwjacks. The weapon can be brought into action in 15 to 20 seconds but can, if required, be fired with the wheels in the travelling position. The ZPU-4 is manufactured in China as the Type 56 and is currently being produced in North Korea, as is the ZPU-2.

Late production model ZPU-2 (Franz Kosar)

SPECIFICATIONS

Model	ZPU-1	ZPU-2 (early)	ZPU-2 (late)	ZPU-4
CALIBRE	14.5 mm	14.5 mm	14.5 mm	14.5 mm
BARREL LENGTH	1.348 m	1.348 m	1.348 m	1.348 m
CARRIAGE	2-wheeled	2-wheeled	2-wheeled	4-wheeled
WEIGHT				
travelling order	413 kg	994 kg	649 kg	1810 kg
firing position	413 kg	639 kg	621 kg	1810 kg
LENGTH (travelling)	3.44 m	3.536 m	3.871 m	4.53 m
WIDTH (travelling)	1.62 m	1.92 m	1.372 m	1.72 m
HEIGHT (travelling)	1.34 m	1.83 m	1.097 m	2.13 m
AXIS OF BORE (firing)	0.635 m	0.8 m	n/a	1.02 m
GROUND CLEARANCE (travelling)	0.28 m	n/a	0.27 m	0.458 m
TRACK	1.384 m	n/a	1.1 m	1.641 m
TYRES	4.50 × 16	6.50 × 20	6.50 × 20	6.50 × 20
ELEVATION/DEPRESSION	+88°/-8°	+90°/-7°	+85°/-15°	+90°/-10°
TRAVERSE	360°	360°	360°	360°
RATE OF FIRE PER BARREL				
cyclic	600	600	600	600
practical	150	150	150	150
MAX RANGE				
horizontal	8000 m	8000 m	8000 m	8000 m
vertical	5000 m	5000 m	5000 m	5000 m
EFFECTIVE VERTICAL RANGE	1400 m	1400 m	1400 m	1400 m
UNIT OF FIRE	1200 rounds	2400 rounds	2400 rounds	4800 rounds
CREW	4	5	5	5

USSR / TOWED AA GUNS

ZPU-4 anti-aircraft machine gun deployed in firing position and showing outriggers either side (US Army)

14.5 mm ZPU-2 light anti-aircraft gun defending Soviet radar station

Status: Production complete. Known users include the following countries:

Country	Quantity	User	Comment
Afghanistan	n/av	army	ZPU-1, ZPU-2, ZPU-4
Algeria	50	army	ZPU-2, ZPU-4
Angola	n/av	army	ZPU-1, ZPU-2, ZPU-4
Benin	n/av	army	ZPU-4
Bulgaria	n/av	army	ZPU-2, ZPU-4, not front line
Burkina-Faso	50	army	ZPU-4
Burundi	15	army	ZPU-4
Cameroon	15	army	Chinese Type 58 (ZPU-2 copy)
Cape Verde Islands	n/av	army	ZPU-2, ZPU-4
Chad	n/av	army	ZPU-1, ZPU-2, ZPU-4
China	n/av	army, militia and marines	locally built ZPU-1, ZPU-2 and ZPU-4
Congo	n/av	army	ZPU-4
Cuba	n/av	army	ZPU-1, ZPU-2 and ZPU-4
Czechoslovakia	n/av	army, militia	ZPU-4 not front line use
Egypt	n/av	army	ZPU-2, ZPU-4
Germany, East	n/av	army, frontier troops, Ministry for State Security, militia	ZPU-2, ZPU-4, not front line
Ethiopia	n/av	army	ZPU-1, ZPU-2, ZPU-4
Guinea	n/av	army	ZPU-4
Guinea-Bissau	n/av	army	ZPU-4
Hungary	n/av	army, militia	ZPU-2, ZPU-4, not front line
Iraq	n/av	army	ZPU-1, ZPU-2, ZPU-4
Korea, North	n/av	army	ZPU-1, ZPU-2, ZPU-4 (locally built)
Laos	n/av	army	ZPU-1, ZPU-2, ZPU-4
Libya	n/av	army	ZPU-2, ZPU-4
Madagascar	50	army	ZPU-4
Malawi	n/av	army	ZPU-4
Mali	n/av	army	ZPU-4 from North Korea
Malta	50	task force	ZPU-4 from North Korea
Mauritania	n/av	army	ZPU-1, ZPU-2, ZPU-4
Mongola	n/av	army	ZPU-2, ZPU-4
Morocco	15	army	ZPU-2, ZPU-4
Mozambique	n/av	army	ZPU-1, ZPU-2, ZPU-4
Nicaragua	100	army	ZPU-1, ZPU-2, ZPU-4
Pakistan	n/av	army	ZPU-2, ZPU-4 from China
Poland	n/av	army, Troops of Territorial Defence	ZPU-2, ZPU-4, not in front line
Romania	n/av	army, MoD Security Troops, Patriotic Guard, Border Guards	ZPU-2, ZPU-4
São Tomé & Principe	n/av	army	ZPU-4
Seychelles	n/av	army	ZPU-4
Somalia	n/av	army	ZPU-1, ZPU-2, ZPU-4
Sudan	n/av	army	ZPU-2, ZPU-4
Syria	n/av	army, militia	ZPU-2, ZPU-4, not front line
Tanzania	240	army	ZPU-1, ZPU-2, ZPU-4, some reports state 160
Togo	38	army	ZPU-4 from North Korea
Uganda	n/av	army	ZPU-1, ZPU-2, ZPU-4
USSR	n/av	army, KGB, MVD, militia and Naval Infantry (reserve)	ZPU-1, ZPU-2, ZPU-4, not front line
Vietnam	n/av	army	ZPU-1, ZPU-2, ZPU-4
Zambia	n/av	army	ZPU-4
Zaire	n/av	army	ZPU-4
Zimbabwe	n/av	army	ZPU-1, ZPU-2, ZPU-4

Manufacturers: Chinese, North Korean and Soviet state factories. Details of the Chinese built versions of the ZPU series are given in this section under China.

UNITED KINGDOM

3.7 Inch Anti-aircraft Gun

Development
In 1933 a requirement was issued for a 3.7 in anti-aircraft gun which would fire a projectile weighing 25 lb (11.34 kg) to a maximum altitude of 28 000 ft (8534 m). After studying proposals put forward by Vickers-Armstrong and Woolwich Arsenal the former design was selected in 1934. The first prototype was completed in 1936 and production was authorised the following year. First production 3.7 in anti-aircraft guns were completed in January 1938 and production continued until 1945. The weapon was also manufactured in Canada. The 3.7 in anti-aircraft gun remained in service with the British Army until the 1950s when it was finally replaced by the Thunderbird I surface-to-air missile system, in turn replaced by the Thunderbird II which has now been withdrawn from service leaving the British Army with no medium/high level SAM system.

As with most guns there were a number of different types of ordnance and carriage, the latter including the Mk 1 series (mobile), Mk 2 series (static), Mk 3 series (mobile) and the Mk 4 series (mobile). The 3.7 in anti-aircraft gun was normally used in conjunction with an off-carriage fire control system. Later developments included a fuze setter and an automatic loader, both of which increased rate of fire to 20 to 25 rds/min.

In the post-war period the 3.7 in anti-aircraft gun has seen service with a number of countries including Australia, Burma, Canada, Cyprus, Egypt, India, Malaysia, Pakistan, South Africa, Sri Lanka and Yugoslavia. The only known users today are India, Sri Lanka and possibly Yugoslavia and in all of these it is probably held in reserve. The United Kingdom has not made ammunition for this weapon for many years.

Although the 3.7 in anti-aircraft gun had a very high success rate towards the end of the Second World War when used in conjunction with radar, predictors and the proximity fuze, it has very limited effectiveness against high speed jet aircraft.

Also in service at this time was the Ordnance QF (Quick Firing), 3.7 in Mark 6, this being a 4.5 in gun lined down to 3.7 in, this had an higher effective ceiling but as far as it is known none remain in service today although they were not declared obsolete by the British Army until 1959.

3.7 in anti-aircraft gun Mk 3 in travelling order

Description
As far as is known there are no longer any static models of the 3.7 in anti-aircraft gun in existence, the most common mounting today being the Mk 3. When travelling the four outriggers are raised into the vertical position, two either side of the carriage. In the firing position the outriggers are swung through 90° into the horizontal and the screw jacks at the end of each outrigger are screwed down so as to raise the wheels off the ground. The wheels are then removed and the carriage lowered to the ground

The 3.7 in anti-aircraft gun fired the following types of ammunition, which was fed to the breech from the left:
AP projectile weighing 12.7 kg with a muzzle velocity of 792 m/s, which would penetrate 117 mm of armour at an incidence of 0° at a range of 914 m.
HE projectile weighing 12.7 kg with a muzzle velocity of 792 m/s.

SPECIFICATIONS
(Mark 3 ordnance on Mark 3 carriage)

CALIBRE	94 mm (3.7 in)
BARREL LENGTH	4.699 m
LENGTH OF RIFLING	3.787 m
MUZZLE BRAKE	none
BREECH MECHANISM	horizontal sliding block, semi-automatic, percussion fired
RECOIL SYSTEM	hydropneumatic
SHIELD	none
CARRIAGE	4-wheeled
WEIGHT	9325.6 kg
LENGTH TRAVELLING	8.687 m
WIDTH TRAVELLING	2.438 m
HEIGHT TRAVELLING	2.502 m
TRACK	2.057 m
WHEELBASE	3.505 m
ELEVATION/DEPRESSION	+80°/-5°
TRAVERSE	360°
RATE OF FIRE	10 rpm (hand loading)
	25 rpm (automatic loading)
EFFECTIVE ANTI-AIRCRAFT RANGE	9760 m
MAX ANTI-AIRCRAFT RANGE	12 497 m
MAX GROUND RANGE	18 836 m

Status: Production complete. In service with India (500), Sri Lanka (24) and possibly Yugoslavia.

---

40 mm Automatic Anti-aircraft Gun Mk 1

Development
In 1937 the British Army placed an order with the Swedish Bofors company for a batch of 100 m/36 40 mm automatic anti-aircraft guns plus a large quantity of ammunition. Shortly afterwards a licence was obtained to undertake production of the weapon in the United Kingdom and additional weapons were ordered from Poland which was already producing the 40 mm for its own use and for export.

The 40 mm Bofors automatic anti-aircraft gun became the standard light anti-aircraft gun of the British Commonwealth during the Second World War and was also manufactured in Canada and in the USA where it was known as the 40 mm Automatic Anti-aircraft Gun M1 for which there is a separate entry in this section. The 40 mm gun was also used by the Royal Navy in both single and twin mounts the latter of which were normally water cooled. The weapon was finally replaced in the British Army in the late 1950s by the 40 mm L/70 automatic anti-aircraft gun.

The original Swedish-designed carriage, designated the Mk 1 in British use, was too complicated to produce on a large scale so a new carriage was designed called the Mk 2 with tubular rather than box type outriggers which was cheaper to manufacture. The Mk 3 carriage was almost identical to the Mk 2. Other more specialised carriages were developed but the Mk 2 and the Mk 3 were the most common and were distinguishable from American weapons by their longer carriage, tubular outriggers, rearward sloping shield and a vertical rather than angled travelling lock.

Description
In the firing position the wheels are normally removed and the carriage is supported on four jacks, one at each end of the carriage and one each side on outriggers. During the Second World War the 40 mm Bofors was normally used in conjunction with a No 3 (Kerrison) predictor. Ammunition is fed to the breech vertically in clips of four rounds and the empty cases are ejected under the forward part of the mount. The following types of ammunition can be fired:
AP with the projectile weighing 0.89 kg and a muzzle velocity of 853 m/s, which will penetrate 52 mm of armour at an incidence of 0° at a range of 457 m or 42 mm of armour at 0° at 914 m.
HE projectile weighing 0.9 kg with a muzzle velocity of 853 m/s.

Variant
Details of the Royal Thai Air Force 20 mm systems based on a 40 mm carriage are given in this section under Thailand.

UK-USA / **TOWED AA GUNS**

Original British 40 mm Bofors with riveted carriage and box type outriggers (via Terry J Gander)

British 40 mm Bofors with new carriage with tubular outriggers and different travelling lock for ordnance

SPECIFICATIONS

CALIBRE	40 mm
BARREL LENGTH (overall)	2.249 m
OPERATION	recoil
RECOIL SYSTEM	hydro-spring
BREECH MECHANISM	vertical sliding block
CARRIAGE	4-wheeled with outriggers
SHIELD	yes
WEIGHT	
travelling order	2288 kg
firing position	2034 kg
LENGTH (travelling)	6.248 m
WIDTH (travelling)	1.92 m
HEIGHT (travelling)	2.438 m
ELEVATION/DEPRESSION	+90°/-10°
TRAVERSE	360°
RATE OF FIRE	
cyclic	120 rpm
practical	60 rpm
MAX RANGE	
horizontal	4750 m
vertical	4660 m
EFFECTIVE VERTICAL RANGE	2560 m
FEED	4 round clip
UNIT OF FIRE	200 rounds
CREW	4-6
TOWING VEHICLE	2½ ton (6 × 6) truck

Status: Production complete. In service with a number of countries including:

Country	Quantity	User	Comment
Cyprus	20+	army	probably phased out of service
India	1245	army	used with Super Fledermaus FCS, may use US M1 rather than UK Mk 1
Pakistan	n/av	army	
Yugoslavia	n/av	army	status uncertain, may be US M1 and not UK Mk 1

UNITED STATES OF AMERICA

90 mm Anti-aircraft Gun M118

Development
In 1940 the 90 mm Gun T2 and the 90 mm Anti-aircraft Mount T1 were standardised as the 90 mm Gun M1 and the 90 mm Anti-aircraft Gun Mount M1. After the end of the Second World War the complete weapon was redesignated the Gun, Anti-aircraft Artillery Towed: 90 mm M117. The main disadvantage of the M117 was the time that it took to bring into action and it was not suitable for use against tanks or in coastal defence.

In June 1941 a new requirement was established that all anti-aircraft guns should be capable of use against ground and water borne targets so the development of the 90 mm Gun T4 on Mount T2 began. The 90 mm Gun T4 was first fitted with a T1E1 rammer and became the T4E1, then modified to operate with the M20 (T7) Fuze Setter-Rammer and became the T4E2. The T2 Mount was designed to permit a depression of -5° with Fuze Setter-Rammer M20 and Recoil Mechamism T17. The gun and mount were standardised in May 1943 as the 90 mm Gun M2 and 90 mm Anti-aircraft Gun Mount M2. In the post Second World War period the complete weapon was redesignated the Gun, Anti-aircraft, Towed: 90 mm; M118.

The weapon was often called the 'Triple Threat' gun as it could be used as an anti-aircraft and anti-tank gun as well as a field artillery piece. It remained in service with the United States Army until the late 1950s when it was replaced by the Raytheon HAWK SAM system.

After the Second World War the United States supplied numbers of 90 mm M117 and 90 mm M118 towed anti-aircraft guns to other countries under the Military Aid Programme. These included Argentina (12), Brazil (40), Greece (61), Japan (120), Pakistan (15), Spain (40), Taiwan (24) and Turkey (116). The only front-line users known today are Greece and Turkey.

As the 90 mm M118 was designed to engage relatively slow aircraft flying at medium to high altitudes, it is ineffective against today's low flying jet aircraft and must be considered obsolete. No known upgradings of the 90 mm M118 weapon have been carried out.

Description
The M118 consists of the 90 mm Cannon M2A1 or M2A2, Recoil Mechanism M17 Series, Fuze Rammer M20 and Mount Gun M2A1.

The cannon consists of a gun tube and breech mechanism. The former includes the support assembly and the recoil side rails, the breech mechanism includes the breech ring, breech-block and breech closing mechanism. The breech is opened automatically in counter-recoil after firing the first round and closed automatically when the round is rammed. The gun is loaded and fired manually.

The combination Fuze Setter-Rammer M20 functions as a unit to set projectile fuzes automatically according to fire control system or director data and to ram rounds into the gun chamber at high speeds. AP ammunition is rammed manually and when the fuze setter-rammer is not operating rounds can also be hand-rammed.

TOWED AA GUNS / USA

90 mm anti-aircraft guns M118 on Todendorf range in West Germany in 1956 (US Army)

90 mm anti-aircraft gun M118 of Japanese Ground Self-Defence Force in travelling order (Kensuke Ebata)

The gun is positioned in elevation and traverse either manually or by remote-control according to the fire control system. For surface targets and when required gun elevation is less than 15° the gun is directed by a periscope-type telescope sighting system.

The mount consists of the equilibrators, elevating, traversing and levelling mechanisms, top carriage, pedestal and outriggers. In action the bogies are removed and the pedestal is emplaced on the ground; for firing in an emergency the gun can be fired from the bogies. The pedestal forms the base of the mount and chassis for attaching the bogies. It supports the top carriage and the levelling mechanism. The cradle of the recoil mechanism suports all the tipping parts, the cannon assembly, recoil mechanism, counter-recoil buffer, and combination fuze setter-rammer. Spring equilibrators mounted on the top carriage counterbalance the overhanging weight of the cannon. The recoil mechanism, installed on the mount, is of the hydro-pneumatic type that decreases the energy of recoil gradually and so avoids violent movement of the cannon or mount.

The M118 fires the following types of fixed ammunition:
APHE with the projectile weighing 10.9 kg and a muzzle velocity of 854 m/s, which will penetrate 147 mm of armour at an incidence of 0° at a range of 1000 m.
HE (M58) with the projectile weighing 10.6 kg and a muzzle velocity of 824 m/s.
HVAP-T with the projectile weighing 7.63 kg and a muzzle velocity of 1022 m/s, which will penetrate 252 mm of armour at a range of 1000 m.

The 90 mm Anti-aircraft Gun M118 was normally used in conjunction with the M33 series anti-aircraft fire control system which consisted of acquisition radar, tracking radar and fire control system trailer containing the control equipment.

SPECIFICATIONS

CALIBRE	90 mm
BARREL LENGTH	4.496 m
MUZZLE BRAKE	none
RECOIL	hydro-pneumatic
BREECH MECHANISM	vertical sliding
CARRIAGE	4-wheeled with outriggers
SHIELD	yes
WEIGHT (travelling order)	14 650 kg
LENGTH (travelling)	8.99 m
WIDTH (travelling)	2.62 m
HEIGHT (travelling)	3.073 m
TYRES	14.00 × 20
ELEVATION/DEPRESSION	+80°/-10°
TRAVERSE	360°
RATE OF FIRE	
rapid	28 rpm
sustained	23 rpm
MAX RANGE	
vertical	10 980 m
horizontal	19 000 m
EFFECTIVE VERTICAL RANGE	8500 m
CREW	10-12
TOWING VEHICLES	M4 Tractor 7½ ton (6 × 6) truck

Status: Production complete. In service with Brazil (reserve), Greece, and Turkey.

90 mm Anti-aircraft Gun M117

Development

By the late 1930s it had become evident that the 3 in anti-aircraft gun was incapable of combating the faster and higher flying aircraft then coming into service. The Chief of Coast Artillery subsequently recommended a gun with a calibre of 90 mm, a muzzle velocity of 2800 ft/s (853 m/s), weighing no more than 10 tons, with the complete round of ammunition weighing no more than 40 pounds (18.14 kg) and a rate of fire of 25 rpm.

The project to meet this requirement began in June 1938 under the designation 90 mm Gun T2 and the 90 mm Anti-aircraft Mount T1. Design work was completed in December 1938 and the first prototype was completed and tested at Aberdeen Proving Grounds late in 1939. Early in 1940 the weapon was standardised as the 90 mm Gun M1 and the 90 mm Anti-aircraft Gun Mount M1. Watertown undertook the production of the carriages and Watervliet produced the ordnance. In an effort to speed up production, contracts were subsequently awarded to York, Allis-Chalmers and Worthington Pump to produce the carriages with Watervliet still supplying the ordnance. Other companies were however awarded contracts for the ordnance including the Chevrolet Division of General Motors Corporation, the Wheland Company and the Oliver Machinery Company. Production was very slow to start with and by the end of 1941 only 171 had been built with few actually being issued to units. The following year production rapidly built up.

To increase the rate of fire from 14/15 rpm a mechanical rammer was developed and standardised as the Spring Rammer M8. To accommodate the rammer slight changes were made and the modified gun was then designated the M1A1. The M8 proved unsuccessful and was subsequently abandoned. A combination fuze setter and rammer was then successfully developed and standardised as the M20.

The basic mount was used in conjunction with a director and required manual pointing of the gun. With the development of the M2 Remote Gun Control Equipment the electric and hydraulic equipment on the mount automatically pointed the gun in both elevation and traverse, with provision for manual pointing if necessary. The M1 mount with this equipment was called the M1A2 and standardised in 1941.

In June 1941 a new requirement was established that all anti-aircraft guns should be capable of use against ground and waterborne targets

USA / **TOWED AA GUNS** 219

90 mm anti-aircraft gun M117 in travelling order

Brazilian Army 90 mm anti-aircraft gun M117 in firing position (Ronaldo S Olive)

so the development of the 90 mm Gun T4 on Mount T2 began. It eventually became the 90 mm Gun M2 and the 90 mm Anti-aircraft Gun Mount M2 and after the Second World War the 90 mm M118 for which there is a separate entry.

In the post-Second World War period the 90 mm anti-aircraft gun was redesignated the Gun, Anti-aircraft Artillery Towed: 90 mm, M117, which was finally replaced in the early 1960s by the Raytheon HAWK SAM system.

After the Second World War the United States supplied numbers of 90 mm M117 and 90 mm M118 towed anti-aircraft guns to other countries under the Military Aid Programme (MAP). These included Argentina (12), Brazil (40), Greece (61), Japan (120), Pakistan (15), Spain (40), Taiwan (24) and Turkey (116). The only known users today are Argentina (reserve), Brazil (reserve), Greece, Spain (reserve), Turkey and Yugoslavia.

As the 90 mm M117 was designed to engage relatively slow flying aircraft flying at medium to high altitudes, it is ineffective against todays low flying jet aircraft and must be considered obsolete. No known upgradings of the 90 mm M117 weapon have been carried out.

Description
M117 consists of the 90 mm Cannon M1A2 or M1A3, Recoil Mechanism M1 series and the Mount M1A2. The composition of the steel is the only difference between the M1A2 and the M1A3 cannon as the latter meets requirements for cold weather operations and can be retubed.

The mount M1A2 is of the trailer type with a two-wheel bogie for supporting the weight when travelling. In the firing position the mount is lowered to the ground and the bogie detached and rolled forward. The recoil mechanism is hydro-pneumatic with variable recoil that absorbs the energy of the recoil gradually and so avoids violent movement of the cannon or mount. The mount has electric brakes that are operated from the prime mover and handbrakes. When travelling the platform is dismantled and stowed vertically on the towing bar on the carriage.

Ammunition is of the fixed type and with exceptions is interchangeable with that of the M36 tank destroyer and can also be fired by the M47 tank, although ammunition used by the M47 cannot be fired by the M117. The following types of fixed ammunition can be fired:

APHE projectile weighing 10.9 kg with a muzzle velocity of 854 m/s, which will penetrate 147 mm of armour at an incidence of 0° at a range of 1000 m.

HE projectile weighing 10.6 kg with a muzzle velocity of 824 m/s.

HVAP projectile weighing 7.63 kg with a muzzle velocity of 1022 m/s, which will penetrate 252 mm of armour at an incidence of 0° at a range of 1000 m.

SPECIFICATIONS

CALIBRE	90 mm
BARREL LENGTH	4.728 m
MUZZLE BRAKE	none
RECOIL	hydro-pneumatic
BREECH MECHANISM	vertical sliding wedge
CARRIAGE	2-wheeled with outriggers
SHIELD	no
WEIGHT	
travelling order	8626 kg
firing position	6646 kg
LENGTH (travelling)	6.35 m
WIDTH (travelling)	2.586 m
HEIGHT (travelling)	2.845 m
GROUND CLEARANCE (travelling)	0.305 m
TRACK	2.222 m
TYRES	10.00 × 22
ELEVATION/DEPRESSION	+80°/-5°
TRAVERSE	360°
RATE OF FIRE	22 rpm
MAX RANGE	
horizontal	17 879 m
vertical	10 980 m
EFFECTIVE VERTICAL RANGE	8500 m
CREW	10
TOWING VEHICLES	5 to 7½ ton (6 × 6) truck

Status: Production complete. In service with Argentina (reserve), Brazil (reserve), Greece, Pakistan, Spain (reserve), Turkey and Yugoslavia.

75 mm Anti-aircraft Gun M51

Development
Development of a 75 mm anti-aircraft gun with a muzzle velocity of 3000 ft/s (914.4 m/s) and an automatic loader began in 1944. The first two prototypes were delivered to the US Army in June 1948 and limited procurement was authorised in December 1948. After much further development work and redesign it was finally type classified in October 1955 as the M51, or Skysweeper, but even then it had a muzzle velocity of only 2800 ft/s (853 m/s).

Carriage machining and complete assembly were carried out by Aetna-Standard. The M51 Skysweeper was replaced in the US Army from the early 1960s by the Raytheon HAWK surface-to-air missile. Quantities of the M51 Skysweeper were also supplied to West Germany, Greece (52), Japan (20) and Turkey (110) but Greece and Turkey are now the only known operators.

As the weapon was originally developed to engage aircraft flying at medium altitudes, the M51 Skysweeper is ineffective against today's low flying high performance aircraft.

Description
The Gun, Anti-aircraft Artillery, Towed: 75 mm Weapons System, M51, consists of the 75 mm Automatic Gun M35, Recoil Mechanism M29 and Mount M84.

The M35 cannon consists of a steel tube screwed into a breech ring that is locked to the tube with a key. Support and alignment for this

220 TOWED AA GUNS / USA

75 mm anti-aircraft gun M51 in travelling order (US Army)

assembly in the body of the cradle of the recoil mechanism are provided by rails fastened to the breech ring and the tube support on each side of the cannon. The latter has an automatic breech mechanism that utilises the force of the counter-recoil to cam the vertically sliding breech-block to the open position and wind the breech-closing torsion spring. This spring is released and raises the breech-block to the closed position when the round is rammed home, thereby chambering the round and aligning the percussion mechanism for firing the gun.

The recoil mechanism is installed in the cradle of the mount and is a variable hydro-pneumatic shock absorber that decreases the energy of the recoil gradually and so avoids violent movement of the cannon or carriage.

The mount is a mobile four-wheel assembly which incorporates a rigid pedestal assembly, stabilised by four retractable outrigger assemblies, a rotating top carriage that permits full 360° traverse and an equilibrator assembly of the torsion spring type between the top carriage transoms that balances the cannon. A hydraulic lifting mechanism assembly permits lowering or raising of the mount in conjunction with removal or attachment of the front and rear bogie assemblies.

Ammunition is of the fixed type and is fed manually to two revolver type magazines each of which holds six rounds. The HE projectile weighs 5.7 kg and has a muzzle velocity of 854 m/s.

75 mm anti-aircraft gun M51 in firing position showing M4 tracking radar antenna aligned with gun (US Army)

The M51 is used in conjunction with the M38 Fire Control System, which consists of the M15 Director, M4 Tracking Radar (with a maximum range of 21 945 m and mounted on the left side of the carriage), M10 Ballistic Computer (mounted on the right side of the carriage), M16 Control Power and an M22 periscope which is kept continually aligned with the antenna of the radar scanner except in search. The gun may also be positioned on the target manually by means of handwheels, sighting being done by an auxiliary telescope M96 (azimuth) and M96C (elevation) which are parts of the M37 auxiliary sighting system. The M5 Target Selector is an auxiliary sighting device which is used to spot visible targets that present more of a threat than the one being engaged. A warning horn is sounded on the mount and the radar beam is automatically aligned to the new target.

SPECIFICATIONS

CALIBRE	75 mm
BARREL LENGTH	4.495 m
RECOIL	hydro-pneumatic, variable
BREECH MECHANISM	vertical sliding
CARRIAGE	4-wheeled with outriggers
WEIGHT	
travelling order	9480 kg
firing position	8750 kg
LENGTH TRAVELLING	6.603 m
WIDTH TRAVELLING	2.509 m
HEIGHT TRAVELLING	2.133 m
TYRES	11.00 × 20
ELEVATION/DEPRESSION	+85°/-6°
TRAVERSE	360°
RATE OF FIRE	45 rpm
MAX RANGE	
horizontal	13 000 m
vertical	9000 m
TOWING VEHICLE	M8 full tracked tractor

Status: Production complete. In service with Greece and Turkey.

40 mm Automatic Anti-aircraft Gun M1

Development
Before the Second World War the USA made a number of unsuccessful attempts to obtain a Swedish Bofors 40 mm anti-aircraft gun which had already been adopted by the British Army. Late in 1940 Bofors guns were obtained by the Ordnance Department and the Bureau of Ordnance of the Navy.

Trials showed that the 40 mm gun was superior to the 37 mm anti-aircraft gun which had been adopted in 1940 and was already entering production by Colt's Patent Fire Arms Manufacturing Company. At that time the United States Army did not adopt the Bofors although production was allowed in the USA to meet British requirements. Late in 1941 the 40 mm Automatic Gun T1 and the 40 mm Automatic Gun Carriage T1 were standardised as the 40 mm Automatic Gun M1 and the 40 mm Automatic Gun Carriage M1 as the replacement for the 37 mm weapon. In February 1941 Chrysler was awarded a contract to build two guns and the Firestone Tyre and Rubber Company was awarded a contract for two carriages. The carriage was very complicated to manufacture so the company redesigned it for large-scale manufacture as the M2. By late 1941 the 40 mm Bofors was in production in the USA and first production weapons were delivered early in 1942.

Further development of the M2 carriage to increase the tracking rate and improve the outriggers and the sight resulted in the M2A1, and later other minor changes were made to both the carriage and the gun.

A special model for air transport was developed called the M5 but none are known to be in service today. Late in the Second World War the M19 twin 40 mm self-propelled anti-aircraft gun based on the chassis of the M24 light tank was developed but none remain in service today. The M19 was replaced in the early 1950s by the M42 self-propelled anti-aircraft gun, which is essentially the same turret as mounted on the M19 fitted to a new chassis which shares many common components with the M41 light tank. Full details of the M42 are given in the *Self-propelled anti-aircraft guns* section.

Description
In the firing position the carriage is supported on four jacks, one at the front and one at the rear, and one each side on outriggers. During the Second World War the 40 mm anti-aircraft gun was normally used in conjunction with the British-designed Kerrison predictor which was also manufactured in the United States by the Singer Manufacturing Company of Elizabethport, New York, under the designation M5. The following types of ammunition, which are fed to the breech vertically in clips of four rounds, can be fired:

AP-T (M81 series) with the complete round weighing 2.077 kg, projectile weighing 0.89 kg and a muzzle velocity of 872 m/s. This will penetrate 52 mm of armour at an incidence of 0° at a range of 457 m, or 42 mm of armour at an incidence of 0° at a range of 914 m.

40 mm anti-aircraft gun M1 in travelling order

HE-T with the complete round weighing 2.15 kg, projectile weighing 0.935 kg, muzzle velocity of 880 m/s.
HEI-T with complete round weighing 2.15 kg and a muzzle velocity of 880 m/s.
TP-T(M91) with the complete round weighing 2.14 kg and a muzzle velocity of 872 m/s.

40 mm anti-aircraft gun M1 of Brazilian Army in firing position with wheels raised and 4-round clip ammunition in position above breech (Ronaldo S Olive)

SPECIFICATIONS

CALIBRE	40 mm
BARREL LENGTH (overall)	2.49 m
OPERATION	recoil
RECOIL	hydro-spring
BREECH MECHANISM	vertical sliding block
CARRIAGE	4-wheeled with outriggers
SHIELD	optional
WEIGHT (travelling order)	2656 kg
LENGTH (travelling)	5.728 m
WIDTH (travelling)	1.829 m
HEIGHT (travelling)	2.019 m
GROUND CLEARANCE	0.359 m
TYRES	6.00 × 20
ELEVATION/DEPRESSION	+90°/−11°
TRAVERSE	360°
RATE OF FIRE cyclic	120 rpm
practical	60 rpm
MAX RANGE horizontal	4753 m
vertical	4661 m
EFFECTIVE VERTICAL RANGE	2742 m
FEED	4 round clip
UNIT OF FIRE	200 rounds
CREW	4-6
TOWING VEHICLE	2½ ton (6 × 6) truck

Status: Production complete. In service with many countries including

Country	Quantity	User	Comment
Argentina	n/av	army	
Brazil	60	army	
Burma	18	army	status uncertain
Chile	n/av	army	status uncertain
Colombia	30	army	
Dominican Republic	10	air force	
Ecuador	30	army	
Greece	60	army	may now be in reserve
Guatemala	12	army	
India	1245	army	used with Super Fledermaus FCS, may use UK Mk 1 rather than M1
Indonesia	90+	army	
Iran	20-40	army	also used by Air Force, status uncertain
Korea, South	80+	army	
Peru	28	army	
Malaysia	24	army	may have been replaced by L/70
Norway	132	army	may be in reserve, 32 Air Force
Pakistan	60	army	
Paraguay	12	army	
Portugal	20-30	army	may be Swedish L/60
Taiwan	200	army	
Thailand	80	army	
Turkey	70	army	
Yugoslavia	128	army	may be UK Mk 1, status uncertain

M167 20 mm Vulcan Anti-aircraft Gun

Development

Development of the Vulcan Air-Defense system began under the direction of the United States Army Weapons Command at Rock Island Arsenal, Illinois, in 1964. Two versions of the Vulcan were subsequently developed, a self-propelled model called the M163 (development designation XM163) and a towed model called the M167 (development designation XM167). Prime contractor for both models is the Armament Systems Department of the General Electric Company of Burlington, Vermont.

After trials carried out by the United States Army Air Defense Board at Fort Bliss, Texas, and at Aberdeen Proving Ground, Maryland, in 1965, the system was accepted for service as the replacement for the 12.7 mm (quad) M55 anti-aircraft gun system. First production M167s were delivered to the United States Army in 1967 and since then the system has been adopted by a number of other countries. The current service model is the M167A1 which incorporates no fundamental changes from the M167. By early 1988 a total of 626 M167s had been built.

The M167 is deployed in the United States Army with the airborne and airmobile division, each of which has one battalion of M167s consisting of an HQ and HQ battery and four batteries. Each battery has a battery HQ and three firing platoons each with four M167 systems, giving the battalion 48 Vulcan weapons.

Description

The towed version of the Vulcan air-defence system is mounted on the M42A1 two-wheeled carriage and is a lightweight version of the M163 self-propelled system that is fully described in the *Self-propelled anti-aircraft guns* section. The M167 has the advantage of being helicopter

TOWED AA GUNS / USA

M167 20 mm Vulcan anti-aircraft gun, twin wheel configuration, in firing position showing generator on forward part of carriage, this model is fitted with Lockheed Electronics Company Product Improved Vulcan Air Defense System kit

transportable and can therefore be used in tactical situations where the tracked version cannot be employed.

The M167 consists of a 20 mm Vulcan gun, a linked ammunition feed system and a fire control system, all mounted in an electrically-powered turret. The towed M42A1 carriage has its own power generator for recharging mounted on the forward part of the carriage.

The six-barrelled 20 mm M168 cannon has two rates of fire, 1000 rds/min, normally used against ground targets and 3000 rds/min, normally used against aircraft. Maximum effective anti-aircraft range is 1200 m and maximum effective ground range is 2200 m. The gunner can select either 10, 30, 60 or 100 round bursts and the dispersion pattern can be increased by fitting a special muzzle spread which results in an increased hit probability. The ammunition container is on the left side and holds 300 or 500 rounds of ammunition. The 20 mm M168 cannon can fire the following types of fixed ammunition:

M53 (APT) with the projectile weighing 0.1 kg and a muzzle velocity of 1030 m/s.
M54 (HPT) with the projectile weighing 0.127 kg.
M55A2 (TP) with the projectile weighing 0.098 kg and a muzzle velocity of 1030 m/s.
M56A3 (HEI) with the projectile weighing 0.103 kg and a muzzle velocity of 1030 m/s.
M220 (TPT) with the projectile weighing 0.097 kg and a muzzle velocity of 1030 m/s.
M242 (HEIT) with the projectile weighing 0.094 kg and a muzzle velocity of 1030 m/s.

The fire control system consists of a gyro lead-computing gunsight, an EMTECH range-only radar (on the right side) and a sight current generator. The gunner visually acquires and tracks the target. The radar supplies range and range-rate data to the sight generator. These inputs

Basic Vulcan Air Defense System which has no range-only radar

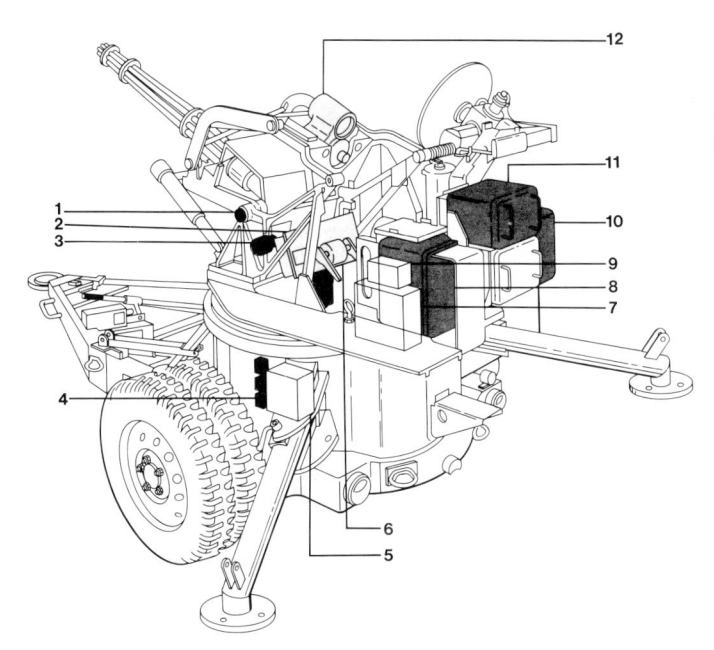

USA / **TOWED AA GUNS** 223

Key components of Lockheed Electronics Product Improved Vulcan Air Defense System (PIVADS) are (1) Elevation synchro (2) Control panel (3) Elevation drive (4) Servo amplifiers (three) (5) Distribution box (6) Azimuth drive (7) Electronics unit (8) Radar power supply (9) Voltage converter (10) Radar unit 2 (11) Radar unit 4 (12) Director gunsight

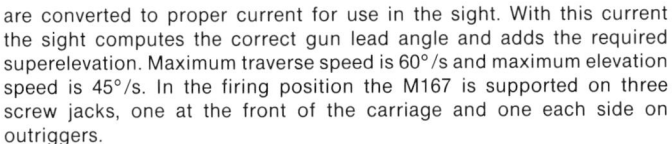

Basic Vulcan with dual wheels on tow by M715 (4 × 4) truck

are converted to proper current for use in the sight. With this current the sight computes the correct gun lead angle and adds the required superelevation. Maximum traverse speed is 60°/s and maximum elevation speed is 45°/s. In the firing position the M167 is supported on three screw jacks, one at the front of the carriage and one each side on outriggers.

The M167 system in US Army service is towed by the M561 (6 × 6) vehicle but trials have shown that it can also be towed by the M1069 High Mobility Multi-purpose Wheeled Vehicle.

Variants

PIVADS

Lockheed Electronics Company has developed an improved fire control system for the Vulcan system which includes a new optical sight, a digital processor and harmonic drives for azimuth and elevation. A director-type optical sight is provided as the angle tracking device which permits rapid acquisition and accurate tracking when turret disturbances are present. The sight contains integrating rate gyros for azimuth and elevation tracking, in conjunction with proportional hand-grip controls. A new digital processor replaces the existing analogue computer to improve weapon tracking and operational capabilities. The system also includes built-in test equipment and permits multiple ballistics selection via the operator control panel. System response and point accuracies are also improved with the new Lockheed Electronics system. Harmonic drives replace older azimuth and elevation gear trains to improve stiffness, backlash and power consumption characteristics. A test prototype, designated Product Improved Vulcan Air Defense System (PIVADS) was tested extensively by the US Army at Fort Bliss in June 1979. Late in 1982 the US Army awarded Lockheed Electronics a $19 million contract for the supply of 285 PIVADS kits for the 20 mm Vulcan Air Defense System in both towed and self-propelled configurations. Final deliveries were made in 1988. Of the 285 systems, 122 were for the towed M167 series and the remaining 163 for the M167 self-propelled systems.

Vulcan Stinger Hybrid

This private venture development is a Vulcan carriage carrying not only the 20 mm Vulcan anti-aircraft gun but also a pod mounted on the right-hand side of the carriage carrying four Stinger ground-to-air guided missiles. The fire control for this Vulcan Stinger Hybrid is based on the use of the Hughes Aircraft Company's Integrated Fire Control electro-optical sensor system instead of the usual Vulcan radar fire control. The Hughes system combines existing components from the M1 Abrams Thermal Imaging Sensor (TIS), a Maverick Missile Autotracker and a laser rangefinder already in production for the M65 Laser Augmented Airborne TOW anti-tank missile fire control system which includes a solid-state TV camera. This Integrated Fire Control Sensor is mounted in a

Basic Vulcan with dual wheels deployed in firing position

Phalanx stabilised gimbal platform produced by General Dynamics. The complete system allows day and night operation while the gunner has a video display for use as a sight. The video image control unit incorporates a laser rangefinder 'ARM' switch and the gun or missiles are fired using a foot pedal. It is possible that the current Nd/YAG laser will be replaced by an eyesafe laser.

The Vulcan Stinger Hybrid is still in the development stage and may also be used with the M163 self-propelled version of the Vulcan.

Basic Vulcan

This is a simplified version of the M167 Vulcan produced for commercial export sales. The basic changes are to the fire control system which does not use the range-only radar of the M167 but a range update computer, lead-computing gunsight and a control panel which includes burst length, estimated range and target speed settings, mode selection, and controls for positioning the electrically-powered turret.

Four operating modes are available to the gunner, range update, external range, fixed mode and ground.

With range update the gunner identifies the target visually, estimates the target speed, selects the burst length and predicted range at which he intends to open fire. These settings are made on the control panel.

TOWED AA GUNS / USA

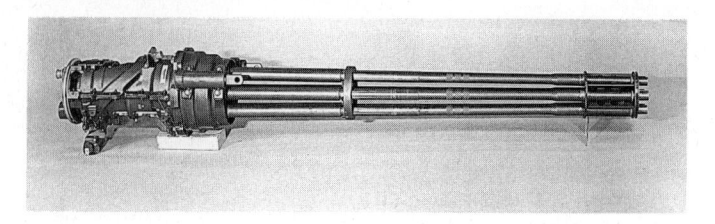

20 mm M168 Vulcan cannon which is used in both the M167 towed and M163 self-propelled air defence systems

Using the hand controls he moves the turret to acquire the target in the sight, keeping the sight gyro caged by using a button on the left hand grip. On acquisition, he releases the cage button and tracks the target using the centre of the sight graticule. After tracking the target to the pre-selected range the gunner opens fire. The computer then updates the range data automatically and supplies the system with the lead angles and super-elevation throughout the engagement.

In the external range mode an extra crew member signals the predicted range and signals the gunner to open fire. The extra crew member then updates the range setting via a hand-held external range unit.

In the fixed mode the lead computing gun sight is fixed with preset range and target speed.

In the ground mode the lead computing sight is mechanically caged so that the system is set for use at 1000 m range.

The rest of the Basic Vulcan is the same as the normal M167. The only data change is that the combat weight is reduced to 1406 kg.

Dual Wheel Vulcan

All US Army M167 Vulcans have been modified by the addition of a second road wheel on each side of the carriage. This increases cross-country performance. The extra wheel is available as a modification kit, and when fitted the combat weight of the M167A1 is increased to 1732 kg. The outside wheel track is then 2.271 m and the inside track 1.76 m.

SPECIFICATIONS

CALIBRE	20 mm
BARREL LENGTH	1.524 m
OPERATION	externally powered
CARRIAGE	2-wheeled with outriggers
SHIELD	no
WEIGHT	
travelling order	1588 kg
firing position	1565 kg
LENGTH (travelling)	4.9065 m
WIDTH (travelling)	1.98 m
HEIGHT	
travelling	2.038 m
firing	1.651 m
TRACK	1.7526 m
ELEVATION/DEPRESSION	+80°/-5°
TRAVERSE	360°
CYCLIC RATE OF FIRE	
low	1000 rpm
high	3000 rpm
MAX EFFECTIVE RANGE	
anti-aircraft	1200 m
ground	2200 m
CREW	1 (on mount)
TOWING VEHICLES	M715 (4 × 4) truck
	M561 (6 × 6) truck

Status: Production as required. In service with:

Country	Quantity	User	Comment
Belgium	36	army	without radar
Ecuador	28	army	
Israel	100	air force	airfield defence
Jordan	n/av	army	
Korea, South	66+	army	has been built locally
Morocco	70	army	delivered early 1980s
Somalia	n/av	army	
Sudan	n/av	army	
USA	220	army	122 being upgraded with PIVADS

Manufacturers: Armament Systems Department, General Electric Company, Lakeside Avenue, Burlington, Vermont 05401-4985, USA.
Telephone: (802) 657-6000
Telex: 510 299 0028

Daewoo Heavy Industries Limited, 6 Manseog-Dong, Dong-Gu, Inchon, South Korea.
Telephone: (132) 72-1011
Telex: K23301

12.7 mm (Quad) Anti-aircraft Machine Gun M55

Development
Development of the 12.7 mm (0.50) (Quad) Anti-aircraft Machine Gun M55 was begun in 1942 by the Kimberly-Clark Corporation and it entered service the following year. About 10 000 M55s were delivered to the US Army between 1943 and 1953, with the final contractor being the Bowen and McLaughlin Corporation. It has been replaced in the United States Army by the 20 mm M167 Vulcan anti-aircraft gun system.

Description
The full designation of the M55 is the Mount, Gun: Trailer, Multiple Calibre .50 Machine Gun, M55, and is composed of two main parts, the M45C Mount and the M20 Trailer.

The M45C Mount is a power-driven semi-armoured gun mount with a self-contained power unit. A power charger produces electrical current to be stored in two 6 V storage batteries on which the electrical system operates. The mount has four 12.7 mm (0.50) M2 HB machine guns, two each side. The early models have two M2 ammunition chests each side, but later mounts have the chests replaced by ammunition box trays.

Power is directed by a pair of control handles immediately in front of the operator's seat on the mount. The machine guns are fired by a solenoid and will continue to fire and load automatically as long as the gunner applies pressure to both the triggers on the control handles.

The gunner aims the weapons using an M18 reflex sight which projects a graticule image, focused at infinity, on an inclined glass plate. The graticule image consists of four concentric circles, corresponding to various aircraft speeds, and three dots on a vertical line in the centre of the field of view are used to determine line of sight and to compensate for gravity pull on the projectile. As the gunner looks through the plate he sees the target super-imposed on the graticule image. Turret traverse and gun elevation speeds are 60°/s.

The machine guns fire the following types of fixed ammunition:

Type	Designation	Projectile Weight	Muzzle velocity
AP	M2	45.88 or 46.53 g	885 m/s
API	M8	42.06 g	888 m/s
API-T	M20	39.66 g	888 m/s
Ball	M2	46.1 or 46.79 g	858 m/s
Ball	M33	42.9 g	888 m/s
Incendiary	M1	41.02 g	901 m/s
Incendiary	M23	33.18 g	1036 m/s
Training	M10	41.67 g	873 m/s
Training	M17	14.67 g	873 m/s
Training	M21	45.3 g	867 m/s

In the firing position the wheels are removed by using the three lifting jacks (one at the front and two at the rear of the carriage) and the complete unit is then lowered to the ground to provide a stable firing platform. The two-wheeled trailer M20 can be towed by a light 4 × 4 Jeep-type

USA / TOWED AA GUNS

12.7 mm (Quad) anti-aircraft machine gun M55 in firing position (US Army)

Belgian MAN (4 × 4) truck with 12.7 mm (quad) anti-aircraft machine gun M55 installed for airfield defence (C R Zwart)

vehicle, but its small diameter tyres allow it to be towed on roads at a maximum speed of only 16 km/h. Normally the trailer is carried in the rear of a 2½ ton (6 × 6) truck which is equipped with special loading and unloading equipment.

Variants
During the Second World War the M45 Mount was mounted on Trailer Mount M17 which in turn was mounted on the M51 four-wheel carriage, which could be towed by a 4 × 4 or 6 × 6 truck. Two self-propelled models were also built, the M16 which was based on the M3 half-track and the M17 based on the M5 half-track.

The MBT Division of Israel Aircraft Industries has developed a new model armed with twin 20 mm cannon called the TCM-20, details of which are given in this section under Israel.

Brazil has developed a modernised version of the M55, now in production. See entry under Brazil in this section.

SPECIFICATIONS

CALIBRE	12.7 mm
BARREL LENGTH	1.143 m
MUZZLE BRAKE	none
OPERATION	recoil, automatic
CARRIAGE	2-wheeled
SHIELD	yes
WEIGHT	
travelling order with trailer	1338 kg
firing position	975 kg (M45C only)
LENGTH (travelling)	2.89 m
WIDTH (travelling)	2.09 m
HEIGHT	
travelling	1.606 m
firing	1.428 m
GROUND CLEARANCE (travelling)	0.178 m
TRACK	1.524 m
ANGLE OF APPROACH/DEPARTURE	10°/20°
FORDING	0.457 m
ELEVATION/DEPRESSION	+90°/−10°
TRAVERSE	360°
RATE OF FIRE PER BARREL	
cyclic	450/550 rpm
practical	150 rpm
EFFECTIVE RANGE	
horizontal	1500 m
vertical	1000 m
FEED (per barrel)	210 round belt
CREW	4 (1 on mount)
TOWING VEHICLE	4 × 4 Jeep (normally carried on rear of 6 × 6 truck)

Status: Production complete. In service with the following countries:

Country	Quantity	User	Comment
Belgium	56	army	airfield defence
Brazil	n/av	army	some locally modified
Chile	n/av	army	
Denmark	n/av	army	status uncertain
Italy	109	army	status uncertain
Japan	280	army	some also used for airfield defence
Jordan	36	army	
Korea, South	n/av	army	locally built, also truck mounted
Mexico	40-50	army	
Norway	n/av	army	some used for air defence
Pakistan	45	army	
Portugal	18	army	
Spain	132	army	also Marines, some truck mounted
Thailand	n/av	army	
Turkey	160	army	
Yugoslavia	n/av	army	probably now in reserve

YUGOSLAVIA

20/3 mm M55 A2 Anti-aircraft Gun

Development
The 20/3 mm M55 A2 anti-aircraft gun forms the 'base' component of a family of three similar weapons all based on the same triple-gun mounting; the other two weapons are the M55 A3 B1 and the M55 A4 B1 (see following entries). The first 20/3 mm M55 guns were produced in 1955.

20/3 mm M55 A2 anti-aircraft gun in firing position

Description
Although many local modifications have been introduced since 1955, the 20/3 mm M55 A2 is basically a licence-built weapon comprising three Hispano-Suiza HSS-804 20 mm L/70 guns mounted on the HSS 630-3 towed carriage. (Hispano-Suiza is now part of the Oerlikon-Bührle Group.) The three guns are arranged on the mounting horizontally with the central gun positioned slightly to the rear of the two outboard guns; this allows the three 60 round drum magazines to be positioned close together for loading, and concentrates the three barrels. In action the carriage rests on three outrigger legs that are folded outwards into place, with the two carriage wheels raised off the ground. In an emergency the guns can be fired directly from the towed carriage. A spring suspension is used on the carriage which is equipped with a hydraulic system for the parking and automatic towing brakes. The weapon can be towed at speeds of up to 80 km/h by a light 4 × 4 truck.

The gunner, positioned behind the guns, aims manually with elevation and traverse handwheels and fires via a foot pedal. Two equilibrators are provided. For fire control the M55 A2 is fitted with a PANS-20/3 optical-mechanical automatic sight. The gunner inserts the target information which includes target range, course angle, angles of dive and climb, and target speed which is inserted in increments of 50 m up to 300 m/s. With the target information inserted the gunner can then track the target directly using the sight graticule. Targets flying at speeds up to 1000 km/h can be engaged at ranges up to 1500 m although for slower targets the effective range is 2000 m.

The ammunition used with the M55 gun family includes the following types:

TYPE	HEI-T	HE-T	HEI	HE	API	API-T	AP-T
DESIGNATION	M57	M57	M57	M57	M60	M60	M60
WEIGHT OF PROJECTILE	137 g	137 g	132 g	132 g	142 g	142 g	142 g
TYPE OF BURSTING CHARGE	TNT or RDX/Alum	TNT or RDX/Alum	TNT + Inc	TNT or RDX/Alum	nil	nil	nil
TOTAL WEIGHT OF ROUND	261 g	261 g	257 g	257 g	274 g	274 g	274 g
MUZZLE VELOCITY	850 m/s	850 m/s	850 m/s	850 m/s	840 m/s	840 m/s	840 m/s

Additional rounds include TP-T (M57), TP (M57), Blank (M77) and drill. All of the above have brass cartridge cases 110 mm long with propellant being NC powder.

SPECIFICATIONS
CALIBRE	20 mm
BARREL LENGTH	1.956 m
CARRIAGE	2-wheeled
SHIELD	no
WEIGHT	
with loaded drums	1100 kg
with empty drums	970 kg
LENGTH (travelling)	4.3 m
WIDTH (travelling)	1.27 m
HEIGHT (gun, travelling)	1.47 m
GROUND CLEARANCE	0.23 m
ELEVATION/DEPRESSION	+83°/-5°
TRAVERSE	360°
RATE OF FIRE PER BARREL (cyclic)	700 rpm
RATE OF FIRE (total, cyclic)	2100 rpm
FEED (per barrel)	60 round drum magazine
MAX RANGE	
horizontal	5500 m
vertical, under 80°	4000 m
EFFECTIVE RANGE	
horizontal	2500 m
vertical	2000 m
CREW	6
TOWING VEHICLE	AR-51 (4 × 4) truck

Status: In production. In service with Angola, Cyprus, El Salvador, Honduras, Lebanon, Mozambique, Yugoslavia, Zimbabwe and possibly some other countries.

Manufacturer: Federal Directorate of Supply and Procurement (SDPR), PO Box 308, 9 Nemanjina Street, Belgrade, Yugoslavia.
Telephone: 621 522
Telex: 11360

20/3 mm M55 A3 B1 Anti-aircraft Gun

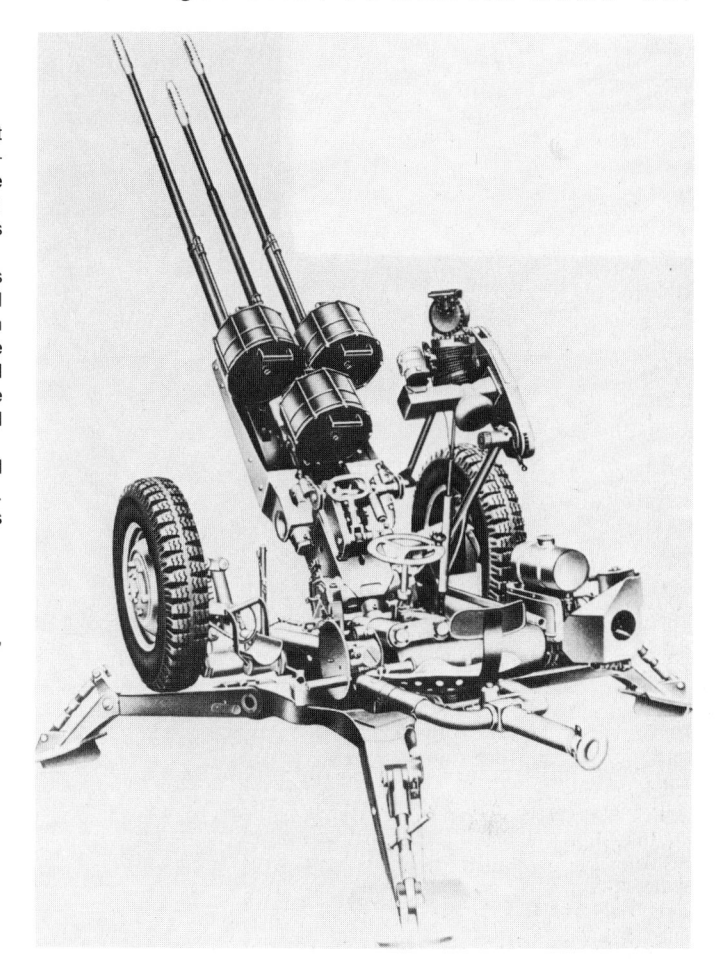

Development/Description

The 20/3 mm M55 A3 B1 anti-aircraft gun is a Yugoslavian-derived variant of the basic M55 A2 weapon. It uses the same locally-produced Hispano-Suiza HSS-804 20 mm L/70 guns in a triple arrangement and the carriage is derived from the HSS 630-3. The main change on the M55 A3 B1 is that a small Wankel engine has been added to the right of the gunner's position to provide power for both elevation and traverse.

The Wankel engine has a power output of 8 hp. Each chamber has a capacity of 160 cm^3 and consumes, on medium load, 2.4 litres of fuel an hour (the petrol/oil mix is 50:1). The power unit has three main components; the control unit which the gunner operates via a single joystick for both traverse and elevation, the transmission system, and the Wankel engine. In traverse the power unit can move the carriage at rates between 0.3 and 70°/s. In elevation the barrel can be moved at rates between 0.3 and 50°/s. Manual control is available.

In all other respects the M55 A3 B1 is the same as the M55 A2 and uses the same PANS-20/3 sighting system and ammunition types (qv). The only change is that the weight without the ammunition drums is 1150 kg and with all three loaded drums fitted the weight is 1235.5 kg.

Status: In production. In service with Yugoslavia.

Manufacturer: Federal Directorate of Supply and Procurement (SDPR), PO Box 308, 9 Nemanjina Street, Belgrade, Yugoslavia.
Telephone: 621 522
Telex: 11360

20/3 mm M55 A3 B1 anti-aircraft gun in firing position

20/3 mm M55 A4 B1 Anti-aircraft Gun

Development/Description

With the 20/3 mm M55 A4 B1 the Yugoslavian weapon designers have combined the established M55 triple-gun mounting with a local adaptation of the carriage and sighting system of the Hispano-Suiza HSS 666A (now the Oerlikon twin 20 mm GAI-D01 automatic anti-aircraft gun). While the three licence-built HSS-804 20 mm barrels have been retained, the M55 carriage has been much revised to accommodate a Wankel engine under the gunner's seat, a licence-built version of the Italian Officine Galileo P56 computer sight, a small shield and a compressed air system for firing the guns. The engine provides the power for a hydraulic drive system to move the carriage in both elevation and traverse. In action the maximum rate of motion of the carriage in both modes is up to 80°/s. Acceleration in traverse is 120°/s^2, and in elevation 60°/s^2.

Before the computer sight is used the target range and speed are inserted into the sight computer, the latter in speeds of up to 350 m/s, while the maximum range that can be inserted is 1200 m. The computer sight will then lay off automatically for traverse and angle of lead (up to 21°). The gunner controls the weapon aim by a joystick mounted on the console under the sight unit. For ground targets, the sight unit uses a separate sight with range divisions of 100 to 2500 m. The ground sight has a magnification of ×4 (the aircraft sight has a magnification of ×1.1). For rough alignment of the barrels with a target the gunner uses an open horizontal grid sight over the sight unit. Once the gun is roughly aligned he then uses the optical system of the computer sight.

The maximum towing speed of the M55 A4 B1 is 70 km/h.

The ammunition types used with the M55 A4 B1 are the same as those used with the M55 A2 (qv).

Although the M55 A4 B1 is intended for use as an autonomous weapon unit, it would require little modification to adapt it for use with a central fire control system.

The BOV-3 triple 20 mm self-propelled anti-aircraft gun system uses the 20/3 mm M55 A4 B1 system on a 4 × 4 armoured chassis. Details of this are given in the *Self-propelled anti-aircraft guns* section.

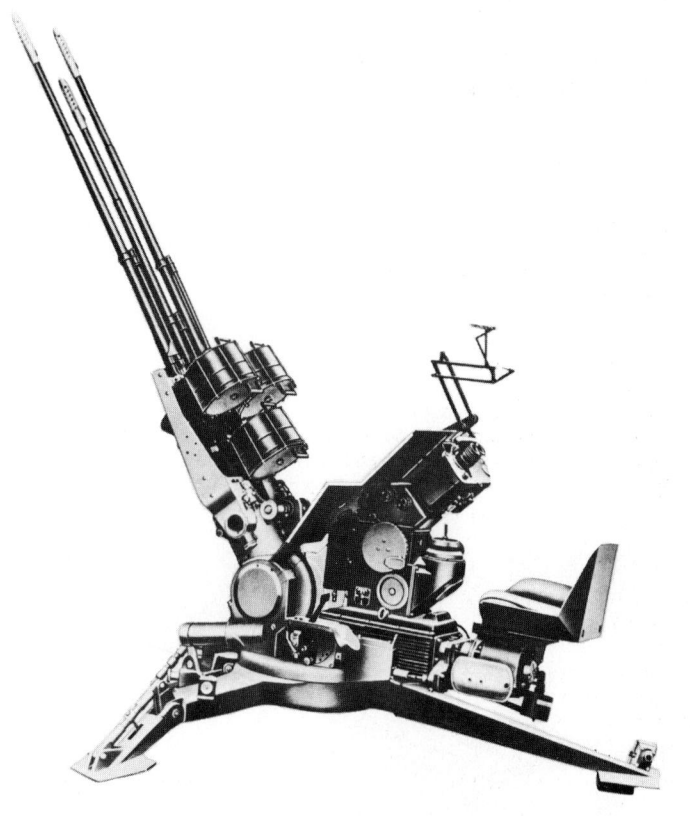

20/3 mm M55 A4 B1 anti-aircraft gun in firing position

TOWED AA GUNS / Yugoslavia

20/3 mm M55 A4 B1 anti-aircraft gun in travelling position

SPECIFICATIONS

CALIBRE	20 mm
BARREL LENGTH	1.956 m
CARRIAGE	2-wheeled
SHIELD	yes
WEIGHT	
travelling, less drums	1350 kg
in action loaded	1095.5 kg
carriage	300 kg
ELEVATION/DEPRESSION	+83°/-5°
TRAVERSE	360°
RATE OF FIRE PER BARREL (cyclic)	700 rpm
FEED (per barrel)	60 round drum magazine
MAX RANGE	
horizontal	5500 m
vertical, under 80°	4000 m
EFFECTIVE RANGE	
horizontal	2500 m
vertical	2000 m
CREW	6
TOWING VEHICLE	AR-51 (4 × 4) truck

Status: In production. In service with Yugoslavia.

Manufacturer: Federal Directorate of Supply and Procurement (SDPR), PO Box 308, 9 Nemanjina Street, Belgrade, Yugoslavia.
Telephone: 621 522
Telex: 11360

20/1 mm M75 Anti-aircraft Gun

Development
The 20/1 mm M75 anti-aircraft gun is a simple lightweight weapon mounting a single licence-produced HSS-804 20 mm L/70 gun and intended for infantry use against both air and ground targets. Although it looks like other similar weapons, the M75 is believed to be a completely Yugoslavian-designed product and mentions of its derivation from the Yugoslavian naval M74 20 mm gun have been made.

Description
The M75 is transported on a two-wheeled bogie which also carries ammunition and sight boxes. In action, the M75 can be emplaced by two men, and when the bogie is removed the gun rests on a tripod mounting with the actual carriage height being varied by the mounting feet angles; the rear tripod leg foot angle adjustment doubles as a variable height towing eye. For traverse the gunner pushes the gun round with his feet but for elevation a small handwheel is provided. The M75 is light enough to be carried in or on vehicles but can be stripped down for pack carriage on four animals in only 60 seconds. As the heaviest sub-assemblies weigh no more than 55 kg man-pack carriage is possible. Assembly and disassembly require no tools. The M75 may be fired direct from the bogie if necessary.

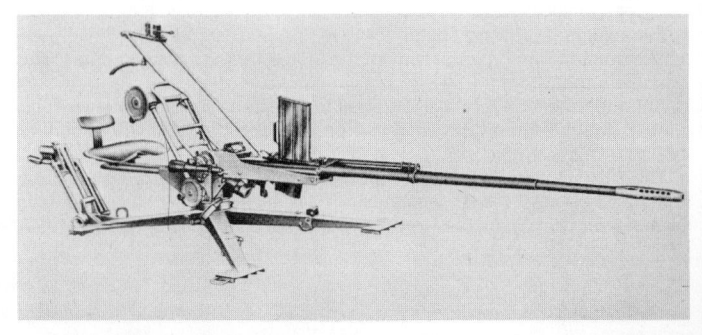

20/1 mm M75 anti-aircraft gun in travelling position

20/1 mm M75 anti-aircraft gun with box magazine in direct fire against ground target configuration

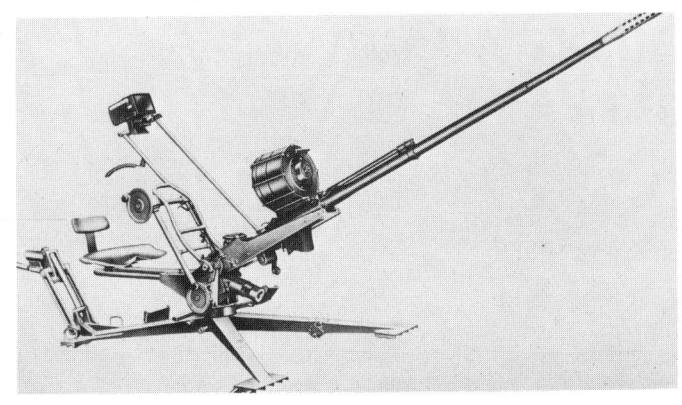

Yugoslavia / TOWED AA GUNS

The M75 can be fitted with a simple cartwheel sight for anti-aircraft use but the more usual sight is the M73, a reflex sighting device with a tritium source providing scale illumination. The M73 is calibrated for an average target range of 800 m and target speeds of 50, 100, 150, 200, 250 and 300 m/s, and uses an elliptical grid. For use against ground targets at ranges up to 1000 m a ×3.8 magnification sighting telescope is used.

The normal ammunition feed used on the M75 is a 60 round drum magazine but when using armour-piercing ammunition a 10 round box magazine may be used. The same ammunition as that used on the M55 family is fired:

TYPE	HEI-T	HE-T	HEI	HE	API	API-T	AP-T
DESIGNATION	M57	M57	M57	M57	M60	M60	M60
WEIGHT OF PROJECTILE	137 g	137 g	132 g	132 g	142 g	142 g	142 g
TYPE OF BURSTING CHARGE	TNT or RDX/Alum	TNT or RDX/Alum	TNT + Inc	TNT or RDX/Alum	nil	nil	nil
TOTAL WEIGHT OF ROUND	261 g	261 g	257 g	257 g	274 g	274 g	274 g
MUZZLE VELOCITY	850 m/s	850 m/s	850 m/s	850 m/s	840 m/s	840 m/s	840 m/s

Additional rounds include: TP-T (M57), TP (M57), Blank (M77) and drill. All of the above have brass cartridge cases 110 mm long with propellant being NC powder.

20/1 mm M75 anti-aircraft gun, with drum magazine, in normal firing position

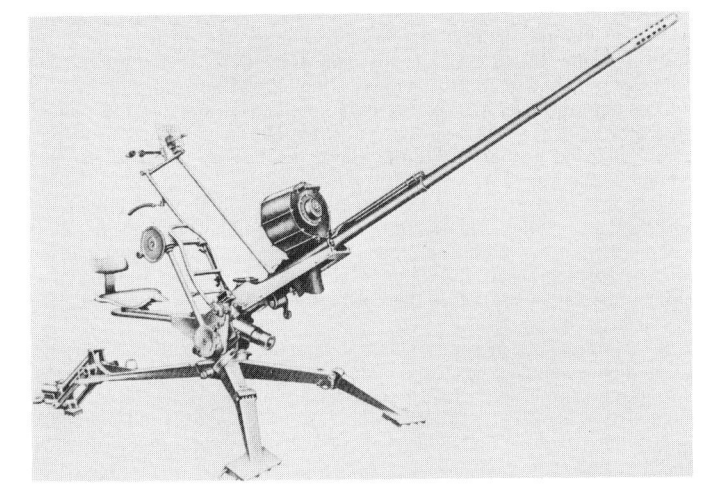

20/1 mm M75 anti-aircraft gun with carriage legs raised and fitted with drum magazine

SPECIFICATIONS

CALIBRE	20 mm
BARREL LENGTH	1.956 m
CARRIAGE	2-wheel bogie/tripod
SHIELD	no
WEIGHT (total)	260 kg
WIDTH	1.51 m
TRACK WIDTH	1.215 m
GROUND CLEARANCE (bogie)	0.215 or 0.315 m
ELEVATION/DEPRESSION	+83°/−10°
TRAVERSE	360°
RATE OF FIRE (cyclic)	700 rpm
FEED	60 round drum or 10 round box magazine
MAX RANGE	
horizontal	5500 m
vertical, under 80°	4000 m
EFFECTIVE RANGE	
aerial targets	2000 m
ground targets	1000 m plus
CREW	4-6
TOWING VEHICLE	light 4 × 4 truck or pack carriage

Status: In production. In service with Yugoslavia and Zambia.

Manufacture: Federal Directorate of Supply and Procurement (SDPR), PO Box 308, 9 Nemanjina Street, Belgrade, Yugoslavia.
Telephone: 621 522
Telex: 11360

Towed Anti-Aircraft Gun Sights

ITALY

Contraves Gun King Sight

Development

The Gun King computerised multi-divergence laser sighting system was developed as a private venture by Contraves for installation on a wide range of small- to medium-calibre air defence guns as well as self-propelled air defence systems. The Gun King can be installed on new weapons such as the Oerlikon-Bührle twin 35 mm GDF series or twin 25 mm Diana weapons, or retrofitted to older weapons such as the Soviet ZU-23 and Chinese twin 37 mm systems. By early 1989 over 300 Gun King sights had been ordered.

Description

The Gun King sight has five key components: a periscope with a laser rangefinder as a tracking unit; a collimator for autonomous target acquisition; an operator's control unit; a sight electronics unit with a computer and the servo system and drives.

Once the target has been found by means of an external search radar or the collimator, the operator tracks it through the periscope. The integrated laser rangefinder measures the target distance continuously to provide three-dimensional information to the computer system.

There is a common optical path in the periscope for the laser beam and for the operator's line-of-sight. Spectral beam splitting is effected by a system of lenses and prisms, specially coated to ensure operator safety. For engaging ground targets, the laser beam is narrowed to eliminate terrain clutter and for training purposes a TV camera may be mounted on a periscope. All information relating to meteorological parameters and muzzle velocity is entered into the computer via a keyboard and an alphanumeric display to compensate for its influence on the intercept calculation point. This enables the operator to concentrate on target tracking once the weapon is in position.

The gun and sight are operated by a control yoke which provides full hands-on control since all actuators are integrated in the yoke grips. The Gun King allows computer assisted tracking of the target and the operator only has to control the gun if the target manoeuvres.

The high speed computer not only calculates all of the fire control data and ballistics, but also the gun drive electronics. At the moment of optimum hit probability, the operator receives an acoustic alarm to commence firing.

For control, modern DC power electronics and high performance DC servo drives are used. The DC power supply is fitted with buffer batteries to smooth out transient peak loads. The battery capacity ensures full operational readiness of the complete system and up to five combat cycles can be accomplished before the power supply engine has to be started to recharge the batteries.

Monitoring of the system function is effected on-line, even during the combat phase and a quick test enables functional checking of the system during start up. When a fault does occur, the faulty Line Replacement Unit (LRU) is localised with the memory resident functional and diagnostic unit without external aids. The faulty LRU is then substituted in the field and returned to the rear for repair.

Close up of Contraves Gun King sight installed on Oerlikon-Bührle GDF series twin 35 mm anti-aircraft gun system

Close up of Contraves Gun King sight from front

Italy / TOWED AA GUN SIGHTS

Status: In production. In service with undisclosed countries.

Manufacturer: Contraves Italiana SpA, Via Affile, 102, 00131 Rome, Italy.
Telephone: (06) 43611
Telex: 610166 CONITA I

Egyptian built ZU-23 twin 23 mm light anti-aircraft gun system fitted with Contraves Gun King sight

Officine Galileo P56 Optical Sight and Fire Control System

Development
In 1960 Officine Galileo started development work on a new anti-aircraft fire control system called the P36. Development was completed in 1962, with first production systems being completed in 1963 and a total of 800 units were subsequently built before production ended.

The P36 was replaced by the P56, on which development work commenced in 1970. Development was completed in 1972 and production commenced the same year. By early 1989 a total of 3800 units had been completed. Further development of the P56 has resulted in the Galileo Vanth MA and MB systems for which there are separate entries.

Description
The P56 is a computing sight designed for installation on light anti-aircraft guns to enable them to engage accurately low and very low flying targets attacking at high speed (up to 350 m/s). In addition it is suitable to engage ground targets at a range of up to 4000 m.

The P56 has been installed on a wide range of weapons including GIAT twin 20 mm 76T2, Bofors 40 mm L/60, Oerlikon-Bührle GAI-D02, Rheinmetall Rh 202, ESD twin 20 mm turret on Panhard M3 (4 × 4) chassis and on some Yugoslav 20 mm weapons.

The P56 system is directly mounted on the gun and as it has its own power supply, it is a fully autonomous weapon.

The P56 comprises an open sight for the acquisition of the target, an optical sight for tracking, a joystick, a panel on which the estimated parameter of target speed and crossing range are introduced to feed

Yugoslav triple 20 mm anti-aircraft gun Type 20/3 M55 A4 B1 showing P56 sight and engine mounted under gunner's seat

Officine Galileo P56 sight showing gunner's eye piece and joystick

232 TOWED AA GUN SIGHTS / Italy

the computer, an electronic computer for continuous computation of lead angles, both in azimuth and elevation and an AC generator which is driven by an engine mounted under the gunner's seat.

With an optional kit, crossing range is automatically computed and as a consequence, only one parameter – the speed of the target – must be estimated and introduced.

The gunner tracks the target in the centre of the graticule by moving the joystick, and the computer controls both the line of sight and the line of fire, computing the lead angles continuously. The target is aligned with the centre of the graticule, while the gun is aiming at the future point.

A typical target engagement sequence is as follows. The gunner estimates the target parameters and acquires the target. Target parameters are introduced into the P56; he then tracks the target and opens fire.

Officine Galileo P56 sight from front

SPECIFICATIONS

MAGNIFICATION	×5
FIELD OF VIEW	12°
MAX LEAD ANGLES	21°
COMPUTER TARGET SPEED	up to 350 m/s
COMPUTER CROSSING RANGE	up to 1500 m for 40 mm gun
COMPUTER RANGE GROUND TARGETS	
20 mm gun	up to 2500 m
40 mm gun	up to 4000 m
HYDRAULIC SERVOS	
elevation	-3.5° to +81.5°
azimuth	360°
MAX SPEED	
elevation	up to 55°/s
azimuth	up to 80°/s
MAX ACCELERATION	
elevation	75-120°/s^2
azimuth	120-180°/s^2
ENGINE POWER	7 hp
WEIGHT	250 kg

Status: Production as required. In service with many countries.

Manufacturer: Officine Galileo, Military Systems Division, Via A Einstein, 35 - 50013 Campi Bisenzio (Florence), Italy.
Telephone: (055) 89501
Telex: 570126 GALILE I
Fax: (055) 8950600

Officine Galileo Vanth MA/40 Optical Sight and Fire Control System for Bofors 40 mm L/60 Gun

Development
Development of the Vanth MA/40 started in 1984 and was completed in 1985. Production commenced in 1986 and by early 1989 some 510 units had been completed, with production continuing. This sight forms part of the FN HERSTAL (S.A.) upgrade package for the Bofors 40 mm L/60 anti-aircraft gun which is fully described in the *Towed anti-aircraft guns* section under Belgium.

The Vanth MA/40 is essentially a technically modernised Officine Galileo P56 sight (qv) for installation on the well known Bofors 40 mm L/60 towed anti-aircraft gun.

Description
As originally built, the Bofors 40 mm L/60 towed anti-aircraft gun has a very low hit probability against aircraft flying at speeds of 150 to 350 m/s.

Its manual operation is not only too slow, but its accuracy is poor due to the mechanical aiming system being continuously adjusted by the gun layer during tracking. The four people required on the weapon during operations are yet a further complication to the already complicated slow gun motions.

When fitted with the Officine Galileo Vanth MA/40 fire control system, the Bofors 40 mm L/60 is provided with speed in elevation and traverse to permit tracking of the fastest aerial targets with the best aiming and firing accuracy.

The optics of the Vanth MA/40 allows for continuous target aiming in the centre of the optical field with provision being made for an independent line of sight.

Hydraulics controlling elevation and traverse allow for very good acceleration and gun motion accuracy, while the electronics provide a precise computation of the lead angles. According to Officine Galileo, the upgrading cost of eight Bofors 40 mm L/60 guns fitted with the Vanth MA/40 is definitely lower than purchasing a brand new 35 mm or 40 mm fire control system. In addition, the defence provided by a battery of Bofors L/60 guns upgraded with the Vanth MA/40 may be considered more convenient than a number of weapons controlled by a single fire control system.

The main advantages of the upgraded Bofors 40 mm L/60 weapon can be summarised as follows: reduction in time needed to bring the weapon into action, greater survivability of the weapon and greater possibility of engaging multiple threats. It also has reduced manning requirements as only one man is required to control the weapon and another to act as loader.

The main components of the Vanth MA/40 are the optical sight, data introduction panel, electronic computer and hydraulic drive.

Target acquisition is made by the operator with the aid of an open sight which is mechanically connected with the gun elevation. Once the target is aimed at through the open sight, it is acquired in the optical sight, which permits a magnified field-of-view of the target. As it is provided with an independent line-of-sight, it keeps the target aiming in the centre of the optical field, even during lead angle computation and firing.

Two knobs are provided on the data introduction panel for target speed and crossing range introduction into the computer, according to the data provided for the gunner by the search radar, or estimated by the commander. A third knob permits target range to be introduced when engaging ground targets.

Lead angles are computed according to target speed, and crossing range either comes from a search radar or are estimated as constant parameters, rate of change of the line of sight and range table.

The hydraulic drive consists of two independent channels providing for local power control of the gun traverse and elevation angles. The rate of change of traverse and elevation angles is controlled by a joystick that is provided with 2° freedom. In an emergency, hand wheels are used to move the weapon manually in both elevation and traverse.

The Vanth MA/40 has been designed for installation on the weapon to be independent of any external power sources with the petrol engine, which is on the right side of the mount, being mechanically linked to the Vanth MA/40 hydraulics.

The modifications to the Bofors 40 mm L/60 to install the Vanth MA/40 system include reinforcement of the platform on which the Vanth MA/40 and loader protection have to be installed, two reduction gears and

Italy / **TOWED AA GUN SIGHTS** 233

Officine Galileo Vanth/MA system installed on platform of Bofors 40 mm L/60 weapon with sight on left and petrol engine on right

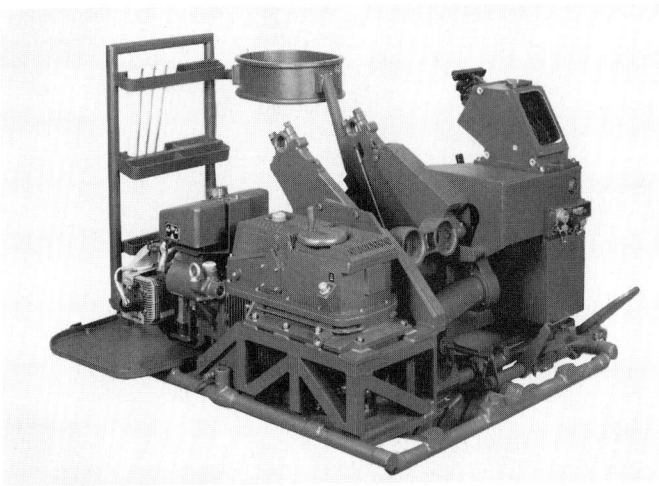

Officine Galileo Vanth/MA system installed on platform of Bofors 40 mm L/60 weapon from front with sight on right

relevant boxes for mechanical connection of the fire control systems outputs with the elevation and traverse gun movements, modification to the fire pedal, installation of a metal bar to stop the loader from falling during accelerations in target tracking or target designation and finally two electrical connection boxes. Options include an ammunition reservoir and protection shields.

The Vanth MA/40 can be automatically designated by a search radar, as provision is made for an electronic interface. According to the type of radar, the sight can automatically receive the crossing range and target speed parameters required for lead angle computation. This information can be provided by radio or phone or supplied directly to the computer.

Bofors 40 mm L/60 anti-aircraft gun upgraded by FN HERSTAL (S.A.) and fitted with Officine Galileo Vanth/MA system

SPECIFICATIONS
MAGNIFICATION	×5
FIELD OF VIEW	12°
MAX LEAD ANGLES	21°
COMPUTER TARGET SPEED	
min	60 m/s
max	350 m/s
COMPUTER CROSSING RANGE	
min	100 m
max	1500 m
HYDRAULIC SERVOS	
elevation	−3.5° to +81.5°
azimuth	360°
MAX SPEED	
elevation	up to 55°/s
azimuth	up to 70°/s
MAX ACCELERATION	
traverse	95°/s^2
elevation	80°/s^2
WEIGHT	250 kg

Status: Production. In service with undisclosed countries.

Manufacturer: Officine Galileo, Military Systems Division, Via A Einstein, 35 - 50013 Campi Bisenzio (Florence), Italy.
Telephone: (055) 89501
Telex: 570126 GALILE I
Fax: (055) 8950600

Officine Galileo Vanth/MB Optical Sight and Fire Control System for Anti-aircraft Guns

Development
In 1975 Officine Galileo started development of a new anti-aircraft sight called the P75. Development of this was completed in 1977 and it entered production the following year. Further development of this from 1986 resulted in the Vanth/MB whose development was completed in 1987 with production commencing in 1988. By early 1989 over 80 units had been completed and production was continuing.

The Vanth/MB system has been designed for installation on towed anti-aircraft guns with calibres from 20 to 40 mm, including the Rheinmetall Rh 202 (twin 20 mm), Oerlikon-Bührle Diana (twin 25 mm), Bofors 40 mm L/60 and L/70, Chinese single and twin 37 mm and the Breda Sentinel (twin 30 mm).

Description
The base model of the Vanth family consists of three main sub-assemblies; optical head, main structure and electro-hydraulic servo system. This enables fully automatic computation to take place, based on laser ranging, local control with remote designation (radar or optical) and integrated autotest.

The optical head integrates the visual and laser (plus optional TV) channels into a single input/output optical path to ensure the necessary parallelism. The independent line-of-sight is an important advantage as it allows the operator to keep the target in the centre of the reticle at all times, while the gun leads automatically. The laser rangefinder

234 TOWED AA GUN SIGHTS / Italy-Sweden

incorporated is of the Nd/YAG type with high repetition and accuracy.

The main structure is located below the optical head and comprises a control joystick, manual manoeuvring and a microprocessor computer. The latter performs all the fire computations at high speed as well as taking into account the ballistic data when required. It controls and manages the operation of all the basic functions (optical sight, laser rangefinder and servos) as well as of the optional sensors and accessory functions (BITE, training and taboo arcs).

In addition, it permits the reconfiguration of system operation from the basic level, both upwards, by addition of optional modules and downwards, as a back-up in case of partial failures. In the event of a laser failure, effective fire is still possible by using the estimated target speed.

The electro-hydraulic servo system is mounted below the main structure and ensures very high performance in terms of speed, acceleration and aiming accuracy, which means very small dynamic error, even during firing.

Sight and gun control is done by the operator through a 2° of freedom joystick. In the back-up mode, control is manual by means of hand wheels.

As the Vanth/MB is modular, it can be easily expanded to meet specific user requirements. Options include remote control by an external fire control system, firing taboo arc setting, parallax and ballistic introduction, integrated training system, automatic TV tracking and a night operation capability using an infra-red module.

Officine Galileo Vanth/MB sight installed on Breda twin 30 mm Sentinel mount before installation on trailer carriage

Status: In production. In service with undisclosed countries.

Manufacturer: Officine Galileo, Military Systems Division, Via A Einstein, 35 - 50013 Campi Bisenzio (Florence), Italy.
Telephone: (055) 89501
Telex: 570126 GALILE I
Fax: (055) 8950600

SWEDEN

Bofors Aerotronics UTAAS Fire Control System for Anti-aircraft Guns

Development

The UTAAS fire control concept is a further development of well proven fire control systems produced by Bofors Aerotronics for the home and export markets. According to Bofors, the prime objective has been to increase cost-efficiency by maintaining a high degree of performance at reduced cost.

The first self-propelled application for this system is the 40 mm air defence version of the Combat Vehicle 90 family of vehicles being developed to meet the requirements of the Swedish Army.

Description

Like all Bofors Aerotronic systems, the UTAAS is based on the principle of an independent line-of-sight. This means that the gunner only has to control the line-of-sight. The gun is aimed-off with reference to the line-of-sight, the aiming mark remains steady on target, while the gun moves to the correct superelevation and lead angles.

UTAAS is especially suitable for the retrofit of guns and armoured fighting vehicles. The towed application of the system is in the upgrade kits for the Bofors 40 mm L/60 and L/70 guns, but it can be fitted on a wide range of other air defence weapons, towed and self-propelled, including 37 mm Chinese weapons.

The main components of the UTAAS are the U-sight (U for universal), operator's panel, operator's handle and the U-fire control computer.

The U-sight itself is fitted with a top mirror which is servo-controlled from the fire control computer to accomplish the independent line-of-sight. The weapon is automatically laid with no re-aiming required.

The full ballistic solution is computed based on range to the target, speed and elevation, including compensation for meteorological conditions and barrel wear. During tracking, target range is repeatedly updated.

The UTAAS anti-aircraft version significantly increases hit probability and final intercept range is further extended when used to upgrade in-service weapons, such as Bofors 40 mm L/60 and L/70 weapons. Kill probability increases by about 50 per cent at an intercept range of 3000 m when firing a two second burst with Bofors PFHE (Pre-formed High Explosive) ammunition at an attack aircraft crossing at a range of 2000 m.

The UTAAS fire control system provides search radar interface, optical target designator interface and magnification, with field-of-view optimised for easy target detection and target acquisition, line-of-sight aiming and laser ranging via a servo-controlled mirror, automatic gun

Bofors Type U Universal fire control system installed on a towed anti-aircraft gun with sight on top and operator's console below

laying to aim-off direction, digital computation of the ballistic equations and track-while-fire capability.

The system has been designed for ease of operation and once the system has entered into its target-acquisition mode, either by the gunner's designation of the target directly to the system or by using input from a radar or optronic sensor, the gunner only has to make minor corrections and start lasing. Lasing continues as the gun lays automatically. Indicators in the eyepiece tell the gunner when to open fire. Typical target engagement time is normally six seconds.

As UTAAS is a modular design, several options are available. These include video output from the sight, night capability by using thermal imaging or image intensification, stabilisation to compensate for ship or vehicle movement and alternative laser rangefinders.

A training facility forms an integral part of the fire control system software to provide the operator with a means to improve his tracking skill.

SPECIFICATIONS

OPTICAL UNIT
magnification ×7
field of view 8°

MIRROR HEAD
elevation −10° to +60°
lead angle ±20°

LASER UNIT
type Nd/YaG
repetition rate 5 pps
range 300-9995 m

U-FIRE CONTROL COMPUTER
range 300-9995 m (autofed input)
number of ammunition types 6 (manual input)
muzzle velocity, relative nominal −120 to +70 m/s (manual/autofed input)
air temperature −40 to +60°C (manual/autofed input)
air pressure −30 to +10 kPa (manual/autofed input)
powder temperature −40 to +60°C (manual/autofed input)
wind 0 to 30 m/s (manual/autofed input)

Status: Development complete. Ready for production.

Manufacturer: Bofors Aerotronics AB, S-181 81 Lidingo, Sweden.
Telephone: (46) 87316000
Telex: 19188 bofaero s
Fax: (46) 7659265

Saab LVS-A Anti-aircraft Gun Sight

Development

The LVS-A anti-aircraft gun sight has been developed as a private venture by Saab Instruments, part of the Combitech Group, to enable existing anti-aircraft guns to be upgraded at a low cost. Two versions have been developed; the LVS-A for installation on servo-controlled guns and the LVS-M for manually directed guns.

The main features of the Saab LVS-A can be summarised as follows; it measures the 3D target trajectory independently from gun movements, computes aim-off angles digitally, controls gun direction automatically and has a short reaction time. Little modification is required in order to fit the anti-aircraft sight system and little training required.

Description

The LVS-A anti-aircraft gun sight comprises two main components; the target acquisition and tracking unit (TAU) and the computer control unit (CCU).

The operator acquires and tracks the target using the TAU and during this phase all of the data required to determine the 3D target trajectory and velocity is collected.

During the coarse initial tracking phase, the gun is automatically slaved to the TAU sight line and in the final tracking phase, when the target is normally within range, the gun is automatically steered to computed aim-off angles relative to the actual sight line.

Status: Prototypes.

Manufacturer: Saab Instruments AB, Box 1017, S-551 11, Jonköping, Sweden.
Telephone: (46) 36 19 40 00
Telex: 7005 saabjkg s
Fax: (46) 36 16 41 06

Weibull Anti-aircraft Sights

Development

J L Weibull started development work on sight systems in 1970, although well before this date they had become involved in power-laying systems for various weapons. Today, the company manufactures two types of reflex sights; a small one with one graticule and a larger one with four different graticules. These sights can also form part of the company's upgrade packages for anti-aircraft guns such as the Bofors 40 mm L/60, which is fully covered in the *Towed anti-aircraft guns* section.

According to the manufacturer, the Swedish Coastal Artillery has mounted J L Weibull sights on all of their anti-aircraft guns from the 7.62 mm machine gun up to the Bofors 40 mm (both L/60 and L/70). Training of the gunners is so similar as their sights are similar, that gunners can easily be transferred from one type of weapon to another with little additional training being required. The Swedish Army also uses a J L Weibull reflex sight on the 20 mm turret fitted to its Pbv 302 armoured personnel carriers.

Description

Ring Sight

A typical ring sight system for example, that fitted to the Bofors 40 mm L/70 weapon consists of a diopter with a diameter of approximately 3 mm and a sight with four concentric rings which have a radius of 15, 25, 50 and 100 mm each for the measurement of angles.

When aiming at a moving target, the eye, the diopter, the chosen set-

Pbv 302 APC with 20 mm turret fitted with J L Weibull anti-aircraft sight

forward point in the sight and the target must be aligned in order to get a hit. For the choice of the correct set-forward point in the sight, the gunner must consider the course, speed and distance of the target as well as the parameters of the weapon.

Speed and distance must be estimated by the gun-layer himself and he must then calculate the set-forward point in the sight. The course is obtained by letting the target fly towards the centre of the sight. This is correct when the firing distance is equal to the adjustment distance.

236 TOWED AA GUN SIGHTS / Sweden-Switzerland

J L Weibull reflex anti-aircraft sight

J L Weibull reflex anti-aircraft sights on 40 mm anti-aircraft gun

Reflex Sight

This is equipped with four different graticules mounted on a revolving disc. Two of these are intended for air combat, one for fast moving targets and the other for slow moving targets. One is designed for sea target combat (and is also suitable for ground targets) and one graticule corresponds to the standard ring sight.

Centre-aimed Sight System

In the centre-aimed sight system, the Reflex sight (with cross-hairs graticule) is mounted onto a rotating table on a sight arm on the gun. The rotating table supports the sensors measuring the movement vertically and laterally. The sensors transmit the data to an onboard computer that also receives data from a rangefinder (radar or laser) mounted on the gun. As the gunner aims at the target, keeping it in the centre of the sight, the computer processes the sensor data and range data to calculate the required lead angle and drive the rotating table in both axes to the correct aim-off point. The gunner then places his cross-hairs (the centre of the sight) back over the target and fires.

Status: Production. In service with Sweden and other armed forces.

Manufacturer: J L Weibull AB, PO Box 43, S-232 02, Akarp, Sweden.

SWITZERLAND

Kern Block Sight FERO-Z 13

Development

The Block Sight FERO-Z 13 has been developed by Kern and Co for installation on light anti-aircraft guns such as the Norwegian 20 mm automatic anti-aircraft gun FK 20-2 used by the West German and Norwegian armed forces, although it is also suitable for a wide range of similar weapons including 25 mm types.

Description

The Kern Block Sight FERO-Z 13 is a combined sighting telescope that is equally suitable for engaging both air and ground targets.

On the front of the sight is the ground/air target firing changeover lever and the actuation of this causes the block sight to change over from the ground target firing mode to the air target firing mode or vice versa, with the optical data and graticule image being changed each time.

On the left side of the sight is the flying speed changeover lever. The flying speeds determined by the gunner are pre-selected on the changeover lever and fixed with a detent. With the speed settings at 0 in the case of a dive approach, 250, 600 and 900 km/h, the lead curve moves downwards with increasing barrel elevation.

With the upper air target ocular, the target image appears 1.5 times magnified in the ocular image plane. The ocular can be adjusted by ±3 diopters to compensate for subjective ametropia.

In the lower ground target ocular, the target image is magnified five times in the ocular image plane and the ocular can be adjusted by ±3 diopters to compensate for subjective ametropia.

For infantry applications, the magnification and light gathering power of the optical system simplifies firing at poorly visible targets. The graticule of the ground target sight consists of simple cross wires with lead marks for firing distances of 500, 1000 and 1500 m with the horizontal axis having mm graduation.

The graticule of the air target sight consists of a system of fixed flight direction lines together with a lead line that is functionally related to flying speed and barrel elevation. This principle provides a simple sight image and optimum sighting accuracy for aimed firing bursts at approaching aircraft.

The lead curve moves as a function of barrel elevation and flying speed and is produced by a control cam. This allows for the variable parameters of differing flight situation as well as for ballistic values. The approximately elliptical lead curve is computed from the variable parameters of differing flight situations.

Switzerland-UK / TOWED AA GUN SIGHTS

The graticule of the ground sight can be illuminated by means of an attachable illumination device.

The sight is also provided with an easily exchangeable desiccant cartridge which is screwed into a flange and this prevents condensation inside of the instrument.

SPECIFICATIONS

	ground target	air target
MAGNIFICATION	×5	×1.5
ENTRANCE PUPIL DIAMETER	35 mm	10.5 mm
EXIT PUPIL DIAMETER	7 mm	7 mm
DISTANCE OF EXIT PUPIL	32.5 mm	32.5 mm
FIELD-OF-VIEW AT 1000 m	200 m	700 m
FIELD-OF-VIEW	11.3°	39.4°
ELEVATION RANGE	−10 to +80°	−10 to +80°
OPERATING RANGE	−54 to +60°	
WEIGHT	18 kg	
HEIGHT	463 mm	
WIDTH	183 mm	
LENGTH	395 mm	

Status: In production. In service with West German and Norwegian armed forces.

Manufacturer: Kern and Company Limited, CH-5001 Aarau, Switzerland. Telephone: (064) 251111

Norwegian 20 mm automatic anti-aircraft gun FK 20-2 fitted with the Kern Block Sight FERO-Z 13

UNITED KINGDOM

British Aerospace (Dynamics) Air Defence Gun Sight

Development

The Air Defence Gun Sight has been developed as a private venture by British Aerospace (Dynamics) and was shown for the first time in 1988. It has been designed as a low cost computer-controlled gun sight which can be easily fitted to existing weapons in the 20 mm to 57 mm range, for example the Bofors 40 mm L/70 used by many countries around the world.

The sight is capable of being operated by one man and can be fitted with minor modifications to most servo-assisted and manually operated ground or naval guns that use a single layer.

The sight is designed for engagements against crossing or directly attacking aircraft at speeds of up to 300 m/s at ranges out to 4000 m.

Description

The fire control system consists of the following major components; laser rangefinder/sight, sight platform, electronic unit, control and display unit, operator controls and training simulator.

The laser rangefinder/sight serves three functions; ranging the target, providing the aiming mark and providing quality optics and magnification for smoother tracking.

The rangefinder is a modified handheld monocular unit which is of modular design, making it possible to use a thermal imager/rangefinder combination for 24 hour clear weather operation.

The rangefinder is a modified hand-held monocular unit which is of modular design, making it possible to use a thermal imager/rangefinder combination for 24 hour clear weather operation.
the existing sight arm and sight.

The platform contains a two axis rate-gyro, two angle pick-offs, an elevation sensor, two gearboxes and their associated servo motors. The rate-gyro is mounted with its spin axis parallel to the laser axis and provides the computer with target angular rates. The gyro is also used to maintain a measure of elevation and bearing of the barrel for wind drift and gravity drop compensation.

The electro unit contains the power supplies, servo electronics, microprocessor and signal processing electronics.

Bofors 40 mm L/70 anti-aircraft gun fitted with British Aerospace (Dynamics) Air Defence Gun Sight on left side of mount

The control and display unit is small and is used for mode selection, data entry and calibration and allows for the following major items of data to be inserted: ammunition type, air temperature, barometric pressure, wind direction, wind speed, humidity and variations in muzzle velocity.

The operator controls are used for setting of the main operational modes and for changing the target.

The simulator injects the image of a target into the sight. Sight super-elevation and aim-off are generated to give a realistic engagement sequence. A more sophisticated digital simulator is available if required.

A typical target engagement sequence is as follows:
1) Target is detected
2) Layer lays the gun using a wide angle mechanical sight mounted on the laser rangefinder/sight

TOWED AA GUN SIGHTS / UK

3) Layer tracks the target through the rangefinder/sight and identifies aircraft as hostile
4) Layer fires the laser rangefinder and range data is obtained
5) Aim-off is automatically applied to the gun barrel and when applied is confirmed to the layer by a light indication
6) A flashing light in the sight indicates to the layer that the target is in range
7) Layer fires the gun.

The accuracy of the total weapon system is a function of ballistic dispersion, performance of the layer and the inherent accuracy of the sight. The accuracy of the sight alone, against an aircraft at a range of 4000 m is such that 95 per cent of the rounds will fall within 2 mils of the desired point of impact.

Engagement time against an aircraft flying at a range of 4000 m will be approximately four seconds (ie, from the time the laser fire button is first pressed to the time when the aim-off applied indicator is lit).

Status: Demonstration prototype. Not yet in production or service.

Manufacturer: British Aerospace (Dynamics) Limited, Downshire Way, Bracknell, Berkshire RG12 1QL, UK.
Telephone: (0344) 483222
Telex: 848129
Fax: (0344) 58900

Ferranti GSA 200 Series Anti-aircraft Sight

Development
The GSA 200 series of anti-aircraft sights are the latest in a long line of gun sights developed by the Electro-optics Department of Ferranti Defence Systems for a variety of naval and ground-based air defence guns. They have been designed to provide a lead computing optical tracking facility for medium calibre guns and by early 1989 several thousand had been built for a wide range of weapons with ground-based guns including the Oerlikon-Bührle GDF series of twin 35 mm systems and the Bofors 40 mm L/70.

In mid-1987 Ferranti announced that the Japanese Ground Self Defence Force had selected the Ferranti GSA 202 series for installation on its towed 20 mm Vulcan air defence guns.

Description
All the variants in this series compute the gyroscope sensitivity for two optimum ranges selected by the gunner. These can be calibrated to accommodate distances of around the maximum accurate range of the gun and also approaching the minimum range at which the target can still be manually tracked.

Many users prefer the simplicity of this setting procedure so that full attention can be given to the task of smooth and accurate tracking which is obviously the prime consideration of successful gun-laying.

As an alternative, the two range settings can be preset to provide one computed track mode and a preliminary slew mode in which the gyroscope is heavily caged for rapid traversing movements. Selection of the alternative range setting is provided on different GSA 200 series variants either by means of a three position off/min/max switch on the GSA control panel, or via a separate push-button when the gun-mounting is rotated by electrical hand controls.

The GSA variants embody two graticule patterns, one a fixed pattern for use in surface-to-surface targets which can be augmented together with the target by use of a telescope. The second is the gyro controlled air defence graticule.

The GSA series can also be supplied with different graticule patterns, mounting arrangements and paint finishes and the sunscreen position control can be fitted to either side of the unit.

Front and rear protective visors, standby peep-sights and brackets for foldaway telescopes for target identification purposes are available as optional extras.

The power supply of 24 V DC is supplied via a 14-12P bulkhead connector.

The GSA series is compatible with any 20 mm, 30 mm, 35 mm or 40 mm gun with the required ballistic data being inserted into the computation by means of an adjustment of trim potentiometers on the electronic card module of the unit. This gives the user the flexibility of having one gun sight for a number of guns of different calibre.

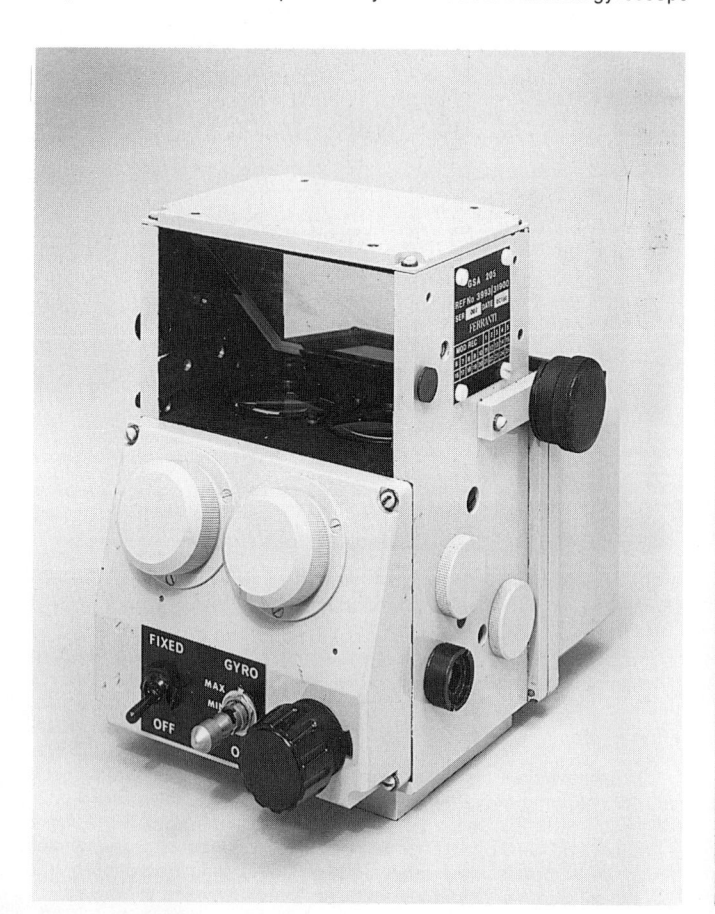

Ferranti GSA series anti-aircraft sight from operator's side showing position of controls

Oerlikon-Bührle GDF series twin 35 mm towed anti-aircraft gun system showing Ferranti GSA series sight on right

UK / TOWED AA GUN SIGHTS

SPECIFICATIONS
LENGTH 233.6 mm
WIDTH 153.9 mm
HEIGHT 233.6 mm

Status: In production. In service with many countries including Japan.

Manufacturer: Ferranti Defence Systems Limited, Electro-optics Department, St Andrews Works, Robertson Avenue, Edinburgh, EH11 1PX, UK.
Telephone: (031) 337 2442
Telex: 72529

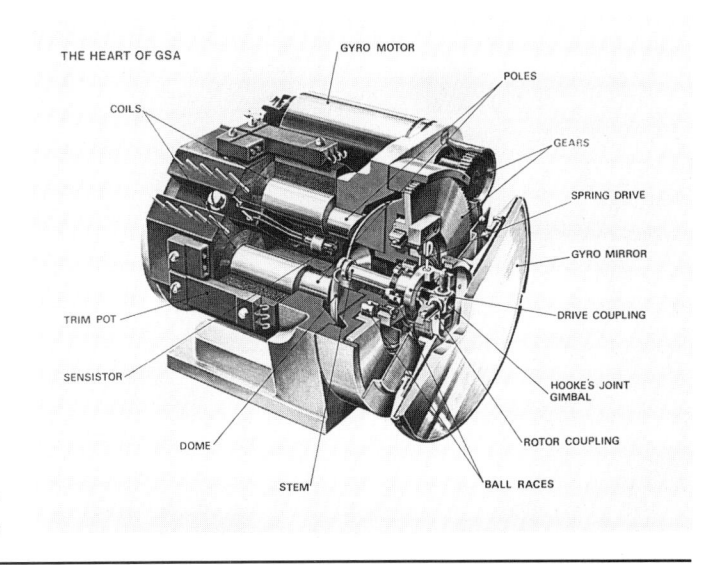

Heart of the Ferranti GSA series air defence sight showing position of main components

---

Hall & Watts RC25 Low Level All Arms Air Defence Sight (LLAAADS)

Development
This sight was originally developed as a private venture by Ring Sights, but was subsequently taken over by Hall & Watts who have continued to develop it and are now responsible for both marketing and manufacture.

The first prototype of the RC25 Low Level All Arms Air Defence Sight (LLAAADS) was completed in 1985, with first production sights being completed for the export market in 1987. In early 1989 it was adopted by the British Army for its All Arms Air Defence (AAAD) system requirement.

This consists of the RC25, a 12.7 mm MG (the L1A2 in British Army service), weapon cradle provided by Fenlow and a vehicle interface. The RC25 can, however, be fitted to other weapons such as the 7.62 mm GPMG. A total of 1050 AAAD systems are to be procured for the British Royal Artillery and fitted to a number of in service vehicles including the FV432 APC, FV436 command post vehicle, 155 mm M109A2 self-propelled howitzer and the Tracked Rapier Support Vehicle.

Description
The RC25 has no magnification, so making it user-friendly by allowing the gunner to keep both eyes open during operation, thereby giving him an extensive field-of-view.

The sight picture is a graticule seen in space in the viewing window which the gunner overlays on the target.

This graticule gives aim-off and attack approach angles. For operation in low light conditions, tritium illumination can be introduced.

Hall & Watts have designed a variety of graticule patterns to address different applications, including a combined air defence and ground role graticule.

Successful trials have also been carried out by helicopter air gunners using the RC25 in the air-to-air and air-to-ground combat role.

It is a self-illuminated sight designed to increase the hit probability of both static and moving targets, with a strike ratio of at least 60 per cent being claimed for the latter.

A diffused graticule is available for bright daylight in both arctic and desert conditions.

Future developments of the RC25 include aim read-out linked to a video monitor and recorder as a training aid, alternative graticules and retrofit kits to suitable weapon systems.

Hall & Watts RC25 Low Level All Arms Air Defence Sight

Hall & Watts RC25 Low Level All Arms Air Defence Sight fitted to a 12.7 mm M2 machine gun during British Army trials

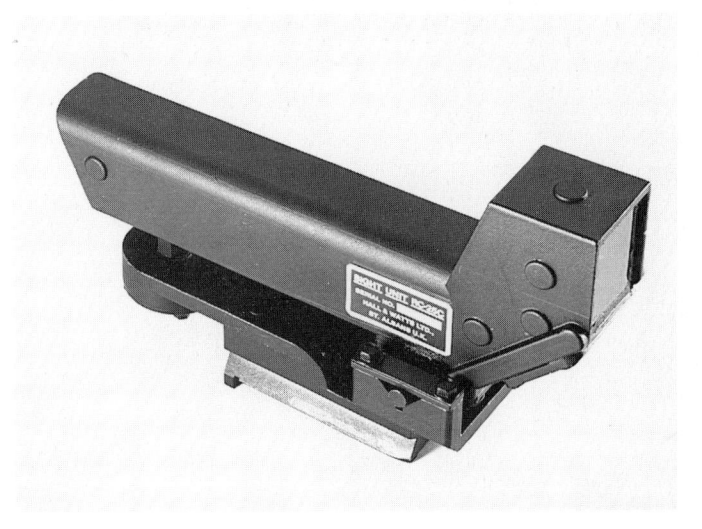

Close up of Hall and Watts RC25 Low Level All Arms Air Defence Sight

TOWED AA GUN SIGHTS / UK

SPECIFICATIONS

FIELD OF VIEW	14.25° × 14.25° (250 × 250 mils)	LENGTH	190 mm
APERTURE	25 mm	WEIGHT	625 g including zeroing mount
FOCAL LENGTH	122 mm	TEMPERATURE RANGE	−40° to +55°C

Status: In production. In service with four countries and under evaluation by many others. Selected by the British Army in early 1989.

Manufacturer: Hall & Watts Limited, 266 Hatfield Road, St Albans, Hertfordshire, AL1 4UN, UK.
Telephone: (0727) 59288
Telex: 267001 Watts G
Fax: (0727) 35683

Static and Towed Surface-to-Air Missile Systems

(Including tactical anti-ballistic missile systems currently under development)

BRAZIL

AVIBRAS Solar Low Altitude Surface-to-air Missile System

Development/Description
The Brazilian company AVIBRAS Industria Aerospacial SA is at the prototype stage for a four-round mobile/static missile system known as Solar by the Brazilian Army. Similar in many respects to the Euromissile Roland, the weapon is likely to be integrated with the company's EDT-FILA anti-aircraft fire control system which is used with the army's Bofors 40 mm L/70 air defence guns.

Status: Prototype.

Manufacturer: AVIBRAS Industria Aerospacial SA, Marketing Division, Caixa Postal (PO Box) 229, Sao José dos Campos-SP, Brazil.
Telephone: 123 21 7433
Telex: 123 3793 AIAE

CHINA, PEOPLE'S REPUBLIC

FM-80 All-weather Low Altitude Surface-to-air Missile System

Development/Description
At the Dubai 1989 Aerospace show the FM-80 all-weather low and very low altitude surface-to-air missile system was revealed for the first time.

The FM-80 has been developed over the period 1978-79 to 1988 and is designed as a self-propelled vehicle or static trailer-mounted point defence system for use around airfields, oil fields, army field units and other Vital Point (VP) military and strategic installations.

The command guided missile itself is mounted in four side-by-side cylindrical container-launchers and appears to be a reverse engineered version of the French Crotale system.

Flight control is by cruciform canard fins. The effective range is believed to be from 800 to 10 000 m between altitude limits of 15 to 4000 m.

Target acquisition and tracking is performed by an indigenous shelter-mounted low altitude surveillance radar.

Status: Entering production. On order for People's Republic of China Armed Forces with first deliveries due in 1990.

Manufacturer: Chinese state factories.
Enquiries to: Chinese Precision Machinery Import and Export Corporation (CPMIEC), 17 Wenchang Hutong Xidan, Beijing, People's Republic of China.
Telephone: 895012
Telex: 22484 SPMC CN

HQ-61 Low to Medium Altitude Surface-to-air Missile System

Development
The HQ-61 SAM system has been designed to meet the requirements of both the Chinese People's Liberation Army and Navy and in many respects the missile is similar to the US Sparrow family design but is larger and heavier.

The army version was first seen in public during the November 1986 Beijing defence exhibition, by which time it had been under development for some years to meet a projected service date in the late 1980s.

The system has been designed to engage targets flying at low to medium altitudes with a minimum range of 3 km and a maximum range of 10 km in the horizontal plane, extending in an arc to an altitude of around 8000 m.

Description
Ths missile itself is single stage with a solid propellant rocket motor, a chain type high explosive warhead, dual fuze system, homing head using a continuous wave semi-active homing guidance system which is said to have an anti-jamming feature, autopilot, airborne power supply using a combustion turbine generator to supply AC and DC power for all missile components and four hydraulic servo-operated canard fins.

A typical army battery of HQ-61 launchers consists of four 6 × 6 trucks each with two rail-mounted missiles on a turntable at the rear of the vehicle, mobile generators, command post vehicle, tracking and illuminating radar vehicle and a target indicating radar vehicle. This last is also based on a 6 × 6 chassis which is similar in appearance to the

Close-up of two missiles on HQ-6l launcher (Christopher F Foss)

Soviet-designed Flat Face target acquisition radar used with the Soviet SA-3 Goa SAM system.

The launcher vehicle has a fully enclosed forward control cab with an anti-blast shield to its immediate rear. When in the firing position the launcher is supported on four stabilisers, two each side. Reload missiles are brought up by a missile resupply truck and loaded with the aid of a crane.

242 STATIC & TOWED SAM SYSTEMS / China

CESIEC Model 571 C-band radar deployed in field showing two elliptic parabolic net reflectors one above the other. A similar vehicle carries generator

Scale model of HQ-61 launcher with stabilisers lowered and missiles in elevated position (Christopher F Foss)

HQ-61 missile being launched during trials in 1986

HQ-61 SAM system with stabilisers lowered and launcher traversed to left

A typical target engagement would take place as follows. The target is first detected by the target indication and radar vehicle and after confirmed as hostile, tracked and illuminated by the tracking and illuminating radar vehicle. When the target is within range a missile is launched. It appears that the system can engage only one target at a time.

No details of the tracking and illuminating radar system have been disclosed, although the single photograph released shows a dish-type antenna with a TV camera mounted coaxially to the right for use in an ECM environment, or passive operations during clear weather engagements.

The target indication and radar vehicle is based on a different CA-30 (6 × 6) 2500 kg cross-country truck, as is the power supply truck.

The C-band radar system has the Chinese designation Model 571 and has two elliptic parabolic net type reflectors. The speed of rotation is 3 or 6 rpm. Other features include moving target indication and frequency hopping agility. According to the Chinese, the Model 571 radar has been designed specifically for low altitude warning and displays both the slant range and azimuth of aircraft targets detected.

SPECIFICATIONS (missile)

TYPE	single stage, low to medium altitude	WARHEAD	HE fragmentation
LENGTH	3.99 m	MAX SPEED	Mach 3.0
DIAMETER	0.86 m	MAX RANGE	10 000 m
MAX SPAN	1.166 m	MIN RANGE	3000 m
LAUNCH WEIGHT	300 kg	MAX ALTITUDE	8000 m
PROPULSION	solid fuel sustainer	LAUNCHER TYPE	mobile twin rail
GUIDANCE	command with semi-active radar terminal homing		

China / STATIC & TOWED SAM SYSTEMS

Status: Development of the army version of the HQ-61 SAM system is understood to be complete but it has yet to enter service with the Chinese Army. It is expected to enter production in the near future.

Manufacturer: Chinese state factories with export marketing carried out by Chinese Precision Machinery Import and Export Corporation, 17 Wenchang Hutong Xidan, Beijing, People's Republic of China.
Telephone: 895012
Telex: 22484 SPMC CN
The Model 571 radar is marketed by China National Electronics Import & Export Corporation, 49 Fuxing Road, Beijing, People's Republic of China.
Telephone: 810910
Telex: 22475 CEIEC CN

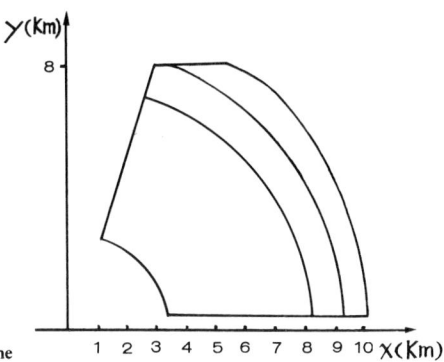

Typical target envelope of HQ-61 SAM system in vertical plane

Vertical plane of combat zone

HQ-2 Medium to High Altitude Surface-to-air Missile System

Development
Following the supply of the Soviet SA-2 (Guideline) SAM system in the 1960s, China reverse-engineered this system and it is now produced in China under the designation HQ-2. It has also been referred to in the West as CSA-1.

The latest version is the HQ-2J which has been supplied to Pakistan whose air force operates several batteries each with six launchers. The system has also been supplied to Iran and North Korea. An earlier version of the HQ-2 was supplied to Albania during the 1960s and early 1970s.

The HQ-2 series has seen combat use with the Chinese Air Force, shooting down a number of Taiwanese flown Lockheed U-2 high altitude reconnaissance aircraft over mainland China during 1962-70, and the Iranian Armed Forces from 1985 onwards in the Gulf War.

Description
As far as is known, the missile system is virtually identical in detail and performance to the Soviet SA-2 for which full details are given later in this section. The later versions, such as the HQ-2J, have had minor modifications made as a result of operational use.

The HQ-2 missile comprises two stages in tandem, the sustainer stage (stage II) and the booster (stage I). The warhead in these versions has an improved design with multiple fragments and a large scattering angle.

The complete HQ-2J system comprises missiles, a Gin Sling A (NATO designation) locally built copy of the Soviet Fan Song guidance radar which has been upgraded in terms of electronic counter countermeasures (ECCM) capability, fire control system, six single rail launchers and ground support equipment, with Chinese trucks used in place of Soviet trucks.

Chinese Gin Sling A equivalent of Soviet Fan Song A radar which is used to track target and guide one or more HQ-2J missiles against it

Latest version HQ-2J SAM being launched from its single rail launcher

HQ-2B mobile surface-to-air missile system with missile elevated (Eric Ditchfield)

Probable Gin Sling B HQ-2B missile guidance radar

STATIC & TOWED SAM SYSTEMS / China-France

Variants

HQ-2B Mobile Surface-to-air Missile System

The HQ-2B is a mobile launched version of the HQ-2J. It is carried on a single rail launcher mounted on the rear decking of a lengthened Type 63 light tank chassis. All the firing controls and system electronics are located in the hull area with access provided by side panels.

The launcher vehicle simply takes the place of the semi-static model to allow greater unit flexibility in deployment and tactical positioning both before and after engagements.

Further improvements to the system's guidance and ECCM capabilities have also resulted in the Gin Sling B digital guidance radar, which is thought to be equivalent in capabilities to the Soviet Fan Song E missile guidance radar set from the SA-2 Guideline family.

Status: In production. In service with Albania, People's Republic of China, Iran, North Korea and Pakistan.

Manufacturer: Chinese state factories with export marketing carried out by China Precision Machinery Import and Export Corporation, 17 Wenchang Hutong Xidan, Beijing, People's Republic of China.
Telephone: 895012
Telex: 22484 SPMC CN

FRANCE

Aerospatiale/Thomson-CSF SAMP Low to Medium Altitude Surface-to-air Missile System

Development

The feasibility studies for the French SYRINX programme (système rapide interarmées à base d'engins et fonctionnant en bande X: X-band fast tri-service missile system) were carried out from 1982-1984. Pre-development contracts were awarded in 1984 to Thomson-CSF for the Arabel radar and fire control system, and to Aerospatiale for the ASTER missile family. These were followed by full development contracts in 1988. The SYRINX system is designed to defend against aircraft, air-to-surface missiles, surface-to-surface missiles and cruise misiles, with the possibility of further development to defend against short-range ballistic missiles.

The Arabel fire control I/J-band radar is a 3D phased array system scanning 360° in azimuth and 70° in elevation, capable of both surveillance and tracking functions, as well as passing update information to missiles in flight. There are planned to be four ASTER missile versions; SAAM (système naval d'autodéfense moyen portée: naval surface-to-air anti-missile system) to be met by the ASTER 15, SAMP terrestre (système d'autodéfense moyen portée: land-based medium-range surface-to-air missile) and SAMP naval (système d'autodéfense moyen portée: ship-based medium-range surface-to-air missile) which will both be met with the ASTER 30, and finally a fourth version to be capable of intercepting tactical ballistic missile targets.

The SAMP land and naval versions will have additional sensors to augment the Arabel radar, including a secondary search radar and optical systems to assist with identification and provide better performance in heavy ECM environments. It is planned for the SAMP fire control system to be able to handle up to 10 simultaneous missile interceptions, in a largely automatic system.

The full-scale development contract, signed in 1988, only covered work on the radar, fire control system and ASTER 15 missile for short-range ship defence. The medium-range SAMP systems, using the ASTER 30 missile version, are potential I-HAWK, Standard and Sea Sparrow missile replacements being proposed for the European Medium-Range Surface-to-Air (MSAM) and NATO Anti-Air Warfare System (NAAWS) requirements.

France and Italy have agreed to co-operate on a joint ASTER/Idra missile programme, where it is believed that Selenia will utilise the Idra missile seeker with EMPAR radar and fire control system components for the Italian Navy. This French/Italian co-operative agreement may be enlarged to embrace the UK and Spain as a four nation study called 'Family of Anti-Air Missile Systems' (FAAMS) and is examining possible local area missile defence for ships.

Description

The all-weather SAMP missile system will be used for area defence on the battlefield and the protection of Vital Points against mass strikes by aircraft and/or missiles at all altitudes.

The basic SAMP has an inherent anti-tactical ballistic missile (ATBM) interception capability against various types of missiles (eg SRBMs of the SS-21 Scarab type, diving Anti-Radiation Missiles (ARMs) and very low altitude cruise weapons). The engagement range is between 10 and 20 km depending upon the missile's characteristics.

Against highly manoeuvrable Mach 2.5 aircraft targets at various altitudes the range increases to around 30 km, whilst for slow and poor manoeuvring targets like stand-off jammers (SOJ) and other similar battlefield/strike support aircraft, the engagement range can further be increased to approximately 90 km by the use of a semi-ballistic flight trajectory.

The heart of the system is the 60 rpm Arabel 3D frequency-agile radar already mentioned. This scans electronically, both in azimuth and elevation, to provide both multi-target tracking and missile guidance data channel uplinks on a time-share basis.

Arabel can accurately track up to 100 targets at any one time and provide the necessary information for the simultaneous engagement of at least 10 of them.

The minimum reaction time from initial radar detection to first missile launch is only four seconds.

The operational engagement sequence is:
(a) first detection plus immediate detection confirmation leads to a track initialisation
(b) target identification via IFF subsystem and, if hostile, track formation
(c) threat evaluation (and priority assigned if more than one)
(d) target designation and missile launch
(e) inertial midcourse missile guidance
(f) active radar terminal missile guidance
(g) target interception.

The ASTER 30 missile used is vertically launched and has a tandem first stage solid propellant booster that is jettisoned in flight.

The missile itself can manoeuvre at up to 50 g and has four long rectangular wings, and four moving clipped-tip control fins at the rear. Additional manoeuvrability in the terminal flight phase is provided by a gas generator exhausting through four lateral nozzles close to the missile's centre of gravity (this system is known as Pilotage en Force - PIF).

Guidance in the midcourse phase is inertial, with the addition of commands from the fire control centre being sent via the Arabel's antenna and the uplink data channel. This flies the missile out on a reciprocal course to the target's vicinity where the active radar seeker is activated.

This is derived from the Electronique Serge Dassault AD4A homing head design of the Matra MICA air-to-air missile and uses a centimetric

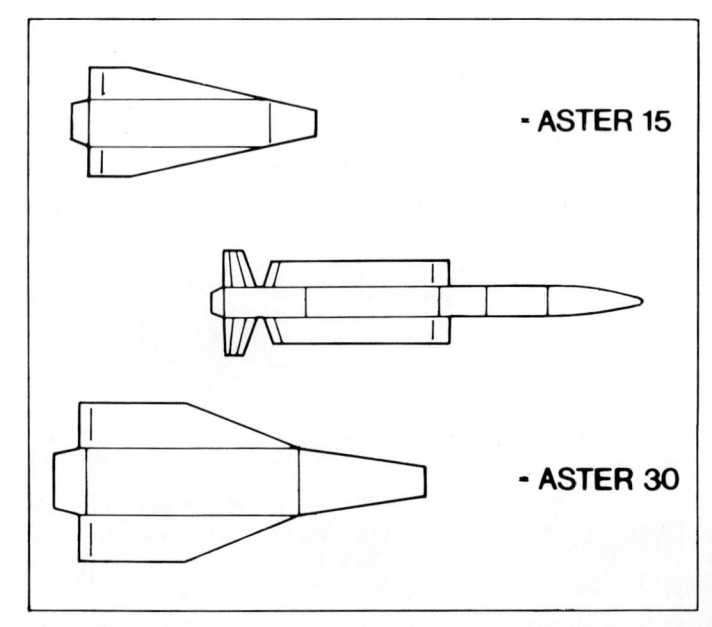

The Aerospatiale ASTER missile, which has different boosters to meet different requirements of SA-90 (DB/JDW)

J-band pulse Doppler seeker to guide the missile on an optimised, proportional navigation low flight path to the target.

A HE-blast fragmentation warhead with parallel distribution characteristics is then triggered by the weapons calculated proximity delay fuzing circuit. This ensures that the missile is in very close to the target when the warhead detonates so as to guarantee its structural destruction. It is also the reason for the additional PIF flight control system used just before impact, as this enables targets performing up to 15 g evasive manoeuvres to be successfully destroyed.

The SAMP fire unit is expected to be truck-mounted on Renault TRM 10 000 (6 × 6) vehicles with a two-station automatic fire control module vehicle, an Arabel radar vehicle with retractable antenna, optional secondary radar, electro-optronics and communications/IFF subsystem vehicles and four to six missile transporter-erector-launcher (TEL) vehicles.

The TEL will have eight canisterised ready-to-fire vertically launched ASTER 30 missiles. Distance of the launchers from the radar will be up to 5 km in order to increase the fire unit's survivability.

The complete fire unit is airportable and can be deployed in combat configuration in 10 minutes.

The launchers will also be able to fire the ASTER 15 missile, which is the same as the ASTER 30 weapon but with a smaller booster section. The ASTER 15 has an effective engagement range of 15-17 km against aircraft and subsonic missiles and between 8-10 km against head-on or crossing low altitude supersonic missiles.

To cope with steeply diving tactical ballistic missiles, the ASTER 30 and the Arabel fire control technology is being modified to produce an ATBM missile variant.

SPECIFICATIONS

TYPE	ASTER 15 two-stage short-range	ASTER 30 two-stage medium-range
LENGTH		
missile	2.6 m	2.6 m
booster	1.6 m	2.2 m
total	4.2 m	4.8 m
DIAMETER		
missile	0.18 m	0.18 m
booster	0.36 m	0.54 m
WEIGHT		
missile	100 kg	100 kg
booster	300 kg	450 kg
total	400 kg	550 kg
PROPULSION	two-stage solid propellant booster rocket and ramjet sustainer motors	
GUIDANCE	inertial midcourse with command update and terminal active J-band radar	
WARHEAD	HE-blast fragmentation with calculated delay proximity fuzing	
SPEED	Mach 2 plus	
MAX RANGE	see text	
LAUNCHER	8-round semi-mobile vertical launch	

Status: ASTER 30 under full scale development to meet French Army and Air Force requirements.

Prime contractor: Thomson-CSF, Division Systèmes Electroniques, 116 Avenue Aristide-Briand, NP 10, 92223 Bagneux Cedex, France.
Telephone: (1) 46 64 14 30
Telex: 204 780 F

Aerospatiale, Division Engins Tactiques, 2 rue Béranger, 92322 Chatillon Cédex, France.
Telephone: (1) 47 46 21 21
Telex: 250 881 F

GERMANY, WEST

BGT AIM-9L Sidewinder/AIM-132A Low Altitude Surface-to-air Missile System

Development/Description
In order to provide additional low altitude air defence of its airfields and other sites, the West German Luftwaffe requested that Bodenseewerk Gerätetechnik GmbH (BGT) develop a fire-and-forget trailer-mounted surface-to-air missile system, based on its license-built version of the Ford Aerospace and Communications Corporation/Raytheon Company Missiles Division AIM-9L Sidewinder air-to-air missile.

The result was a trailer unit which mounts four ready to fire missiles and a remotely operated TV camera. The missile used is a slightly modified AIM-9L round with an all-aspects argon-cooled indium-antimony (InSb) passive infra-red seeker head with fixed reticule and tilted mirror guidance. The warhead is of the annular blast/fragmentation type enclosed in a skin of prefragmented rods and is triggered by an active laser proximity fuze which utilizes eight gallium-arsenic (Ga-As) diodes in a ring to emit the laser illumination and a further ring of photodiodes to receive any reflected light.

The definite trailer unit will also be equipped to fire the AIM-132A Advanced Short-Range Air-to-Air Missile (ASRAAM).

SPECIFICATIONS (AIM-9L missile)

TYPE	single stage, low altitude
LENGTH	2.85 m
DIAMETER	0.127 m
WING SPAN	0.63 m
LAUNCH WEIGHT	85.3 kg
PROPULSION	solid fuel sustainer rocket motor
GUIDANCE	passive infra-red homing with active laser proximity fuze
WARHEAD	11.4 kg HE blast-fragmentation
MAX SPEED	Mach 2.5
MAX RANGE	10 000 m
MAX EFFECTIVE RANGE	around 6000 m
MIN RANGE	around 500 m
MAX EFFECTIVE ALTITUDE	3000 m
MIN EFFECTIVE ALTITUDE	50 m
LAUNCHER	trainable four-round trailer

Status: Development complete. Programme for acquisition of 100 launcher units on hold until funding is provided. Not expected until 1990s when the ASRAAM is deployed.

Manufacturer: Bodenseewerk Gerätetechnik GmbH (GBT), D-7770 Uberlingen/Bodensee, Federal Republic of Germany.

BGT AIM-9L Sidewinder low altitude surface-to-air missile deployed in typical operational environment

MBB/AEG/Siemens TLVS Low to Medium Altitude Surface-to-air Missile System

Development/Description
The TLVS (Taktisches LuftVerteidigungsSystem) is a concept development study for an indigenous medium-range surface-to-air missile system, to meet the West German Air Force's MSAM requirement for an I-HAWK replacement to defend airfields and other high value targets.

The system will use a 30 km range all-weather truck-mounted supersonic weapon to counter aircraft, tactical SRBMs, cruise missiles and low observable (ie stealth equipped) targets.

The MBB developed missile will use inertial guidance first and then switch in its midcourse phase, either on command or automatically, to an AEG J-band active radar seeker for the terminal guidance stage. The latter will have the ability both to discriminate rapidly between targets and to pick out low level targets from ground clutter in what is virtually a look-down mode.

The associated Siemens ground radar is to be a multi-function phased array system operating in the H/I-band region. It will scan electronically in both azimuth and elevation with coverage in the former being up to 100° at any one time during a single rotation. This maximises the dwell time spent on the target.

If the TLVS is adopted then full scale engineering development will start in 1994 and initial production in 1999-2000. Operational deployment would follow with the I-HAWK systems being replaced by around 2005.

Status: Concept development phase. Study to be submitted in 1990.

Manufacturers: Prime contractor (and for missile and launch unit): Messerschmitt-Bölkow-Blohm GmbH (MBB), Dynamics Group, PO Box 801149, D-8000 Munich 80, Federal Republic of Germany.
Telephone: (89) 6000-2206
Telex: 52870 mbbd

Active radar seeker: AEG Aktiengesellschaft, Theodor-Stern-Kai 1, D-6000 Frankfurt/Main, Federal Republic of Germany.
Telephone: (69) 6001
Telex: 411076
Cable: ELEKTRON WEST

Radar and fire control system: Siemens AG, Radio and Radar Systems Division, Landshuter Str 26, D-8044 Unterschleissheim, Federal Republic of Germany.

INDIA

Static Surface-to-air Missile Systems

Development/Description
As part of the Indian plan to become self-sufficient in weapon production by the year 2002, three surface-to-air missile systems are being developed by the Defence Research and Development Organisation.

The heavy long-range system is known as Agni (Fire). It is believed to be in the engineering design phase and will probably replace the SA-2 Guideline.

The medium system is the 27 km range Akash (Space) which will probably supplant the SA-3 Goa and use a fire control system capable of engaging multiple targets.

The final system is the truck-mounted low level quick reaction Trishul (Trident) weapon with a maximum range of 9000 m. This was first tested in April 1987 and is currently undergoing user trials with production due to start in the early 1990s.

Status: Agni and Akash are in the development phase. Trishul is at the prototype stage.

INTERNATIONAL

Medium Surface-to-air Missile (MSAM) System

Development/Description
For some time there have been a number of studies underway on a follow-on medium-range surface-to-air missile system to the I-HAWK. In October 1987 eight European nations - Belgium, France, Italy, the Netherlands, Norway, Spain, the United Kingdom and West Germany - signed an agreement under the auspices of the International European Programme Group (IEPG) for a 12 month study of the subject.

In addition MBB, AEG and Siemens have been co-operating with the West German MoD on the TLVS concept (see this section) as a possible successor to replace the Luftwaffe I-HAWK batteries by 2005. The West Germans have also entered into a bilateral study with the US DoD on such a system. This programme is usually referred to as the Medium Surface-to-air Missile System (MSAM).

In addition to engaging aircraft targets, MSAM would have to engage cruise missiles and tactical ballistic missiles. As well as being a new start, some, such as Raytheon, believe that the current HAWK system could be the basis for further development.

The US Army's 1989 budget request released early in 1988 included $3 million for the MSAM programme, but this could be supplemented by funding from other air defence programmes.

Raytheon is proposing a development of the existing HAWK air defence system. The modular steps would include an Agile Continuous-Wave Acquisition Radar (ACWAR), modified HAWK missile and a new vertical launched multi-mode missile.

The ACWAR would provide accurate all-altitude 3D data, detect small targets in severe clutter, be inherently anti-radiation missile survivable without decoys, have a capability in advanced electronic counter countermeasures (ECCM) and be applicable to the Forward Area Air Defense System (FAADS).

The current HAWK missile would have improved effectiveness against stealth aircraft and cruise missiles, full range simultaneous target engagement, ECCM diversity, be able to counter stand-off jammers and complement Patriot anti-tactical ballistic missile capability through interoperability.

International / **STATIC & TOWED SAM SYSTEMS** 247

The vertical launched multi-mode missile would be transported and launched from a cross-country truck and have autonomous or netted operation, passive surveillance and remasked target engagement.

In March 1988 the British MoD placed a 15 month study contract worth £500 000 with the British Aerospace Dynamics Division to establish feasible and cost-effective ways of meeting the UK's perceived needs for a future MSAM system.

The study will examine the stretch potential of existing UK systems and address the possibilities of using foreign equipments and the feasibility of mixing and matching UK and foreign equipments into the MSAM system.

All major aspects of an MSAM system will be addressed and some contracts for subsystems will be let.

The study will support current multi-national initiatives in the field and will complement the planned multi-national studies in which the UK intends to participate.

According to British Aerospace, the information derived from the study will reinforce the UK's position, ensuring it will have a leading role in the development and manufacture of an MSAM system in the 1990s.

Skyguard/Sparrow Air Defence System

Development

This air defence system is a joint development between Contraves of Switzerland and Raytheon of the United States and combines two proven systems, the Skyguard fire control system, normally used to control Oerlikon-Bührle twin 35 mm GDF series towed anti-aircraft guns and the Raytheon AIM-7E/AIM-7F/AIM-7M Sparrow missile, which in its normal application is air-launched.

Typically, the missile would be used to engage targets at long range with the guns used at ranges of 4000 m or less.

A variant of the AIM-7E, designated RIM-7E-5, is used in the surface-to-air role with the US Navy as part of its Basic Point Defense System. Another variant, the RIM-7H-5, is used in the NATO Sea Sparrow Surface Missile System. More recently, the RIM-7M has been adopted by the US Navy with the RIM-7P under development.

In 1982 the Egyptian Air Defence Command ordered 18 battery sets of the Skyguard/Sparrow air defence from Contraves (Italy) to equip three autonomous air defence brigades. The first deliveries were made in December 1984 and final deliveries were in 1987. Egypt calls the system Amoun and a typical section consists of one Skyguard fire control system, two Oerlikon-Bührle GDF-003 twin 35 mm towed anti-aircraft guns and two four-round Sparrow SAM launchers. One section can engage three targets at once, two with missiles and one with guns. Reaction times are 4.5 seconds for the guns and eight seconds for the Sparrows.

The system delivered to Egypt has some 16 modifications, including a new search antenna unit to reduce the effects of clutter, a new computer and software, and a revision of the operator's console to incorporate three operators. Optical target detection range is 15 km and radar range 20 km.

Egypt is understood to have a requirement for additional Amoun sections so that the remaining obsolete Soviet-supplied systems can be phased out of service. Further orders would involve a more significant proportion of local production which was minimal in the initial order.

Prior to this, Greece selected the system under the name Velos in 1983 using RIM-7M missiles. The first was delivered in October 1984 and in October 1985 Spain ordered 13 Italian Selenia Spada launchers and 200 Aspide missiles for integration with existing Skyguard fire control systems and Oerlikon-Bührle twin 35 mm GDF-005 towed anti-aircraft gun

Typical Skyguard/Sparrow/twin 35 mm air defence battery with Contraves Skyguard fire control system centre, flanked by two twin 35 mm Oerlikon-Bührle GDF series anti-aircraft guns with four-round Sparrow launcher in background

Close-up of launcher showing two Sparrow missiles in their transport/launcher containers each side of the operator's position with illuminator antenna mounted forward and below his position

Rear view of four-round launcher for Sparrow missiles. Carriage is identical to that employed in twin 35 mm Oerlikon-Bührle anti-aircraft gun which is also deployed in battery

Raytheon AIM-7E Sparrow being launched during trials conducted at China Lake Naval Weapons Centre, California (US Department of Defense)

STATIC & TOWED SAM SYSTEMS / International-Iraq

batteries. The Aspide missiles were already used by the Spanish Navy on its frigates. Total value of this contract was $150 million and included Spanish co-production.

The first battery was delivered direct from Italy by Contraves with the remaining six assembled at the Bazan factory in Spain. Marconi Spain is responsible for modification kits and the launcher electronic groups and EISA will manufacture the electrical cables. Bazan will also produce the missile container and the launcher's electrical and mechanical components.

The Spanish name for this system is Toledo. All systems are expected to be delivered by the end of 1989. As the Spanish Skyguard fire control systems were delivered in the late 1970s, the contract also covered the supply of seven modification packages to bring these up to the latest configuration.

Each Toledo battery will consist of one Skyguard fire control system, two twin 35 mm GDF-005 towed anti-aircraft guns and two four-round launchers. It was stated that seven batteries would enter service which gives a total of 14 launchers with no launchers for training or war reserve, but only 13 have been ordered.

Tactical firing trials of the Skyguard/Sparrow were carried out in October 1980 at the Naval Weapons Center, China Lake, California. Three missiles, one AIM-7E and two AIM-7Fs, were fired against remotely controlled aircraft targets, Northrop QT-38 Talon for the AIM-7E and North American QF-86 Sabre for the AIM-7F.

The AIM-7E was not fitted with a warhead, but intercepted the target and passed well within the lethal radius of the warhead. The first AIM-7F was fitted with a telemetry pack in place of the warhead, but scored a direct hit on the right underwing fuel tank. The second AIM-7F hit the front fuselage of the target causing extensive damage to the air intake and cockpit. The drone aircraft then went out of control and subsequently crashed.

In 1980 a demonstration of the Skyguard/Sparrow took place at the NATO Missile Firing Range (NAMFI) in northern Crete using production equipment that had already been delivered to a customer.

A remotely piloted Chuka II target drone, which has roughly the dimensions and speed of some cruise missiles, was used as a target. The drone approached the weapon position at an angle from the front, flying 700 m over the weapon site at a speed of more than 200 m/s. The first launch scored a physical hit at more than 12 km range sending the drone into the sea. In the second intercept the missile flew past the new drone at a 1 m distance; since the Sparrow missile would have been triggered by its proximity fuze in a real engagement this was considered a kill.

Description

The Contraves Skyguard (additional details of which are given in the entry for the Oerlikon-Bührle twin 35 mm GDF towed anti-aircraft gun) carries out search and identification using a 20 km I/J-band radar, tracks

Sparrow missile being launched during trials of the Skyguard/Sparrow system at the NATO Missile Firing Range in northern Crete during 1980. The top right-hand missile has already been launched

the selected target by radar using a pulse Doppler K-band set or TV, computes intercept to facilitate the engagement and then aims the launcher at the target via digital data cable transmission.

The four-round launcher is mounted on the carriage of the Oerlikon-Bührle twin 35 mm GDF towed anti-aircraft gun system and the missiles are fired through the covers. The folded wings deploy after separation.

Two rounds are mounted each side of the operator's position with the illuminator antenna mounted forward and below his position.

The I-band illuminator provides continuous wave illumination of the target out to 13 km (20 km in the case of Egyptian systems) and the missile's seeker homes on the reflected signal.

Variants

Skyguard/Aspide

This is similar to the Skyguard/Sparrow but uses the four-round Aspide launcher used in the Spada air defence system in service with Italy and Thailand. The system was successfully demonstrated in 1981 and subsequently adopted by Spain under the name Toledo, which already has the Skyguard and twin 35 mm guns in service.

SPECIFICATIONS (AIM-7F) (missile)

TYPE	single stage, low altitude	MIN ALTITUDE	15 m
LENGTH OF MISSILE	3.66 m	LAUNCH WEIGHT	233.6 kg
BODY DIAMETER	0.203 m	PROPULSION	single stage, solid propellant
WINGSPAN	1.02 m	GUIDANCE	I-band semi-active radar homing
MAX RANGE	13 000 to 20 000 m (depending upon illuminator radar range)	WARHEAD	39 kg HE fragmentation with contact and proximity fuzing
MAX ALTITUDE	5000 m	SPEED	Mach 2.5

Status: In production. In service with Egypt (18 batteries, Air Defence Command), Greece (20 batteries, air force manned) and Spain (6 batteries, army manned with Aspide missiles).

Manufacturers: Contraves AG, Schaffhauserstrasse 580, CH-8052, Zurich, Switzerland.
Telephone: 01 306 2211
Telex: 52517

Raytheon Company, Missile Systems Division, Bedford, Massachusetts 01730, USA.
Telephone: 617 274 222

IRAQ

Iraqi Surface-to-air Missile System

Development/Description

During the latter part of 1988 the Iraqi MoD revealed that its defence research unit was developing a number of missile systems, amongst which was a surface-to-air missile system. No other details are available at present.

Status: Development.

ISRAEL

Israel Aircraft Industries Chetz (Arrow) Anti-tactical Ballistic Missile (ATBM) System

Development/Description
As part of the US Department of Defense (DoD) Strategic Defense Initiative (SDI) research and development effort, a $158 million initial demonstrator contract was placed with Israel Aircraft Industries (IAI) Electronic Division in July 1988 to develop, manufacture, integrate and flight test the 90 km range solid propellant Chetz (Arrow) ATBM early warning, guidance and proximity fuzed warhead subsystems.

Total cost is estimated at $400 million with the US DoD funding 80 per cent and the Israeli MoD the other 20 per cent. The system is designed to counter SRBMs of up to 1000 km in range by intercepting them in the final stage of their flight trajectory.

In January 1989 it was announced that Lockheed Missiles and Space Company had signed an agreement with IAI to involve itself in the follow-up full-scale development and production phases following a successful completion of the demonstrator test programme.

The first flight trials are due to be flown at an Israeli test range in late 1990/early 1991. If full scale development is approved, an in-service date of 1998 is likely.

Status: Development phase.

Manufacturer: Israel Aircraft Industries (IAI) Ltd, Electronic Division, Yahud Industrial Zone, I-56000 Yahud, Israel.
Telephone: (3) 357211
Telex: 341450
Cable: ISRAELAVIA

ITALY

Selenia Spada Low Altitude Surface-to-air Missile System

Development
In the 1960s the Indigo short-range surface-to-air missile system was developed by Sistel with a typical firing unit consisting of a Contraves Superfledermaus fire control centre, Contraves LPD-20 acquisition radar and two Sextuple Indigo towed missile launchers. This was never placed in production, nor was a self-propelled version on an M548 tracked carrier which used the same missiles, but a new fire control system with Officine Galileo acquisition and tracking radars.

The Spada point defence missile system was developed in the 1970s to meet an urgent Italian Air Force requirement for a low level air defence system to defend air bases and other key areas.

To reduce both development time and costs, it was decided to use components already proven in other applications. For example, the Aspide missile is identical to that used in the naval air defence role, the SIR is a modified Selenia Pluto E/F-band radar system and the TIR pulse Doppler radar has been developed from the naval Selenia Orion 30X G/HI- band radar tracker incorporating an I-band illuminator which has been in widespread service for some years.

Trials with the first prototype system were completed in 1977 with full technical and operational evaluations undertaken by the Italian Air Force during 1982 and 1983.

By 1986 a total of four battery sets totalling 12 systems had been ordered by the Italian Air Force with the first battery becoming operational in 1983.

In 1986 the Royal Thai Air Force ordered one complete Spada battery which was delivered in 1988. The Royal Thai Navy already has the Aspide missile used in its Albatros naval point defence system.

Key features of the Spada point defence system have been summarised by Selenia as large area of cover with high single shot kill probability, flexibility in system configuration, deployment and sighting, good co-ordination, reliable target identification capability, high resistance to enemy ECM and the possibility of being integrated into a national air defence system.

Description
A typical Spada battery has two main components, the detection centre (DC) and the firing sections (FS). The detection centre consists of the Search and Interrogation Radar (SIR) which comprises the SIR antenna pedestal and its equipment shelter and the Operational Control Centre (OCC) shelter, plus a generator.

One DC controls two firing sections, each of which comprises the Fire Control Centre (FCC) comprising the Tracking and Illuminating Radar (TIR) antenna pedestal with its TV sensor, Control Unit (CU) shelter for the TIR and firing control equipment, a generator and two Missile Launchers (ML) each with six missiles in the ready to fire position.

The firing sections can be up to 5 km from the DC and the configuration of the battery is flexible from one to four firing sections, each equipped with up to three six-round missile launchers.

The Aspide missile has an intercept envelope extending out to a range of 15 000 m to an altitude of 5000 m with an SSKP of not less than 70 per cent. Overall reaction time on first target is in the order of 10 to 15 seconds and of about five seconds on the following target.

The largest size battery can cover an area of up to 800 km^2 with a maximum of 72 missiles in the ready to launch position which can be fired singly or in salvoes of two.

The task of the DC is to search for targets, identify, evaluate and designate them to the FS. Through the SIR, targets in the area covered are searched for, detected, plot extracted and selectively IFF interogated.

Six-round Aspide missile launcher in travelling configuration being towed by truck fitted with hydraulic crane for missile resupply

Six-round Aspide missile launcher in firing position with outriggers deployed

STATIC & TOWED SAM SYSTEMS / Italy

All shelters used in Spada low level air defence system can be quickly fitted with mobilisers for rapid redeployment

Heart of Spada low level air defence system is the detection centre with its Pluto SIR which is modified Selena Pluto E/F-band radar

Tactical control of the battery is achieved by means of the associated OCC. Plot initiation, track-while-scan and data updating of a number of tracks, their identification, threat evaluation and target designation to the FS for engagement are carried out.

All the operations listed above are carried out automatically by the system.

The SIR consists of a low altitude search radar, particularly suitable for dense clutter environments, and advanced ECM and an interrogation radar with decoding capability on IFF answers.

The OCC consists of three operational consoles, a data processing system with two NDC-160 interconnected computers and a number of digital and phonic operational communication links.

The main tasks of the three OCC operators are checking for correctness of the various automatic operations, setting up the zones in which automatic plot extraction and track initiation should or should not take place, manual intervention to substitute for or correct automation, particularly in the presence of ECM, and selection of battery intervention criteria.

SPECIFICATIONS (search radar)
FREQUENCY BAND	F
ANTENNA TYPE	supercosecant square
TRANSMITTER	coherent chain, TWT final stage
WAVEFORM	coded
PRF	staggered
FREQUENCY AGILITY	pulse-to-pulse or burst-to-burst
MTI	double canceller, frequency agility compatible

SPECIFICATIONS (tracking and illuminating radar)
ANTENNA	integrated with the search radar antenna
SLS	included
SIF modes	1, 2, 3/A
MARK XII IFF	compatible

SPECIFICATIONS (operational console in OCC)
16 in CRT display for synthetic and raw radar data
7 in CRT display for alphanumeric data
Man/machine interfaces (keyboard, control panel, trackball on-line and off-line BITE)

SPECIFICATIONS (NDC-160 computer)
MAGNETIC CORE MEMORY	32 K words of 16 bits plus 2 bits parity
CYCLE TIME	1.10 s
ARITHMETIC	binary, parallel two-complement
INSTRUCTIONS	121
INPUT/OUTPUT INTERFACE	synchronous
Operational digital communications	
Serial link in full duplex with four wires	
EXCHANGE SPEED	up to 50 kbit/s for direct links, 600/1200 bit/s for modem link
OPERATIONAL PHONIC COMMUNICATIONS	(inside the system) up to 4 lines (outside the system) up to 2 lines (logistics) up to 6 lines

The task of the FS, which represents the reaction centre of the system, is to acquire and destroy assigned targets. At the FCC, TIR performs target acquisition, tracking and illumination for missile guidance. As an additional mode of operation, the TIR provides for target search (all round or sectorial scan), detection and self-designation. The TV set is used both as a back-up to the radar and as an aid for target identification and discrimination and for kill assessment. The associated CU supervises the above-mentioned functions. Automatic or manual control of the firing action by means of displays and communications equipment is also monitored.

The MLs provide for missile storing, aiming, selection and setting to fire, as well as for automatic launching sequence of the six missiles on each launcher.

The TIR consists of a tracking pulse radar, a CW transmitter for illumination and a common antenna with its own pedestal.

The CU consists of an operational console, a data processing system making use of an NDC-160 computer and a number of digital and phonic operational communication links.

The ML consists of a slewable stand, which supports a frame type structure on which two rows of three missile canisters each are located. This structure can be moved in elevation, both for positioning to the firing angle and for canister loading/unloading operations.

The main tasks of the FCC are setting the FS in stand-by status, checking for correctness of the various automatic operations, providing manual intervention when required, missile firing according to the criteria selected by the OCC, and kill assessment.

SPECIFICATIONS (tracking radar)
FREQUENCY BAND	I
ANTENNA TYPE	monopulse
TRANSMITTER	coherent chain, TWT final stage
PRF	staggered
FREQUENCY AGILITY	pulse-to-pulse or burst-to-burst
MTI	quintuple canceller, frequency agility compatible

SPECIFICATIONS (illuminator)
FREQUENCY BAND	J
ANTENNA	same as for tracking
TRANSMITTER	klystron oscillator
OPERATIONAL CONSOLE	same as for OCC plus A/R presentation on 7 in CRT and fire pushbutton
NDC-160 COMPUTER	same as for OCC
OPERATIONAL DIGITAL COMMUNICATIONS	same as for OCC
OPERATIONAL PHONIC COMMUNICATIONS	(inside system) 1 line (outside system) 1 line (logistics) up to 4 lines

Derived from the US Raytheon AIM-7H Sparrow air-to-air missile, the Aspide missile is a J-band semi-active homing weapon able to guide itself onto the target by sensing the CW electromagnetic energy, either reflected by the illuminating target or emitted by a self-screening jammer.

Italy / **STATIC & TOWED SAM SYSTEMS** 251

The Selenia Aspide multi-role missile

Selenia Aspide missile being fired from Spada system launcher

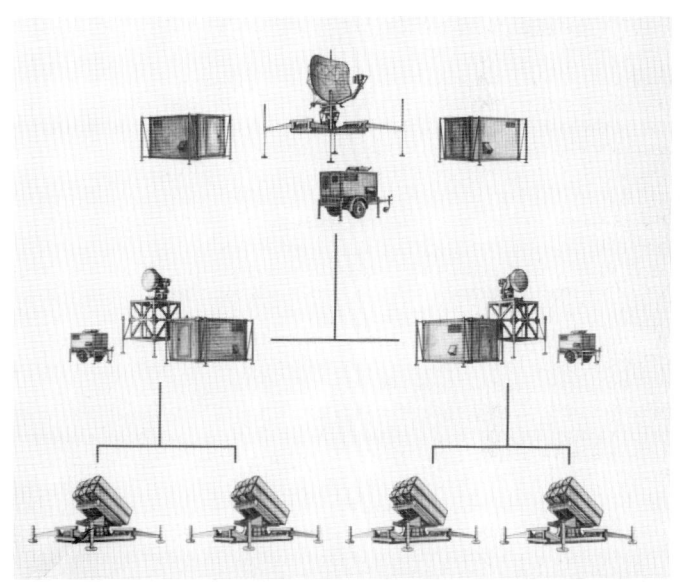

Close-up of Selenia TIR used at each firing section with TV sensor to its left

Typical Spada low altitude SAM battery configuration showing main components minus support and missile resupply vehicles

Propelled by a Difesa e Spazio single-stage solid propellant rocket motor, the missile uses proportional navigation to direct itself through the collision course towards the target.

According to Selenia, the guidance accuracy (due to the adoption of a monopulse inverse type radar receiver) and the active radar proximity fuze and the sizeable Difesa e Spazio 33 kg prefragmented type warhead assure a very high SSKP, even in the presence of a dense and sophisticated ECM environment and at very low altitude.

The electrical and hydraulic power generator of the Aspide missile has been developed by Microtecnica and is powered by a solid propellant gas generator. It consists of a high-speed gas turbine, reduction gears, an alternator and a hydraulic pump. The hydraulic system is a closed-loop, ensuring the availability of full hydraulic power for the entire duration of guided flight.

The missile is housed and fired from a canister which is also used for transportation and stowing.

In addition to engaging aircraft and helicopters, Spada has a capability against RPVs and air-to-surface missiles.

The Aspide has a high thrust single-stage solid propellant rocket motor. The air-to-air version is hypersonic and the surface-to-air version is supersonic. They have many common components although their fore and aft fins are different, the former being movable and the latter fixed.

The launcher has six rounds in the ready to launch position and when in the firing position is supported on four outriggers that can be adjusted for height. The launcher can be traversed through 360° at a slew rate of 50°/s with elevation up to 30°.

New missiles in the containers are loaded with a hydraulic crane carried on the missile resupply vehicle.

The main components of the Spada point defence system, such as the shelters and fire units, are coupled to a mobiliser wheeled system with the units then towed behind trucks. The mobiliser basically consists of two pairs of wheels which are connected to the ends of the shelters as well as both the SIR antenna and the missile launchers.

In addition the shelters and SIR antenna platform can be autonomously loaded/unloaded from a truck by means of a positioning device that consists of four lifting legs which are fitted as standard.

Variants
The Skyguard/Aspide point defence system is an integration between the Contraves Skyguard fire control system, Oerlikon-Bührle twin 35 mm towed anti-aircraft guns and the Selenia Aspide missile. The tracker and illuminator radar installed on the launcher were developed by Selenia. (There is a separate entry in this section for the Skyguard/Aspide (or Sparrow) point defence system.)

Status: In production. In service with the Italian Air Force. One battery delivered to the Royal Thai Air Force in 1988.

Manufacturer: Selenia, Industrie Elettroniche Associate SpA, Defence Systems Division, Via Tiburtina Km 12.400 2 - 00131 Rome, Italy. PO Box 7083 - 00100 Rome, Italy.
Telephone: (0039-6) 43601
Telex: (43) 613690 SELROM 1

SPECIFICATIONS (missile)

TYPE	single stage, low altitude
LENGTH OF MISSILE	3.7 m
BODY DIAMETER	203 mm
WINGSPAN	680 mm
LAUNCH WEIGHT	204 kg
PROPULSION	single stage, solid propellant
GUIDANCE	semi-active radar homing
WARHEAD	33 kg HE fragmentation with contact and proximity fuzing
SPEED	Mach 2.5
MAX RANGE	18 000 m
MAX ALTITUDE	6000 m
MIN ALTITUDE	15 m

JAPAN

Type 81 Tan-SAM Low Altitude Surface-to-air Missile System

Development
The requirement for the Tan-SAM missile system (Tan is the Japanese word for short) was generated in 1966 when a replacement for the US-supplied divisional level static 75 mm M51 Skysweeper and self-propelled M15A1 37 mm/12.7 mm anti-aircraft guns was requested by the Japanese Ground Self Defence Force (JGSDF).

System research and fabrication of basic prototype systems was undertaken in 1967-68 with actual construction of experimental units taking place in 1969-70. The first complete prototype systems were built between 1971-76 with the technical testing of the individual system components taking place during 1972-77. In 1978-79 the operational tests of the complete system were undertaken and upon their successful conclusion the JGSDF standardised the Tan-SAM as the Type 81 short-range surface-to-air missile system in late 1980 and began placing yearly production contracts with its manufacturer Tokyo Shibaura Denki Company (Toshiba Electric).

As part of the current JGSDF plans, each of its divisional groups will be assigned four fire units of Tan-SAM systems with the first deployments already made to the four divisions located on the northern island of Hokkaido.

A fire unit comprises one fire control system (FCS) vehicle, two quadruple-round launcher vehicles and a few support vehicles with a total team of 15.

During the mid-1970s, the Japanese Air Self Defence Force (JASDF) began a project to increase the survivability of its airfields in terms of both active and passive defences. The Tan-SAM was chosen to provide the outer defence ring against enemy aircraft that had 'leaked' through the forward interceptor and area defence SAM barriers whilst the General Dynamics FIM-92A Stinger and the Nippon Steel Works Company licence-built 20 mm M167 Vulcan Air Defence System provided the progressively shorter-ranged second and third line point defence rings.

The first JASDF bases to be so equipped are the five interceptor airfields which are being assigned two fire units of Tan-SAM systems each. Both the JGSDF and the JASDF have also taken delivery of two additional fire units which have been exclusively assigned to the training role.

The total requirement for Tan-SAM systems currently stands at 27 fire units for the JASDF and 47 fire units for the JGSDF, for which 1212 missiles will be procured. The last order for both services should be placed under the FY88 defence budget requirements. No export orders for the system are envisaged.

Description
The missile is of the single-stage fire-and-forget type with four cruciform centrebody wings and four movable tail-mounted cruciform control fins. Propulsion is by a Nissan Motor solid-fuel rocket which exhausts an excessive amount of white smoke that both visually marks the launch site and allows an observant target to evade the oncoming weapon. The missile is also not kept in a controlled environment launch-container, which means it requires very careful and continuous maintenance practices for its sophisticated electronic components. The guidance system uses an autopilot for the first part of the flight and then switches to an infra-red (IR) passive homing seeker in the missile nose compartment.

Before launch, the scanning angle (in degrees) of the seeker head is pre-programmed by the FCS computer to avoid the missile tracking the sun. This data is calculated from the continuously updated information on the target position. The FCS also controls the launcher movements so that a round cannot be fired directly at the sun by accident.

Once the missile is in flight and has reached the point at which the seeker is activated, the IR head starts to scan the pre-programmed area of the sky to find the target. The guidance unit then locks on and the missile continues to follow the shortest course-to-intecept. At the target, either the HE-fragmentation warhead's contact or radar proximity fuze is activated to detonate the explosive. The lethal radius of the warhead is 5-15 m depending on the target type. No self-destruct circuit is fitted.

Although adverse weather conditions affect the missile performance, it is still said to be comparable to that of the Euromissile Roland under the same conditions. The intercept capabilities in cloud remain good. However, although no IR filters are fitted, targets employing IR decoy systems or manoeuvring within or near to the sun's disc as viewed from the missile stand a good chance of defeating its seeker by simply overwhelming it with spurious heat sources. Some protection is provided by the special electronic precautions incorporated into the design of the search pattern scanning programme (Intermediate Frequency - IF).

For operations against extremely low altitude targets in a heavy electronic jamming environment or against targets approaching from the rear of the launcher where the radar coverage is of marginal effect, control can be switched from the FCS vehicle to a tripod-mounted off-vehicle optical sight/control unit which is carried by each of the launchers. Once this is activated, the electronic link between the FCS and the launcher unit is automatically disengaged and the module is slaved to the sight.

At a fire unit position the personnel responsible for an engagement consists of the commander, radar operator and two launch operators. Each vehicle has to be levelled and stabilised by its hydraulically operated jacks and interconnected by electric cables and the field telephone/data

Close-up of four-round missile launcher of Type 81 Tan-SAM low altitude surface-to-air missile system in travelling configuration (K Nogi)

Type 81 Tan-SAM low altitude surface-to-air missile launcher in travelling configuration. When in firing position four jacks, two on each side, are lowered to the ground to provide a more stable firing platform (Kensuke Ebata)

Japan / **STATIC & TOWED SAM SYSTEMS** 253

Fire control system of Type 81 Tan-SAM low altitude surface-to-air missile in travelling configuration (Kensuke Ebata)

Fire control system of the Type 81 Tan-SAM low altitude surface-to-air missile in operating configuration and stabilisers deployed (Kensuke Ebata)

link system. The normal distance between the FCS and the two launchers is around 300 m. The total time for these preparations is about 30 minutes.

Once these have been completed the surveillance radar on the FCS commences searching its assigned defence area. If only a single target is found, the engagement is relatively simple but for multiple targets priorities have to be assigned. When a designated target comes into effective range of the chosen missile on its launcher a visual signal is lit in the FCS and a weapon is launched using the guidance technique described.

The in-flight seeker lock-on feature allows a Tan-SAM fire unit to launch either two missiles simultaneously or successively while the first is still homing on to the target. Thus, theoretically, up to four targets can be engaged by a single fire unit. However, in practice this is doubtful as a single missile cannot be guaranteed a 100 per cent hit probability. The actual hit probability of a Tan-SAM missile is officially stated to be 75 per cent, even in cloud.

If required, the FCS module, the two launcher modules and their associated generators can be removed from their vehicles and used either for a fixed static site or as a helicopter-transported unit by JGSDF Kawasaki/Vertol V-107II-4/IIA-4 or Kawasaki/Vertol CH-47J Chinook for distances of up to 100 km and over. In either case a small dozer tractor is required to set up the launch site.

Fire Control System (FCS)

The approximately 3054 kg FCS module is mounted on the rear of a modified Isuzu Motors Ltd Type 73 (6 × 6) 3000 kg truck and consists of a 30 kW generator unit immediately aft of the driving cab with the system control cabin to the rear. On top of the cabin roof is a 1 m wide, 1.2 m high 3D phased array pulse Doppler radar antenna which is mechanically steered in azimuth and elevation. The vehicle is stabilised on site by three hydraulically operated outriggers. No armour or NBC protection is provided. The radar search range is around 30 000 m and an integral IFF interrogation facility is fitted. The antenna rotates at 10 rpm and sweeps 360° in azimuth and 15° in elevation during a full rotation. In a sector search it automatically sweeps 110° in azimuth and 20° in elevation. The system has a multi-target capability with each threat being assigned its own number by the FCS computer. The future position and elevation of an individual threat is calculated, then all the information on the various targets is displayed on the three CRT scopes below the antenna in the form of a target symbol, range, altitude and direction data. The unit commander assigns target priorities and indicates those which he intends to engage to the radar operator, who then moves a cursor onto each of the designated targets and presses a button to select it for precise tracking by the radar. Up to six targets can be tracked in this manner at any one time, each one being displayed on a CRT together with its continuously updated evaluation data. The launch data is fed into the selected weapon's onboard guidance system by the FCS computer which also directs the appropriate launcher to turn and elevate according to the position of the target. Once in range the missile is fired.

Launcher

The launcher/generator system weighs approximately the same as the FCS and is mounted on the same type of truck chassis. It has no armour or NBC protection but has four hydraulically operated stabiliser jacks. The module is rectangular with two arms that have launcher rails on their upper and lower sides. On the front ends of each are two IR seeker covers which can be rotated through 180° to protect the missile heads during transit.

Each missile is loaded onto the launcher by hydraulically operated loading platforms mounted on each side of the vehicle. The missile, which

Type 81 Tan-SAM low altitude surface-to-air missile launcher with missiles on upper arm only and stabilisers lowered (Kensuke Ebata)

arrives in a simple box-like container, is manually picked up and placed on the loading platform by the fire unit's crew after removing the container's cover. The loader hydraulically lifts the round into the loading position where the aft end of the launcher rail is slid back to reveal two latches which are then inserted into a slit on the missile body to hold it in place. The rail is moved back to its original position which automatically advances the round into the launch position. This process is repeated four times until all four launch rails are loaded. The total time taken for this action is approximately three minutes.

Variants

Type 81 Tan-SAM Kai Low Altitude Surface-to-air Missile System

In early 1981 the Japanese Defence Agency awarded a Yen 3.14 billion contract to Toshiba for initial research and development work on an improved Tan-SAM Kai (Kai being a Kaizo or modification symbol) missile. This incorporates a strap-down active radar homing seeker, intermittent direction command/programme guidance and mid-course lock-on after launch capabilities into the weapon.

Full scale development, if authorised, will be funded from FY89 onwards. The improvements are to enhance the missile's current areas of weakness: namely its range, hit probability and ECCM performance.

Status: In production. In service with the Japanese Ground Self Defence Force and Japanese Air Self Defence Force.

Manufacturer: Prime contractor and system integration: Toshiba (Tokyo Shibaura Electric) Company Limited, 1-6 Uchisaiwacho, 1-Chrone, Chiyoda-ku, Tokyo 100, Japan.

Main subcontractors: Vehicles: Isuzu Motors Limited, 22-10 Minami-oi, 6-Chrone, Shinagawa-ku, Tokyo, Japan.

Rocket motor: Nissan Motor Company Limited, Aerospace Division, 5-1 3-Chrome, Momoi, Suginami-ku, Tokyo, Japan.

STATIC & TOWED SAM SYSTEMS / Japan-Norway

SPECIFICATIONS (missile)

TYPE	single stage, low altitude	MAX SPEED	Mach 2.4
LENGTH	2.7 m	MAX EFFECTIVE RANGE	7000 m
DIAMETER	0.16 m	MIN EFFECTIVE RANGE	about 500 m
WING SPAN	0.60 m	MAX EFFECTIVE ALTITUDE	around 3000 m
LAUNCH WEIGHT	100 kg	MIN EFFECTIVE ALTITUDE	15 m
PROPULSION	solid fuel sustainer rocket motor	LAUNCHER	trainable four-round static or vehicle-mounted module
GUIDANCE	pre-programmed autopilot with passive IR terminal homing		
WARHEAD	HE-fragmentation with contact and radar proximity fuzes		

NORWAY

Norwegian Advanced Surface-to-air Missile System (NASAMS) for Low to Medium Altitude

Development

In January 1989 the Royal Norwegian Air Force (RNoAF) awarded a $12.5 million Phase I study contract to Hughes Kongsberg Våpenfabrik (HKV) – a joint venture company formed by Norsk Forsvarsteknologi (NFT, formerly Kongsberg Våpenfabrik) and Hughes Aircraft Company Missile Systems Group.

The contract provides for the development of a short- to medium-range semi-mobile ground-launched version of the Hughes AIM-120A Advanced Medium-Range Air-to-Air Missile (AMRAAM) under the designation NASAMS, two batteries of which will be initially fielded to replace the four obsolete Nike Hercules SAM batteries currently deployed in southeast Norway to defend the Gardemoen and Sergye air bases near Oslo. Two of the Nike Hercules batteries will have disbanded by the end of 1989 and the other two are due to go in 1992.

Ultimately, it is envisaged that by the end of the 1990s all six of the Norwegian Adapted HAWK (NOAH) batteries currently in service will also have been upgraded to the NASAMS configuration.

The initial work covers definition of the system specification, study of the software changes required in the systems adopted radar (the Hughes AN/TPQ-36A Low Altitude Surveillance Radar (LADR) of which 24 are currently in Norwegian service for use with the NOAH batteries) and the Fire Distribution Centre (FDC, of which NFT has produced 24 for the NOAH batteries).

The development team will also define the configuration of the launcher and conduct two unguided test launches of AMRAAM rounds to evaluate the weapon's initial launch ballistics during the first 0.5 second of flight before the full aerodynamic control is effected.

Phase 2 of the project is to be full-scale development of the system and will involve three launches of guided rounds at the White Sands Missile Range, New Mexico to evaluate the complete integrated system.

Phase 3 is the production stage with the six year programme due to culminate in the delivery to the RNoAF of an initial 18 launchers and 118 missiles for the first two batteries.

Description

A NASAMS fire unit (FU) consists of three truck mobile 6-round launcher platform subsystems, an FDC and a 3D AN/TPQ-36A radar. The FU composition allows for up to 60-80 targets to be independently handled.

Three fire units are linked together in a triangular command network to form the battery, so that if required, any of the three radars can provide targetting data to any of the nine available launcher platforms.

The gimballed missile launcher is pallet-mounted on a truck and off-loaded at a launch site where it is levelled by adjusting four hand operated jacks. The missile pallet can be raised to point the missile at an acute nose-up angle and slewed in azimuth to the desired launch bearing.

The six missiles are attached to standard LAU-129 aircraft launcher rails and protected by hinged weather covers. The missiles are standard solid-state AIM-120A all-weather all-aspect air-to-air rounds which use a Nortronics strap-down inertial guidance unit for the mid-course flight phase and a Hughes I/J-band active radar seeker for terminal homing. It also has a home-on-jam capability. Flight control is by cruciform rear fins. The HE blast-fragmentation warhead is detonated either by the proximity delay or contact fuzing circuits.

In operation the missiles will be maintained in an unpowered condition until a firing command is initiated for the selected weapon at the FDC. Once this is received at the launcher, the missile start sequence is activated and boost motor ignition starts the launch 1.4 seconds later.

Initial position data is fed into the AIM-120A inertial guidance unit prior to launch by an indigenous designed and built navigation system mounted on the launcher. This guides the weapon towards the predicted target location during the early part of the flight trajectory.

Upon approaching the location the active seeker is switched on in a high pulse repetition frequency (PRF) mode to acquire and track the target. The missile then changes to its medium PRF mode for the terminal attack phase.

The AN/TPQ-36A low altitude search and track radar uses 3D pencil beams and frequency agile phase beam scanning to provide accurate target range, bearing and elevation cueing data to the manned field mobile FDC shelter. The radar antenna rotates mechanically in azimuth to provide 360° coverage with a variable rate azimuth scan. Beam scheduling is computer-controlled and adaptive to mission requirements. Elevation coverage has been successfully demonstrated between 3 and 1800 m on fixed and rotary wing aircraft operating from the hoverto 724 km/h.

The FDC contains a command/control processor and display subsystem, a digital radar signal processor and a radar control computer.

Although having a shorter engagement range than the NOAH systems, the NASAMS battery more than compensates for this by having an acquisition range which is a greater percentage of its total fly-out range. This, plus the weapon's relatively short reaction time and autonomous launch-and-leave capability, allows multiple-engagements which could have up to 18 independently targetted AMRAAMs in the air at any one time from a fire unit, thus considerably increasing the enemy's perceived problems in trying to overwhelm the RNoAF air defence network.

SPECIFICATIONS (Missile)

TYPE	single-stage low to medium altitude	GUIDANCE	inertial mid-course with active radar terminal homing
LENGTH	3.655 m	WARHEAD	20.4 kg HE-fragmentation with proximity and contact fuzing
DIAMETER	0.178 m	MAX SPEED	Mach 2-3
MAX SPAN	0.627 m	MAX RANGE	not available
LAUNCH WEIGHT	152.05 kg	MIN RANGE	not available
PROPULSION	single-stage solid propellant rocket motor	MAX ALTITUDE	not available
		MIN ALTITUDE	not available
		LAUNCHER TYPE	6-rail trainable pallet system

Status: Development. On order for the Royal Norwegian Air Force (2 batteries).

Manufacturers: Norsk Forsvarsteknologi A/S, N-36000 Kongsberg, Norway.

Hughes Aircraft Company, Missile Systems Group, 8433 Fallbrook Avenue, Canoga Park, California 91304, USA.
Telephone: (213) 883 2400
Telex: 910 4944 997

TAIWAN

Tien Kung I Low to High Altitude Surface-to-Air Missile System

Development
In the mid to late 1970s the Sun-Yat-sen Institute of Science and Technology began work on a new surface-to-air missile system for the Taiwanese Army that was based on the I-HAWK missile. A higher thrust rocket motor was to be installed to increase both the speed and maximum engagement altitude. The airframe and control surfaces were to be redesigned to cope with the higher velocities and to increase the weapon's manoeuvring capabilities and a new guidance system was fitted. This combined mid-course command guidance with a terminal semi-active radar (SAR) seeker head which allowed the missile to fly an energy-efficient flight path to the vicinity of the target where the seeker head would take over for the final attack. The theory was that the actual radar illumination of the target to produce the reflected electromagnetic energy signals for the seeker to home on would be initiated only during the last seconds of the engagement to give the target the minimum amount of time either to evade or commence ECM. Ultimately this project produced a missile design that resembled a scaled-up Hughes AIM-54 Phoenix.

However, due to the acquisition of more sophisticated missile technology in the form of an 85 per cent transfer from Raytheon and the US Government of the MIM-104 Patriot design, the Sun-Yat-sen Institute was directed to stop work on the above and, in 1981, start development of the Tien Kung I (Sky Bow I) missile system based on the Patriot. Various combinations of different components and aerodynamic configurations to suit local production needs were tried, using computer-aided design techniques coupled with an exhaustive scale model wind tunnel test programme and, in the final stages of the work, full-scale test firings that included one missile configuration fitted with much larger tail surfaces than Patriot. Firing trials were completed in March 1985.

Description
In the end, however, the Tien Kung I's physical appearance and basic operational parameters remained similar to those of Patriot (see entry in this section). For the target acquisition, tracking and mid-course missile guidance requirements the army deployed, in mid-1987, a 4 × 4 truck-mounted container with four planar multi-element phased array antennas mounted on each face of a retractable 'tower' to provide 360° coverage. The 'tower' is elevated for use only when the vehicle is placed at a missile site. For illumination of targets during the terminal attack phase the Institute developed the CS/MPG-25 continuous wave illuminator radar set which is believed to be tied into the weapon's phased array system on a similar time-share manner to that employed by the US Navy's shipborne AEGIS air defence system in order to allow multi-engagement capability.

Prior to these Sun-Yat-sen Institute developments, operational Tien Kung I batteries were fitted with interface electronics to operate with the fire control systems of I-HAWK batteries. Post deployment of the radars, it is believed that interfaces now exist for both systems to co-ordinate their actions during an engagement.

There is no track-via-missile (TVM) homing capability as this technology was not included as part of the package released to Taiwan. Despite this, the basic SAR seeker-equipped version is being supplemented in service by a variant fitted with a passive all-aspects liquid nitrogen cooled infra-red indium actinide seeker. This provides the battery with the option of firing more than one missile type during a single or multiple target engagement. This variant was tested successfully in April 1985 against a HAWK missile target.

The trailer-mounted launcher station is almost identical to that used for Patriot except in minor details such as the frangible covers on the four container-launcher boxes.

Status: In production. In service with the Taiwanese Army.

Note: In 1988 it was reported that both the Tien Kung I and Tien Kung II had been renamed the Chungcheng 100 series.

Tien Kung II Low to High Altitude Surface-to-air Missile System

Development/Description
Using the technology and experience gained from its previous surface-to-air missile development projects, the Sun-Yat-sen Institute of Science and Technology is engaged in the development of a ramjet-propelled replacement for the Taiwanese Army's MIM-14 Nike Hercules systems. Known as Tien Kung II (Sky Bow II), the first test firings apparently took place in late 1988 with operational deployment due in the early 1990s.

Status: Development phase.

Note: In 1988 it was reported that both the Tien Kung I and Tien Kung II had been renamed the Chungcheng 100 series.

Sky Sword I Low Altitude Surface-to-air Missile System

Development
In mid-1988 the Taiwanese Cabinet, in its report to the Taiwanese Legislate, revealed that the Ministry of National Defence had successfully undertaken modification of the Chung San Institute of Technology Sky Sword I infra-red passive homing air-to-air missile for mobile, naval and static ground launch applications.

It is envisaged that the Sky Sword I will eventually replace the MIM-72 Chaparral/Sea Chaparral weapons.

Description
The all-aspects Sky Sword I is similar in physical appearance to the AIM-9G/H Sidewinder. Flight control is by cruciform canard fins. Maximum range is estimated to be 10 000 m within altitude limits of 20 to 3000 m.

SPECIFICATIONS (missile – provisional)

TYPE	single stage low altitude
LENGTH	2.87 m
DIAMETER	0.127 m
MAX SPAN	0.64 m
LAUNCH WEIGHT	90 kg
PROPULSION	solid fuel rocket motor
GUIDANCE	passive infra-red homing
MAX SPEED	Mach 1 plus
MAX RANGE	10 000 m
MAX ALTITUDE	3000 m
MIN ALTITUDE	20 m
LAUNCHER	4-round trainable static (or mobile)

Status: Entering production. On order for the Taiwanese Army and Air Force.

SA-1 Guild Medium Altitude Surface-to-air Missile System

Development
Development of the R-113 (NATO designation SA-1 Guild) guided air defence missile system was begun in 1950 by the Lavochkin OKB design bureau with the first trial launches in 1951. By 1952 the initial trial units were formed in the Moscow PVO-Strany (*Voyska Protivovozdushnoy Oborony Strany* — Troops of the National Air Defence) district. Between 1954 and 1958, their strength was increased to several Air Defence Force Armies, Corps and independent Brigades and Regiments totalling some 3200 launchers in battalions of six static launcher rails.

Each site was constructed in a characteristic herring-bone pattern. So many were built round the Moscow area, in three concentric circles, that the Soviet Union had to build the two outer Moscow ring roads to support them.

The SA-1 missile was first shown in public during the 7 November 1960 Red Square Parade in Moscow and has remained in continuous front line service until the mid-1980s when reports have indicated that numbers have begun to decline due to the introduction of more capable weapons.

The SA-1 Guild was used on a number of occasions during the late-1950s against CIA-flown high altitude overflights of the Soviet Union by Lockheed U-2s without success.

Description
The R-113 (SA-1) is a longer and more streamlined version of the R-101E surface-to-air missile which was a Soviet copy of the Second World War German Wasserfall design. It is a single stage weapon which uses an Isayev storable liquid fuel rocket motor with a turbo-pump fuel feed system. Steering is by four canard fins on the nose.

During its service life the weapon has undergone a number of internal improvements to increase its reliability. The maximum slant range is 55 km and the maximum engagement altitude is around 30 000 m, although its maximum effective altitude is thought to be around 20 000 m. The single rail launcher is semi-fixed and lifts the missile into the vertical for firing.

Initial target detection is usually carried out by the elderly A-band medium to high altitude (up to 45 720 m) P-14 (NATO designation Tall King) 600 km range fixed site peripheral early warning radars which hand the contact over to the 300 km range E/F-band target acquisition radar of the R-113 system known by the NATO designation Gage. This is usually used in conjunction with a D/E-band nodding heightfinder radar such as the 200 km range PRV-9 (NATO designation Patty Cake) set to gain additional target data before the central guidance radar of the R-113 battalion is locked on. Known by the NATO designation Yo-Yo, this 150 km E/F-band radar is unique in having six antennas, each rotating about 70 × 70°. Using 'flapping' beams it can track 24-30 targets simultaneously and guide two to three missiles at any one time at a single target.

For the whole flight, the R-113 is command guided with the 250 kg HE-fragmentation warhead detonated either by its proximity fuze or a command signal. Its manoeuvring capabilities at the upper part of its flight envelope are considerably limited by its low fuel supply and small control surfaces.

Close-up of SA-1 (Guild) surface-to-air missile on its semi-trailer (US Army)

SA-1 (Guild) surface-to-air missiles on semi-trailers being towed by ZIL-137 (6 × 6) tractor trucks through Red Square, Moscow, in November 1982

SA-1 (Guild) surface-to-air missiles being launched from their single rail launchers

SPECIFICATIONS (missile)

TYPE	single stage, medium altitude
LENGTH	12 m
DIAMETER	0.7 m
MAX SPAN	2.7 m
LAUNCH WEIGHT	3500 kg
PROPULSION	storable liquid fuel rocket motor
GUIDANCE	command
WARHEAD	250 kg HE-fragmentation with proximity and command fuzing
MAX SPEED	Mach 2.5+
MAX RANGE	55 km
MAX ALTITUDE	30 000 m
MIN ALTITUDE	4000 m
LAUNCHER	single rail semi-fixed vertical

Status: Production complete. In service only with the Soviet Union.

Manufacturer: Soviet state factories. Designed by Lavochkin OKB design bureau.

SA-2 Guideline Medium to High Altitude Surface-to-air Missile System

Development
Development of the V-75 Dvina (Soviet river name, NATO designation SA-2 Guideline) system began during 1953 at the Lovochkin OKB design bureau as a medium to high altitude SAM system for use against non-manoeuvring targets such as bombers. It was also designed to be more suitable for nation-wide deployment than the R-113 (SA-1 Guild).

In 1957 the first operational PVO-Strany (*Voyska Protivovozduchnoy Oborony Strany* — Troops of the National Air Defence) V-75 missile regiments of three six-rail launcher battalions were formed with one of the initial deployments near the strategically important city of Sverdlovsk. On 1 May 1960 the Sverdlovsk units fired a total of 14 V-750s against a Lockheed U-2 high altitude reconnaissance aircraft flown by Gary Powers of the CIA. The subsequent detonation of the missiles at high altitude not only forced the U-2 to crash, thereby precipitating an international crisis, but also destroyed a Soviet PVO-Strany MiG-19 interceptor. The end result of the incident was that the USA ceased all further U-2 overflights of Soviet territory, losing a valuable strategic intelligence source.

The next incident involving the V-750 was when Chinese People's Liberation Army Air Defence Missile units shot down a Taiwanese-flown Lockheed U-2 over Narching in September 1962. The V-750 and its locally built derivative, the HQ-2, were subsequently used on many occasions throughout the 1960s against further Taiwanese-flown U-2s and American Ryan pilotless reconnaissance drones, scoring at least another eight U-2s by 1970.

The initial Chinese incident was rapidly followed by the 1962 Cuban missile crisis during which a US Air Force U-2 was lost on 27 October to a V-750 whilst flying over the Cuban naval base at Banes. In mid-1965 the Guideline was introduced into the North Vietnamese Air Defence Network, claiming its first victim, a US Air Force McDonnell Douglas F-4C Phantom, on 24 July. By the end of 1965, 194 V-750s had been fired to destroy five US Air Force (two F-4s and three F-105s) and six US Navy aircraft (one F-4, one A-4, two F-8, one A-6 and one RA-5C).

In 1966 the total rose to 1096 for 34 kills (18 US Air Force, 15 US Navy, one US Marine Corps). In 1967, 3202 fired for 60 kills (28 US Air Force, 30 US Navy, two US Marine Corps) and from January to the bombing halt in March 1968, 322 for three kills. From the beginning of 1968 to the end of 1971 an unknown number of SAMs were fired to destroy a total of 16 US aircraft (seven US Air Force, eight US Navy and one US Marine Corps). During the 1972 invasion of South Vietnam until the January 1973 ceasefire, the total number of SAMs fired was 4244 (including numbers of SA-3 Goas and SA-7 Grails). This resulted in the loss of 76 aircraft (54 US Air Force, 22 US Navy) and seven helicopters (six US Army, one US Marine Corps). Among the US Air Force losses were 16 Boeing B-52 Stratofortresses, one of which was hit by a V-750 over Vinh on 22 November; the others were lost to the V-750 during the Linebacker 2 raids of late 1972. To destroy these aircraft and damage at least four others, the North Vietnamese were logged as firing 1242 Guidelines at them using both individual guided launchers and shotgun-like unguided salvoes using MiG-21s which shadowed the bomber cells to provide the necessary height and bearing data to the fire control teams.

Surprisingly, despite the initial uses of the V-750, it was not until the Vietnam War that the Americans gained the necessary raw intelligence data on the weapon's proximity fuzing system, its terminal phase guidance signals and the warhead's overpressure charactistics at detonation to enable them to design suitable ECM systems to counter it. This was obtained on 13 February 1966 during a flight over North Vietnam by specially radar enhanced high altitude Ryan 147E ELINT pilotless drone which relayed the information back to a monitoring station until a V-750 destroyed it. This was followed on 22 July 1966 by another special flight involving a Ryan 147F drone protected by onboard ECM equipment. A total of 11 V-750s were fired at the drone before one managed to defeat the ECM coverage and hit it.

In the same year as the V-750 entered the Vietnam War, the Indian Air Force used it operationally during the 1965 Indo-Pakistan War. Obtained in 1963, the first examples of an eventual 25 battalion force were deployed around New Delhi and several of the key airfields in that area. Their only confirmed kill was near Delhi on 6 September when an Indian Air Force Antonov An-12 Cub transport was shot down in mistake for a Pakistan Air Force Lockheed C-130 Hercules. However, during the later stages of the war, the Pakistan Air Force sole high altitude Martin RB-57F reconnaissance aircraft was bracketed by two V-750s at about 15 850 m altitude causing sufficient damage for it to crash land on return to its base.

Egypt began receiving the V-750 at the same time as the Indians and had 18 battalions in service by the 1967 June war with Israel. They fired only 22 missiles without success and one complete battery including radars was captured by the Israeli Army. During the 1968-70 War of Attrition that followed, hundreds of V-750s were supplied to Egypt and the weapon finally scored its first kill over the Middle East on 9 March 1969 when an Israeli Piper Cub observation aircraft was destroyed. Between then and the 1973 war the number of kills it made increased to about 10, including several F-4E Phantoms, A-4 Skyhawks and a specially configured ELINT Boeing C-97 Stratocruiser.

The V-750 was also used in the 1971 Indo-Pakistan war (no kills scored), the 1973 Yom Kippur War (by both Egypt and Syria), the Gulf War (by both sides), by Syria during the 1982 Bekaa Valley air defence battle, by Libya during the March/April 1986 incidents with the Americans, and by Angola against the South African Air Force. It has also been used by North Korea and Cuba on numerous occasions to try and hit American Lockheed SR-71 high-speed high altitude reconnaissance aircraft.

SA-2 Guideline surface-to-air missile on its single rail launcher installed in a revetment and showing stabilisers deployed

SA-2 Guideline surface-to-air missile partly elevated

SA-2 Guideline surface-to-air missile on its single rail launcher before elevation into the launch position

STATIC & TOWED SAM SYSTEMS / USSR

ZIL-157 (6 × 6) truck towing semi-trailer carrying SA-2 Guideline surface-to-air missile for loading directly onto the launcher

Soviet missiles on parade in Moscow, with four SA-2 Guidelines centre, FROG-7s in foreground and SA-3 Goas top left side

Although when the performance of the weapon is analysed a high number of launches per kill is found, the missile has proved its worth by reducing the accuracy and effectiveness of the enemy's air power by diverting valuable effort to SAM suppression missions, restricting the use of reconnaissance assets and, most importantly, forcing enemy aircraft to adopt tactics or fly lower where other air defence systems such as guns, interceptors or different missile types can prey on their increased vulnerability.

By 1988 the number of V-750 launchers in V-PVO (*Voyska Protivovozdushnoy Oborony* — Troops of the Air Defence) regiments had declined to around 2500 from the PVO-Strany peak of over 4600 in the late 1960s. During its long life the weapon had been subjected to numerous modifications, both internally and to its guidance systems. Most of these were prompted by combat experience and the need to rectify problems.

The original V-750 missile (Soviet system designation V-75, US/NATO missile codename SA-2a/Guideline Mod 0) was first seen in public during the 1957 Red Square parade. The associated E-band missile guidance radar was allocated the NATO codename Fan Song A.

The system was quickly superceded in 1958 by the V75SM system with the marginally longer V-750VK missile (US/NATO codename SA-2b/Guideline Mod 1) and the NATO codename Fan Song B radar set. The main improvements were incorporated within the missile itself and on the radar with the deletion of the original upper parabolic antenna fitted to the vertical orthogonal antenna.

In 1959-60 the V-75M system with the V-750M missile (US/NATO codename SA-2c/Guideline Mod 2) and its NATO codename G-band Fan Song C radar entered operational service. The V-750M is identical in appearance to the V-750VK but has a greater maximum engagement range and lower minimum engagement altitude.

During the early 1960s two other Fan Song G-band radars were developed, the Fan Song D (which never actually entered operational service) and the Fan Song E. The latter was associated with the US/NATO codename SA-2d/Guideline Mod 3 weapon which appeared around 1961 but is more readily identified with the improved guidance US/NATO codename SA-2e/Guideline Mod 4. The SA-2d differed significantly from the SA-2a in having four enlarged dielectric up-link guidance receiver strip antennas under prominent covers on the forward side of the missile instead of the usual two sets of four. It also has a longer barometric nose probe and several other differences associated with the sustainer motor casing. The SA-2e is essentially the same in external layout as the SA-2d but has upgraded internal components and a larger, more bulbous warhead section for either a conventional HE-fragmentation or command detonated nuclear warhead. Unlike the SA-2d the SA-2e was not exported and has remained a solely Soviet operated weapon.

The Fan Song E radar has two parabolic antennas added above the horizontal orthogonal antennas to provide a Lobe-On-Receiver-Only (LORO) Electronic Counter Counter Measure (ECCM).

During 1967-68, following the extensive combat experience gained on Guideline during the Vietnam War and the loss of at least 12 SA-2b missiles with associated Fan Song B radar equipment to Israel in the 1967 Six Day War, the V-75 system design bureau undertook a crash programme to improve the ECCM capabilities and engagement envelope of the Dvina.

Using technology drawn from the more advanced S-125 Pechora, the bureau produced the US/NATO codename SA-2f/Guideline Mod 5 missile and Fan Song F radar. Prototype trials were undertaken in late 1968, with the first production battalions being operationally deployed in early 1970. A number of the SA-2f systems were rushed to Egypt for use along the Suez Canal in the latter part of the War of Attrition. Further deliveries were made to Vietnam during 1970-71 for incorporation into its air defence network.

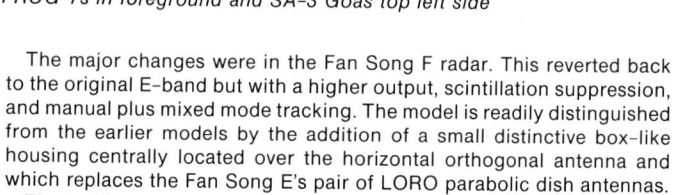

The major changes were in the Fan Song F radar. This reverted back to the original E-band but with a higher output, scintillation suppression, and manual plus mixed mode tracking. The model is readily distinguished from the earlier models by the addition of a small distinctive box-like housing centrally located over the horizontal orthogonal antenna and which replaces the Fan Song E's pair of LORO parabolic dish antennas.

The 'cab' contains the necessary electro-optical tracking and guidance equipment for a two-man team to track a target in a severe ECM environment where the normal automatic electronic tracking mode has been jammed. The optical systems allows target acquisition and missile guidance using the C-band UHF command link at altitudes down to approximately 90 m.

The other significant change in the SA-2f is in the missile guidance package, which now has a capability to home on targets using strobe jamming.

It is expected that the SA-10 Grumble family will totally replace the SA-2 Guideline in Soviet service by the turn of the 20th Century.

Description

The V-750 is a two stage weapon with a large solid propellant booster stage fitted with four very large delta fins. The missile itself has a storable liquid fuel sustainer rocket motor which uses a nitric acid/hydrocarbon fuel mix. Towards the mid-section is a set of four cropped delta-shaped wings with a second in-line set of small fixed fins at the nose and a third in-line set of slightly larger powered control fins at the tail. The warhead of the SA-2a/b/c/d/f weighs 195 kg (130 kg of which is HE) and is an HE internally grooved fragmentation type with proximity, contact and command type fuzing available. The warhead has a lethal burst radius of 13.5 m against F-4 sized targets at low altitude and around 61 m against large targets such as bombers at high altitude. Maximum blast radius is about 125-135 m. The 295 kg nuclear warhead for the SA-2d variant is believed to have a yield of 25 kt. The conventional warhead weighs the same.

The whole V-75 system, including the launcher, is designed to be simple and easy to operate with the minimum of specialised training. In practically all user countries the pattern of a battalion site is as follows: six semi-fixed trainable single rail launchers are deployed in a hexagon arrangement, about 60-100 m apart. They can either be dug into pits, left at ground level or hardened by being dug in and surrounded by concrete revetments. In the centre of the launchers is the battery command post with the fire control team and its computer, the Fan Song missile control radar, the P-12 (NATO designation Spoon Rest-A truck-mounted or Spoon Rest-B) early warning radar and usually six reload rounds on their articulated trailers. Again, the fire control team, its equipment and the radars can either be van-mounted above ground, simply dug in or located underground in hardened concrete bunkers. Camouflage is used as required.

The battalion's early warning and target acquisition Spoon Rest A-band radar has a range of 275 km using a large Yagi antenna array.

At regimental HQ there is a fourth Spoon Rest, a van-mounted P-15 (NATO Codename Flat Face) 250 km range C-band search and tracking radar with two elliptical parabolic reflectors and a PRV-11 (NATO codename Side Net) 180 km range E-band nodding heightfinder radar mounted on a box-bodied trailer. There is also a radar control truck and a Mercury Grass truck-mounted command communications system for linking the HQ to the three battalions.

Once the P-12 and P-15 radars detect a target entering the regiment's assigned defence zone, it is interrogated by the HQ's IFF system (NATO codename Score Board). If designated hostile, the regimental HQ identifies which of its three battalions is the most suitable one for the engagement and transmits the contact details in the form of range, altitude

USSR / STATIC & TOWED SAM SYSTEMS

Heart of the SA-2 Guideline surface-to-air missile system is this Fan Song Radar (E version) system which is deployed together with six launchers (US Department of Defense)

Close-up of SA-2 Guideline on its semi-trailer which transfers the missile directly onto the launcher in 12 mins

and bearing either by radio or land line from the Mercury Grass command station to the battalions radar elements.

The Fan Song A through to E are normally operated by a four man crew (the Fan Song F has six); a range tracking officer and three enlisted men who serve as angle track operators.

The Fan Songs operate in two basic modes (except the Fan Song E and F systems which have a third intermediate mode for low altitude searching).

In the target acquisition zone the radar searches for the target to which it has been alerted by the P-12 battalion set. The track-while-scan capability in this mode allows it to transfer the data on one target's bearing, altitude and velocity to the fire control computer whilst continuing the scanning to acquire other targets for follow-up tracking. The Fan Song E is able to track up to six targets simultaneously.

Maximum radar range of the E-band Fan Song A/B/F models varies between 60-120 km depending upon target type, altitude and operating conditions. The G-band Fan Song D/E maximum range is extended to between 75-150 km under the same parameters.

The main element of a Fan Song is the pair of orthogonal trough antennas, one horizontal and one vertical, which emit two 'flapping' fan-shaped radar beams in their respective planes.

As already stated the Fan Song E set has an additional LORO ECCM facility built in, whilst the Fan Song F has had this replaced by an electro-optical guidance mode option for use in heavy ECM environments.

In some countries which only deploy early versions of the SA-2, the elderly ground-mounted P-8 Dolphin (NATO codename Knife Rest-A) or truck-mounted P-10 (NATO codename Knife Rest-B/C) radars may be used in lieu of Spoon Rest. They are A-band sets and have an operating range in the order of 150-200 km.

As soon as the computer has a firing solution on a target, a launcher is brought to bear, elevated to between 20 and 80° and blast deflectors erected. Up to three missiles can be fired and controlled against a single target. Launch interval is six seconds.

Once a missile is fired its solid fuel booster is ignited and this burns for 4.5 seconds to take the weapon away from the launch site. After five seconds it is jettisoned. Once a missile is on its way the fire control computer continues to receive target data from the Fan Song which is now tracking the missile as well. The computer continually generates commands to guide the missile at the target and these are transmitted over a C-band UHF radio beam up-link to four (or eight depending upon missile model) strip antennas mounted forward and aft of the missile's centrebody wings. The onboard guidance unit accepts these and adjusts the missile's trajectory using the moveable control fins aft. A V-750 must pick up its narrow UHF line-of-sight guidance beam within six seconds of launch otherwise it goes ballistic and does not guide. The liquid fuel sustainer burns for a total of 22 seconds with the V-750 attaining its maximum velocity only when it reaches around 7630 m altitude.

This means that the missile has limited capability and manoeuvrability when engaging tactical aircraft. Once guided to the vicinity of its target, the weapon's fuzing system is activated and this detonates the warhead either by proximity or command signal. A self-destruct unit detonates the warhead after 60 seconds of unguided flight time following launch or after 115 seconds, if closure with the target during guided flight has not been made. Reloading a launcher takes about 12 minutes using the articulated reload trailer and its ZIL-151 (6 × 6) truck.

Over the years various defence techniques have been developed to counter the V-75 models. These include ECM systems, the deployment of large quantities of chaff to confuse the Fan Song guidance radar, and actually outmanoeuvring the missile in flight. However, the best to date has proved to be the use of specialist aircraft to suppress the SAM system by electronically and physically attacking it.

Variants

The People's Republic of China has developed its own reverse engineered version of the V-750 under the designation HQ-2, details of which appear earlier in this section.

Arab British Dynamics reverse engineered the V-750 Guideline to meet the requirements of the Egyptian Air Defence Command, but it was not placed in production. It had the local name Early Bird.

A navalised version, the M-2 (US designation SA-N-2), was tried from 1961 onwards, but proved unsuccessful.

SPECIFICATIONS (missile)	
TYPE	two-stage medium to high altitude
LENGTH	
SA-2a	10.6 m
SA-2b/c/e/f	10.7 m
SA-2d	11.2 m
DIAMETER	
booster	0.65 m
missile	0.50 m
MAX SPAN	
booster	2.5 m
missile	1.7 m
LAUNCH WEIGHT	
SA-2a/b/c/f	2287 kg
SA-2d/e	2450 kg
PROPULSION	solid fuel booster with storable liquid fuel sustainer rocket motor
GUIDANCE	command type
WARHEAD	
SA-2a/b/c/e/f	195 kg HE-fragmentation with proximity and/or command fuzing systems
SA-2d	Optional 295 kg HE-fragmentation with proximity and/or command fuzing or 25 kt nuclear warhead with command fuzing system
MAX SPEED	
SA-2a/b/c	Mach 3.0
SA-2d/e/f	Mach 3.5
MAX EFFECTIVE RANGE	
SA-2a/b/f	35 000 m
SA-2c	44 000 m
SA-2d/e	50 000 m
MIN EFFECTIVE RANGE	
SA-2a/b/c	9300 m
SA-2d/e/f	7000 m
MAX EFFECTIVE ALTITUDE	27 400 m
MIN EFFECTIVE ALTITUDE	
SA-2a/b	450 m
SA-2c	300 m
SA-2d/e	150 m
SA-2f	90 m
LAUNCHER	single rail semi-fixed trainable
RELOAD TIME	12 mins

260 STATIC & TOWED SAM SYSTEMS / USSR

Status: Production complete. In service with the following countries:

Country	No of launchers	Operator
Afghanistan	120	Air Force (20 battalions)
Albania	30	Air Force (5 battalions including HQ-2)
Algeria	42	Air Force (2 battalions), army (5 battalions)
Angola	12	Air Force (2 battalions)
Bulgaria	132	Air Force (22 battalions)
China, People's Republic	not known	Air Force (mostly HQ-2)
Cuba	144	Air Force (24 battalions)
Czechoslovakia	120	Air Defence Command (20 battalions)
Egypt	390	Air Defence Command (65 battalions)
Ethiopia	36	Army (6 battalions)
Germany, East	88	Air Defence Command (22 battalions)
Hungary	96	Air Force (16 battalions)
India	100	Air Force (25 battalions)
Iran	60+	Air Force (HQ-2 only)
Iraq	120	Army (20 battalions)
Korea, North	270	Air Force (45 battalions in 15 Regiments, including HQ-2 model)
Libya	108	Air Defence Command (6 brigades each with 18 launchers)
Mongolia	6	Army (1 battery)
Pakistan	6	Air Force, HQ-2 version (1 battery)
Peru	18	Air Force (3 battalions)
Poland	240	Air Defence Command (40 battalions)
Romania	108	Air Force (18 battalions)
Somalia	36	Army (6 battalions)
Sudan	18	Army (1 brigade of 3 battalions)
Syria	138+	Air Defence Command (minimum 23 battalions)
USSR	2730	Air Defence Troops
Vietnam	360	Air Defence Force (20 Regiments with 18 launchers each)
Yemen, North	18	Army (1 battalion), Air Force (1 Regiment with 12 launchers)
Yemen, South	54	Army (1 battalion), Air Force (1 Regiment with 8 battalions each with 6 launchers)
Yugoslavia	48	Air Defence Force (8 battalions)

Manufacturer: Soviet state factories. Designed by Lavochkin OKB design bureau.

SA-3 Goa Low to Medium Altitude Surface-to-air Missile System

Development

Known by the name Pechora (Soviet river), the S-125 (NATO designation SA-3 Goa) was developed from around 1956 by the Lavochkin OKB as a low to medium altitude complement to the larger R-113 (SA-1), S-75 (SA-2) and S-200 (SA-5) medium to high altitude surface-to-air missile systems.

Prototype trials began in 1959 with initial deployment beginning in 1961 at static sites on trainable twin launchers. The missile entered operational service with the PVO-Strany (*Voyska Protvovozdushnoy Oborony Strany* — Troops of the National Air Defence) missile units for use in airfield defence, low level air defence around long-range SAM systems and the rear area protection of Soviet Army fronts in conjunction with the S-75 (SA-2) system. In this last role the missile units are not subordinate to the ground forces but are integrated into the overall front air defence network. At the same time as the S-125 entered service a navalised version, M-1, achieved operational status with the Soviet Navy aboard cruisers and destroyers. In 1973 a quadruple rail launcher was introduced into service with Soviet Air Defence forces to replace the twin launcher in areas of strategic importance.

The first recorded combat use of the S-125 was in 1970 when Soviet PVO-Strany units, including several Goa missile regiments, were deployed to Egypt with twin launchers to form a joint Egyptian-Soviet air defence network to cover the Suez Canal Zone during the last phase of the 1968-70 Egyptian-Israeli War of Attrition.

Although losing a large number of men and much equipment to Israeli air attacks, the Soviet Union shot down three McDonnell Douglas F-4E Phantoms in four days with the S-125 and were instrumental in forcing on the Israelis the 7 August 1970 UN ceasefire.

The next combat use came in late 1972 when the North Vietnamese used small numbers of S-125s against American aircraft during the Linebacker raids. Their first recorded kill was also against an F-4 Phantom. However its major combat test came during the 1973 Yom Kippur War when both Syria and Egypt used large numbers against the Israeli Air Force. The Egyptians started the war with an air defence network of

ZIL 131 (6 × 6) truck carrying two SA-3 Goa SAMs

SA-3 Goa SAM twin-round launcher of the East German Air Force.

USSR / STATIC & TOWED SAM SYSTEMS

SA-3 Goa SAM four-round launcher deployed in the field

ZIL-131 (6 × 6) trucks carrying two SA-3 Goa SAMs

Older ZIL-157 (6 × 6) truck carrying two SA-3 Goa SAMs

146 SAM batteries of which approximately a third used S-125s. The Syrians deployed a total of 34 SAM batteries, of which some 15 (including three S-125s) were located between Damascus and the Golan Heights.

The Arab Air Defence networks of both fronts fired around 2100 missiles of the SA-2/SA-3 and SA-6 types to destroy some 46 Israeli aircraft as confirmed kills. However in return the Egyptians lost a number of SA-2, SA-3 and SA-6 batteries which were captured intact by the Israelis and subsequently made available to US Intelligence experts.

Since 1973, the S-125 has been used in combat by Iraq (during the Gulf War), Syria (two batteries in the 1982 air-to-ground Bekaa Valley Air Defence War), Libya (during the April 1986 US Navy and Air Force raids) and Angola (against South African aircraft during various battles in Southern Angola).

By late 1986 the Soviets had over 300 S-125 battalion sites in operation, using either four twin or 5P73 quadruple rail launchers. The missile was still in production and had been exported to 26 countries world-wide.

Description

The S-125 has a large 2.6 second burn jettisonable solid fuel Isayev OKB booster section fitted with rectangular fins that rotate through 90° at launch. The smaller missile body has an 18.7 second burn Isayev OKB solid fuel sustainer rocket and is fitted with four fixed fins aft and four movable control surfaces forward. After booster jettison the second stage is captured in the radar beam and guidance signals are sent via antenna on the rear fins to place the missile on an intercept trajectory. In the initial 1961 version, US designation SA-3a (NATO designation Goa Mod 0), guidance is by command throughout the flight, while in the definitive version introduced into service in 1964 and known by the US designation SA-3b (NATO designation Goa Mod 1), this has been improved.

Long-range early warning and target acquisition is usually handled by a van-mounted P-15 (NATO designation Flat Face) C-band 250 km range radar with two stacked elliptical parabolic antennas. In many Warsaw Pact S-125 battalions the P-15 has been replaced by the P-15M set (NATO designation Squat Eye) which has the same performance but has had its antenna mounted on a 30 m mast to improve the low altitude coverage. A PRV-11 (NATO designation Side Net) 180 km range 32 000 m altitude E-band heightfinder radar is also used.

All target data generated is passed onto the S-125 battalion's organic trailer mounted fire control radar known by the NATO designation Low Blow. Wherever possible, the four launchers at an S-125 site are positioned in a hand-shaped pattern with the thumb consisting of the revetted long-range search and the palm the Low Blow radar. The latter is controlled from a van or bunker and is optimised for low to medium target monitoring using an unusual antenna configuration of two electro-mechanically scanned parabolic dishes set above each other and optimised to pick objects out of the ground clutter. Maximum acquisition range is 100 km and tracking range of the I-band system is between 45-80 km depending on the target size, altitude and operational conditions. It can track six aircraft simultaneously and guide one or two missiles at once. For operating in a heavy ECM environment, late production Low Blow radars have been fitted with 25 km range TV cameras to give the fire control team the same data as from the emitting radar and allow a command guidance interception only to be performed. Against F-4 sized targets at low level the 60 kg HE-fragmentation warhead has a lethal burst radius of 12.5 m. The warhead is armed after the missile has travelled 50 m with the Doppler radar fuze being activated by command signal when the weapon is 300 m from the launcher. If the missile fails to intercept, another signal is sent to either change the trajectory or self-destruct. The trainable launchers are ground-mounted but can be relocated. S-125s are normally transported in pairs from battalion storage areas on modified ZIL-131 (6 × 6) or ZIL-157 (6 × 6) trucks and loaded onto the launchers with the aid of a conveyor. It takes only a minute to load the missiles onto the rails, but the duration between missile launches is about 50 minutes due to missile preparation, truck transit and other reloading procedures.

The missile's ability to dive also allows it to be used against surface targets and naval vessels.

SPECIFICATIONS (missile)

TYPE	two stage, low to medium altitude
LENGTH	6.1 m
DIAMETER OF BOOSTER	0.55 m
DIAMETER OF MISSILE	0.37 m
MAX SPAN	1.22 m
LAUNCH WEIGHT	
SA-3a	946 kg
SA-3b	950 kg
PROPULSION	solid fuel booster with solid fuel sustainer rocket motor
GUIDANCE	
SA-3a	command
SA-3b	command improved
WARHEAD	60 kg HE-fragmentation with Doppler radar proximity and contact fuzes
MAX SPEED	Mach 3.5
MAX EFFECTIVE RANGE	
SA-3a	22 200 m
SA-3b	18 300 m
MIN EFFECTIVE RANGE	
SA-3a	6000 m
SA-3b	2400 m
MAX ALTITUDE	
SA-3a	12 200 m
SA-3b	18 300 m
MIN ALTITUDE	
SA-3a	1500 m
SA-3b	45 m
LAUNCHER	twin or quadruple rail semi-fixed trainable ground mount
RELOAD TIME	50 mins (quadruple launcher)

STATIC & TOWED SAM SYSTEMS / USSR

Status: In production. In service with:

Country	No of launchers	Operator
Afghanistan	120	Air Force (30 battalions with quad launchers)
Algeria	20	Air Force (1 battalion), Army (4 battalion)
Angola	44	Air Defence Force (11 battalions)
Bulgaria	136	Air Force (34 battalions)
Czechoslovakia	120	Air Defence Command (30 battalions)
Cuba	48	Air Force (12 battalions)
Egypt	220	Air Defence Command (55 battalions)
Ethiopia	32	Army (8 battalions)
Finland	12	Army (3 battalions with quad launchers, as SAM-79)
Germany, East	48	Air Defence Command (3 Regiments)
Hungary	24	Air Force (6 battalions)
India	48	Air Force (12 battalions with quad launchers)
Iraq	100	Army (25 battalions)
Korea, North	32	Air Defence Command (8 battalions in 2 Regiments)
Libya	132	Air Defence Command (9 brigades of 12 launchers and 6 battalions of 4 launchers)
Mali	16	Army (independent batteries)
Mozambique	12	Army (3 battalions)
Peru	24	Air Force (6 battalions)
Poland	200	Air Defence Command (50 battalions)
Somalia	8	Army (2 battalions)
Syria	160	Air Defence Command (40 battalions)
Tanzania	12	Army (3 four launcher batteries)
USSR	1250	Air Defence Troops, 300 sites
Vietnam	160	Air Defence Force (10 Regiments)
Yemen, South	12	Army (3 batteries)
Yugoslavia	140	Air Defence Force (35 battalions)
Zambia	12	Air Force (1 battalion of 3 batteries)

Manufacturer: Soviet state factories.

SA-5 Gammon Medium to High Altitude Surface-to-air Missile System

Development

Development of the S-200 Volga (Soviet river), US/NATO designation SA-5 Gammon, was begun in the early 1950s by the PVO-Strany (*Voyska Protivovozdushnoy Oborony Strany* — Troops of the National Air Defence) Voisko design bureau to meet a requirement for a long-range medium to high altitude surface-to-air missile to complement the R-113 (SA-1) and V-750 (SA-2) weapons, as neither was considered sufficient to deal with the projected new generation of American high-speed high altitude penetrating strategic bombers such as the North American B-70.

By 1960 an interim deployment of a 30 launcher complex had begun around Leningrad, apparently using pre-production model S-200 missiles. This proved unsuccessful and the network was dismantled by the mid-1960s.

The first authentic deployment of the basic missile, NATO designation SA-5a, occurred in 1963-65 around Tallinn in Estonia. By the late 1960s the S-200 force had grown to some 26 sites, each with a Square Pair engagement radar and two to three six rail launcher battalions. Deployments continued throughout the Soviet Union during the 1970s and early 1980s and in 1981 the PVO-Strany was reorganised as the V-PVO *(Voyska Protivovozdushnoy Oborony* — Troops of the Air Defence).

However, the R-113 (SA-1), S-75 (SA-2), S-125 (SA-3), S-200 (SA-5) and later missile systems remained under the control of the ZRV (*Zenitayye Raketnyye Voyshky* — Zenith Rocket Troops) component with the addition of all mobile surface-to-air systems from the former troops of Troop Air Defence of the Ground Forces.

Over the years a number of SA-5s have apparently been fired by Soviet Air Defence Troops against Lockheed SR-71 strategic reconnaissance aircraft without success.

The missile has gone through periodic updates with a nuclear warhead equipped version, the SA-5b, entering service in 1969-70. This was followed by the definitive version, the SA-5c, in 1975-76 with improved terminal guidance and dual nuclear or conventional warhead capability. Partially to counter NATO's AWACS type aircraft, the Soviet Union fielded the SA-5e variant fitted with a passive anti-radiation seeker head designed to home onto emitting airborne radars such as those carried by the AWACS aircraft. The missing SA-5d designation was misapplied in the late 1970s to what is now known to be the SA-12 Gladiator. By 1984 the US DIA indicated that the number of SA-5 complexes had risen to around 1300 with approximately 2000 launchers. The 1987 *Soviet Military Power* handbook revealed that although the launcher numbers remained constant, further system improvements were being made so the SA-5 could be used in conjunction with the SA-10a Grumble that was replacing the SA-1. In 1989 the number of launchers was revised to 1930.

In the same year as the SA-5e was deployed (1983) the Soviets first began to establish Gammon sites in Warsaw Pact territory with battalions positioned in East Germany (near Rostock and Rudolstadt), Czechoslovakia (near Plzen) and western Hungary (near Szombathely). Before this, the only known site outside official Soviet borders was in Mongolia. By the mid-eighties the number of sites in East Germany had risen to at least six.

Also in the wake of the Syrian Air Defence débâcle in the Lebanese Bekaa Valley during 1982, the Soviets sent four six launcher battalions to Syria in late 1982-early 1983. Two sites were activated: Dumayr (40 km east of the capital Damascus) and Sharsar (in northeast Syria to the southeast of Homs). Initially manned by Soviet V-PVO troops, they were turned over to the Syrian Air Defence Command in 1985 to form initially two, then four two-battalion Independent Air Defence Missile Regiments with the additional sites located at As Suwayda and Mesken.

Following the Syrian success in obtaining S-200s, Libya began negotiations for some in 1984 with the first of three brigades delivered the following year. Operated by the Libyan Arab Air Defence Command, each brigade comprises two six launcher S-200 battalions and two four quadruple launcher S-125 battalions. On 24 March 1986 the S-200 brigade at Sirte on the Gulf of Sidra launched at least five missiles at US Navy aircraft operating in international airspace. All missed and the brigade's radars were subsequently attacked by US Navy aircraft firing ARMs on at least two occasions during the 'mini-war' of 24/25 March. The other two sites are at Benghazi and Oka Ben Nafi.

Artist's impression of the SA-5 Gammon single static launcher which can be traversed through 360° (US Department of Defense)

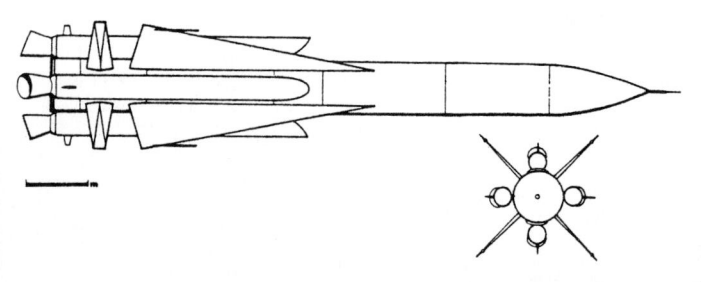

Provisional drawing of the SA-5 Gammon SAM (Steven Zaloga)

In the Soviet Union the S-200 has, for a number of years, been organised into Air Defence Rocket Brigades, each of two or three Regiments with two S-200 battalions of six launchers each (arranged in circles around the battalion's Square Pair radar) and two or three battalions of S-125s each with four quadruple launchers to provide low altitude cover of both the installations being guarded and the S-200 battalions. In addition, each of the SAM battalions has a sub-unit of automatic anti-aircraft (AAA) guns of either light (23 mm ZU-23) or medium (57 mm S-60) calibre.

In late 1987 North Korea took delivery of SA-5 systems for use in the Korean People's Air Force (KPAF) Air Defence Command.

The first SA-5 regiment of two 6-launcher battalions was deployed to the Sarlwon-Pyonsan area, some 40-100 km north of the DMZ, with the second regiment located on the east coast in the Wonsang-Hamhung region. Both units can reach into the northern sectors of South Korea's airspace threatening both AWACS aircraft and strategic stand-off reconnaissance assets like the Lockheed TR-1/U-2R and Boeing RC-135 ELINT/COMINT aircraft.

The regiments are integrated with the advanced 1980s technology Soviet Tin Shield early warning (EW)/ground control intercept (GCI)/target acquisition jam-proof radar system supplied at the same time. The radars also serve the four SA-2 Guideline brigades (with a total of 15 regiments) and the two independent SA-3b Goa regiments already in service with the KPAF.

The entire country comprises a single air defence district with all operations controlled from the Combat Command Post (CCP) located at the KPAF HQ, Pyongyang.

The district is sub-divided into three Sector Commands: Northwest, Northeast and Southern and the Pyongyang air defence subsector.

Each Sector consists of a HQ, an air direction control centre (ADCC), EW radar regiment(s), air defence fighter division(s), SAM regiment(s), an AAA division and other independent AAA units.

When a target is detected, fighters are alerted and launched whilst the SAM and AAA units initiate tracking. Any subsequent SAM or AAA engagement is then co-ordinated with the fighter division's HQ and the CCP. The idea being that if the aircraft are unable to engage or are unsuccessful in their interception then the SAMs deployed in 'belts' will either destroy the target or force it, by virtue of making it take evasive action, into a position where covering AAA in 'ambush' positions are able to effect its destruction.

The SA-2 regiments of three 6-launcher battalions each are deployed mainly in a west coast 'belt' that runs along the Kaesong-Sarlwon-Pyongyang-Pakch'on-Sinuljus axis and two east coast 'belts' that lie along the Wonsan-Hamhung-Sinp'o and Chongjin-Najin lines. A number of independent Guideline regiments are located in 'dead' areas and around strategic areas between these 'belts'.

The SA-5 regiments are used to support these 'belts' as are the two SA-3b units of four four-quadruple launcher battalions each, one in the west and the other in the east.

The SAM force, based on the Soviet practice of three ready missiles per launcher, disposes of a total of over 1200 missiles - 810 SA-2, 384 SA-3 and 72 SA-5. With the strategic war storage stock added the grand total is increased to the 2500-3000 round level.

The individual SA-2/3/5 sites generally follow the Soviet patterns except that the majority of their EW, target acquisition and GCI radars are located either in large underground concrete-reinforced NBC protected bunker complexes or dug into mountains. The sites comprise a tunnel, control room, crew quarters and steel blast-proof doors. An elevator raises the radar to the surface when required. There are also many dummy radar and SAM sites together with genuine alternative site positions for the SAM launchers.

Description

The Gammon is known to be a two stage missile with four strap-on solid fuel booster packs and a storable liquid fuel rocket sustainer. The minimum range is around 80 km due to the boost requirements which limits it to engagements against relatively large unmanoeuvrable targets at ranges out to around 240-300 km. It is very sluggish when the cruciform and rear wings respond to the aerodynamic control directives sent over the command guidance link. Terminal homing, except on the SA-5e which has a passive radar seeker, is conducted by a semi-active radar head using reflections from the continuous wave fire control radar.

Initial target acquisition is performed for the S-200 brigades by either the 320 km range P-50 (NATO designation Bar Lock) E/F-band set or the similarly ranged earlier P-80 (NATO designation Back Net) E-band radar. The long-range early warning radars associated with SA-5 are the Big Back and the E-band Back Trap systems. Co-located with the acquisition radar is a PRV-11 (NATO designation Side Net) E-band 180 km range heightfinder radar. The H-band 170 km range NATO designation Square Pair fire control radar are located at the battalion launcher sites. Initial versions of the fire control system have been described by US sources as antiquated and very susceptible to ECM techniques, as was demonstrated by the US Navy over the Gulf of Sidra.

SPECIFICATIONS (missile)
TYPE	two stage, medium to high altitude
LENGTH	10.9 m
DIAMETER	0.86 m
MAX SPAN	2.9 m
LAUNCH WEIGHT	7900 kg
PROPULSION	four solid fuel strap on boosters with storable liquid fuel rocket motor
GUIDANCE	SA-5a/b/c command with semi-active radar terminal homing seeker SA-5e command with passive radar terminal homing seeker
WARHEAD	HE-fragmentation (SA-5a/c/e) or 25 kt yield nuclear (SA-5b/c) with proximity and command fuzing
MAX SPEED	Mach 4 plus
MAX RANGE	240-300 km
MIN RANGE	80 km
MAX ALTITUDE	30 480 m
MIN ALTITUDE	3000 m
LAUNCHER	static semi-fixed single rail trainable

Status: In production. In service with:

Germany, East	6+ sites
Korea, North	Air Defence Command 4 × 6 launcher battalions
Libya	6 × 6 launcher battalions
Poland	2-3 sites
Syria	4 × 6 launcher battalions
USSR	130 sites with total of 1930 launchers

Manufacturer: Soviet state factories. Designed by the PVO-Voisko design bureau.

STATIC & TOWED SAM SYSTEMS / UK

UNITED KINGDOM

British Aerospace Rapier Low Level Surface-to-air Missile System

Development

The Rapier low level surface-to-air missile system was developed by the then British Aircraft Corporation, Guided Weapons Division, from the early 1960s onwards to meet the requirements of the British Army and Royal Air Force Regiment for a missile system to replace the obsolete 40 mm L/70 Bofors air defence guns then in use.

The operational requirements laid down for Rapier can be summarised as short reaction time with the ability to be taken into and out of action quickly, compactness and low weight, high rate of fire and kill potential, good defence coverage with maximum/minimum range performance, and the ability to engage targets with speeds from zero to Mach 1.5 from ground level up to at least 3000 m.

Before receiving MoD funding for the ET-316, the British Aircraft Corporation invested its own money in a simpler weapon then called Sightline which eventually became ET-316, or Rapier as it was officially named in January 1967.

Rapier was preceeded by the PT-428 which was a self-propelled surface-to-air missile system with both day and night capability. This was being developed by the British Aircraft Corporation but was cancelled in 1962 because it was becoming too complex and expensive.

At one time the British MoD was considering purchasing the Mauler self-propelled air defence system from the USA, but this was considered too expensive and was itself soon cancelled.

Design studies began in 1963 and Rapier was announced for the first time in September 1964 with the first unguided firing trials carried out in 1965.

In April 1967 the first successful guided engagement of a live target took place at the RAE range at Aberporth. This was a drone Meteor representing a crossing target and was flying at an altitude of 3000 ft at a range of 10 000 ft from the firing site. The target was hit and destroyed. Joint Services evaluation trials of the Rapier at the Woomera range commenced in 1968.

The Rapier, together with the Thunderbird high altitude surface-to-air missile, was ordered by Libya in 1967, but the order was subsequently cancelled by the new regime when it seized power.

The first production order was placed by the British MoD in June 1967 and the first production units delivered in July 1970. The system achieved initial operational capability with the British Army and Royal Air Force in 1973. In addition to extensive trials in the UK, cold weather trials were carried out at Cold Lake in Alberta, Canada, and hot and wet trials were carried out in Australia.

Troop trials of towed Rapier were carried out by 9 (Plassey) Light Air Defence Battery, Royal Artillery, based at Kirton-in-Lindsey, which also included a flight from No 63 Squadron, Royal Air Force Regiment. (Kirton-in-Lindsey was the base of the Royal Artillery's first Rapier regiment, 12 Light Air Defence Regiment.)

The British Army has three air defence regiments equipped with Rapier, of which two are in BAOR and one in the UK. Originally, each regiment had three batteries, each battery with three troops of four Rapier fire units to give a total of 36 per regiment. But the Regiments in BAOR

Royal Air Force Regiment Rapier deployed in the field with Rapier launcher in background, optical tracker centre and Marconi Command and Control Systems Blindfire tracker in foreground

Four-round Rapier missile launcher deployed ready for action with wheels removed and supported on four jacks (MoD)

British Aerospace Rapier SAM leaves its four-round launcher

British Aerospace Rapier fire unit deployed in Oman with optical tracker in foreground and four-round launcher in background

UK / STATIC & TOWED SAM SYSTEMS

defence is used to give localised protection to small sized target location such as HQs, vehicle choke points and logistic dumps. Each VP is allocated either four or six launchers. They are deployed in such a manner as to give mutual support and to try to destroy an attacker before it releases weapons. The Battery Command Post (BCP) normally co-ordinates the VP defences, but if a troop is allocated an independent VP task, command and control devolves to the troop commander.

The second mission role is route defence of main supply or unit withdrawal routes. A battery can protect up to 30 km although this depends greatly on the local terrain. Two fire units are normally located at each end of the route to be defended in 'blocking' positions, and the other eight are deployed between 1-2 km off the line of march in alternate positions either side of the route.

However, it is the third mission role which is used most often as it covers the largest area of battlefield. The Air Defended Area (ADA) can be used to cover both VPs and routes with a battery's tactical area of responsibility (TAOR). Once assigned this task, the troop commanders and their staff reconnoitre likely firing positions within their TAORs and send the details back to the BCP either by burst transmission radio message or courier.

The Battery Commander and his Command Post officer feed the information into the BCP processor which selects the best 12 sites and a number of reserve sites according to firing arcs and radar coverage.

When this is finished the fire units are moved to their new locations. For a Tracked Rapier battery the same three mission roles can be assigned but because of increased mobility the individual fire unit commanders have much more latitude and can move on their own initiative when the position they are occupying becomes undefendable. For support of armoured units in direct combat with the enemy, the Tracked Rapier elements will be located a number of kilometres behind in order to remain out of range of enemy fire weapons.

Rapier was used by 'T' Battery of 12 Air Defence Regiment, Royal Artillery, during the 1982 Falklands campaign. A total of 12 launchers were deployed with reduced logistic support and no Blindfire radars.

At the time of the Falklands conflict the UK Rapier force was undergoing a systems upgrade to improve its performance, but the Rapier unit deployed to the Falklands was the original Field Standard A model.

Rapier was in action from the first day of the landings in San Carlos water on 21 May through to the end of hostilities, by which time the official UK Government White Paper (*The Falklands Campaign: The Lessons*) stated that at least 14 Argentine aircraft were destroyed by Rapier with another six possibles. However, other sources have since suggested that Rapier actually shot down only one IAI Dagger A and assisted in the destruction of a McDonnell Douglas A-4C Skyhawk.

'T' Battery of 12 Air Defence Regiment was followed by four Blindfire radars from the Royal School of Artillery, eight Rapiers and Blindfire radars from 63 Squadron, Royal Air Force Regiment and finally 9 Battery, 12 Air Defence Regiment. The Blindfire radar was never used in action.

Rapier was, however, first used in combat by Iran in the second half of 1972 when it shot down an Iraqi Air Force Tu-22 Blinder supersonic bomber attacking Kurdish rebels in the Iran/Iraq border region. During the Iran/Iraq War Rapier saw action and claimed a number of Iraqi Air Force aircraft.

A typical fire unit consists of a one tonne Land Rover carrying the optical tracker and towing the four-round launcher and generator power supply, a one tonne Land Rover towing Blindfire radar (if used), and generator power supply and a 3/4 ton Land Rover carrying nine reserve missiles.

Each battery also has a battery HQ and a repair section which has a ¾ ton Land Rover equipped with diagnostic and performance test gear and tows a trailer carrying a quantity of ready use spares. There is also a battery repair team with two vehicles, one for optical and hydraulic repairs, and the other for major electronic repairs, and an ordnance spares vehicle.

The first Royal Air Force Regiment unit to receive Rapier was No 63 Squadron based at North Luffenham, UK, and this subsequently deployed at Gutersloh, West Germany, in mid-1974.

The second unit to be equipped was No 58 Squadron which was deployed to RAF Laarbruch, West Germany. No 27 Squadron was the first to receive the Blindfire radar in late 1977.

A Royal Air Force Low Level Air Defence (LLAD) Rapier squadron comprises an HQ flight, an engineering flight of four forward repair teams (of which two are for Rapier) and a second echelon maintenance section and two Rapier flights, each with four fire units. The latter comprise eight men, a towed Rapier launcher, a Blindfire radar tracker, two 1 tonne 4 × 4 light vehicles and an LWB Land Rover with missile resupply trailer. A basic load of 17 missiles for the unit is carried.

Since it was introduced into the British Army and Royal Air Force Regiment in the early 1970s, there have been a series of phased developments not only to improve the performance of the system but also to maintain the system ahead of the threat which is constantly changing.

For example, in mid-1987 the British MoD placed an order with British Aerospace worth over £5 million for the supply of new digital computers

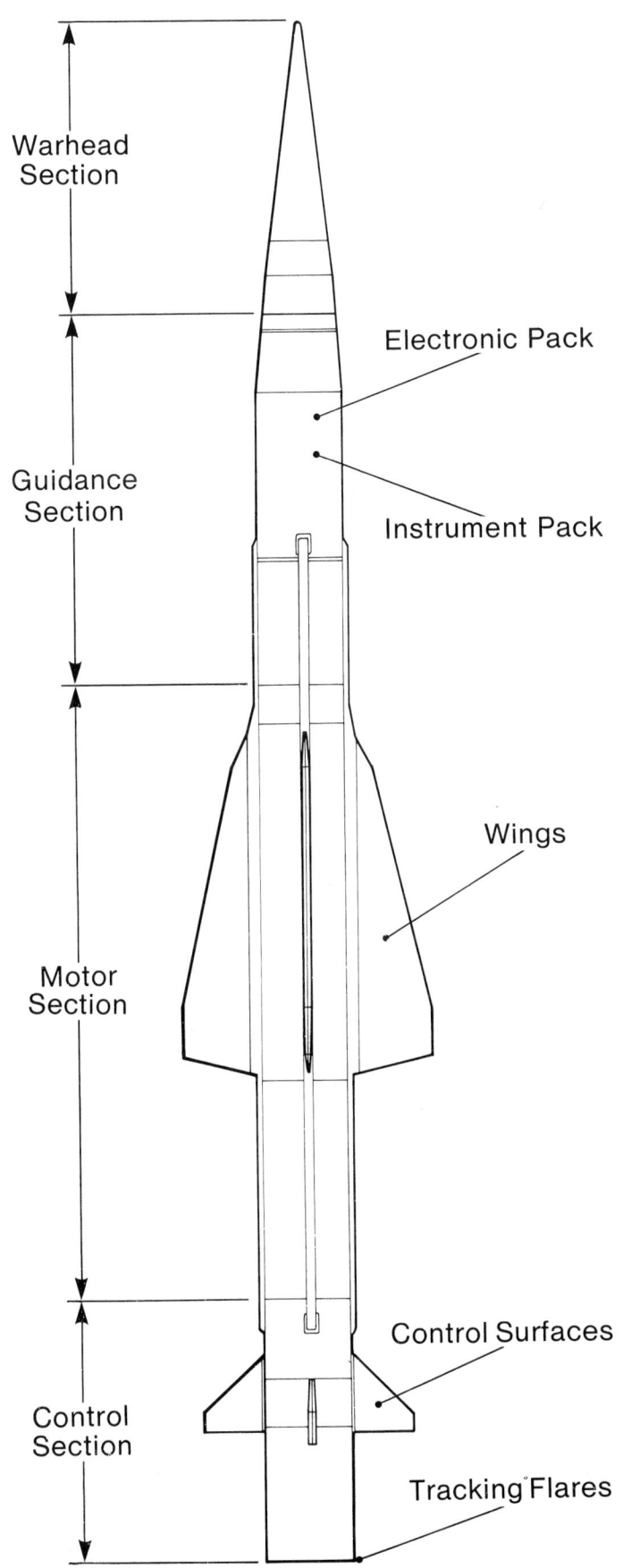

Drawing of the BAe Rapier Mk 1 SAM showing position of key components

(12 and 22) have been re-equipped to field two batteries with towed Rapier and two batteries with Tracked Rapiers.

In the British Army Rapier is used as the second and third line of battlefield air defence. The first is the Javelin manportable system which is used as a gap filler for the Rapiers, as a vital point (VP) defence system and as a route defence system. The second line is provided by Tracked Rapier Vehicles and the third by the Towed Rapier systems.

Towed and Tracked Rapiers are employed in three main roles. VP

266 STATIC & TOWED SAM SYSTEMS / UK

Reloading a Rapier launcher with a new missile

Land Rover 1 tonne (4 × 4) vehicle of Royal Air Force Regiment towing Marconi Command and Control Systems Blindfire radar system

Marconi Command and Control Systems Blindfire radar deployed in the field

for the Rapier air defence systems to replace older computers. By 1987 more than 50 per cent of the launcher's major assemblies comprised 1980s technology including the key areas of computing and radars. This has had a significant effect on Rapier system reliability as well as increasing system automation.

These modifications are incorporated into current production systems and are offered to current Rapier users as part of a programme of modifications.

By early 1989 the total signed orders for towed Rapier and Tracked Rapier exceeded 7000 fire units and 25 000 missiles, of which more than 12 000 missiles have been fired during development, training and combat.

Individual parts of the towed Rapier air defence system can be carried slung under medium or heavy lift helicopters such as the Aerospatiale SA330 Puma and Boeing Vertol CH-47 Chinook, and a C-130 Lockheed Hercules transport can carry one complete system with Blindfire radar tracker or two optical systems with vehicles.

For the export market, Rapier is tailored to meet the specific requirements of each customer, but the British armed forces use designations to avoid confusion.

The basic Rapier, together with its Blindfire radar, is called Field Standard A (FS A). This was followed in 1979/80 by Field Standard B1 (FS B1) which has a free-standing tripod-mounted 'pointing stick', which, when pointed at a target and activated by pressing a trigger, aligns the optical tracker automatically. There are also improvements to both ECCM and ECM including an improved planar array antenna and an automatic code changer for the IFF.

In 1985 troop trials began, of the Field Standard B2 (FS B2) electro-optical system, known as Rapier Darkfire. This involves the introduction of an infra-red tracker which replaces the optical unit, a new six-round launcher incorporating an improved planar array Racal-Decca surveillance radar with a 50 per cent range increase, an automatic code changer for IFF and the Console Tactical Control system for the fire unit commander.

By using an analogue digital interface unit a standard Blindfire radar tracker can also be used with Rapier 90 where an all-weather capability is required.

The Field Standard C Rapier 2000 has a separate entry.

Description

The main component of the towed Rapier system is the launcher which is carried on a two-wheeled A-frame trailer. When in the firing position the wheels are removed and it is stabilised on four adjustable legs. The engagement envelope is from −5 to +60° in elevation and 360° in traverse. The Racal-Decca 15 km maximum range 3000 m altitude capability F-band surveillance radar aerial, on which the Cossor IFF aerials and interrogator are mounted, is housed under the radome and rotates once every second. The radar transmitter receiver is mounted in the lower part of the launcher.

The radar, together with the IFF, provides for the early detection and warning of approaching aircraft and helicopters. The launcher turntable rotates through 360° and carries four missiles in the ready-to-launch position, two on each side. The command transmitter and aerial which provides the link between the computer, in the base of the launcher, and the missiles in flight is located between the two banks of two missiles.

The optical tracker stands on a tripod which has a levelling jack on each leg and consists of a static column with a rotating head providing 360° coverage in azimuth. Elevation coverage between −10 to +60° is provided by movable prisms in the rotating head. The wide field-of-view is 20° and the narrow field-of-view 4.8°. Operation is normally controlled by the computer with operator override at any time to select the narrow option.

The manual tracking system is optical, with the operator using a joystick operated servo-driven unit to track the target. The guidance system uses a fully automated TV system that gathers the missile in flight after launch using an 11° field-of-view, then automatically switches over to a 0.55° field-of-view to guide it to interception with the target.

The operator is provided with biocular sight for target tracking and has a few simple controls to operate the system. A second monocular sight is provided at the rear of the static column which an instructor can use to monitor students' performances during field training.

The Tactical Control Unit (TCU) provides tactical control facilities and is connected by cable between the launcher and optical tracker. It is divided into 32 sectors in azimuth, each sector covering 11.25°. By operating sector switches blind arcs can be built up as required to provide 'safe' channels for friendly aircraft or to set in priority arcs of fire.

The Rapier missile has a streamlined monocoque body of circular cross-section and consists of four main sections: warhead, guidance, propulsion unit and control.

The 1.4 kg warhead section contains the semi-armour piercing warhead, with 0.4 kg of explosive, a safety and arming unit and crush fuze. A collapsible plastic nose cone is fitted to the penetration head to provide optimum aerodynamic shape.

The guidance section is in two parts: the electronic pack and the instrument pack. The Imperial Metal Industries Troy propulsion unit is an integral dual thrust two stage rocket motor and gives the missile a maximum speed of around 650 m/s. The control section contains the hot gas-driven control surface actuation mechanism, which controls the missile in flight, and pyrotechnic flares to facilitate TV gathering and tracking. The same Mk 1 missile is used for both the optical and Blindfire guidance modes and for Tracked Rapier. A missile flying to maximum range takes 13 seconds with a minimum time of flight (required to arm) being three seconds. The single shot kill probability is stated to be over 70 per cent.

Rapier is manufactured as a round of ammunition and requires no maintenance testing or servicing once it has left the ordnance depot except for routine changing of desiccators. When stored in controlled conditions the missile has a shelf-life of 10 years.

British Aerospace is now developing the Rapier Mk 2 missile which will be introduced in the early 1990s and will be compatible with all versions of the Rapier missile system including Optical Rapier, Blindfire Rapier, Tracked Rapier, Rapier Darkfire and Rapier 2000.

The Mk 2 missile will exist in two versions and have a 15 to 20 per cent increase in range. One version will retain the semi-armour piercing warhead of the original, the other will have a combined fragmentation and armour piercing warhead and dual crush and proximity fuzes. It will also incorporate a number of other refinements.

The DN181 Blindfire K-band 10 km range radar was developed by Marconi Command and Control Systems to enable Rapier to cope with the night and all-weather threat. The non-coherent frequency-agile radar was designed to meet the same characteristics of size, light weight and mobility as the rest of the system; it is therefore trailer mounted and can be simply plugged into any Rapier system.

In operation, the monopulse radar employs differential tracking of both the missile and target using a very narrow pencil beam to achieve the accuracy required.

Marconi commenced development of the Blindfire radar under contract to the MoD in 1968 with first prototypes completed in 1970. The first pre-production system was handed over in 1973 and the main production order was placed the same year, with Iran placing its first order in 1974. The Blindfire radar has also been successfully tested with the US Chaparral SAM system during trials in the USA. By 1989 over 350 had been built for the home and export markets with production continuing.

The Blindfire radar is mounted on a chassis which is similar to the launcher and when deployed for action the wheels are removed and it is supported on four adjustable legs. The base housing contains the electrical, electronic and hydraulic power assemblies and is static during operation.

The upper assembly carries the main reflector and sub-reflector assembly, the TV gathering unit with its power supply and the RF unit. This assembly rotates in azimuth and the aerial system in elevation.

The addition of Blindfire allows Rapier to engage targets successfully in darkness and poor visibility. As it is autonomous the target tracking and acquisition process decreases system reaction time, increases kill probability and reduces human operations to a monitoring role. Once a target has been picked up by the surveillance radar, the azimuth bearing is passed automatically to the Blindfire tracking radar which slews rapidly onto this bearing. A high speed search pattern is carried out and the precise position of the target is established.

As soon as the tracking radar is locked onto the target, the operator is informed by an audio tone that the radar is tracking and then he switches to the radar mode to allow the tracking radar to control the Rapier system. Immediately the target comes within range, a lamp indicator tells him he is free to launch a missile. All the operator has to do is to press the launch button.

Once the Rapier missile is launched, the tracking radar tracks both the target and the missile. Error signals are derived automatically within the radar system and passed to the command guidance unit which uses encoded signals to direct the missile flight path to reduce the error angle to zero.

Blindfire uses a standard Rapier generator and requires only the cable connection to the launcher unit and to the lamp indicator system control switch on the optical tracking unit.

The system control switch enables the operator to select either radar or optical guidance for the engagement at any point up to the moment of firing.

A mobile optical fire unit consists of two Land Rovers (or similar vehicles), the launcher and a light trailer.

The first Land Rover carries the optical tracker, four missiles in their travelling boxes, and tows the launcher with its generator set rear mounted. The second Land Rover carries stores and supplies for the fire unit and tows the missile resupply trailer, carrying a further nine missiles in their travelling boxes. The fire unit can be brought into and out of action in under 20 minutes and can be manned by three men, although five are normally used for sustained operations. Rapier can also be integrated into an overall air defence system.

An optical fire unit can be converted into a Blindfire unit simply by the addition of a Blindfire Radar towed by a third Land Rover, which is similar to that which tows the launcher. It carries four missiles in their travelling boxes and tows the Blindfire unit with its generator set rear mounted.

A fully mobile Blindfire fire unit thus consists of three light vehicles, three light trailers, with a total of 17 ready use/reload missiles. In terms of capabilities, it has its own surveillance radar, IFF system, guidance computer, day, night and all-weather tracking systems, ready use and resupply missiles and power supply units. It can thus operate autonomously or be integrated, with the necessary communications system, as part of an air defence network.

A typical Rapier target engagement takes place as follows:

The surveillance radar is continuously rotating through 360° looking for aircraft or helicopters which come within range. When detected, a target is automatically interrogated by the Cossor IFF system. If no friendly reply is received the operator is alerted by an audible signal in his headphones. At the same time, the rotating head on the optical tracker and radar tracker automatically lines up with the target in azimuth followed by the launcher. The radar tracker then begins its automatic elevation search while the operator undertakes a manual visual search. If a radar tracker is available it will be used as the prime means of target engagement and the procedure will be as described, however an alternative manual engagement procedure can be used. The operator then undertakes an elevation search to acquire the target, after which he switches to the track mode and begins to track the aircraft visually using a joystick control.

He is then able to identify the aircraft visually. Information from the optical tracker and the surveillance radar are fed into the system computer in the launcher and this data is used to calculate whether or not the aircraft is within effective range of the system.

When the aircraft comes within firing range a visual signal appears in the operator's field of view and he immediately presses the firing button to initiate a missile launch.

The computer calculates toe in and turns the launcher towards the optical line of sight. The missile is automatically gathered along the sight line by the TV system until impact. During the missile flight the only task of the operator is to keep tracking the target.

The missile has a semi-armour piercing warhead which penetrates the aircraft skin. The crush fuze detonates the high explosive inside the aircraft, causing the target to be destroyed. This contact technique has caused Rapier to be known as a 'hittile' system.

Once the target has been engaged the operator can switch back to search so that another engagement sequence can be immediately started, or a second missile may be launched at either the same target or another target in the operator's field of view.

Four replacement missiles can be reloaded by a trained crew in less than 2.5 minutes. The surveillance radar can detect low-flying targets in the presence of heavy ground clutter out to a range of more than 15 km and the missile itself can engage targets at 7000 m, giving an overall intercept coverage of 150 km² per fire unit. Numerous firings have demonstrated that the system reaction time (from when the target is detected until a missile is launched) is about six seconds.

Variants

Variants

Rapier Darkfire

Known by the British MoD as Electro-Optical Rapier this was being delivered to the British Army in 1988. It uses data highways throughout and a distribution data processing system.

The launcher has six missiles in the ready-to-fire position, compared to four in the current system and has a new STC surveillance radar which provides increased acquisition accuracy, considerably improved ECM and enables a radar display to be provided for the operator.

The new distributed processor greatly increases the computing and data storage capacity offering more automation, improved threat

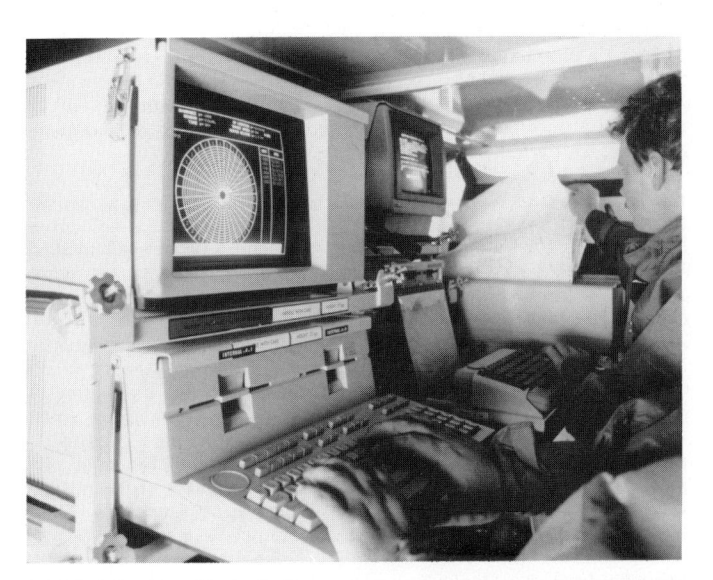

British Aerospace Rapier battery command post processor which assists the battery commander by automating planning, deployment and management duties. It is used by British armed forces and Indonesia

268 STATIC & TOWED SAM SYSTEMS / UK

assessment and the instant retrieval of system data for testing and diagnostic purposes.

The standard Rapier optical tracker has been replaced by an electro-optical tracker (or thermal/video) providing a day/night and poor visibility capability. The complete system can be plugged into the standard radar tracker using an interface box when all-weather capability is required.

The new tactical control unit provides a TV display of surveillance radar data including aircraft tracks with their identification and electronic interference. Also on the display are range intervals and a number of functional markers. The operator therefore has a complete picture of the air scenario from which to conduct threat assessment routines and fight the air battle. The display's secondary function is to display test and diagnostic data stored in the processor.

It will not be issued to the Royal Air Force Regiment as they have chosen to wait for Rapier 2000.

Rapier 2000

Details of this system, currently under development for the British Army and Royal Air Force Regiment and expected to enter service in the 1990s, are given in the following entry.

Tracked Rapier

This is covered in the *Self-propelled surface-to-air missiles* section and is deployed only by the British Army.

Rapier Laserfire

Details of this private venture system, which can be mounted on a variety of tracked and wheeled chassis, is given in the *Self-propelled surface-to-air missiles* section.

Rapier Darkfire deployed in field with operator and electro-optical tracker (left), which provides a day/night and poor visibility capability and six-round launcher centre

SPECIFICATIONS

Rapier launcher
WEIGHT	1227 kg
LENGTH	4.064 m
WIDTH	1.765 m
HEIGHT	2.134 m

Optical tracker
WEIGHT DEPLOYED	119 kg
HEIGHT	1.549 m
TRIPOD DIAMETER	1.828 m

Tactical control unit
WEIGHT	19 kg
LENGTH	457 cm
WIDTH	33 cm
DEPTH	24.1 cm

Generator
WEIGHT	243 kg
LENGTH	0.991 m
WIDTH	0.832 m
HEIGHT	0.914 m

Blindfire tracker
WEIGHT	1186 kg
LENGTH	4.14 m
WIDTH	1.753 m
HEIGHT TRAVELLING	2.032 m
HEIGHT DEPLOYED	3.378 m

Missile
TYPE	single stage, low altitude
LENGTH	2.24 m
DIAMETER	0.133 m
WING SPAN	0.381 m
LAUNCH WEIGHT	42.6 kg
PROPULSION	two stage, solid propellant
GUIDANCE	semi-automatic optical command-line of sight, or thermal, command-line of sight or automatic command-line of sight using Blindfire radar
WARHEAD	1.4 kg HE, semi-armour piercing with crush fuze
MAX SPEED	650 m/s
MAX RANGE	7000 m
MIN RANGE	500 m (optical/Blindfire Rapier)
MAX ALTITUDE	around 3000 m
MIN ALTITUDE	less than 15 m
LAUNCHER	mobile trainable four-round trailer mounted

Status: In production. In service with:

Abu Dhabi: This country placed its first order, then worth £35 million, late in 1974. It originally deployed an optical version but subsequently deployed Blindfire.

Australia: A contract for 20 optical Rapier systems was signed in December 1975, with the first optical Rapier fire unit accepted in October 1978. The contract included test equipment and a base repair facility. In January 1977 an order was placed through British Aerospace worth £13 million for 10 Blindfire radars to give the system an all-weather capability. Rapier became operational with the 16 Air Defence Regiment, Australian Army, in 1980. The Australian Government and private industry are involved in the manufacture of various Rapier equipments which include the specially designed Australian generator and the supply of optical and other components for Rapier tracker sights and fire units. The Rapier contract required that 30 per cent of the value was to be placed with Australian industry, and this was met in full. Australia now makes the rocket motor and undertakes final assembly of the missile with a complete Rapier magazine constructed at the Munitions Filling Factory at St Mary's, Sydney. The 16 Air Defence Regiment deploys 12 of the launchers with two at the RAEME School at Albury, four at the School of Artillery in Manly, Sydney and the remaining two in operational reserve.

Brunei: The government of Brunei announced its intention to purchase Rapier Blindfire in late 1978 with the contract, worth over £30 million, being signed in 1979 and first units delivered in 1983. Late in 1980 British Aerospace was awarded a contract worth more than £3 million by Brunei for construction of a missile firing range on its coast. It is understood that a total of 12 Rapier fire units and four Blindfire radars were delivered.

Indonesia: Late in 1984 Indonesia signed a contract worth £100 million for optical Rapier air defence systems for use by the army. The contract also covered the transfer of technology to Indonesia. A second order, valued at over $100 million, was announced in December 1985. The third order, worth £40 million, was signed in December 1986, to bring the total to 51 optical systems. In early 1987 Indonesia became the first export customer for the British Aerospace Battery Command Post Processor System for Rapier. Total value of the contract, for five systems plus spares, was half a million pounds.

The Battery Command Post Processor, which is already used by the British armed forces, links by radio all elements of the battery. Data can be passed using tactical data entry devices coupled to existing combat radio which permits the automatic transmission of data to and from the command post. Messages can also be passed in voice to the command post radio operator who enters the data, using a keyboard, into the battery command post processor. All relevant data can be received, stored, processed and displayed on request. By rapidly speeding up management and computation tasks which have previously been carried out manually, the assessment times for deployment are much reduced.

Iran: The first order, placed in June 1970 and worth some £47 million, covered technical, maintenance and support training. It originally deployed an optical version but subsequently deployed Blindfire. In Iran, Rapiers are manned by the air force and a total of 45 launchers to equip five batteries were originally procured, although substantially fewer are now operational due to non-availability of spare parts owing to the British Government Gulf War arms embargo.

Oman: An order was placed in mid-1974 for 28 fire units valued, with spares and training, at $47 million. These were delivered in 1977. Oman purchased 12 Blindfire radars in 1980. The Rapiers are operated by the Omani Air Force with two squadrons deploying a total 24 launchers. The remainder are used for training and war reserve.

Qatar: The army ordered Rapier in 1981 and now operates 12 Rapier fire units of which six are equipped with Blindfire radars that were acquired as part of the original order. They are used to defend the Doha Air Base.

Singapore: The air force deploys one squadron with 12 Rapier launchers which were ordered in 1981 at a cost of $60 million. They are used in conjunction with six Blindfire radars.

Switzerland: The Swiss Government formally proposed the purchase of 60 Rapier units in June 1980 at an initial cost of SFr1.2 billion (£315 million) which included £50 million for Blindfire radars which are issued on the scale of one per Rapier launcher. The order was finally placed with British Aerospace in December 1980 with a proportion of the equipment built in Switzerland shared between Government Factories and private industry. This included the licensed manufacture of missiles and other parts of the Rapier system.

F+W are responsible for final assembly of the missile and licensed manufacture of the parts, minus the motor, warhead and safety and arming unit which are subcontracted to M+FA and made under licence from Imperial Metal Industries, Royal Ordnance and Marconi Command and Control Systems. F+W and M+FA in turn subcontract to some 14 other Swiss companies.

Firing trials of the first Swiss Rapier units were completed in the UK in 1982. The Swiss use Pinzgauer (6 × 6) 2000 kg light vehicles to tow their Rapier systems.

The Swiss Rapier systems have a number of modifications to meet their unique operational environment, including an improved acquisition and tracking capability in mountainous terrain, improved ECCM capability, PPI tactical display and Swiss IFF system.

The new target display and control system allows the operator to select automatic or manual target designation, threat assessment, effective countermeasures against electronic jamming as well as fast identification of defects in the system.

Each Swiss Army mechanised division has one battalion with 20 mm LAAGs and a second with Rapier SAM systems. The latter has an HQ battery and two Rapier batteries. A total of three Rapier battalions have been formed, all of which are militia, one French speaking and two German speaking. The 60th Rapier system was handed over on 1 May 1986.

Turkey: In August 1983 Turkey placed a $146 million order for 36 Rapier launchers and 12 Blindfire radars. These were delivered between November 1983 and later 1985 and used by the air force. In mid-1985 a second contract of similar size was placed but, due to financial problems, was not implemented until December 1985. This contract also involved the co-assembly of the Rapier missile.

United Kingdom: Army — Three regiments are deployed by the Royal Artillery, one regiment in the UK (16) and two at Dortmund, BAOR (12 and 22). It originally deployed an optical system but subsequently ordered Blindfire which is issued on a scale of one per three towed Rapier launchers.

The RAF Regiment man four optical Rapier units deployed in Belize, as well as the systems deployed in the Falkland Islands.

Royal Air Force — There are six Royal Air Force Regiment squadrons of which four are deployed in West Germany and two in the UK. It originally deployed an optical system but subsequently ordered Blindfire, which is issued on the scale of one per launcher. When defending an airfield, the Rapiers are normally located in a double interlocking ring so they are both in-depth and mutually supporting. They are normally positioned at pre-surveyed sites within 4 to 6 km of the airfield. To set up for optical firing a flight takes 20 minutes, for secondary radar capabilities 60 minutes, for full all-weather capability 90 minutes. The current RAF Rapier squadrons are:

No 16 Squadron, RAF Wildenrath, West Germany
No 26 Squadron, RAF Laarbruch, West Germany
No 27 Squadron, RAF Leuchars, Scotland
No 37 Squadron, RAF Bruggen, West Germany
No 48 Squadron, RAF Lossiemouth, Scotland
No 63 Squadron, RAF Gutersloh, West Germany.

United States of America: (Turkey) — In October 1985 it was announced that the US Government had placed an order under the US European Air Defense Initiative programme for 14 Rapier launchers with 11 Blindfire systems to defend two USAF bases in Turkey, these are manned by Turkish military personnel.

(UK) — Early in 1981 it was announced that an agreement had been reached between the USAF and the British Government for the supply of 32 Rapier systems to defend seven USAF air bases in the UK. These are manned by the Royal Air Force Regiment and became operational in 1985. Each launcher has one Blindfire radar. Total value of the contract was about $327.5 million. Of the total of 32 launchers, 28 are for operational use and four for training. The first Rapier fire unit was handed over in October 1983 and the same year the assembly of 200 Rapier missiles commenced at the Chemical Systems Division of United Technologies in the USA. The following Rapier squadrons are formed in 6 Wing, Royal Air Force Regiment:

No 19 Squadron, based at RAF Brize Norton will defend RAF Upper Heyford and RAF Fairford
No 20 Squadron, based at RAF Honington, will defend RAF Alconbury and RAF Bentwaters, with RAF Woodbridge close by
No 66 Squadron, based at RAF West Raynham, will defend RAF Lakenheath and RAF Mildenhall

These three squadrons are under the operational command of the Commander-in-Chief, RAF Strike Command, acting in his NATO capacity as Commander-in-Chief, UK Air.

Zambia: This country was supplied with 12 optical Rapiers in 1971 to defend the country against Rhodesian air attack, but they rapidly became unserviceable.

Manufacturer (prime): British Aerospace (Dynamics) Limited, Six Hills Way, Stevenage, Hertordshire SG1 2DA, UK.
Telephone: (0438) 312422
Telex: 825125/825126

British Aerospace Rapier 2000 Low Level Surface-to-air Missile System

Development

In November 1986 British Aerospace Stevenage was awarded a contract worth around one billion pounds for the design, development and initial production of the Rapier 2000 air defence weapon for delivery to the British Army and Royal Air Force Regiment in the mid-1990s and beyond.

Development of Rapier 2000 (which is also known as Field Standard C or FS C) actually started in 1983 as part of the continuing Rapier improvement programme contract for the British Ministry of Defence.

While the present Rapier system is considered to be effective against the current low level air threat, a major improvement programme was thought necessary if the system was to remain effective in the 1990s.

According to British Aerospace, the major areas of threat are expected to include a severe electronic countermeasures environment with heavy jamming, multiple pop-up helicopter attack, anti-radiation missiles, smaller battlefield targets such as remotely piloted vehicles, surveillance tasks, cruise missiles, chemical attack that will inhibit crew performance and exo-atmospheric devices that create massive electro-magnetic pulses for the destruction of electronic communications and weapon systems.

Major subcontractors to British Aerospace for Rapier 2000 include: Plessey Radar (surveillance radar), THORN EMI Electronics (proximity fuze and telemetry), Cossor Electronics (IFF), GEC Avionics (Class II common modules), Marconi Command and Control Systems (tracker radar and missile safety and arming system), Ferranti Computer Systems (Argus M700/40 processor), Wallop Industries (rocket missile flare), RO Patricroft (missile warhead), Keelavite (primary power supply), Racal Radar Defence (command transmitter) and Royal Ordnance Westcott (rocket motor).

For this contract, British Aerospace have agreed with the UK MoD an incentive pricing arrangement bounded by a maximum price for the whole package. The contract, as announced in late 1986, covers an initial production order sufficient to replace two of BAOR's towed Rapier air defence batteries and three squadrons of the Royal Air Force Regiment Rapiers also deployed in West Germany. It is envisaged that further orders will be placed at a later date so additional units can be re-equipped.

Description

The key element of the Rapier 2000 air defence system is an eight-missile launcher with automatic infra-red tracking which, with manual acquisition and computerised tactical control facilities, provides an engagement capability by both day and night. Its engagement zone is -5 to +60°

STATIC & TOWED SAM SYSTEMS / UK

Marconi Command and Control Systems Blindfire 2000 tracking radar for the Rapier 2000 air defence missile system

British Aerospace eight-round launcher for the Rapier 2000 air defence system with the tracker mounted on top between the two banks of four missiles and the transmitter mounted below

in elevation and 360° in traverse. Mounted on the turntable is a transmitter which sends guidance commands to the missile in flight.

By day an optical acquisition facility can be used to acquire and designate targets for engagement. The infra-red tracker has a passive scanning mode which can be employed to search for, acquire and track targets by day or night. A remote viewing console allows the operator to work from a protected position.

To this basic system can be added a Plessey Radar J-band 3D surveillance radar to provide a fully automatic engagement capability and a Marconi Command and Control Systems radar tracker to provide for all-weather operations.

The three separate elements of Rapier 2000 are all mounted on monocoque two-wheel trailers each with its own built-in power supply and with a much smoother shape than the existing Rapier system. This shape serves two functions, firstly to offer a greater degree of protection against nuclear blast and secondly, to provide a faster decontamination time in the event of chemical attack.

The trailer inter-connections incorporate fibre optics and nuclear hardened micro-chips, offering increased resistance to nuclear radiation and Electro Magnetic Pulse effects.

Each trailer also incorporates built-in test equipment, offering an automatic diagnosis of faulty line replaceable units (LRUs) which can then be easily exchanged.

The new Plessey surveillance radar features a high power-output transmitter to minimise the effectiveness of electronic countermeasures with separate narrow search beams in elevation to minimise the effect of jamming signals. The set has an integrated Mk 12 IFF system from Cossor and will detect, identify and display all air movements within its range. It also has a high elevation guard beam which, when an anti-radar missile is detected, inhibits the radar transmissions. This portion of the contract is worth an initial £75 million to Plessey.

The Marconi Command and Control Systems dual tracking radar generates enough power to break through most jamming systems effectively. It uses a Ferranti M700 processor with frequency management software techniques to evade jamming signals. The radar gathering beam replaces the earlier TV gathering unit and ensures missile acquisition in extreme weather conditions. It has a separate missile guidance transmitter which enables a single Rapier fire unit with a radar tracker to engage two separate targets simultaneously. This new radar is called Blindfire 2000 with the initial contract valued at over £100 million.

In addition to firing the current Rapier Mk 1 missile, Rapier 2000 will fire the new Rapier Mk 2 missile which will enter production in the early 1990s.

The Rapier Mk 2 missile features an increased range due to the use of an improved Royal Ordnance Thermopalae rocket motor. Two versions are under development. One retains the semi-armour piercing warhead of the original triggered by an impact fuze, the other is fitted with a combined armour piercing and fragmentation warhead. It will have a dual crush and proximity fuze and a number of other refinements, and will be used with existing Rapier air defence systems.

The current Rapier air defence system is towed, in the British Army and Royal Air Force Regiment, by a one tonne Land Rover, but it is envisaged that a larger and more powerful vehicle will be used for Rapier 2000. Early in 1988 the UK RAF issued a requirement for a new 4 × 4 vehicle with a payload of 1.5 tonnes and capable of towing a 1.5 tonne trailer for use with the Rapier air defence system.

SPECIFICATIONS (Mk 1 missile)

TYPE	single stage, low altitude	MAX SPEED	650 m/s
LENGTH	2.24 m	MAX RANGE	7000 m (Mk 2 8000 m)
DIAMETER	0.133 m	MIN RANGE	500 m
WING SPAN	0.381 m	MAX ALTITUDE	around 3000 m
LAUNCH WEIGHT	42.6 kg	MIN ALTITUDE	less than 15 m
PROPULSION	two stage solid propellant rocket motor	LAUNCHER	mobile, eight round trainable, trailer-mounted
GUIDANCE	optical or automatic		
WARHEAD	1.4 kg HE- semi-armour piercing, crush fuze		

Status: Under development to meet the requirements of the British Army and Royal Air Force Regiment.

Manufacturer (Prime): British Aerospace (Dynamics) Limited, Six Hills Way, Stevenage, Hertfordshire SG1 2DA, UK.
Telephone: (0438) 312422
Telex: 825125/825126

UK / STATIC & TOWED SAM SYSTEMS

British Aerospace Wolverine Anti-tactical Ballistic Missile (ATBM) System

Development/Description
The Wolverine ATBM concept is based on the use of a modified vertical launch Seawolf missile with a low risk guidance system to deal with battlefield missile threats.

The highly automated guidance type under consideration for Wolverine is known as Missile Reference Command-to-Line-Of-Sight (MRCLOS) which relies principally upon an inertial reference within the weapon to keep it on course for intercepting the threat.

This minimises the command link update transmissions and allows a single fire control system to guide several missiles at once on a time-shared basis thus boosting the target-handling rate.

The MRCLOS guidance is able to cope with all current and projected upgraded versions of Soviet SRBMs such as the SS-21 Scarab and SS-1 Scud B/C/D.

The missile itself is to use a flechette type warhead and, if served by the correct radar type, could engage aircraft as well as missile targets.

A typical role for Wolverine could be the close area defence of an airbase using a 32-round vertical launch container, a 2D surveillance radar and an I/J-band fire control radar.

It would also be possible to network a Wolverine launch complex to the radars of a Patriot area defence system so as to provide terminal air defence of the Patriot launchers themselves against SRBM attack whilst they engage aircraft of missiles targeted at higher value or time urgent targets.

In 1988 the US Army Strategic Defence Command placed a contract with British Aerospace to evaluate the Wolverine ATBM using advanced seeker, warhead and fire control radar technology concepts.

Status: Concept study. Deliveries could be made within five years of a development go-ahead decision.

Manufacturer: British Aerospace (Dynamics) Limited, Six Hills Way, Stevenage, SG1 2DA, UK.
Telephone: (0438) 312422
Telex: 825125/825126

Shorts Tigercat Low Altitude Surface-to-air Missile System

Development
In the late 1950s Shorts Precision Engineering Division at Castlereagh developed the SX-A5 surface-to-air missile system using manual-command-link control. The company was awarded a development contract early in 1958 for a small SAM to provide close defence of Royal Navy warships.

The missile system was originally called Green Light but was renamed Seacat in 1959 and by 1961 acceptance trials were under way with first production missiles completed in 1962. In addition to the Royal Navy, Seacat has been purchased by at least 16 other navies all over the world. By 1987, total sales of Seacat and Tigercat systems amounted to some £650 million.

Although originally intended for naval applications, early consideration was given to developing a land-based version for defence of airfields and other high value targets and this was subsequently called Tigercat.

Tigercat was purchased by the Royal Air Force Regiment as its first SAM system and became fully operational in 1970. These have now been replaced by the British Aerospace Rapier.

The Tigercat SAM system has been exported to Argentina, India, Iran, Jordan, Qatar and Zambia. During the 1982 Falklands War both the Argentinian Army and Marine Corps deployed Tigercat systems to the area of Port Stanley. The Marines unit, the 1st Marine Anti-Aircraft Regiment, had three firing units whilst the Army unit, the 601st Anti-Aircraft Defence Group, had four. Although a number of Tigercats were fired, none scored any hits on British aircraft or helicopters. All the launchers were used in conjunction with 20, 30 and 35 mm anti-aircraft cannon and ground radar control units. Following the Argentinian defeat, all seven firing units were apparently captured in fairly intact condition.

The systems originally sold to Jordan have found their way to South Africa, but it is understood that they are no longer operational.

Description
A Tigercat Mk 1 SAM system consists of three main components: the missile, launcher trailer and director trailer. Each trailer is towed by a Land Rover (4 × 4) light vehicle with the system normally having a five-man crew, of whom one is the gunner. Tigercat can be operational within 15 minutes of coming to a halt.

The launcher trailer consists of a two wheel chassis integral with a three-missile, two axes rotatable launching platform. In the firing position the trailer is supported on three outriggers. The launcher incorporates an electro-hydraulic system which moves it to the correct bearing and elevation as determined by the aimer's sight.

The gunner, or aimer, is seated in the director trailer which is supported on four jacks. Attached to his seat is a structure with binoculars, firing button, thumb-operated joystick and fixed transmitting aerial for the guidance system.

The aimer acquires the target using his binocular sight and when the target comes within range the aimer starts the firing sequence which launches a missile from the three-round launcher two seconds later.

At a range of approximately 300 m the missile appears in the aimer's sight and is guided visually along the line of sight to the target. Fin-mounted flares ensure that the missile is visible all the way. The aimer flies the missile along the line of sight to the target by means of a thumb joystick.

The guidance and control system translates the thumb joystick movements into radio commands and transmits them to the missile via an aerial on top of the three-round missile launcher.

When the missile hits or passes close to the target the contact/proximity fuze is activated.

The missile itself is a small single stage subsonic unit with a relatively large high explosive blast warhead fitted with a contact/proximity fuze. Its Imperial Metal Industries motor is the tandem type, boost and sustainer.

The missile has four movable wings swept back at an angle of 60° and four fixed fins at the rear. The fuze is mounted at the front of the

Three-round Tigercat launcher deployed in firing position with trailer supported on three jacks and missile covers removed

Shorts Tigercat operator in director trailer

272 STATIC & TOWED SAM SYSTEMS / UK

Shorts Tigercat surface-to-air missile system deployed in field with launcher on left, director in centre and Marconi Radar Systems ST850/M radar on right

Tigercat three-round launcher with all three missiles protected by their rigid transport covers, removed prior to action

Tigercat missile being launched showing the flare tubes in the fins which are used by the operator to track the missile (Ministry of Defence)

missile followed by the warhead, electronic pack, control surface (wing) actuator assembly and finally the rocket motor assembly. The fixed rear fins are set at 45° to the wings to reduce downwash effect of control movements and each fin incorporates flare tubes, although only two contain tracking flares.

No pre-firing 'warm-up' sequences are required and auxiliary power services within the missile are activated at launch.

Since it was first introduced, the missile itself has been constantly updated and today's version is much more reliable and lethal than the original. According to Shorts, two Tigercat fire units would have an equal attrition rate to 12 Bofors 40 mm L/70 guns and save over 70 per cent in manpower and 90 per cent in airlift weight.

Target detection is provided either from forward observation posts to surveillance post or by a surveillance radar, and gives the gunner the direction of attack. The gunner acquires the target visually and when within range a missile is launched and guided to the target by him.

Tigercat can be integrated with fire control radar units to give dark fire or even blind fire capability for all-weather use.

The launcher takes about three minutes to be reloaded with new missiles which are provided with rigid covers for transport. The covers are removed manually once the missile has been placed on the launcher.

As far as is known only one export customer, Zambia, has the all-weather Radar Enhanced Mk 2 Tigercat version which uses the Marconi Radar Systems ST850/M radar with its associated TV system. The ST850/M is mounted in a fully enclosed mobile cabin and could also be integrated with the I/J-band Marconi S860 mobile surveillance radar.

The ST850/M gives Tigercat an all-weather capability as well as enhancing the clear weather performance via a TV auto-gather facility. In conditions where the missile is visible, it is automatically gathered within a few seconds of launch after which the engagement is completed automatically or manually using the TV monitor.

The radar may assume control of either of two Tigercat units, providing fully automatic control of the channel while the second channel reverts to optical control.

The fully enclosed cabin is air-conditioned with the director mounted on the roof. This carries a 1 m diameter antenna and the TV camera and covers an elevation arc from -25 to +85°.

SPECIFICATIONS (missile)

TYPE	two stage, low altitude	GUIDANCE	command-to-line-of-sight
LENGTH		WARHEAD	17.2 kg HE blast fragmentation with contact and proximity fuzing
missile	1.480 m		
missile in canister	1.548 m	MAX SPEED	Mach 0.9 approx
DIAMETER		MAX RANGE	5500 m
missile body	0.191 m	MIN RANGE	300 m approx
missile in canister	0.711 m	MAX ALTITUDE	4000 m plus
WING SPAN OF MISSILE	0.65 m	MIN ALTITUDE	30 m
LAUNCH WEIGHT	62.7 kg	LAUNCHER	mobile, triple trainable mount
PROPULSION	dual solid fuel booster/sustainer		

Status: Production as required. In service with:

Country	No of launchers	Operator
Argentina	10	Army, Marine Corps
India	40	Army
Iran	15	Air Force
Qatar	5	Air Force (1 battery)
Zambia	3	Army (1 battery)

Manufacturer: Short Brothers Limited, Missile Systems Division, Montgomery Road, Belfast BT6 9HN, Northern Ireland.
Telephone: (0232) 458444
Telex: 74688
Fax: (0232) 732974

UK / STATIC & TOWED SAM SYSTEMS

Bloodhound Mk 2 Surface-to-air Missile System

Development
Shortly after the end of the Second World War the Royal Air Force issued a requirement for a medium/high altitude surface-to-air missile system which was subsequently given the code name Red Duster.

Prime contractor was the Bristol Aeroplane Company and after extensive trials, production of the missile commenced at Filton in 1957. This entered service with the then Royal Air Force Fighter Command as the Bloodhound Mk 1 pulse radar semi-active homing missile with the first squadron becoming operational in 1958.

Bloodhound was deployed between 1958 and 1961 at RAF Woolfox Lodge, Watton, Woodhall Spa, Dunholm Lodge and North Coates and used mainly to defend the V-bomber and Thor IRBM bases in Lincolnshire and the East Midlands.

Sales of the Bloodhound Mk 1 were also made to Australia (one squadron in 1959) and a trials quantity to Sweden in 1958, but none is now operational. The Australians used their Bloodhounds at sites in Sydney, Darwin and North-West Cape for 15 years.

Between 1951 and 1959 over 500 test vehicles were built and delivered with a total of 300 production Bloodhound Mk 1s delivered between 1958 and February 1960.

The Bloodhound Mk 1 was followed by the Bloodhound Mk 2 on which design work commenced in 1958. This entered service in 1964 and has an improved warhead, longer range, is more effective at low level and has greater resistance to ECM.

Production of the Bloodhound Mk 2 missile was undertaken at Cardiff in South Wales and a total of 783 were built with final missiles built for Switzerland in late 1966.

Bloodhound Mk 2 is slightly longer than the Mk 1 with more powerful Thor ramjets and larger boost motors. There was also a project for the Bloodhound Mk 3, or Blue Envoy as it was also called, but this was cancelled in 1962.

The Bloodhound Mk 2 was originally deployed by the Royal Air Force in the UK (25 Squadron at North Coates and 41 Squadron at West Raynham), Cyprus (112 Squadron), Malaysia and Singapore, with some retained in the UK as a strategic reserve.

Bloodhound Mk 2 became operational in the Far East in 1964 with No 65 Squadron at Seletar and No 33 at Butterworth, Malaysia, the former being in mobile configuration.

In 1970 the UK-based Bloodhounds were all redeployed to West Germany with No 25 squadron, with one flight each at Laarbruch, Bruggen and Wildenrath with support from RAF West Raynham.

In 1977 it was announced that the Bloodhound Mk 2s were to be withdrawn from West Germany and redeployed in the United Kingdom with No 11 Group, Royal Air Force Strike Command, for use by Nos 25 and 85 squadrons. The move was completed by March 1983.

The HQ of No 25 Squadron is at RAF Wyton with A Flight at Barkson Heath, B Flight at Wyton and C Flight at Wattisham. No 85 Squadron has its HQ at RAF West Raynham which also houses A Flight, with B Flight at RAF Bawdsey and C Flight at RAF North Coates. Both squadrons have their administrative centre and engineering base at RAF West Raynham.

The Bloodhound Mk 2 was phased out of service in 1974 with the Royal Swedish Air Force which purchased it in 1964 and called it the Rb 68, but it remains in service with the Singapore Air Force (one squadron with a total of 24 launchers taken over from the RAF, ex-No 65 Squadron, originally 28 launchers) and the Swiss Air Force (two battalions each with two batteries with a total of 64 launchers).

The Swiss Air Force designation is BL-64. They also have two Ferranti training simulators. The remaining Swedish Bloodhound Mk 2 Missiles were purchased by Switzerland and the UK.

Early in 1984 British Aerospace was awarded a contract by Switzerland for the further supply of Bloodhound boost motors, indicating a significant continuation of the system's life.

Late in 1986 a series of firings of Bloodhound Mk 2 SAMs was carried out at the Royal Aircraft Establishment's range at Aberporth by the RAF. Under the auspices of the Swiss Air Force and BAMF (Swiss Maintenance Organisation) the Royal Air Force also supported firing trials of Bloodhound missiles taken from the Swiss weapon stock.

The aim of these trials, which were carried out successfully, was to:
a) prove the continuing operational reliability of Bloodhound missiles of varying age
b) check the interception by Bloodhound of air targets (radar augmented Jindivik drones) operating under different ECM conditions
c) confirm the correct functioning of the Bloodhound tracker radar and weapon launch post following a recently completed equipment upgrading programme.

In 1987 British Aerospace, Naval and Electronic Systems Division, was awarded a £4 million contract from the Swiss Government to update Bloodhound SAM Launch Control Posts in conjunction with Ferranti Computer Systems.

Late in 1969 British Aerospace, which had taken over the Bristol Aeroplane Company some years before, was awarded a £10 million contract from the Singapore Government to refurbish the Bloodhound Mk 2 systems operated by the RAF in the Far East.

In March 1987, the Naval and Electronic Systems Division of British Aerospace announced that it had been commissioned by the UK MoD to carry out a technical evaluation of the Bloodhound Mk 2 SAM system to assess the changes required to maintain its effectiveness as an area anti-aircraft weapon past 1995 and until the turn of the century. The study was completed late in 1987.

Royal Air Force Bloodhound operations rooms, Launch Control Posts (LCPs) and the Target Illuminating Radar (TIR) have all been updated in the last few years. The re-equipping of the LCPs with more powerful computers has enabled new facilities to be added to the system. Engagements can now be simulated for training purposes using a record/playback facility. Additional details of the Bloodhound automatic operations room are given in the description of the system.

Description
A basic Bloodhound Mk 2 SAM section usually comprises four to eight launchers, each with a Bloodhound Mk 2 in the ready to launch position, a TIR, an LCP and associated power supplies. Most RAF flights have two such sections. Usually there is at least one reload round per launcher.

In the case of all Bloodhound Mk 2 operators, it is integrated into an overall air defence system, although it can operate independently if required by the tactical situation.

The missile is launched with the scanner pointed to the predicted target direction at the end of boost. The steering system is locked until the end of the boost phase.

The TIR searches for, acquires, then automatically tracks and illuminates the target. It also interrogates the target via IFF for positive

A standard Lancer Boss 700 sideloader (foreground) and a sideloader with the BAe-designed attachment for the Bloodhound Mk 2 SAM. The missiles are of No 85 Squadron, RAF

Bloodhound Mk 2 SAMs deployed at RAF base somewhere in the UK

274 STATIC & TOWED SAM SYSTEMS / UK

Bloodhound Mk 2 immediately after launch from its single round static launcher with power provided by the four boosters

Bloodhound Mk 2 of No 85 Squadron at RAF West Raynham, stripped of its booster motors, is taken from its storage site by a specialised lifting vehicle (Royal Air Force)

Interior of first Automated Operations Room for the Royal Air Force Bloodhound air defence system which became operational in 1987. This is the first stage of a computer network designed to automate distribution and presentation of information in all the Bloodhound air defence ORs of the RAF

identification and transmits the appropriate information to the LCP.

When the target is within the effective range, a Bloodhound is launched with the receiver in the missile nose detecting and following the radiation reflected by the target as it is illuminated by the TIR.

The engagement controller in seated in the LCP which is the control centre of the missile section. A computer in the LCP processes the output data from the TIR to determine the optimum conditions for the target engagement. The computer also performs routine tasks concerned with the state of readiness of the system and its missiles.

Both the engagement controller and the technical supervisor are provided with displays and communications equipment to enable the former to take rapid operational decisions and the latter to maintain maximum equipment serviceability. No missile can be launched until the engagement controller and the technical supervisor have turned separate keys to release the firing circuit.

The types of TIR radar developed for Bloodhound were: Radar Type 87 – Blue Anchor (RAF), Scorpion (Swiss AF version of Type 87), Radar Type 86 – Indigo Corkscrew (RAF) and Firelight (Swedish AF version of Type 86).

In RAF service the Type 87 radars have all been phased out in favour of an all Type 86 fleet.

The Type 86/Firelight is air-transportable and can be rapidly brought into action. The whole system is contained in a single cabin with the 2.1 m diameter antennas mounted on a retractable pedestal on the roof. It can also carry out an autonomous search in a specified area.

The Scorpion was designed for static operations or where system mobility is not a prime consideration. It has a number of transportable units and has a larger 4.2 m diameter antenna providing a longer range of 400 km. The target range does, of course, depend on the target radar cross-section; for a typical Soviet fighter bomber a range of 200 km is more realistic.

Both the Type 86/Firelight and Scorpion are CW Doppler systems operating in the I/J-bands and are said to have good performance in the presence of natural or ECM interference. The missile is mounted on the launcher at an angle of 34° and is slaved in azimuth to the TIR via offsets in the LCP.

The Bloodhound is boosted to supersonic speed by four Gosling solid propellant rocket boost motors which develop 45 360 kg of thrust and burn for four seconds by which time the two Rolls-Royce Thor ramjets have reached ignition speed.

As the missile builds up velocity it flies out of the ring of four expended boosters which are then discarded together with the fins; the Thor ramjets then take over.

When the boosters have been jettisoned, the central pivoting wings are unlocked and the missile becomes steerable.

When engaging low level targets it flies downwards to pick up the radiation generated by the TIR and reflected by the target, but when intercepting a target at medium or high altitude it initially cruises at a pre-set height (12 192 m or 15 240 m), then climbs or dives during the terminal stage to attack the target. The HE warhead is mounted to the rear of the nose mounted semi-active radar receiver and guidance electronics and has a THORN EMI proximity fuze.

Reserve missiles are kept on trailers hooked up to an air-conditioning unit and are loaded onto the launcher using a fork lift truck.

Missile Detail

The missile is a ramjet-powered monoplane with moving wings. It is boosted to supersonic speed by four solid boost motors with fins that are linked to a common thrust ring and discarded when the missile has achieved operational speed.

The missile manoeuvres by means of twist and steer in the same way as a bird in flight. A twist and steer missile rolls so as to align to normal to the wings with the vector direction in which the manoeuvre is required and then pitches in that direction to complete the manoeuvre. The wings rotate together to produce pitch manoeuvres and in opposite directions to produce roll.

The missile homes onto a target following a proportional navigation course (a line of sight to the target is maintained by the missile's receiving aerial, whilst the axis of the missile is aligned towards the predicted interception point). The rate of turn of the missile is therefore proportional to the rate of change of sight-line angle.

UK / STATIC & TOWED SAM SYSTEMS

At the same time more powerful hydraulic servos are energised in order to position the wings to steer the missile. The required pitch and yaw components are compared to obtain a roll signal, and the required pitch signal is passed to the wing servos while the missile rolls to the required altitude. A feedback circuit ensures that, in the absence of any guidance demand, the missile remains stabilised.

The missile has five main units: forebody, mainbody, ramjet engines, boost motors and control surfaces.

The zero type launcher has three main functions: firstly to support the missile at the firing elevation, secondly to provide or route all the necessary facilities to the missile in preparation for firing and thirdly to turn the missile to the correct launch bearing.

The missile is supported on the launcher beam at the front end of the boosts and at the rear end of the missile mainbody. The rear connection is made through shear pins which are broken at launch under the force generated by the boosts.

Late in 1987 British Aerospace, completed installation of the first Bloodhound automated operations room. This was the first stage of a computer network designed to automate the distribution and presentation of information in all the Bloodhound SAM operations rooms of the RAF.

The network handles two main classes of information, both of which are continuously updated: operational engagement data and engineering status data. Identical information will be presented, or available for retrieval, in each operations room. Typical data presented in real-time includes details of potential targets acquired, individual weapon readiness and engagement status plus essential engineering information such as spares provisioning.

Each RAF Bloodhound flight has three or four Bloodhound LCPs which are linked to and in direct control of up to eight Bloodhound missile launchers. Each RAF Bloodhound flight also has its own automated control room.

A Bloodhound squadron operations room has a computer and four consoles, while a flight operations room has one computer and one console. All the computers and consoles having a similar design.

The computer used in the system is the Hewlett Packard HP1000AA. All the computers are interconnected by landlines with the data held in store by each common to all and constantly updated.

In the event of an equipment failure or action damage, the status of the entire UK Bloodhound air defence system will be available to all the operations rooms remaining on line, both at squadron and flight level. The system is capable of automatic reconfiguration of data links.

Each console has two video screens. The larger screen, which is associated with a tracker ball, displays a map of the UK airspace defended by Bloodhound and shows the positions and tracks of potential targets, together with the identities of those LCPs capable of engaging them. In a column on the left-hand side of the screen, supplementary operational information is presented in alphanumeric form. The smaller screen, with which a keyboard is associated, shows Bloodhound engineering status data. Any one of more than 100 pages of information held in a databank in the computer's store can be accessed and presented.

Bloodhound Mk 2 SAM deployed on its launcher which can be traversed through a full 360°

Throughout the flight, the missile's guidance takes into account variables such as missile altitude, target course and speed, and variation in the reflected signal from the target. A gyro is employed as a space reference to determine dish position.

Error signals proportional to the difference between gyro and dish orientation are used to operate hydraulic valves which control a pair of double acting jacks; these in turn position the dish in pitch and yaw.

SPECIFICATIONS (missile)

TYPE	two stage, low to high altitude
LENGTH	8.46 m (including boosters)
DIAMETER OF MISSILE	0.546 m
MAX SPAN	2.83 m
LAUNCH WEIGHT	2270 kg
PROPULSION	four disposable solid-fuel Gosling boosters with paired set of Thor ramjet liquid kerosene fuelled sustainers
GUIDANCE	continuous-wave semi-active radar homing
WARHEAD	HE continuous rod fragmentation
MAX SPEED	Mach 2 plus
MAX RANGE	160 km
MIN RANGE	est 5 km
MAX ALTITUDE	17 000 m
MIN ALTITUDE	50 m
LAUNCHER	single rail semi-fixed or mobile trainable ground mount
RELOAD TIME	20 mins

Status: Production complete. In service with Singapore, Switzerland and the United Kingdom.

Manufacturers: Co-contractors for the UK are British Aerospace (Dynamics) Limited, PO Box 5, Filton, Bristol BS12 7QW, UK.
Telephone: (0272) 693831
Missile, launcher, operations rooms and site installation: British Aerospace (Dynamics) Limited.
Guidance and LCP: Ferranti International Dynamics Ltd, Oldham.
Ramjet propulsion system: Rolls-Royce.
Missile fuze: THORN-EMI.
Scorpion TIR: Marconi Radar Systems.
Type 86/Firelight TIR: Ferranti, Edinburgh.
Launcher/trailers: ML Aviation.
For overseas customers, British Aerospace is the prime contractor.

UNITED STATES OF AMERICA

Raytheon MIM-23 HAWK Low to Medium Altitude Surface-to-air Missile System

Development

The HAWK (Homing All the Way Killer) semi-active radar seeking medium-range SAM system commenced development in 1953 with the US Army awarding a full-scale development contract to Raytheon for the missile in July 1954 and Northrop providing the launcher and ground equipment.

The first test firing took place in June 1956 with its development phase completed in July 1957. Initial operational capability (IOC) of the Basic HAWK, MIM-23A, took place in August 1960 when the first US Army battalion was activated. In the same year a NATO Memorandum of Understanding (MoU) was signed between France, Italy, the Netherlands, Belgium, West Germany and the United States for co-production of the system in Europe. In addition, special grant aid arrangements were made to deliver European-built systems to Spain, Greece and Denmark and direct sale arrangements of US-built systems were made with Japan, Israel and Sweden. The Japanese sale soon expanded into a country-to-country co-production agreement. In the same region, the United States also made grant aid deliveries of HAWK to Taiwan and South Korea.

However, in order to counter advanced threats, especially at low altitude, in 1964 the US Army initiated a modernisation programme known as the HAWK/HIP (HAWK Improvement Program). This involved a number of changes to the basic system, of which the most important were the addition of a central information co-ordinator with a digital automatic data processor at the battery HQ for target processing, threat ordering and target intercept evaluation, and updating of the missile to the Improved-HAWK, MIM-23B, configuration with a larger warhead (54 kg versus 45 kg), an improved small guidance package and a higher performance rocket motor. The system modifications allowed both the missile and its continuous wave (CW) illuminating radar to discriminate a target from ground-clutter by using its velocity, ensuring low altitude coverage. Type classified in 1971, all US Army and Marine Corps HAWK battalions were subsequently retrofitted to the I-HAWK standard by 1978 and in 1974 an enlarged NATO consortium (including Denmark and Greece but excluding Belgium, which eventually rejoined in 1979) awarded Raytheon a contract for co-production of I-HAWK components in Europe. All NATO users then brought their batteries up to this status. Japan followed suit with an I-HAWK co-production agreement in 1977.

In September 1977 the US armed forces started a second modernisation effort under the designation HAWK-PIP (Product Improvement Program). This involved three phases, the PIP Phase I being fielded with the US forces in 1979. This included an Improved CW Acquisition Radar (ICWAR) transmitter to double the output power and increase detection range, the addition of digital Moving Target Indication (MTI) to the Pulse Acquisition Radar (PAR) and the inclusion of Army Tactical Data Link (ATDL) communications within the system.

The Phase II upgrade modifications were approved for production in 1983. These greatly improved the reliability of the High Powered Illumination (HPI) radar by replacing vacuum-tube circuits with modern solid-state technology and added the Tracking Adjunct System (TAS) optical tracking system for operation in an ECM environment to the HPI, the Battery Control Center (BCC) and the Platoon Command Post (PCP).

Belgium, Denmark, France, Italy, Greece, the Netherlands and West Germany have implemented Phase I and are currently embodying Phase II. Other countries are following suit.

The Phase III upgrade programme, which started development in 1983 and is currently in production for the US armed forces for deployment in 1989, makes major modifications to many of the system's major items. The Range Only Radar (ROR) and Information Co-ordination Center (ICC) have been deleted from the system and the BCC replaced by a Battery Command Post (BCP). Major electronic modifications, which included the addition of distributed microcomputers and greatly improved computer software, were made to the BCP, PCP, CWAR and HPI.

However, the major system operational change made by Phase III is the addition of a single scan target detection capability and a low altitude simultaneous HAWK engagement (LASHE) system to the HPI by employing a fan beam antenna to provide a wide angle, low altitude illumination pattern to allow multiple engagements against saturation raids.

Until the Phase III modifications have been fielded, the HAWK system exists as two battery configurations: the standard Phase II PIP battery for normal field army operations and the Triad battery for situations requiring increased fire power, which is peculiar to the US Marine Corps. The standard battery includes an HQ with an AN/MPQ-50 pulse/acquisition radar, an AN/MPQ-48 ICWAR, an AN/MPW-51 range only radar, an AN/MWS-11 Improved Platoon Command Post (IPCP) and an AN/TSW-8 BCC, and two firing platoons each with an AN/MPQ-46 tracking/illuminating radar (HPI) and three M192 triple missile launchers.

The Triad battery comprises three firing platoons. One is as the standard battery configuration and the other two are usually configured as Assault Fire Units (AFU) containing an ICWAR, an HPI, a PCP and three launchers. The AFUs can be detached from the batteries and operated autonomously when greater mobility or dispersion is required.

The Phase III HAWK System will be fielded in three configurations: an Assault Fire Platoon (AFP), an Assault Fire Platoon Plus (AFP+) and a Battery. The AFP will consist of a CWAR, PCP and HPI and four to six launchers. The AFP+ has the same complement as the AFP with a PAR added. The Battery has a CWAR, PAR, BCP, two HPIs and six launchers.

A minimum HAWK force of 19 batteries (65 AFU or AFPs) will remain under US Army control in the field indefinitely with six batteries in three battalions being transferred to the US National Guard by the mid-1990s.

Norway has developed its own HAWK upgrade scheme known as the Norwegian Adapted HAWK (NOAH) which involved the lease of I-HAWK launchers, HPI radars and missile loaders from the USA and their integration with Hughes-Kongsberg Vaapenfabrik (HKV) Acquisition Radar and Control Systems (ARCS) in place of the normal search, acquisition and ranging radars. The ARCS is a combination of the Hughes 3D AN/TPQ-36A Low Altitude Surveillance Radar (LASR) and the NFT fire control system. The passive TAS is also being modified to incorporate a thermal imaging system based on that used on the M1 Abrams MBT. A total of six batteries was procured from 1983 onwards.

During the early 1970s to early 1980s, the I-HAWK system was also sold to a number of countries in the Middle and Far East. To maintain

Improved HAWK air defence missile site of the US Army in West Germany showing the four missile launchers deployed in the foreground

Three-round HAWK missile launcher deployed in the field (US Army)

USA / STATIC & TOWED SAM SYSTEMS

HAWK missile leaves its three-round launcher during US test in April 1988 on Patriot/HAWK interoperability

US Army personnel setting up their AN/MPQ-50 Improved Pulse Acquisition radar set

Close up of the Northrop Corporation's Tracking Adjunct System (TAS) which is mounted on top of the HAWK's high-powered radar system

HAWK missile shoots down short-range tactical ballistic missile target while interoperating with Raytheon's Patriot air defence system

their HAWK system's viability, the Israelis have upgraded it to the PIP Phase II standard with the addition in the mid-1970s of a Super Eye electro-optical TV system for detection of aircraft at 30 to 40 km and identification at 17 to 25 km. They have also modified their I-HAWK systems for use at altitudes up to 24 384 m and used one from an Israeli Air Force battery located in southern Lebanon to shoot down on 31 August 1982 a Syrian Air Force MiG-25R Foxbat-B photo-reconnaissance aircraft flying at Mach 2.5 on a high level 21 336 m plus sortie near Jouniehj, north of Beirut.

Not surprisingly, Israel was also the first country to use the Basic-HAWK in combat when, during the 1967 June war, it had destroyed one of its own Dassault Mirage IIICJ fighters with an incapacitated pilot on board to prevent it crashing into the nuclear weapons facility at Dimona. They followed this by the first true combat launch on 24 May 1969, when an Egyptian MiG-21 flying near Kantara, over the Suez canal, was hit at about 6700 m altitude. By the end of the War of Attrition in August 1970, Basic-HAWK had accounted for 12 Egyptian aircraft (one Ilyushin IL-28 Beagle, four Sukhoi Su-7 Fitters, four MiG-17 Frescoes and three MiG-21 Fishbeds).

During the 1973 Yom Kippur War around 75 HAWK rounds were used against Syrian, Iraqi, Libyan and Egyptian aircraft and destroyed four MiG-17s, one MiG-21, three Sukhoi Su-7s, one Hawker Hunter, one Dassault Mirage V and two Mil Mi-8 helicopters. Included amongst the kills were several multiples using just one missile.

Its next use by the Israelis was in its modified I-HAWK configuration during the June 1982 Peace for Galilee war when a Syrian MiG-23 was destroyed. This was followed by the MiG-25 incident.

However, before these last two Israeli uses, Iran's armed forces started using I-HAWKs against the Iraqi Air Force following the 1980 invasion and to date is believed to have shot down at least 20 aircraft with the weapon.

The latest combat user of the I-HAWK is France which deployed one battery to Chad to defend the capital, N'Djamena. On 7 September 1987 it shot down a Libyan Air Force Tupolev Tu-22 Blinder bomber which was trying to bomb the airport.

For the future a programme known as HAWK IV will further enhance system mobility and acquisition. The salient features of this programme are discussed below

Among the HAWK items designed and developed by Northrop are the loader/transporter, crane attachment, ramps, winter kits, hoisting beam, hoist adapter, track cleats, wings/elevons, actuator and the tracking adjunct system.

By 1988 Northrop had built some 750 loader/transporters, 1700 three-round launchers, 35 000 sets of wings/elevons, 35 000 actuators and over 300 tracking adjunct systems with production continuing.

STATIC & TOWED SAM SYSTEMS / USA

Patriot/HAWK Interoperability Development

Patriot/HAWK interoperability is being considered to gain the benefits of effective air defence co-ordination when these two systems occupy the same defence area. The functional capabilities for improved performance are being addressed by two new concepts, the brigade operations centre and a composite battalion.

A capability for centralised battle management through a brigade operations centre will allow data sharing between separate Patriot, HAWK or even composite battalions.

Information will be combined in one Patriot Information Co-ordination Central (ICC) from which engagement assignments are sent to other battalions as well as its own fire units.

The composite battalion capability will allow local commanders the choice of using a single Battalion ICC to direct fire from both HAWK and Patriot fire units. In this mode, Patriot and HAWK units will function as if assigned to the same battalion. Because surveillance data will be shared, the battalion's tactical director will be able to choose Patriot or HAWK weapons for specific engagements.

HAWK Mobility

For further development and exploitation of the HAWK system and its evolution into a system for the early 2000s, the first step foreseen by the manufacturer is the HAWK mobility programme. The goal of this near-term future development by the US and the Netherlands is to improve the system's overall mobility and reduce both the emplacement and march order times. Full-scale development is due to start in 1989.

There are four major features of this upgrade. Firstly, the launcher will be modified to remove its remaining vacuum-tube circuits and replace them with a modern digital micro-computer. This change permits improved computation of missile launch obstruction avoidance and provides full duplex serial data link communications between each launcher and the PCP. This last change replaces the current large, heavy, multi-conductor data cables with a telephone type field wire interconnector to the PCP.

Secondly, mechanical modifications will be made to the launcher to allow it to move during road march, with three ready to fire HAWK missiles mounted in place. The change greatly reduces launcher emplacement and march order times by eliminating the requirement to load missiles during emplacement and remove missiles during march order.

Thirdly, a new Loader-Transporter vehicle will be developed to replace the existing truck transported M501E1 tracked missile loader. This new vehicle will be a flat bed truck with an integral hydraulic hoist crane. The truck can carry three ready to fire missiles on a triple missile pallet and tows the fully loaded Launcher-Transporter behind. The crane can be used to lift either one or three missiles from the pallets and place them directly on the launcher. The Loader-Transporter and Launcher-Transporter combination provides immediate access to six ready-to-fire missiles, reducing the number of supporting transport trucks from four to one.

The fourth modification is the incorporation of a North Orientation Module (NOM) into the system. This device contains a north seeking gyroscope and a digital computer. When mounted on a HAWK radar or launcher, the NOM can provide rapid determination of the unit's azimuth alignment with respect to the true north reference. With this device, each unit of the HAWK system can be independently and accurately aligned day or night in all-weather conditions without using the existing optical telescope and the need for line-of-sight between units.

Agile Continuous Wave Acquisition Radar (ACWAR)/Multiple Role Survivable Radar (MRSR)

The next change is expected to be the introduction of Agile CW Acquisition Radar (ACWAR).

The agile continuous wave acquisition radar (ACWAR) is an evolution of the HAWK CW radar technology. It performs full 3D target acquisition over a 360° azimuth sector and large elevation angles.

The ACWAR programme was initiated to meet increasingly severe tactical air defence requirements, and the equipment is designed for operation in the 1990s and the 21st century. ACWAR replaces two current HAWK radars to reduce vehicle, manpower and logistics needs. At the same time, the system provides full 3D track information on a large number

Type 63 (6 × 6) truck of the Japanese Ground Self Defence Force towing three-round HAWK loader (Kensuke Ebata)

Nine-round Sparrow HAWK launcher deployed in the field

Northrop Tracking Adjunct System (TAS) mounted between the HPI

of targets to accuracies sufficient for cueing and control of other remote weapons as well as data netting. ACWAR is mobile, helicopter and C-130 transportable, and can be vehicle- or trailer-mounted.

ACWAR consists of all solid-state exciter/transmitter, all digital radar control, row board transmit and receive antenna construction for precise sidelobe control, mechanical steering in azimuth and electronic steering in elevation. ACWAR uses a CW frequency agile, phase-coded waveform. Digitised target data is sent from the radar to the HAWK PCP or equivalent. The antenna assembly is mast-mounted with a hydraulic arm elevation system.

ACWAR technologies are being used in the US Army/Raytheon Multiple Role Survivable Radar (MRSR) Program. Major purposes of this advanced development programme include survivability from anti-radiation missiles (ARMs) without decoys or EMCON, robust ECM performance against the increasing threat while continuously providing an accurate 3D air picture.

Description

The I-HAWK missile is a certified round requiring no field maintenance or testing. The certification is maintained through periodic batch acceptance testing, annual service firing and periodic batch sampling at special maintenance facilities operated by the contractor.

It is the single stage cruciform configuration type with a dual-thrust Aerojet M112 solid propellant rocket motor. Control is achieved by the use of elevons on the trailing edges of the four wings. In operation, the acquisition radar sweeps the I-HAWK's battery's area of operation and when a target is detected, its position is relayed to the illuminating radar. This illuminates the target with electro-magnetic energy which is reflected back to the array seeker antenna of the missile-in-flight which then uses proportional navigation to intercept it. Once within range the proximity fuzed HE-blast fragmentation warhead is detonated to destroy it.

The major components of the ground equipment are:

AN/MPQ-50 Pulse Acquisition Radar (PAR)

The PAR is the primary source of high to medium altitude aircraft detection for the battery. The C-band frequency allows the radar to perform in an all-weather environment. The radar incorporates a digital MTI to provide sensitive target detection in high clutter areas and a staggered pulse repetition rate to minimise the effects of blind speeds. The PAR also includes several ECCM features and uses off-the-air tuning of the transmitter. In the Phase III configuration the PAR is not modified.

AN/MPQ-48 Improved CW Acquisition Radar (ICWAR)

Aircraft detection at the lowest flyable altitudes in the presence of heavy clutter is the primary feature the ICWAR brings to HAWK. The ICWAR and PAR are synchronised in azimuth for ease of target data correlation. Other features include FM ranging, built-in test equipment (BITE) and band frequencies. FM is applied on alternate scans of the ICWAR to obtain target range information. During the CW scan, range rate minus range is obtained. The Automatic Data Processor (ADP) in the ICC processes this information to derive target range and range rate. This feature provides the necessary data for threat ordering of low altitude targets detected by the ICWAR.

The Phase III programme makes some major modifications to the ICWAR. The basic function of the ICWAR as the system's low altitude acquisition sensor remains unchanged, however the transmitted waveform was changed to permit the radar to determine both target range and range rate on a single scan. A digital signal processor (DSP) using a Fast Fourier Transform (FFT) was added to digitally process target Doppler into detected target data. The DSP provides this digital data to a new microcomputer located in the ICWAR. The microcomputer performs much of the ICWAR target processing formally done by the ADP in the ICC and transmits the processed target track data to the PCP/BCP in serial digital format over a field telephone wire interconnection. The full-duplex digital link eliminates the need for a large heavy multi-conductor cable between the ICWAR and PCP/BCP.

AN/TSW-8 Battery Control Centre (BCC)

The BCC provides the facilities for the man-to-machine interface. The tactical control officer (TCO) is in command of all the BCC operations and maintains tactical control over all engagement sequences. The TCO monitors all functions and has the authority and facilities to enable or pre-empt any engagement or to change established priorities. The tactical control assistant assists the TCO in detection, identification, evaluation and co-ordination with higher commands. The tactical control console gives these two operators the necessary target and battery status information and controls required.

The azimuth-speed operator has the sole mission of earliest possible detection of low altitude targets. The azimuth-speed indicator console, a separate radar B-scope display, provides ICWAR target data for this purpose. Targets selected for manual engagements are assigned to one of the two fire control operators. Each operator uses the fire control console displays and controls for rapid HPI target lock, target track, missile launch and target intercept evaluation.

In the Phase III configuration the BCC is removed from the system and replaced by the BCP described below.

Information Co-ordination Central (ICC)

The ICC is the fire control data processing and operational communications centre for the battery. It provides rapid and consistent reaction to critical targets. Automatic detection, threat ordering, the IFF followed by automatic target assignment and launch functions are provided by the ICC. The ICC contains an ADP, IFF, battery terminal equipment and communications equipment.

The ADP comprises an electronic data processor (EDP) and a data take-off unit (DTO). The DTO forms the interface between the other system equipment and EDP. With the exception of inputs from a solid-state reader and outputs to a printer, all communications with the ECP are through the DTO. The EDP is a militarised, general-purpose digital computer especially adapted to this role.

Phase III eliminates the ICC and transfers its data processing and communications functions to the Phase III PCP and BCP described below.

AN/MSW-11 Improved Platoon Command Post (IPCP)

The IPCP is used as the fire control centre and command post for the AFU. It can also be used to replace an ICC. The IPCP provides manual and automatic target processing, IFF, intra-unit, intra-battery and army air defence command post communications and the displays and fire control equipment for the three-man crew. It is essentially an ICC with tactical display and engagement control console, a central communications unit, status indicator panel and an automatic data processor. The tactical display and engagement control console provides the man/machine interface for the AFU. The interior of the shelter is divided into two compartments: the tactical officer, radar operator and communications operator occupy the forward compartment with the display console, status panel, power distribution panel and communications equipment; the rear compartment contains the ADP, air-conditioning unit and IFF equipment.

Phase III Platoon Command Post (PCP)

The Phase III PCP performs most of the same functions for Phase Assault Fire Platoon (AFP) as the PCP performed for the AFU. The new PCP uses the same shelter as the original PCP and is also operated by a crew of three consisting of Tactical Officer (TO), Radar Operator (RO) and Communications Operator. Some of the original equipment is retained in the new PCP, however a large proportion is replaced by the newly designed Phase III equipment.

The interior layout of the shelter is considerably changed with the communications operator, radios, computers, IFF set and air-conditioning equipment both relocated and changed. The entire shelter interior is air-conditioned with the larger relocated air-conditioner supplying cooling for the shelter as well as all the electronic equipment. The addition of a Nuclear, Biological and Chemical (NBC) Gas-Particulate Filter Unit (GPFU) and an entryway air lock provides positive air pressurisation of the shelter for protection of the crew and equipment from NBC effects.

Phase III electronic equipment modifications replaced the ADP with modern high-speed microcomputers and more densely packed memories; replaced the TO's, RO's and TAS display with two new computer-driven display systems; and provided full-duplex serial digital data link communications from the PCP to both the CWAR and HPI.

The PCP features an Integral Operator Trainer (IOT) that provides an on-site capability for HAWK Operational Training. This trainer, housed within the Automatic Data Processor, provides the realistic target simulation necessary to enable all of the fire control capabilities inherent to a fire unit to be exercised. Twenty-five simulated target scenarios, including multiple, manoeuvring and ECM targets, are contained in its software memory.

When the AFP is configured as an AFP+ which includes a PAR, the PCP used is the same as before except that an additional microcomputer is placed into the digital computer rack. This additional computer capacity is used to process PAR data and interface the PAR with the PCP.

Battery Command Post (BCP)

In Phase III battery configuration both the BCC and ICC are replaced by a single BCP. This reduces the operating crew from six personnel to the following four operators: a TO, two ROs and a Communications Operator. The physical configuration of the BCP is identical to that of the Phase III PCP described above with the exception that a Second Radar Operator's (SRO) console is placed in the left corner adjacent to the Tactical Display and Engagement Control Console (TDECC) and additional microcomputers are placed into the digital computer rack.

STATIC & TOWED SAM SYSTEMS / USA

AN/MPQ-46 High Power Illuminator (HPI)

The HPI automatically acquires and tracks designated targets in azimuth, elevation and range rate. It serves as the interface unit supplying azimuth and elevation launch angles computed by the ADP to up to three launchers. The HPI J-band energy reflected off the target is also received by the HAWK missile for guidance. A missile reference signal is transmitted directly to the missile by the HPI. Target track is continued throughout missile flight, and after intercept HPI Doppler data is used for kill evaluation. The HPI receives target designations from the BCC and automatically searches a given sector for rapid target lock-on. The HPI incorporates ECCM and BITE.

The Phase II programme includes two major modifications to HPI. One is the addition of a wide beam transmitting antenna which is used to illuminate a much larger volume for missile guidance during use of the Low Altitude Simultaneous HAWK Engagement (LASHE) mode of operation against multiple target attacks. The second is the addition of a digital microcomputer which processes HPI target data and provides full-duplex serial digital communications between the HPI and the PCP.

AN/MPQ-51 Range-only Radar (ROR)

This is a K-band pulse radar that provides quick response range measurement when the other radars are denied range data by enemy countermeasures. During a tactical engagement, the radar is designated to obtain ranging information which is used in the computation of the fire command. The ROR reduces its vulnerability to jamming by transmitting only when designated. The ROR is not retained in the Phase III system.

M192 Launcher (LCHR)

The LCHR supports up to three ready-to-fire missiles and is activated only on the initiation of the fire cycle. When the fire button is activated in the BCC or PCP, several launcher functions occur simultaneously: the launcher slews to designated azimuth and elevation angles, power is supplied to activate the missile gyros, electronic and hydraulic systems, the launcher activates the missile motor and launches the missile. The launcher is equipped with electronic cut-outs and sensing circuits that allow firing in all emplacement situations.

Variants

Self-propelled HAWK

To increase the mobility of some of its Basic-HAWK batteries, the US Army at one stage fielded several self-propelled HAWK platoons.

These consisted of three tracked M727 vehicles, based on the M548 tracked cargo carrier, each carrying three ready to fire missiles and towing one piece of ground equipment. They have now been withdrawn from service.

HAWK on Dragon Wagon

As a private venture, Raytheon developed a version of the I-HAWK mounted on the Lockheed Dragon Wagon (8 × 8) high mobility vehicle. Announced in 1978, the I-HAWK self-propelled wheeled assault fire platoon would have consisted of an ICWAR, IPCP, IHPI and three launcher vehicles each with three ready to fire missiles. This version was not placed in production.

Sparrow HAWK

Another HAWK project is a system called Sparrow HAWK. It combines elements of both these Raytheon-produced missile systems. The standard HAWK three-round launcher is modified to allow nine Sparrow missiles to be placed on the same launcher. In January 1985 at the Naval Weapons Center, China Lake, California, a modified three-round HAWK missile launcher was used for field demonstration tests. A HAWK fire unit was manned by a US Marine Corps team which successfully fired Sparrow missiles, when two unmanned aircraft targets were intercepted. Earlier tests on the mobility of the system were carried out at the US Marine Corps Air Station, Yuma, Arizona.

SPECIFICATIONS (missile)

TYPE	single stage low to medium altitude
LENGTH	5.08 m
DIAMETER	0.37 m
WING SPAN	1.19 m
LAUNCH WEIGHTS	
MIM-23A	584 kg
MIM-23B	627.3 kg
PROPULSION	dual-thrust solid fuel booster-sustainer rocket motor
GUIDANCE	semi-active radar homing with proportional navigation
WARHEAD	MIM-23A 45 kg
	MIM-23B 54 kg
	both are HE-blast fragmentation with proximity and contact fuzing
MAX SPEED	Mach 2.5
MAX RANGE	
MIM-23A	35 000 m
MIM-23B	40 000 m
MAX ALTITUDE	
MIM-23A	11 000 m
MIM-23B	18 000 m
MIN ALTITUDE	30 m
LAUNCHER	mobile, triple round trainable, trailer mounted

Status: Basic HAWK: production complete. A few may still be in service.
I-HAWK: in production and in service with the following:

Country	No of launchers	PIP/Phase	Service
Belgium	36	2	Army (6 battalions)
Denmark	48	2	Air Force (8 batteries)
Egypt	72	2	Air Defence Command (12 batteries)
France	66	2	Army (11 batteries)
Germany, West	216	2	Air Force (36 batteries)
Greece	36	2	Army (6 batteries)
Iran *	222	—	Army (37 batteries)
Israel	180	2	Air Force (15 battalions)
Italy	60	1	Army (2 regiments)
Japan	192	2	Army (32 batteries)
Jordan	56	2	Army (14 batteries)
Korea, South	164	1	Army (28 batteries)
Kuwait **	27	2	Air Force (4 battalions)
Netherlands	72	2	Air Force (12 squadrons)
Norway	54	NOAH	Air Force (6 batteries)
Portugal	6	2	Air Force (1 battery)
Saudi Arabia **	90	2	Air Force (10 Triad batteries)
Singapore	18	1	Air Force (1 squadron)
Spain	48	2	Army (2 battalions)
Sweden	12	—	Army (1 battalion, known as Rb67)
Taiwan	78	1	Army (13 batteries)
UAE	42	2	Air Force (7 batteries)
USA **	unknown	2/3	Army (11 battalions) Marine Corps (4 battalions)

Notes

* Exact status of numbers in service for Iran is unknown

** These countries are known to have procured AN/TSQ-73 Missile Minder fire control systems for their I-HAWK batteries.

The US FY86 DoD budget showed scheduled and planned HAWK procurement and expenditure for 1984/85/86/87 as follows (quantities in brackets and funding in $million): (400) 97, (500) 126.1, (550) 140.1 and (550) 156.6. In 1987 it was stated that the United States Army National Guard was to receive at least six HAWK battalions as part of its ongoing modernisation programme.

Contracts: For European manufacture of the Improved HAWK air defence system Raytheon is systems contractor under the direction of the NATO HAWK Management Office (NHMO) in Paris, France. In the USA, Raytheon produced the missile guidance and control units and limited quantities of ground equipment, certain missile parts, final missile assembly and overhaul and conversion of the basic HAWK equipment. A Raytheon subsidiary, Raytheon European Management and Systems Company (REMSCO), Oversees major European industrial activities. NATO nations participating in the programmes are Belgium, Denmark, France, West Germany, Greece, Italy and the Netherlands.

Complete system development and US Production: Raytheon Company, Missile Systems Division, Bedford, Massachusetts 01730, USA.
Telephone: 617 274 2222
Rocket motors: Aerojet General Corporation, El Monte, California, USA.
Wings and elevons: Northrop Corporation, Beverley Hills, California, USA.
Warheads: Iowa Ordnance Depot.
NATO Improved HAWK: Belgium - ACEC: France - SNPE, SODETEG, Thompson-CFS; West Germany-AEG-Telefunken, MBB;
Italy - Aeritalia, Aerochemi, Selenia, Sigme, MES, FIAR.
Japanese production: Mitsubishi Electric Corporation Toshiba.

Raytheon MIM-104 Patriot Low to High Altitude Surface-to-air Missile System

Development

The concept of a mobile all-weather air defence missile was started in 1961 by the US Army Missile Command (MICOM) Research and Development Directorate as the Field Army Ballistic-Missile Defence System (FABMDS), then became the Army Air Defence System-1970 (AADS-70). By 1965 the design had been specified and the missile assigned the designation XMIM-104 Surface-to-air Missile/Development (SAM-D) before project management was placed under MICOM direction. Shortly after this, in April 1966, the US Department of Defense (DoD) issued contract definition awards to Raytheon, Hughes and RCA with Raytheon receiving a full missile development contract in May 1967. The first test launch occurred in February 1970 and in 1972 the initial engineering development programme commenced. This consisted of two phases, the first being a nine-round flight series in 1973 to test the missile systems, then a 14-round series in 1974-75 to evaluate the Track-via-Missile (TVM) guidance system concept. The success of these tests led in 1976 to the DoD initiating the Full Scale Engineering Development phase of what was then called in the MIM-104 Patriot missile system. By July 1980 all the development and operational evaluation trials were complete and limited production by Raytheon had commenced. The first production systems were delivered to the US Army in June 1982 and a follow-on test and evaluation programme was conducted in 1983. This, however, uncovered a number of hardware and training problems which were subsequently resolved with Patriot undergoing a further series of firings in 1984. Following the successful completion of these the US Army declared Patriot to be fully operational.

Despite this the US Army has a continuous Patriot Improvement Research and Development programme under way. This currently consists of three development items and the US/West German component development of the Advanced Tactical Patriot missile.

The first, known as Phase 1B, consists of a radar enhancement design and software development for jammer engagements, guidance ECCM, a 16-missile launch capability and better battalion resource management, which was completed in 1986.

The second, Phase 1A, started in 1986 and was a radar enhancement software development by Raytheon for a Patriot out-of-sector launch capability. It was completed in 1989.

The last is the Anti-Tactical Missile (ATM) programme which consists of two parts. The Patriot Level-1 ATM (or PAC-1) requires only software changes to the ground radar itself (ie, does not require destruction of the target's warhead) for it to achieve a mission kill capability against short-range ballistic missiles such as the SS-12M Scaleboard, the SS-21 Scarab and SS-23 Spider by giving it an upward trajectory and a high-angle sector search capability to track them in flight. The idea is to protect the Patriot system itself. This ability was successfully demonstrated on 11 September 1986 when a modified production line Patriot intercepted a Lance missile at the White Sands Missile Range and knocked it off its intended course. The Patriot Level-2 ATM (or PAC-2) was also successfully tested at White Sands on 4 November 1987 when a suitably modified Patriot destroyed another Patriot in flight, together with its warhead, which was simulating a Soviet SRBM. The PAC-2 modification involves further software changes, a new missile warhead casing with enhanced explosives and a fuzing system with a second set of forward-angled beams designed to optimise warhead detonation against targets with a very high closing rate so as to increase sensitivity and reduce the system's reaction time. This then allows the larger 45.4 g size of the fragmentation pattern splinters produced in the explosion to perform a catastrophic kill of the target by destroying both the missile body and its warhead and is an overall improvement to system's area defence role.

Raytheon Patriot surface-to-air missile leaves its launcher during trials

Four-round Raytheon Patriot surface-to-air M901 missile launcher is trailer-mounted and towed by a 6 × 6 truck

282 STATIC & TOWED SAM SYSTEMS / USA

Patriot AN/MPQ-53 radar set camouflaged in its field environment

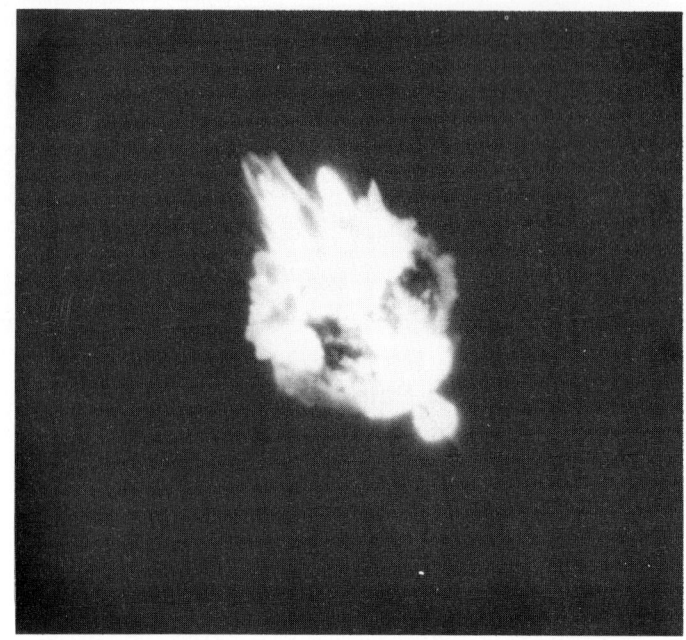

Patriot PAC-1 missile destroying Lance surface-to-surface missile in September 1986 test firing

Four-round Raytheon Patriot surface-to-air M901 missile launcher deployed in the field

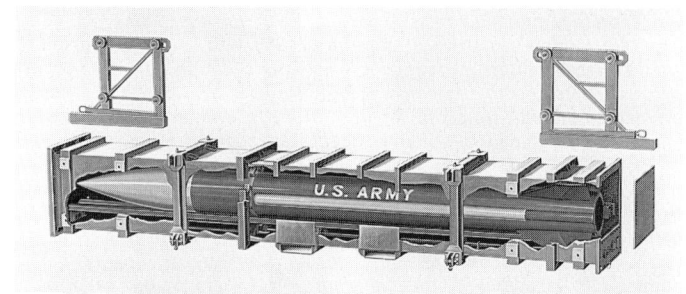

Cutaway view of the Patriot missile sealed in its container which serves as the launch tube for the missile when it is fired. The missile and its canister are manufactured by Martin Marietta Orlando Aerospace under contract to Raytheon

The Level-1 ATM capability was deployed with the US Army in Europe in July 1988. Level-2 ATM capability will be deployed in the near future. Israel is also evaluating Patriot as an interim ATM system.

As an adjunct to the Patriot system MICOM awarded a $2.7 million contract in May 1983 to the General Instrument Corporation's Government Systems Division to develop and build a decoy unit that could entice attacking Anti-radiation Missiles from Patriot air defence missile sites. The technological challenge in the programme was the size of the decoy which apparently became a two-man portable device. In December 1987 MICOM started seeking bids from industry to undertake a two-year Full Scale Engineering Development (FSED) programme which involves the development, production and qualification of five decoy units. The contract will also include an option for the production of an initial 72 decoys to be built over a two-year period.

In February 1989 the $4.715 million FSED contract was awarded to Brunswick Corporation's Defense Division. The system is known as an Anti-Radiation Missile Decoy (ARM-D) and will transmit an RF signal of similar frequency and amplitude to the AN/MPQ-53 radar in order to divert the track point of the incoming threat weapon.

Under current planning the US Army procurement objective for Patriot is 104 batteries and 6077 missiles. Of these 84 batteries will be in the field and the remainder for training and reserve. By December 1988 nine battalions had been activated with six out of nine planned for West Europe deployed to West Germany as part of the 32nd Air Defense Missile Command. Currently the West European battalions have three fire units each instead of the six in their TOE, but they will be brought up to the current strength as production continues. When eventually re-equipped the 32nd will comprise two three-battalion Patriot Brigades, one three-battalion Vulcan gun Brigade and one mixed Brigade with two I-HAWK/PIP Phase III battalions and three Patriot battalions. Each 600 man Patriot battalion comprises six batteries each of two firing platoons and four launchers. Each battery HQ and firing platoon also includes an FIM-92A Stinger man-portable SAM two-man team-set of equipment for close-range low level air defence. At battalion level there is also a 6 × 6 truck mounted Information Co-ordination Central (ICC) which provides battalion command and control and the interface with other air defence assets. This is performed by 6 × 6 truck mounted communications relay units and attendant 6 × 6 truck mounted Antenna Mast Groups (AMG).

The US DoD has also promoted Patriot as a NATO follow-on system for the MIM-14 Hercules and some MIM-23 HAWK systems. In February 1979 the USA, Belgium, Denmark, France, West Germany, Greece and the Netherlands signed a NATO Memorandum of Understanding (MoU) for a two year study on the most practical and economical ways to acquire and produce the Patriot system. This was itself a follow-on study to Project Successor, a joint US-German analysis, concluded in 1978, to evaluate Patriot's suitability for a European Air Defence role.

By early 1988 only two of the MoU signatories had actually procured the system. In 1984 the Netherlands ordered four squadrons totalling 20 launchers and 160 missiles. The first of these, the 502nd Anti-aircraft Squadron of the Royal Netherlands's Air Force 5th Guided Weapons Group, became operational in April 1987 with a second squadron of the Group attaining operational status in July 1988. By 1990 the remaining two squadrons will be operational with the 3rd Guided Weapons Group. A follow-on order for four more fire units, 32 launchers and 256 missiles has been approved by the Dutch Government.

In place of US 6 × 6 trucks the Netherlands use the new DAF YTZ 2300 (6 × 6) truck to tow the four round Patriot launcher and the AN/MPQ-53 radar set, and YAZ 2300 (6 × 6) 10 000 kg trucks will carry the engagement control station.

In the same year as the Dutch ordered their systems West Germany agreed to buy the system and in 1985-86 ordered the first 16 of 28 squadrons it is going to purchase and accepted, through a supplementary compensation agreement with the USA, an additional 12 squadrons to be supplied from US Army stocks and manned by German personnel. The 40 Luftwaffe squadrons will be used to form two training squadrons, two reduced strength squadrons to act as float units and six Wings (*Geschwader*) each of six air defence squadrons (*Flugabwehr-raketenstaffeln*), one HQ squadron, a direct support unit and four radio relay groups. The major difference between this patriot equipment and the US Army systems is that the prime German contractor, Siemens AG, is using German MAN (8 × 8) vehicles and accessories wherever possible. The first Luftwaffe firing trials were completed in November 1987 at the

White Sands Missile Range using its own training equipment. The first operational units will be handed over in August 1989.

In 1984 Patriot was also selected by the Japanese Defence Agency as its long-term replacement for the Nike Hercules-J. In 1986 Mitsubishi started producing the missile under a licensed agreement from Raytheon. An initial buy of two batteries (one in knock-down form for local assembly) was made in 1985 to form training units. A total of six Japanese Air Self Defence Force missile groups are being re-equipped at the rate of one per year between 1986 and 1991 with four batteries each of five launchers and a total of 1000 missiles (980 of which will be produced locally).

In 1987 the Italian Government after long debate decided to purchase 20 Patriot batteries of 100 launchers and 1280 missiles at a cost of around $3 billion. After suitable offset agreements have been made these will enter service in the 1990s.

Early in 1988 it was disclosed that under the outline plan, Italy would purchase the Patriot missiles for the 20 fire units while the USA purchased the launchers and radars. The missiles would eventually be made in Italy. In return, the Italians would provide short-range air defence, including the Spada surface-to-air missile system, for the protection of key US bases in Italy.

Description

The MIM-104A Patriot missile is certified round which is shipped, stored and fired from its Martin Marietta rectangular box-like container-launcher. It requires no testing or maintenance in the field, periodic lot sampling of missiles on launchers, and in storage provides assurance of the weapon's capability. In configuration it is a single stage missile with four sections. At the front is the Raytheon guidance and radome compartment containing the autopilot controls, guidance electronics and the monopulse seeker unit with its steerable 30.5 cm diameter antenna. Next is the warhead section made by Picatinny Arsenal which contains four flush mounted guidance antennas, inertial sensors and the E/F-band fuzing (M818E1), arming and blast fragmentation warhead devices. This is followed by the high strength steel propulsion section which contains a Thiokol 11.5 second burn 10 909 kg thrust TX-486 solid propellant rocket motor. At the tail is the Martin Marietta control section which supports the control actuation system, four aerodynamic control surfaces and two further flush-mounted guidance antennas.

Velocity at motor burn out is 1700 m/s with the missile able to undertake 20 g continuous manoeuvres and 30 g short term manoeuvres. This allows it to cope with targets performing continuous 6 g evasive manoeuvres.

Maximum flight time is 170 seconds and minimum flight time (ie time required to arm) is 8.3 seconds.

In the field the Patriot battery consists of an AN/MPQ-53 phased array radar mounted on a two-axle M860 semi-trailer with a 5 ton (6 × 6) M818 truck as the tractor, a 6 × 6 truck mounted AN/MSQ-104 Engagement Control Station (ECS), an AN/MSQ-24 6 × 6 power plant truck with two 150 kW diesel powered gas turbine AC generator units, two firing platoons each with four four-tube M901 launching stations on M860 trailers with their own individual 15 kW generators and secure VHF data links to the ECS and M818 tractors. There is also support equipment in the form of missile reload trailer transporters and their tractors, a maintenance centre truck and trailer, a battery replaceable unit small truck transporter, and a large battery replaceable unit semi-trailer transporter with a maintenance vehicle tractor. There can also be a 6 × 6 truck with a GTE/Sylvania extendable AMG for communications with battalion HQ, other units and higher echelons.

Communications within the battalion is via voice and digital data. Six operational nets, two data and four voice, are used with at least 50 km between the Battalion's Command and Co-ordination ICC and up to six ECSs, 40 km between each ECS and at least 1 km between the ECS and M901s in a typical deployment pattern.

AN/MSQ-104 Engagement Control Station (ECS)

This is the only manned station in the Patriot battery and requires three operators. Inside are two operator console positions, one communications station, the digital weapons control computer, the VHF data link terminal, three radio relay terminals and the battery status panel with a hard copy unit beneath. In operation it sequences the battery through all tactical engagement procedures, monitors the operational status of the various systems, conducts automatic fault finding and location as required, and provides the human control part of the man-machine interface for the battery.

A typical engagement involves the radar being assigned its search sector then automatically adapting itself via the ECS's No 2 operating station with its environmental control panel to both the natural and hostile electronic environments it finds. It then modifies its operational functions as required. The radar search is carried out by the surveillance and detection beam with the radar informing the ECS when a detection occurs. The ECS then verifies the track by looking at several returns and at the appropriate time initiates IFF interrogation using the target track and illumination beam. The ECS then orders all tracks, establishes their engagement priorities and schedules the engagement. When an engagement decision is made, either in the manual, semi-automatic or fully automatic mode, the ECS selects the launcher to be used and sends any pre-launch data to the chosen missile through the VHF data link.

Patriot AN/MPQ-53 radar set which is built by Raytheon

The four-round Patriot launcher used by the West German Air Force mounted on the rear of a MAN (8 × 8) truck for improved cross-country mobility

(Background) Patriot trailer-mounted radar set. (Foreground left) the engagement control station and (right) the electrical power unit which is mounted in the rear of a 6 × 6 truck

284 STATIC & TOWED SAM SYSTEMS / USA

West German Air Force telescopic antenna mast system for Patriot has been designed by Dornier and is carried on rear of MAN (6 × 6) truck

Electrical power unit used by West German Air Force is mounted on MAN (6 × 6) truck with capacity of 2 × 150 kw

The West German Air Force AN/MPQ-53 radar set for Patriot is mounted on the rear of a MAN (8 × 8) truck and is shown here in the travelling configuration

It also notifies the radar at the time of launch as to where to look for the missile. The initial coarse turn executed by the weapon is either commanded by the simple, self-contained guidance system aboard or by the pre-set launch instructions from the ECS. Once in the air the missile is acquired by the radar and this initiates a missile track and command uplink beam to monitor its flight and command it to follow, using instructions from the ECS computer, an efficient energy saving trajectory to the vicinity of the designated target. At this point the TVM terminal homing technique, described below, using the missile's onboard TVM track and downlink systems is initiated by the EEC. Just before the missile's closest approach to the target, the warhead is detonated, to produce a fragmentation pattern of 1.94 g splinters, by the E/F-band proximity fuzing device.

AN/MSQ-53 Multi-function Phased Array Radar

The AN/MPQ-53 G-band frequency agile phased array radar is automatically controlled from the ECS by the digital weapons control computer. Mounted on a trailer it has a 5161 element array for the search and detection, target track and illumination and missile command and uplink beams. At any one time the system can handle between 90-125 target tracks and be able to support up to nine missiles in their final moments of engagement using TVM terminal homing. This technique involves the missile's passive monopulse seeker array being directed by the ECS to look in the direction of the target. This then begins to intercept increasingly precise returns from the reflected electro-magnetic energy signals. This in turn triggers the G/H-band onboard downward data link which is offset in frequency from the target track and illumination beam and which transmits target data from the missile guidance package to the ECS computer via the circular 251 element TVM receive-only array at the lower right of the antenna group. The ECS uses this information to calculate guidance instructions which are passed to the missile by the radar's G/H-band command and uplink beam. The phase coded information is received on the missile by the two sets of guidance antennas which transmit it to the guidance electronics which in turn use it to move the control surfaces. This procedure is repeated until the point of closest approach when the warhead is detonated. At no time throughout the engagement is any data actually processed on the missile itself.

Radar interrogation of a target is carried out by an AN/TPX-46(V)7 IFF system using a linear antenna array set below the main array position. There are also five diamond-shaped 51-element arrays: two individual ones above the IFF array set at the bottom corners of the main array and a set of three centred below the level of the TVM receiver array near the lower edge of the front face of the planar radar housing. These are side-lobe cancellers used to reduce the effects of enemy jamming. In a jamming environment the TVM technique is still usable because the system can measure range difference and as it already has the angular measurement of the target it can determine the difference in path length without loss of range resolution. It has the same range resolution as a non-jamming target engagement.

The 3 to 170 km range radar performs its surveillance, tracking, guidance and ECCM functions in a time-shared manner by using the weapon's computer to generate 'action-cycles' that last in milliseconds. Up to 32 different radar configurations can be called up with the beams tailored for long-range, short-range, horizon and clutter, guidance and ECCM functions in terms of their power, waveform and physical dimensions. The data rate for each function can also be independently selected to give 54 different operational modes so that, for example, a long-range search can be conducted over a longer time period than a horizon search for low altitude pop-up targets. None of the functions requires any given time interval which therefore allows a random sequence of radar actions at any one time considerably adding to an attacker's ECM problem. The search sector is 90° and the track capability 120°.

When emplaced the radar is connected to both the ECS and generator vehicles by cabling.

AN/MSQ-24 Electrical Power Plant

This comprises two turbine-driven Deko Products 150 kW AC generator units with power cable reels, control panel and fuel tank transported on the rear of a standard US Army 5 ton 6 × 6 truck. Either generator can supply the required power for both the ECS and radar.

M901 Launcher Station

This is a remotely operated traversable four-round launcher station mounted on the rear of an M860 two-axle semi-trailer with its own 15 kW generator, data link terminal and electronics pack.

Time required to reload the full basic 20 missile complement of a five launcher battery is 60 minutes.

USA / STATIC & TOWED SAM SYSTEMS

Variants

Advanced Tactical (AT) Patriot Programme

The AT Patriot is the subject of a US/West German component demonstration project to provide a low risk but much improved tactical air defence against SRBMs, low observable cruise missiles and aircraft and stand-off jammers (SOJs). The current Phase I AT Patriot work is using funds from the original US/West German Roland-Patriot agreement and involves Raytheon, AEG, Martin Marietta, MBB and Siemens.

The US DoD and West German MoD are also formulating the Memorandum of Agreement which is defining Phase 2 AT Patriot. This will result in prototype flights tests in 1990. Phase 3 would follow as a three year full scale development effort from 1990 with Phase 4, actual production of the weapon, starting in 1993.

The main changes involved are improvements to the radar by introducing both a dual travelling-wave-tube transmitter and hardware design changes to reduce the system's internal noise and modifying the missile.

The radar changes are to enhance the effective radiated power level and reduce the signal-to-noise ratio components of the radar range equation in order to offset the reduction in the anticipated target's radar cross-section component.

The modified AT Patriot missile has a 0.76 m long rocket motor extension and an AEG K-band active radar seeker in addition to the normal TVM guidance system. Under certain circumstances the motor extension is expected to double the range of the weapon so it can engage Warsaw Pact AWACS aircraft flying over territory deep in the rear of an Army's sphere of operations. In the ATM role the motor will also allow the weapon to increase its engagement altitude so as to provide more time in engaging a multiple incoming SRBM raid.

The combination of the improvements will also give Patriot fire units the capability of driving SOJ aircraft over the horizon thus improving all the divisional and Corps level communications assets and the effective range of all radar-based systems within its vicinity which the jammers would otherwise have seriously degraded had they remained in line-of-sight to them.

The seeker itself uses a 0.406 m aperture and is designed to give considerable improvements in the missile's engagement envelope against low observable targets. It will also allow the weapon to attack low altitude threats even if they remask themselves behind terrain features in trying to escape a missile.

West German Air Force Patriot missile resupply vehicle which carries four missiles and tows a trailer carrying a further four missiles

One other area of improvement includes incorporating on the launchers of a fire unit the ability to allow them to be placed under the control of a neighbouring ECS whilst their own ECS and radar are being moved to another location.

Patriot-HAWK Phase III Interoperability

With the introduction of the HAWK Phase III it will become possible for the Patriot ICC to supply target data to HAWK Assault Fire Units. This allows the HAWK to engage targets more quickly without the need for them to search for them in elevation and to share the more sophisticated IFF of the Patriot to clarify their identities.

They can also be used together in the ATM role with an April 1988 demonstration programme test using a Patriot radar to cue the High Powered Illuminator (HPI) radar of a HAWK III system onto a Patriot missile simulating a SRBM target. The HAWK then successfully destroyed it at 8000 m altitude and 8000 m downrange.

The HAWK/Patriot interoperability is already part of US Army air defence doctrine.

SPECIFICATIONS (missile)

TYPE	single stage, low to high altitude	WARHEAD	91 kg HE-blast fragmentation with proximity fuzing
LENGTH	5.18 m	MAX SPEED	Mach 3.7
DIAMETER	0.41 m	MIN RANGE	3000 m
WING SPAN	0.92 m	MAX RANGE	160 000 m
LAUNCH WEIGHT	about 1000 kg	MAX ALTITUDE	24 240 m
PROPULSION	single stage solid propellant rocket motor	MIN ALTITUDE	60 m
GUIDANCE	command with TVM semi-active homing	LAUNCHER	mobile trainable four-round semi-trailer

---

Status: In production. In service with or on order for the following countries:

Country	No of launchers needed	Service
Germany, West	320	Air Force (40 squadrons)
Italy	100	Air Force (20 batteries)
Japan	130	Air Force (26 batteries)
Netherlands	64	Air Force (8 squadrons)
USA	832	Army (104 batteries)

Manufacturers: Prime System Contractor: Raytheon Company, Missile Systems Division, Bedford, Massachusetts 01730, USA. Telephone: 617 274 2222.
Principle Sub-contractor: Martin Marietta Aerospace, Orlando, Florida, USA.
Principle German Patriot contractor: Siemens AG, Postfach 70074, 8000 Munich, Federal Republic of Germany.
Principle Japanese Patriot contractor (licence builder): Mitsubishi Heavy Industries, 5-1, Marunouchi 2-chrome, Chiyoda-ku, Tokyo, Japan.
ARM-D System: Brunswick Corporation, Brunswick Defense Division, Skokie, Illinois 60077, USA. Telephone: (312) 470 4797.

Nike-Hercules (MIM-14B) Surface-to-air Missile System

Development

Development of the Nike-Hercules SAM system commenced in 1954 with prime contractor being Western Electric Company of Burlington, North Carolina.

The Nike-Hercules was developed as the replacement for the older Nike-Ajax (MIM-3) which was range limited and had only an HE warhead. A total of 15 000 Nike-Ajax missiles were produced but none remain in service. The Nike-Ajax was also suplied to Belgium, Denmark, France, West Germany, Greece, Italy, Japan, the Netherlands, Norway, Taiwan and Turkey.

Delivery of production Nike-Hercules systems to the US Army commenced in January 1958 and was completed in March 1964, although production for export continued after this date. Three different models of the Nike-Hercules were produced: the MIM-14A, MIM-14B and MIM-14C, the MIM-14B being the most common. Total production amounted to over 25 500 missiles of which 2650 were exported under the Foreign Military Sales programme and 1764 under the Military Aid Program (MAP). Production of the missile was undertaken at the US Army Ordnance Missile Plant at Charlotte, North Carolina, run by the then Douglas Aircraft company.

STATIC & TOWED SAM SYSTEMS / USA

Nike-Hercules on its launcher ready for launch (US Army)

Nike-Hercules missile showing four boosters at rear (US Army)

The Nike-Hercules was deployed by the US Army in the static role in the United States (including Alaska) as well as in West Germany and South Korea.

In the Continental United States (CONUS) static versions were employed to provide defence of critical installations and urban population centres while semi-mobile units were deployed to protect field armies and theatres of operation.

In the US Army each air defence battalion consisted of a headquarters battery and four firing batteries. Each battery can operate as part of an air defence network or as an autonomous unit and is capable of multiple launches during a single engagement.

It was designed to engage aircraft flying at altitudes up to about 45 000 m and at ranges of up to 145 km and during trials successfully intercepted short-range ballistic missiles such as Corporal and other Nike-Hercules missiles. The missile can also be used in the ground-to-ground role with a contact fuzed nuclear warhead.

It has been supplied to a number of NATO countries and a non-nuclear version was produced under licence for the Japanese Air Force by Mitsubishi Heavy Industries. This version is known as the Nike-Hercules-J.

Deployment of the Nike-Hercules in the US Army reached its peak in 1963 when no fewer than 134 batteries were operational in the CONUS as well as Alaska, Okinawa, Taiwan and West Germany. By 1974 they had all been disbanded in the CONUS apart from those retained for training. The successor to Nike-Hercules is the much more capable Patriot system.

Description

The actual Nike-Hercules missile is two-stage consisting of a solid-propellant, computer controlled missile body and a cluster of four solid propellant booster rockets. The missile airframe, wings and booster clustering hardware are made of aluminium and the booster cases are steel.

The missile body is sharply tapered at the nose and is faired back to a maximum diameter of 800 mm and the rear end of the body is faired back to a maximum diameter of 538 mm. The missile has four delta-shaped wings, with elevons to control roll and steering. Four small linearisation fins are attached forward of the wings.

The booster cluster is composed of four individual booster rockets and has a cross-sectional width of 877 mm with the four trapezoidal fins attached to the aft end of the cluster.

The Nike-Hercules is launched by remote control, normally at an angle of about 85°, and when the booster is jettisoned the guidance system is activated, programming the missile to roll toward the target and dive into the intercept plane. Steering orders direct the missile to the optimum burst point. The warhead is either the high explosive or nuclear type. The latter is designated W31 with some 2550 being produced.

Two separate time-fuzed tritium boosted orallloy W-31 Mod 2 nuclear warhead sections were deployed, the 510.5 kg M22 and M97, which are interchangeable. They have two yield options: 1-2 kt and 40 kt. All US nuclear warheads were returned by 1984 and by mid-1987 there were only 75 NATO dedicated W31 warheads left for Nike-Hercules and these are to be returned as the Patriot system is fielded. Nike-Hercules has an electronic countermeasures capability.

In addition to the missile itself, key components of Nike-Hercules are a low power acquisition radar, high power acquisition radar, target tracking radar, missile tracking radar, electronic data processing equipment and remote controlled launchers.

Nike-Hercules 1-J of the Japanese Air Force on its two-axle M529 transport-trailer being towed by a Type 73 (6 × 6) 3500 kg truck (Kensuke Ebata)

After the system was in service for some years a later development, the high power acquisition radar (HIPAR), enabled mobile versions of the Nike-Hercules to get the same full target detection capability as the batteries at fixed sites.

The HIPAR has three vans housing radar transmitter, receiver and control equipment and one of the two semi-trailers hauls the 13.1 m wide fan-shaped antenna while the other carries the generators. Before the introduction of HIPAR some 20 vehicles were required to move the radar system.

In operation the target is first detected by the acquisition radar and is then interrogated by the associated AN/TPX-46 IFF Mk XII interrogator, and if confirmed as hostile its location is transferred to the target tracking radar which pin-points it for intercept purposes.

When the target is within range a missile is launched and the missile tracking radar issues guidance and orders to the missile until it reaches the target.

The system operators are located in a battery control trailer, a tracking control trailer and a launcher control trailer.

In 1981 contracts were placed for a number of improvements to the system with McDonnell Douglas refurbishing and modifying NATO Nike-Hercules missiles.

Norden Systems has provided the Digital Computer System which is based on the PDP-11/34M mini-computer. This receives missile and target position inputs from tracking radars, solves the intercept problem and issues guidance commands to the missile. In addition it performs various routines such as fault diagnosis.

Variants

South Korea is known to have produced a version of the Nike-Hercules optimised for the ground-to-ground role. At least two batteries are believed to have been converted to this configuration.

USA / **STATIC & TOWED SAM SYSTEMS**

SPECIFICATIONS (missile)
TYPE	two stage, medium to high altitude
SHAPE	symmetrical cruciform
GROSS WEIGHT	4858 kg
first stage	2350 kg
second stage	2509 kg
LENGTH	12.141 m
first stage	4.34 m
second stage	8.19 m
DIAMETER	
min	538 mm
max	800 mm
SPAN	
first stage	8.191 m
second stage	2.286 m
GUIDANCE	command
STEERING	hydraulically actuated control surfaces
PROPELLANT TYPE	solid
PROPELLANT CONFIGURATION	
first stage	rod and tube charge
second stage	internal burning star
MAX SPEED	
MIM-14A	Mach 3.35
MIM-14B/C	Mach 3.65
MAX ALTITUDE	45 720 m (approx)
MIN ALTITUDE	1000 m (approx)
MAX RANGE	145 km (approx)
IN FLIGHT POWER SOURCE	battery
LAUNCHER TYPE	monorail
WARHEAD	nuclear or HE
LAUNCH CREW	45 men

Status: Production complete. In service with:

Country	No of launchers	Operator
Belgium	36	Air Force, two wings with 4 squadrons, all in West Germany and to be phased out by 1990 without replacement
Germany, West	108	Air Force, three battalions each of 4 batteries, being replaced by Patriot
Greece	36	Air Force, 1 group
Italy	96	Air Force, 8 groups, to be replaced by Patriot
Japan	180	Air Force, 6 groups of 19 squadrons, being replaced by Patriot
Korea, South	90	Army, 2 battalions, with 10 batteries (also used in surface-to-surface role)
Norway	18	Air Force, 1 battalion with two batteries, to be replaced by NASAMS
Spain	9	Army, 1 battalion
Taiwan	96	Army, 2 battalions
Turkey	72	Air Force, 8 squadrons each with 9 launchers

Manufacturer (prime): Western Electric Company (now AT & T Technologies), Burlington, North Carolina.
Major subcontractors: AAI Incorporated, Bell Telephone Laboratories, General Electric Company, McDonnell Douglas Astronautics, Raytheon Company.

Inventory

This excludes weapons operated by local resistance and guerilla units and in some cases updates that in the main text.

AFGHANISTAN

Air Force
20 battalions SA-2 (Guideline) SAM (120 launchers)
30 battalions SA-3 (Goa) SAM (120 × 4 round launchers)
37 mm M1939 AAG
57 mm S-60 AAG
85 mm KS-12 AAG, with Fire Can radar

Army
SA-7 (Grail) manportable SAM
14.5 mm ZPU-1, ZPU-2 and ZPU-4 LAAG
23 mm ZSU-23-4 SPAAG (20)
23 mm (twin) ZU-23 LAAG, also truck-mounted for convoy escort
57 mm S-60 AAG
85 mm KS-12 AAG, with Fire Can radar
100 mm KS-19 AAG

ALBANIA

Air Force
5 battalions (SA-2 or HQ-2) SAM (30 launchers)

Army
23 mm (twin) ZU-23 LAAG, from China
37 mm M1939 AAG (50)
57 mm S-60 AAG (unconfirmed)
85 mm KS-12 AAG (unconfirmed)
100 mm KS-19 AAG (unconfirmed)

ALGERIA

Air Force
2 battalions SA-2 (Guideline) SAM (12 launchers)
1 battalion SA-3 (Goa) SAM (14 launchers)
85 mm KS-12 AAG (30+), with Fire Can radar
100 mm KS-19 AAG (150)

Army
SA-7 (Grail) manportable SAM
5 battalions SA-2 (Guideline) SAM (30 launchers)
4 battalions SA-3 (Goa) SAM (16 launchers)
40 SA-6 (Gainful) SAM
30 SA-8 (Gecko) SAM
36 SA-9 (Gaskin) SAM
32 SA-13 (Gopher) SAM
14.5 mm ZPU-2 and ZPU-4 LAAG (50)
23 mm (twin) ZU-23 LAAG (50 to 60)
23 mm ZSU-23-4 SPAAG (110)
37 mm M1939 AAG (190)
57 mm S-6 AAG (60)
57 mm ZSU-57-2 SPAAG (100)
85 mm KS-12 AAG (20+), with Fire Can radar

ANGOLA

Air Defence Force
2 battalions SA-2 (Guideline) SAM (12 launchers)
11 battalions SA-3 (Goa) SAM (44 launchers)
24 SA-6 (Gainful) SAM
30 SA-8 (Gecko) SAM
30 SA-9 (Gaskin) SAM
30+ SA-13 (Gopher) SAM
23 mm (twin) ZU-23 LAAG

Army
SA-7 (Grail) manportable SAM
SA-14 (Gremlin) manportable SAM
SA-16 manportable SAM
14.5 mm ZPU-1, ZPU-2 and ZPU-4 LAAG

Army (continued)
23 mm (twin) ZU-23 LAAG
23 mm ZSU-23-4 SPAAG (20+)
37 mm M1939 AAG
57 mm S-60 AAG
57 mm ZSU-57-2 SPAAG (40)

ARGENTINA

Air Force
20 mm (twin) TCM-20 LAAG, (24+), used with Elta EL/M 2106 point defence alert radar
20 mm Rheinmetall (Twin) LAAG

Army
Blowpipe manportable SAM (also Special Forces)
SA-7 (Grail) manportable SAM system and Air Force
10 Short Tigercat SAM (some also used by Marines)
4 shelter-mounted Roland 2 SAM systems
Rheinmetall 20 mm (twin) LAAG used with Elta early warning radar, at least 30 systems in service and Air Force may use similar number
35 mm (twin) Oerlikon-Bührle AAG, 100 system total for use by Army (Skyguard FCS,) Air Force (Super Fledermaus FCS) and Marines
40 mm M1 AAG
40 mm Bofors L/60 AAG (may have been replaced by Bofors L/70)
40 mm Bofors L/70 AAG (built under licence)
90 mm M117 AAG (12 held in reserve)

Marines
Blowpipe manportable SAM system
RBS 70 SAM
Short Tigercat SAM
30 mm Hispano-Suiza AAG
35 mm (twin) Oerlikon-Bührle AAG

AUSTRALIA

Army
FIM-43 Redeye manportable SAM, being replaced by RBS 70
RBS 70 short range SAM system selected after competition in 1985, 60 launchers plus missiles ordered to replace Redeye FIM-43 manportable SAM at present in use
Rapier SAM, 20 optical systems ordered in 1975, first deliveries 1978, Blindfire radars ordered 1978

Australian Army crew reloading their Rapier SAM launcher during trials

AUSTRIA

Air Force
35 mm (twin) Oerlikon-Bührle GDF-002 AAG (18) (with Super Fledermaus FCS)

Army
20 mm (single) Oerlikon GAI-BO1 LAAG (552), including some mounted on rear of Pinzgaurer (6 × 6) truck
35 mm (twin) Oerlikon-Bührle GDF-002 AAG (74) (with Super Fledermaus FCS)
40 mm (twin) M42 SPAAG (38)
40 mm Bofors L/70 AAG (60) with Skyguard and Super Fledermaus FCS
Note: GDF-002 have been upgraded to GDF-005 standard; weapons are called the 3.5 cm Zwillings FlaMK 75 bzw 79 while Skyguard is known as the Feuerleitgerät 75 bzw, 79

Austrian Army Steyr-Daimler Puch (6 × 6) Pinzgaurer vehicle fitted with 20 mm Oerlikon-Bührle cannon on rear deck

M42 twin 40 mm SPAAG of the Austrian Army (Austrian Army)

BAHRAIN

Army
60 B RBS 70 SAMs in service since 1980
Stinger FIM-92A manportable SAM

BELGIUM

Air Force
Nike-Hercules SAM, 2 wings with 4 squadrons, to be phased out by 1990 without replacement, although in February 1988 a number of NATO countries were said to be working out a cost sharing package that would allow Belgium to purchase Patriot
2 battalions of HAWK SAM (36 launchers)

Army
Late in 1988 Belgium placed an order for 714 Mistral SAMs worth an estimated $93 million with deliveries to take place from 1992. The Belgian Air Force may order 300 Mistral systems for air base protection

Army (continued)
12.7 mm (quad) M55 LAAG, 56 supplied, airfield defence
Rheinmetall 20 mm (twin) LAAG (56)
20 mm M167 VADS (towed) (36)
35 mm Gepard SPAAG (55)

BENIN

Army
SA-7 (Grail) manportable SAM system
4 SA-9 (Gaskin) SAM
14.5 mm ZPU-4 LAAG

BOTSWANA

Army
SA-7 (Grail) manportable SAM
Javelin manportable SAM
20 mm M167 AAG
(ordered 1989)

BRAZIL

Army
A competition for manportable SAM system is underway while AVIBRAS is designing the Solar air defence missile system to meet requirements of Brazilian Army, Orbita is proposing a system using technology from the BAe Thunderbolt SAM
4 Roland SAM on Marder chassis
12.7 mm M55 towed anti-aircraft gun system (including modernised)
35 mm (twin) Oerlikon-Bührle GDF-001 AAG (38) with Super Fledermaus FCS, AVIBRAS has developed FILA (Fighting Intruders At Low Altitude) FCS for use with Brazilian AAGs
40 mm M1 AAG (40)
40 mm Bofors L/60 AAG (may have been replaced by L/70)
40 mm Bofors L/70 AAG (36+), some with BOFI
90 mm M117 AAG (40 held in reserve)

Brazilian AVIBRAS FILA fire control system being used to control Bofors 40 mm L/70 anti-aircraft guns

BRUNEI

Army
Rapier SAM ordered in 1978, first deliveries 1983, believed 12 launchers plus 4 Blindfire radars in service

BULGARIA

Air Force
22 battalions SA-2 (Guideline) SAM (132 launchers)
34 battalions SA-3 (Goa) SAM (136 launchers)

Army
SA-7 (Grail) manportable SAM
27 SA-4 (Ganef) SAM
30 SA-6 (Gainful) SAM
60+ SA-9 (Gaskin) SAM
14.5 mm ZPU-2 and ZPU-4 LAAG (held in reserve)
23 mm (twin) ZU-23 LAAG (300)
23 mm ZSU-23-4 SPAAG (35)
37 mm M1939 AAG (reserve)
57 mm S-60 AAG
57 mm ZSU-57-2 SPAAG (60) (reserve)
85 mm KS-12 AAG, with Fire Can radar
100 mm KS-19 AAG

BURKINA FASO

Army
SA-7 (Grail) SAM
14.5 mm ZPU series LAAG (50)

290 INVENTORY

BURMA

Army
40 mm M1 AAG (18 received but status uncertain)

BURUNDI

Army
14.5 mm ZPU-4 LAAG (15)

CAMEROON

Army
14.5 mm Type 58 LAAG (copy of Soviet ZPU-2) (18)
35 mm (twin) Oerlikon-Bührle AAG (6) with Super Fledermaus FCS
37 mm M1939 AAG (18) (from China)

CANADA

Armed Forces
Blowpipe manportable SAM (first order placed in 1973)
On order are 36 Oerlikon-Bührle ADATS, 20 GDF-005 twin 35 mm towed anti-aircraft guns and 10 Skyguard fire control systems
First systems were delivered in 1988. Four GDF-005s are at the Low Level Air Defence School at Chatham, with eight each at Baden (128 Air Defence Battery) and Lahr (129 Air Defence Battery), West Germany. Of the 30 ADATS systems, 24 will be deployed in Europe to provide mobile air defence to field units. Final deliveries 1991
40 mm Bofors AAG in static role defending 2 air bases in West Germany (being replaced by twin 35 mm GDF-005)

CAPE VERDE ISLANDS

Army
SA-7 (Grail) manportable SAM
14.5 mm ZPU-2 and ZPU-4 LAAG

CHAD

Note: French air defence systems deployed to Chad in the last two years include GIAT 20 mm anti-aircraft guns (both towed and ACMAT truck-mounted), Crotale SAMs and HAWK SAMs. The latter have protected the main airbase at the Chadian capital of N'Djamena, while the Crotale have also defended the airstrip at Abeche in the northeast of the country

Army
SA-7 (Grail) manportable SAM
FIM-92A Stinger manportable SAM
FIM-43 Redeye manportable SAM
14.5 mm ZPU-1, ZPU-2 and ZPU-4 LAAG
23 mm (twin) ZU-23 LAAG
Note: Some LAAG have been mounted on rear of cross-country trucks for increased mobility

CHILE

Air Force
Blowpipe manportable SAM (also operated by Marines)
Javelin SAM underwent trials in early 1988
2 Crotale acquisition and 4 Crotale SAM firing units
12.7 mm (twin) LAAG
12.7 mm (quad) M55 LAAG
20 mm FAM-2M twin 20 mm LAAG
20 mm Rheinmetall (twin) LAAG (total of 40+ used by Air Force and Army)

Army
20 mm (single) Oerlikon-Bührle GAI-CO4 LAAG
20 mm Rheinmetall (Twin) LAAG
35 mm (twin) Oerlikon-Bührle AAG (24) operated by Army/Air Force
40 mm M1 AAG, status uncertain
40 mm Bofors L/70 AAG (use unconfirmed)

CHINA, PEOPLE'S REPUBLIC

Air Defence Force
SA-2 (Guideline) SAM (and Chinese HQ-2)
23 mm (twin) LAAG (also Marines and Militia)
57 mm S-60 (Type 59) AAG
85 mm Type 56 AAG
100 mm Type 59 AAG (copy of Soviet KS-19)

Army
SA-7 (Grail) manportable SAM and Chinese HN-5/HN-5A versions, truck-mounted 4 round HN-5C under test

Army (continued)
HQ-61 SAM (twin launcher) under test
FM-80 SAM (twin launcher) under development
14.5 mm Type 56 LAAG (copy of Soviet ZPU-4)
14.5 mm Type 58 LAAG (copy of Soviet ZPU-2)
14.5 mm Type 75-1 LAAG (improved version of Soviet ZPU-1)
14.5 mm Type 75 LAAG (copy of Soviet ZPU-1)
14.5 mm Type 80 LAAG (improved version of Soviet ZPU-1)
23 mm (twin) LAAG (copy of Soviet ZU-23)
25 mm Type 85 LAAG (service use not confirmed)
37 mm (twin) Type 55 AAG (copy of Soviet M1939)
37 mm (twin) Type 65 AAG
37 mm (twin) Type 74 AAG
37 mm Type P793 AAG
All Chinese 37 mm AAGs can be used in conjunction with Type 311 series radar fire control system
57 mm Type 59 AAG (copy of Soviet S-60) used together with GW-03 fire control director
57 mm (twin) Type 80 SPAAG
57 mm ZSU-57-2 SPAAG
85 mm Type 56 AAG (copy of Soviet KS-12)
100 mm Type 59 AAG (copy of Soviet KS-19)

Chinese HQ-2J in self-propelled configuration on tracked chassis (Eric Ditchfield)

COLOMBIA

Army
40 mm M1 AAG (30)

CONGO

Army
14.5 mm ZPU-4 LAAG
23 mm ZSU-23-4 SPAAG (8)
37 mm M1939 AAG (28)

CUBA

Army
SA-7 (Grail) manportable SAM
SA-14 (Gremlin) manportable SAM
12 SA-6 (Gainful) SAM
60 SA-9 (Gecko) SAM
40 SA-13 (Gopher) SAM
12.7 mm (quad) AA MG (believed to be in reserve)
14.5 mm ZPU-1, ZPU-2 and ZPU-4 LAAG
23 mm (twin) ZU-23 LAAG (400)
23 mm ZSU-23-4 SPAAG (36)
30 mm (twin) M53 AAG, status uncertain (100)
30 mm SPAAG (local modification, BTR-60P (8 × 8) APC with twin Czech 30 mm automatic anti-aircraft gun system M53) installed
37 mm M1939 AAG (300)
57 mm S-60 AAG (200)
57 mm ZSU-57-2 SPAAG (25)
85 mm KS-12 AAG, and Fire Can radar (100)
100 mm KS-19 AAG (75)

CYPRUS

SA-7 (Grail) manportable SAM
20/3 mm M55 A2 LAAG
35 mm (twin) Oerlikon-Bührle GDF-005 AAG with Skyguard FCS
40 mm MK 1 AAG (20+)

INVENTORY

CZECHOSLOVAKIA

Air Defence Command
23 mm (twin) ZU-23 LAAG
30 mm (twin) M53 AAG (some of which are held in reserve)
20 battalions SA-2 (Guideline) SAM (120 launchers)
30 battalions SA-3 (Goa) SAM (120 launchers)

Army
SA-7 (Grail) manportable SAM (local production)
SA-14 (Gremlin) manportable SAM
120 SA-6 (Gainful) SAM
40 SA-8 (Gecko) SAM
80+ SA-9 (Gaskin) SAM
100+ SA-13 (Gopher) SAM
14.5 mm ZPU-4 LAAG, not in front line service, also used by Militia
23 mm (twin) ZU-23 LAAG
23 mm ZSU-23-4 SPAAG (100)
30 mm (twin) M53 AAG
30 mm (twin) M53/59 SPAAG
57 mm S-60 AAG (600)

DENMARK

Air Force
8 batteries of HAWK SAM (48 launchers)
40 mm Bofors L/70 AAG (Super Fledermaus FCS by TERMA and SATT)

Army
FIM-92B Stinger manportable SAM
FIM-43 Redeye manportable SAM
12.7 mm (quad) M55 LAAG, status uncertain
40 mm Bofors L/60 (36), plus Super Fledermaus FCS
Note: There is a requirement to replace the Redeye manportable SAM system and a decision is expected sometime in 1989. Contenders are Shorts Starstreak, Bofors RBS 90, General Dynamics Stinger and Matra Mistral. Requirement is believed to be for 80 launchers and over 800 missiles with a cost of over $60 million. An early warning and control system will also form part of the package selected

DJIBOUTI

Army
20 mm (twin) Tarasque 53T2 LAAG
23 mm (twin) ZU-23 LAAG

DOMINICAN REPUBLIC

Army
40 mm M1 AAG (10)

ECUADOR

Air Force
35 mm (twin) Oerlikon-Bührle GDF-003 AAG

Army
Blowpipe manportable SAM
20 mm Oerlikon-Bührle GAI-C01 LAAG
20 mm M167 VADS (towed) (28)
40 mm M1 AAG (30)
40 mm Bofors L/70 AAG (24)

EGYPT

Air Defence Command
60 SA-6 (Gainful) SAM system
12 batteries of HAWK SAM (total of 72 launchers)
65 SA-2 (Guideline) battalions (total 390 launchers)
55 SA-3 (Goa) battalions (total 220 launchers)
12 Crotale acquisition units and 24 Crotale firing units
18 Amoun batteries delivered 1984/1987 each with one Skyguard fire control system, two twin 35 mm Oerlikon-Bührle towed anti-aircraft guns and one four-round Sparrow SAM launcher
23 mm (twin) ZU-23 LAAG, and locally built version
37 mm M1939 AAG (400)
57 mm S-60 AAG (600)
85 mm KS-12 AAG, with Fire Can radars (400)
100 mm KS-19 AAG (300)

Army
SA-7 (Grail) manportable SAM system
20 SA-9 (Gaskin) SAM system
26 Chaparral SAM system (delivered 1988) (used in conjunction with seven M577A2 vehicles fitted with TRACKSTAR radar system)

Soviet supplied SA-6 Gainful SAM of Egyptian Air Defence Command (Egyptian MoD)

Thomson-CSF Crotale SAM firing unit of Egyptian Air Defence Command (Egyptian Army)

Army (continued)
Sakr Eye manportable SAM system
12.7 mm (quad) M53 AAG (reserve)
14.5 mm ZPU-2 and ZPU-4 LAAG
23 mm (twin) ZU-23 LAAG, and locally built version
23 mm (twin) ZU-23 SPAAG on order (M113A2 chassis)
23 mm ZSU-23-4 SPAAG (150)
57 mm S-60 AAG
57 mm ZSU-57-2 SPAAG (110)

EL SALVADOR

Army
20 mm Rheinmetall (twin) LAAG
20/3 mm M55 A2 LAAG
40 mm Bofors L/60 AG (small number)

ETHIOPIA

SA-7 (Grail) manportable SAM
6 SA-2 (Guideline) SAM battalions (total 36 launchers)
8 SA-3 (Goa) SAM battalions (total 32 launchers)
20+ SA-6 (Gainful) SAM system
14.5 mm ZPU-1, ZPU-2 and ZPU-4 LAAG
23 mm (twin) ZU-23 LAAG
23 mm ZSU-23-4 SPAAG (60)
37 mm M1939 AAG
57 mm ZSU-57-2 SPAAG (40)

FINLAND

Army
SA-7 (Grail) manportable SAM (called SAM-78)
SA-14 (Gremlin) manportable SAM and used with Finnish made FCS that includes a surveillance radar
SA-16 manportable SAM (called 86 Ilga)

292 INVENTORY

SISU XA-180 (6 × 6) APC of the Finnish Army fitted with Swedish Ericsson Giraffe surveillance radar. The Finnish company of Jantronic OY fitted out this vehicle and also manufactured the radar mast, electric system, heating system, raising and lowering system and additional armouring

FINLAND (continued)

3 battalions SA-3 (Goa) SAM (12 × 4-round launchers) (called SAM-79)
23 mm (twin) ZU-23 LAAG
35 mm (twin) Oerlikon-Bührle upgraded to GDF-005 standard and used with Super Fledermaus FCS
40 mm Bofors L/60 AAG (has purchased Gather modernisation kits)
40 mm Bofors L/70 AAG (60+)
57 mm ZSU-57-2 SPAAG (12)
Late in 1988, the Finnish MoD placed an order worth FIM75 million (£10 million) for an initial quantity of Marconi Command and Control Systems Marksman twin 35 mm anti-aircraft turrets, training, spares, test equipment and on-site support. The initial contract is for a straight buy but it also includes an option for a further quantity in 1992.
In 1988 Finland also ordered an improved version of the Thomson-CSF Crotale SAM system. This will be based on the Finnish SISU XA-180 (6 × 6) APC chassis and carry the US LTV VT-SAM, rather that the Crotale missiles

FRANCE

Air Force
400 Mistral launchers, 4000 missiles (total requirement, not yet in service)
24 Crotale SAM acquisition units and 48 firing units
SA-90 SAM under development
20 mm (twin) Cerbere 76T2 LAAG (299)

Army
FIM-92A Stinger manportable SAM (small number)
90+ SANTAL SP air defence systems to be delivered from 1990 onwards on Panhard ERC (6 × 6) chassis
500 Mistral launchers + 5000 missiles (total requirement, not yet in service)
30 mm AMX-13 DCA SPAAG (60) (these will eventually be replaced by the SANTAL on 6 × 6 chassis)
Roland 2 SAM on AMX-30 MBT chassis (176)
11 HAWK SAM batteries (66 launchers)
20 mm (twin) Tarasque 53T2 LAAG
20 mm (single) 53T1 LAAG

French Army Euromissile Roland 2

GABON

Army
37 mm M1939 AAG (10) (from China)
In 1988 1 Mygal and 5 Aspic on Panhard VBL 4 × 4 light vehicles were ordered
Kriss (6 × 6) on ERC Sagaie chassis (4)

GERMANY, EAST

Air Defence Command
22 SA-2 (Guideline) SAM battalions (total 88 launchers)
3 regiments SA-3 (Goa) SAM (48 launchers, 6 sites for SA-5 Gammon) SAM
23 mm (twin) ZU-23 LAAG

Army
SA-7 (Grail) manportable SAM
SA-14 (Gremlin) manportable SAM
27 SA-4 (Ganef) SAM
120 SA-6 (Gainful) SAM
40 SA-8 (Gecko) SAM
60 SA-9 (Gaskin) SAM
40+ SA-13 (Gopher) SAM
14.5 mm ZPU-2 and ZPU-4 LAAG, no longer in front line service but still used by Frontier Troops, Ministry for State Security and Militia
23 mm (twin) ZU-23 LAAG, also Militia, Frontier Troops and Ministry for State Security
23 mm ZSU-23-4 SPAAG (100)
37 mm M1939 AAG (reserve)
57 mm ZSU-57-2 SPAAG (reserve)
57 mm S-60 AAG (reserve)
100 mm KS-19 AAG (reserve)

GERMANY, WEST

Air Force
FIM-92A Stinger manportable SAM
FIM-43 Redeye manportable SAM
68 Roland SAM on MAN (8 × 8) chassis, delivery 1986 to 1990
36 HAWK SAM batteries (total 216 launchers)
3 battalions of Nike-Hercules SAM, with each having 4 batteries being replaced by Patriot
Patriot SAM system, total requirement is 40 squadrons with a total of 32 launchers, of which 12 squadrons will be supplied by US but manned by West Germans. The 40 squadrons which comprise 2 training squadrons, 2 reduced strength squadrons to act as float units and 6 wings each with 6 missile squadrons
20 mm (twin) Rheinmetall LAAG (1670 systems)
21 fire control and co-ordination systems on order, first deliveries late 1988 on 8 × 8 MAN chassis. Provides target information to SAM or AAG

Army
FIM-92A Stinger manportable SAM (local production now underway with total requirement being for 12 500 missiles)
FIM-43 Redeye manportable SAM
20 mm (single) FK 20-2 (from Norway)

Gepard twin 35 mm SPAAG system of the West German Army with tracking and surveillance radars retracted (Michael Green/US Army)

The Siemens TUR system based on a Marder armoured chassis is being evaluated by the West German Army. Radar used is the MPDR 3002-S

Army (continued)
35 mm (twin) Gepard SPAAG (420)
40 mm Bofors L/70 AAG (Super Fledermaus FCS)
144 Roland 2 SAM systems on Marder chassis (3 regiments each with 36 launchers)

Navy
20 Roland on MAN (8 × 8) chassis, delivery 1988 to 1990

GHANA

Army
SA-7 (Grail) manportable SAM

GREECE

Air Force
35 mm (twin) Oerlikon-Bührle AAG with Skyguard FCS
20 batteries of Skyguard/Sparrow delivered from 1984, called Velos
1 group of 36 Nike Hercules SAM launchers

Army
FIM-43 Redeye manportable SAM
Stinger manportable SAM (member of European consortium making Stinger under licence from USA)
6 batteries HAWK SAM (36 launchers)
20 mm (twin) Rheinmetall LAAG (30+)
30 mm (twin) Artemis AAG, first production systems completed by late 1988, used with Philips fire control system. Some will also be used by Air Force for air base defence
40 mm Breda L/70 AAG (50 were built by Breda of Italy and delivered to Greece)
40 mm Bofors L/70 AAG (50)
40 mm (twin) M42 SPAAG (101 delivered)
40 mm M1 AAG, 60 supplied but may now be in reserve
75 mm M51 (61 supplied)
90 mm M117 AAG (91 supplied)

GUATEMALA

Army
20 mm (twin) Oerlikon-Bührle GAI-D01 LAAG
40 mm M1 AAG (12)
40 mm (twin) M42 SPAAG (small number)

GUINEA

Army
SA-7 (Grail) manportable SAM
4 SA-6 (Gainful) SAM
16 SA-9 (Gaskin) SAM
14.5 mm ZPU-4 LAAG
30 mm (twin) M53 AAG (unconfirmed user)
37 mm M1939 AAG (8) (from China)
57 mm S-60 AAG (12)
100 mm KS-19 AAG (4)

GUINEA-BISSAU

Air Defence Command
8 SA-6 (Gainful) SAM

Army
SA-7 (Grail) manportable SAM
8 SA-6 (Gainful) SAM
32 SA-9 (Gaskin) SAM
14.5 mm ZPU-4 LAAG
23 mm (twin) ZU-23 LAAG
37 mm M1939 AAG (6)
57 mm S-60 AAG (12)

GUYANA

Army
SA-7 (Grail) manportable SAM

HAITI

Army
20 mm (twin) TCM-20 LAAG (6)

HONDURAS
20/3 mm M55 A2 LAAG

HUNGARY

Air Defence Command
23 mm (twin) ZU-23 LAAG
16 battalions SA-2 (Guideline) SAM (96 launchers)
6 battalions SA-3 (Goa) SAM (24 launchers)

Army
SA-7 (Grail) manportable SAM
SA-14 (Gremlin) manportable SAM
27 SA-4 (Ganef) SAM
80 SA-6 (Gainful) SAM
20 SA-8 (Gecko) SAM
50 SA-9 (Gaskin) SAM
14.5 mm ZPU-2 and ZPU-4, not in front line service, also used by militia
23 mm (twin) ZU-23 LAAG
23 mm ZSU-23-4 SPAAG (50)
57 mm ZSU-57-2 SPAAG (30)
57 mm S-60 AAG (100)
100 mm KS-19 AAG

294 INVENTORY

SA-2 (Guideline) SAMs of the Hungarian Air Defence Command on their resupply trailers being towed by 6 × 6 tractor trucks

ZSU-23-4 self-propelled anti-aircraft guns of the Hungarian Army on parade

INDIA

Air Force
25 battalions SA-2 (Guideline) SAM (150 launchers)
12 battalions SA-3 (Goa) SAM (48 4-round launchers)

Army
SA-7 (Grail) manportable SAM
SA-14 (Gremlin) manportable SAM
40 Tigercat SAM
185 SA-6 (Gainful) SAM
100 SA-8 (Gecko) SAM
200 SA-9 (Gaskin) SAM
50+ SA-11 (Gadfly)
The Indian defence research and development organisation is now developing 3 missiles, the Agni (Fire) long-range, Akash (Space) medium-range and Trishul (Trident) short-range
23 mm (twin) ZU-23 LAAG
23 mm ZSU-23-4 SPAAG (75)
40 mm Mk 1 AAG used with Super Fledermaus, 1245 believed to be in service but some of these may be US M1 40 mm gun
40 mm Bofors L/70 AAG (800+) with Super Fledermaus FCS but being replaced by Flycatcher (first order comprised 40 systems plus option on 212)
3.7 inch (94 mm) AAG, 500 but most are thought to be in reserve

INDONESIA
20 mm (twin) Rheinmetall LAAG, small quantity believed used (10)
40 mm M1 AAG (90+)
40 mm Bofors L/70 AAG (40) (some used by Marines)
Rapier SAM ordered in 1984, 3 orders placed to date
RBS 70 surface-to-air missile system

IRAN

Air Force
15 Tigercat SAM (not all operational)
Rapier SAM plus Blindfire radars (45 launchers delivered)

Air Force (continued)
HQ-2 SAM (Chinese SA-2) reported to be in service (60+ launchers)
23 mm (twin) ZU-23 LAAG
40 mm M1 AAG (20 to 40 may still be in service)
40 mm Bofors L/70 AAG
57 mm S-60 AAG

Army
FIM-92A Stinger (small number obtained in 1987)
SA-7 (Grail) manportable SAM
HN-5A manportable SAM
37 batteries HAWK SAM (222 launchers) (original number supplied, less than this are now operational)
23 mm (twin) ZU-23 LAAG, (and Revolutionary Guard Corps) (300)
23 mm ZSU-23-4 SPAAG (100+)
35 mm (twin) Oerlikon-Bührle AAG with Skyguard FCS (100)
37 mm M1939 AAG (300)
40 mm Bofors L/70 AAG
57 mm S-60 AAG (200)
57 mm ZSU-57-2 SPAAG (80)
85 mm KS-12 AAG (unconfirmed user)

IRAQ

Air Defence Troops
23 mm (twin) ZU-23 LAAG
20 battalions SA-2 (Guideline) SAM (120 launchers)
25 battalions SA-3 (Goa) SAM (100 launchers)
During late 1988 the Iraqi MoD revealed that it was developing a SAM system

Army
SA-7 (Grail) manportable SAM
HN-5A manportable SAM
180 SA-6 (Gainful) SAM
50 SA-8 (Gecko) SAM
100+ SA-9 (Gaskin) SAM
60 SA-13 (Gopher) SAM
Roland 2 SAM AMX-30 (13)
Roland 2 SAM shelter (100)
14.5 mm ZPU-1, ZPU-2 and ZPU-4 LAAG
23 mm (twin) ZU-23 LAAG
23 mm ZSU-23-4 SPAAG (200+)
37 mm M1939 AAG (250)
57 mm S-60 AAG (500)
57 mm ZSU-57-2 SPAAG (100+)
85 mm KS-12 AAG, with Fire Can radar (200)
100 mm KS-19 AAG (200)
130 mm KS-30 AAG (200)

IRELAND

Irish Army RBS 70 SAM (Raymond Maloney)

Army
40 mm Bofors L/70 (2)
40 mm Bofors L/60 (24)
RBS 70 SAM (4)

INVENTORY

ISRAEL

The Israeli Air Force operate some 15 battalions of Raytheon HAWK SAMs

Army
FIM-43 Redeye manportable SAM

Air Force
Chaparral SAM (52)
15 battalions HAWK SAM (180 launchers)
20 mm (twin) TCM-20 LAAG in both towed and self-propelled (half track) configurations, used with Elta EL/M 2106 point defence radar (370)
20 mm M167 VADS (towed) (106)
20 mm M163 VADS SPAAG (48)
23 mm (twin) TCM Mk 3 LAAG on half track
40 mm Bofors L/70 AAG (Super Fledermaus FCS, upgraded locally)

ITALY

Air Force
4 battery sets of Selenia Spada SAM with more being delivered
Nike Hercules SAM, 8 groups with a total of 96 launchers, to be replaced by Patriot SAM with requirement being for 20 Patriot battery fire units. Missiles will be provided by Italy, while launchers and radars will be purchased by the US. In return, Italy will provide short-range air defence, including the Spada SAM system, for the protection of key US bases in Italy

Army
Mistral manportable SAM (selected in 1988 with 600 launchers and 5000 missiles to be made under licence)
FIM-92B Stinger manportable SAM
2 regiments of HAWK SAM (60 launchers)
12.7 mm (quad) M55 LAAG, 109 supplied, status uncertain
25 mm SIDAM SPAAG (310 required)
40 mm L/70 AAG, Breda delivered 230 to the Italian Army from 1969

OTO Melara is now producing the 25 mm quad SIDAM SPAAG for the Italian Army

IVORY COAST

Army
Panhard M3 VDA SPAAG (6)

JAPAN

Air Force
FIM-92A Stinger manportable SAM
Type 81 Tan-SAM (27 units)
20 mm M167 Vulcan AAG
26 Patriot batteries are to be fielded, with two of these ordered direct from the US in 1985 and the remainder made under licence at the rate of about 4 batteries each with 5 launchers per year. These will replace Nike Hercules units
6 groups of 19 squadrons of Nike Hercules (180 launchers), to be replaced by Patriot

Army
FIM-92A Stinger manportable SAM
Type 81 Tan-SAM (47 units)
32 HAWK SAM batteries (192 launchers)
12.7 mm (quad) M55, 280 supplied, some still operational for airfield defence
35 mm AWX SPAAG (under development)
35 mm (twin) Oerlikon-Bührle AAG (56) with Super Fledermaus FCS
40 mm (twin) M42 SPAAG (phasing out)

Twin 35 mm Oerlikon-Bührle towed anti-aircraft gun system of the Japanese Ground Self-Defence Force (Kensuke Ebata)

JORDAN

Army
SA-7 (Grail) manportable SAM
SA-14 (Gremlin) manportable SAM
FIM-43 Redeye manportable SAM
Mistral manportable SAM (reported ordered in 1988)
Javelin manportable SAM (reported)
14 HAWK SAM batteries (56 launchers)
12.7 mm (quad) M55 LAAG, 36 supplied
20 mm M167 VADS (towed)
20 mm M163 VADS (100)
40 mm (twin) M42 SPAAG (222) (not all operational)

Air Force
23 mm ZSU-23-4 SPAAG (36)
50 SA-8 Gecko
40 SA-13 Gopher

KAMPUCHEA

Army
37 mm M1939 AAG
57 mm ZSU-57-2 SPAAG (10)
57 mm S-60 AAG
100 mm KS-19 AAG
SA-7 (Grail) manportable SAM

KENYA

Army
20 mm (twin) TCM-20 LAAG, 50 towed systems in service

296 INVENTORY

Kenya has some 50 Israeli TCM-20 twin 20 mm LAAGs

KOREA, NORTH

Air Defence Command
45 SA-2 (Guideline) SAM battalions (270 launchers) some may be HQ-2 from China
8 SA-3 (Goa) SAM battalions (32 launchers)
4 SA-5 (Gammon) SAM battalions (24 launchers)

Army
HN-5A manportable SAM
SA-7 (Grail) manportable SAM
14.5 mm ZPU-1, ZPU-2 and ZPU-4 LAAG which are now locally built and have also been exported (eg Malta)
14.5 mm M-1983 SPAAG (tracked chassis fitted with radar controlled ZPU-4 system which is manufactured in South Korea)
23 mm (twin) ZU-23 LAAG (1500)
23 mm ZSU-23-4 SPAAG (100+)
37 mm M1939 AAG (1000)
37 mm SPAAG
57 mm ZSU-57-2 SPAAG (100+)
57 mm S-60 AAG (600)
85 mm KS-12 AAG, with Fire Can radar (400)
100 mm KS-19 AAG (500)

KOREA, SOUTH

Army
Shorts Javelin manportable SAM (may involve some local assembly work)
FIM-92A Stinger manportable SAM
28 batteries HAWK SAM (164 launchers)
2 battalions with 10 batteries of Nike Hercules (90 launchers) some used in surface-to-surface role
12.7 mm (quad) M55 LAAG, locally built, some now mounted on rear of 6 × 6 trucks
20 mm M167 VADS (towed), local production (66+)
30 mm twin SPAAG under development
35 mm (twin) Oerlikon-Bührle GDF-003 AAG (18+)
40 mm M1 AAG, 80+ in service
40 mm Bofors L/70 AAG
Super Fledermaus FCS

KUWAIT

Air Force
4 battalions HAWK SAM (27 launchers)

Army
SA-7 (Grail) manportable SAM
20 SA-8 (Gecko) SAM
In June 1988 it was announced that Kuwait had signed an agreement with Egypt for the supply of a quantity of Amoun air defence systems.

Army (continued)
These consist of the Contraves Skyguard FCS, twin 35 mm GDF anti-aircraft cannon and Sparrow 4-round SAM launchers. Amoun is already used by the Egyptian Air Defence Command

LAOS

Army
SA-7 (Grail) manportable SAM
14.5 mm ZPU-1, ZPU-2 and ZPU-4 LAAG
23 mm (twin) ZU-23 LAAG
23 mm ZSU-23-4 SPAAG (10+)
37 mm M1939 AAG
57 mm S-60 AAG

LEBANON

Army
20/3 mm M55 A2 LAAG
23 mm (twin) ZU-23 LAAG, also used by various Militias
40 mm (twin) M42 SPAAG (small number)

LIBYA

Air Defence Force
6 SA-2 (Guideline) SAM brigades (each with 18 launchers)
9 SA-3 (Goa) SAM brigades (each of 12 launchers)
6 SA-3 (Goa) SAM battalions (each of 4 launchers)
6 SA-5 (Gammon) SAM battalions (total of 36 launchers)
9 Crotale SAM acquisition units and 27 firing units
50 SA-8 (Gecko) SAM
23 mm (twin) ZU-23 LAAG

Army
SA-7 (Grail) manportable SAM
160 SA-6 (Gainful) SAM
40 SA-8 (Gecko) SAM
60 SA-9 (Gaskin) SAM
60+ SA-13 (Gopher) SAM
14.5 mm ZPU-2 and ZPU-4 LAAG
23 mm (twin) ZU-23 LAAG (100)
23 mm ZSU-23-4 SPAAG (250)
30 mm M53/59 SPAAG
40 mm Bofors L/70 AAG (small number?)
57 mm S-60 AAG (150)

MADAGASCAR

Army
4 SA-9 (Gaskin) SAM
14.5 mm ZPU-4 LAAG (50)

MALAWI

Army
Blowpipe manportable SAM
14.5 mm ZPU-4 LAAG (from North Korea)

MALAYSIA

Army
40 mm M1 AAG, 24 supplied but believed to have been replaced by Bofors
40 mm Bofors L/70 AAG (36) (some BOFI)
Late in 1988 an agreement was signed between the UK and Malaysia for a wide range of defence equipment including 12 Rapier and 48 Javelin SAM launchers plus 2 Marconi Martello radars

MALI

Army
16 SA-3 (Goa) SAM launchers
8 SA-9 (Gaskin) SAM
SA-7 (Grail) SAM
14.5 mm ZPU-4 LAAG (from North Korea)
37 mm M1939 AAG (6)
57 mm S-60 AAG (6)

MALTA

Army
14.5 mm ZPU-4 LAAG (50 from North Korea)
40 mm Bofors L/70 AAG (6)

INVENTORY

One of the 50 ZPU-4 14.5 mm LAAG supplied to Malta by North Korea, shown being used in coast defence/anti-aircraft role

MAURITANIA

Army
SA-7 (Grail) manportable SAM
SA-9 (Gaskin) SAM
14.5 mm ZPU-1, ZPU-2 and ZPU-4 LAAG
23 mm (twin) ZU-23 LAAG
37 mm M1939 AAG (6)

MAURITIUS

Army
SA-7 (Grail) manportable SAM

MEXICO

Army
12.7 mm (quad) M55 LAAG (40 to 50 supplied)

MONGOLIA

Army
SA-7 (Grail) manportable SAM
1 SA-2 (Guideline) SAM battalion (6 launchers)
14.5 mm ZPU-2 and ZPU-4 LAAG
23 mm (twin) ZU-23 LAAG
37 mm KS-12 AAG
57 mm S-60 AAG

MOROCCO

Army
SA-7 (Grail) manportable SAM
37 Chaparral SAM
14.5 mm ZPU-2 and ZPU-4 LAAG (15 in service)
20 mm M167 VADS (towed) (70 delivered in early 1980s)
20 mm M163 VADS SPAAG (60)
23 mm (twin) ZU-23 LAAG (35)
37 mm KS-12 AAG
57 mm S-60 AAG (60)
100 mm KS-19 AAG (? still operational)

MOZAMBIQUE

Army
SA-7 (Grail) manportable SAM
3 battalions SA-3 (Goa) SAM (12 launchers)
12 SA-6 (Gainful) SAM
32 SA-9 (Gaskin) SAM
20/3 mm M55 A2 LAAG
14.5 mm ZPU-1, ZPU-2 and ZPU-4 LAAG
23 mm (twin) ZU-23 LAAG (120)
23 mm ZSU-23-4 SPAAG (25)
37 mm M1939 AAG
57 mm ZSU-57-2 SPAAG (20)
57 mm S-60 AAG (70)

NEPAL

Army
40 mm Bofors L/60 AAG (2)
Reported that China supplied a quantity of LAAG in 1987 and 1988

NETHERLANDS

Air Force
40 mm Bofors L/70 AAG (72) with Flycatcher FCS
12 squadrons of HAWK SAM (72 launchers)
Patriot SAM, 4 squadrons with a total of 20 launchers and 160 missiles have been ordered with first squadron becoming operational in 1987, second in 1988 and remaining 2 in 1990. Last of Nike Hercules SAMs were disbanded in West Germany in 1988 and in the same year the Patriot SAM system was declared operational with No 3 and No 5 Guided Missile Groups at Blomberg and Stolzenau in West Germany, with each group having 2 squadrons with five 4-round launchers each. Eventually each Group will comprise 2 Patriot and 4 HAWK fire units with Stingers for close defence. By 1990 the Guided Missile Group Netherlands (GMGN) will be deployed near major sea and airports in the western Netherlands. At present, the HAWKs defend Dutch air bases but this role will be taken over by a new SAM system (short-range) in 1990. Four additional Patriot squadrons will be allocated to the GMGN after 1991 at the rate of one squadron a year. Eventually all Patriot units will be brought up to the standard of 8 launchers per unit.
In April 1989 the Netherlands selected the French Crotale New Generation using the VT-1 missile to meet this requirement.

Army
FIM-92A Stinger manportable SAM (member of European consortium making Stinger with total requirement being 90 for Navy/Marines, 944 for Army and 675 for the Air Force)
35 mm (twin) SPAAG (95)
40 mm Bofors L/70 AAG (60) with Flycatcher FCS. Late in 1987 it was announced that these would be upgraded, 6 being done by Bofors in Sweden and the remainder by RDM in the Netherlands. Early in 1987 30 Flycatcher FCS were ordered, 27 for use by 3 L/70 units in West Germany and 3 in reserve. All will be delivered by 1990

NICARAGUA

Army
SA-7 (Grail) manportable SAM
SA-14 (Gremlin) manportable SAM
12 SA-9 (Gaskin) SAM
14.5 mm ZPU-1, ZPU-2 and ZPU-4 LAAG (100 in service)
20 mm GAI-C01 LAAG
23 mm (twin) ZU-23 LAAG
37 mm M1939 AAG (56)
57 mm S-60 AAG
100 mm KS-19 AAG

NIGERIA

SA-7 (Grail) manportable SAM
Blowpipe manportable SAM
Roland 2 SAM on AMX-30 chassis (16)
23 mm ZSU-23-4 SPAAG (30)

NORWAY

Air Force
6 batteries of improved HAWK NOAH SAM (54 launchers)
1 battalion of Nike Hercules with 2 batteries, total 18 launchers, being replaced by NASAMS
40 mm M1 AAG (32)
40 mm Bofors L/70 AAG (64), Super Fledermaus FCS, being upgraded by SATT
40 mm Bofors L/60 AAG (32), Super Fledermaus FCS, being upgraded by SATT
In January 1989 contracts were signed for the Norwegian Advanced SAM System (NASAMS) which will replace remaining Nike Hercules missiles

Army
RBS 70 SAM used with Giraffe radar (first order was for 110 launchers plus 27 radars)
12.7 mm (quad) M55, some used for airfield defence
20 mm (single) FK 20-2 LAAG
40 mm M1 AAG, (132 supplied but some in reserve)
40 mm Bofors L/60 AAG

OMAN

Air Force
2 squadrons of Rapier ordered in 1974 and delivered from 1977, Blindfire radars ordered in 1980; 28 launchers purchased, 24 operational, remainder training/war reserve

298 INVENTORY

Omani National Guard VAB (6 × 6) vehicles fitted with ESD TA-20 twin 20 mm anti-aircraft turret

Army
Blowpipe manportable SAM
23 mm (twin) ZU-23 LAAG Javelin manportable SAM

National Guard
20 mm (twin) SPAAG on VAB (6 × 6) chassis (9)

PAKISTAN

Air Force
12 Crotale acquisition units and 24 firing units
1 battalion of HQ-2 SAM (from China) 6 launchers

Army
HN-5A manportable SAM
Blowpipe manportable SAM
FIM-92A Stinger SAM
RBS 70 SAM, 140 launchers plus Giraffe radars
12.7 mm (quad) M55 LAAG, 45+ supplied
14.5 mm ZPU-2 and ZPU-4 LAAG (from China)
23 mm (twin) ZU-23 LAAG (from China)
35 mm (twin) Oerlikon-Bührle AAG (also used for airfield defence) (up to 100 have been ordered with Skyguard FCS)
37 mm (twin) AAG (from China) (700) (same as M1939 of USSR) competition to provide new FCS underway
40 mm Mk 1 AAG
40 mm M1 AAG (60)
57 mm S-60 AAG (from China)
90 mm M117 (15 supplied and now in reserve)
Anzi manportable SAM
Anzi/14.5 mm SPAA system

PARAGUAY
40 mm M1 AAG (12)

PERU

Air Force
6 battalions of SA-3 (Goa) SAM (24 launchers)
3 battalions of SA-2 (Guideline) SAM (18 launchers)

Army
SA-7 (Grail) manportable SAM
23 mm (twin) ZU-23 LAAG
23 mm ZSU-23-4 SPAAG (35)
40 mm M1 AAG (28)
40 mm Bofors L/60 AAG (40)
40 mm Bofors L/70 AAG (40)

POLAND

Air Defence Command
40 battalions SA-2 (Guideline) SAM (240 launchers)
50 battalions SA-3 (Goa) SAM (200 launchers)
23 mm (twin) ZU-23 LAAG

Army
SA-7 (Grail) manportable SAM
SA-14 (Gremlin) manportable SAM
120 SA-6 (Gainful) SAM
60 SA-8 (Gecko) SAM
160 SA-9 (Gaskin) SAM
20+ SA-11 (Gadfly) SAM
SA-13 (Gopher) SAM
14.5 mm ZPU-2 and ZPU-4 LAAG, not in front line service, also used by Troops of Territorial Defence
23 mm (twin) ZU-23 LAAG, also used by Troops of Territorial Defence (450)

Army (continued)
23 mm ZSU-23-4 SPAAG (150)
57 mm ZSU-57-2 SPAAG (100 in reserve)
57 mm S-60 AAG (200)
100 mm KS-19 AAG (reserve) (90)

PORTUGAL

Air Force
1 Improved HAWK battery

Army
Blowpipe manportable SAM
5 Chaparral SAM delivered in 1987
12.7 mm (quad) M55 LAAG (18)
20 mm M163 VADS SPAAG (10 ordered in 1987)
20 mm (twin) Rheinmetall LAAG, 36 believed used by Army
40 mm M1 AAG (20 to 30 in service, but may be Bofors L/60)
40 mm Bofors L/60 AAG (20) (see above)

QATAR

Army
Rapier SAM, 12 ordered in 1981, also has Blindfire radar
Blowpipe manportable SAM
Stinger FIM-92A manportable SAM
5 Tigercat SAM (1 battery)
3 Roland 2 on AMX-30 chassis
6 Roland 2 shelter on 8 × 8 MAN chassis

ROMANIA

Air Force
18 battalions SA-2 (Guideline) SAM (108 launchers)

Army
SA-7 (Grail) manportable SAM
60 SA-6 (Gainful) SAM
14.5 mm ZPU-2 and ZPU-4 LAAG, also used by MoD Security Troops, Patriotic Guard and Border Troops
23 mm ZSU-23-4 SPAAG (50) (unconfirmed)
30 mm (twin) M53 AAG (300)
37 mm M1939 AAG (100)
57 mm S-60 AAG (150)
57 mm ZSU-57-2 SPAAG (60)
85 mm KS-12 AAG, with Fire Can radar (75)
100 mm KS-19 AAG (30)

SÃO TOMÉ & PRINCIPE

Army
14.5 mm ZPU-4 LAAG

SAUDI ARABIA

Air Force
16 Crotale SAM acquisition units and 48 Crotale firing units
10 batteries HAWK SAM (90 launchers)
35 mm Oerlikon-Bührle AAG with Skyguard FCS

Saudi Arabian National Guard is sole user of Commando V-150 fitted with Vulcan 20 mm air defence system

INVENTORY

Army
FIM-92A Stinger manportable SAM
FIM-43 Redeye manportable SAM
16 Shahine SAM acquisition units on AMX-30 chassis
40 Shahine SAM firing units on AMX-30 chassis
16 Shahine SAM acquisition units shelter mounted
32 Shahine SAM firing units shelter mounted
20 mm M163 VADS SPAAG (60 to 104 and may include 20 VADS on V-150 Commando operated by National Guard
30 mm (twin) AMX-30 DCA SPAAG (53)
35 mm (twin) Oerlikon-Bührle AAG with Skyguard FCS (up to 200 may be in service, some used by Air Force for airfield defence)

SENEGAMBIA

Army
20 mm (twin) Tarasque 53T2 LAAG
40 mm Bofors L/60 AAG (small number)

SEYCHELLES

Army
SA-7 (Grail) manportable SAM
14.5 mm ZPU-4 LAAG

SIERRA LEONE

Army
SA-7 (Grail) manportable SAM

SINGAPORE

Air Force
20 mm GAI-C01 LAAG
35 mm (twin) Oerlikon-Bührle GDF-002 AAG with Super Fledermaus FCS, but upgraded with SATT modernisation package (34)
40 mm Bofors L/60 AAG (16)
RBS 70 SAM (1 squadron) mounted on Commando V-200 (4 × 4) armoured car
1 squadron of Rapier 12 SAM ordered in 1981, also uses 6 Blindfire
1 squadron of HAWK SAM (18 launchers)
1 squadron Bloodhound SAM (24 launchers)

Army
RBS 70 SAM

SOMALIA

Air Defence Forces
6 battalions SA-2 (Guideline) SAM (36 launchers)
2 battalions SA-3 (Goa) SAM (8 launchers)
12 SA-6 (Gainful) SAM

Army
FIM-43 Redeye manportable SAM
SA-7 (Grail) manportable SAM
14.5 mm ZPU-1, ZPU-2 and ZPU-4 LAAG
20 mm M167 VADS (towed)
20 mm (twin) Cerbere 76T2 LAAG (40)
23 mm (twin) ZU-23 LAAG
23 mm ZSU-23-4 SPAAG (4)
37 mm M1939 AAG (120)
57 mm S-60 AAG (50)
100 mm KS-19 AAG (45)

SOUTH AFRICA

Air Force
7 Crotale SAM acquisition and 14 Crotale firing units

Army
20 mm (single) SPAAG called the Ystervark. This is an armoured SAMIL 20 (4 × 4) truck fitted with an Oerlikon-Bührle 20 mm GAI-C01 cannon on the rear
20 mm (single) Oerlikon GAI-C04 and GAI-C01 LAAG
20 mm (single) Oerlikon GAI-B01 LAAG
35 mm twin Oerlikon GDF-002 AAG (150) with Super Fledermaus FCS
40 mm Bofors L/60 (reserve)
LPD-20 radars

SPAIN

Army
Mistral manportable SAM. Late in 1988 the Spanish Government decided in principle to order the French Matra Mistral manportable SAM with possible co-production with Belgium and France
6 batteries of Toledo air defence systems, each has 1 Skyguard fire control system, 2 twin Oerlikon-Bührle 35 mm GDF-005 anti-aircraft guns and two 4-round Spada SAM launchers
2 battalions HAWK SAM (48 launchers)
1 battalion Nike Hercules SAM (9 launchers)
12.7 mm (quad) M55 LAAG, 132 supplied, some have been mounted on rear of 6 × 6 truck, also used by Marines
20 mm (single) Oerlikon GAI-B01 LAAG
35 mm (twin) Oerlikon-Bührle GDF-002 AAG (96) with Super Fledermaus and Skyguard FCS
40 mm Bofors L/70, 243 were built under licence in Spain by SA Placencia de las Armas, getting FELIS FCS
18 Roland SAM systems on Spanish built AMX-30E chassis and 414 missiles ordered in 1984 with first of these being delivered in November 1988. Of these, 9 are clear weather systems and 9 all-weather. Used by 71st Independent Air Defence Regiment
90 mm M117 AAG (40 supplied and now in reserve)

SRI LANKA

Army
24 3.7 inch (94 mm) AAG may be in service

SUDAN

SA-7 (Grail) manportable SAM
FIM-43 Redeye manportable SAM
3 battalions SA-2 (Guideline) SAM (18 launchers)
14.5 mm ZPU-2 and ZPU-4 LAAG
20 mm M163 VADS SPAAG (8) (delivered 1981/1982)
20 mm M167 VADS (towed)
23 mm (twin) ZU-23 LAAG (from Egypt)
37 mm M1939 AAG (60)
40 mm Bofors L/60 AAG (60, ? still operational)
85 mm KS-12 AAG, with Fire Can radar
100 mm KS-19 AAG

SWEDEN

Swedish Army using Ericsson Giraffe radar system to provide early warning and control facility to its RBS 70 SAMs

Army
RBS 70 SAM system with Giraffe radar
RBS 90 SAM on order
Lvrbv 701 vehicle mounted RBS 70 system
1 HAWK SAM battalion (12 launchers) (called Rb 67)
20 mm LAAG
40 mm Bofors L/60 AAG
40 mm Bofors L/70 AAG

SWITZERLAND

Air Force
2 Bloodhound (BL-64) SAM battalions, each with 2 batteries (total 64 launchers)
35 mm (twin) Oerlikon-Bührle AAG (see below)

Army
FIM-92 RMP Stinger manportable SAM (in 1988 the Swiss MoD announced that it would acquire a minimum of 2500 missiles valued at $315 million)
Rapier SAM, 60 launchers in service plus Blindfire radars, final deliveries 1986
20 mm (single) Oerlikon GAI-B01 AAG
35 mm (twin) Oerlikon-Bührle AAG (260) (used by Army and Air Force with Super Fledermaus and Skyguard FCS)

SYRIA

Air Defence Command
40 battalions SA-2 (Guideline) SAM (138 launchers)
23 battalions SA-3 (Goa) SAM (160 launchers)
4 battalions SA-5 (Gammon) SAM (24 launchers)
27 battalions SA-6 (Gainful) SAM (108 launchers)
23 mm (twin) ZU-23 LAAG

Army
SA-7 (Grail) manportable SAM
SA-14 (Gremlin) manportable SAM
150 SA-9 (Gaskin) SAM
108 SA-6 (Gainful) SAM
160 SA-8 (Gecko) SAM
20+ SA-11 (Gadfly) SAM
60 SA-13 (Gopher) SAM
14.5 mm ZPU-2 and ZPU-4 LAAG, but not in front line service, also used by Militia
23 mm (twin) ZU-23 LAAG
23 mm ZSU-23-4 SPAAG (100+)
37 mm M1939 AAG
57 mm ZSU-57-2 SPAAG (100+)
57 mm S-60 AAG
85 mm KS-12 AAG, with Fire Can radar
100 mm KS-19 AAG

TAIWAN

Army
Tien Kung I SAM
Tien Kung II SAM (under development)
Sky Sword I SAM (under development)
13 HAWK SAM battalions (78 launchers)
2 Nike Hercules battalions (96 launchers)
Chaparral SAM (52)
12.7 mm (quad) M55 LAAG
35 mm (twin) Oerlikon-Bührle GDF AAG and Skyguard FCS
40 mm M1 AAG (200)
40 mm Bofors L/70 AA (use unconfirmed)
40 mm (twin) M42 SPAAG (295 delivered)

TANZANIA

Army
SA-7 (Grail) manportable SAM
3 SA-3 (Goa) battalions (12 launchers)
12 SA-6 (Gainful) SAM
40 SA-9 (Gaskin) SAM
14.5 mm ZPU-1, ZPU-2 and ZPU-4 LAAG (160/240)
23 mm (twin) ZU-23 LAAG
37 mm Type 55 AAG (120) (from China)

THAILAND

Air Force
Blowpipe manportable SAM
One Spada SAM battery delivered in 1988 (4 four-round launchers)
20 mm M39 (twin and triple LAAG)
20 mm M163 VADS SPAAG (24)

Air Force (continued)
30 mm (twin) Arrow AAG, first deliveries 1988 from West Germany, used with Contraves Skyguard FCS
37 mm (twin) Type 74 AAGs supplied by China in 1987/1988 (40)
40 mm M1 AAG (80)
40 mm Bofors L/70 AAG (48 delivered from UK in 1987)
40 mm (twin) M42 SPAAG (16)

Army
FIM-43 Redeye manportable SAM
12.7 mm (quad) M55 LAAG
20 mm M167A1 VADS (towed) (24 ordered in 1982)

TOGO

Army
14.5 mm ZPU-4 LAAG (38 from North Korea)
37 mm M1939 AAG (6)

TUNISIA

Army
60 RBS 70 Launchers and 12 Giraffe radars
Charappal SAM (26)
37 mm Type 55 (M1939) AAG (18) (from China)
40 mm (twin) M42 SPAAG (16)

TURKEY

Air Force
Rapier SAM, 36 ordered in 1983 and another 36 in 1985, also uses Blindfire
8 squadrons of Nike Hercules SAM each with 9 launchers (total 72 launchers)

Army
FIM-92A Stinger manportable SAM (member of European consortium making Stinger with total Turkish requirement being for 4500 missiles)
FIM-43 Redeye manportable SAM
12.7 mm (quad) M55 LAAG (160)
20 mm (twin) GAI-D01 LAAG (licenced production)
20 mm (twin) Rheinmetall LAAG (300+ in service)
35 mm (twin) Oerlikon-Bührle GDF AAG (140 ordered with Gun King) (believed licenced production)
40 mm M1 AAG (70)
40 mm Bofors L/70 AAG (also Air Force)
40 mm (twin) M42 SPAAG (153 supplied by West Germany)
75 mm M51 AAG (110 delivered)
90 mm M117 AAG (116 delivered)
90 mm M118 AAG (above figures include this version)
The Turkish Army has a requirement for a new low level air defence system and in late 1988 the choice was narrowed to 3, ADATS, Crotale and Roland
Super Fledermaus FCS

UGANDA

Army
SA-7 (Grail) manportable SAM system
14.5 mm ZPU-1, ZPU-2 and ZPU-4 LAAG
23 mm (twin) ZU-23 LAAG (20+)
37 mm M1939 AAG (20)

USSR

Air Defence Troops
SA-1 (Guild) SAM (3200 launchers, being reduced)
SA-2 (Guideline) SAM (2730 launchers)
SA-3 (Goa) SAM (1250 launchers at 300 sites)
SA-5 (Gammon) SAM (2000 launchers at 130 sites)
SA-10a/b (Grumble) SAM
SA-12a/b (Gladiator/Giant) SAM
23 mm (twin) ZU-23 LAAG
57 mm S-60 AAG
85 mm KS-12 AAG (reserve)
100 mm KS-19 AAG (reserve)
130 mm KS-30 AAG (reserve)

Naval Infantry
SA-7 (Grail) manportable SAM
SA-14 (Gremlin) manportable SAM
SA-16 manportable SAM
SA-8 (Gecko) SAM
SA-9 (Gaskin) SAM
SA-13 (Gopher) SAM
23 mm ZSU-23-4 SPAAG

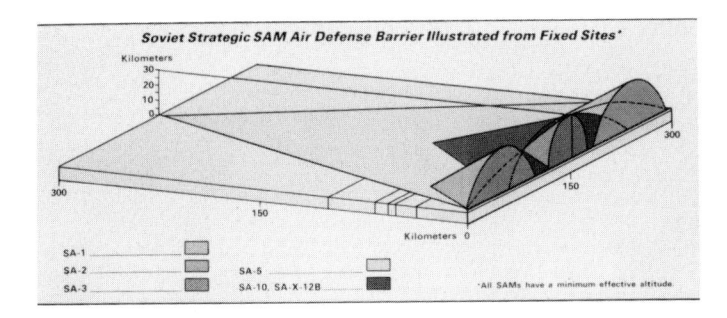

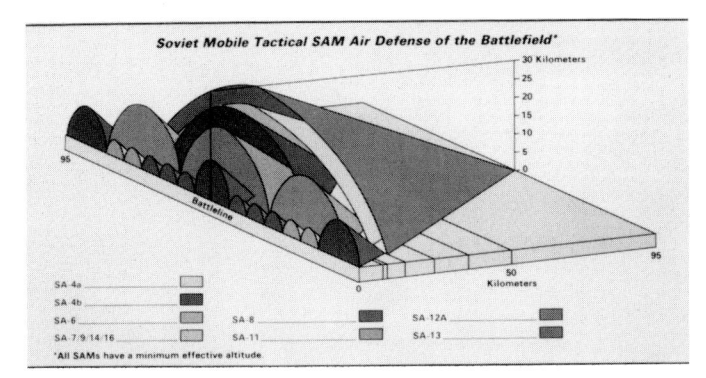

Army

SA-4 (Ganef) SAM
SA-6 (Gainful) SAM
SA-7 (Grail) manportable SAM
SA-8 (Gecko) SAM
SA-9 (Gaskin) SAM
SA-10 (Grumble) SAM
SA-11 (Gadfly) SAM
SA-12a (Gladiator) SAM
SA-13 (Gopher) SAM
SA-14 (Gremlin) manportable SAM
SA-X-15 SAM, troop trials
SA-16 manportable SAM
SA-X-17 SAM
14.5 mm ZPU-1, ZPU-2 and ZPU-4, not in front line service, also used by KGB, MVD, Militia and Naval Infantry (reserve)
23 mm (twin) ZU-23 LAAG, also used by KGB, MVD and Militia
23 mm ZSU-23-4 SPAAG
30 mm 2S6 SPAAG
37 mm M1939 AAG (reserves and militia)
57 mm ZSU-57-2 SPAAG (mainly reserve)
57 mm S-60 AAG

Three SA-4 (Ganef) systems re-deploying

UNITED ARAB EMIRATES

Air Force
7 HAWK SAM batteries (42 launchers)

Army
RBS 70 SAM delivered from 1980 onwards
Rapier SAM ordered by Abu Dhabi in 1974, later ordered Blindfire radars
3 Crotale SAM acquisition and 9 Crotale firing units
20 mm (twin) Panhard M3 VDA SPAAG (42)
35 mm (twin) Oerlikon-Bührle GDF series AAG (30) with Skyguard FCS
Javelin manportable SAM (Dubai)

UNITED KINGDOM

Air Force
35 mm (twin) Oerlikon-Bührle GDF series AAG (12) with Skyguard FCS (captured from Argentina in Falklands)
Rapier SAM, 6 regiments, 4 in West Germany and 2 in UK, Blindfire radar issued on scale of 1 per launcher
2 squadrons of Bloodhound SAM at 6 sites

THORN-EMI Air Defence Alert Device in tripod-mounted configuration providing target information for Shorts Javelin manportable surface-to-air missile system. The ADAD will also be fitted to the Shorts Starstreak HVM system mounted on the Alvis Stormer vehicle to enter service with the British Army in the early 1990s

Army
Rapier SAM, 3 regiments (2 in BAOR, 1 in UK), plus Blindfire radars (but on 1 per 2 launcher basis and issued as required) Rapier is also deployed in Belize (4) (RAF) and Falkland Islands (RAF). Army is getting Rapier Darkfire while RAF will wait for Rapier 2000 which will also go to British Army
130 to 150 Starstreak SPAAM on order
Tracked Rapier SAM (72)
Blowpipe manportable SAM (TA only)
Javelin manportable SAM (Army and TA)
FIM-92A Stinger manportable SAM (SAS)

Marines
Shorts Javelin manportable SAM

British Aerospace Rapier SAM system defending an RAF airfield. Marconi Command and Control Systems Blindfire radar (left), optical tracker (centre) and four round launcher (right)

302 INVENTORY

UNITED STATES OF AMERICA

Air Force
FIM-92A/B/C Stinger manportable SAM
27 Roland SAM on MAN (8 × 8) chassis in FGR, manned by West Germany and delivered 1987 to 1989
Rapier SAM plus Blindfire radar (1 per launcher), 14 in Turkey manned by Turkish military personnel, 32 in UK manned by Royal Air Force Regiment to protect USAF basis, (28 launchers operational and remaining 4 for training)

Army
FIM-43 Redeye manportable SAM (training)
FIM-92A/B/C Stinger manportable SAM (by FY85 a total of 11 650 Stingers had been procured with the total procurement objective being 50 664 missiles)
Pedestal Mounted Stinger, 20 ordered in 1987 with deliveries late 1988, total requirement 173 systems over 5 year period with total requirement to be 1200 units
600+ Chaparral SAMs, being improved, total procurement objective in 1987 was stated to be 632 units. National Guard fielded its first battalion in November 1987 with second following in early 1988
ADATS, 4 ordered with FY88 funding, total requirement 562
31 Roland SAM systems, 1 battalion, may be deactivated
20 mm M167 VADS (towed) AAG (some being upgraded to PIVADS)
20 mm M163 VADS SPAAG (360) (some being upgraded to PIVADS)
40 mm (twin) M42 SPAAG (300, but declining)
11 battalions of Raytheon HAWK SAM
The National Guard is to receive at least 3 HAWK battalions
Raytheon Patriot SAM, total procurement objective is 104 fire units (batteries) of which 58 had been procured through FY85 with 3 of these procured with NATO air base air defence funds. Of these 84 will be in the field and remainder for training and war reserve. By 1988, 6 battalions had been deployed to Europe

Marine Corps
FIM-92A/B/C Stinger manportable SAM
4 battalions Raytheon HAWK SAM

Navy
FIM-92A/B/C Stinger manportable SAM

US Army Roland 2 fire unit being transported under a CH-47 Chinook helicopter

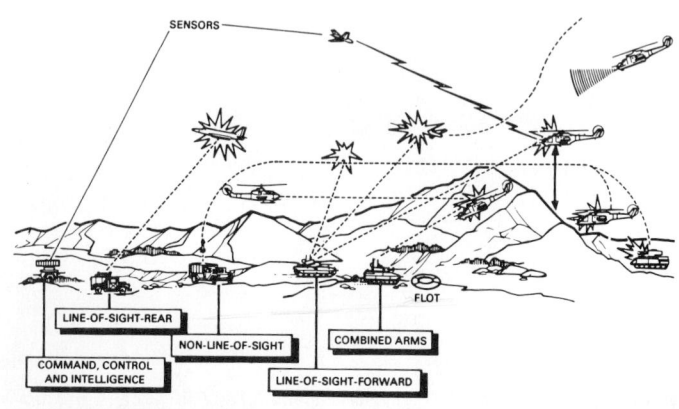

Main components of US Army's Forward Area Air Defense (FAAD) system (US Army)

URUGUAY

Army
20 mm M167 VADS (towed)
40 mm Bofors L/60 (2)

VENEZUELA

Army
36 40 mm (twin) Breda 40L70 field mountings were delivered in early 1980s and these, together with 18 Signal Flycatcher radar FCS, form the Guardian air defence system
40 mm Bofors L/70 AAG (18)
40 mm Bofors L/60 AAG (60 but some may be L/70)
6 Roland 2 SAM shelter-mounted
RBS 70 surface-to-air missile system

Marines
40 mm (twin) M42 SPAAG (30)

Venezuela is the only known user of the Breda 40 mm (twin) 40L70 field mounts which are used in conjunction with Flycatcher FCS

VIETNAM

Air Defence Forces
20 regiments SA-2 (Guideline) (each with 18 launchers)
10 SA-3 (Goa) regiments (total 160 launchers)
85 mm KS-12 AAG
100 mm KS-19 AAG
130 mm KS-30 AAG

Army
SA-7 (Grail) manportable SAM
80 SA-6 (Gainful) SAM
100+ SA-9 (Gaskin) SAM
12.7 mm (quad) M53 AAG, probably now held in reserve
14.5 mm ZPU-1, ZPU-2 and ZPU-4 LAAG
23 mm (twin) ZU-23 LAAG (900)
23 mm ZSU-23-4 SPAAG (100+)
30 mm (twin) M53 AAG, probably now held in reserve (150)
37 mm M1939 AAG
40 mm M42 SPAAG (130, probably non operational)
57 mm ZSU-57-2 SPAAG (50+)
57 mm S-60 AAG

YEMEN (NORTH)

Air Force
1 regiment SA-2 (Guideline) SAM (12 launchers)

Army
SA-7 (Grail) manportable SAM
1 battalion SA-2 (Guideline) SAM (6 launchers)
12 SA-6 (Gainful) SAM
20 mm M163 VADS SPAAG (20)
23 mm ZSU-23-4 SPAAG (20+)
23 mm (twin) ZU-23 LAAG
37 mm M1939 AAG
57 mm S-60 AAG

YEMEN (SOUTH)
1 battalion SA-2 (Guideline) SAM (6 launchers)
3 battalions SA-3 (Goa) SAM (12 launchers)
SA-7 (Grail) manportable SAM
20+ SA-9 (Gaskin) SAM
23 mm (twin) ZU-23 LAAG
23 mm ZSU-23-4 SPAAG (30+)
37 mm M1939 AAG
57 mm S-60 AAG
85 mm KS-12 AAG, with Fire Can radar

YUGOSLAVIA

Protective Air Defence Force
8 battalions SA-2 (Guideline) SAM (48 launchers)
6 battalions SA-3 (Goa) SAM (24 launchers)
SA-11 (Gadfly) SAM
SA-6 (Gainful) SAM
SA-9 (Gaskin) SAM
Above three form total of 6 regiments

Army
SA-7 (Grail) manportable SAM
80 SA-6 (Gainful) SAM
20+ SA-8 (Gecko) SAM
100 SA-9 (Gaskin) SAM
12.7 mm (quad) M55 LAAG, probably now in reserve
20/3 mm M55 A2 LAAG
20/3 mm M55 A3 B1 LAAG
20/3 mm M55 A4 B1 LAAG
20/1 mm M75 LAAG
20 mm BOV-3 SPAAG
23 mm ZSU-23-4 SPAAG
30 mm (twin) M53 AAG, probably now held in reserve
30 mm M53/59 SPAAG
30 mm (twin) BOV SPAAG
37 mm M1939 AAG (400)
40 mm Bofors L/70 AAG
40 mm AAG, both UK Mk 1 and US M1 have been in service, but present status of these is uncertain, some sources state 128 40 mm M1s supplied
57 mm S-60 AAG
57 mm ZSU-57-2 SPAAG (50+)
85 mm KS-12 AAG, with Fire Can radar (260)
90 mm M117 AAG, probably now non-operational
3.7 inch (94 mm) AAGs are now believed to have been phased out of service

ZAIRE

Army
14.5 mm ZPU-4 LAAG
37 mm M1939 AAG
40 mm Bofors L/60 AAG (status uncertain)

ZAMBIA

Air Force
1 SA-3 (Goa) battalion of 3 batteries (12 launchers)

Army
Rapier, 12 supplied in 1971, but believed no longer operational
SA-7 (Grail) manportable SAM
3 Tigercat SAM (1 battery)
14.5 mm ZPU-4 LAAG
20 mm M75 LAAG
37 mm M1939 AAG (40)
57 mm S-60 AAG (55)
85 mm KS-12 AAG with Fire Can radar (16)

ZIMBABWE

Army
SA-7 (Grail) manportable SAM
14.5 mm ZPU-1, ZPU-2 and ZPU-4 LAAG
20/3 mm M55 A2 AAG
23 mm (twin) ZU-23 LAAG
37 mm M1939 AAG

INDEX

306 INDEX

2S6 2×30mm Self-propelled AA Gun System, 84
3.7inch AA Gun (UK), 216
10 ILa/5TG *see* GAI-B01 20mm Automatic AA Gun
12.7mm M55 Quad 12.7mm Self-propelled AA Gun System, 79
12.7mm Modernised AA Machine Gun M55, 155
12.7mm NORINCO AA Machine Gun Type 54, 158
12.7mm NORINCO Type 77 AA Machine Gun, 159
12.7mm NORINCO Type W-85 AA Machine Gun, 160
12.7mm (Quad) AA Machine Gun M55, 224
12.7mm Quad M53 AA Machine Gun, 166
12.7mm Twin AA Gun, 157
14.5mm AA Guns (Chinese), 164
14.5mm BTR-40A Twin Self-propelled AA Gun System, 89
14.5mm BTR-152A Twin Self-propelled AA Gun System, 89
14.5mm M1938 Self-propelled AA Gun, 78
14.5mm ZPU Series of AA Machine Guns, 213
20/1mm M75 AA Gun, 228
20/3mm M55 A2 AA Gun, 226
20/3mm M55 A3/A4 B1 AA Gun, 227
20mm 53T1 Single Light AA Gun, 170
20mm 53T4 Twin Automatic AA Gun, 168
20mm AA Twin Gun Air Defence System, 173
20mm AML S530 Twin Self-propelled AA Gun, 67
20mm Automatic AA Gun FK 20-2, 184
20mm BOV-3 Triple Self-propelled AA Gun System, 104
20mm Cerbere 76T2 Twin Automatic AA Gun, 169
20mm FAM-2M Twin Light AA Gun, 157
20mm GAI-B01 Automatic AA Gun, 201
20mm GAI-C01/GAI-C04 Automatic AA Guns, 200
20mm GAI-C03 Automatic AA Gun, 202
20mm GAI-D01 Twin Automatic AA Gun, 199
20mm High Mobility Vulcan Wheeled Carrier (VWC) AA Gun System, 103
20mm M3 VDA Twin Self-propelled AA Gun System, 65
20mm M163 Vulcan Self-propelled AA Gun System, 100
20mm M167 Vulcan AA Gun, 221
20mm Meroka Multi-barrel AA Gun System, 186
20mm Mobile Gun Platform, 72
20mm Tarasque 53T2 Automatic AA Gun, 170
20mm TCM-20 Twin AA Gun System, 178
20mm VDAA Twin Self-propelled AA Gun System, 65
20mm Vulcan-Commando Self-propelled Air Defense System, 102
20mm Ystervark Self-propelled AA Gun System, 79
23mm Light AA Gun (Chinese), 163
23mm Nile 23 Twin Self-propelled AA Gun, 59
23mm Sinai 23 Twin Self-propelled AA Gun, 58
23mm ZSU-23-4 Quad Self-propelled AA Gun System, 86
23mm ZU-23 Twin Automatic AA Gun, 211
23mm ZU-23M Twin Automatic AA Gun, 168
25mm GBF-BOB Diana LAAG, 196
25mm GBI-A01 Automatic AA Gun, 198
25mm Infantry Gun Iltis, 197
25mm Light AA Gun (China), 163
25mm Quad Self-propelled AA Gun System, 73
25mm SIDAM 25 Self-propelled AA Gun System, 73
30mm 2S6 Self-propelled AA Gun System, 84
30mm AMX-13 DCA Twin Self-propelled AA Gun System, 62
30mm AMX-30 DCA Twin Self-propelled AA Gun System, 62
30mm Arrow AA Gun, 171
30mm Artemis Light AA Gun System, 174
30mm Automatic AA Gun M53, 166
30mm M53/59 Twin Self-propelled AA Gun System, 57
30mm SABRE Twin Self-propelled AA Gun System, 60
30mm Sentinel Twin AA Gun, 183
30mm Twin Self-propelled AA Gun System, 78
35mm AW-X Twin Self-propelled AA Gun System, 77
35mm CA 1 Twin Self-propelled AA Gun System, 69
35mm Eagle Twin Mobile Air Defence System, 96
35mm GDF-002 & GDF-005 Twin Automatic AA Guns, 193
35mm GDF-DO3 Escorter 35 Twin Self-propelled AA Gun System, 81
35mm Gepard Twin Self-propelled AA Gun System, 69
35mm Marksman Twin AA Turret, 91
37mm AA Guns (China), 161
37mm Automatic AA Gun M1939, 209, 288
37mm Twin Self-propelled AA Gun System, 55
37mm Type 55 AA Gun, 161
37mm Type 63 Twin Self-propelled AA Gun System, 56
37 mm Type 65 AA Gun, 161
37mm Type P793 AA Gun, 161
40L70 Breda Twin Field Mounting, 180
40mm AA Gun (Italy), 180
40mm AA Gun Update (Sweden), 192
40mm Automatic AA Gun M1, 220
40mm Automatic AA Gun Mk1, 216
40mm FN Herstal (SA) Bofors 40mm L/60 Upgrade Kit, 154
40mm L40/60 Boffin Automatic AA Gun, 156
40mm L/60 Bofors Gun, 232
40mm L/70 Bofors AA Guns, 186, 187
40mm M42 Twin Self-propelled AA Gun System, 93
40mm m/36 L/60 Automatic AA Gun, 191
40mm Self-propelled AA Gun System (Brazil), 54
40mm Trinity Self-propelled Air Defence System, 79
53T1 Single 20mm Light AA Gun, 170
53T2 Tarasque 20mm Automatic AA Gun, 170
53T4 Twin 20mm Automatic AA Gun, 168
57mm Automatic AA Gun S-60, 207, 288
57mm Type 80 Twin Self-propelled AA Gun System, 54
57mm Type 59 AA Gun, 160
57mm ZSU-57-2 Twin Self-propelled AA Gun System, 82
75mm M51 AA Gun, 219
76mm Self-propelled OTOMATIC Air Defence Tank, 75
76T2 Cerbere 20mm Twin Automatic AA Gun, 169
85mm M1939 and M1944 AA Guns, 206
90mm M117 AA Gun, 218
90mm M118 AA Gun, 217
100mm KS-19 AA Gun, 205
130mm KS-30 AA Gun, 203

A

AATCP Mistral Air-to-air System, 31
ACF Industries Inc, Self-propelled AA Guns, 93
ACWAR Agile Continuous Wave Acquisition Radar, 278
ADAMS Vertical Launch Low Altitude SAM System, 119
ADATS Missile System, 122
ADI Air Defence Initiative, 25
ADSM Air Defence Suppression Missile, 51
AEG Aktiengesellschaft, Static & Towed SAM Systems, 246
AIM-9L Sidewinder AIM-132A Low Altitude SAM System, 245
ALB1 Mistral Lightweight Twin-round-Mobile System, 31
AML S530 Twin 20mm Self-propelled AA Gun, 67
AMX-13 DCA Twin 30mm Self-propelled AA Gun System, 62
AMX-30 DCA Twin 30mm Self-propelled AA Gun System, 62
AMX-30 SABRE, 64
AN/FPS-115 Pave Paws SLBM Detection System, 23
AN/MPQ-46 High Power Illuminator (HPI), 280
AN/MPQ-48 Improved CW Acquisition Radar (ICWAR), 279
AN/MPQ-50 Pulse Acquisition Radar (PAR), 279
AN/MPQ-51 Range-only Radar (ROR), 280
AN/MSQ-4 Electrical Power Plant, 284
AN/MSQ-53 Multi-function Phased Array Radar, 284
AN/MSQ-104 Engagement Control Station (ECS), 283
AN/MSW-11 Improved Platoon Command Post (IPCP), 279
AN/TPS-59 and 63 Air Defence System, 6
AN/TSQ-143 Air Defence System, 6
AN/TSW-8 Battery Control Centre (BCC), 279
ARE Atelier de Construction Roanne, Self-propelled AA guns, 62
ARES Inc, Self-propelled AA Guns, 96
AT (Advanced Tactical) Patriot Programme, 285
ATBM Anti-tactical Ballistic Missile Systems, 249, 271
AVIBRAS Industria Aerospacial SA, Static & Towed SAM Systems, 241
AW-X Twin 35mm Self-propelled AA Gun System, 77
Abu Dhabi, Air Defence Systems, 1
Abu Zaabal Engineering Industries Company, Towed AA Guns, 168
Advanced Tactical (AT) Patriot Programme, 285
Aerospatiale,
  Self-propelled SAM Missiles, 113
  Static & Towed SAM Systems, 244
Afghanistan, Inventory, 288
Agile Continuous Wave Acquisition Radar (ACWAR), 278
Air Defence Gun Sight, 237
Air Defence Initiative, 25
Air Defence Suppression Missile (ADSM), 51
Albania, Inventory, 288
Algeria, Inventory, 288
Angola,
  Air Defence Systems, 2
  Inventory, 288
Anti-tactical Ballistic Missile Systems, 271
Argentina,
  Air Defence Systems, 2
  Inventory, 288
Arrow 30mm AA Gun, 171
Arrow (Chetz) Anti-tactical Ballistic Missile (ATBM) System, 249
Artemis 30mm Light AA Gun System, 174
Atelier de Construction Roanne (ARE), Self-propelled AA guns, 62
Australia,
  Air Defence Systems, 2
  Inventory, 288
Austria,
  Air Defence Systems, 3
  Inventory, 289
Avenger Pedestal Mounted Stinger Self-propelled Air Defence System, 145
Avia Zavody, Self-propelled AA guns, 57

B

BADGE Base Air Defence Ground Environment, 10
BCC Battery Control Centre AN/TSW-8, 279
BCP Battery Command Post, 279
BMEWS Ballistic Missile Early Warning System, 22
BOFI Gun Systems, 189
BOV-3 Triple 20mm Self-propelled AA Gun System, 104
BTR-40A Twin 14.5mm Self-propelled AA Gun System, 89
BTR-152A Twin 14.5mm Self-propelled AA Gun System, 89
Bahrain, Inventory, 289
Ballistic Missile Early Warning System (BMEWS), 22
Base Air Defence Ground Environment (BADGE), 10
Battery Command Post (BCP), 279
Battery Control Centre (BCC) AN/TSW-8, 279
Belgium,
  Inventory, 289
  Towed AA Guns, 154
Benin, Inventory, 289
Blazer Air Defence Turrets, 99
Block Sight FERO-Z 13, 236
Bloodhound Mk2 SAM System, 273
Blowpipe Low Altitude SAM System, 45
Bodenseewerk Geratetechnik GmbH (GBT), Static & Towed SAM Systems, 245
Boeing Aerospace, Self-propelled Surface-to-Air Missiles, 145, 149
Boffin 40mm L40/60 Automatic AA Gun, 156
Bofors AB,
  SAM systems, manportable, 32
  Self-propelled AA Gun Systems, 79
  Self-propelled Surface-to-Air Missiles, 120
  Towed AA Guns, 186, 187
  Towed AA Gun Sights, 234
Botswana, Inventory, 289
Brazil,
  Air Defence Systems, 4
  Inventory, 289
  SAM systems, manportable, 26
  Self-propelled AA guns, 54
  Static & Towed SAM Systems, 241
  Towed AA Guns, 155
Breda 40L70 Twin Field Mounting, 180
Breda M42 Upgrade (USA), 95
Breda Meccanica Bresciana SpA, Towed AA Guns, 180
British Aerospace (Dynamics) Ltd,
  Self-propelled Surface-to-Air Missiles, 140
  Static & Towed SAM Systems, 264, 273
  Towed AA Gun Sights, 237
Brunei, Inventory, 289
Bulgaria, Inventory, 289
Burkina Faso, Inventory, 289
Burma, Inventory, 290
Burundi, Inventory, 290

C

CA 1 Twin 35mm Self-propelled AA Gun System, 69
CATRIN Air Defence System, 10
CETME Compana de Estudios Tecnicos de Materiales Especiales SA, Towed AA Guns, 186
COMCO Electronics Corporation, Air Defence Systems, 16
CONUS OTH-B radar system, 24
CPMIEC Chinese Precision Machinery Import & Export Corporation, Static & Towed SAM Systems, 241
CRIS Coastal Radar Integration System, 5
Cactus Low Altitude SAM System, 119
Cameroon, Inventory, 290
Canada,
  Air Defence Systems, 5, 23
  Inventory, 290
  Towed AA Guns, 156
Cape Verde Islands, Inventory, 290
Caribbean, Air Defence Systems, 5
Centre-aimed Sight System, 235
Cerbere 76T2 Twin 20mm Automatic AA Gun, 169
Chad, Inventory, 290
Chang Bai SAM system, 18
Chaparral M48A1 Low Altitude Self-propelled SAM System, 150
Chetz (Arrow) Anti-tactical Ballistic Missile (ATBM) System, 249
Chile,
  Inventory, 290
  Towed AA Guns, 157
China,
  Air Defence Systems, 5
  Inventory, 290
  SAM systems, manportable, 26-7
  Self-propelled AA guns, 54-7
  Static & Towed SAM Systems, 241
  Towed AA Guns, 158
China North Industries Corporation,
  Self-propelled AA guns, 54
  Towed AA Guns, 158
Chinese Precision Machinery Import & Export Corporation (CPMIEC),
  Static & Towed SAM Systems, 241
Coastal Radar Integration System (CRIS), 5
Colombia, Inventory, 290
Combat Grande Air Defence System, 16
Compana de Estudios Tecnicos de Materiales Especiales SA (CETME),
  Towed AA Guns, 186
Congo, Inventory, 290
Contraves AG, Static & Towed SAM Systems, 247
Contraves Italiana SpA, Towed AA Gun Sights, 230

INDEX 307

Crossbow Pedestal-mounted Weapons System, . . 147
Crotale Air Defence System, ... 6
Crotale Low Altitude SAM System, ... 109
Cuba, Inventory, ... 290
Cyprus, Inventory, ... 290
Czechoslovakia,
Self-propelled AA guns, ... 57
Towed AA Guns, ... 166

D

DACTA Air Defence Systems, ... 4
DEW Distant Early Warning *see* North Warning System
Datasaab AB, Air Defence Systems, ... 16
Denmark,
Air Defence Systems, ... 5
Inventory, ... 291
Djibouti, Inventory, ... 291
Dominican Republic, Inventory, ... 291

E

ECS Engagement Control Station AN/MSQ-114, . 283
Eagle Twin 35mm Mobile Air Defence System, . . . 96
Ecuador, Inventory, ... 291
Egypt,
Air Defence Systems, ... 6
Inventory, ... 291
SAM systems, manportable, ... 27
Self-propelled AA guns, ... 58
Towed AA Guns, ... 168
El Salvador, Inventory, ... 291
Electrical Power Plant AN/MSQ-4, ... 284
Electronique Serge Dassault, Self-propelled AA guns, ... 58, 65
Engagement Control Station (ECS) AN/MSQ-104, 283
Ericsson Radar Electronics AB, SAM systems, manportable, ... 32
Escorter 35 GDF-D03 Twin 35mm Self-propelled AA Gun System, ... 81
Ethiopia, Inventory, ... 291
Euromissile Roland Low Altitude SAM System, . . 113

F

FAM-2M Twin 20mm Light AA Gun, ... 157
FAMIL SA, Towed AA Guns, ... 157
FERO-Z 13 Block Sight, ... 236
FIM-43 Redeye Low Altitude SAM System, ... 51
FIM-92 Stinger Low Altitude Surface-to-air Missile, 48
FK 20-2 20mm Automatic AA Gun, ... 184
FM-80 All-weather Low Altitude SAM System, . . 241
FMC Corporation,
Self-propelled AA Guns, ... 99
Self-propelled Surface-to-Air Missiles, ... 120
FN Herstal (SA), Towed AA Guns, ... 154
FOG-M Fibre Optic Guided Missile System, ... 149
Ferranti,
Static & Towed SAM Systems, ... 273
Towed AA Gun Sights, ... 238
Fibre Optic Guided Missile (FOG-M) System, ... 149
Finland,
Air Defence Systems, ... 6
Inventory, ... 291
Fire Control Systems (Chinese), ... 162
Florida Air Defence System, ... 18
Ford Aerospace & Communications, Self-propelled Surface-to-Air Missiles, ... 150
France,
Air Defence Systems, ... 6
Inventory, ... 292
SAM systems, manportable, ... 29
Self-propelled AA guns, ... 60
Self-propelled Surface-to-Air Missiles, ... 106
Static & Towed SAM Systems, ... 244
Towed AA Guns, ... 168

G

GAI-B01 20mm Automatic AA Gun, ... 201
GAI-C01 20mm Automatic AA Guns, ... 200
GAI-C03 20mm Automatic AA Gun, ... 202
GAI-C04 20mm Automatic AA Guns, ... 200
GAI-D01 20mm Twin Automatic AA Gun, ... 199
GBF-BOB Diana 25mm LAAG, ... 196
GBI-A01 25mm Automatic AA Gun, ... 198
GBT Bodenseewerk Geratetechnik GmbH, Static & Towed SAM Systems, ... 245
GDF-002 35mm Twin Automatic AA Guns, ... 193
GDF-005 35mm Twin Automatic AA Guns, ... 193
GDF-D03 Escorter 35 Twin 35mm Self-propelled AA Gun System, ... 81
GEADGE German Air Defence Environment, ... 7
GEODSS Ground Electro-Optical Deep Space Surveillance, ... 24
GIAT Groupement Industriel Des Armements Terrestres,
Self-propelled AA guns, ... 62
Towed AA Guns, ... 168
GSA 200 Series AA Sight, ... 238
Gabon, Inventory, ... 292
Gadfly SA-11 Low to Medium Altitude SAM System, ... 136
Gainful SA-6 Low to Medium Altitude SAM System, ... 127
Gammon SA-5 Medium to High Altitude SAM System, ... 262
Ganef SA-4 Medium to High Altitude SAM System, ... 125
Gaskin SA-9 Low Altitude SAM System, ... 134
Gecko SA-8 Low Altitude SAM System, ... 131
General Dynamics,
SAM systems, manportable, ... 48
Self-propelled AA Guns, ... 103
General Electric,
Air Defence Systems, ... 6
Self-propelled AA Guns, ... 99
Towed AA Guns, ... 221
General Motors Corporation, Self-propelled AA Guns, ... 93
Gepard Twin 35mm Self-propelled AA Gun System, ... 69
German Air Defence Environment (GEADGE), ... 7
Germany, East, Inventory, ... 292
Germany, West,
Air Defence Systems, ... 7
Inventory, ... 292
Self-propelled Surface-to-Air Missiles, ... 113
Static & Towed SAM Systems, ... 245
Towed AA Guns, ... 171
Ghana, Inventory, ... 293
Giant SA-X-12b/Gladiator SA-12a Low to High Altitude Missile Systems, ... 137
Gladiator SA-12a/Giant SA-X-12b Low to High Altitude Missile Systems, ... 137
Goa SA-3 Low to Medium Altitude SAM System, 260
Gopher SA-13 Low Altitude SAM System, ... 138
Grail SA-7 Low Altitude SAM System, ... 39
Greece,
Inventory, ... 293
Towed AA Guns, ... 174
Gremlin SA-14 Low Altitude SAM System, ... 38
Ground Electro-Optical Deep Space Surveillance (GEODSS), ... 24
Groupement Industriel Des Armements Terrestres (GIAT),
Self-propelled AA guns, ... 62
Towed AA Guns, ... 168
Grumble SA-10 Low to High Altitude SAM System, ... 135
Guatemala, Inventory, ... 293
Guideline SA-2 Medium to High Altitude SAM System, ... 257
Guild SA-1 Medium Altitude SAM System, ... 256
Guinea, Inventory, ... 293
Guinea-Bissau, Inventory, ... 293
Gun King Sight, ... 230
Guyana, Inventory, ... 293

H

HAWK Homing All the Way Killer SAM System, . 276
HN-5 Series Manportable AA Missile System, ... 26
HPI High Power Illuminator AN/MPQ-46, ... 280
HQ2B Mobile SAM System, ... 244
HQ-2 Medium to High Altitude SAM System, . . . 243
HQ-61 Low to Medium Altitude SAM System, . . . 241
HS 639-B4.1 *see* GAI-C03 20mm Automatic AA Gun
HS 693-B3.1 *see* GAI-C01 20mm Automatic AA Guns
HSS 639-B5 *see* GAI-C04 20mm Automatic AA Guns
HSS 666A *see* GAI-D01 20mm Twin Automatic AA Gun
HVSD High Value Site Defense System, ... 103
Hagglund Vehicles, Self-propelled Surface-to-Air Missiles, ... 121
Haiti, Inventory, ... 293
Hall & Watts Ltd, Towed AA Gun Sights, ... 239
Hellenic Arms Industry SA, Towed AA Guns, ... 174
High Energy Laser Air Defence Armoured Vehicle, 113
High Mobility 20mm Vulcan Wheeled Carrier (VWC) AA Gun System, ... 103
High Power Illuminator (HPI) AN/MPQ-46, ... 280
High Value Site Defense System (HVSD), ... 103
Hispano-Suiza, AA Guns, ... 202
Hollandse Signaalapparaten,
Air Defence Systems, ... 13
SAM systems, manportable, ... 32
Honduras, Inventory, ... 293
Hotspur Armoured Products, Self-propelled AA guns, ... 72
Hub Cap Air Defence System, ... 2
Hughes Aircraft Company,
Air Defence Systems, ... 6, 9, 12, 18
Self-propelled Surface-to-Air Missiles, ... 149
Static & Towed SAM Systems, ... 254
Hungary, Inventory, ... 293

I

IADGES Indian Air Defence Ground Environment System, ... 10
IADS NATO-Icelandic Air Defence System, ... 9
IAI Israel Aircraft Industries Ltd,
Static & Towed SAM Systems, ... 249
Towed AA Guns, ... 177
ICC Information Co-ordination Central, ... 279
ICCE Iceland Command and Control Enhancement, . 9
ICWAR Improved CW Acquisition Radar AN/MPQ-48, ... 279
IPCP Improved Platoon Command Post AN/MSW-11, ... 279
IUKADGE Improved United Kingdom Air Defence Ground Environment, ... 21
Iceland, Air Defence Systems, ... 8
Iceland Command and Control Enhancement (ICCE), . 9
Igla SA-16 Low Altitude SAM System, ... 37
Iltis 25mm Infantry Gun, ... 197
Improved Chaparral M48A2 Low Altitude Self-propelled SAM System, ... 150
Improved CW Acquisition Radar (ICWAR) AN/MPQ-48, ... 279
Improved Platoon Command Post (IPCP) AN/MSW-11, ... 279
Improved United Kingdom Air Defence Ground Environment (IUKADGE), ... 21
India,
Air Defence Systems, ... 9
Inventory, ... 294
Static & Towed SAM Systems, ... 246
Indian Air Defence Ground Environment System (IADGES), ... 10
Indonesia,
Air Defence Systems, ... 9
Inventory, ... 294
Information Co-ordination Central (ICC), ... 279
International,
Self-propelled AA guns, ... 69
Self-propelled Surface-to-Air Missiles, ... 113
Static & Towed SAM Systems, ... 246
Iran, Inventory, ... 294
Iraq,
Inventory, ... 294
Static & Towed SAM Systems, ... 248
Ireland, Inventory, ... 294
Israel,
Air Defence Systems, ... 9
Self-propelled Surface-to-Air Missiles, ... 119
Static & Towed SAM Systems, ... 249
Towed AA Guns, ... 177
Israel Aircraft Industries (IAI) Ltd,
Static & Towed SAM Systems, ... 249
Towed AA Guns, ... 177
Italy,
Air Defence Systems, ... 10
Inventory, ... 295
Self-propelled AA guns, ... 73
Static & Towed SAM Systems, ... 249
Towed AA Guns, ... 180
Towed AA Gun Sights, ... 230
Ivory Coast, Inventory, ... 295

J

JSS Joint Surveillance System, ... 23
Japan,
Air Defence Systems, ... 10
Inventory, ... 295
SAM systems, manportable, ... 32
Self-propelled AA guns, ... 77
Static & Towed SAM Systems, ... 252
Javelin Low Altitude SAM System, ... 43
Jindalee Air Defence System, ... 3
Joint Surveillance System (JSS), ... 23
Jordan,
Air Defence Systems, ... 10
Inventory, ... 295

K

KS-19 100mm AA Gun, ... 205
KS-30 130mm AA Gun, ... 203
KUKA Wehrtechnik GmbH, Towed AA Guns, ... 171
Kampuchea, Inventory, ... 295
Keiko Low Altitude SAM System, ... 32
Kenya, Inventory, ... 295
Kern & Company Ltd, Towed AA Gun Sights, . . . 236
Korea, North,
Air Defence Systems, ... 11
Inventory, ... 296
Self-propelled AA guns, ... 78
Korea, South,
Air Defence Systems, ... 11
Inventory, ... 296
Self-propelled AA guns, ... 78
Krauss-Maffei Wehrtechnik GmbH, Self-propelled AA guns, ... 69
Kuwait,
Air Defence Systems, ... 11
Inventory, ... 296

L

L40/60 40mm Boffin Automatic AA Gun, ... 156
L/60 40mm Bofors Gun, ... 154, 232
L/60 m/36 40mm Automatic AA Gun, ... 191
L/70 Bofors 40mm AA Guns, ... 186, 187
LASS Low Altitude Surveillance System, ... 11
LAV Light Armoured Vehicle Air Defence, ... 99
LCHR M192 Launcher, ... 280
LLAAADS RC25 Low Level All Arms Air Defence Sight, ... 239

308 INDEX

LML Lightweight Multiple Launcher, ... 44
LTV, Self-propelled Surface-to-Air Missiles, . 118, 147
Lvrbv 701 RBS 70 Low Altitude SAM System, . . 121
LVS-A AA Gun Sight, ... 235
LYSAM, Towed AA Guns, ... 155
Laos, Inventory, ... 296
Laser Air Defence Weapons (USSR), ... 125
Launcher Station M901, ... 284
Lebanon, Inventory, ... 296
Libya,
Air Defence Systems, ... 11
Inventory, ... 296
Light Armoured Vehicle (LAV) Air Defence, ... 99
Lightweight Multiple Launcher (LML), ... 44
Long White SAM system, ... 18
Low Altitude Surveillance System (LASS), ... 11

M

M1 40mm Automatic AA Gun, ... 220
M3 VDA Twin 20mm Self-propelled AA Gun
System, ... 65
m/36 L/60 40mm Automatic AA Gun, ... 191
M42 40mm Twin Self-propelled AA Gun System, . 93
M42 Breda Upgrade (USA), ... 95
M48A1 Chaparral Low Altitude Self-propelled SAM
System, ... 150
M48A2 Improved Chaparral Low Altitude Self-propelled SAM System, ... 150
M51 75mm AA Gun, ... 219
M53 12.7mm Quad AA Machine Gun, ... 166
M53 30mm Automatic AA Gun, ... 166
M53/59 Twin 30mm Self-propelled AA Gun
System, ... 57
M55 12.7mm Modernised AA Machine Gun, . . . 155
M55 12.7mm (Quad) AA Machine Gun, ... 224
M55 A2 20/3mm AA Gun, ... 226
M55 A3/A4 B1 20/3mm AA Gun, ... 227
M55 Quad 12.7mm Self-propelled AA Gun
System, ... 79
M75 20/1mm AA Gun, ... 228
M113 with SHORAR, ... 75
M113/RBS 70 Low Altitude SAM System, ... 120
M113A2 Mounted Sakr Eye, ... 29
M117 90mm AA Gun, ... 218
M118 90mm AA Gun, ... 217
M163 20mm Vulcan Self-propelled AA Gun
System, ... 100
M167 20mm Vulcan AA Gun, ... 221
M192 Launcher (LCHR), ... 280
M901 Launcher Station, ... 284
M1938 14.5mm Self-propelled AA Gun, ... 78
M1939 37mm Automatic AA Gun, ... 209, 288
M1939 and M1944 85mm AA Guns, ... 206
MA/40 Vanth Optical Sight and Fire Control
System, ... 232
MADGE Malaysian Air Defence Ground
Environment, ... 12
MATRA,
SAM systems, manportable, ... 29
Self-propelled Surface-to-Air Missiles, . . . 107, 112
MBB Messerschmitt-Bolkow-Blohm GmbH,
Static & Towed SAM Systems, ... 246
Self-propelled Surface-to-Air Missiles, ... 113
MIM-14B (Nike-Hercules) SAM System, ... 285
MIM-23 HAWK Low to Medium Altitude SAM
System, ... 276
MIM-104 Patriot Low to High Altitude SAM
System, ... 281
Mk1 40mm Automatic AA Gun, ... 216
MRSR Multiple Role Survivable Radar, ... 278
MSA-3.1 Low Altitude Surface-to-air High Velocity
Missile System, ... 26
MSAM Medium SAM System, ... 246
Machine Tool Works Oerlikon-Buhrle Ltd, Towed AA
Guns, ... 192
Madagascar, Inventory, ... 296
Malawi, Inventory, ... 296
Malaysia,
Air Defence Systems, ... 12
Inventory, ... 296
Malaysian Air Defence Ground Environment
(MADGE), ... 12
Mali, Inventory, ... 296
Malta, Inventory, ... 296
Marconi,
Air Defence Systems, ... 14
Self-propelled AA Guns, ... 91
Marksman Twin 35mm AA Turret, ... 91
Mauritania, Inventory, ... 297
Mauritius, Inventory, ... 297
Mauser-Werke GmbH, Towed AA Guns, ... 171
Meroka 20mm Multi-barrel AA Gun System, ... 186
Mexico, Inventory, ... 297
Mistral AATCP Air-to-air System, ... 31
Mistral ALB1 Lightweight Twin-round-Mobile
System, ... 31
Mistral SADRAL Naval System, ... 31
Mistral SATCP Low Altitude SAM System, ... 29
Mongolia, Inventory, ... 297
Morocco,
Air Defence Systems, ... 12
Inventory, ... 297
Mozambique, Inventory, ... 297
Multi-function Phased Array Radar AN/MSQ-53, 284
Multiple Role Survivable Radar (MRSR), ... 278
Mygale Air Defence System, ... 31, 106

N

NAADM North American Air Defence Modernization, 5
NADGE NATO Air Defence Ground Environment, . 10, 12, 14, 15
NALLADS Norwegian Army Low Level Air Defence
System, ... 14
NASAMS Norwegian Advanced SAM System for Low
to Medium Altitude, ... 254
NATO Air Defence Ground Environment
(NADGE), ... 10, 12, 14, 15
NATO-Icelandic Air Defence System (IADS), ... 9
NOAH Norwegian Adapted Hawk, ... 14
NORAD North American Air Defense Command, . . 24
NORINCO China North Industries Corporation,
Towed AA Guns, ... 158
Navspur, ... 24
Nepal, Inventory, ... 297
Netherlands,
Air Defence Systems, ... 13
Inventory, ... 297
Nicaragua, Inventory, ... 297
Nigeria,
Air Defence Systems, ... 13
Inventory, ... 297
Nike-Hercules (MIM-14B) SAM System, ... 285
Nile 23 Twin 23mm Self-propelled AA Gun, ... 59
Norsk Forsvarsteknologi AS,
Static & Towed SAM Systems, ... 254
Towed AA Guns, ... 184
North American Air Defence Modernization
(NAADM), ... 5
North American Air Defense Command (NORAD), . 24
North Warning System, ... 23
Norway,
Air Defence Systems, ... 14
Inventory, ... 297
Static & Towed SAM Systems, ... 254
Towed AA Guns, ... 184
Norwegian Adapted Hawk (NOAH), ... 14
Norwegian Advanced SAM System (NASAMS) for
Low to Medium Altitude, ... 254
Norwegian Army Low Level Air Defence System
(NALLADS), ... 14

O

OTO Melara SpA, Self-propelled AA guns, ... 73
OTOMATIC 76mm Self-propelled Air Defence Tank, 75
Oerlikon-Buhrle Ltd,
Self-propelled AA Gun Systems, ... 81
Self-propelled Surface-to-Air Missiles, ... 122
Towed AA Guns, ... 192
Officine Galileo, Towed AA Gun Sights, ... 231
Oman,
Air Defence Systems, ... 14
Inventory, ... 297
Orbita Sistemas Aerospaciais SA, SAM systems,
manportable, ... 26

P

P56 Optical Sight and Fire Control System, ... 231
PAR Pulse Acquisition Radar AN/MPQ-50, ... 279
PCP Platoon Command Post, ... 279
PIVADS Product Improved Vulcan Air Defense
System, ... 101, 223
PVO Strany, ... 21
Pakistan,
Air Defence Systems, ... 14
Inventory, ... 298
Panhard, Self-propelled AA guns, ... 65
Paraguay, Inventory, ... 298
Patriot MIM-104 Low to High Altitude SAM
System, ... 281
Patriot-HAWK Phase III Inter-operability, ... 285
Pave Paws AN/FBS-115 SLBM Detection System, 23
Peace Shield Air Defence System, ... 15
Pedestal Mounted Sakr Eye, ... 28
Peru, Inventory, ... 298
Phase III Platoon Comman Post (PCP), ... 279
Philippines, Air Defence Systems, ... 15
Platoon Command Post (PCP), ... 279
Poland, Inventory, ... 298
Portugal,
Air Defence Systems, ... 15
Inventory, ... 298
Product Improved Vulcan Air Defense System
(PIVADS), ... 101, 223
Pulse Acquisition Radar (PAR) AN/MPQ-50, ... 279

Q

Qatar, Inventory, ... 298
Quad 12.7mm M53 AA Machine Gun, ... 166
Quad 25mm Self-propelled AA Gun System, ... 73

R

RAMTA Structures and Systems, Towed AA
Guns, ... 177
RBS 70 series Low Altitude SAM System, . . 32, 121
RBS 70/M113 Low Altitude SAM System, ... 120
RBS 90 Low Altitude SAM System, ... 32
RC25 Low Level All Arms Air Defence Sight
(LLAAADS), ... 239
REPORTER radar system, ... 36
ROR Range-only Radar AN/MPQ-51, ... 280
ROTHR Relocatable Over-the-horizon Radar, ... 24
Rafael, Self-propelled Surface-to-Air Missiles, . . . 119
Range-only Radar (ROR) AN/MPQ-51, ... 280
Rapier 2000 Low Level SAM System, ... 269
Rapier Laserfire Low Altitude SAM System, ... 143
Rapier Low Level SAM System, ... 264
Raytheon Company, Static & Towed SAM
Systems, ... 246
Redeye FIM-43 Low Altitude SAM System, ... 51
Reflex Sight, ... 235
Relocatable Over-the-horizon Radar (ROTHR), ... 24
Rheinmetall GmbH,
Self-propelled AA guns, ... 72
Towed AA Guns, ... 173
Ring Sight, ... 235
Roland Low Altitude SAM System, ... 113
Romania, Inventory, ... 298

S

S-60 57mm Automatic AA Gun, ... 207, 288
SA Placencia de las Armas, Towed AA Guns, . . . 186
SA-1 Guild Medium Altitude SAM System, ... 256
SA-2 Guideline Medium to High Altitude SAM
System, ... 257, 288
SA-3 Goa Low to Medium Altitude SAM
System, ... 260, 288
SA-4 Ganef Medium to High Altitude SAM
System, ... 125
SA-5 Gammon Medium to High Altitude SAM
System, ... 262
SA-6 Gainful Low to Medium Altitude SAM
System, ... 127
SA-7 Grail Low Altitude SAM System, ... 39
SA-8 Gecko Low Altitude SAM System, ... 131
SA-9 Gaskin Low Altitude SAM System, ... 134
SA-10 Grumble Low to High Altitude SAM
System, ... 135
SA-11 Gadfly Low to Medium Altitude SAM
System, ... 136
SA-12a Gladiator/SA-X-12b Giant Low to High
Altitude Missile Systems, ... 137
SA-13 Gopher Low Altitude SAM System, ... 138
SA-14 Gremlin Low Altitude SAM System, ... 38
SA-16 Igla Low Altitude SAM System, ... 37
SA-19 Low to Medium Altitude SAM System, . . . 140
SA-X-12b Giant/SA-12a Gladiator Low to High
Altitude Missile Systems, ... 137
SA-X-15 Low to Medium Altitude Self-propelled
SAM System, ... 139
SA-X-17 Low to Medium Altitude SAM System, . 140
SABRE 30mm Twin Self-propelled AA Gun
System, ... 60
SABRE AMX-30, ... 64
SADA Sistema Semi-Automatico de Defensa
Aerea, ... 16
SADRAL Mistral Naval System, ... 31
SAKR Factory for Developed Industries,
SAM systems, manportable, ... 27
SAMP Low to Medium Altitude SAM System, . . . 244
SANTAL Low Altitude SAM Self-propelled
System, ... 112
SATCP Mistral Low Altitude SAM System, ... 29
SHORAR Short-Range-Acquisition Radar, ... 75
SIDAM 25 Self-propelled AA Gun System, ... 73
SLBM Detection System, ... 23
SPADOC Air Defence System, ... 24
STRIDA Systeme de Traitement et de Representation
des Informations de Defense Aerienne, ... 6
STRIL Swedish automatic air surveillance and
operational control system, ... 16
Saab Instruments AB, Towed AA Gun Sights, . . . 235
Sakr Eye Low Altitude SAM System, ... 27, 28, 29
Santal Armoured Vehicle Turret System, ... 31
Sao Tome & Principe, Inventory, ... 298
Saudi Arabia,
Air Defence Systems, ... 15
Inventory, ... 298
Selenia Industrie Elettroniche Associate SpA,
Air Defence System, ... 3, 4, 13
Static & Towed SAM Systems, ... 249
Senegambia, Inventory, ... 299
Sentinel Twin 30mm AA Gun, ... 183
Seychelles, Inventory, ... 299
Shahine Low Altitude SAM System, ... 107
Short Brothers Limited,
SAM systems, manportable, ... 41
Self-propelled Surface-to-Air Missiles, ... 144
Short-Range-Acquisition Radar (SHORAR), ... 75
Sidewinder AIM-9L AIM 132A Low Altitude SAM
System, ... 245
Siemens AG,
Air Defence Systems, ... 9
Static & Towed SAM Systems, ... 246
Sierra Leone, Inventory, ... 299

INDEX

Simbad Mistral Lightweight Twin-round Naval System, ... 31
Sinai 23 Twin 23mm Self-propelled AA Gun, ... 58
Singapore,
    Air Defence Systems, ... 15
    Inventory, ... 299
Sistema Semi-Automatico de Defensa Aerea (SADA), ... 16
Sky Net Air Defence System, ... 18
Sky Sword I Low Altitude SAM System, ... 255
Skyguard Gun Missile System, ... 195
Skyguard/Aspide Air Defence System, ... 248
Skyguard/Sparrow Air Defence System, ... 247
Societe d'Applications des Machines Motrices, Self-propelled AA guns, ... 60, 67
Solar Low Altitude SAM System, ... 241
Somalia, Inventory, ... 299
South Africa,
    Inventory, ... 299
    Self-propelled AA guns, ... 79
    Self-propelled Surface-to-Air Missiles, ... 119
Southern Africa, Air Defence Systems, ... 1
Spacetrack, ... 24
Spada Low Altitude SAM System, ... 249
Spain,
    Air Defence Systems, ... 16
    Inventory, ... 299
    Towed AA Guns, ... 186
Sparrow HAWK, ... 280
Spartan Javelin, ... 44
Spider II, ... 177
Sri Lanka, Inventory, ... 299
Standard Manufacturing Company, Self-propelled AA Guns, ... 103
Starstreak Close Air Defence Weapon System, . . . 41
Starstreak Low Altitude Self-propelled High Velocity Missile System, ... 144
Stinger, ... 101
Stinger FIM-92 Low Altitude Surface-to-air Missile, 48
Sudan, Inventory, ... 299
Sweden,
    Air Defence Systems, ... 16
    Inventory, ... 299
    SAM systems, manportable, ... 32
    Self-propelled AA guns, ... 79
    Self-propelled Surface-to-Air Missiles, ... 120
    Towed AA Gun Sights, ... 234
    Towed AA Guns, ... 187
Switzerland,
    Air Defence Systems, ... 18
    Inventory, ... 300
    Self-propelled AA guns, ... 81
    Self-propelled Surface-to-Air Missiles, ... 122
    Towed AA Gun Sights, ... 236
    Towed AA Guns, ... 192
Syria,
    Air Defence Systems, ... 18
    Inventory, ... 300
Systeme de Traitement et de Representation des Informations de Defense Aerienne (STRIDA), ... 6

T

TADOC, Air Defence Systems, ... 16
TCM Mk3 Light Air Defence Artillery System, . . . 177
TCM-20 20mm Twin AA Gun System, ... 178
TLVS Low to Medium Altitude SAM System, . . . 246
TLVS Taktisches Luftverteidigungssystem, ... 7
TMLD Low Level Reporting and Control System, . 9
TRS 2230 surveillance radar, ... 4
TRS-2215D Air Defence System, ... 10
Taiwan,
    Air Defence Systems, ... 18
    Inventory, ... 300
    Static & Towed SAM Systems, ... 255
Taktisches Luftverteidigungssystem (TLVS), ... 7

Tan-SAM Type 81 Low Altitude SAM Systems, . . 252
Tanzania, Inventory, ... 300
Tarasque 53T2 20mm Automatic AA Gun, ... 170
Thailand,
    Air Defence Systems, ... 18
    Inventory, ... 300
    Towed AA Guns, ... 203
Thomson-CSF,
    Air Defence Systems, ... 6, 11
    Self-propelled AA guns, ... 59
    Self-propelled Surface-to-Air Missiles, ... 106, 118, 119
    Static & Towed SAM Systems, ... 244
Tien Kung I & II Low to High Altitude SAM System, ... 255
Tigercat Low Altitude SAM System, ... 271
Tin Shield radar system, ... 11
Togo, Inventory, ... 300
Toshiba Corporation,
    SAM systems, manportable, ... 32
    Static & Towed SAM Systems, ... 252
Tracked Rapier, ... 268
Tracked Rapier Low Altitude SAM System, ... 140
Trinity 40mm Self-propelled Air Defence System, . 79
Tunisia,
    Air Defence Systems, ... 18
    Inventory, ... 300
Turkey,
    Air Defence Systems, ... 19
    Inventory, ... 300
    Towed AA Guns, ... 203
Type 54 12.7mm NORINCO AA Machine Gun, . 158
Type 55 37mm AA Gun, ... 161
Type 56 LAAG, ... 164
Type 58 LAAG, ... 164
Type 59 57mm AA Gun, ... 160
Type 65 37mm AA Gun, ... 161
Type 75 LAAG, ... 164
Type 77 12.7mm NORINCO AA Machine Gun, . 159
Type 80 LAAG, ... 164
Type 80 57mm Twin Self-propelled AA Gun System, ... 54
Type 81 Tan-SAM Low Altitude SAM Systems, . . 252
Type P793 37mm AA Gun, ... 161
Type W-85 12.7mm NORINCO AA Machine Gun, 160

U

UKADGE United Kingdom Air Defence Ground Environment, ... 21
UKADR United Kingdom Air Defence Region, . . . 21
UTAAS Fire Control System for AA Guns, ... 234
Uganda, Inventory, ... 300
United Arab Emirates,
    Air Defence Systems, ... 21
    Inventory, ... 301
United Kingdom,
    Air Defence Systems, ... 21
    Inventory, ... 301
    SAM systems, manportable, ... 41
    Self-propelled AA guns, ... 91
    Self-propelled Surface-to-Air Missiles, ... 140
    Static & Towed SAM Systems, ... 264
    Towed AA Gun Sights, ... 237
    Towed AA Guns, ... 216
United Kingdom Air Defence Ground Environment (UKADGE), ... 21
United Kingdom Air Defence Region (UKADR), . . . 21
United States,
    Air Defence Systems, ... 22
    Inventory, ... 302
    SAM systems, manportable, ... 48
    Self-propelled AA guns, ... 93
    Self-propelled Surface-to-Air Missiles, ... 145

SLBM Detection System, ... 23
Static & Towed SAM Systems, ... 276
Towed AA Guns, ... 217
Uruguay, Inventory, ... 302
USSR,
    Air Defence Systems, ... 19
    Inventory, ... 300
    Laser Air Defence Weapons, ... 125
    SAM systems, manportable, ... 37
    Self-propelled AA guns, ... 82
    Self-propelled Surface-to-Air Missiles, ... 125
    Static & Towed SAM Systems, ... 256
    Towed AA Guns, ... 203

V

VDAA 20mm Twin Self-propelled AA Gun System, 65
VT-1 Low Altitude SAM System, ... 118
VWC Vulcan Wheeled Carrier AA Gun System, . . 103
Vanth MA/40 Optical Sight and Fire Control System for Bofors 40mm L/60 Gun, ... 232
Vanth/MB Optical Sight and Fire Control System for AA Guns, ... 233
Venezuela,
    Air Defence Systems, ... 25
    Inventory, ... 302
Vietnam, Inventory, ... 302
Vulcan M163 20mm Self-propelled AA Gun System, ... 100
Vulcan M167 20mm AA Gun, ... 221
Vulcan Stinger Hybrid, ... 223
Vulcan Wheeled Carrier (VWC) AA Gun System, . 103
Vulcan-Commando 20mm Self-propelled Air Defense System, ... 102

W

Watchdog Air Defence System, ... 13
Weibull, J L AB, Towed AA Gun Sights, ... 235
Western Electric Company, Static & Towed SAM Systems, ... 285
Westinghouse, Air Defence Systems, ... 11
Wolverine Anti-tactical Ballistic Missile (ATBM) System, ... 271

Y

Yemen (North), Inventory, ... 302
Yemen (South), Inventory, ... 303
Ystervark 20mm Self-propelled AA Gun System, . . 79
Yugoslavia,
    Air Defence Systems, ... 25
    Inventory, ... 303
    Self-propelled AA guns, ... 104
    Towed AA Guns, ... 226

Z

ZPU Series of 14.5mm AA Machine Guns, ... 213
ZSU-23-4 23mm Quad Self-propelled AA Gun System, ... 86
ZSU-57-2 57mm Twin Self-propelled AA Gun System, ... 82
ZU-23 23mm Twin Automatic AA Gun, ... 211
ZU-23M 23mm Twin Automatic AA Gun, ... 168
Zaire, Inventory, ... 303
Zambia, Inventory, ... 303
Zimbabwe, Inventory, ... 303

For Reference

Not to be taken from this room